Multi-Agent Systems

Multi-Agent Systems

An Introduction to Distributed Artificial Intelligence

JACQUES FERBER

 Addison-Wesley

An imprint of PEARSON EDUCATION

Harlow, England · London · New York · Reading, Massachusetts · San Francisco · Toronto · Don Mills, Ontario · Sydney
Tokyo · Singapore · Hong Kong · Seoul · Taipei · Cape Town · Madrid · Mexico City · Amsterdam · Munich · Paris · Milan

Pearson Education Limited

Head Office:
Edinburgh Gate
Harlow CM20 2JE
Tel: +44 (0) 1279 623623
Fax: +44 (0) 1279 431059

London Office:
128 Long Acre
London WC2E 9AN
Tel: +44 (0) 171 447 2000
Fax: +44 (0) 171 240 5771

Website: *www.awl-he.com/computing*
www.awl. com/cseng

First Published in Great Britian 1999

ISBN 0-201-36048-9

British Library Cataloguing-in-Publication Data
A catalogue record for this book is available from the Britich Library.

Library of Congress Cataloging in Publication Data
Applied for.

10 9 8 7 6 5 4 3

Translated and typeset by Arrow Applied Languages, Kent.
Printed and bound in Singapore
Cover designed by Designers and Partners, Oxford.

The publishers' policy is to use paper manufactured from sustainable forests.

Contents

Foreword

This book responds to a need: that of giving a precise computer science content to the expression 'multi-agent system'. What ideas, what trends, what new possibilities are hidden within this fashionable term? Above all, it is a question of modelling. The current languages oblige applications programmers to describe the phenomena they handle in a strictly mechanistic and hierarchised way. At the very best, an application is constructed on the basis of independently constructed modules – like a modern building made from prefabricated elements, instead of from stone blocks shaped on site. The procedure is perfect for a program handling the functioning of a building. But what of the life of its inhabitants? The handsome layout which explains, for example, the complex structure of a storey as a composition of rooms and walls, considered as being simpler elements, clearly no longer applies. We must take into account the operational independence of individuals (and not just their conceptual independence), together with phenomena relating to communication, free will, belief, competition, consensus – and also discord. This isn't easy. But computers are insatiable! Now that computerised imaging of buildings, blocks of buildings, and even entire developments has almost become commonplace (ask the architects), the next step is to tackle the human beings and societies that inhabit these locations. How can we do this? Through multi-agent systems, of course ...

No doubt several factors have contributed to this development. I believe that the increased importance given to concepts of liberalism and individualism is pushing us more strongly than ever towards the desire to model any situation which is even slightly complicated in economic terms of competition and of the market. When we do this, we have a tendency to prefer those computing models that make use of the same concepts. The same shift in ideas can be viewed with a more optimistic eye if we regard it as a salutary trend towards decentralisation, a corrective tool operating against state control, or if we emphasise the riches of collective creativity. But wherever we choose to put the emphasis, our age likes to think of itself as pluralistic, and it comes as no surprise that this ideology tends to be reflected even in computer models of reality. Machines are evolving in the same direction as ideas: the growth in parallel architectures and networks has dethroned the single processor, the image which faithfully reflected the single brain and the centralised administration system. Here too, pluralism and competition are taking over!

As always, there's many a slip 'twixt cup and lip. The task facing those specialising in multi-agent systems and distributed artificial intelligence systems (two ways of describing the same community) is, firstly, to find the 'right' ways to control the fabulous computing power of our machines (by defining what the jargon refers to as architectures – software and hardware); and, secondly, to explain to users what they can expect the machines to do. The problem which then arises is how to say things in sufficiently clear and evocative ways, without this leading to any concealment of the limitations or insufficiencies of the systems proposed, which can sometimes be enormous: after all, these constructions are based on mere machines! From this point of view, computer science is dependent on the cognitive sciences, as it is necessary to correlate the intellectual processes of the user with those (sic) of the machine. This comparative approach is in turn shedding new light on the study of cognition. Jacques Ferber does this in his book, drawing on both systemic thought and cognitive psychology. This is not a work on programming techniques, although the author is extremely well aware of the possibilities and limitations of current computing resources. His knowledge of these resources forms the implicit background to his analysis of the numerous factors which contribute to the multi-agent systems that can already be constructed. Some of the examples on which his reasoning is based were actually developed by his own team and have been described in doctoral theses.

As will be seen, we are still a long way from using a multi-agent system to produce a complete model of any human society – for reasons which are not all connected with the stupidity of machines. We are not on the threshold of simulating *the life we live*. On the other hand, we can produce models of some activities of human societies – for example, the fisheries system in the central Niger delta – which are influenced by various competing factors which can be climatic, cultural, economic or bound up with the behaviour of the fish. We also know how to represent the characteristics of some ant populations, with each insect being individually treated as a very simple agent. The interaction of these multiple agents on a large scale leads to the emergence of overall patterns of behaviour very similar to those observed by entomologists in their ethology laboratories, a development which opens up new paths for research. And, to return to engineers' preoccupations with systems which can be used for problem solving, Jacques Ferber can offer a whole range of problem-solving techniques which look promising.

This book is a beginning. It will be up to you, its readers, to continue the story!

Jean-François Perrot

Professor, Pierre and Marie Curie University

Preface

Over the past few years, multi-agent systems have become more and more important in many aspects of computer science (artificial intelligence, distributed systems, robotics, artificial life ...) by introducing the issue of collective intelligence and of the emergence of structures through interactions. In focusing on the autonomy of individuals, called 'agents', and on the interactions that link them together, multi-agent systems have raised several questions. What really are the concepts on which this area of study is based? How does it differ from other disciplines, and in particular from the fields of artificial intelligence, distributed systems and robotics? What contributions can it make to the cognitive sciences and to philosophical thought in general?

Research into multi-agent systems demands integrational rather than analytical science, and prompts us to ask a certain number of questions. What is an agent that interacts with other agents? How can they cooperate? What methods of communication are required for them to distribute tasks and coordinate their actions? What architecture can they be given so that they can achieve their goals? These questions are of special importance, since the aim is to create systems possessing particularly interesting characteristics: flexibility, the capacity to adapt to change, the capacity to integrate heterogeneous programs, the capacity to obtain rapid results and so on.

Two major objectives are being pursued by research in the area of multi-agent systems. The first important area is the theoretical and experimental analysis of the self-organisation mechanisms which come into play when several autonomous entities interact. The second is the creation of distributed artefacts capable of accomplishing complex tasks through cooperation and interaction. So these researches have a dual aspect: on the one hand, they are centred in the cognitive and social sciences (psychology, ethology, sociology, philosophy and so on) and the natural sciences (ecology, biology and so on), since they simultaneously model, explain and simulate natural phenomena and provide models for self-organisation. On the other hand, they can be seen as a practical method, a technique, aimed at creating complex computing systems based on the concepts of agents, communication, cooperation and coordination of actions.

This book came out of several years of experience while I was lecturing on multi-agent systems (MASs) in the DEA IARFA at the Pierre and Marie Curie University (Paris 6). As far as I know, no textbooks dealing with MASs exist. The only works available are published theses, work on specific projects or compilations of articles written by specialists for other specialists in this field, which offer no opportunity for a student or a non-specialist to obtain an integrated overall view of the topic. The research carried out into multi-agent systems, stretching back over nearly 20 years, is extremely wide-ranging, and there are (as yet) no foundations for this discipline which are sufficiently simple and precise to make it easy to give a chronological and structured picture of work in this area. So the first step was to bring all the positions together and establish a conceptual framework for the development of theories in future. That is the purpose behind this book – to bring together the main strands of knowledge relating to this area and to begin to lay down the foundations for a science of interaction, which I have called *kenetics* (from the Greek term *koïnon*, that which is common).

For the present, this remains a somewhat timid and tentative approach, essentially based on the definition of conceptual frameworks, on certain classifications and formalisations, and on the presentation of a modular method for constructing multi-agent systems. There is a twofold interest in bringing all these areas together. It means that we can eventually escape from the problems caused by differences in notation and by the legitimate meanderings of researchers exploring their field of study, and jointly arrive at a clear view of the issues which can be expressed precisely and simply. We are not there yet, but I hope that the unified language offered in this book will help the non-specialist reader to understand the results achieved by multi-agent systems and the issues involved therein; and that at the same time the book will provide some solid bases which may enable the student or researcher in pursuit of new knowledge to contribute a stone of his or her own to the foundations of this discipline.

Contents of the book

This book contains:

(1) a survey of the state of the art in relation to the subject;

(2) a viewpoint on multi-agent systems, presented as a new systemics, which puts the emphasis on the issues of interaction and its consequences;

(3) a conceptual analysis of the field, based on a classification of the main problems and results and, above all, a functional and structural analysis of the organisations within which all the work being done in this field is carried out;

(4) a formal system, BRIC, making possible the modular and incremental conception of MASs through the modelling of behaviours, communication structures and the main forms of interaction, which are the allocation of tasks and the coordination of actions;

(5)   an attempt to formalise MASs and interaction, using an action model based on an influence/reaction pairing.

To whom is it addressed?

This book is addressed, first of all, to computer professionals not specialising in this field, who are interested in obtaining an integrated view of it. It is also intended for readers who are not computer scientists, but who specialise in social sciences or natural sciences and want to use multi-agent systems to model natural behaviours and study the emergence of complex phenomena. It is also addressed to readers who are not computer specialists, but who want to obtain some knowledge of the essential concepts which will allow them to understand what is meant by a 'collective intelligence' and to obtain a general view of the issues raised by multi-agent systems. And finally, it is intended as a study resource for second- or third-year computer science students who would like to specialise in this area.

How this book is organised

This book has deliberately been constructed in such a way that the full picture emerges gradually. After a brief introduction to the field and an outline of a general analysis framework for multi-agent systems, the concepts and mechanisms brought into play in multi-agent systems are progressively studied and analysed. The first part of the book deals with the basic concepts. Chapter 1 contains a general outline of the field, the most important aspects and their relationship to other disciplines. Chapter 2 introduces the concept of interaction situation, and puts forward a general framework to help readers to appreciate the various elements involved in cooperation. Chapter 3 offers a functional and structural analysis of organisations, together with the various architectures generally used to form conceptions of them. Chapter 4 is intended to act as a bridge between the generalities of the preceding sections and the more detailed descriptions which follow. It tackles the issues of the formalisation of action and behaviour and of modelling multi-agent systems, and it introduces most of the concepts used in the remainder of the book. It is shown here that the classic concepts of action are not sufficient to provide a clear understanding of interactions. A theory of action is then developed which considers an action as the result of a set of influences generated by agents. This chapter also formalises a system for modelling agents and multi-agent systems, BRIC, which associates Petri nets with a modular structure. Chapter 5 gives an update on the concept of the mental state of an agent (beliefs, intentions, obligations and so on) and suggests a way of representing the agent's mental dynamics, which takes the form of a modular architecture described in terms of BRIC elements. The final section is devoted to the various conceptual methods and tools which are used to construct cooperative organisations. Chapter 6 relates to communications and describes the modelling of the principal communications structures, with the help of Petri nets. Chapter 7 deals with the study of collaborative organisations in which work is dynamically distributed among the agents. Finally, Chapter 8 presents the main models for coordination of action which manage dynamic articulation of planning and of the carrying out of tasks and which attempt to avoid conflicts. It is further explained here that problems can be resolved by interaction between single agents.

Only two research topics have not been tackled in this book. The first is the application of games theory and economic theories to multi-agent systems. An excellent reference work on this subject is that by Rosenschein and Zlotkin (1994). The second area concerns learning how to use multi-agent systems. A very good survey of the state of the art can be found in Weiss and Sen (1996).

Acknowledgements

This book could not have been written without the help of a great many people who assisted me with their comments, their criticisms and above all their support. I am particularly grateful to Jacqueline Zizi both for her friendship and for reading and rereading my book in its entirety. Her strict and exacting standards were a great help to me, and her tact and encouragement assisted me in maintaining my confidence in this project. I am happy to express my gratitude here. My thanks also go to Philippe Laublet, Alexis Drogoul and Anne Collinot for providing me with constructive comments and criticisms when the book existed only in embryonic form. I found their views very helpful.

I am also grateful to the members of the MIRIAD team – Stephane Bura, Thierry Bouron, Patrice Carle, Christophe Cambier, Eric Jacopin, Karim Zeghal and all the others. They brought their skills and their dynamic energy to the creation of this research group – a perfect example of a multi-agent system. They provided continual stimulation while this book was in preparation.

I must also thank the students at the DEA IARFA for putting up with my explanations – which I'm sure were sometimes rather confused – of why MASs are so interesting. They helped me to crystallise certain theories and syntheses which have found their way into this book.

Yves Demazeau, Jean Erceau, Les Gasser, Charles Lenay, Jean-Pierre Müller and Jean-François Perrot gave me their friendship, their help and their encouragement, for which I am profoundly grateful.

I must also pay tribute to Pierre Azema, Jean-Paul Barthès, Paul Bourgine, Jean-Pierre Briot, Christian Brassac, Christiano Castelfranchi, Brahim Chaib-Braa, Bruno Corbara, Pascal Estraillier, Dominique Fresneau, France Guérin, Alain Pavé, Joël Quinqueton, Mario Tokoro, Dominique Lestel, Christian Mullon, Gérard Sabah, Lena Sanders, Luc Steels, Jean-Pierre Treuil and many others too numerous to mention here. Their kindness, and the particularly fruitful scientific discussions we had together, were a great help to me.

And finally, I would like to thank all my companions, my family and friends, for their understanding, their unconditional support and their affection over the past few years, during which they must have become all too familiar with the words 'I'm just about to finish my book'.

1 Principles of Multi-Agent Systems

1.1   In favour of a collective intelligence

1.1.1   From the thinking machine...

For a long time now, computer science in general and artificial intelligence (AI) in particular have considered programs as distinctive entities capable of competing with human beings in specific areas. Conceived as a simple calculating machine, the computer developed to the point where it could undertake increasingly complex tasks, such as managing a company, monitoring and controlling industrial processes, assisting in medical diagnosis or designing new machines. This rivalry between the human being and the machine was accompanied by a tendency to humanise the machine, to think of a program as the direct equivalent of an 'expert', capable of resolving a problem on its own.

It is possible to find signs of this humanisation or individualisation of AI programs, this comparison between the cognitive capacities of a human being and those of a computer, from the earliest developments in artificial intelligence. Indeed, since its very beginnings, with the experimental programs of Newell, Shaw and Simon (Newell *et al.* 1957) on the automatic demonstration of theorems, the term 'artificial intelligence' has been used to refer to research aimed at the creation of an intelligent machine, one capable of performing complex tasks as well as a human being. This work raised a large number of questions, relating not only to the nature of a possible 'artificial intelligence', but also to a crucial problem for the entire human race: does a machine think? Can it be intelligent? Should it be given a legal status similar to that of a human being? All these questions have stimulated a debate which, in recent times, has critically challenged the capabilities of AI.

To illustrate this concept of an intelligent machine, Turing invented a test based on the assumption that a machine is intelligent if it cannot be distinguished from a human being during a conversation. The test consists of placing an experimenter in front of a computer terminal and linking him or her up either to another human operator or to a computer. The operator and the computer both claim to be human. By involving them in a dialogue, the experimenter has to decide if he or she is talking to a human or a machine. If he or she cannot make this distinction, or gives the right answer only half the time, it can be said that the machine has successfully passed the test, and it can be described as intelligent. It should be noted that, for a machine, being considered as intelligent amounts to imitating the behaviour of a human being, and is not based on any intrinsic criteria. Thus, intelligence is being considered as something pertaining to distinct individuals and not to groups, since in no case is a machine (or a group of machines) being asked to take the place of several people.

This way of looking at computer programs as being like 'thinkers', enclosed within their own worlds, is directly reflected in the idea of the *expert system,* that is, computer programs capable of replacing a human being in tasks considered extremely complicated, tasks which call for knowledge, experience and a certain type of reasoning.

This conception is both the root and the result of the development of centralised and sequential systems in which the control, that which decides what is to be done, is defined as the driver of the various activities carried out one after another. However, this concept of centralisation and sequence meets with several obstacles, theoretical as well as practical in nature. On the theoretical level, artificial intelligence has embarked upon a course which is too optimistic, and at the same time too reductive. Intelligence, like science (Latour 1989; Lestel 1986), is not an individual characteristic which can be separated from the social context in which it finds expression. A human being cannot develop properly if he or she is not surrounded by fellow human beings. Without an adequate social environment, his or her cognitive development is very restricted. Simply learning to articulate his or her thoughts in language becomes literally impossible for anyone who has not been immersed in a human culture from earliest infancy onwards. In other words, other people are indispensable to our cognitive development, and what we call 'intelligence' is due no more to the genetic base which defines our general neuronic structure than it is to our interaction with the world that surrounds us, and in particular with human society.

It can thus be said that, from the very start, the artificial intelligence project could be considered as inaccessible, not so much because of the polemics which argued that human intelligence was transcendental in nature and that it was impossible to reproduce consciousness in a computer system, as because of the lack of interaction between the programs and the outside world and the fact that they were not being inserted into a community of other intelligent entities of the same kind. The criticisms of Dreyfus (1979) and Searle (1991) in particular are essentially concerned with the lack of embodiment for the programs, and thus with their incapacity to interact in any significant way with their environment and with their own kind.

This theoretical difficulty later proved to be a real one, giving rise to practical problems caused by the complexity of the questions to be answered. Computer systems are becoming more and more complex, and they have to be broken down into 'weakly coupled' modules, independent units with limited interactions which can be fully controlled. Thus, instead of being in the presence of a 'machine' — an entity with a specific location defined by its structure and its architecture — we now find ourselves, as demonstrated by the development of object-oriented languages, faced with a group of interacting entities, each entity being defined in a local manner, with no detailed overall perception of all the actions of the system. Thinking of programs in this way introduced new software engineering design methods and changed our perspective. We moved from the concept of a program to that of organisation, a concept to which we shall continually return and which we shall develop throughout this work.

For different reasons, the various designers of expert industrial systems arrived at similar conclusions with regard to the difficulties thrown up by the development of knowledge bases. Most of these difficulties are caused by the fact that, in a complex application, the expertise which we are trying to integrate into the knowledge base, that is, the various kinds of know-how, skills and knowledge, is possessed by different individuals who communicate within a group, exchange knowledge and collaborate in carrying out a common task. In this case, the knowledge of the group is not equal to the sum of the knowledge possessed by the individuals: each kind of know-how is linked to a specific point of view, and these different ways of looking at things, which sometimes contradict each other, cannot necessarily be brought together to form a coherent whole. So carrying out a common task will require discussions, adjustments, perhaps even negotiations to resolve any conflicts that may arise.

And finally, problems can sometimes arise naturally in a distributed context. Whether the task is to design a group of explorer robots or to define an air traffic control system, the problem assumes that a certain number of entities are in existence which are capable of acting and interacting. In certain cases, like that of explorer robots, the interactions can be positive, and the agents are able to help each other, whereas in others, like air traffic control, they can be negative, with aircraft interfering with one another, and the difficulty arises from having to act in such a way that there are no collisions. On the basis of all these factors, is it not possible to 'de-individualise' computer science in general and AI in particular? Is it not possible to look at the problem the other way round, and to consider collective phenomena, quite properly, as being both the first signs and the carriers of this intelligence which we have still not managed either to define or truly to understand, or even effectively to reproduce?

1.1.2 ... to artificial organisation

The approach developed here is in fact based on a radical critique of sequential computing and classic AI, which takes into account the fact that simple or complex activities, such as problem solving, the establishment of a diagnostic system, the coordination of actions or the construction of systems, represent the fruits of interaction between relatively independent and autonomous entities, called 'agents', which operate within communities in accordance with what are sometimes complex modes of cooperation, conflict and competition in order to survive and perpetuate themselves. Organised structures emerge from these interactions which in turn restrict and modify the behaviours of the agents.

This scientific project, to which I have given the name of *kenetics* (Ferber, 1994), consists in being able to plan, design and create universes or organisations made up of artificial agents (electronic or computing agents) capable of acting, collaborating in common tasks, communicating, adapting, reproducing, perceiving the environment in which they move and planning their actions to fulfil objectives defined either extrinsically (by a human programmer, for example) or intrinsically on the basis of a general objective of survival.

Kenetics aspires to be both the science and the technology of *artificial organisations*†, whether these organisations are called populations, societies, groups, worlds or universes. It will further be explained that kenetics proceeds by the construction of *multi-agent systems*, that is, by the creation of electronic or computing models made up of artificial entities which communicate with each other and act in an environment. More precisely, kenetics has the following aims:

(1)   To define a scientific discipline which takes account of interaction between agents as the basis for understanding the functioning and evolution of systems.

(2)   To define the various forms of interaction, such as cooperation, competition, collaboration, obstruction etc., and link them to the issues of auto-organisation, performance or the survival of the system.

(3)   To outline the main mechanisms giving rise to auto-organisation, such as grouping, specialisation, distribution of tasks and resources, coordination of actions, conflict resolution and so on.

(4)   To define operational models of these interactions by describing the functioning of agents and of multi-agent systems.

This characteristic of emphasising interactions and, more precisely, of analysing the interaction systems which exist between agents is what distinguishes multi-agent

---

†The term 'artificial system' will be used here only in the sense of 'a device constructed by a human being which is itself made up of artificial elements'. It thus refers essentially to electronic or computer systems which are covered by such terms, and not to enterprises or natural eco-systems developed by people.

systems (or MASs) from the more classical systemic approaches, in that preference is given to emergence, and action and interaction are considered as the motor elements in the structuring of a system taken as a whole.

The method used has affinities with both theoretical and experimental science. Refined analysis of the various types of multi-agent systems will make it possible for us to categorise the various forms of interaction and the various distributed behaviours which can be brought into play to resolve problems of cooperation or competition. Creating mathematical and computing models will also enable us to develop theories relating to this area and to make it into a scientific discipline in its own right. Above all, we must carry out experiments in the construction of collectively organised artefacts which will help us to improve our analysis of the factors required for the description, auto-organisation and evolution of societies composed of agents. But the forms such experiments take are very different from those known from the social sciences or from nature. The universes created by kenetics are purely artificial, and all their parameters can be directly controlled by the designer. The fact that these organisations are constructs in their entirety means that everyone can determine his or her own point of view and select the parameters in which he or she is interested.

The resulting artificial organisation is then dependent only on these selections, and the properties of the structures are not affected by uncontrolled external factors. Indeed, the entities in a multi-agent universe are created entirely by human thought. Such universes represent a deliberate creation with tightly controlled characteristics. In particular, and in contrast to studies carried out on human or animal social systems, everything that goes on inside the 'heads' of these artificial agents is entirely defined. The designer has access to all the nooks and crannies of their 'minds' since, by definition, he or she is their creator.

However, the mere fact that such a universe has been created does not mean that the way it will evolve can always be predicted. Its evolutionary paths are not governed by a pure determinism which would allow us to foresee all future configurations on the basis of the initial situation. On the contrary, multi-agent systems obey the principles that govern chaotic phenomena (Gleick, 1989). Any modification to the initial conditions, however infinitesimal, any introduction of random variables, however restricted, has effects which are amplified by the interactions between the agents, and it is not possible to know in advance what the precise state of the agents will have become after a certain time has elapsed. Phenomena which are known as 'butterfly effects' (a butterfly flapping its wings in Asia may produce a series of amplifications which lead to a tornado in America) then interfere with any precise forecasting and cause anomalies in most results.

This does not mean that there are no laws governing these systems. On the contrary, it is possible to observe auto-organisation effects, and effects causing emergent structures to appear, which develop in ways which are perfectly well understood. Indeed, with a little experience, it is possible to construct systems that produce desired behaviours in a stable situation, while demonstrating the capability to adapt to disturbances which were not initially predicted.

The interesting thing about multi-agent systems is that we can carry out direct tests of the theories we want to develop on reduced models of societies. All theories relating to social or biological evolution are freely admissible in such universes, since they no longer need to be validated by experiments on the ground. The only factor determining whether a theory is valid or not is whether this theory is or is not 'computable', that is, realisable in the context of a computing program. A theory which is inadmissible in the natural world may very well find a place in kenetics. For example, it is possible to create universes in which individuals reproduce in a 'Lamarckian' manner, by making the assumption that acquired behaviours are directly transmitted to the genes of their descendants, which goes against what we know about the evolution of animal species.

However, the absence of the experimental constraints which operate in a real universe is perversely responsible for a great deal of pressure, because every feature of the mechanisms used has to be made explicit. It is no longer possible to allow certain aspects to remain unclear, or even to define a concept in some vague and tortuous way. All elements, all components, all mechanisms defining a system must be thought out in minute detail, and there is no margin for imprecision, the computer being the ultimate censor.

Why distribute intelligence?

The development of these techniques poses a fundamental problem. Why do people want to create collective intelligences? Why such insistence on a local point of view? Quite simply, why try to distribute intelligence?

There are several ways of responding to these questions. The first is to explain that industrial computer systems are becoming more and more complex, and call for a large number of subsystems of widely divergent natures, including numerous functionalities and interacting with several human specialists (operators, experts, technicians and so on), who are often naturally distributed over physical space.

In large-scale industrial applications, such as the supervision of extended networks (telecommunications, transport and distribution of power, raw materials or finished products), the supervision and management subsystems are naturally distributed at the nodes of the network, and call for a large number of technicians and miscellaneous programs which have to work together to accomplish the overall objective – to do what is necessary to make the system function. Each person involved has only a partial view covering what he or she has to do, but the whole system reacts in the desired manner if all actions are efficiently coordinated. The need to distribute activities and intelligence can therefore be explained by the following lines of reasoning:

- *Problems are physically distributed.* In the first place, complex problems are often physically distributed: a transportation network, by its very nature, is distributed over a wide area, but an industrial control system, such as those which are in use in refineries or on assembly lines, also assumes that the activities in question are, to some extent, distributed spatially. The same applies to vehicle traffic management: each car or plane is an autonomous entity, which must reach its destination in the best possible condition.

- *Problems are widely distributed and heterogeneous in functional terms.* Designing an industrial product as complicated as a racing car, an airliner or a satellite launcher requires the intervention of a large number of specialists, who have only a local view of all the problems posed by the creation of the system. No one could possibly be knowledgeable enough, or well enough qualified, to create such a system on his or her own. There are too many problems for a single individual to handle. A Formula 1 car, for example, requires a large number of experts to perfect its design: specialists in engines, chassis and tyres, a chief engineer, a driver. All these people pool their knowledge to try to make the best possible car.

- *Networks force us to take a distributed view.* In the age of interplanetary networks, when all data and processing power are distributed over a considerable number of sites (the Internet already has several tens of thousands of sites all over the world), software engineers must stop 'thinking globally'. As indicated by C. Hewitt (1985), we have to think in terms of open systems, that is in terms of the radical interoperability of computing systems. Mobile remote computing, in particular, calls for a complete overhaul of our assumptions, which are based on Von Neumann's concept of the machine as something sequential, stationary, and managing all the data it needs in an individual fashion. M. Tokoro's suggestion (Tokoro, 1993) concerning the creation of a 'computing field' is in line with current trends. It should be remembered that computing space is only a gigantic spider's web (the Internet's World Wide Web forms a first approach to this) in which any computer, whether it is stationary, portable or mobile, is linked to every other computer in the world. MASs can thus be seen as serious candidates for the construction of open, distributed, heterogeneous and flexible architectures, capable of offering high-quality service for collective work, without imposing any *a priori* structure.

- *The complexity of problems dictates a local point of view.* When the problems are too extensive to be analysed as a whole, solutions based on local approaches often allow them to be solved more quickly. For example, air traffic control is a complex global problem which is difficult to solve because of the large number of parameters which are brought into play and because of all the constraints which must be taken into account. As we shall see in Chapter 8, local approaches make it possible to solve this type of problem elegantly and efficiently. It is obviously more difficult (and frequently impossible) to verify the validity of the solution theoretically. But empirical results show that the solutions are correct and often appear very 'natural'. The habit of thinking locally induced by kenetics thus constitutes a promising approach to the solving of complicated large-scale problems. It makes it simpler to obtain results, by avoiding the difficulties linked to the inefficiency of algorithms functioning over a worldwide system, and at the same time provides comparable results which 'emerge' from local interactions.

- *Systems must be able to adapt to changes in the structure or the environment.* It is no longer enough to know how to design efficient, reliable and accurate computing systems. Faced with the challenges of complexity, we also have to think about how software can adapt to changes in the context of operations (changes in the operating system, in the database manager or the graphics interfaces, addition of other software and so on) and about its necessary evolutionary capacity in the face of ever-growing needs (extra functionalities, changes in use, integration with other types of software etc.). In this context, MASs, because of their distributed nature, because they always assume that reasoning takes place locally, and because they allow for integration and for the appearance or disappearance of agents even while the system is functioning, are architectures which are especially suitable for taking account of the capacity for evolution and adaptation necessary for the functioning of the system.

- *Software engineering is moving towards designs using concepts of autonomous interacting units.* The history of software development shows that the creation of computer programs is following a course intended to lead to systems designed as assemblies of entities which will be more and more widely distributed, and making use of components which are more and more individualised and autonomous. Recent developments in object-oriented languages in all sectors of computing bear witness to this. Software engineering is now involved in creating autonomous modules which can interact with each other even, and especially, when they have been designed by different people, different teams or different companies. So we have to bring together flexibility in computing, distribution in processing and heterogeneous forms of realisation. MASs have an essential role to play here by acting as possible successors to object-oriented systems and combining local behaviours with autonomy and distributed decision making. Thus it is already a good bet that the software engineering of tomorrow will be 'agent-oriented', just as that of today is beginning to be 'object-oriented'.

1.2 Agent and society

All the issues arising from kenetics stand at the crossroads where the concepts of agents and societies meet, or, if you prefer, where individual behaviours meet phenomena observed on a global scale. This is why the concepts of cooperation, conflict, collaboration and coordination of actions can take on their full meaning in the dialectic between the individual and the group. But before going into these issues more deeply, we must attempt to define what we understand by the terms 'agent' and 'multi-agent system'.

1.2.1 Some definitions

What is an agent? As in all carrier sectors, the term 'agent' is used in rather a vague way. However, we can arrive at a minimal common definition which runs approximately as follows:

Definiton

An agent is a physical or virtual entity

    (a)   which is capable of acting in an environment,

    (b)   which can communicate directly with other agents,

    (c)   which is driven by a set of tendencies (in the form of individual objectives or of a satisfaction/survival function which it tries to optimise),

    (d)   which possesses resources of its own,

    (e)   which is capable of perceiving its environment (but to a limited extent),

    (f)   which has only a partial representation of this environment (and perhaps none at all),

    (g)   which possesses skills and can offer services,

    (h)   which may be able to reproduce itself,

    (i)   whose behaviour tends towards satisfying its objectives, taking account of the resources and skills available to it and depending on its perception, its representations and the communications it receives.

Each of the terms in this definition is important. A *physical entity* is something that acts in the real world: a robot, an aircraft or a car are examples of physical entities. A software component and a computing module, on the other hand, are *virtual entities*, since they have no physical existence.

Agents are *capable of acting*, and not just of reasoning, as in the classic AI systems. The concept of action, which is fundamental for multi-agent systems, is based on the fact that the agents carry out actions which are going to modify the agents' environment, and thus their future decision making. They can also *communicate* with one another, and this is, in fact, one of the main ways in which agents interact. They are acting within an environment, except, as we shall see, for purely communicating agents, for which all actions can be condensed down to communications.

Agents are endowed with *autonomy*. This means that they are not directed by commands coming from a user (or another agent), but by a set of *tendencies* (cf. Chapter 5), which can take the form of individual goals to be achieved or of satisfaction or survival functions which the agent attempts to optimise. It could thus be said that the motor of an agent is itself. It is the agent that is active. It can accede to or reject requests coming from other agents. It thus has a certain freedom of manoeuvre, which differentiates it from all other similar concepts, whether they are called 'objects', 'software modules' or 'procedures'. But autonomy is not simply behavioural, it also relates to resources. In order to act, the agent needs a certain number of resources: power, a CPU, a quantity of memory, access to certain sources of information and so on. The agent is at once partially dependent on its environment for the provision of resources, and independent of its environment to the extent that it is capable of managing those resources. The agent is thus simultaneously an open system (it needs elements external to it in order to survive) and a closed system (as the exchanges it has with the outside world are very strictly regulated).

Agents have only a *partial representation* of their environment, that is, they have no overall perception of what is happening. And this is actually also the case in any large-scale human endeavour (the manufacture of an Airbus, for example) in which nobody knows all the details of the project, each specialist having only a partial view corresponding to his or her area of competence.

The agent is thus a kind of 'living organism', whose *behaviour*, which can be summarised as communicating, acting, and perhaps reproducing, is aimed at satisfying its needs and attaining its objectives, on the basis of all the other elements (perceptions, representations, actions, communications and resources) which are available to it.

Figure 1.1 gives an illustration of the concept of a multi-agent system.

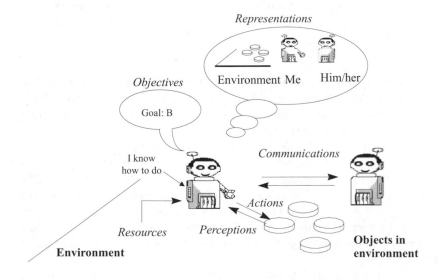

Figure 1.1 Image representing an agent interacting with its environment and the other agents.

The concept of multi-agent systems can be defined as follows:

Definiton

The term 'multi-agent system' (or MAS) is applied to a system comprising the following elements:

(1) An environment, E, that is, a space which generally has a volume.

(2) A set of objects, O. These objects are situated, that is to say, it is possible at a given moment to associate any object with a position in E. These objects are passive, that is, they can be perceived, created, destroyed and modified by the agents.

(3) An assembly of agents, A, which are specific objects (A $\subseteq$ O), representing the active entities of the system.

(4) An assembly of relations, R, which link objects (and thus agents) to each other.

(5) An assembly of operations, Op, making it possible for the agents of A to perceive, produce, consume, transform and manipulate objects from O.

(6) Operators with the task of representing the application of these operations and the reaction of the world to this attempt at modification, which we shall call the laws of the universe (cf. Chapter 4).

A special case exists for systems in which A = O and E is equal to the empty assembly. In this case, the relations, R, define a network: each agent is directly linked to an assembly of other agents, which are called its *acquaintances* (Chapter 5). These systems, which can be referred to as *purely communicating MASs*[†], are very common in distributed artificial intelligence. Their preferred area is cooperation between software modules, the function of which is to resolve a problem or to draw up an expert's report (interpretation of signals or conception of a product, for example) on the basis of specialised modules, as in the case of a distributed control system where E is defined by the structure of the underlying network. These systems are characterised by the fact that the interactions are essentially intentional communications (cf. Chapter 6) and that the working mode resembles that of a social organism (working group, company, administration and so on).

[†]We shall use the term *communicating multi-agent system* or *communicating MAS* as a shorthand notation for what we should refer to as a *multi-agent system whose agents communicate with each other directly by means of messages*. When there is no environment and the agents do nothing except communicate, we shall refer to *purely communicating MASs*. We shall also use the term *situated multi-agent system* or *situated MAS* as shorthand to indicate that this is a *multi-agent system whose agents are positioned in an environment*; and we shall use *purely situated MAS* to refer to a situated MAS in which the agents do not communicate by sending messages but only by the propagation of signals (cf. Chapter 6).

When the agents are *situated*, E is generally a metric space, and the agents are capable of perceiving their environment, that is, of recognising the objects situated in the environment through the functioning of their perceptive capabilities; and of acting, that is, of transforming the state of the system by modifying the positions of, and the relationships existing between, the objects.

We shall see that most reactive multi-agent systems consider that the concept of environment is fundamental to the coordination of actions between several agents. For example, in a universe of robots, the agents, A, are the robots, E is the Euclidian geometrical space in which the robots move, and O is obviously made up of agents, but also of physical objects placed here and there which the robots have to avoid, pick up or manipulate. The operations, Op, are the actions that the robots can take in moving themselves, moving the other objects or communicating, and R is the assembly of relations that link certain agents to others, such as acquaintance relationships (certain agents know some of the others) and communication relationships (agents can communicate with certain agents, but not necessarily with all of them).

For this reason, the agent/environment duality is at the heart of situated multi-agent systems. In acting on the basis of its perceptions of physical space and of the direct communications it receives, the agent defines itself as the dual image of its environment, that is, by what distinguishes it from that which surrounds it. Conversely, the environment of an agent is characterised by everything the agent is not. It is thus impossible to define the concept of a situated agent independently of that of the environment, the two being intrinsically linked and constituting two complementary aspects of a multi-agent universe. The creation of a multi-agent system thus requires the simultaneous definition of the structure of the agents and that of their environment, the actions of the agents having to be carried out within that environment. When agents are purely communicating or purely situated, the definition of multi-agent systems we have given can be adapted.

Definiton

By comparison with the general definition of an agent given above, a purely communicating agent (or software agent) is defined as a computing entity which

(a) is in an open computing system (assembly of applications, networks and heterogeneous systems),

(b) can communicate with other agents,

(c) is driven by a set of its own objectives,

(d) possesses resources of its own,

(f) has only a partial representation of other agents,

(g) possesses skills (services) which it can offer to other agents,

(i) has behaviour tending towards attaining its objectives, taking into account the resources and skills available to it and depending on its representations and on the communications it receives.

Definiton

A purely situated agent is defined as a physical entity (or perhaps a computing entity if it is simulated) which

(a)   is situated in an environment,

(c)   is driven by a survival/satisfaction function,

(d)   possesses resources of its own, in the form of power and tools,

(e)   is capable of perceiving its environment (but to a limited extent),

(f)   has practically no representation of its environment,

(g)   possesses skills,

(h)   can perhaps reproduce,

(i)   has behaviour tending to fulfil its survival/satisfaction function, taking into account the resources, perceptions and skills available to it.

A purely communicating agent is thus distinguished from the concept of an agent in general by the fact that it has no perception of other agents (item (e) no longer exists), that its tendencies take on the appearance of objectives (or intentions, cf. Chapter 5), that it is not acting in an environment[†] and that the context of its evolution is naturally that of computing networks.

Purely situated agents are thus the opposite of software agents as far as their representation capacities are concerned (they are practically non-existent), and in that communications are not generally effected directly but indirectly, through perceptions and through their actions in the environment (cf. Chapter 6).

1.2.2   Levels of organisation

If we take up the classification proposed by G. Gurvitch (1963), which is now traditional in sociology (Rocher, 1968), we can distinguish three levels of organisation in multi-agent systems:

(1)   The *micro-social* level, where we are essentially interested in the interactions between agents and in the various forms of link which exist between two agents or between a small number of agents. It is at this level that most studies into distributed artificial intelligence have been undertaken.

[†]In the sense in which the term is used in this work, that is, a space with a metric space, in which the agents are positioned. Purely communicating agents, on the other hand, live in what is often referred to as a *computer environment*, that is, an assembly of processors, software and resources which they can use and with which they interact.

(2)   The level of *groups*, where we are interested in the intermediary structures which intervene in the composition of a more complete organisation. At this level, we study the differentiations of the roles and activities of the agents, the emergence of organisational structures between agents, and the general problem of the aggregation of agents during the constitution of organisations.

(3)   The level of *global societies* (or *populations*) where interest is mainly concentrated on the dynamics of a large number of agents, together with the general structure of the system and its evolution. Research in relation to artificial life is quite frequently located on this level.

Obviously, as with most classifications, this one should not be considered as a fixed standard for studies, but rather as a guide for us to refer to as we make our own judgements and analyses. It suggests, in particular, that it is possible to analyse and design artificial organisations either on the basis of an overall specification for the society we wish to obtain and the properties we are seeking or, conversely, on the basis of the precise definition of the agents, the society finally obtained being the consequence – whether desired or not – of the interactions between the agents.

The first one is a top-down approach, and is characteristic of the approach of an engineer attempting to obtain a system that responds to a need. The second is more experimental. It fits better with an exploratory project in which an attempt is being made to obtain emergent properties.

Work relating to artificial organisations is thus focused at the centre of an irreducible agent/organisation duality. Any organisation is the result of an interaction between agents, and the behaviour of the agents is restricted by the assembly of organisational structures, as shown by Figure 1.2.

For example, if behavioural differentiation and the constitution of specialists can be viewed as emergent functionalities, the attribution of a role to an agent reduces the margin of manoeuvre of the others to a corresponding extent. This, in turn, imposes restrictions on each of the agents with regard to their possible set of

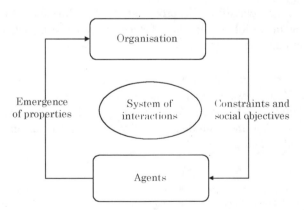

Figure 1.2   The micro–macro relationship in multi-agent systems.

behaviours (cf. Chapter 7). Likewise, if emergent phenomena such as gyratory movements can appear in a very restricted anti-collision system (cf. Chapter 8), any agent wishing to insert itself into this movement must necessarily turn in the gyratory direction imposed by the group.

For this reason, a society is not necessarily a 'given' entity, that is, an object with an existence which pre-dates the actions of its members. If organisations such as public institutions or companies possess an individuality of their own which distinguishes them from the assembly created by the individualities of their members, it is not necessarily the same for simpler collective structures such as working groups or herds of animals. Even societies considered as being complex, such as colonies of bees or ants, should not necessarily be considered as individuals in their own right if we wish to understand their organisation and the regulation and evolution phenomena prevailing there. In terms of multi-agent systems, this means that an organisation can *emerge* from the juxtaposition of individual actions, without its being necessary to define a specific objective (an element from the assembly O) which represents such an outcome.

Conversely, this does not mean that it is impossible or useless, or even unthinkable, to represent societies as entities in their own right. We can of course design an agent in the form of a multi-agent system, and thus consider MASs as Russian dolls, that is, as packages of agents which are themselves represented in the form of MASs. The construction procedure is then recursive, and continues down to the creation of primitive agents which cannot be broken down.

The rapport which exists between agents and organisations is thus a shifting reality. Except in those cases in which the organisation is integrally described by the system designer, the distribution of work, the coordination of actions and the allocation of roles result from the activities of its members. An organisation is therefore not just a static structure such as can be analysed if we are considering a multi-agent system at a given moment, but an organising process, whose structure is merely a resulting effect. This concept has affinities with that of M. Crozier and E. Friedberg in relation to human organizations (Crozier and Friedberg, 1977), where such societies are considered as proceeding from the actors' action systems, that is, from their strategies of taking power, falling back, and negotiating to define the 'local orders' of regulation (Friedberg, 1993).

So an essential duality characterises the processes that take place between the individuals and the organisations which result from them. We are dealing with interaction phenomena, the logic of which depends simultaneously on the capacities of the agents and on the properties and constraints of the system as a whole. Moreover, it is by emphasising the interactions and, more precisely, by analysing the interaction systems which exist between the agents that multi-agent systems are distinguished from the more classical systemic or sociological considerations to which we shall return later. In fact, while many approaches consider systems from a global or even a holistic point of view, analysing them from the top down, multi-agent systems favour emergence, that is, action and interaction, as the motor element in the structuring of the society as a whole. Interaction systems thus constitute the essential area of study for multi-agent systems, and serve to articulate the rapport which exists between the agent on the one hand and the organisation in its entirety on the other.

1.2.3 Social or biological?

Should we consider agents as entities which are already 'intelligent', that is, capable of solving certain problems by themselves, or should they be assimilated to very simple beings reacting directly to modifications of the environment?

Cognitive and reactive agents

These two concepts have given rise to two schools of thought. The first, the 'cognitive' school, is more widely represented in the domain referred to as *distributed artificial intelligence* (DAI), since its origins lie in the focus on communication and cooperation associated with classic expert systems. In this respect, a multi-agent system is made up of a small number of 'intelligent' agents. Each agent has a knowledge base available, comprising all the data and know-how required for the carrying out of its task and for handling interactions with the other agents and with its environment. Agents are also said to be 'intentional', that is, they have goals and explicit plans allowing them to achieve their goals. In this respect, the cooperation problems are astonishingly similar to those of small groups of individuals, who have to coordinate their activities and are sometimes impelled to negotiate with one another to resolve their conflicts (Bond and Gasser, 1988; Demazeau and Müller, 1991; Chaib-Draa *et al.*, 1992). The analogies, then, are social, and numerous researchers in this field base their work on the findings of sociology and, in particular, on the sociology of organisations and of small groups.

By contrast, the other tendency, the 'reactive' school, claims that it is not necessary for agents to be individually intelligent for the system to demonstrate intelligent behaviour overall (Deneubourg *et al.*, 1991; Steels, 1989; Ferber and Drogoul, 1992). Mechanisms of reaction to events, which take into account neither an explanation of the goals nor any planning mechanisms, can then resolve problems categorised as complex. The clearest example of an emergent organisation is that of the anthill (Corbara *et al.*, 1993). Whereas all the ants are on an equal footing and none of them has any strict power of authority over the others. The actions of the ants are coordinated so that the colony can survive, coping with complex problems such as those posed by the search for food, the need to look after the eggs and the larvae, the construction of nests, reproduction and so on.

Intentions, drives and reflexes

In reality, this cognitive/reactive division is sometimes too simplistic. We have to refine it by distinguishing two main themes:

(1)   The conduct of agents is regulated by the opposition between *teleonomic* behaviour, directed towards explicit goals, and *reflex* behaviour, regulated by

Table 1.1   The different types of agent, listed by their representational capacities and their modes of conduct.

Relationship to world / Conduct	Cognitive agents	Reactive agents
Teleonomic	Intentional agents	Drive-based agents
Reflexes	Module-based agents	Agents

perceptions. We have already said that, by definition, all agents are driven by tendencies. But, as we shall see in Chapter 5, certain tendencies may come from the environment, whereas others are explicitly expressed within the agents. We shall use the term 'reflex' behaviour in the first case and the term 'teleonomic' behaviour in the second.

(2)   The relationship between the agent and its environment poses the classic problem of the subject/object pairing, that of knowing whether the agent has available a symbolic and explicit representation of the world, on the basis of which it can reason, or whether its representation is situated at a sub-symbolic level, that is, integrated into its sensory–motor capacities (Piaget and Inhelder, 1966). In the first case, we shall use the term *cognitive agents*, and in the second, the term *reactive agents*.

These two main themes can be combined to distinguish four types of agents which are contrasting in their way of acting and of conceiving of the world, as Table 1.1 shows. Most cognitive agents are *intentional*, which means that they have explicit goals which motivate their actions. They are also referred to as *rational*, that is, the actions they initiate follow a principle of rationality in relation to the goals that direct them. *Module-based agents* (reflex cognitive agents) are at the limits of the concept of an agent. They are sometimes used as auxiliary agents, capable of responding to questions or accomplishing tasks which they are commanded to perform by other agents, without these requests forming part of any explicit goals for the auxiliary agents themselves. We might think of databases or simple computing agents, that is, agents which respond directly to requests addressed to them.

Reactive agents can be directed by motivation mechanisms pushing them towards the accomplishing of a task, such as the satisfaction of an internal need (for example, maintaining their energy level) or the achieving of a goal defined by the designer, in which case they are referred to as *drive-based* agents. They can also be made to respond only to stimuli from the environment, their behaviour being guided integrally by the local state of the world in which they are immersed. They are then described as *tropistic* agents. We shall refer to multi-agent systems comprising nothing but tropistic agents as tropistic multi-agent systems. The difference between these two forms of action is due to the disparity in the origins of the sources of motivation. In the first case, they are located within the agent, whereas in the second they are located in the environment. In reality, this distinction is sometimes difficult to maintain. The behaviours of these agents are often triggered by combinations of internal drives and external stimulations, and the boundary between reflex and drive-based is relatively arbitrary. For this reason, we shall refer essentially to reactive agents in what follows, except where there is a need to do otherwise, without distinguishing between drive-based and tropistic agents.

Cognitive agents, due to their sophistication and their capacity to reason about the world, can operate in a relatively independent way. The tasks they accomplish are complex in relation to the more elementary faculties of the reactive agents. They can thus solve complicated problems in a relatively individual manner. Their internal representation and the inference mechanisms available to them allow them to function independently of other agents, and give them great flexibility in the expression of their behaviour.

Conversely, the cruder structure of reactive agents imposes more rigid behaviour on them. For this reason, reactive agents are not very powerful, as they are reduced to their own resources. But their strength comes from their capacity to form a group, that is, to constitute colonies capable of adapting to their environment. So reactive agents are interesting, not so much at the individual level as at the level of populations, and with regard to the capacities for adaptation and evolution which emerge from the interactions between their members. Reactive agents have little or no individuality. They merge into a mass, but because of their numbers, and the redundancy that flows from them, they can tackle complex tasks and can thus compete, in terms of performance, with agents that are more sophisticated but less numerous.

Anticipation and reaction

Finally – and this is perhaps what constitutes the essential distinction – the cognitive/reactive opposition conceals another duality: *the capacity or lack of capacity to anticipate future events and to prepare for them.* Reactive agents, by the very fact that they have no representation of their environment or of other agents, are incapable of foreseeing what is going to happen, and thus of anticipating by planning what action to take.

Cognitive agents, on the other hand, by their capacity for reasoning based on representations of the world, are capable, at one and the same time, of memorising situations, analysing them, foreseeing possible reactions to their actions, using these to decide on conduct during future events, and so planning their own behaviour (indeed all planning assumes that one is capable of dealing with actions one is not actually carrying out, on the basis of a description of the environment and of these actions). And thus it is thanks to their cognitive capacities, which allow them to construct a virtual world which they can manipulate, that cognitive agents are in a position to produce plans of action.

This capacity for anticipation and planning allows certain agents to optimise their behaviour, and thus to effect only actions which are truly necessary. For example, let us suppose that a robot wishes to go through a door, and that the door is locked. If this is a cognitive agent, it can construct a plan 'in its head', such as:

```
Plan for opening door:
  Go to place where key is
  Take key
  Go to door
  Open door with key
```

In carrying out this plan, the cognitive agent will go directly to the place where the key is and take it, then it will move to the door to open it using the key.

A reactive agent, on the other hand – because it has no representation of the universe in which it is operating – cannot carry out this type of *a priori* reasoning. It merely reacts to the situation. To resolve this problem, we can construct a reactive agent which behaves in the following way:

```
R1 : If I am in front of the door and I have a key,
     then open it
R2 : If I am in front of the door and have no key,
     then try to open it
R3 : If the door does not open and I have no key,
     then go to look for the key
R4 : If I am looking for a key and there is a key in
     front of me, then take the key and go towards the
     door
```

These four rules are sufficient to regulate the behaviour of a reactive robot. If the agent is in front of a locked door, it will try to look for the key, then it will come back to open the door[†].

The difference between the two behaviours is characteristic. Firstly, in the first case the plan is constructed, whereas in the second the rules are laid down by the agent's designer. Secondly, the cognitive agent obviously wins the prize for efficiency in terms of the number of actions carried out. It optimises the number of movements it makes, because it can foresee the consequences of the actions to be undertaken, whereas the reactive agent is obliged first to go towards the door before realising that the key is not there and that it has to go to look for it. On the other hand, the reactive agent is more flexible. If the door is unlocked, it opens it directly, without first going to look for the key.

So we can say that the reactive agent has knowledge compiled from the actions to be carried out. It does not need to construct a mental representation of its world, since it is sufficient for it merely to react to the situations that present themselves to it. But the simplicity of its behaviour is a sign of the intelligence of its designers, rather than of its own.

[†]We shall see in Chapter 4 that there are several ways of defining the behaviour of a reactive agent, the rules given here being characteristic of a technique based on 'situated actions'.

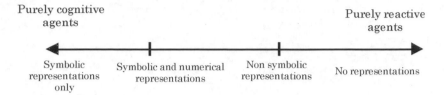

Figure 1.3 The cognitive/reactive distinction defines a practical axis for evaluating the capacity of agents to accomplish complex tasks individually and to plan their actions.

Opposing cognitive and reactive agents may be a good way of seeing where there are problems, but it should not be taken too far. Indeed, where is the boundary between cognitive and reactive? Where is the demarcation line between agents that have explicit models and those that only react to stimuli from their environment? There is actually a continuum between the pure reactive agent, which reacts only to stimuli, and the entirely cognitive agent, which has a symbolic model of the world which it updates continually and on the basis of which it plans all its actions. Between these two extremes, a whole range of possibilities is on offer, from the agent that adapts by memorising certain data in the form of digital parameters to the one that has a 'mental map', that is, an analogue representation of its environment, permitting it to determine trajectories when it is moving. So the cognitive/reactive distinction, although useful to begin with, represents only the extremities of a straight line segment, and not a categorical opposition (Figure 1.3). Indeed, current interest lies, on the one hand, in trying to construct cognitive agents based in reactive organisations, and on the other hand, in creating agents which have both cognitive and reactive capacities at the same time.

In what follows, we shall make frequent references to the cognitive/reactive contrast, but this dichotomy should never be considered as absolute. It should be understood that it is merely a working classification, and that we must be able to go beyond it by synthesising the two terms whenever it becomes necessary.

1.2.4 Architecture and behaviour

An agent is essentially characterised by the manner in which it is designed and by its actions, in other words by its *architecture* and by its *behaviour*. The architecture corresponds to a designer's point of view, which can be summed up in the question: how can the various parts of an agent be assembled in such a way that it accomplishes the actions that we expect it to carry out? Certain other questions then become especially pertinent. Do the agents have a representation of their environment, or are they merely reacting to the stimuli they perceive? Are the agents capable of reasoning on the basis of symbols, or are they merely applying pre-established actions? The replies to these questions are located 'inside' the agents, in their 'guts'. We have to 'lift the bonnet' to know what implementation selections have been made. Thus an agent's architecture characterises its internal structure, that is, the principle of organisation which subtends the arrangement of its various components. We shall see in Chapter 3 that a large number of conceivable architectures exist. Some prove to be more efficient in terms of computing time, others are more flexible and make it possible to encode a huge range of actions, while still others have the advantage of simplicity.

By contrast, behaviour can be analysed without any knowledge of the implementation details. We are dealing here with a phenomenon which can be apprehended by an external observer who looks at the actions the agent undertakes and describes the relationship existing between the agent, its environment and the other agents. For example, for a plane, the fact that it avoids another plane is a characteristic of its behaviour, however this action is implemented. The behaviour thus characterises all the properties that the agent manifests in its environment, that is, what is known in biology as its *function*. To understand the behaviour of an agent, we no longer need to 'lift the bonnet'. We need to observe the way it moves and responds to the stresses of its environment. This approach leads to the creation of behavioural models which are independent of the architecture even if, as we shall see, certain architectures lend themselves more than others to bringing about certain behaviours. The opposition between the viewpoints of the designer and the observer is akin to the debate between structure and function which is a familiar one in biology. For the designer, the problem lies in finding an architecture which allows him or her to implement robots capable of manifesting a certain behaviour. So for the designer the behaviour of the agent is the manifestation of the structure of the agent, that is, of its architecture and its program. The behaviour is then seen as an external specification for the agent, with the architecture defining the internal relationships making it possible to arrive at this specification.

Conversely, the observer perceives behaviour, on the basis of which he or she can induce or specify what an architecture is considered as producing. If the agent is natural, then the architectures we can put forward are only models in relation to reality. On the other hand, if the agent is artificial, behavioural models act as specifications, that is, as design constraints for the realisation of the internal structure of an agent.

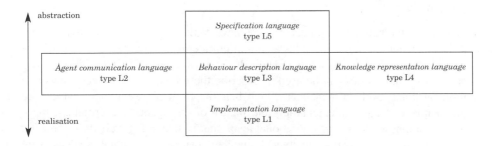

Figure 1.4   The various languages and formalisations involved in the realisation of MASs.

1.2.5 Languages, communications and representations

Computing is above all a matter of language and description. Computing programs cannot be designed without using a set of languages intended to represent, describe and implement computing structures and procedures. Designers of multi-agent systems thus make use of a large number of languages and formalisations in order to encompass all aspects of these systems. They can be grouped into four main categories, depending on whether we are interested in the implementation or formalisation of MASs, in representing the knowledge of agents, in defining their behaviour, or in their communications (Figure 1.4).

Type L1: Implementation languages

These are used for programming the multi-agent system. This covers the computing structures used for agents and for the environment (if it is simulated), the computing mechanisms making possible inter-agent and intra-agent parallelism, the efficient implementation of behaviours, the activities of transmitting and receiving messages, the perception of objects, and all the tools required for finalising an MAS. The languages most frequently used at this level are usually the classic programming languages such as Lisp, C/C++, Prolog, Java or Smalltalk, languages which already carry parallel execution mechanisms such as actors' languages (cf. Chapter 3), or even rules-based systems.

Type L2: Communication languages

These provide for interactions between agents (communicators) by means of data transmissions and reciprocal requests for information and services. For this reason, communication languages constitute the 'glue' making it possible for what may be heterogeneous agents to coordinate their actions, cooperate for a common goal, and come together to form an integrated group of agents. KQML (cf. Chapter 6) is a good example of such a language.

Type L3: Languages for describing behaviours and the laws of the environment

Describing the behaviour of agents or the laws of the universe for the environment in implementation languages adds a certain number of details which are necessary for comprehending the system, and which mask essential principles. This is why adapted formalisations can be used to describe these behaviours or these laws at a more abstract level, in a manner which benefits from representations which are independent of the implementation and nature of the agents. Nevertheless, these formalisations are still at an operational level, that is, they effectively describe *what is happening* in an abstract manner. Languages can be used which are based on production rules or, as we shall see in Chapter 3, benefit from the capacities for abstraction provided by the formalisations arising from automata or from distributed systems such as Petri nets. In Chapter 4, we shall be presenting the BRIC model in order to describe the behaviour of agents in a modular manner.

Type L4: Languages for representing knowledge

Languages for representing knowledge are used by cognitive agents to describe internal models of the world in which they move and to allow them to reason and to make predictions about the future on the basis of the data available to them. These languages are most frequently associated with logical systems, that is, with formal systems which have a syntax and semantics rigorously defined to make their inferences explicit. They serve not only to express the mental states of the agents and, in particular, to represent the content of their goals and their beliefs, but also to describe agents' behaviour. When the agents are simple and reactive, we may perhaps be able to do without this layer of language. But for cognitive agents, or for agents which are even slightly complex, the use of languages of this type is almost imperative. In this family, we essentially find AI languages, such as rules-based or blackboard-based languages, and languages for the structured representation of knowledge such as semantic nets (Lehmann, 1992) or 'frames' (Masini *et al.*, 1989).

Type L5: Formalisation and specification languages

On the most abstract level are the languages used on the one hand to formalise what is understood by multi-agent systems, by the notion of interaction, by the concept of intention and so on; and on the other hand to specify the conditions that have to be respected in the modelling and implementation of such systems. Languages of this type, which have developed from mathematics, thus have a 'meta' perspective in relation to other language families. We shall see in Chapter 4 in particular a formalisation of the notion of action and interaction in MASs and in Chapter 5 how certain formalisations arising out of modal logics make it possible to specify the conditions that should be fulfilled for intentional cognitive agents.

All these languages are obviously connected: a negotiations protocol, for example, will use a type L2 language, that is, a communications language, as a carrier for conversations, and a type L3 language to describe the mechanisms for the interpretation of messages and the functions of evaluating proposals put forward from one side or the other, with the second interpreting the statements of the first. The cognition elements and the reasoning mode of the agents can be represented in a type L1 language, the interpreter of this language being generally written in a type L3 language. Finally, the general functioning of the system, together with the conversational structure utilised, should respect specifications written in L4.

These languages need not be similar in form. The type L3 language can be C++; the type L1 language a rules-based language; the type L2 language may have a very special syntax; and the type L4 language may be a modal language arising from modal logic. But they may also resemble one another. If the type L3 language is Prolog, the type L1 and L4 languages ones arising from the logic of first order predicates, and the type L2 language one with a predicative syntax, then the general impression will be one of handling the same language all the time. However, this impression will be only very superficial, as all these forms of expression can be distinguished quite easily by their semantics, that is, by what they designate. In effect, while a programming language describes sequences of instructions enabling agents to execute their behaviour, a representation language takes its references from things the agent can know, and a communications language designates speech acts, as we shall see later. Finally, a specification language represents the conditions which must be respected by the entities present in the multi-agent universe.

1.3 A little history

The multi-agent approach lies at the crossroads of several disciplines. The two most important ones are *distributed artificial intelligence* (DAI), the purpose of which is to create organisations of systems capable of solving problems by means of reasoning most generally based on the manipulation of symbols; and *artificial life* (or AL), which seeks to understand and model systems possessing life, that is, capable of surviving, adapting and reproducing in sometimes hostile surroundings.

1.3.1 The early years

DAI was born in the United States, and took many forms. The first systems essentially explored the relationship existing between architecture and reasoning mode, and distinguished two types of control:

1. The first was organised around communication by the sharing of data, and gave rise to the drawing up of the model of the blackboard system. The work of F. Hayes-Roth, L. Erman and V. Lesser (Erman *et al.*, 1980) with Hearsay II formed the basis for all the later research in relation to this type of system. Starting from an automatic word comprehension application, they developed the metaphor of the blackboard, based on the idea that problem solving could result from the opportunistic activation of specialists, the KSs (knowledge sources), without its being necessary to define a control structure *a priori*. The activity of the KSs consists of putting down, modifying and withdrawing objects within a common working area, the blackboard, which structures the modelling of the application domain as the space available for hypotheses and solutions. A control device manages conflicts of access between the agents and organises their functioning. We shall give a slightly longer description of these architectures in Chapter 3.

Of the same order of ideas, the work of Kornfeld and Hewitt on Ether (Kornfeld, 1979) related to problem solving starting from the metaphor of scientific communities. Sprites, which have many points in common with the KSs of the preceding systems, put down facts, hypotheses and demonstrations in a common area similar to that of a blackboard. The difference essentially results from the fact that the sprites can be broken down into two categories, the defenders and the sceptics, with the first attempting to demonstrate that a hypothesis is true, and the second attempting to show that it is false by displaying examples that tell against it. Finally, there are sponsors which regulate the amount of time to be allocated to each sprite.

Although the general idea is very attractive, the resources brought to bear did not allow the general objectives to be met, as a certain confusion reigned between the architecture and the coordination technique. In effect, there was no definition of an organisation capable of demonstrating or rejecting hypotheses on the basis of considerations relating to architectural models and modes of communication. Since that time, DAI work relating to cooperation, the coordination of action and negotiation has liberated itself more and more from architectural constraints. However, these limitations should not mask the considerable influence of these systems on subsequent research in this field.

2. Work on the second type of control was originated by Lenat and Hewitt. In the 1970s, D. Lenat, the future author of the AM and Eurisko systems (Lenat and Brown, 1984) and the instigator of the CYC project (Lenat and Guha, 1990), developed a system called PUP6, which included a host of ideas, most of which were subsequently developed by other systems (Lenat, 1975). For perhaps the first time, PUP6 implemented the idea of problem solving by a community of specialists, called 'beings', working on the synthesis of a specific specialist – Concept Formation – capable of handling a task by itself. The user responds through a specialist to questions that cannot be resolved by the assembly. These specialists are not KSs, as they are continuously modified during execution. Each specialist is made up of an assembly of attribute/value pairings, similar to those of 'frames', and can ask for information from other specialists without having to know them. Actually, Lenat produced only a model of the general Beings system, the PUP6 application being limited to being capable of recognising an arch by using the program of P. H. Winston, which was particularly well known at the time.

Hewitt's work on actors, although initially done in relation to artificial intelligence, has, like many other projects, turned to programming. At the start of the 1970s, having designed a system, Planner, dedicated to demonstrating theorems, he realised that the issue of control was central to an understanding of the progression of a line of reasoning. Rather than considering this reasoning process as a sequence of choices, he tended to think in terms of distributed systems, considering control structures as patterns of message passing (Hewitt, 1977) between active entities called *actors*. So he had the idea of viewing problem solving as the activity of an assembly of experts, considering a reasoning process as a confrontation of points of view. These ideas gave birth to a whole range of languages for actors, characterised by their mode of communication through buffered asynchronous messages and continuation passing style. These languages are still considered as being good bases for the creation of multi-agent platforms. But the influence of this work extended well beyond DAI. Because of the impact of his actor model of computation on the development of concurrent programming and his visionary work on *open systems* (Hewitt, 1991), C. Hewitt is one of the most brilliant figures in the landscape of computer science in general and artificial intelligence in particular.

1.3.2 The classical age

In the phase that followed, which we might describe as the *classical age of DAI*, three systems had a considerable impact. The first, DVMT (Distributed Vehicle Monitoring Test), which was developed by V. Lesser's team at Massachusetts University (Lesser and Corkill, 1983), is a big research project on the perception and recognition of distributed situations. Sensors transmit data to processing agents, implemented in the form of blackboards. The problem for the agents consists of obtaining a coherent view of a road traffic situation, and thus of identifying and following vehicles on the basis of data – diffuse, contradictory and with sound effects – which they receive from the sensors. The interest of this study is particularly concentrated in the fact that a large number of configurations between the sensors and the processing agents have been examined, the issues of multi-agent planning have been analysed with the aid of partial plans, and the bases for cooperation and negotiation mechanisms have been defined. It also contributed in a general manner to the definition of DAI as a field of study in its own right. However, if DVMT had a considerable influence on the American community, it caused less of a stir in Europe than Mace.

Another of DAI's 'sacred monsters', the Mace system, developed by L. Gasser, had a considerable impact on all subsequent DAI research (Gasser *et al.*, 1987). For the first time, a clear explanation was given of how to create a DAI system, and what the essential components of a generic platform for developing DAI systems were. By linking his work to that done by Hewitt on actors, L. Gasser demonstrated not only that it was possible to create an MAS based on the concept of message transmission, but also that this was not enough, as a social organisation could not be condensed into a simple communications mechanism. It is also necessary to introduce concepts such as representations of others, and to arrange matters so that an agent can reason about its skills and its beliefs. Moreover, one should distinguish – as Mace did – between efficient skill, directly applicable know-how, and the knowledge an agent can have concerning its own skill. One can say that most current platforms for the development of MASs are direct or indirect descendants of Mace.

At the beginning of the 1980s, R. Smith developed a model for the distribution of tasks and problems called the *contract net*, which still has a lot of repercussions today. This was an opportunistic system for the allocation of tasks, based on the protocol of requests for bids for public contracts. By allowing each agent to be a manager or an executive, and by distributing requests over a net, R. Smith resolved the problem of task distribution without utilising a common memory area, as in the blackboard, and without having any need to identify the recipient of the message specifically, as in systems based on actors (Smith, 1979). Today, the contract net is a part of the traditional landscape of DAI studies. Its functioning is examined in Chapter 7.

In addition to these projects, we might also mention the work done by Steeb, Cammarata and F. Hayes-Roth at Rand Corporation (Cammarata *et al.*, 1983), where they studied the impact of several organisations on the resolution of cooperation problems, such as air traffic control, and especially the abundant harvest from the formalisation of cooperative action through concepts of belief intentions and obligation intentions, to which we shall return later.

A very good summary of DAI research carried out up to 1988 can be found in Bond and Gasser (1988).

1.3.3   The influence of artificial life

The history of artificial life is both longer and more recent. Longer, because its bedrock foundations go back into the history of computer science itself, with Von Neumann's work on cellular automata, Grey Walter's work on reactive robots, Warren McCulloch's work on the creation of formal neurones, or that of Ross Ashby on homeostasis (Dupuy, 1994); but also more recent in that it has existed as a field of study for only a few years. So we shall confine ourselves to giving a brief description of some key points in connection with artificial life, and leave readers to refer to Langton (1988); Langton *et al.* (1990); Langton (1994), Varela and Bourgine (1992), Meyer and Guillot (1989), Meyer *et al.* (1993) and Meyer and Wilson (1991) if they wish to know more about the topic, and to Heudin (1994) for a good introduction to the area. The issues of artificial life were introduced by C. Langton as 'the study of life as it might be and not of life as it is' – the latter being the preserve of classical biology. It was therefore a question of 'abstracting the underlying principles of the organisation of living things and implementing them in a computer so as to be able to study and test them' (Langton *et al.*, 1990). Nowadays, the field of artificial life extends over several main research topics, the most important of which can be listed as follows:

- analysis of the dynamics of complex phenomena with the aid of cellular automata or non-linear differential equations, carried out by Wolfram, Kaufman and Langton;

- evolution of populations through the use of genetic algorithms, the principal leaders in this area being Wilson and Koza;

- creation of animats, that is, autonomous creatures capable of acting, and thus of surviving, in a not entirely specified environment, the main representatives in this area being Brooks, Meyer and Husbands;

- study of collective phenomena based on the interaction of an assembly of reactive agents, the essential names here being Steels, Deneubourg, Mataric, Ferber and Drogoul.

This fourth topic is evidently the one most closely connected with the problems of kenetics, and we shall return to it repeatedly in this book, but all the others, in a general way, include work in which the idea of 'collective' figures.

In contrast to the work on DAI, which follows the cognitivist paradigm and considers that intelligence proceeds from the manipulation of symbols, artificial life puts the emphasis on behaviour, autonomy and, above all, the issue of viability.

J. P. Aubin, P. Bourgine and F. Varela have developed the idea of viability. For a being to remain alive, its state must remain within its area of viability, K, during its evolution; that is, if f is its evolution function, then:

$$s(t+1) = f(s(t)) \ with \ \forall s, f(s) \subseteq K$$

This can happen only for one of two reasons: either the entity is never in a configuration for which it was not created; or it can adapt as its evolution progresses, and can thus envisage viable behaviours by 'guessing' the subsequent state, that is, by being capable of displaying *abduction behaviour* (Varela and Bourgine, 1992).

In contrast to the cognitive approaches characteristic of DAI, those taken up by supporters of artificial life are minimalist and *sub-cognitive*. They are attempting to understand cooperation and coordination mechanisms on the basis of criteria not involving the intervention of symbols. The agents display behaviour of the stimulus/response type, their communications take place with the help of simple propagations of signals with no intrinsic significance, and in general they have no representations. This shows that it is possible to obtain complex collective behaviour without the agents themselves having any advanced faculties. Work in this area has therefore imparted a new vigour to the concept of the multi-agent system by allowing a stimulating dialogue between supporters of the 'cognitivist' and 'reactive' positions, and thus a better understanding to be reached of what belongs to each of them by right. We shall, of course, take account of this in this work, treating these two approaches as being on an equal footing.

To these two important areas we must add the influence of distributed systems on all aspects of communications and models of concurrency, and that of automation and robotics on the regulation of actions in a real universe.

1.3.4 Modern times

It is difficult to give an accurate and comprehensive view of current trends in MASs, as this field is expanding in several directions, with fundamental options which are sometimes very different from one another. We shall make no attempt here to give an exhaustive list of the research being done on this subject. We shall merely give a few reference points to assist in the understanding of current trends in research and of certain 'schools of thought' which are tending to form.

The American DAI school. The dominant school in DAI is certainly the American school, centred around Victor Lesser (Lesser and Corkill, 1983) and his 'disciples', Ed Durfee (Durfee *et al.*, 1987) and Susan Conry (Conry *et al.*, 1988) in particular. In addition to this group, some of the most important independent researchers are L. Gasser (1995), M. Huhns (1987) and K. Sycara (1989). The American DAI school, which tends to concentrate on the analysis of cognitive MASs made up of a small number of agents with very 'artificial intelligence' tendencies, has very few contacts with researchers specialising in reactive agents and, in particular, with the 'artificial life' community, although they are particularly numerous in that country (cf. above). By contrast, very strong links have been forged between DAI and the organisation sciences, especially through the efforts of K. Sycara and L. Gasser (Gasser, 1995) There is an excellent presentation of this school of thought (together with other approaches) and of the research carried out on DAI in this area until 1988 in Bond and Gasser (1988).

Rational agents. In addition to this DAI school, there is a very important school of thought which is essentially interested in the formalisation of autonomous rational agents. This school considers that the problem of interaction comes down to a problem of modifications to the mental states of the interlocutors. This research follows the theoretical trend started by Cohen and Levesque, which formalises intentions and beliefs on the basis of modal logics. The most important current members, Y. Shoham (1993), Georgeff and Rao (Rao and Georgeff, 1992; Rao, 1996), Jennings and Wooldridge (Wooldridge, 1994; Wooldridge and Jennings, 1994), Singh (1994) and Sadek (1992), supplement their theoretical approach with a practical dimension which leads them to create systems that implement their theories. The interaction standards (cf. Chapter 6) KQML (Finin *et al.*, 1994) and ACL came out of this approach. In Europe, this school's leading exponents are J. Galliers (1988), E. Werner (1989), C. Castelfranchi and R. Conte (Conte *et al.*, 1991), Wooldridge and Jennings (1994), and Coelho (Corrêa and Coelho, 1993), together with Chaib-Draa (1989) in Quebec.

Speech acts and MASs. The links between speech acts (cf. Chapter 6) and communications in multi-agent systems are very close. While theoretical work on the links between these two fields is being pursued (Moulin and Cloutier, 1994; Brassac, 1992), there is a very clear trend towards defining communications protocols efficiently with the help of the theory of speech acts, as shown by all the work done on the KQML standard (Finin *et al.*, 1994).

DAI and games theory. Essentially represented by J. Rosenschein (Zlotkin and Rosenschein, 1992) and by researchers who were his students, such as G. Zlotkin and S. Klaus, this school of thought was initially Israeli, but has since been the inspiration for quite a widespread trend in research from a point of view based on games theory and economic theories. A summary of this approach can be found in Rosenschein and Zlotkin (1994).

Petri nets and MASs. Essentially French, this research trend aims at making use of the theoretical tools of distributed systems, and of Petri nets in particular, for the analysis, design and validation of MASs. It includes notably the teams headed by P. Estraillier (Bachatène and Estraillier, 1992), J. Ferber (Ferber and Magnin, 1994), S. Pinson and S. Haddad (El Fallah-Seghrouchni and Haddad, 1994) and P. Azema (Vernadat and Azema, 1993).

Actors' languages and MASs. In the same vein as the preceding research, this trend is best exemplified by M. Tokoro (Maruichi *et al.*, 1990), T. Ishida (1989) and A. Yonezawa (1990) in Japan; S. Giroux (1993) in Réunion (initially in Quebec);

and P. Carle and J. Ferber (Ferber *et al.*, 1993) in France. It attempts to integrate research on parallelism in general and on actors' languages in particular with concepts and objectives connected with MASs.

Reactive agents. From R. Brooks to L. Steels via J.-L. Deneubourg, J. Ferber and A. Drogoul, Y. Demazeau, P. Bourgine and J. A. Meyer, those favouring this approach form part of the 'artificial life' scene referred to above.

Learning in multi-agent systems. While still a relatively new area in the field of multi-agent studies, learning and adaptation have developed considerably in recent years and have become an area of research in their own right. These aspects should become even more important in the years to come, since adaptation is so much a core characteristic of MASs. For a collection of recent articles, see Weiss and Sen (1996).

Scientific activities are concentrated in international conferences and workshops: the DAI Workshop in the United States, MAAMAW (Modelling Autonomous Agents in Multi-Agent Worlds) in Europe and MACC (Multi-Agent and Concurrent Computing) in Japan. These three conferences have come together to create an international conference, ICMAS (International Conference on Multi-Agent Systems). The first three ICMAS conferences were held in San Francisco (1995), Kyoto (1996) and Paris (1998). All the papers read at MAAMAW have been published in works which are easily obtainable (Boman and Van de Velde, 1997; Castelfranchi and Werner, 1994; Demazeau and Müller, 1990, 1991; Werner and Demazeau, 1992; Perram and Müller, 1996; Van de Velde and Perram, 1996). Only two of the American workshops have been the subject of publications (Gasser and Huhns, 1989; Huhns, 1987). There are also national conferences in most European countries. As regards the French-speaking countries, a conference known as French-Language Seminars on Distributed Artificial Intelligence and Multi-Agent Systems (Journées Francophones sur l'Intelligence Artificielle Distribuée et les systèmes Multi-Agents) brings the French-speaking scientific community together every year. Apart from the French representatives, this includes people from Belgium, Switzerland and Quebec, with individual researchers from Western Europe (Italy, Spain, Portugal), from West African countries (Senegal, Cameroon, Benin, Mali, Ivory Coast) and from Eastern Europe (especially Poland), all of whom speak French.

1.4 Areas of application

Areas of application for multi-agent systems are particularly numerous. We shall refer only to the main trends, as any attempt at an exhaustive list could only end in ossification, this being an area of research which is evolving all the time. We can divide applications for multi-agent systems into five main categories: problem solving in the broadest sense, collective robotics, multi-agent simulation, the construction of hypothetical worlds and kenetic design of programs (Figure 1.5).

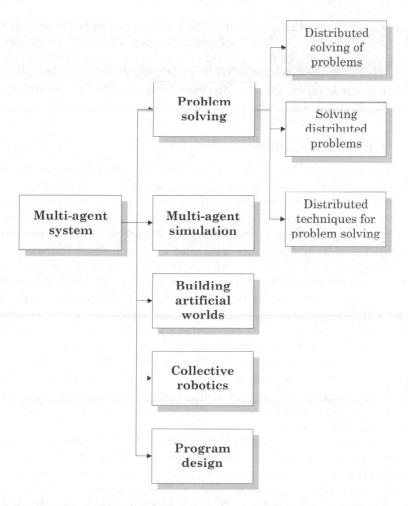

Figure 1.5   A classification of the various types of application for multi-agent systems.

1.4.1   Problem solving

Problem solving, in the broadest sense, actually concerns all situations in which software agents accomplish tasks which are of use to human beings. This category can be contrasted with the applications for collective robotics in the sense that the agents are purely computing agents, and have no real physical structure.

The Anglo-Saxon term for such techniques – 'distributed problem solving' – remains rather ambiguous. There are in fact two different meanings which translate differently into French – either 'résolution distribuée de problèmes' (distributed solving of problems) or 'résolution de problèmes distribués' (solving distributed problems). These two translations refer to two large classes of applications. In the first, the total expertise is distributed among all the agents, each having only restricted skills in relation to the complete problem to be solved. This form of application is also called 'cooperation between specialists'. In the second, it is the problem itself that is distributed, and the agents can have similar skills. Finally, another class of problem exists in which agents are used in interaction to solve classic problems, and I shall discuss these problems under the name of solving by coordination (cf. Chapter 8).

Distributed solving of problems

All applications covered by distributed solving of problems assume that it is possible to carry out a complex task by calling upon an assembly of specialists possessing complementary skills. So in this case the expertise or the solving mode is distributed, while the area of operations is not. When expertise is in fact so wide and complex that one person cannot possess it all, it is necessary to call upon several specialists, who must work together in pursuing a common objective.

For instance, when several specialists are required to build a racing car, one will be particularly well informed about engines, another will handle the selection and testing of the tyres, a third will concentrate on the chassis and the suspension, a fourth will know where to find the right fuels, and the last will be responsible for the race strategy and for defining the interfaces with the driver. These specialists cooperate with one another to solve a general problem such as a medical diagnosis, the design of an industrial product (Iffenecker and Ferber, 1992), the acquisition of knowledge, fault finding in nets (Jennings *et al.*, 1995), the recognition of shapes (Demazeau *et al.*, 1994), the understanding of natural language (Sabah, 1990), or the control and monitoring system for a telecommunications network (Weihmayer and Brandau, 1990).

The Condor system designed by C. Iffenecker at Télémécanique as an aid to the designing of electro-mechanical products provides a good example of an MAS oriented towards cooperation between specialists (Iffenecker, 1992). Specialists in specifications, design, assembly, materials, planning, marketing and many other things, who are taking part in the design of an industrial product, are represented in the form of an assembly of agents in the Condor system. These agents, which are of course cognitive, are designed to operate in a blackboard architecture (cf. Chapter 3) with three boards: knowledge of the field, control and communications.

All these agents have their own expertise and intervene at different stages in the creation of the product. The special feature of this system lies in its general organisation, which itself takes the form of a blackboard architecture. We can thus represent operational groups such as the 'qualification' group, the 'decision-making' group, or the 'drawing office' group, whose work is based on their own protocols for automation of the data flow, in the manner of current workflow systems.

The KBS-Ship system, which developed from an Esprit programme, is designed as a platform integrating several experts working on a common task. This system is dedicated to monitoring and maintaining equipment on a cargo vessel. It integrates several separate expert systems (piloting, freight loading, maintenance of electronic equipment, fault finding in case of failure and so on), which operate within a multi-agent architecture under the control of an expert responsible for managing communications via an Ethernet net and for resolving conflicts between agents.

In the field of industrial process control, the Flavors Paint Shop system used in the painting of lorries provides a fairly simple example of the interest multi-agents can have for industry (Morley, 1993) (the interesting features of this system were described in Parunak (1993)) and of their competitiveness by comparison with centralised approaches. When they leave the assembly line, the lorries have to be painted in a particular colour, depending on the customers' wishes. There are fewer paint stations than there are colours available. For this reason, it is sometimes necessary to change the colour at a paint station, which uses up a lot of time, and also a lot of paint.

Initially, the colour optimisation system was using a classic program which was very expensive to adjust and maintain. Moreover, very detailed planning was required which left little margin for any failures at these stations. The system was then rewritten in the form of a multi-agent system, in which each paint station was represented as an agent. When a station is free, it accepts a new lorry from a queue containing about a hundred lorries waiting to be painted. This selection is made on the basis of the following three rules:

(1)   Take the first lorry in the queue needing the colour that is currently available.

(2)   If there is no lorry that needs this colour, take the lorry with the highest priority and switch the station to the colour that lorry needs.

(3)   If no lorries have priority, take the next lorry in the queue and switch the station to the colour that lorry needs.

In spite of the simplicity of this system, it reduced the number of paint-change operations by half in comparison with the centralised system, which led to a saving of more than a million dollars a year. In addition, the system has no difficulty in allowing for failures at paint stations.

Solving distributed problems

If in addition the area in question is itself distributed, we refer to *(distributed) solving of distributed problems*. This refers essentially to applications such as analysis, identification, fault finding and the control of physically distributed systems for which it is difficult to obtain a totally centralised overall view. For example, if the task is to control a communications or energy network, the domain, which is represented by the network itself, constitutes a distributed system which needs to be monitored, indeed supervised, by decentralising the monitoring tasks within the nodes of the network as much as possible. Distributed perception, as it has been initiated by DVMT, where the monitoring of energy or telecommunications networks is distributed to each of the nodes, constitutes a good example of the solving of distributed problems.

The Ideal system, designed by Onera and Alcatel-Alsthom, is a characteristic example of an MAS dedicated to monitoring and fault finding in a telecommunications network. It comprises three sorts of agent: supervisors, with the task of locating failures and fault finding; follow-up agents, which have to maintain coherence between the real state of the network and the agents' view of it; and maintenance operators with the task of carrying out tests and repairs on elements of the network. The agents, which operate within a blackboard architecture (Chapter 3), consist of five modules: a communications module which manages the communications protocols; an expert module which contains knowledge concerning the supervision of the network; a cooperation module which manages the contacts tables (Chapter 5), the representation of themselves and model dialogues (Chapter 6); a module for the graphics interface enabling a user to follow the functioning of the agent and to intervene if necessary; and a control module which manages all the agent's activities.

Distributed techniques for problem solving

Agents can also be used, in a much more elementary way, for problem solving in the classic sense of the term, that is, for attempting to find a solution to a problem which has been well formulated and on which all the data is fully available: allocating tasks to a machine tool, for example, or defining how time should be used in a school, determining the sequence of actions to be carried out to get out of a labyrinth or to launch a rocket, assembling cubes or mechanical components, solving a puzzle or demonstrating a theorem.

In this case, the domain is not distributed. Nor is the expertise. And yet the multi-agent approach can impose a new mode of reasoning by breaking the problem down in a totally different way. For example, if the task is to stack cubes or to assemble mechanical components, the cubes or the components can be considered as agents which have to fulfil precise objectives laid down by the plan imposed by the designer, with the links as constraints which the agents must respect. This is exactly the type of problem that can be solved very efficiently by the eco-problem solving approach described in Chapter 8.

Likewise, if the task is to solve a constraints-based problem, we could adopt the view put forward by K. Ghedira (1993) and K. Sycara (Liu and Sycara, 1993) that the tasks and resources are agents which are trying to attain their own objectives: a task wants to be allocated, and a resource wants to be used to the best effect, without having too much or too little work. By adopting a technique similar to that used in eco-problem solving, and combining it with the principle of simulated annealing, K. Ghedira was able to solve constraints problems very rapidly and to limit the number of modifications involved in changing data.

These approaches to problems to be processed involve such a change in attitude that even specialists in problem solving are thrown completely off course by them at first. Moreover, they often do not exist in a very formal version, and it is therefore difficult to know *a priori* whether they are valid: are they decidable, semi-decidable, incomplete? Even if partial results are available, it is still difficult to decide in many cases. Their fundamental advantage lies in their speed of execution. Based on considerations which are very different from those adopted in classic approaches through state space exploration, they make far greater use of certain structural characteristics of problems, which often makes them more efficient. They have been utilised in particular in the field of collective robotics (cf. Section 1.4.4). We shall be considering some of these techniques in more detail in Chapter 8.

1.4.2   Multi-agent simulation

Simulation is a very active branch of computer science which consists of analysing the properties of theoretical models of the surrounding world. Physics, chemistry, biology, ecology, geography and the social sciences make particularly frequent use of simulations to try to explain or forecast natural phenomena. To do this, researchers in these various disciplines construct models of reality and then test their validity by 'running' them on computers. Generally, these models are set up in the form of mathematical relationships between variables representing physical values which can be measured in reality. The most frequently used models are differential equations, transition matrices and so on. They are based on the definition of a cause and effect relationship between the input variables and output variables. One of the famous examples used in ecology is that of the mathematical model of the dynamics of populations introduced by Lotka and Volterra (Volterra, 1926), which expresses the growth rates for populations of prey animals and predators occupying the same territory.

$$\frac{dN_1}{dt} = r_1 N_1 - P N_1 N_2 \qquad \frac{dN_2}{dt} = a P N_1 N_2 - d_2 N_2$$

where P is the coefficient of predation, N_1 and N_2 are the numbers of prey animals and predators, a is the efficiency with which the predators convert food into offspring, r_1 determines the fecundity of the prey animals and d_2 is the mortality rate of the predators. Although they have made numerous advances possible both in theory and practice (Pavé, 1994), these models and the associated numerical simulation techniques nevertheless do present certain problems, of which the main examples are listed here:

- *Sealed-off nature of level of analysis.* The mathematical models link up parameters which are all on the same level of analysis. For example, it is not possible to link the size of a population to the decisions taken by individuals. It can be said that these levels of analysis are 'sealed off', since it is not possible to make the behaviours executed at the 'micro' level correspond with the global variables measured at the 'macro' level.

- *Complexity and realism of parameters.* Considered in terms of usability and correspondence to reality, these equations often contain a large number of parameters which are difficult to estimate, and above all they lack realism.

For example, in the prey animal–predator model in the preceding equation, the coefficient, a, which indicates the efficiency with which the predators convert food into offspring, appears decidedly oversimplified when we think of all the complex behaviours (hierarchies and dominance, sexual strategies, use of territory and construction of shelters) that can have a direct impact on their fecundity.

- *Difficulty of modelling action.* Perhaps the most serious criticism which can be levelled at the current mathematical models is that it is difficult (or even impossible) to take into account the actions of individuals, and thus the effective modifications to the environment which flow from their behaviour. Most collective phenomena (consider stock exchange phenomena, for example) are the result of a set of decisions taken by individuals who take into account the behaviour of other actors in the system. If we consider actions only in terms of their measurable consequences at the global level, or of their probability of appearance, it will be difficult to explain phenomena emerging from the interaction of these individual behaviours, in particular all those relating to intra- and interspecific cooperation.

- *Qualitative deficiency.* By their very nature, digital simulations can consider only quantitative parameters, and seem helpless when faced with the host of qualitative data collected by researchers on the ground – by naturalists in particular. Faced with the intricacies involved in the balancing of relations between the behavioural habits of species and their mechanisms of reproduction and occupancy of space, mathematical models give up the struggle, and thus leave many fields of research unable to benefit from the advantages that simulation can confer.

Multi-agent systems bring a radically new solution to the very concept of modelling and simulation in environmental sciences, by offering the possibility of directly representing individuals, their behaviour and their interactions. Multi-agent simulation is based on the idea that it is possible to represent in computerised form the behaviour of entities which are active in the world, and that it is thus possible to represent a phenomenon as the fruit of the interactions of an assembly of agents with their own operational autonomy. For example, in a multi-agent population model, individuals will be directly represented in the form of agents, and the number of individuals in a given species will be the result of the confrontations (cooperation, struggle, reproduction) of the behaviours of all the individuals represented in the system.

The interest that these simulations hold is that of being able to consider both quantitative parameters (that is, digital parameters) and qualitative parameters (individual behaviours which may call on strategic reasoning). We therefore sometimes use the term *micro-analytical models* (Collins and Jefferson, 1991) or *individual-centred simulation* to indicate clearly that the representations are at the level of the individual, and that individuals are interacting both with one another and with the simulated environment. These are constructions producing 'artificial micro-worlds', for which it is possible to control all their characteristics and to reproduce series of experiments, as if we were dealing with laboratory situations. We are thus in the presence of analogue modelling, similar to the small-scale models used in aeronautics or shipbuilding, the essential difference stemming from the fact that the small-scale model takes the form of a computing entity and not of a physical structure.

For this reason, anyone using such a simulator has an active role. The researcher employs a multi-agent system as if it were a miniature laboratory, moving individuals around, changing their behaviour and modifying the environmental conditions. Each agent is of course 'tagged', as a natural being could be, but tagging is obviously easier, since the individual can be followed up at any moment in its evolution in as much detail as is desired. So we are making use of the capacities of computers to process the data obtained, bringing them together and utilising them with the aid of statistical techniques in order to verify the hypotheses put forward. Thus, in contrast to the classic approaches, multi-agent simulation does not boil down to implementing a model and then analysing the response from this model as against the input parameters, but participates in the process of searching for models.

The main qualities of multi-agent modelling are its capacity for integration and its flexibility. It is in fact possible to integrate within the same model quantitative variables, differential equations and behaviours based on symbolic rules. It is also very easy to integrate modifications, each enhancement of the model being brought about by adding behavioural rules which operate at the individual level. In addition, as individuals are always different from one another, it is possible to add new types of agents with their own model of behaviour, who come to interact with the agents already defined. For example, in a forest model, we can introduce new animal or vegetable species and analyse their interactions with those already modelled.

Finally, multi-agent systems make it possible to model complex situations whose overall structures emerge from interactions between individuals, that is, to cause structures on the macro level to emerge from models on the micro level, thus breaking the level barrier which is so flagrant in classical modelling. Let us take a look at two characteristic multi-agent simulation systems which are the result of collaboration between computer specialists and ecological researchers. It is of course obvious that there are a great many other applications for behavioural simulation, but these two, together with the Manta system developed in Chapter 7, provide a glimpse of the varied domains in which MASs can be employed.

SIMDELTA

The Simdelta simulator has been used to summarise the knowledge of a set of specialists (experts on fish, ecologists, pedologists, biologists, anthropologists and so on) who have spent many years studying the fisheries of the central Niger delta in Mali. The idea was to find a way of modelling both quantitative data (concerning the evolution of the Niger's floods, for example) and qualitative data (such as fishing techniques).

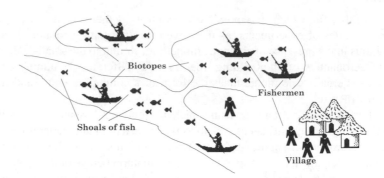

Figure 1.6 The artificial world of Simdelta.

This simulator, created by F. Bousquet and C. Cambier (Cambier *et al.*, 1992) makes it possible to simulate both the dynamics of the fish population – taking into account the numerous biological and topological factors which may affect its evolution – and the decision making of the fishermen. The agents here are the shoals of fish and the fishermen. The technique employed brings into being three types of agents (Figure 1.6): the biotopes, which represent portions of the environment; the fish, which exhibit behaviour that tends to be reactive; and the fishermen, who behave like cognitive agents. The environment is made up of biotopes, the links between which can be dynamically modified when the water level changes. For each biotope, a resource function indicates the amount of food available for a population of fish, plotted against time. The shoals are agents which represent assemblies of fish, and whose parameters (size and number of eggs, migration process, diet, and so on) characterise their adaptation strategy.

Each fisherman is represented in the form of a cognitive agent, and his behaviour is described by a system based on knowledge put together from a database which contains his fisherman's beliefs and memory and from a system of rules which represents his cognitive strategy for exploiting the biotopes.

Two series of experiments were carried out. The first related to the study of the population dynamics of the fish, plotted against the continuous growth in fishing. The simulation of the dynamics of these fish was based on the behaviour of Sahelian fresh-water fish, in particular on what biologists knew of their reproduction, growth, migration and mortality. This simulation made it possible to reproduce a curve divided into three characteristic phases showing the evolution of a restricted fishing system and, above all, to bring out variations relating to the specific composition of the fish population and the size of the fish.

The second series of experiments was intended to model the fishermen who were taking decisions and acting on the renewable resource. This model demonstrated the importance of the decision-making mechanism in relation to the dynamics of the fish. Strategies based on criteria of economic rationality are notably less effective overall in the long term than those that integrate rules for access to space (Bousquet *et al.*, 1993; Cambier, 1994).

SIMPOP

If mobile entities can naturally profit by the advantages of multi-agent simulations, the same is true for fixed agents. The example of the Simpop system is a good illustration of this (Bura *et al.*, 1993). The plan here was to create a model of the dynamics of evolution of a system of towns and, more specifically, of the genesis, development and concentration of urban functions at different levels over a long period of time (about 2000 years).

The environment is represented by a set of 'places' of various sizes and shapes (essentially squares and hexagons). They are characterised by their nature (plains, mountains, sea, marsh), their natural resources (agriculture, fishing, minerals) and miscellaneous elements such as the presence of a means of communication (river, road and so on). The resources correspond to the potential that a population can exploit, productivity depending on factors such as technical possibilities or the activity of a neighbouring centre of population.

Each place comprises a 'populated area' agent which is frequently referred to as a town (in fact these 'towns' can be anything from a simple hamlet to a great metropolis). The towns are characterised by the size of their populations, their economic wealth and the functions they have (agriculture, economy, industry, administration). The behaviour of a town is determined from the sum of the behaviours of its inhabitants, the latter being represented by economic functions corresponding to the principal social groups. For example, the majority of the population in the hamlets is associated with the agricultural function.

The towns are therefore the main agents in the system and, because they do not move, interactions take place essentially through transfers of goods, money,

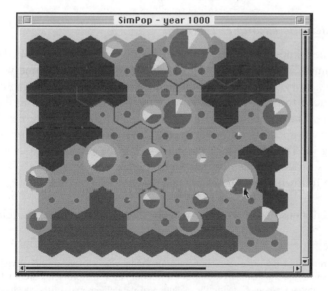

Figure 1.7 State of a populated area after a thousand simulated years in Simpop.

services and inhabitants, which are expressed in the form of mechanisms of supply and demand between towns. As a result, certain towns tend to expand, and numerous local phenomena come into play to reinforce the differences appearing between them in such a way as to form what is referred to as a 'hierarchy' of towns, affecting their size and wealth, as shown in Figure 1.7.

1.4.3 The construction of synthetic worlds

Although we are not talking here about applications in the strict sense, as they do not enable anyone to solve specific problems, do not use physical agents and do not simulate any real world, the construction of synthetic worlds plays a big part in research into multi-agent systems because it makes it possible to analyse certain interaction mechanisms in a more detailed way than a real application could do. For example, the analysis of a cooperation protocol, or the understanding of the influence of behaviour on the regulation of a society, can often be more thorough in 'virtual' worlds than in applications which are of immediate benefit.

In addition, because of the diversity of multi-agent systems and the number of fields in which they can be used, it is very important to define situations demonstrating the problems dealt with and the difficulties encountered by a kenetic approach. Some of these situations are *toy situations*, that is, situations which, in extreme cases, have been stripped of all the rough aspects of reality but which, because of their austerity, provide ideal conditions for a good understanding of the mechanisms brought into action. Others correspond to real situations, even if their expression is often simplified so that we can grasp what is at issue in, and understand the use of, multi-agent systems in full-size applications.

A characteristic example: the hunt

One of the best-known examples is that of the hunt (which is also called the problem of prey animals and predators[†]). This problem comes from a game which is itself taken from a story, *Red October*, in which a Soviet submarine has to try to escape from American torpedo boats. Of course, the situation analysed in the game is a little simpler. The agents, that is, the prey animals (submarines or herbivores), like the predators (torpedo boats or carnivores), move over a space represented in the form of a grid. The objective of the game is for the predators to capture the prey animals by surrounding them, as shown by Figure 1.8.

The following hypotheses are laid down:

(1)   The dimensions of the environment (that is, of the grid) are finite.

[†]There is a problem of the same name in population ecology, as we saw in the previous section. But although predators and prey animals are involved in both cases, the problems are totally different: in theoretical ecology, we are interested in the evolution of the demography of the agents, whereas in the hunt version we are studying the mechanisms whereby predators cooperate to surround the prey animals.

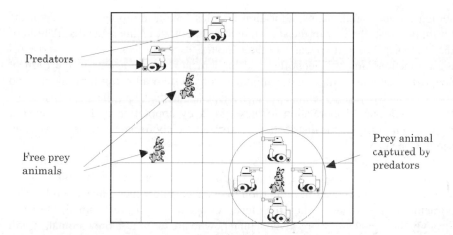

Figure 1.8 The hunt game: the predators have to surround the prey animals in order to capture them.

(2) The predators and prey animals move at fixed speeds and generally at the same speed.

(3) The prey animals move in a random manner by making what are called Brownian movements, that is, they select a random position at each moment.

(4) The predators can use the corners and edges to block a prey animal's path.

(5) The predators have a limited perception of the world that surrounds them, which means that they can see the prey animal only if it is in one of the squares at a distance within their field of perception.

There are obviously several variations of this game. The world can be made unlimited, for example by folding back the edges in such a way that an agent leaving the board to the east comes back from the west; or the speeds of movement of the prey animals and the predators can be made different; or again the prey can be made to move in a less random way, for example in trying to reach a specific square. With any of these variations, the predators' strategies will be comprehensively modified. Finally, the respective numbers of prey animals and predators, and of course the predators' quality of perception, are also important parameters for success in making captures (Benda *et al.*, 1986; Gasser *et al.*, 1989; Bouron, 1992).

The problem consists in coordinating the actions of the predators so that they can surround the prey animals as fast as possible, a surrounded prey animal being considered as dead. The interesting thing about this problem is that it is very well defined and yet leaves open all possible modes of cooperation. In fact, several strategies can be brought to bear, and this example provides a good illustration of the differences in approach between cognitive systems and reactive systems.

Cognitive strategies generally proceed from a top-down analysis by defining the different functions that the system has to carry out: detection of prey animals, setting up of hunting teams, allocation of roles (taking the prey animal from the north, the west, the east or the south), reorganisation of teams if the distribution of the hunters is wrong (two teams of three hunters each, for example), and so on. All these functions are well identified and implemented in the agents in the form of adapted behaviours requiring a communications system allowing for dialogue and for distributed decision making. We then suppose that the agents have goals and that they act reasonably in relation to these goals by appointing a 'leader' agent if necessary to organise the distribution of work and to coordinate actions, as we shall see in Chapter 8.

The creation of a reactive system to solve this problem starts from a completely different approach. Let us suppose that the prey animals emit a signal, whose intensity decreases in proportion to distance, and which plays the role of an attractor for the hunters. Then the closer an agent is to a prey animal, the more strongly the signal will be received. Hunters who are close to a prey animal, P, will therefore be more likely to move towards P than towards any more distant prey animal whose emissions they might register. In addition, so that the hunters shall not all find themselves at the same place, and so that they shall effectively surround the prey animal, we arrange for each hunter to emit a signal which acts a repellant for the other hunters. Thus each hunter is at one and the same time attracted by the prey animals and (weakly) repelled by the other hunters (Figure 1.9). The capture of the prey animals thus emerges from the combination of these different reactions to the stimuli sent out by the prey animals and the hunters. We can say that, while the cooperation induced by cognitive agents is of the *intentional* type, since they are capable of dialogue and of allocating explicit tasks, reactive agents introduce another type of cooperation which can be described as *reactive* and which appears as a simple side effect of the individualistic behaviour of each agent.

The animat: half robot, half animal

These hypothetical worlds are often based on two metaphors which are virtually interchangeable: that of the robot and that of the animal. In the first case, we

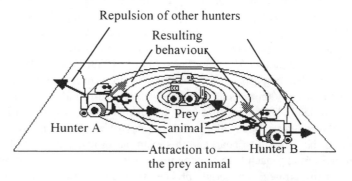

Figure 1.9   The hunters are attracted by the prey animals and repelled by the other hunters.

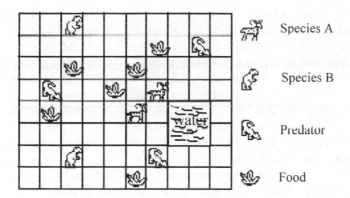

Figure 1.10   A world characteristic of the animat approach: an assembly of individuals of different species are trying to survive.

suppose that the agents are robots which are accomplishing their actions in a virtual world. But these robots have no physical reality, and calling them robots is therefore misleading. Moreover, they are given the possibility of accomplishing actions such as reproducing with other robots, which it would be very difficult to ask real beings made of metal and electronics to carry out! From another angle, calling these creatures animals is no more realistic than calling a character in an adventure game 'human', since these pretend animals bear only a distant relation to those we meet in nature. This is why J.-A. Meyer and S. Wilson invented the term *animat* – a contraction of the words 'animal' and 'artefact' (Meyer and Guillot, 1989) – to indicate clearly both that these agents are metaphorically descended from animals and that they have only a virtual existence, the one with which they are kindly provided by the imagination of their creator (and of his or her colleagues) as displayed by the visual traces of some computing procedures.

So there are a large number of situations which can feature an assembly of animats in an environment generally represented in the form of a set of squares, with no other objective than to satisfy their needs to consume food, to drink and to reproduce. Figure 1.10 represents a typical snapshot of such a world. We shall see further examples of the behaviour of animats – in Chapter 5 in particular – as they explore their space in order to extract from it the nutritive elements necessary for their survival while avoiding the predators.

Explorer robots descending on Mars

If the metaphor is used to highlight the 'robot' side rather than the 'animal', it is possible to invent a whole range of behaviours which differ from the survival of an animal, such as the action of collecting ore.

To begin with, this all started with a real application. When NASA decided to invest in a space project with the aim of exploring the planet Mars, it was clear that this exploration could first be carried out only with the aid of robots. But radio transmissions take at least 3 to 5 minutes[†] to travel from Mars to the Earth because of the distance involved – much too long a time for it to be possible to operate the robots by remote control from the Earth. The robots would therefore have to be autonomous, that is, capable of winning through by using their own resources in a universe which might be hostile. NASA then decided to finance some research making it possible to design and build such autonomous robots.

At this point, Brooks came upon the scene and put forward the idea of an invasion of Mars by a large number of inexpensive little robots with very simple capabilities (Brooks, 1990). In this case, the coordination of actions between the robots becomes crucial, and can therefore be envisaged from a multi-agent perspective. J.-L. Deneubourg (Deneubourg *et al.*, 1986) and L. Steels (1989) then advanced the idea, each on his own behalf, that it was possible to carry out tasks efficiently using robots whose behaviour resembled that of ants. By first simulating them and then building real robots, they showed that it was indeed possible to create groups of reactive robots, whose behaviour was an exact copy of animal behaviour. The collaboration between L. Steels and D. McFarland, a well-known ethologist (McFarland, 1990), like that undertaken by A. Drogoul and myself with biologists specialising in animal behaviour (Drogoul *et al.*, 1992), is characteristic of the fusion of viewpoints that can occur between the life sciences and the sciences of the artificial, notably computer science and robotics. Since that time, many laboratories connected with these last two sciences have taken up the challenge, and are working on the definition of societies of autonomous robots which would be effective in conditions similar to those of Martian exploration.

The problem of collecting ore samples particularly caught the attention of researchers, as it defines an immediately comprehensible toy situation, one for which it is possible to compare different types of cooperative organisation. The general problem can be described like this. We suppose that a base exists which is fixed (or has very little mobility), from which several mobile robots have to set out to explore a space which is *a priori* unknown (we are supposing that no maps of the terrain exist) in order to find and recover ore, and transport this ore back to the base. So the problem consists in defining the structure and behaviour of the robots, together with the organisation of the society, in such a way as to obtain the best possible results in terms of the time taken by the set of robots to collect as much ore as possible (Figure 1.11).

To solve such a problem, we have to go through the following stages:

(1) Defining the different types of robot to be built: should it be supposed that they are identical or should it be supposed that they are specialised? It is perhaps preferable to define specialist ore-transporting robots whose detection capacities are weaker than those of generalist robots, but which can transport larger loads.

[†]This takes into account only travel in one direction. If the reaction to a dangerous situation came from the Earth, the time between the moment when the situation was perceived by the robot and the time it received its commands would at least double.

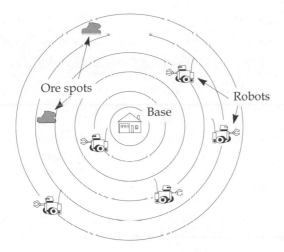

Figure 1.11   The explorer robots.

(2)   Determining the cognitive capacities of the agents: can they memorise the terrain they cross and make maps? Are they purely reactive, and capable only of local perceptions, or can they communicate with one another by sending messages over long distances?

(3)   Describing the collective work structures: do they work in a group or on their own? Are the teams fixed or dynamic? Can they obtain assistance, and if so how? Or do they have to rely exclusively on their own resources?

(4)   Defining the cooperation mechanisms and the interaction protocols allowing the agents to accomplish their work collectively and reducing the number of potential conflicts. For example, what happens when two robots discover a heap of ore at the same time?

(5)   Being capable of evaluating the choices made and comparing them with other types of organisation.

The idea of this 'application' is therefore to raise all the problems that might be posed during the creation of a multi-agent system within the context of a situation which is easy to apprehend and evaluate. We shall return to this example in Chapter 3 and analyse some possible types of organisation for solving this problem. As well as problems of hunting and exploration, numerous situations exist which bring into operation the robot animals called animats, which can act as a point of departure for the analysis and comprehension of multi-agent systems. We shall refer to three types: house-moving robots, the production workshop, and builder robots. All these examples except the last one have more to do with science fiction than with industrial reality at present, but they offer the advantage of presenting relatively complex situations which handle problems of cooperation and coordination of actions.

House-moving robots

Let us suppose that you wish to move house and go to live somewhere else. You have at your disposal a team of robots capable of carrying furniture and transporting fragile objects, as well as a certain number of autonomous vehicles. How can the robots be programmed in such a way that you move house under good conditions, that your movers do not drop your grand piano and do take good care of your china vases? The type of behaviour required is very similar to that required for the exploration of Mars. To this we can add some constraints relating to the nature of the objects (some furniture may be too heavy for one robot to carry alone) and to the topology of the environment (the corridors are narrow and it is sometimes impossible for two robots to pass each other; the layout of the rooms in the house and of the road system can be complicated, and so on). These constraints apply even if the problem of exploring the terrain can be done away with by supposing that the location and topology of the two houses are known.

An autonomous production workshop

Building an autonomous production cell is a particularly interesting means of testing hypotheses relating to the different ways of designing multi-agent systems. The problem can be defined like this. Let us suppose that we have to create manufactured products, $A_1,...,A_k$, using a set of machine robots, $M_1,...,M_n$, and batches of raw material, $P_1,...,P_j$, and that we have a set of transporter robots, $T_1,...,T_m$, to carry the intermediate products from one machine to another. If we know that the raw material arrives at one end of the production workshop, and that the manufactured products leave at the other end, how do we organise this production unit so that it can react to any modification in demand? Even if this problem closely resembles an operational research problem, it is nevertheless different in that it is necessary not just to predict the best way of arranging the various units in the workshop, but also to define the programs for each of these units in such a way that they can work together, and thus coordinate their work by reacting to any failures, while causing the fewest possible problems for overall production.

1.4.4 Collective robotics

Collective robotics relates to the creation not of a single robot, but of an assembly of robots, which cooperate to accomplish a mission. Collective robotics differs from the field covered by the previous application (the construction of hypothetical worlds) in using concrete agents which move in a real environment. The domain of distributed robotics actually takes in two very distinct types of robotics, cellular robotics and mobile robotics:

1. *'Cellular' robotics* relates to building robots on a modular basis. In this context, a robot will be considered as a multi-agent system, and each of its constituent parts will be regarded as an agent. The creation of a movement will thus be the result of

coordination involving an assembly of agents. Techniques similar to those which we shall look at in connection with eco-solving (Chapter 8) make it possible to accomplish complex gestures with a minimum of computation. On the basis of similar ideas, the research carried out in parallel by J. Perram's team in Denmark (Overgaard *et al.*, 1994) and D. Duhaut's team in France (Regnier and Duhaut, 1995) has produced models for the movement of manipulating arms in which each element in the arm is considered as an agent, with the articulations describing constraints on the set of acceptable movements (Figure 1.12). The head agent attempts to achieve the goal which has been set for it, for example to weld two components together or to pick up an object on a table. If it can do it itself, it makes the movement and the system comes to a halt. If not, it brings in the next agent (agent A on the diagram), giving it goals which will help the head agent to get nearer to its objective. The process is repeated recursively, each agent trying to achieve the goals set for it by transmitting its desiderata to the next agent.

The computations can be simply expressed and are carried out very rapidly. In addition, the increase in the number of degrees of freedom (that is, the number of articulations), as against the classical techniques used in robotics, means the problem can be solved more quickly. This type of model is sufficiently flexible to be used efficiently in industrial environments. J. Perram's system, for example, is used to program welding robots in the Odense shipyards.

2. *Mobile robotics* uses at least two robots, which have to coordinate their movements and cooperate in accomplishing tasks such as cleaning the floor, monitoring buildings, intervening to help people, repairing ducts or exploring distant or dangerous spaces. For the moment, all these projects tend to be at the research stage, but numerous contributions have been made in this field, in particular by M. Mataric (1994), L. Steels (1994) and J.-L. Deneubourg (Beckers *et al.*, 1994).

The coordination of vehicles, whether they be aircraft, cars or ships, also falls within this area of application. When several vehicles are on the move, there is

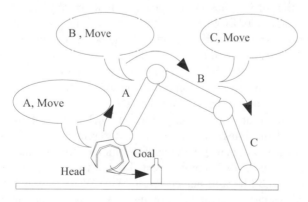

Figure 1.12   A manipulator arm considered as a multi-agent system.

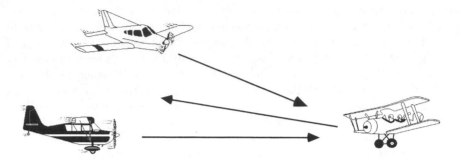

Figure 1.13 The problem of avoiding collisions. How can these aircraft cross each other's paths without a smash-up, while still preserving their initial objectives?

a risk that they will get in each other's way. For example, two aircraft moving in adjacent sectors, or two cars on the same road, have to be careful not to run into each other. The risk of a collision grows greater the nearer the vehicles are to each other and the more their trajectories lead them to cross each other's paths. It then becomes a question of coordinating their movements in such a way that each of them can go where it wants to go without having a collision (Figure 1.13).

In a variation of this problem, some vehicles are requested to advance in formation, in the manner of wild geese or squadrons of aircraft. The problem then becomes more complicated, since the vehicles have to move together in such a way that the structure of the formation remains constant. The first attempts to find a solution were made in the field of air traffic control and made use of cognitive agents (Cammarata *et al.*, 1983; Chaib-Draa, 1989), but with very limited results. The more up-to-date approaches (Zeghal *et al.*, 1993) use reactive agents and field force mechanisms, as we shall explain in Chapter 8.

1.4.5   Kenetic program design

Thus the ambition of kenetics is to advocate a new mode of design for computer systems which attempts to go beyond the current data processing techniques to create distributed software functioning with great flexibility and with a great capacity to adapt to the environment. So the objective of what I shall call *kenetic software design* is to give birth to computing systems capable of evolving through the interaction, adaptation and reproduction of relatively autonomous agents functioning in physically distributed universes.

The spread of large-scale computing nets such as the Internet, the extension of local nets and the integration of data as different as text, images, sound or animation still leave untouched the crucial question of the automated utilisation of this information. It is really becoming very difficult to know where you are in this gigantic spider's web (the well-named World Wide Web), in which every node is a computing and resources server functioning in a relatively autonomous way with regard to the others. No one is in overall charge of the whole system – which is anyway unmanageable – but each node is responsible for its own data and for the links it may have with other nodes.

Kenetics proposes a new technology for creating software, based on the concepts of agents and interaction. For example, each program unit can take the form of an agent which has its own autonomy and its own objectives and which 'lives' on the net, like an animal in a natural ecosystem, and cooperates or negotiates with other units of the same kind. The users then become 'shepherds', giving instructions to their flock of agents and subsequently harvesting the fruits of their labour. This metaphor, which still sounds like science fiction, has every chance of becoming a reality in the near future, as the basic technologies needed for this evolution in programming already exist. So we shall soon see 'agents' appearing – simple ones at first, still with little autonomy but quickly becoming more elaborate and complex – to help users in their daily tasks by gathering data, managing encounters and administering common tasks, offering services to and requesting services from other agents, and doing all this in an integrated and natural way.

The concept of an agent circulating in a net constitutes only one of the facets – perhaps the most visible – of kenetic program design. The other important area is the architecture of the programs themselves. If, for the moment, design by objectives appears to be the universal panacea for the writing of programs (Booch, 1991; Ferber, 1990), it is in fact only a step towards an even more 'modular' conception of writing software. Each component of a program can be envisaged as an agent, with its own skills and its own goals, and with all the agents attempting to respond to the needs of the user and to the new extensions that continually appear.

One of the systems best known in Europe for having tried to provide an operational framework for these ideas is the Archon system (Architecture for Cooperating Heterogeneous On-line Systems), which grew out of an Esprit project that puts forward a general multi-agent system architecture for integrating different programs which have to cooperate with one another (Burg and Arlabosse, 1994; Wittig, 1992). The general architecture of the system is shown in Figure 1.14. The 'head' of an agent comprises a high-level communications manager which is based on the recommendations of the OSI standard, a model of its own and others' skills in the form of a contacts manager (cf. Chapter 5) and a planning and coordination system. A monitor provides the interface and the management functions between the 'head' and the body of an agent consisting of a set of tasks, each corresponding to a pre-existing software module. It is thus possible to encapsulate existing programs with the help of Archon agents and so forge cooperation between heterogeneous programs which initially did not cooperate. The Archon system has been tested in numerous industrial configurations, in particular for the monitoring of electrical power distribution networks and the analysis of particle accelerator failure. There is now a truly industrial software, marketed by the French company Framentec. The reference (Jennings, 1994) gives a detailed presentation of how this system functions[†].

[†]Although the system presented in this work is called Grate, it can be used as a description of Archon.

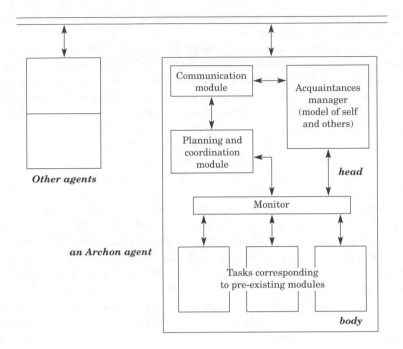

Figure 1.14 General architecture of the Archon system.

1.5 Principal aspects of kenetics

Designing a multi-agent system consists primarily in analysing and solving a very large number of problems. Designing an anti-collision system, for example, raises a large number of questions which relate to very diverse fields. How do the agents perceive their environment and the other agents? How do they cooperate? Can they ensure their viability? Are they capable of adapting their behaviour to modifications in the ambience in which they move? Are they arranged in a hierarchy, or do some of them have authority over others? These different questions can be classified into five main categories: the issues of action, the agent and its relationship to the world, interaction, adaptation, creation and implementation of MASs.

1.5.1 The issues of action

Problems of action are often not considered in much detail, as they involve a subtle question which gives the impression of being easy to solve, whereas it actually raises numerous difficulties. The question can be put like this: how can several agents act simultaneously, and what are the consequences of their actions on the environment? The answer looks obvious. The state of the environment is the direct consequence of the combination of actions carried out by the agents. But how are these agents combined? How does it happen that an agent which decides to advance and finds an obstacle in its way cannot move? How can two agents come into collision or, conversely, avoid a collision? How do environmental constraints combine with the actions of agents? All these questions raise important theoretical problems, which have to be brought up as soon as situated agents are put to work, or as soon as there is any attempt at multi-agent planning.

1.5.2 The individual and its relationship with the world

The different topics concerning the individual relate on the one hand to its architecture and its internal organisation, and on the other hand to all the means it uses to ensure its viability and meet its objectives. These are obviously essential topics, since the creation of a multi-agent system necessarily involves the description of the architecture of the agents and the functionalities available to them for accomplishing their tasks.

It is at this level that we are interested in the cognitive elements, the organisation of which makes it possible to set up adapted behaviour. Except for simple reactive agents, any agent will, at a certain time, be in a certain 'mental state' which results from its own history, its perception of the world, and its interactions with the world and with other agents. These mental states are often very complex and involve a large number of elements, the combination of which explains the behaviour of an agent 'from within'.

These cognitive elements, which we shall refer to as *cognitons* in Chapter 5, are to the mental states of the agents what the elementary corpuscles are to physical bodies: basic components, the combination of which makes it possible to express the mental state of an agent, and the laws governing the interaction of which serve to describe the future evolution of the behaviour of an agent and its subsequent mental states. They govern all aspects of the internal activity of an agent: perception and execution of actions, beliefs, desires and tendencies, intentions, methods and plans, and so on. It is at this level too that obligations are described. By undertaking to carry out an action for a third party, the agent restricts the set of actions it can perform and gives the third party the possibility of planning its own behaviour by reducing its uncertainty about future states.

1.5.3 Interaction

For an agent, interacting with another is at once the source of its power and the origin of its problems. It is in fact because they cooperate that agents can accomplish more than the sum of their actions, but it is also because there are so many of them that they have to coordinate their actions and resolve conflicts. For an agent, the other is simultaneously the worst and the best of things.

Handling the problem of interaction means providing oneself with the means not only of describing the elementary mechanisms allowing agents to interact, but also of analysing and designing the different forms of interaction that agents can execute to accomplish their tasks and achieve their goals. First of all, agents have to be capable of using communication not just to transmit information but, most importantly, to induce specific behaviour in others. Communicating is thus a special form of action which, instead of being applied to the transformation of the environment, tends to modify the mental state of the recipient. For example, asking another to carry out a task tends to create in the other an intention to accomplish this task, and thus constitutes a way of achieving a goal without carrying out the task oneself.

The different forms of interaction which we shall be studying in greater detail are collaboration (cf. Chapter 7) and coordination of actions (cf. Chapter 8). In respect of the former, we are concerned with the manner in which work is distributed among several agents, whether the techniques in question are centralised or distributed. In respect of the latter, we analyse the way in which the actions of the different agents have to be organised in time and space so as to achieve goals. Finally, when conflicts arise, it is important to be able to limit the effects. Negotiation techniques thus serve to satisfy the parties involved by establishing compromises or by transcending the conflict.

Cooperation is the general form of interaction studied most in multi-agent systems (Ferber, 1995). Crucially, we shall see that, in contrast to the common-sense view of cooperation as the prerogative of beings capable of having an explicit project, and thus of cognitive agents, it is possible to talk about cooperation in both a reactive and a cognitive manner if we look only at the result of actions and not at the intention of the agents. To put it more simply, the problem of cooperation can be condensed down to determining who does what, when, by what means, in what way and with whom; to solving, in other words, the different sub-problems which make up collaboration by task distribution, coordination of actions and resolution of conflicts. We can sum this up through the formula:

$$\text{Cooperation} = \text{collaboration} + \text{coordination of actions} \\ + \text{resolution of conflicts}$$

1.5.4 Adaptation

We can see the problem of the structural and behavioural adaptation of an assembly of agents in two different ways: either as an individual characteristic of the agents – and we then talk of *learning* – or as a collective process bringing reproductive mechanisms into play, which we call *evolution*. Although the two approaches are generally treated in different ways, it is possible to take an overall view of them as an adaptation process which is simultaneously individual and collective. These problems are the subject of important research in the fields of distributed artificial intelligence and artificial life, the former naturally focusing more on learning by symbolic or neuronal techniques, and the latter on evolution, using genetic algorithms. Although adaptation is a particularly important theme in the study of multi-agent systems (Lestel *et al.*, 1994), we shall develop it only to a very partial extent, tackling it only by way of collective behaviour and the resulting adaptation of regulation mechanisms developing from the combined actions of a set of agents (cf. Chapter 7).

1.5.5   The creation and implementation of MASs

Finally, there remains one large area which will not be dealt with in this book, and which is relevant to the implementation of multi-agent systems. This topic, which takes in implementation languages (type L1 languages, using the classification from Section 1.2.5), computing architectures, development platforms and the methodological aspects of putting these systems into operation, is so wide-ranging that it would need a book of its own. It will be touched on only briefly here.

1.6   Areas related to multi-agent systems

Kenetics is related to a large number of other scientific fields, though this does not mean it is not a separate discipline on its own. We are essentially talking here about artificial intelligence, systemics, distributed systems and robotics.

1.6.1   Artificial intelligence

In contrast to artificial intelligence, and to most computer programs, multi-agent systems are no longer 'thinkers' sealed within their own reasoning, and ignorant of their environment, but constitute veritable societies of beings which have to move, plan, communicate, perceive, act and react and, in a general fashion, 'live' and work in a milieu in which they sometimes come into conflict with other agents.

In relation to AI, kenetics calls into play a large number of concepts which are new to the field, such as cooperation, coordination of action, negotiation, conflicts, satisfaction, obligation, action and reaction or perception. These concepts are no longer grounded in individual cognitive psychology alone, as in classic AI, but also draw on sociology and biology, and even ethology.

Whereas for AI it is the individual that is intelligent, for kenetics it is the organisation that displays functionalities that can be characterised as intelligent. Designing intelligent beings is not a goal for kenetics, since it is essentially interested in the relations between individuals and the consequences of their interactions, but merely a means of developing artificial organisations which perform better by reducing the redundancy and increasing the efficiency of the actions carried out.

By the way, there is a joke in the multi-agent systems field that AI is a single-agent form of DAI! Although this is a jest, it is a good way of expressing the fact that AI and kenetics work on different levels of study, a little like psychology and sociology.

1.6.2   Systemics

Although systemics has always accepted the importance of interactions in systems definition, the current trends in this area put more emphasis on the analysis of the input and output flows than on the behavioural aspect of interactions. Indeed, the strictly operative part of systemic analysis, since its origins with V. Bertalanffy (1968), N. Wiener (1948) and above all J. W. Forrester (1980), has dedicated itself mainly to the analysis of biological, economic and artificial systems in relation to the transfer of flows of materials, energy, data or money between different storage, command or regulation elements. Even the early work by J.-L. Le Moigne (1977) on general systems theory, and that of P. Delattre (1971) on organised structures took up what had become the classic notion of a system as an assembly of subsystems, interconnected by links for transferring flows or controlling their activity. Although this approach is very useful in many fields, such as business organisation or the creation of electronic devices, it is actually restrictive – in spite of its vaunted universality – since the only truly fruitful concepts it contains are those of regulation, stabilisation and transfer function. As is in fact indicated in a recent work on systems analysis (Lapierre, 1992), 'The concept of systems as we are thinking of it here is not a concept of an objective, it's a concept of tools. These systems are abstract entities, not concrete parts of this totality.'

In this approach a system, whether it is a human being, a company or any kind of organisation, is broken down into subsystems, each subsystem responding to a specific function of the system such as consumption, production, research, design, exchange and management (Charest, 1980). These subsystems bring together the characteristics of the system being studied through an approach which is analytical, but which has been challenged, as it does not enable us to understand the evolution of the system or the internal factors of an organisation. Systemics then becomes a 'portmanteau' concept, which sometimes is really a disguised functionalism.

Nevertheless, there is a second tendency which is very popular at the moment, represented by researchers ranging from E. Morin (1977) to F. Varela (1989) and including H. Atlan (1979), I. Prigogine (Prigogine and Stengers, 1979) and E. Bernard-Weil (1988), which consists in understanding systems as self-organising entities, whose functioning and evolution are the products of the behaviour of an assembly of entities in interactions. However, apart perhaps from the concept of autopoïesis developed by Maturana and Varela (1987), which postulates that a self-organising system has no other function than that of maintaining its organised structure, the emphasis is still on interconnection flows and on the modelling of retroaction loops.

Some remarkable work such as that by F. Le Gallou (1992) or E. Schwartz (1993) attempts to combine these two approaches. But these projects, which are more about trying to explain phenomena in a qualitative way than providing an operational model of them, approach systems in a holistic manner (a system is a whole) and pay only marginal attention to the behaviour of the entities that make them up. Now, defining a system in terms of its global relationships does not explain the genesis of its structure, but only the general forms of its evolution from a macroscopic point of view. This approach ignores the importance of the individual actions which contribute to setting up the structure and thus to the organisation of the system as such.

In contrast, kenetics is more interested in local interactions and the emergence phenomena resulting from them. So what we are dealing with is a form of systemics, or more precisely a *neo-systemics*, based on the analysis of the behaviours of interacting agents, the self-organisation of systems then being the product of the conversion actions of these agents.

1.6.3   Distributed systems

There are numerous points in common between the problems raised by kenetics and questions related to distributed systems. But these two fields are nevertheless distinct from each other. Distributed systems are attempting to design computer systems capable of managing the carrying out of tasks by making the best use of physically distributed resources (memory, processor, data managers). The techniques brought into service (customer/server, distribution of applications) are more specifically linked to computing practice, or more precisely to the operationalisation of computer systems, than kenetics is. For example, distributed systems try to create distributed operating systems in which the user does not have to specify the processor on which the user's program is to run, or verify that the resources needed to run it are in fact present on the machine. It is left to the system to manage these details. The problems which then arise require an ability to design, specify and validate distributed applications by defining protocols allowing several distributed computing modules to have mutual use of their services.

The issues of kenetics are much more open. It is not confined to the management of computing applications or to the definition of operating systems that are transparent for the user. MASs attempt to take a general and abstract view of the problem of interaction between individual entities, considering distributed systems as being merely one possible application or realisation (although a particularly important one) of this general concept. Fundamental to this approach are the problems of autonomy, of cooperation (in the true sense of the term, and not in the restricted sense of the distribution of tasks or of computing resources) and of the setting up of emergent artificial organisations capable of accomplishing work which a single entity would be incapable, or barely capable, of doing. Hence, the 'problem solving', 'coordination of actions' or 'knowledge sharing' type of perspective inherent in multi-agent systems does not correspond to distributed systems at all.

The connection between process and agent is particularly interesting in this respect. While the concept of a process is related to that of execution, that of an agent corresponds to an individualisation of skills and objectives, an autonomy of the capacities for action and interaction. An agent can therefore be implemented in the form of several processes without losing its individuality – we should not confuse the conceptual level with the physical level of its implementation. Nevertheless, these two domains are very closely linked. MASs use a large number of techniques taken from distributed systems, while being situated at a more conceptual and methodological level. Certain algorithms that MASs use, such as task-allocation algorithms, and certain representational formalities, such as Petri nets, form part of the natural baggage of distributed systems. For this reason, there is more of a synergical relationship than a true opposition between MASs and distributed systems. Distributed systems contribute their rigour and their algorithms while the MASs provide conceptualisation and a more general approach less centred on execution mechanisms. We should therefore not find it surprising that current research is moving towards closer and closer collaboration between specialists in distributed systems and those studying multi-agent systems.

1.6.4 Robotics

Multi-agent systems also have very many links with robotics. But in this case the relationship is very clear. Robotics, and especially distributed robotics, is one possible application of multi-agent systems, as the latter describe what robots have to be capable of accomplishing in order to cooperate on tasks that bring several robots into action.

Conversely, robotics studies a whole set of problems connected with mechanics, electronics, geometry and, in a general way, movement commands, which do not form part of the interests of kenetics. For this reason, and apart from very rare applications which involve breaking a manipulator robot down into an assembly of agents (Overgaard *et al.*, 1994 and Regnier and Duhaut, 1995), kenetics turns to robotics only when it is necessary to make a set of mobile robots interact with one another. It is in this sense that the problems tackled in Chapters 7 and 8 may concern robotics.

1.6.5 What is not covered by kenetics

To avoid any misunderstanding, here are some factors which will help us to determine what is not not covered by kenetics. In a general way, we can say that anything that can be classed as an individualistic conception of systems does not fall within the area of MASs. Nor does any system broken down into an assembly of subsystems fall within the area of kenetics. For a system to be considered as a multi-agent system, the following conditions must apply:

(1)   It must have autonomous agents functioning in parallel and attempting to achieve a goal or to fulfil a satisfaction function (what we shall refer to as tendencies in Chapter 5).

(2)   These agents must possess a high-level interaction mechanism independent of the problem to be solved (communication protocols or mechanisms for interaction with the environment).

We can therefore reply to certain questions as follows:

Are networks multi-agent systems?

No, since the network nodes generally have neither goals nor satisfaction functions. Nevertheless, networks are well placed to evolve towards a multi-agent concept, as they are already distributed and have management problems which call for a local approach. This is why many multi-agent applications use networks as carriers for their activity.

Does a modular breakdown of a program constitute a multi-agent system?

No, for the same reasons as before (modules have neither goals nor satisfaction functions) and also because the interaction mechanisms which are implemented in modules are low-level mechanisms (for example, procedural calls or transmission of messages requesting a service which the modules are obliged to render because otherwise they would risk creating an error).

Is an AI program which is being executed in parallel a multi-agent system?

No, for the same reasons as before.

The following question is one which comes up fairly frequently:

What is the difference between an object, an actor and an agent?

The answer is simple. In the field of computer science, the terms object and actor refer to computing entities characterised by their structure and by their execution mechanisms. The notion of an *object* is defined by three concepts: the class/instance relationship, which describes the class as a structural and behavioural model and the instance as a representation of a model; inheritance, which allows one class to be derived from another and the former to benefit from the characteristics of the latter; and message transmission, which authorises the definition of polymorph procedures, that is, procedures whose code depends on the recipient of the message. Objects are thus positioned, on the one hand, on an implementation level with object languages and, on the other hand, on a logical level, within the framework of analysis and design by object. In no case are objects agents, for they do not fulfil the two criteria mentioned above. They have no goals and they do not search for satisfaction, and the message transmission mechanism comes down to a procedural call. The interaction mechanisms are thus the programmer's responsibility. *Actors* in computing terms are entities which perform in parallel, which communicate by transmitting asynchronous buffered messages and which, in general, do not wait for a computation to return, but ask the recipient of the message to send the response to another actor called the local computation continuation (Agha, 1986). Although we are dealing here with parallel models of execution, for the same reasons which apply to objects actors cannot be identified as agents. The essential difference between objects and (purely communicating) agents is illustrated in Figure 1.15. An object is defined by a certain number of services (its methods), which it cannot refuse to carry out if another object asks it to, and the messages are thus necessarily invocations of methods. The developer of object-oriented software should therefore verify that all the objects will in fact receive sensible commands which they will effectively be capable of carrying out. In relation to objects, *agents* can receive messages which are not confined to execution requests but can also consist of information or of requests for information – on their capacities, for example. For

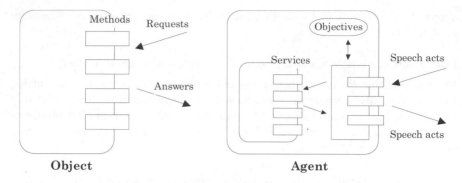

Figure 1.15   An object responds directly to requests corresponding to its methods, while an agent encapsulates its skills (or services) through supplementary mechanisms which 'filter' external communications and manage dialogues. Agents are also driven by personal objectives (or tendencies).

this reason, the services an object can provide are filtered by a software layer, which decouples the requests and the internal functioning of the agent. Finally, as we have said, agents attempt to attain objectives, which gives them more autonomy than objects. In fact the agent, unlike the object, can refuse to carry out a given job, such refusal being explicable by its lack of skill (it does not have the required know-how) or by the fact that it is too busy with another task, or for any other reason. Figure 1.15 illustrates the fundamental difference between an agent and an object. An agent encapsulates the methods an object can offer, in the form of a set of services which can be accessed only by using a special language known by all the agents, and which generally utilises the theory of language acts (cf. Chapter 6). But the link which exists between objects and agents must not be underestimated either. If a purely communicating agent can be considered as a sort of improved object, then conversely an object can be seen as a degenerate agent, that is, an agent whose language of expression can be summarised as the use of key words corresponding to its methods. Finally – and this adds yet more possibilities of confusion – agents are often implemented in the form of objects or actors, for practical reasons. However, this is only one of the possible implementations. Agents can be implemented in the same way in Fortran, C or Lisp, which are not naturally object-oriented languages, without modifying their nature as an agent in any way.

To sum up, then, we can say that agents are defined on a conceptual level and objects or actors on the implementation and execution levels. Incidentally, it is to avoid this confusion that there will be hardly any references to objects or actors in this work.

2 Interactions and Cooperation

2.1 Interaction situations	2.4 Forms of cooperation
2.2 Components of interactions	2.5 Methods of cooperation
2.3 Types of interaction	2.6 Organisations and cooperation

2.1 Interaction situations

The concept of interaction is central to the issue of multi-agent systems and kenetics. But what is an interaction?

An interaction occurs when two or more agents are brought into a dynamic relationship through a set of reciprocal actions. Thus interactions develop out of a series of actions whose consequences in turn have an influence on the future behaviour of the agents. The agents interact through a series of events, during which they are in contact with each other in some way, whether this contact is direct or takes place through another agent or through the environment.

Interaction situations are numerous and varied: one robot helping another, an exchange of data between servers, several specialists sharing their skills to support a fault-finding system, the use of a printer by two programs simultaneously, the distribution of loads over several processors, the collision of two vehicles – all of these are examples of interaction situations.

Interactions are not only the consequences of actions carried out by several agents at the same time but are also the element necessary for the setting up of social organisations. It is through the exchanges they undertake, the obligations that bind them, the influences they exert on one another, that agents become social entities and new functionalities can emerge from these reciprocal action systems. Groups are thus both the results of interactions and the preferred locations in which interactions take place. This is why it is generally impossible to analyse social organisations without taking account of the interactions between their members.

If we take the example of transporter robots: in order to move a mass of 300 kg when none of them can carry more than 100 kg supposes (1) that there are enough robots to carry this load, and (2) that their actions are going to be coordinated in such a way that the load is efficiently moved and arrives safe and sound. The same applies to vehicles moving over a network of roads: their actions must be coordinated so that they can reach their destinations without having a collision. More precisely, the concept of interaction assumes:

(1)   the presence of agents capable of acting and/or communicating;

(2)   situations which can serve as a meeting point for agents: collaboration, movement of vehicles leading to a collision, use of limited resources, regulation of group cohesion;

(3)   dynamic elements allowing for local and temporary relationships between agents: communication, impact, field of attraction or repulsion, and so on;

(4)   a certain amount of 'slack' in relationships between agents, enabling them not only to sustain a relationship but also to detach themselves from it, that is, to have a certain amount of autonomy. If agents are bound completely by a fixed link, their interaction becomes rigid and they are no longer interacting in the full sense of the term.

Interaction forms the basis of the constitution of organisations (Morin, 1977), and at the same time interactions assume the definition of a space, and generally of a pre-established organisation, within which they can take place. For this reason, interaction is the crucial element in every organisation, simultaneously the source and the product of the permanence of the organisation; and the dissolution of an organisation is concomitant with the disappearance (or at any event the reduction) of interactions among the individuals present in that organisation.

Finally, interaction is the consequence of the plural aspect of multi-agent societies, bringing in a dimension which goes beyond the individual. The latter is no longer the centre of the universe, as in the 'ego-centred' concepts characteristic of classic artificial intelligence in which intelligence can be understood from the point of view of the individual alone, but the node of an assembly of exchanges and interdependencies which, in turn, mould it and give it its whole meaning. An agent without any interaction with other agents is nothing more than an isolated body, a computing system, stripped of any adaptive characteristics.

Paying so much attention to interaction as an essential and basic element in forms of intelligence may appear innovative for the cognitive sciences, but it is not actually a novelty. Ethology, which is interested in animal and human behaviour, demonstrates that the appearance of cognitive forms is the product of a series of complex behaviours in which exchange and interaction with individuals

of one's own species play an essential role in the development of a living
being (McFarland, 1990; Lannoy and Feyereisen, 1987; Cyrulnik, 1989). When this
exchange does not exist, individuals cannot reach their full potential, and remain in
a 'primitive' state.

The interactions between agents are expressed in various forms. But beyond
the superficial diversity, it is possible to detect differences and points in common at
a deeper level. But how do you actually compare the interactions of sailors in the
process of manoeuvring a vessel and those of workers building a house? Or those of
car drivers passing each other on the road and of robots searching for and collecting
ore? The first stage consists in considering different situations in which several
agents are in interaction. In order to describe these activities, we shall make use of
the concept of an *interaction situation*, which allows us to describe types of
interaction by linking them to the elements of which they are composed.

Definiton
We shall consider an interaction situation as being an assembly of behaviours resulting from the grouping of agents which have to act in order to attain their objectives, with attention being paid to the more or less limited resources which are available to them and to their individual skills.

For example, the building of a house is an interaction situation (in this instance, a
cooperation situation requiring a certain coordination of actions), defined by the
assembly of behaviours of the agents (the workforce, the architect, the owner, the
project manager) characterised by their objectives (the creation of the house looked
at from the various points of view of the agents) and their skills (the know-how of
the architect and of the various groups of skilled workers), with attention being paid
to the available resources (the construction materials, financing, tooling, the
building site, the weather).

This concept of an interaction situation serves to define abstract categories
independent of their concrete realisations, by distinguishing between, on the one
hand, the main invariables which we find everywhere and, on the other hand, the
differences which show up between situations. Starting from this definition of the
categories, it is possible to classify them, that is, arrange them in accordance with
their relationships with one another. However, we shall not become too attached to
the idea of considering all the possible interactions. We shall look only at those
which are characteristic of kenetics at the present time. For example, in spite of their
importance in human interactions, we shall not take into account the phenomena
arising from the emotions and from relationships involving tenderness or love.

2.2 Components of interactions

What are the different types of interaction? Is it possible to define interaction parameters allowing us to classify situations? In subsequent sections, we shall describe several criteria by means of which it will be possible to classify different types of interaction and thus arrive at a better comprehension of both the potentialities and the problems involved in this concept. The main interaction situations can be classified in relation to three criteria: the objectives or intentions of the agents, the relationships of these agents to the resources they have available, and the means (or skills) available to them to achieve their ends.

2.2.1 Compatible and incompatible goals

The agents' objectives and interactions are obviously central to the issues of interaction. Do the agents have concurrent goals – that is, going in the same direction – or are their objectives contradictory, or even opposed?

For example, if a couple want to go on holiday, and one spouse wants to go to the mountains while the other wants to go to the seaside, the goals are contradictory. There is also a contradiction of objectives when two business associates are not in agreement on the strategy to be followed to develop their company, one wishing to increase productivity by making employees redundant while the second, in contrast, wants to take more employees on because he or she considers that the market is in a growth phase. Likewise, most sports and games are based on a competition situation, that is, on the fact that the goals of the participants are incompatible. They all want to win, but there will be only one victor. In other words, there are several local objectives which cannot be merged into a single objective at the global level.

In a general manner, we say that goals are incompatible if achieving one means another cannot be achieved, the converse being automatically true.

This distinction between compatible and incompatible goals forms the basis of an initial classification. We shall say that agents are in a situation of *cooperation* or indifference if their goals are compatible, and in a situation of *antagonism* in the opposite case.

Although the concept of a goal is characteristic of cognitive agents, it is possible to extend this concept of compatibility to reactive agents. When we are dealing with *drive-based agents* (cf. Chapter 1), it is permissible to distinguish between

---

Definiton

The goal of an agent, A, is incompatible with that of another agent, B, if agents A and B have, as their respective goals to be achieved, the states described by p and q respectively, and if $p \Rightarrow \neg q$, that satisfies is:
$(goal(A, p)) \Rightarrow \neg \text{ satisfies } (goal (B, q))$.

compatible and incompatible drives by defining whether or not the desires of these agents can be co-satisfied. In the case of *tropistic agents*, we shall consider only their viability, and we shall say, by extension, that the objectives of two such agents are compatible if the survival behaviour of the one does not entail the death of the other. For this reason, situations of cooperation (or of indifference) are those in which the viability of the one is not negatively affected by that of the other. In situations of indifference, the viability of the one is not affected at all (either negatively or positively) by the behaviour of the other, whereas in situations of cooperation, the viability of the one is reinforced by the viability of the other. In the animal and vegetable kingdoms, cases of symbiosis are characteristic of reactive cooperation. For example, in certain cases of animal symbiosis, when an organism, A, nourishes another organism, B, which in turn defends A from predators, it can be said that the two animals cooperate, since the viability of each is reinforced by the presence and behaviour of the other. Group survival and cooperation situations thus go hand in hand.

The example of the prey animal–predator model is a good illustration of the mechanisms of cooperation and antagonism. By forming a group, the predators are cooperating to hunt their prey, but they are in an antagonistic relationship with the prey animals. The satisfaction of the predators entails the death of the prey animals, and the survival of the prey animals entails the failure of the predators.

2.2.2 Relation to resources

Another important factor in interactions relates to the external resources available to the agents. By resources we mean all the environmental and material elements which can be used in carrying out an action. It may be a matter of energy values, financial options, tools or raw materials, but also of taking into account more general concepts such as the space and time available for accomplishing a task. Any agent needs resources to carry out its actions, which take place in four-dimensional space–time, consume energy (and money) and require instruments as catalysts of activity.

This quantity of resources, necessarily limited, leads to conflicts. In this case, the interactions are disruptive. From the point of view of each agent, the other is an intruder interfering with the accomplishment of its own actions. Essentially, conflicts arise when several agents need the same resources at the same time and in the same place, that is, when the zones corresponding to the resources they need intersect (Figure 2.1). Two workers needing the same tool, two robots needing to re-energise themselves from the same power source, two people wanting to print at the same time, or two programs sharing the same processor are all examples of conflicts caused by lack of resources.

Another example is provided by traffic on the roads, where the mere presence of others causes problems. In a traffic jam, I am in conflict with the other driver because he or she is blocking my path. If there were more space, or if there were fewer vehicles, the conflicts would disappear. So the problem comes from the number of vehicles and the available space, that is, from the resources available to each driver. If the traffic is moving freely, that is, if the cars are not too densely packed together, then all goes well, but if the density of the traffic increases too

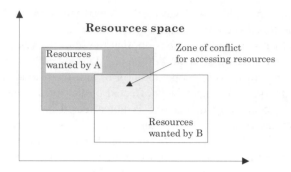

Figure 2.1   Agent A wants resources some of which are also desired by B, generating a conflict.

rapidly the traffic is immobilised, the actions of each car driver being thwarted by those of the others.

Conflict situations can be resolved in one way or another through mechanisms of coordination of actions and conflict resolution. Some of these methods are particularly crude: for example, the law of the strongest is a technique for conflict resolution which defines an order of priority based on the agent's 'strength', the stronger dominating the weaker in respect of access to resources. Other methods are more elaborate. Negotiation techniques, for example, are used to get out of a conflict situation by way of compromises which moderate the satisfactions and the frustrations of both sides.

Finally, techniques for coordinating actions are utilised to anticipate conflicts which are yet to come and to ensure that they can be managed even before they break out. They comprise a set of devices, regulations and supplementary actions which have to be implemented for the actions of the various agents to be possible. Traffic lights and the Highway Code are examples of devices and regulations making it possible to regulate road traffic and reduce the risks of conflicts between motorists. For example, a red light at a crossroads serves to coordinate the actions of the vehicles and ensure that there are no conflicts of passage between the vehicles. In the absence of any traffic-regulation system, if each car tries to pass without worrying about the difficulties it may cause for other cars, conflicts will break out which may go as far as causing an accident. A jointly agreed statement for insurance purposes (negotiation) or going to court (arbitration) will then serve to resolve the conflicts of interest provoked by the accident.

Conflicts may arise even if all the agents are in the best possible frame of mind and decide in advance to collaborate. For example, when several friends come to give you a hand to move house and to carry the furniture from your sitting room, their actions don't worry you. On the contrary, they are welcome! However, because your flat isn't very big and several people have volunteered to act as porters, the comings and goings of your friends have to be more or less coordinated for the furniture to arrive safe and sound and in good condition, and for this assistance not to be transformed into disruptive disorder. We shall discuss coordination problems in greater detail in Chapter 8. It is sufficient here to understand that limitations on resources may be causes of conflict which can be avoided to a certain extent by coordinating the actions of agents.

2.2.3   Capacities of agents in relation to tasks

The relationship between the capacities of agents and the tasks to be accomplished constitutes the third fundamental factor in interactions between agents. Can an agent carry out a task alone, or does it need others to achieve its goal? In many situations, an isolated agent proves capable of coping with achieving its goal on its own. For example, going to get a beer from the fridge or some bread from the bakery are simple tasks which can be carried out by one person alone. Other more complex tasks can still be carried out by a single individual, even if their accomplishment is facilitated by the presence of other people in a situation of mutual support. Sailing across the Atlantic, producing a medical diagnosis or repairing a car are examples of such situations. Finally, there are certain tasks for which the capacities of several people are absolutely necessary. Putting up a monument or constructing a space shuttle requires the coordinated efforts of several individuals to accomplish a common task which none of them could accomplish alone. Without the others, the mason, the electrician and the plumber in the one case, or the propulsion engineer and the aerodynamics expert in the other, are incapable of attaining the objective they have set for themselves.

In these last two situations, the interactions are beneficial, and people are helping each other by their actions. The resulting system then possesses new properties, which are sometimes expressed as an emerging functionality. A house is not simply a matter of 'construct walls, plus lay water pipes, plus connect electricity'. An aircraft cannot be reduced to the bringing together of a fuselage and some engines. In all these cases, the thing produced is greater than the simple sum of the skills of each of the agents, and it is the interactions between the latter that account for the transformation.

2.3   Types of interaction

These three main elements in interaction, namely the nature of the goals, access to resources and the skills of the agents, can be used to create an initial typology of interaction situations, as shown in Table 2.1, providing for all the possible cases.

2.3.1   Independence

Compatible goals, sufficient resources, sufficient skills. The situation of independence poses no problems from the multi-agent point of view, and can be

Table 2.1 Classification of interaction situations.

Goals	Resources	Skills	Types of situation	Category
Compatible	Sufficient	Sufficient	*Independence*	Indifference
Compatible	Sufficient	Insufficient	*Simple collaboration*	
Compatible	Insufficient	Sufficient	*Obstruction*	Cooperation
Compatible	Insufficient	Insufficient	*Coordinated collaboration*	
Incompatible	Sufficient	Sufficient	*Pure individual competition*	
Incompatible	Sufficient	Insufficient	*Pure collective competition*	Antagonism
Incompatible	Insufficient	Sufficient	*Individual conflicts over resources*	
Incompatible	Insufficient	Insufficient	*Collective conflicts over resources*	

summarised as the simple juxtaposition of actions carried out by agents independently, without any effective interaction. For example, people who pass each other in the street, knowing that there is enough room for them to pass, or engineers who are not working on the same project, are in a situation of total independence. We are dealing with a neutral situation, which in fact lays no claim to any specific interaction from the kenetics viewpoint. We shall therefore not discuss it.

2.3.2 Simple collaboration

Compatible goals, sufficient resources, insufficient skills. Simple collaboration consists of the simple addition of skills, requiring no supplementary coordination actions between those involved. This situation is characteristic of communicating systems in which all the interaction is expressed in the form of the allocation of tasks and the sharing of knowledge. Multi-specialist systems (cf. Chapter 1), in which the agents merely share knowledge to arrive at a solution for a problem, generally involve only simple collaboration. Chapter 7 essentially deals with these scenarios.

2.3.3 Obstruction

Compatible goals, insufficient resources, sufficient skills. Obstruction is characteristic of all situations in which agents get in each other's way in accomplishing their tasks, and do not need one another. Typical examples are cars on the road, air traffic control, optimal use of resources such as scheduling use of time, stock management, placing tasks on a processor, etc. Solving this type of problem calls for specific techniques for the coordination of actions, some of which are presented in Chapter 8.

2.3.4   Coordinated collaboration

Compatible goals, insufficient resources, insufficient skills. Complex collaboration supposes that the agents have to coordinate their actions to procure the synergic advantages of pooled skills. Coordinating collaboration is implicated in almost all industrial activities requiring a distributed approach, such as network control, the design and manufacture of industrial products or the distributed regulation or implementation of even slightly complicated societies of autonomous robots. Coordinated collaboration is the most complex of cooperation situations, since it combines task allocation problems with aspects of coordination shaped by limited resources. In tackling the problem of coordination of actions, Chapter 8 will be shedding some light on the resolution of this type of situation.

2.3.5   Pure individual competition

Incompatible goals, sufficient resources, sufficient skills. When goals are incompatible, agents have to struggle or negotiate in order to achieve them. 'Sporting' competition assumes that agents all have the same resources at their disposal, and that they are placed in identical initial situations. We refer to pure competition when the resources are not limited – more precisely when access to resources is not what the conflict is about. A running race is an example of pure competition. Each competitor has enough space, and each can make use of a similar amount of space. Only the competitors' intrinsic athletic ability will make a difference. There are no specific interaction problems linked to this type of situation. Quite simply, may the best competitor win.

2.3.6   Pure collective competition

Incompatible goals, sufficient resources, insufficient skills. When agents do not have sufficient skill, they have to group themselves together into coalitions or associations to be able to achieve their goals. This formation of groups is carried out in two successive phases. The first phase tends to ally individuals within groups united by the ties of coordinated collaboration, and the second tends to set one group against another. A characteristic example of this type of situation is team competitions such as relay races or the Americas Cup sailing competition, that is, opposition situations in which the teams (usually) do not obstruct each other.

2.3.7   Individual conflict over resources

Incompatible goals, insufficient resources, sufficient skills. When resources cannot be shared, we have a typical conflict situation in which a person wishes to acquire the resources for himself or herself alone. The object of conflict may be, say, a territory or a dominant financial position. There are a large number of examples of this type of situation in the animal and human worlds, from animals' defence of their territory to the obtaining of a job which means a step up in the hierarchy for humans.

2.3.8 Collective conflicts over resources

Incompatible goals, insufficient resources, insufficient skills. This type of situation combines collective competition with individual conflicts over resources. Coalitions struggle against each other to obtain a monopoly of a good, a territory or a position. All forms of war, hunting, industrial competition and other kinds of collective conflicts where the objective is to obtain possession of a territory or a resource are characteristic examples of this.

2.3.9 Level of analysis of interaction situations

Obviously, this classification constitutes only an initial approach to the analysis of situations. It would be possible to refine it by describing other parameters to take certain cases into account in greater detail. In particular, we could take account of characteristics such as the cognitive recognition of common goals; the desire to modify the cognitive state of other agents (for instance, by trying to convince them); the existence of a structure of authority and influence mechanisms allowing an agent to make other agents act in the way it desires; types and modes of communication; the cognitive capacities of agents to anticipate the actions of others; the availability of a reward following an action (or during it); the presence of repetitive or isolated actions, and so on.

Situations can be analysed on different levels. A complex interaction situation is made up of more elementary situations. For example, the activity of a company results from a whole series of simpler situations in which the company's employees interact to produce goods and services. We can thus distinguish between interaction *macro-situations*[†], which are characteristic of a global analysis of an activity, and *micro-situations*, where there is a stronger focus on detail. From a systemic point of view, the relationship between micro- and macro-situations is that of the parts to the whole. The macro-situation, while remaining the product of the micro-situations which make it up, introduces a set of problems whose solution involves the creation of a number of micro-situations which themselves bring problems, as shown in Figure 2.2. Thus a situation considered at the macroscopic level as a collaboration situation may produce local competition and obstruction situations at the microscopic level. And conversely, a territorial conflict situation may result in local collaboration situations.

[†]The terms 'macro' and 'micro' do not refer here to fixed points on a scale, but merely describe relative positions. A situation may thus appear to be 'macro' from a certain point of view (for example, a company is considered as 'macro' in relation to the interactions of its employees) and 'micro' from another point of view (a company interacts with other companies to make up larger economic structures).

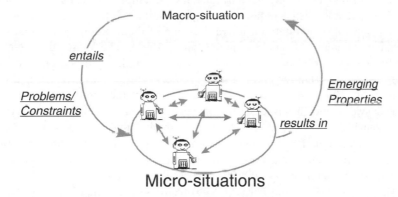

entails

Macro-situation

Emerging
Properties

Problems/
Constraints

results in

Micro-situations

Figure 2.2   The actions of agents situated on the micro level of a system produce relative
macro-situations engendering constraints on the micro level.

In particular, we shall see in Chapter 8 that certain methods used to manage
collaboration and obstruction situations involve the definition of local competition
situations. And this is why, even if we are interested only in situations with
compatible objectives, we must not neglect the study of situations in which the
agents have incompatible goals. It is none the less true that cooperation situations
constitute a major part of interaction situations, and we shall not deal in this
book with the problems associated with situations in which antagonistic goals
are involved.

For the purposes of what follows, we shall assume

(1)   that the agents' goals are compatible;

(2)   that the agents are benevolent and that they try to help each other, or to reach
a compromise, if interests relating to resources are involved.

Although the problem of cooperation between agents was raised long ago, few
theories (before the appearance of multi-agent systems) attempted to describe the
various forms of cooperation in an operative manner, or to show the relationships
between individuals, the tasks they accomplish and the overall interests of the
group[†]. Most work on cooperation relates to whether or not it is in someone's
interests to cooperate with others, as in the context of the prisoner's dilemma
(Axelrod, 1992), or to ways of communicating within groups with restricted social
psychologies (Stoetzel, 1978). But while this work emphasises either decisions to
cooperate out of self-interest, or relationships of authority and the affective
relationships which lead individuals to cooperate and work together, multi-agent

[†]Nevertheless, there are quite a number of philosophical works relating to cooperation and collective
action within a cognitive perspective. For a recent French-language presentation of these reflections, see
Livet (1994).

systems reformulate the problem by placing the emphasis on the cognitive and behavioural characteristics required for implementing a collective operation.

Cooperation is often put forward as one of the key concepts in distributed artificial intelligence (Demazeau and Müller, 1991). The most advanced work currently being carried out on cooperation within multi-agent systems is that of Lesser and Durfee (Durfee *et al.*, 1987), Galliers (1991), Castelfranchi and Conte (Conte *et al.*, 1991) and Bouron (1992). But most of these projects provide only partial answers, and in any case are interested only in cognitive agents, that is, agents capable of having representations and planning their actions. Work on reactive cooperation, that is, on cooperation by agents which do nothing but react to stimuli from their environment, is still in the early stages. However, the work of Deneubourg (Deneubourg *et al.*, 1993), Theraulaz (Theraulaz *et al.*, 1991), Steels (1994), Drogoul (1993) and Ferber (1995) testifies to the importance of the area.

2.4 Forms of cooperation

There are several points of view on cooperation, depending on whether one considers that cooperation is the attitude of agents that decide to work together, or whether one places oneself in the position of an observer and interprets behaviours *a posteriori* by qualifying them as cooperative or not on the basis of social (or physical) criteria, such as the interdependence of actions or the number of communications effected.

2.4.1 Cooperation as an intentional posture

In the first case, cooperation is characteristic of a *posture* of the agents. We say that agents are cooperating if they engage in a common action after identifying and adopting a common goal. The creation of an association, such as an environmental defence association, for example, corresponds to this blueprint. The members of the association have identified a common objective, to fight against sources of pollution, and they have committed themselves to taking part in a common task, the defence of nature. The association has been set up as a result of its members' becoming aware of the existence of a common goal, and of their commitment.

Likewise, when individuals agree to work for a company, they undertake to take part in a common task, considering, not only that their goals are compatible with those of the company, but also that the employees, like the body which is employing them, can pursue their interests in this context; the company will use the skills of those it hires and the employees will receive remuneration.

The problem of commitment to a collective goal is called *goal adoption* by J. Galliers (1991), C. Castelfranchi and R. Conte (Conte *et al.*, 1991), and is considered as being an essential element in social activity. For J. Galliers in particular, cooperation exists if the agents undertake an action and identify a common goal, that is, recognise that the other agents are committed to the same goal.

But are all forms of cooperation the result of an intention to cooperate, and do all intentions to cooperate necessarily lead to cooperation? Consider the following story:

Gaétan wishes to help Ambroise, who is building a stone garage for his car. But Gaétan isn't very good with his hands, and he doesn't place the stone blocks the way Ambroise asks him to. This means Ambroise has to follow Gaétan around to do his work again, and his efficiency is therefore reduced by comparison with what it was when he was on his own.

Can we say that Gaétan and Ambroise are in a cooperation situation? According to Galliers (and most DAI researchers working on cognitive agents), Gaétan and Ambroise are cooperating, because they are aware that their actions are undertaken with a common goal or a common intention.

There are two difficulties with this idea. Firstly, even if the result of the cooperation is not as good as the performance of the agents looked at individually, it is claimed that cooperation exists. And secondly, all possibility of cooperation on the part of reactive agents (who have no explicit intentions, and absolutely no models of others) is eliminated. However, it is often recognised (in ethology, in particular) that social insects such as ants, which work together to gather food outside their nest, do cooperate, even if they are not aware of it (Fresneau, 1994). In a more general way, can reactive agents which manage to accomplish complex tasks be cooperative? If the answer is that they can, then we must assume that cooperation does not result solely from a posture, even if a cooperative posture can be a very good catalyst for cooperation, but that it should be understood in terms of behaviour and results. In this case, cooperation is no longer directly the product of an *intention to cooperate*, but is *the positive benefit* obtained thanks to the interaction of the agents.

2.4.2   Cooperation from the observer's point of view

This is why certain authors, Durfee *et al.* (1989) and Bouron (1992) in particular, consider cooperation as a description of the activity of an assembly of agents by an external observer who need have no access to the mental states of the agents. For example, if the behaviour of ants is described as cooperative, this is because, when we observe them, we observe a certain number of phenomena which are used as indicators of cooperative activity. The idea of a *cooperation indicator* (MIRIAD, 1992) is of particular interest, for it allows us to get away from the internal characteristics of the agents and consider only their observable behaviour. For example, here is a set of indicators put forward by T. Bouron to describe cooperative activity:

(1)   the coordination of actions, which concerns the adjustment of the direction of agents' actions in time and space;

(2)   the degree of parallelisation, which depends on the distribution of tasks and their concurrent execution;

(3)   the sharing of resources, which concerns the use of resources and skills;

(4)   the robustness of the system, which concerns the system's aptitude for making up for any failure by an agent;

(5)   the non-redundancy of actions, which characterises the low rate of redundant activities;

(6)   the non-persistence of conflicts, which testifies to the small number of blocking situations.

The definition of such an assemblage of criteria rests, in the first instance, on considerations of observability and quantifiability. It must be possible to examine and measure such indicators so that we can identify the degree of cooperation existing between different agents. But it is not obvious that such procedures could be applied here. What importance should be attached to the coordination of actions? How can the robustness of a system be quantified? Proposing objective and measurable criteria is fundamental if we wish to give cooperation a precise status. Otherwise, we run the risk of specifying the concept in terms of other concepts just as vague and never achieving any sort of reliable definition.

Such a set of indicators also has to be coherent. A robustness characteristic is really a characteristic of a system's capacity to adapt, and the non-redundancy of activities is in conflict with the degree of parallelisation of tasks. The more we parallelise, the greater the tendency for tasks to be duplicated so that they may be accomplished more rapidly, and the more redundancy is introduced. Finally, these indicators have to be placed in a hierarchy. The degree of parallelisation and the coordination of actions are the consequences of more fundamental indices such as the distribution of resources or the avoidance of conflicts.

So can we give a minimum set of indicators, on the basis of which it would be possible to construct other, more complex ones? We think this is possible, and in what follows we shall retain only two indices, which appear necessary and sufficient to determine whether cooperation activity exists or not: first, the efficiency of group work, and second, the existence of mechanisms for resolving conflicts over access to resources. These criteria can easily be measured, and can be integrated naturally into the typology of the interaction situations set out above.

Definiton

We shall say that several agents are cooperating, or that they are in a cooperation situation, if one of the following two conditions is verified:

(1)   The addition of a new agent makes it possible to increase the performance levels of the group differentially.

(2)   The action of the agents serves to avoid or to solve potential or actual conflicts.

The first index presents a differential criterion: if the agents are cooperating, a new agent is considered as an aid for the group as a whole. When this criterion is verified, we say that the agents *are collaborating*, or that they are in a *collaboration situation*. The objective of an increase in performance levels may be simply to improve a certain parameter, such as the amount of ore brought back to base in the case of the explorer robots. But more fundamentally the improvement in performance has the underlying primordial objective of survival. Survival, whether that means the preservation of a species, of an ecosystem, of a group, or of each of its members, constitutes the ultimate purpose of natural systems in which there are problems of adaptation and reproduction, and in particular that of all biological systems. For example, the members of a horde cooperate because it is easier for them to survive and develop in common than individually. In fact, ethologists consider that specialisation in the individuals in a group and the cooperation which underlies this are good indices of how far they have developed on the evolutionary scale. For example, the most primitive ant colonies generally inhabit nests of a few units, whereas the most highly evolved ants may have several million individuals in one nest (Corbara, 1991).

If, on the other hand, the introduction of an agent does not improve the performances of the group, this agent will be considered as a disruptive factor in collective activities. In this case, the second criterion still allows us to recognise that there is cooperation, even if there is no differential improvement in performances. The agents are then cooperating to ensure that the reduction in performance levels is not too drastic. This is generally the case when there is a limited quantity of resources. The introduction of new agents may have negative consequences on the functioning of the group, in which case cooperative actions such as avoidance, the establishment of conflict resolution techniques, the setting up of organisations for production and resource transportation, or quite simply the formation of queues, then become collective responses to limit the deterioration of individual and collective performances. In this case, we shall say that we are in a *conflict resolution situation*. This type of situation is characteristic of obstruction situations, such as those involving road or air traffic, access to a photocopier for a group of people, trying to get a taxi at an airport, access to a watering place, or to a processor for an assemblage of tasks, etc. Numerous ways of resolving conflicts exist. Some are based simply on the definition of actions to pre-empt the appearance of any conflicts, such as avoidance behaviours, the establishment of dominance, or the definition of rules of priority; while others are directed at cancelling out any conflicts that appear, through arbitration, negotiation, the use of dominance relationships, or the destruction, pure and simple, of the participants in the conflict.

Nevertheless, although a distinction is made here, collaboration situations and conflict resolution situations are often very closely connected. If problems of survival arise, improving performances will generally make it possible to survive better in a difficult universe[†]. Likewise, avoiding conflicts makes it possible either

---

[†]In certain cases, an improvement in individual performances can have a negative effect on the group. If, for example, herbivores can exploit their territory better, they may finally exhaust their resources and bring about their own destruction.

for the members of the group to survive (for example, by avoiding collisions or struggles) or for performances to be improved by comparison with a system without coordination. For example, a group of furniture removers *a priori* forms a collective in a collaboration situation, since the addition of a new furniture remover generally improves their performances. If they are very numerous, they may end up getting in each other's way on staircases and in narrow passageways. They are then in a conflict resolution situation, and they have to cooperate to resolve conflicts of access to space and to ensure that their overall performances are not too badly affected by these problems. This definition of cooperation, which is based totally on the point of view of the observer, makes it possible to characterise objectively what a cooperation situation is in terms of the improvement of performances, without bringing in any considerations of what is going on in the minds of the agents. Cooperation is then reduced to simple and observable criteria. On this basis, if we can define *intentional cooperation* as a cooperation situation in which the agents have the intention of cooperating – which quite obviously assumes that these are cognitive agents and are capable of having intentions – we shall refer to *reactive cooperation* when the agents have no explicit intentions but their collective behaviour satisfies at least one of the two criteria mentioned above. We can thus speak of cooperation even if the agents have no representation of the world in which they move or of other agents, and thus have no knowledge of the consequences of their acts, and quite frequently no knowledge even of the presence of other agents. For example, termites build a nest by simple actions of response to the various stimuli they receive. Their building technique is based simply on perceptive phenomena. The workers deposit pellets of earth and dung, preferably in places where other such pellets have already been put down. In this way, columns are developed. Next, by giving preference to places where they find the scent of other termites, they manage to form arches (Wilson, 1971). In this case, they go about their business without there being any intention to cooperate, and even without any direct interaction between termites, cooperation occurring as a *secondary effect* of the actions of the termite population as a whole (see Theraulaz (1991) for a similar development in the context of the construction of bees' hives).

It is possible to characterise three families of indicators corresponding to the three major functions of cooperation, which are increasing survival capacity, improving performances and resolving conflicts.

2.4.3   Increasing survival capacity

Survival indicators reflect the capacity of an individual or a group to maintain its functional unity when confronted by forces which tend to destroy that unity. We can distinguish between two types of survival – the survival of an individual, that is, the capacity of an agent to persist in its being, and collective survival, which corresponds to the maintenance of the group. If the first is relatively easy to identify, the second appears to be less amenable to verification and definition. By collective survival do we understand the survival of all its members, or the survival of the organisation which has originated from the gathering (perhaps temporary) of an assembly of agents? In the first case the situation is simple, as it can be brought down to an analysis in terms of individual survival, while in the second case it is sometimes difficult to be sure of the moment at which the collective organisation disappeared. Nevertheless, we can sometimes adopt arbitrary criteria for decreeing that a collective organisation has ceased to exist. We can say, for example, that a company is surviving as long as it has not gone bankrupt, or that a group of robots exists as long as at least two of them are left.

It is possible to define an agent's individual survival capacity in two ways – either by considering the probability of its survival in a given environment or by analysing its energy efficiency-sheet, that is, the ratio between the amount of energy it absorbs and that which it expends per unit of time. When this ratio exceeds 1, the individual or the group is capable of surviving and even perhaps of investing its surplus energy in supplementary tasks which are not immediately profitable, but which will subsequently allow energy efficiency to be further improved. The first definition is better adapted to the differential analysis of behaviours of very simple agents, while the second is more general, but also more complicated to handle, since it brings in economic factors and assumes that we are capable of estimating the amounts of 'energy' taken in and given out.

We shall now demonstrate, using the example of hunter agents, how simple cooperation mechanisms can lead agents to increase their survival capacity. Let us suppose that the predator agents can survive if they are capable of finding one prey animal per unit of time. The probability of finding a prey animal is given by P_{ind} for a given species of predator and a given environment. If individual predators are isolated, the survival probability is then directly equal to the probability of finding a prey animal:

$$\sigma_{ind} = P_{hunt}$$

By forming a group, the predators increase their survival probability if the prey animals they bring home can nourish more agents than there are hunters. Thus, the survival probability for an agent if grouping takes place is equal to:

$$\sigma_{group} = P_{hunt} * k / n * c$$

where k represents the number of agents a prey animal can nourish, n is the number of agents the group contains, and c is the number of hunters. Survival as a group is thus an improvement on individual survival if $\sigma_{group} > \sigma_{ind}$, that is, if $k * c > n$ or, in other words, if the amount of food is more than sufficient for the number of agents concerned. So, by making it possible to share the prey, forming a group has increased the survival capacity of the agents. While all the agents consume, only the hunters are producers. Such a system can profit from increased productivity, as the hunters are able to catch larger prey than an isolated agent could, and are more likely to locate a prey animal in the first place.

2.4.4 Improving performances

Performance indicators translate the capacity of an agent or a group of agents to accomplish tasks defined by third parties. The observer may belong to the group – for example, may be the financial analyst of a company – or may be external to the group as in the case of a programmer observing his or her robots. There are various performance indicators, but they have to translate the intrinsic characteristics of a collective. For example, for a group of explorer robots, the performance indicator set may be the amount of ore brought back per unit of time, or else the number of actions (movements) required to bring back a given amount of ore. For an action coordination system allowing aircraft to avoid any collisions, the indicator given can be the discrepancy between the trajectories followed and the ideal trajectories taken from the flight plans (Zeghal *et al.*, 1993). And finally, if possible, it is always worth coming back to considerations of energy and interpreting performance indicators as energy efficiency indicators.

In the case of explorer robots, forming a group associated with communication can improve their productivity by comparison with an identical assembly of robots which are not cooperating. To bring back ore, the robots first have to find the ore deposits and then return with samples. Let us suppose that initially we have only one robot. To start with, it looks for ore deposits on a random basis. Then, if it detects one, it goes towards it, fills its bucket with ore and returns to base. We can improve its efficiency by increasing the number of agents. With several robots which are not cooperating, each robot merely improves the performance levels of the group linearly. There is no improvement in productivity. If, on the other hand, as soon as a robot finds ore it alerts the others to the fact – either by giving the position directly or by leaving marks on the ground (cf. Chapter 8) – then a larger number of robots can be mobilised for the task of transporting the ore, and thus the productivity of each of them can be improved.

Qualitative and quantitative amplification

Cooperation therefore consists in amplifying the capacities of the agents taken in isolation, and improving their performances. This improvement can be *quantitative*, as we have just seen, but it can also be *qualitative*, that is, make actions possible which it would be impossible for isolated agents to carry out.

Collaborations allowing the performances of agents to be qualitatively improved are essential, for without them action is quite simply not possible. Let us suppose, for example, that we want to create a magazine. Someone who knows only how to write articles without knowing anything about page make-up or printing cannot obtain the desired result on his or her own. He or she needs the help of someone who can produce a page mock-up, and also the help of a printer. And this is also true for computing agents: software that knows how to compute but does not know how to print will need the services of a printer and printing software.

The qualitative performances of agents are therefore fundamental in making possible the qualitative performance of the group. But we must not neglect

Table 2.2 The four forms of collaboration, depending on the amplification produced and the advantages obtained.

Advantages Amplification	Qualitative	Quantitative
Qualitative	Qualitative collaboration	Catalysis
Quantitative	Mass effect	Quantitative collaboration

quantitative performances, for they sometimes make possible qualitative results which are impossible without this collaboration. For example, if a transporter robot wishes to carry an object which weighs 100 kg, and it has only the strength to carry 70 kg, it will be totally incapable of accomplishing its action. If the object is all in one piece, it is impossible to carry only 70% of it! For this reason, the assistance of other robots, although initially they contribute only a quantitative amplification, makes an action possible, transforming quantitative assistance into qualitative collaboration. We then say that we are faced with a *mass effect*, linked to a critical quantity of agents. These phenomena are due to non-linear characteristics of collaboration obtained by adding up the capacities of different agents. This concept is well known in chemistry and in nuclear physics, where certain reactions can take place only if concentrations reach a certain threshold.

Conversely, it is possible to obtain quantitative advantages based on qualitative amplification. Thus, the presence of a supplementary agent endowed with new skills can lead to an overall improvement in the performances of the organisation. For example, the presence of a police officer at a crossroads generally makes it possible to improve the flow of traffic. It is the control skill possessed by this officer that makes it possible to ensure an improvement in the system's capacities. Likewise, in the case of the explorer robots, the introduction of a robot capable of building roads will make it possible to increase the speed at which the robots move, and thus to improve the group's performances. We shall refer here to a *catalysis* phenomenon, by analogy with the chemical phenomena where the mere presence of certain chemical constituents – catalysts – makes possible an improvement in reaction speeds, although these catalysts do not play any direct part in the reactions.

Consequently, we can note that amplifications obtained through cooperation can be quantitative or qualitative, and that the advantages obtained can also be qualitative or quantitative. We then obtain Table 2.2, which represents the four possible collaboration situations, depending on the amplification and advantage parameters.

2.4.5   Conflict resolution

By reason of their autonomy, that is, their capacity to determine their own behaviour, agents are led into situations where their interests may be contradictory. They are then, objectively, in conflict situations. These situations essentially arise from a problem of access to limited resources. Two agents simultaneously desire something which cannot be shared, or for which any sharing reduces what one of the agents could have obtained if the other had not been present. For example, when two people want to make their photocopies on the same machine at the same time, they are in a conflict situation. The same applies to vehicles passing each other at a crossroads, to aircraft at risk of colliding, to people who want to acquire the same good, to nations that wish to acquire the same territory, to teachers who want to teach the same course at the same time in the same classroom, or to companies that want to obtain bigger shares of markets. In all these cases, resources are limited and it will be necessary to use conflict resolution techniques to manage the confrontation.

Situations of conflict are simultaneously the effect and the cause of interactions. They have their origins in a lack of resources, and they call for supplementary interactions so that a way out of conflict can be found, whether by techniques of negotiation or arbitration, or the use of a regulation, or even recourse to competition and force.

Although purely conflictual or synergic situations do exist, most natural situations display both conflictual and synergic features at the same time. For example, in an ecological niche, individuals of different species cooperate, since their survival depends on nutrition cycles which involve the other species in the niche; but they are also adversaries, since there is competition between neighbouring species to acquire the resources of the ecosystem. In a general fashion, complex systems are founded on an integration of synergic situations and situations of conflict, with the former providing for the improvement of performances and the latter making possible the selection of the agents concerned.

Conflict indicators very simply translate the number of agents in a conflict situation (the effective number of collisions between aircraft can be counted – preferably in a simulator – with and without coordination of actions) or the number of individuals wishing to gain access to the same resource at the same moment (the number of processes waiting to be carried out on a processor, for example).

2.5 Methods of cooperation

How is cooperation to take place? Although we have studied the conditions of cooperation, we have so far said nothing about the means available for its realisation. We can classify these means into six categories that we shall call *methods of cooperation*: grouping and multiplication, communication, specialisation, collaboration by sharing tasks and resources, coordination of actions, conflict resolution by arbitration and negotiation.

2.5.1 Grouping and multiplication

The first method is clearly the most obvious, and for that very reason is often forgotten. It consists very simply in arranging for the agents to draw physically closer together, that is, to form either a more or less homogeneous unit in space or a communications network allowing several agents to behave as if they were physically side by side. For example, the animal world uses grouping to provide for a large number of needs. In particular, the safety of each of the group members is increased by the implementation of a group defence (the mass is more solid, more difficult to attack), by a greater degree of vigilance (some stand guard while others can go about other business without risk) and finally by the enhanced probability that, should a predator attack, it will be one of the other members of the group that succumbs.

Living as a community also makes it easier to obtain food, since it only needs one member of the group to find something interesting for all the others to profit from it. For example, as soon as one seagull dives and brings back fish (or scraps of food thrown overboard from a boat), the other seagulls form a group around the first and benefit from its discoveries. As regards the chances of finding a sexual companion for reproduction, these improve as well. Living in a group also makes it easier to acquire complex behaviours by allowing the young to compare themselves with adults and to have a large number of behavioural models available to them which they can then imitate.

Lastly, groups simplify navigation problems, as is shown by migrating bird formations, shoals of fish or herds of elephants. The overall effort involved in navigation is reduced if a single agent (or a small number of agents) alone decides where to go and the others follow the movement.

Finally, we can consider a group as acting like a distributed organism. There are specialists in finding food, and specialists in defence or hunting. There are those that provide for reproduction and those that guide the group in finding habitats to suit its needs. All the members act both for their own good and for that of the group, for by looking after society as a whole, they are looking after themselves and their progeny.

On the other hand, multiplication, the simple quantitative increase in the number of individuals in a given system, offers considerable advantages from the point of view of both the improvement of performances and their reliability. For example, in the case of the explorer robots, the fact that a large number of robots is available is not a neutral factor as regards the reliability of the system. If the overall performance in the absence of breakdowns is equal to the sum of the individual performances, that is, if the differential improvement of performances is zero, this is no longer the case if agents do have breakdowns. If we have only one agent available, any breakdown can have troublesome consequences, for the task cannot be accomplished. If, on the other hand, we have several agents available, redundancy will make it possible to improve the reliability of the system (without there necessarily being any improvement in individual productivity).

2.5.2   Communication

The communication system which connects up an assembly of agents acts as a sort of nervous system, which brings individuals that are sometimes separated into contact. In effect, communication expands the perceptive capacities of agents by allowing them to benefit from the information and know-how that other agents possess. Communications are indispensable to cooperation, and it is difficult to conceive of a system of cooperating agents if no system exists which allows the agents to exchange information or make requests. In cognitive systems, communications take place through the sending of messages, while in reactive systems they result from the diffusion of a signal in the environment. Communication constitutes one of the fundamental means of providing for the distribution of tasks and the coordination of actions. Its different aspects will be studied in Chapter 6.

2.5.3   Specialisation

Specialisation is the process through which agents become more and more adapted to their tasks. It is often difficult to create agents that can specialise in all tasks. Carrying out a task to a high performance level often assumes the presence of structural and behavioural characteristics which cannot allow for other tasks to be carried out efficiently. For example, a robot which is very well adapted for excavating and carrying out deep searches for ore, and whose entire structure is dedicated to the boring of holes, will not necessarily be very well adapted to transporting or detecting ore, which requires robots that can go anywhere to cut the transport time. Specialisation is not necessarily the result of an *a priori* choice. Agents which are originally totipotent can progressively specialise in carrying out a temporarily allocated role, through a kind of individual adaptation. This specialisation can well be beneficial to the collective, by increasing the group's capacity to solve a similar problem more quickly. For example, in the collective sorting problem (Deneubourg *et al.*, 1991), in which agents have to place 'blue' or 'red' objects in piles, starting from a random distribution, their behaviour essentially consists of simply moving in a random manner and, if they find a pile of objects, picking one up and putting it down again near a pile of the same colour. A. Drogoul has shown that, if agents are used which are capable of reinforcing their tendency to prefer one colour to the other, then such a specialised society is more efficient than a society of totipotent agents (Drogoul, 1993), owing to the reduction in random wanderings resulting from greater sensitisation to a particular type of object.

2.5.4   Collaborating by sharing tasks and resources

Collaboration consists in several agents working together on a project, a common task. We shall consider collaboration techniques as being all those that enable agents to distribute tasks, information and resources (among themselves) in the advancement of a common labour. Resolving a collaboration problem therefore consists in answering the question 'Who does what?' in respect of a given piece of work. There are numerous ways of distributing tasks and means.

In cognitive agent systems, tasks are distributed by means of supply and demand mechanisms. We can then distinguish between centralised distribution mechanisms in which a coordinating agent centralises the supply and demand and then distributes them to the best advantage; and distributed approaches in which all agents can be offering supplies and making demands at the same time without any centralising organ. There are then two contrasting techniques: those based on acquaintance networks (Gasser *et al.*, 1987), that is, on mutual representations of the capacities of each agent; and those based on the market concept, with requests for bids protocols, the best known of which is the 'contract net' (Davis and Smith, 1983).

It may come as a surprise that it is possible to speak of the allocation of tasks in the case of reactive agents. One might indeed suppose that their limited capacities would not allow them to put into operation mechanisms as complex as the algorithms we have just analysed. However, it is possible both for tasks to be distributed to agents and for the agents themselves to become specialised in the accomplishment of particular tasks.

Chapter 7 is entirely devoted to the issues of collaboration, and develops the different techniques for allocating and distributing tasks, information and resources in both cognitive and reactive multi-agent systems.

2.5.5 Coordination of actions

Managing an assembly of agents presupposes the carrying out of a certain number of supplementary tasks which are not directly productive, but which simply serve to ensure that the productive actions can be accomplished under the best conditions. In the case of a monolithic system, these supplementary tasks form part of the organisational system, but in the case of a multi-agent system, where work is necessarily distributed, we speak of *coordination tasks*. The latter are indispensable as soon as we have an assembly of autonomous agents pursuing their own goals. The carrying out of productive tasks entails a whole range of coordination tasks without which the former could not be accomplished.

The action coordination phase is directly implicated in the definition of the order in which the actions are to be carried out. Chapter 8 is entirely devoted to the issues of the coordination of actions in cognitive or reactive multi-agent systems.

2.5.6 Conflict resolution by arbitration and negotiation

Arbitration and negotiation are two of the means used by multi-agent systems to resolve conflicts, to stop disagreements between individuals from turning into open struggles, and to prevent the performance levels of the system as a whole from deteriorating. Arbitration leads to the definition of rules of behaviour, which act as constraints on the assembly of agents. Their overall effect is to limit conflicts and preserve individuals and societies.

In human societies, behaviour is subject to a body of laws and regulations which govern social activities and restrict the activities of individuals (ideally) for the good of all. There exists an organ of arbitration, the justice system, whose function is to ensure that these collective rules are respected and to supervise their application. This organ also acts to determine responsibilities in conflicts and to decide on the punishments that people judged to be guilty should suffer. In multi-agent systems, the body of social rules acts as a set of behavioural constraints, more or less internalised by the agent. Obviously, these 'laws' can be applied only to very highly developed cognitive agents, which have a kind of 'free will' and are capable of weighing the pros and cons in assessing the consequences of their actions.

When cognitive agents engage in conflict over objectives or resources, we often prefer not to have recourse to an arbitrator, but rather to allow the agents to resolve the conflict themselves by seeking a bilateral agreement through a negotiation process. This form of resolution has been studied in particular by the American school grouped around V. Lesser (Conry *et al.*, 1988), E. Durfee (Durfee *et al.*, 1989) and K. Sycara (1989). In spite of the obvious interest of this problem, we shall not develop it further in this work.

But if negotiation techniques take pride of place in cognitive multi-agent systems, the same cannot be said of reactive systems which cannot go into conflict resolution phases of this type. The behaviour of the agent is 'wired up', so that it is prevented from exceeding the limits which have been assigned to it by the designer, and thus from contravening the social laws. So it is as if these laws had been directly 'compiled' in the behaviour of the agents, in the form of inhibition or avoidance mechanisms (cf. Chapters 3 and 8).

2.6   Organisations and cooperation

2.6.1   The cooperation activities system

Functions and methods of cooperation are interconnected, of course. Certain methods are more applicable to certain functions, others resolve intermediate problems such as the distribution of tasks or the coordination of actions. It is possible to give an integrated view of these different elements in the form of a systemic diagram, shown in Figure 2.3. This diagram shows on the one hand their interdependence, and on the other how objectives connected with survival, performance levels, reliability and conflict resolution are secured by using elementary methods which themselves cause problems that can be dealt with only by more complex levels of techniques. Increasing the survival probability of agents pre-eminently involves improving the performance levels of the group, which requires the application of methods such as grouping, increasing the number of agents and differentiating their roles. But these methods themselves raise other problems, such as the distribution of tasks and an increase in the number of conflicts owing to problems over access to resources and to a lack of coordination. The methods employed in task allocation, communication, coordination of actions and conflict resolution (arbitration, negotiation, hierarchisation) serve to solve these problems and so contribute to improving the performance levels of the group. All these techniques need to be structured within organisations which describe the way

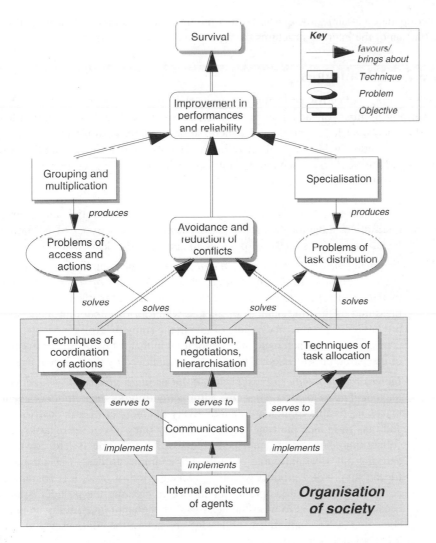

Figure 2.3   Cooperation activities system. Organisations emerge from the interactions originating in techniques for allocating tasks (collaboration), arbitration, negotiation and coordination of action.

in which agents are positioned in relation to each other, and how they can effectively work together. These organisations can be predefined by the designer, or else can emerge from the interactions between agents, as we shall see in Chapter 3. Cooperation thus requires the implementation of mechanisms to improve the performance levels of the group in order that more of its members shall survive, but as a counterpart to this it requires social structures that have both positive and negative consequences for the agents. Finally, the efficient creation of these methods of cooperation assumes the existence of communication mechanisms, as well as the definition of the internal structures the agents need if they are to interact.

2.6.2 Advantages

By favouring collective performances from the agents, cooperation thus offers a certain number of advantages which are expressed either in individual improvements, such as a productivity increase or an increase in the probability of survival for individuals, or by collective improvements, such as the accomplishment of tasks which would have been impossible otherwise. Here is a list (not exhaustive) of the advantages of cooperation[†]:

(1) *Accomplishing tasks impossible to perform alone.* This entails an essential qualitative advantage, as we have seen. In this type of situation, collaboration alone makes it possible to carry out the desired action.

(2) *Improving the productivity of each of the agents.* This quantitative advantage makes it possible to obtain what are called *economies of scale* in business management. Production then increases in a better than linear way, measured against the number of agents, which brings about an increase in productivity. We saw an example of this in the study of explorer robots. This is an essential characteristic of collaboration in that it favours the emergence of new structures, thanks to the economies achieved by the different agents.

(3) *Increasing the number of tasks carried out within a given time or reducing the time it takes to carry out a task.* Simply multiplying the number of agents makes it possible to increase quantitatively the number of tasks carried out and thus to reduce the time required to carry out a given set of tasks. But collaboration may prove indispensable if a limited time is laid down for carrying out a certain quota of tasks. For example, to carry out a contract for the supply of a product within a precise period of time, it is sometimes necessary for several people to collaborate in creating the product, simply because of the need to meet the deadline. This quantitative improvement is converted into a qualitative benefit, since breach of the contract would have led to a whole series of difficulties.

(4) *Improving the use of resources.* By managing the use of certain resources better through collaboration, it is possible to reduce functioning costs by balancing requirements, which then comes down to either increasing the system's productivity (a second advantage) or improving performance levels and making actions possible (a third advantage). For example, if a program functions on a multi-processor, it can be useful for the processors to collaborate, so that the agents can balance their workload on different machines through a dynamic load balancing mechanism.

[†]Durfee, Corkill and Lesser (Durfee *et al.*, 1989) propose a similar classification in the context of distributed problem solving, but they do not differentiate between the qualitative advantages and the quantitative benefits.

There is quite obviously a very close link between collective performance levels and individual survival capacities. The action of the agents contributes to the collective performance which, in return, ensures that more individuals survive. However, gaining this advantage imposes constraints on individuals by limiting their margin for manoeuvre.

2.6.3 Social constraints and emergence of structures

Structures emerge from interactions. We have seen that these structures are necessary for the survival of the group, for they amplify its capacity. For example, the line of explorer robots emerges simply from the interactions tending to improve the performance levels of the group. But it is these structures which, through the effect of a social feedback loop, define individual constraints. In fact, the cooperation mechanisms, by increasing the performance levels of the group and by improving the survival capacities of individuals, are translated into the establishment of a certain number of social standards and constraints tending to restrict the range of possible behaviours for an individual and integrate it into a more and more rigid social organisation. For example, improving performance levels through specialisation of agents, as in the case of the Manta system (cf. Chapter 7), leads to an impoverishment of their totipotence capacities, and thus reduces their margin for manoeuvre. They then become more dependent on others, and therefore less and less capable of surviving alone. Specialisation confines them to a role from which they are less and less capable of liberating themselves, and on which they become more and more dependent. The social mechanisms put into place to ensure the viability of the group impose further constraints on the individual options for agents by restricting their behaviours and forcing them to become even more socialised, that is, more and more specialised and dependent on others. There is thus a positive feedback effect between improved performance levels, increased chances of individual survival, and establishment of social constraints tending to limit individual options for action, as we saw in the previous chapter.

3 Multi-Agent Organisations

Multi-agent systems can make one's head spin when one starts to analyse them. The parameters that can be varied are so numerous that one has the impression of facing an infinity of special cases, which it will therefore be impossible to analyse exhaustively. And indeed, simple variations in agents' capacities of representation, in the way they coordinate their actions, or in their estimation of their own ability or inability to undertake tasks, will produce very diverse multi-agent systems, whose general properties are very difficult to define.

However, in spite of this diversity, it is possible to devise appropriate methods for analysing the organisation of an MAS, and thus to be in a position to bring order to what at first appears to be a product of chaos.

3.1　What is an organisation?

Together with interaction, organisation is one of the basic concepts for multi-agent systems. When we speak of organisation, we assume that an assembly of entities already exists and has a certain unity, that some of the different interdependent elements of this assembly are subordinated to others, and that they share a convergent activity. Organisation therefore requires a certain amount of order among entities which may be heterogeneous, and this order contributes to the coherence of the whole.

Definiton
An organisation can be defined as an arrangement of relationships between components or individuals which produces a unit, or system, endowed with qualities not apprehended at the level of the components or individuals. The organisation links, in an interrelational manner, diverse elements or events or individuals, which thenceforth become the components of a whole. It ensures a relatively high degree of interdependence and reliability, thus providing the system with the possibility of lasting for a certain length of time, despite chance disruptions (Morin, 1977).

In a multi-agent system, numerous interrelationships exist among the agents, through the delegation of tasks and the transferring of data, through obligations, through synchronisation of actions, and so on. These interrelationships are possible only within an organisation but, reciprocally, organisations require these inter-relationships in order to exist. So organisations are simultaneously the support for these interrelationships and the manner in which they manifest themselves, that is, the way in which tasks, data, resources and the coordination of actions are distributed.

In addition, and this is what makes it so difficult to define, the term *organisation* designates both the process of building up a structure and the actual result of this process. This duality of meaning points up the dynamic aspect of all organisations. Strictly speaking, there are no static organisations. Organisation is necessarily dynamic, and is always in the process of reorganising the assembly of entities and the links uniting them.

3.1.1　Organisational structures and concrete organisations

But beyond this dynamic, something persists which is unvarying, which we shall call the *organisational structure* (or simply *structure*, if there is no ambiguity). The organisational structure is what characterises a class of organisation on the abstract plane. Conversely, the *concrete organisation* (or simply organisation) is one possible

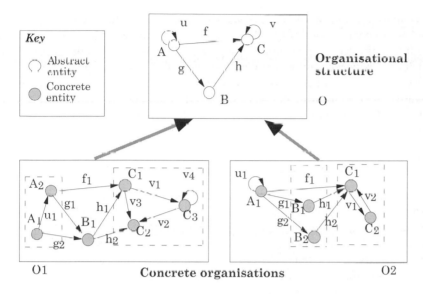

Figure 3.1   Organisations and organisational structures.

instantation (in the sense used in object-oriented languages) of an organisational structure, an implementation comprising the assembly of entities which effectively take part in the organisation, together with all the links which bring these agents into association at any given moment[†]. It is possible to associate an organisational structure with any concrete organisation, but the same organisational structure can act as a base for the definition of a multitude of concrete organisations. If we apply to organisations the definition laid down by P. Delattre (1968) for structures, we can say that an organisational structure is defined through these two data:

(1)   an assembly of classes of agents characterised by the roles allocated to the agents;

(2)   a set of abstract relationships existing between these roles.

Finally, these organisational structures will be classified on the basis of their capacity for adapting and evolving according to requirements. To obtain a concrete organisation, we have to add the assembly of agents belonging to the different classes, and describe the concrete relationships which exist between the agents, that is, to instanciate the abstract organisation. Figure 3.1 illustrates the abstract/concrete duality. The organisational structure, O, is described by the set of roles which can

---

[†]These terms are not standardised. We should point out, in particular, that Maturana and Varela (1987) use the term 'organisation' to refer to what is here termed 'organisational structure' and 'structure' to refer to what is here termed 'organisation'. P. Delattre puts forward another definition, referring to 'relational structure' instead of 'organisational structures' and 'total structure' instead of 'concrete organisations'.

be contained within it (A, B, C), whereas concrete structures comprise a large number of concrete entities $(A_1, A_2, B_1,$ etc.), the A_i being associated with role A. The links between concrete entities $(g_1, g_2, h_1,$ etc.) correspond to the abstract links which exist between abstract entities $(g, h,$ etc.). For example, the abstract link g, which links the abstract entity A to B, is expressed concretely in the concrete organisation O_1 in the form of two links, g_1 and g_2, which respectively link A_2 to B_1 and A_1 to B_1 while in O_2 similar links, g_1 and g_2, respectively link A_1 to B_1 and A_1 to B_2.

3.1.2   Levels of organisation

The interesting thing about the concept of organisation is that we can simultaneously integrate the concept of an agent and that of a multi-agent system. Indeed, from the designer's point of view, an agent is not merely an individual, but also an assembly of components. Likewise, a multi-agent system can be considered simultaneously as a composition of agents and as a unit, when we study the interactions of this system with another technical device.

The concept of levels of organisation makes it possible to consider the embedding of one level into another. In the same way that, in biology, a cell is considered as being an organisation of macromolecules and at the same time an individual being for the multicellular organism of which it forms a part, we can similarly consider that an organisation is an aggregation of elements of a lower level and a component in organisations of a higher level (Figure 3.2).

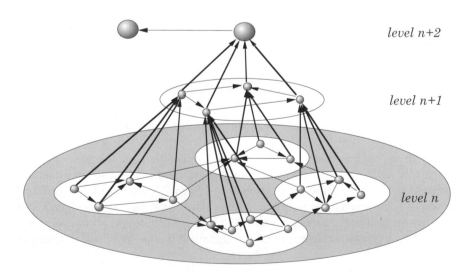

level n+2

level n+1

level n

Figure 3.2   Agents at level n are grouped into organisations which can be considered at level $n + 1$ as individual entities. Inversely, individual entities at level $n + 1$ can be seen at level n as organisations. The process can be repeated on any number of levels.

We shall use the term *elementary component* (or *module*) to refer to units of a lower level considered as being impossible to break down further (by means of this analysis, at least), and the term *general multi-agent system* to refer to an organisation not (from a certain point of view) forming part of an organisation at a higher level than itself. Finally, we can make a distinction between *individual organisations* (or *individual entities*), which are considered from without as individuated beings (that is, as agents), and *collective organisations* (or *collective entities*), which are made up of an assembly of individuated beings without necessarily being individuated themselves.

The difference between individual and collective entities lies above all in the existence of what biologists call a *membrane*: the fact that an individual entity separates its internal space from the external space in such a way that interactions between the internal components and external entities can be effected only within very precise limits dictated by specific components responsible for inputs and outputs. Collective entities do not make distinctions of this kind (or make them rarely), and they cannot naturally appear as constituting an individual.

Agents are thus, first and foremost, individual entities, whereas multi-agent systems are essentially collective entities. Nevertheless, an agent which is itself made up of an assemblage of agents will be considered at a certain level as an individual organisation and, at the next lowest level, as a collective organisation.

3.1.3 How should an organisation be studied?

Faced with all the possible organisations, the analytical approach adopted should be structured. This is why we shall distinguish three elements:

(1)   *Functional analysis*, which describes the functions of a multi-agent system in its different dimensions.

(2)   *Structural analysis*, which distinguishes between the various possible forms of organisation and identifies some essential structural parameters.

(3)   *Concretisation parameters*, which deal with the transition from an organisational structure to a concrete organisation, and raise the difficult question of the effective realisation of a multi-agent organisation.

3.2   Functional analysis

The functional analysis of an organisation leads to the identification of the principal functions that the components of this organisation should fulfil. In the context of such an analysis, an organisation can be seen as a system of roles, each role being defined by the set of properties exhibited within the organisation by the agents having that role. We shall see that it is possible to make this analysis more precise, developing these functions in several dimensions corresponding to the different points of view from which an organisation can be studied.

3.2.1   The functions of an organisation

The roles describe the position of the agents within an organisation, together with the set of activities that they are supposed to carry out in order that the organisation may achieve its objectives. They thus characterise the functions that the agents fulfil, independently of their internal structure and of the mechanisms brought into play. For example, an agent that manages execution requests and distributes them to competent agents will have a *mediator* role; an agent that determines the actions to be undertaken will have the role of a *planner;* an agent that chooses between a number of possible actions will be called a *decision-maker;* an agent that performs a service for another, considered as a *customer*, will have the role of a *supplier;* and an agent whose main function is executive will be an *executive.* These roles are defined with reference to the functions required for an organisation to shape itself in accordance with its aims (and, more particularly, with the objectives and needs of its designer) and to adapt to its environment.

Such roles are not necessarily fixed, but can evolve with the dynamics of the organisation. For example, an executive, through the evolution of the organisation, may become a mediator, a decider or a customer. Likewise, a supplier for a given set of activities can be considered as a customer for other tasks. So each agent has a set of roles available which are characteristic of the different abstract services it can carry out within an organisation, and which determine its position in relationships with other agents. The roles are grouped into subsystems†, that is, into sub-organisations of the main organisation, characterised by their functions which can be either centralised or distributed among the components of the organisation. Here are the six main functions of an organisation and some of the associated roles:

(1)   The *representational function* comprises the generality of functions for modelling the environment and other organisations, as well as the memorisation of any events which may have affected the organisation. This function is particularly well developed in individual cognitive organisations (that is, cognitive agents), which have an internal representation of their environment which they can manipulate in order to plan the actions they have to undertake. In a collective organisation, the representational function, like the other functions, can be distributed among a whole group of agents. In companies' information systems, for example, this function is particularly well developed, since it corresponds to the preservation and filing of all the information carried within the company. Electronic document management systems only improve this function. The role associated with the representational function is that of *archivist*.

(2)   The *organisational function* relates to everything concerning the management of the activity of an organisation, and in particular to the planning, allocation and following up of tasks, the coordination of actions and the

---

†The terms 'system' and 'subsystem' should be understood here as having the same meaning as when they refer to the circulatory, respiratory or vegetative systems of the human body.

management of obligations. This function is obviously essential, and it is the one that has been studied in the greatest detail in the domain of multi-agent systems. A large number of roles are associated with this function, in particular those of *customer*, *mediator*, *planner* and *coordinator*. This function, together with the associated roles, will be dealt with in greater detail in Chapter 7.

(3)   The *conative function* (from the Latin *conari*, to prepare oneself for, to undertake) refers to the sources, limits and selection of the activities of organisations. This function is itself divided into three sub-functions: that of motivations, or the *motivational function*, which describes how goals or tendencies are formed, whether in connection with internal demands (needs, desires, drives) or external ones (requests from other agents, social pressures); that of the building up of *constraints*, which describes the standards and inhibitions which place limits on the organisation's possible range of actions; and finally that of decision making, through the *decision function* which, in combination with the organisational system, handles the evaluation and selection of goals to be achieved and tasks to be undertaken. Each sub-function defines a set of associated roles, the most common being that of *decision-maker*, which is associated with the decision function.

(4)   The *interaction function* serves to create the link between an organisation and that which surrounds it. This is what manages interaction activities between the organisation and its environment, as well as all communications with other organisations. It thus provides for all input–output and interface functions. It is made up of two sub-functions, the perceptive function, which is responsible for the acquisition of data coming from outside, and the executive function, which deals with the carrying out of actions selected by the conative system and set in train by the organisational system. The roles associated with this function are those of *interface* agents (*observer*, *executive* and *communicator*).

(5)   The *productive* or *operative function* concerns the primitive activities which have to be brought into play to solve a problem or carry out a piece of work. This function depends on the application. A MAS dedicated to linguistic analysis, which comprises agents capable of carrying out lexical, syntactic, semantic or pragmatic analysis, will clearly not have the same productive function as a set of explorer robots which have to explore, drill and transport ore samples. There is consequently no characteristic role associated with this function.

(6)   The *vegetative* or (*preservative*) *function* deals with the preservation of both structure and agents, with the acquisition and maintenance of resources, and with the tasks carried out to maintain and reproduce the organisation. For example, for an animat (cf. Chapter 5), eating, looking after itself and reproducing make up the basic behaviours managed by the vegetative system. For a collective organisation, the vegetative function handles both energy replenishment and waste disposal, but also deals with the integration

of new agents, by recruitment or reproduction. This function, which the military refer to as intendancy, also deals with the repairs which have to be undertaken for the organisational structure to endure.

All these functions are obviously linked, like the nervous, circulatory, reproductive and digestive systems of living beings. All are necessary for the satisfactory operation of an organisation, even if some are reduced to their simplest expression, as is the case for the representational function in reactive agents, where it barely exists at all; or distributed over a grouping of agents, like the decision function in a reactive multi-agent system. Figure 3.3 illustrates the main relationships which associate these systems to one another. Let us take a simple example. Let us suppose that we create a robot, Clifford, capable of going to look for objects and bringing them back. Perhaps it is capable of detecting certain stimuli; of recognising tools, such as pliers or a hammer, if they are in front of it; or of identifying the room it is in (on the basis, for example, of an infrared code, or a camera and a shape recognition system). To do this, it must have available organs of perception and shape recognition modules. At the other end of the chain, we find the action primitives (going straight on, turning left, turning right, picking up an object, putting it down, and so on) and mechanisms for receiving and transmitting messages. All this makes up Clifford's interaction function.

If Clifford's role within an organisation at a higher level is to transport objects, its productive function will be made up of a set of transport operations such as 'Go into room X' or 'Bring back object X which is in room P'.

Its organisational function will be responsible for planning tasks. It is this function which will provide for the monitoring of operations, and which will refer them to the conative system if there is a problem. For example, if Clifford is asked to tidy up all the tools, the components responsible for the organisational function

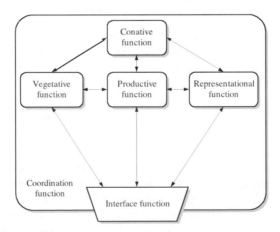

Figure 3.3 Schematic representation of the different functions of an organisation. This diagram applies to both agents and multi-agent systems.

will plan the actions to be accomplished, treating the transport operations of Clifford's productive function as primitives. Clifford may thus be able to break this task down into a set of more elementary actions such as going to look for the pliers which are in the outhouse and bringing them into the shed, then going to look for the hammer which is in the shed and taking it into the workshop. Subsequently, in discharging the organisational function, it will have to follow up on these tasks, making sure that they have in fact been carried out.

The representational function manages Clifford's representations of the world, which are directly utilised by the planning mechanisms. For example, if Clifford is effectively a cognitive agent, its representational function will be characterised by the set of mechanisms which try to match up Clifford's representations with the structure of the environment, by constructing a map of the place it has to go to, showing it the open or closed routes, memorising the positions of the tools, and so on. This function also memorises the agent's various forms of know-how, which it can profit by in making plans. Whereas the productive function is concerned with the carrying out of 'compiled' plans, the representational function has a symbolic description of these operations, so that the components linked to the organisational function can plan new operations.

Finally, the conative function is responsible for evaluating situations and making decisions. For example, it is not certain that Clifford will agree to tidy up all the tools if it is already in the middle of accomplishing other tasks which it considers to be more important. In particular, if its energy level drops too far according to information received from the organs of its vegetative system, it will abandon the tasks in progress to try to return to a correct energy level before carrying on with its productive activity.

This example is not only applicable to a single agent. Let us suppose that a team of agents is responsible for transporting objects. The various functions will be distributed among the agents. Some will have more responsibility for the actual transportation of the objects, and will thus constitute the productive function of the team. The organisational function will be carried out by the set of agents responsible for the planning of actions, the monitoring of their execution, the coordination of transport activities and, in a general way, the team administration in general. The representational function can be either distributed among all the transport agents or else centralised in a few agents which will continually update a map of the area showing the position of the objects and the agents. The agents responsible for the interaction function will devote themselves to communications (radio liaison, management of telecommunications, etc.) with the other teams and with the base. Finally, agents specialising in the conative function will determine the priorities within objectives and decide on the general tasks to be accomplished.

3.2.2   Dimensions of analysis

The study of the preceding functions, and so also that of the roles of the agents, can be considered with reference to several dimensions:

(1) The *physical dimension* (ϕ) deals with implementation, the architecture of the organisation and its personal resources. This dimension responds to the question: 'How is this carried out, explicitly, within the organisation?' While it is not indispensable to be able to answer this question if one is interested only in the behavioural analysis of an organisation, a MAS designer cannot evade it, for the existence of a directly executable operative representation forms the basis of data programming and of all the synthetic sciences aimed at the construction of artefacts.

(2) The *social dimension* (σ) concerns the place and thus the role of an organisation in a higher-level organisation. This dimension is thus also concerned with the social aspect of the activities of an organisation, that is, with its capacity to respond to the general needs of the higher-level organisation of which it forms part, and promote its proper functioning.

(3) The *relational dimension* (α) is concerned with interactions, with the exchanges which an organisation may have with other organisations on the same level, and with its communications and their coordination. This dimension responds to the question: 'Through whom, why, and in what way does an organisation interact with other organisations?' It is at this level that the interaction protocols are defined, that is, the strings of reciprocal behaviours which organisations produce during their exchanges.

(4) The *environmental dimension* (χ) is linked to an organisation's capacities to act, perceive and reason in relation to the surrounding world. It is on this level that are defined its capacities for interactions with the world, strictly instrumental skills. This dimension responds to the question: 'What are the possibilities of action for an organisation, what technical expertise does it possess, and in what way is it capable of acting on the world?'

(5) The *personal dimension*, or *dimension of the self* (ω) represents everything which relates to the essence of the organisation, and in particular to its 'meta' aspects: representation of self, acquisition of knowledge, preservation of structure and auto-poietic activity.

Figure 3.4 expresses these dimensions on two axes. The relational and environmental dimensions lie on the same horizontal plane, for the relationships which an agent has with other agents or with the environment are effected on the same level as the agent itself. The vertical axis corresponds to the social and physical dimensions. These two dimensions are at once opposed and complementary if we consider an agent as a higher-level organisation in relation to components considered as lower-level agents.

In this case, the social dimension of the 'component' agents overlaps the physical dimension of the 'society' agent, as shown in Figure 3.5. In effect, the social function that a 'component' agent provides for within a 'society' agent is a point of view complementary to that of the physical dimension of the 'society' agent, which sees its components as organs providing for its behaviour and ensuring

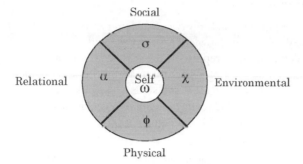

Figure 3.4   An organisation can be analysed with reference to five dimensions: social, relational, physical, environmental and personal (self).

its viability. Finally, the personal dimension is the hub of these oppositions, the reflexive centre from which the agent can construct itself as a subject acting in the midst of other agents.

3.2.3   Dimensional analysis of an organisation

The functional analysis of an organisation along the dimensions we have just mentioned makes it possible to set up analysis grids to give a fairly precise picture of the nature of an organisation. It is in fact possible to project the six functions of an organisation on to these five dimensions.

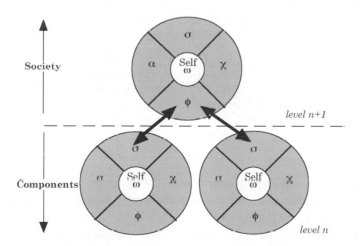

Figure 3.5   'The social dimension of level n is directly linked to the physical dimension of level $n + 1$. The agents of level n are the agent components of level $n + 1$. Conversely, the agents of level $n + 1$ constitute the society in which the agents of level n move.

Representational function

ϕ The *representational/physical dimension* covers everything that relates to the way in which knowledge is represented, together with the inferential architecture used. It represents the way in which the reasoning mechanisms are implemented (inference motors, blackboards which trigger events, programs in Lisp or in C++, and so on). The physical dimension corresponds to what Newell (1982) calls the *symbol level*, as distinct from the *knowledge level*, and thus acts as an implementation dimension, on to which the other dimensions are projected.

σ The *representational/social dimension* concerns the representations which an organisation, and in particular a cognitive agent, makes for itself of the society in which it finds itself, that is, the models enabling it to understand the collective goals, aspirations and social norms which constrain it. Few multi-agent systems implement this dimension.

α The *representational/relational dimension* is concerned with the representations of other organisations. When the organisation is an agent, we then speak of representations of contacts, that is, representations of other agents which the agent knows and with which it can communicate directly. Particular attention has been paid to this dimension in DAI, since L. Gasser's work on Mace (Gasser *et al.*, 1987).

χ The representation of objects in the surrounding world and of the laws of the ambient universe takes place in the *representational/environmental dimension*. When the organisation is an agent, this dimension may be lacking if it is a software agent or, on the other hand, a purely reactive agent. If the organisation is a multi-agent system, the environmental dimension corresponds to the aggregate of interactions which the system maintains with that which is not the system, by means of sensors or interface agents.

ω The *representation/personal dimension* relates to representations of self, that is, the beliefs that an agent has about its own capacities, its know-how, its plans and goals, etc. At this level, everything that is normally unconscious for an organisation becomes explicit, which means that the organisation can then reason about it.

Organisational function

ϕ The *organisational/physical dimension* describes the architecture and implementation of the mechanisms of control, planning and management of the organisation's activities.

σ The *organisational/social dimension* relates to the planning of social tasks, that is, to the definition of the roles allowing a lower-level organisation to accomplish tasks useful to the higher-level organisation.

α The *organisational/relational dimension* has been the subject of much study in connection with DAI, for it deals with the planning of interactions and the coordination of actions and communications. A large part of the work done on cooperation and the coordination of action focuses on this dimension. In particular, requests for bids protocols and for the coordination of actions form part of this dimension.

χ   The *organisational/environmental dimension* handles the planning and control of the execution of actions in the environment, where problems of interaction with other agents are not involved. How are boxes arranged in piles? How do I get from one place to another? are questions that seek responses which have to be built up along this dimension.

ω   The *organisational/personal dimension* corresponds to the problems of meta-organisation, that is, to the control and management of internal tasks. For an agent, this dimension covers what is understood by the term 'meta-level control' (Pitrat, 1990; Maes and Nardi, 1988; Ferber, 1989).

Conative function

φ   The *conative/physical dimension* of the conative function corresponds to the implementation of production and the management of drives, constraints and tendencies or goals.

σ   The *conative/social dimension* corresponds to the collective goals and social constraints which a higher-level organisation gives itself, and which it then retransmits to its members. For example, scoring goals is a collective objective for a football team: each player will try to behave in such a way that the group scores goals, even if he does not try to put the ball in the net himself. By his actions, which form part of a collective approach, he will allow others to score, and thus to achieve the collective aims of the group. The same principle applies to the norms which are generally established on the basis of a collective decision. Laws, for example, apply to everyone, and thus constrain everyone's possible actions. These constraints, which are a secondary effect of the interactions between agents, act as a social amplifier, tending to specialise the roles played by agents within a social organisation (cf. Chapter 7).

α   The *conative/relational dimension* is concerned with demands and constraints from other organisations which entail the production of personal objectives. The demands are generally requests for the recipient organisation to perform actions for, or supply data to, the organisation making the request. When organisations are agents, this type of behaviour is described by communication mechanisms and, in particular, when cognitive agents are involved, by the theory of language acts (cf. Chapter 6).

χ   It is along the *conative/environmental dimension* that are defined the sources of desire and repulsion which an organisation encounters in the surrounding world. The importance of this for animats is especially clear. For a predator, the prey animal is a source of desire; for an explorer robot, ore. It is also possible to induce indirect 'desires'. For a cleaning robot, for example, we could arrange for wastes to be sources of 'desire', so that they would motivate its cleaning action. Conversely, certain objects or agents can be sources of repulsion. The prey flees the predator, an aircraft flees the other plane with which it is at risk of colliding. This means that objectives (both positive and negative) can be located in the environment, while linked to the internal needs and goals related to the following dimension.

ω It is through the *conative/personal dimension* that motivations deriving from the internal needs of the organisation are developed. Such needs are generally based on data coming from its vegetative system and include the need to find energy resources and the need for protection and reproduction.

Interaction function

ϕ The *interaction/physical dimension* describes the implementation of input–output systems made up of mechanisms for communications, perceptions and action. When the organisation is an agent, it is at this level that its sensors and its actuators are described. It is here too that passband problems in communications are dealt with, and in general, everything that relates to the lower levels of communication. This does not form part of the domain of kenetics, but goes back to research done on robotics and on telecommunications networks.

σ The *interaction/social dimension* relates to the primitives of interaction between the individual and the organisation to which it belongs. This dimension, which is generally not implemented in MASs, comprises mechanisms for election, court hearings and so on, and in general, all protocols which, in democratic societies, ensure that individuals have a certain capacity to act on society as a whole.

α The *interaction/relational dimension* deals with the definition of the primitives of communication, that is, with the description of the types of messages transmitted and received by the agents.

χ The *interaction/environmental dimension* describes the primitives of perception and action available for an agent. It is this subsystem that is used (on the conceptual and logical plane, material problems being managed by the physical dimension) to analyse and filter perceptions, and to define possibilities of action.

ω The *interaction/personal dimension* is generally non-existent in current MASs. It would correspond to the possibility (at present only a human one) of talking to oneself and acting on one's own body from outside. One might also think of a robot which would be capable of carrying out repairs on itself or modifying some of its functionalities.

Productive (operative) function

The productive function describes the aggregate of tasks which an organisation is able to accomplish, including all the know-how it can apply in the world as well as all the objects it can produce. The productive function represents the *raison d'être* of an organisation, that is, its function in relation to the project which brought about its creation, or its role in relation to a higher-level organisation.

It is within this dimension that the articulation between the different levels of organisation is particularly clear. A function considered as 'productive' for an organisation on level n often serves to define a function of another nature at level $n + 1$. For example, while we can regard the production function of a group of hunter agents as that of bringing back food, this function can be described at the level of the society to which these agents belong as a vegetative function. Likewise, agents specialising in planning action on behalf of others are described as having a productive planning function, whereas at the level of the society this function is considered as organisational. So the productive functions of level n generally become non-productive roles on level $n + 1$. Only some activities are considered as productive on several levels. For example, an ore-gathering robot on a lunar or Martian base has the productive function of gathering ore which becomes, on level $n + 1$, an element in the fundamental productive function of the society of robots which consists, precisely, in extracting and producing ore. Nevertheless, there is always a level where these functions become an integral part of an organisation on level $n + 1$, and lose their productive character. For example, if we look at things from the level of the totality of all human beings, ore-gathering can be integrated into very high-level vegetative functions (production and consumption of goods allowing a society to survive better).

ϕ The *productive/physical dimension* describes the implementation of productive tasks, the mechanism making their activation possible, and their regulation if necessary. When these tasks produce physical objects, this dimension no longer forms part of the domain of kenetics.

σ The *productive/social dimension* describes the set of tasks carried out on behalf of a higher-level organisation, such as the tasks connected with the direction, management and administration of an organisation.

α The *productive/relational dimension* is concerned with the definition of relational tasks, which provide for cooperation and coordination of actions between organisations on the same level. A word of warning about the relational dimension: we must be careful to distinguish the relational/organisational function from the relational/productive function. The former relates to the way in which the components of an organisation are linked, and thus to the internal communications within an organisation. The latter relates to the set of supplementary functionalities attributed to a component so that the organisation can communicate with other organisations on the same level. For example, in the army, a 'sparks', or communications specialist deals with the processing of messages on a plane that is not accessible to others (use of specialised equipment, coded communications indecipherable for those who do not know the code) and takes responsibility for receiving and transmitting, coding and decoding messages exchanged with other groups.

χ   The *productive/environmental dimension* concerns the set of tasks making it possible for an organisation to be expert in activities relating to its environment, whether such tasks involve fault-finding, design or control. The specialist agents of a multi-expert system are essentially characterised by the productive tasks set out along this dimension.

ω   The *productive/personal dimension* concerns an agent's tasks of self-modification, in particular those that permit the personal acquisition of new expertise or new capacities.

Vegetative (preservative) function

The vegetative function deals with all the means an organisation has available to maintain its organisational structure, that is, to survive by preserving itself and developing its resources. In a certain sense, every task can be brought down to the vegetative function in the last resort, since all the objectives of an organisation participate in its conservation and its reproduction[†].

However, some are more directly implicated than others.

φ   The *vegetative/physical dimension* describes the implementation of the preservation system and of the tasks providing for individual and collective preservation.

σ   The *vegetative/social dimension* describes the set of tasks making possible the preservation of the higher-level organisation and the reproduction of organisations on the same level (procreation, education, etc.).

α   The *vegetative/relational dimension* concerns the preserving and improving of the links existing between several organisations on the same level. When these organisations are agents, it is this dimension which is used for the maintenance of the contact net or the verification of communications and protocols of cooperation.

χ   The *vegetative/environmental dimension* details tasks connected with the conservation of environmental resources and in particular in the event of necessity, with the defence of the territory against any other organisations on the same level that may be considered as intruders.

[†]It might be said that the objectives of the designer of a multi-agent system cannot be brought down to a problem of conservation and reproduction, and that we are dealing with supplementary objectives which cannot be reduced to the vegetative function. I think, on the contrary, that all the skill of the designer of a multi-agent system lies in setting up the system in such a way that the functional (and thus productive) objectives of an organisation are secured as a side effect of the satisfaction-seeking mechanisms of agents acting as if their survival (or the survival of the organisation of which they are members) depended on their actions. This then entails the integration of the external objectives of the designer into the vegetative function of the organisation. It should, however, be pointed out that this conception has been developed mainly by the reactive school (Steels, 1994; McFarland, 1994), and that the cognitive school does not particularly hold to it.

ω   The *vegetative/personal dimension*, for an organisation, implies self preservation, the search for food and the carrying out of repairs and self-maintenance.

Table 3.1 summarises the relationships between systems and dimensions.

3.2.4   Grid for functional analysis of organisations

Not every multi-agent system has all the functions, and not all of them develop their functions in all directions. For example, reactive organisations have no (or at least little) representational function. Likewise, purely communicative organisations (which do not tackle the problem of interaction with an environment) have almost no development at all in their environmental dimension. Finally, most current multi-agent systems, within which socialisation capacities are generally still very poorly developed, provide for practically no social dimension.

Table 3.1 can be understood as a true interpretation grid making it possible to situate organisations in relation to one another by indicating the functions, and thus the roles, effectively developed along the five dimensions. To do this, we indicate, in each box in the table, whether the corresponding function is explicitly implemented in the associated dimension. For example, Table 3.2 shows the analysis grid of a typical reactive organisation, for which social and relational dimensions do not exist, everything being situated along the environmental and physical dimensions.

This organisation has no representation of what surrounds it, and is driven only by the perception of elements in the environment which serve it as stimuli to trigger its actions. It does not communicate directly with other organisations through messages, but indirectly through objects situated in the environment (gradients of smells, for example). It does not plan any tasks, but simply manages environmental actions, and its productive capacities are expressed uniquely in the environment. The cross in the conative/personal box indicates merely that some of these organisations can be motivated by internal stimulations (elementary needs) but that not all have this capacity. In examining this table, we immediately discover that, apart from the column for the physical dimension, which must necessarily be completed if at least one point exists on the corresponding line, only the environmental dimension has been filled in. This type of organisation is entirely oriented towards the environment, and all its behaviours relate to actions and perceptions in the world.

Table 3.3 shows the very different analysis grid for a purely communicative organisation (for example, a purely communicative cognitive agent) which has no mechanisms for action or perception relating to the outside.

Here the environmental column is almost empty, since there is no contact with the environment. On the other hand, if this organisation has any representation of itself and of others, its representational system will be more developed than in the case of reactive organisations. Its conative system is entirely oriented towards the relational, which means that its objectives are the result of demands coming from

Table 3.1 Functions and dimensions of an organisation.

	Physical (φ)	Social (σ)	Relational (α)	Environmental (χ)	Personal (ω)
Representational	Representation structure, models of representation and inference	Representation of roles and functions, representation of group and society	Representation of others (goals, beliefs, skills)	Representation of world, representation of laws of universe	Self-representation of self and own capacities
Organisational	Control of tasks, type of planners	Planning of social actions, distribution of tasks and roles between agents	Control of communications, planning of interactions, coordination of actions and allocation of tasks	Planning of actions in environment, organisation of tasks requiring expertise	Meta-planning, control of planning
Conative	Nature and implementation of objectives, drives and constraints	Demands from society, collective goals and social constraints	Demands from others, demands from self to others, obligations to others	Sources of pleasure and repulsion	Internal drives, desires, internal constraints
Interactional	Implementation of communications primitives, sensors and actuators	Description of interactions between agent and society	Description of communication mechanisms between agents, definition of performatives	Description of perception and action mechanisms	Auto-communication, auto-actions
Productive	Architecture of tasks, regulation of actions	Tasks of management and administration of organisation	Relational coordination and negotiation tasks on behalf of other agents	Expert tasks relating to analysis and design	Auto-modifications, learning
Preservative/ vegative	Implementation of conservation system, individual resources, memory, CPU	Preservation of society, reproduction of species	Preservation of relationships, maintenance of contact net	Conservation of resources, defence and maintenance of territory	Self-preservation (food), repairs and maintenance

Table 3.2   Analysis grid of functionalities of a typical reactive organisation.

	Phys.	Social	Relat.	Env.	Pers.
Representational	—	—	—	—	—
Organisational	●	—	—	●	—
Conative	●	—	—	●	X
Interactional	●	—	—	●	—
Productive	●	—	—	●	—
Preservative	●	—	—	●	—

Key: Systematic presence: ●   Optional: X   Absence: —

other agents (and possibly from a higher-level organisation) and not from internal needs, and even less from environmental signals. The productive system obviously depends on the nature of the agent's speciality. If we are dealing with an observation or execution agent, the productive tasks will be defined in the environmental dimension. On the other hand, if this is a mediator or coordinator agent, the productive system can be developed along the social and/or relational dimensions. Finally, most of these organisations do not (so far) include any ·preservation, maintenance or reproduction tasks. The organisational/personal and conative/personal boxes have been marked with a cross to indicate that it is usual for a cognitive organisation to have functionalities allowing it explicitly to reorganise the tasks to be accomplished and to take account of a set of conditions depending on demands coming from outside and obligations already formulated.

Table 3.4 gives the analysis grid for an agent having characteristics similar to those of a (real) social animal. It has only a minimal capacity for representing the environment and, although it has direct communications mechanisms, these are not very well developed. Its behaviour is entirely determined by environmental stimuli, internal drives, and some direct demands. It is capable of reproducing itself and of having behaviour leading it to try to preserve its identity and that of the group to which it belongs. Obviously, it does not produce anything directly (although its

Table 3.3   Analysis grid for a typical purely communicative organisation.

	Phys.	Social	Relat.	Env.	Pers.
Representational	●	●	—	—	●
Organisational	●	X	●	—	X
Conative	●	X	●	—	—
Interactional	●	—	●	—	—
Productive	●	X	X	X	—
Preservative	—	—	—	—	—

Key: Systematic presence: ●   Optional: X   Absence: —

Table 3.4 Grid for an agent similar to a social animal.

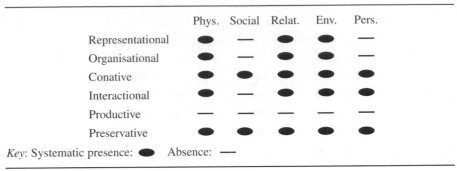

	Phys.	Social	Relat.	Env.	Pers.
Representational	●	—	●	●	—
Organisational	●	—	●	●	—
Conative	●	●	●	●	●
Interactional	●	—	●	●	●
Productive	—	—	—	—	—
Preservative	●	●	●	●	●

Key: Systematic presence: ●   Absence: —

biomass can serve its predators and its parasites). Table 3.5 represents the analysis grid for an organisation which is astonishing, because it is complete. It has all the qualities, and its polyvalent productive system can specialise on the basis of demand. It offers the best representational system known, and it is capable of learning and of planning its actions. This organisation, which appears to be perfect from the point of view of our criteria, represents a human being or a human society ....

3.3   Structural analysis

A multi-agent system appears to be an extremely complex system. Structural analysis attempts to bring order to all possible interactions between agents by isolating the abstract relationships which connect them and the way in which they evolve over time. But before embarking on any detailed analysis, we need to be sure that we understand the various ways of approaching the concept of a multi-agent system.

Table 3.5 Analysis grid for a human organisation.

	Phys.	Social	Relat.	Env.	Pers.
Representational	●	●	●	●	●
Organisational	●	●	●	●	●
Conative	●	●	●	●	●
Interactional	●	●	●	●	●
Productive	✗	✗	✗	✗	✗
Preservative	●	●	●	●	●

Key: Systematic presence: ●   Optional: ✗

3.3.1 Agents and tasks

Breaking down a problem, in multi-agent terms, raises the difficult but crucial question of knowing what an agent really represents in relation to the problem to be solved. More precisely, it is a question of defining the relationship between the individual productive function of the agent and the productive function of the organisation to which it belongs. The definition of a multi-agent system should answer the following questions:

(1)   *What should be considered as an agent for the area in question?* It is necessary to identify what an agent is in relation to a given problem, through an analysis based on a functional approach (an approach centred on the function) or an object approach (an approach centred on the individual and the product).

(2)   *What is the relationship between the agents and the tasks?* What are the tasks to be accomplished, how should they be distributed among the agents, and what is the extent of the redundancy of agents in relation to tasks?

An agent is obviously characterised by its architecture and its behaviour. But, for the designer of a multi-agent system, the agent is characterised above all by what it can do, that is, by its productive function, and thus by its contribution to a multi-agent system. We need, then, to identify what should be regarded as constituting an agent with respect to a given problem, and to address this question from a conceptual and methodological viewpoint applicable to all future questions. This problem can be compared with the analytical phase which is encountered in software engineering methods, and particularly, in object methods, where one has to *reify* the entities which will be represented in the computing system in the form of objects (Ferber, 1990).

Object or functional approach

In the context of the development of computer programs, we can distinguish *functional design* methods, in which the breakdown unit is the function, characterised by its input–outputs and its transfer function; and *object design* methods, which put the emphasis on the entity in question, on the links which it maintains with other entities, and on the operations of which it is capable. It seems natural to think of multi-agent systems as a natural extension of design by objects. Some researchers, in fact, consider the agent to be an object endowed with autonomy, capable of reasoning about its environment and of choosing between several alternatives. But many systems which claim to be using a multi-agent approach nevertheless tend to associate with each agent a precise role characterised by its function in the global organisation.

So it is clear that there is no one universal way of deciding what an agent represents. We can take a variety of approaches to the identification of agents, each leading to the creation of a different multi-agent system. In particular, the work of

Lesser and Durfee (Durfee *et al.*, 1989) and Steeb and Camarata (Steeb *et al.*, 1988) showed that it was possible to analyse the same problem from several different angles by emphasising certain of its characteristics more than others.

The example of an air traffic control system, examined initially by Steeb and Camarata, illustrates this diversity of approaches (Figure 3.6). Which should be the agents responsible for avoidance and for controlling the different operations? The aircraft, the airspace sectors, or the different phases of piloting such as taking off, landing, or following the flight plan?

In the first case, we say that the approach is *object-centred*: it is the aircraft that is responsible for its own movements and that decides on the actions it should undertake, on the basis of interaction with the other planes. Each aircraft then has all the functionalities required for its activity, and in particular the skills to manage the various phases of piloting.

In the second case, the approach is *space-centred*. Each part of the airspace is a portion of environment which controls the movements of all the objects in its sector, the aircraft thus being only passive objects which merely obey orders from the control tower. The operations managing the different piloting phases are no longer associated with the aircraft but with the agents representing the different portions of airspace.

Finally, the third category is characteristic of a *functional approach*: the piloting phases represent the experts who manage the movements of all the aircraft in a centralised manner. As soon as an aircraft is in a specific phase (following a flight plan, waiting, landing, taxiing, taking emergency action, etc.) it is taken charge of by a specialist in the subject.

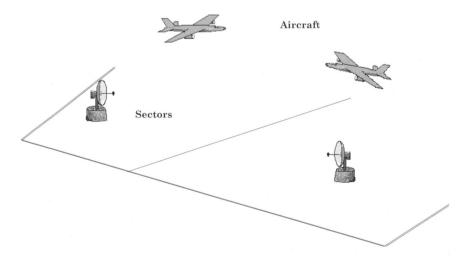

Figure 3.6 In an air traffic control system, we can consider the aircraft, the sectors or the flight phases as agents, depending on whether we emphasise an object, spatial or functional approach.

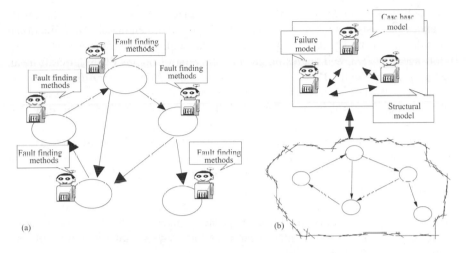

Figure 3.7   Schematic representation of organisations based on the object approach (A) or the functional approach (B) applied to fault-finding in networks.

Only the first and third categories can be applied in almost all scenarios, while the second, representing parts of the environment as agents, cannot. Although it is a possible option for situated agents[†], we shall not deal with it in this chapter, since it is rather infrequent in practice. Functional and object approaches are often antinomic to one another. Let us take another example characteristic of multi-agent systems, such as those for tracing faults in a distribution network. Should the components of this network, that is, the distribution or conversion nodes, be considered as agents (object approach)? Or, on the contrary, should we prefer a functional approach which will consider the agents as being specialists in fault-finding, each using a specific method to solve the problem overall (structuro-functional model, failure model, case base reasoning, and so on)?

Figure 3.7 illustrates these two possibilities.

The functional approach is often considered to be simpler when the agents are not physically situated. The agents then represent specialists characterised by their function and role in the general organisation. This breakdown has affinities with the functional analysis methods of traditional computing and with classic systemic analysis, which identifies the various activities and functions of systems and not the entities on which these functions are applied. On the other hand, the object approach, as used in multi-agent systems, can be seen as an extension of object-oriented analysis and concepts characteristic of the current trend in software engineering.

Nevertheless, the object and functional perspectives can be combined with each other if we view the functional approach as defining a subdivision of the object

[†]We shall return to this approach when dealing with the modelling of the environment in Chapter 4.

approach. For example, we can carry out an object analysis in which the initial breakdown consists in taking the aircraft as agents, and then undertake a functional breakdown of each agent-aircraft by treating the control system of each plane as a multi-agent system, and analysing each of the control organs of the aircraft as an agent in its own right. This possibility results simply from the stratification of the levels of organisation, as we saw above, and from the fact that an object analysis level can itself be broken down into lower-level entities which are then identified as functions.

The question of which perspective is used in designing a multi-agent system is not a neutral one, however. This choice affects every aspect of the creation of the system. Object-centred approaches are generally more 'radical', in the sense that they assume that the agents involved have perfect autonomy. They are almost entirely based on the definition of interaction models and their ability to solve the problem through a totally distributed approach. Functional models, on the other hand, are regarded as being more 'classical', as they do not normally call into question the methods of skill analysis.

Vertical and horizontal breakdowns

A functional approach can be expressed in two different ways, depending on whether preference is given to a *horizontal* or a *vertical* conception of the functions. A vertical functional division associates with each function a complex activity centred on a specific application. In the example of air traffic control, this means linking a function to a phase in the flight plan, as we did above.

By contrast, a horizontal breakdown puts the emphasis on what is shared by the vertical functions. This is the approach we selected for our functional analysis. The six functions (representational, conative, productive, organisational, interactional and vegetative) were cut up horizontally, and thus represent the horizontal functions of an artificial organisation.

Great importance has been accorded to the study of this horizontal/vertical duality in the context of the structuring of agents (Fodor, 1983). For example, for a mobile manipulator robot, a vertical breakdown would require a function to be associated with each of its actions. There would be, for example, the obstacle function of searching for and transporting the object, the function of placing one object on another object, the drilling function, the obstacle-avoiding function, and so on. By contrast, if a horizontal approach is adopted, the functions emphasised will be memorising and inference, perception, coordination of specific actions, and so on, without these functions being defined for precise tasks.

It is of course very rare to see an artificial system organised totally on the basis of only one of these two axes. Hybrid breakdowns are more common than purely vertical or purely horizontal ones. For example, it is possible to design a system in which the initial breakdown is horizontal, distinguishing peripheral activities (interpretation and production of messages, perception, motor mechanisms) from expert cognitive activities (interpretation of situations, know-how), intentional mechanisms and control mechanisms. In the second phase, we would break down each of these modules vertically by distinguishing the different forms of perception and motivity, or the different forms of expertise (for moving in a universe, analysing visual images and carrying out specific tasks) within the domain of competence.

Nevertheless, vertical breakdowns are more closely tied in with the solution of specific problems, whereas horizontal breakdowns are more generic in their approach. This is why reactive agents, or those which are designed using traditional computer science, are more often broken down vertically, whereas more 'AI' agents tend rather to be treated in a horizontal manner.

3.3.2 Abstract relationships

On the abstract level, organisational relationships describe the forms of interrelationships which can occur between functional classes of agents, that is, between roles. We distinguish between two types of organisational relationships: *static relationships*, which form the skeleton of an organisation and characterise the organisational structure predating any functioning, and which are defined without reference to any execution; and *dynamic relationships*, which constitute the flesh of organisations and describe the relationships which are modified during interactions. Table 3.6 describes the principal relationships encountered in multi-agent systems. We can distinguish seven main types of relationships:

(1)   An *acquaintance relationship* between two agents, *A* and *B*, indicates that *A* knows *B*, that *A* has a representation of *B* and that it can address its communications directly to that agent. This is the minimal relationship between two cognitive agents. It generally serves as support for all the other relationships (Figure 3.8(a)).

(2)   The existence of a *communicational relationship* or, more precisely, of a *channel of communication* between two agents, *A* and *B*, indicates that *A* can send messages to *B*. Acquaintance relationships are the preferred supports for channels of communication (Figure 3.8(b)).

Table 3.6 Organisational relationships. A dash indicates that there is no special name to distinguish the static or dynamic forms of a relationship.

Relationships	Static	Dynamic
Acquaintance	—	—
Communicational	—	—
Subordination	Master/slave	Service demand/request
Operative	Dependency between tasks	Obligation to do
Informational	Dependency between knowledges	Validation obligation
Conflictual	—	—
Competitive	—	—

(3)   *Subordination relationships* describe a transfer of execution between a demanding or requesting agent, *A*, and an executive agent, *B*. When this relationship is static, *B* cannot refuse a request from *A*, and *A* and *B* are thus in a master/slave relationship (Figure 3.8(d)). When it is dynamic, this means that *A* merely requests services from *B*, and that *B* can refuse *A* services (Figure 3.8(e)).

(4)   *Operative relationships* represent dependencies linked to tasks. An agent *A*, which has to accomplish a task T_x, may need the results of a task T_y from an agent *B* in order to complete it. In this case, we shall say that *A* depends on *B* for its actions. The dynamic form of these relationships then covers what are called *commitment dependencies*. In undertaking to do something, an agent allows other agents to count on its being done and thus to plan their own actions, on the assumption that the obligation will be discharged. (Figure 3.8(f)).

(5)   *Informational relationships* are concerned with validity dependencies between the various things an agent knows. When the knowledge of an agent *A* depends on that of *B*, this means that *A* has not done any experimenting of

Figure 3.8   Icon chart of principal relationships between agents (informational, conflictual and competitive relationships are not represented).

its own, but that it places its faith in *B* in respect of certain beliefs. These dependencies will be dealt with in Chapter 5.

(6)   *Confidential relationships* indicate that several agents are in conflict over access to resources. The existence of such relationships indicates the need to coordinate access to the resources on the basis of a negotiation between agents, if necessary.

(7)   *Competitive relationships* correspond to a competition situation between agents and are a signal that their goals are incompatible.

3.3.3   Coupling modes

If organisations can be characterised by the quality of the links that unite agents, they are also described by their capacity to modify themselves over time and to adapt to the evolution of needs, whether these needs come from endogenous sources (modification in number of agents, modification of agents' roles) or exogenous ones (modification of environmental characteristics). In order to adapt, organisations have to be capable of modification. In this respect it is possible to characterise three forms of organisation, according to the coupling of the components.

(1)   In an organisation with *fixed couplings*, each component has a role (or perhaps several roles) from which it does not shift. The relationships between agents are frozen too, reorganisations being impossible both on the abstract level of the organisational structure and on the level of concrete organisation. These organisations, which can adapt to their environment only with great difficulty, are more characteristic of classic software engineering than of the kenetic approach. We shall use them only to describe the functioning of agents, that is, as models of agents' architecture (cf. Section 3.6) but not as models of multi-agent systems.

(2)   *Variable couplings* correspond to fixed organisational structures whose specific implementations are variable. The relationships between agents can evolve, but within the framework of very specific mechanisms. This type of coupling is frequently used in multi-agent systems. We shall meet examples of it constantly.

(3)   *Evolutionary couplings* characterise variable organisational structures, the concrete organisation being sometimes variable and sometimes not. Abstract relationships between agents can then evolve, as a function of the performances of the organisation.

3.3.4   Subordination and decision-making structures

Subordination relationships characterise the control structure, that is, the way in which agents can cause other agents to carry out certain tasks. Some structures are particularly classic. We shall essentially distinguish between *hierarchical structures*, which assume that the subordination relationships have a branching structure, and *egalitarian structures*, in which an agent can ask any other agent to carry out a task – something which it may perhaps be able to refuse to do.

Hierarchised organisations, which are associated with a fixed coupling, are characterised by very centralised systems – very 'military', we might say – in which a chief gives commands to a second-in-command, which gives commands to a third-in command, and so on. This organisation can be found in most computer programs, where the subordinate elements are sub-programs. With variable coupling, this subordination structure generally brings about competition between the low-level components, the high-level components taking responsibility for arbitrating and selecting the winners. We thus sometimes talk of *competitive structures* in describing hierarchically structured variable coupling organisations.

Egalitarian structures are more characteristic of organisations in which all agents participate in a uniform way in the final decision. When the coupling is fixed, the components act in a distributed way as regards the decision making. This type of organisation can be found in architectures of the connectionist type (cf. Section 3.6). With variable coupling, this structure generates organisations based on the model of economic markets, where those who have demands and those who can supply eventually come to an arrangement which gives them both what they want.

3.3.5 Ways of setting up organisational structures

Organisational structures can be set up in two ways:

(1) They can be defined *a priori* by the designer, and we then speak of *predefined organisations*, which means that the abstract relationships, whether they are static or dynamic, are determined in advance. In the case of evolutionary organisations, it is the set of possible abstract relationships and the set of transformations which are known in advance. See Le Strugeon (1995) for an initial analysis of predefined evolutionary organisations.

(2) They can also be defined *a posteriori*, and we then speak of *emergent organisations*. These most frequently contain only reactive agents and are characterised by the absence of any predefined organisational structure, their structure being entirely the result of interactions between agents. In this case, positions and relationships are not determined in advance, but appear as the product of the behaviours of each of the agents. More precisely, the distribution of functions and tasks follows an auto-organisation procedure, which permits an organisation to evolve and to adapt easily to modifications in the environment and to the needs of a group of agents.

Although a certain form of emergence also exists in variable or evolutionary predefined organisations, this 'emergence' is always controlled by well-established communication diagrams, and the organisations which result from it are always described by very precise organisational structures, which is not the case for emergent organisations.

3.4 Concretisation parameters

The question which faces the designer of a multi-agent system is as follows: knowing the general task to be carried out, how should the designer distribute the set of skills among the different agents in such a way that the work is effectively executed? Is it preferable to have very specialised agents with only one skill, or is it better to adopt an approach involving *totipotent* agents in which each agent has all the desired skills and only numbers make the difference? For instance, to design a racing car one could call in a set of specialists with different skills (specialists in engines, chassis, tyres, and so on), making it impossible for one agent to replace another in his or her work. We could, however, imagine totipotent agents for transporting objects with different shapes. Each agent could then take the place of another agent if the latter failed, which increases the reliability of the system in case of a breakdown.

To explain more clearly what we mean by specialists and redundancy, it is necessary to go into more detail. To make the presentation simpler, let us suppose that each elementary task can be carried out entirely by one agent alone, and that there is therefore no qualitative improvement if several agents work together. For example, the cleaning of a surface can be carried out by a single agent, and bringing in a group of agents represents an improvement only in quantitative terms. We shall therefore eliminate from this discussion all elementary tasks which explicitly call for several agents to work together if they are to be accomplished[†].

In this case, if we call C_a the set of skills which an agent, a, has available, C^P the set of skills required to carry out a piece of work, P, and C_A the united skills of a set of agents, A, then we can say that the piece of work, P, can be carried out if $C^P \subseteq C_A$, that is, if all the skills required for the accomplishment of a piece of work are at least present in A. We shall say that an agent a is *totipotent* if it has all the necessary skills to carry out this piece of work on its own, that is, if $C^P \subseteq C_a$. We shall use the notation C_a^P for the set of skills which are useful for an agent, a, in carrying out a piece of work P: $C_a^P = C_a \cap C_P$.

On the basis of these definitions, it is possible to characterise the way in which work is distributed in a multi-agent system by two parameters: the degree of specialisation and the degree of redundancy.

(1)   The *degree of specialisation* (H_a^P) of an agent a for a problem P indicates the agent's skill rating in relation to the number of skills necessary to solve a problem. It is defined thus:

$$H_a^P = \frac{card(C^P) - card(C_a^P)}{card(C^P) - 1}$$

[†]This limitation is not too restricting. If a task proves to be too complex for a single agent, it can be broken down into simpler elements, in such a way as to bring it back within the limits. If it is absolutely imperative for two agents to participate in some actions, we shall then consider this as posing a problem of coordination of action, and we shall deal with it in Chapter 8.

If $H_a^P = 0$, the agent is *totipotent* for the problem P since it possesses all the skills required. Conversely, when it has only a single skill the rate is equal to 1, and the nearer this rate is to 1 the more the agent is *specialised*, and the weaker its contribution to the problem as a whole will be. We can generalise this degree of specialisation in a multi-agent system by considering the general degree of specialisation as being equal to the mean value of the specialisations of each of the agents:

$$H^P = \frac{1}{card(A)} \sum_{a \in A} H_a^P$$

(2)   The *degree of redundancy* characterises the number of agents possessing the same skills. If we use P_c to refer to the number of agents with the skill c ($P_c = card(\{a \mid c \in C_a\})$), then the degree of redundancy for a skill may also lie between 0 and 1, if we use the formula:

$$R^c = \frac{P_c - 1}{card(C) - 1}$$

If R^c is equal to 0, this means that there is only one agent capable of carrying out a task which requires a skill, c. The degree of redundancy is equal to 1 when all the agents have this skill, the redundancy being maximal. We can then compute the mean degree of redundancy in the following manner:

$$R = \frac{1}{card(C)} \sum_{c \in C} R_c$$

For example, in the case of a system based on cooperation between specialists, in which the agents cannot replace each other, the specialisation is high (close to 1) and the redundancy low (equal to zero if there is only a single agent per speciality). By contrast, agents of the more multi-purpose type will see their specialisation go down and their redundancy go up. We can sum up the various types of organisation of skills by means of the diagram in Figure 3.9. There are four extreme types:

(1)   *Non-redundant hyper-specialised organisation.* Specialisation 1, redundancy 0: an agent knows how to carry out only one task, and each task is carried out by only one agent. This type of organisation is characteristic of purely functional approaches, in which each function is represented in the form of an agent.

(2)   *Redundant specialised organisation.* Specialisation 1, redundancy 1: each agent knows how to carry out only one task, and each task is carried out by all the agents. This represents a limit case, in which all the agents have precisely one single and unique skill. This type of organisation is sometimes used locally to improve the reliability of a system (for example, a computation system comprising several processors in parallel which are computing the same function and which vote to decide the best result.

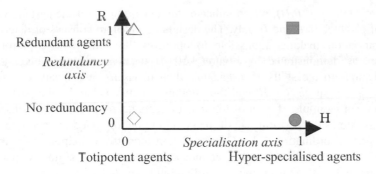

Figure 3.9   The different types of organisation of skills.

(3)   *Redundant generalist organisation.* Specialisation 0, redundancy 1: an agent knows how to carry out several tasks, and each task is carried out by a large number of agents. When the redundancy is equal to the number of tasks, then all the agents are totipotent. The problem then lies in the distribution of tasks among agents which, *a priori*, can do everything. We shall see an example of this in the case of reactive distribution by means of the Manta system (cf. Chapter 7).

(4)   *Non-redundant generalist organisation.* Specialisation 0, redundancy 0: an agent knows how to carry out all the tasks, but each task is carried out by only one agent. This is also a limit case, in which the multi-agent system comes down to a single and unique agent capable of doing everything by itself.

The general case is located towards the centre of the diagram. With a moderate degree of specialisation or redundancy, the agents know how to carry out several tasks, but not all, and each task can be carried out by several agents. The problem for the designer and the organiser of a multi-agent system is to create a high-performance organisation which is capable of displaying adaptability when the environmental conditions come to be modified. To assist him or her in the task, we can define quantitative parameters which take into account the qualities of the solution obtained or the efficiency of the system. In the example of the explorer robots, we may wish to know the time taken by a group of agents to gather a certain amount of ore. In the one where collisions between aircraft are being avoided, we will prefer to know the number of conflicts (the number of times aircraft cross each other's paths at a distance closer than the safety limit), or the divergence from the nominal trajectories laid down by their flight plan.

We can therefore establish a performance function based on several parameters such as the number or density of agents, the passing strip and communication times, individual characteristics, and so on. If we confine ourselves to only two parameters, R and H, that is, the redundancy and the specialisation of the agents, we can define an organisational performance function, to which we shall give the notation $\mu_s(R,H)$, which indicates the performance of the system S on the basis of parameters R and H only. The designer's problem consists of determining an organisation making it possible to optimise the value of the performance function, as demonstrated by Figure 3.10. If the system can evolve, through modifications to the skills of the agents, then it has its own means of changing position in the space $R \times H$, and thus finding a better value for the performance function. For example, if a set of totipotent agents becomes more specialised, this generally allows the performance of the system to be improved, in that it can avoid unnecessary coordinating tasks. Conversely, an increase in totipotency makes the system more adaptable. Finally, redundancy improves the system's qualitative performance, but also means more coordination is needed.

3.5   Analysis of a concrete organisation

How can a concrete organisation be defined on the basis of this set of parameters? All that is needed is to associate the characteristics obtained from functional and structural analyses with the specialisation and redundancy factors corresponding to the instantiation of the organisational structure. An organisation can thus be described through the following data:

(1)   The selected approach (object, vertical functional, horizontal functional) and the productive function of the organisation, that is, the set of technical resources, operations, plans, knowledge and know-how which has to be put to work to achieve the system's global objective and serve its *raison d'être*. This function is linked to the context of the organisation, that is, to the set of

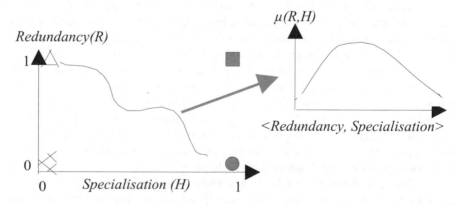

Figure 3.10   The problem for the designer of a multi-agent system is that of optimising the value of the organisational performance function on the basis of the redundancy and degree of specialisation of agents.

constraints and conditions characterising the way in which the multi agent system must operate.

(2)   The analysis grid for the organisation, which describes the way in which the six essential functions are projected along the five analysis dimensions.

(3)   The set of roles associated with the functions, together with the abstract relationships which link these different roles.

(4)   The way in which subordination relationships structure the authority link between the agents.

(5)   The value of the structural parameters, which are the coupling and the constitution.

(6)   The value of the concretisation parameters, that is, specialisation and redundancy.

Figure 3.11 groups all these characteristics together.

3.5.1   The example of explorer robots

To show how these different characteristics can be explained in an example, let us return to the explorer robots (cf. Chapter 1). We shall not deal with this problem in full, since the number of possible organisations is considerable, even for such a simple example. Instead, we shall look at a set of characteristic structures in order to understand how the different parameters we have examined can combine with one another.

Productive function and context

The first question involves knowing what the system does. What is its general objective, and what are its conditions of functioning? Let us suppose that a set of robots are to explore the planet Mars to gather ore. To do this, the robots have to find a place where there is ore, drill down to bring it to the surface, and transport it back to base. Let us suppose that each one of these tasks can be accomplished independently of the others, and that it can be accomplished by one robot alone. The productive function P_{explo} of the organisation then comes down to three tasks:

```
Pexplo = { find-ore, drill, transport-ore}
```

The vertical functional approach has been selected. Each robot has a certain number of skills, allowing it to accomplish at least one of the three tasks. Let us suppose that the system has to operate autonomously, that there are no maps of Mars, and that initially no one knows where there are significant deposits of ore. In addition, let us suppose that robots can be rendered inoperative for various reasons (being struck by a meteorite, falling into a crevasse, succumbing to various types of breakdown, etc.).

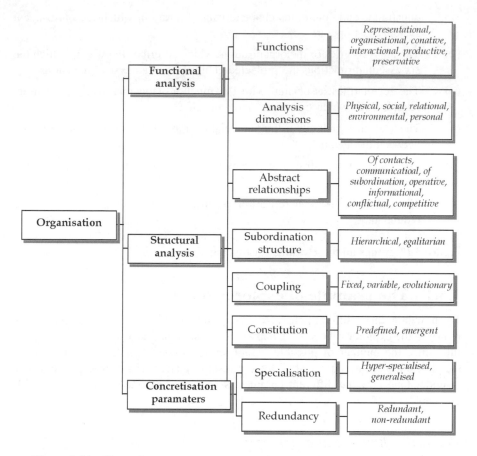

Figure 3.11 The various elements of an artificial organisation: function, structure, concretisation.

Functional analysis

Once we arrive at the functional analysis stage, we have to state our options and choose between cognitive and reactive agents. It is the representational and communicational functions that make the difference here. Cognitive agents will attempt to make a precise map of the terrain and position themselves in relation to it. For example, a cognitive agent, having detected ore, will indicate the position of the site to the others in the form of Cartesian or polar coordinates. On the other hand, a reactive agent will merely send a signal, varying in intensity inversely to distance, to guide agents towards it.

Another concern in functional analysis is to determine the constraints imposed on the vegetative function. To what extent are agents autonomous in regard to energy, and what are the resources available to them to re-energise themselves if necessary? Should supply agents be provided for, at the cost of adding new tasks? We shall not assume it in our structural analysis, but it is a point which would have to be resolved in a real case.

Structural analysis

It is during the structural analysis that the desired form of organisation is selected. In order to demonstrate some of the possible variants, we shall look at the following organisational structures:

- Fixed team organisations (fixed, hierarchical, predefined structure)
- Organisations with a variable, egalitarian, emergent structure
- Organisations using requests for bids (variable, egalitarian, predefined structure)
- Organisations with an evolutionary structure

3.5.2   Organisations with a fixed, hierarchical, predefined structure

In this type of organisation, which is also called a *fixed team organisation*, static roles and relationships can be defined in advance. Figure 3.12 shows one possible organisation, comprising two independent teams in which organisation is fixed and each agent is specialised. Each productive function is carried out by an agent, but several agents can carry out the same function. Each detector robot is associated with a well-defined set of drillers, and each driller is associated with a set of transporters. The detectors are in command of the drillers, and the drillers are in

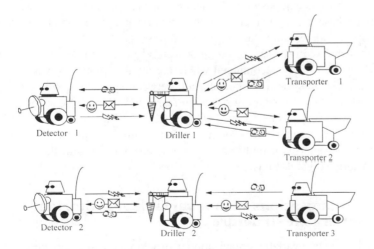

Figure 3.12   A fixed organisation, with static relationships. Here the general structure is also hierarchical.

command of the transporters. The drillers are dependent on the detectors, since the drilling action cannot be carried out unless ore has been detected, and in the same way the transporters are dependent on the drillers.

The subordination structure is hierarchical, the detectors being on the top level and the transporters on the bottom level. Communications go back and forth along this hierarchy defined by acquaintance relationships, but the subordination relationships always follow the same path. The detectors tell the drillers what they have to do, and the drillers give orders to the transporters. So there is necessarily only one detector per team, and the transporters are locked into an association with one driller.

Concretisation parameters

This type of organisation is hyper-specialised, since an agent accomplishes only one action ($H = 1$), but the redundancy is not specified. If the redundancy for detection in a team is 0 (but can be higher, depending on the number of teams), it is entirely a function of the composition of the teams, and thus of the concrete realisation of the organisational structure. One can devise minimal teams comprising only a single driller and a single transporter (and in this case the team's redundancy is equal to 0), or one could have bigger teams if it were thought that there were rich ore deposits and that large-scale operations were needed. The adaptation capacity of a fixed organisation is minimal by definition. If an essential agent happens to disappear, the whole team is lost. Moreover, its performance level is particularly low since, if the detector of a team takes a long time finding ore, its drillers and transporters will remain unused.

Several variants of this type of organisation exist. For example, we could envisage independent coordinating agents in direct charge of operations. These could be robots accompanying the teams on the ground, or software agents remaining at base, receiving reports on the situation and giving orders in return. The same observations remain valid for these variants.

In fact, fixed organisations are not well adapted to the problem of explorer robots. They are usually encountered where the number of agents is not very great and in particular in systems of cooperation between specialists, where each agent 'knows' where it has to obtain information from, and where to send results. So we are dealing with very rigid systems that are really more 'modular' than multi-agent. We shall not encounter these organisations again, except in relation to the constitution of agents, for multi-agent systems are defined with the assistance of more adaptative organisations.

3.5.3   Organisations with a variable, egalitarian, emergent structure

Organisations with a variable organisational structure and an emergent constitution are characteristic of systems peopled by reactive agents which are self-organising. If the explorer robots are totipotent, each agent can detect, drill and gather ore on its own. The problem in this type of organisation consists in making the agents capable of cooperating, so that if one finds ore the others can benefit from this discovery. We shall find out how to deal with this problem in Chapter 8.

The system's redundancy is equal to 1, and so we are looking at a very redundant generalist system. To improve performance levels dynamically, the robots can start to specialise while they are working, so that those that have already transported ore become more and more transporters, and those that drill become more and more drillers. In Chapter 7, we shall see a similar example in the case of a simulated ants' nest.

3.5.4 Organisations with a variable, egalitarian, predefined structure

This structure is typical of organisations based on requests for bids which are characterised by acquaintance relationships with a high degree of variability. Such organisations function in terms of an economic market metaphor whereby an agent with a task to carry out on other agents sends a request for bids. Those interested can respond by putting in bids, and the client agent then decides to which of them it wants to give the contract. This is the type of organisation most used in cognitive MASs.

Concretisation parameters

The specialisation parameter can be varied to obtain some very diverse configurations.

If the degree of specialisation is 0, that is, if the agents are totipotent, each agent can explicitly ask the others for help if the need arises. For example, if a detector agent finds ore, it can give the others the position of the seam so that the ore may be gathered as rapidly as possible. We shall see in Chapter 7 the sort of problems inherent in such an organisation, and how they can be solved.

If, on the other hand, the agents are more specialised, and particularly if the degree of specialisation is close to 1, they can accomplish only one action each. In this case, if we suppose that – as in organisations with a fixed structure – the detectors take the leading role, they can ask driller robots to come and gather ore. Only drillers which are free and close by will respond to this request. The same thing will happen with the transporter robots (Figure 3.13). So this organisation allows us to handle with great efficiency the fact that we are initially ignorant of the topology of the terrain and the site of the ore deposits. In addition, the disappearance of a robot – even of a detector robot – does not penalise the carrying out of operations, since no robot becomes totally indispensable to the project. The degree of redundancy is a guarantor of the system's capacity to function when there are breakdowns.

3.5.5 Organisations with an evolutionary structures

Evolutionary organisations have not received much attention as yet in connection with multi-agent systems. There are essentially two ways of approaching them.

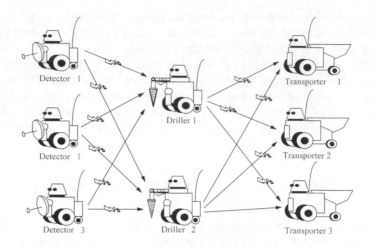

Figure 3.13 A variable-structure organisation with a predefined constitution. The subordination relationships are variable, and tasks can be allocated on the basis of requests. For the sake of clarity, only the subordination relationships have been displayed.

The first solution is to give the organisation predefined mechanisms, so that it can modify its behaviour and its structure when certain organisational parameters reach a critical level. This was the approach selected by E. Le Strugeon (1995) in proposing that an evolutionary organisation should be defined by an assembly of models of fixed or variable organisations, and that the system should decide on the application of one of them, depending on the value of specific internal parameters.

The second solution has mainly been studied in connection with artificial life. By incorporating genetic algorithms into the organisation (or its agents), we allow the society to evolve and adopt the organisation which appears the best adapted to the environmental conditions. C. Delaye (1993) with his Alia system has studied the way in which the introduction of genetic algorithms could affect the structure and functioning of an organisation of reactive and totipotent explorer robots.

3.5.6 Other work on organisations

Relatively little of the research that has been done into the problem of organisations has taken a systematic approach such as ours. We can, however, mention the work of Fox (1981), which classifies organisations ranging from the group, made up of independent non-cooperating agents, right up to the general market in which agents pursue individual goals depending on their decision structures. Mintzberg (1982) put forward a classification which is in fact applied to human organisations, but which has had a certain influence in DAI (Bouron, 1992; Le Strugeon, 1995). He distinguishes five characteristic organisational structures: simple structure (centralisation), mechanistic bureaucracy (hierarchy with limited horizontal decentralisation), professional bureaucracy (vertical and horizontal decentralisation), divisional structure (limited vertical decentralisation) and adhocracy (functioning through mutual adjustments between project groups).

Gasser (1992) proposes classification into four categories: centralised (which corresponds to the fixed adaptation mode, with subordination links of the master/slave type); market-like (which corresponds to variable predefined organisations with calls for tenders); pluralistic community (corresponding to our variable emergent organisations); and community with rules of behaviour (variable predefined organisations with interactions according to explicit protocols). He also maintains that what I have called kenetics ought to integrate developments in the theory of organisations, thereby constituting a field of research on synthetic organisations (computational organisation research) (Gasser, 1995), which would both further the understanding of human organisations and contribute concepts and theories of fundamental value to the design of artificial organisations.

Finally, the work of Pattison, Corkill and Lesser (Pattison *et al.*, 1987) makes use of an approach which is very similar to that proposed here for structural analysis. Organisations are made up of components characterised by different parameters (responsibilities, resources, knowledge) linked to one another by relationships. Accordingly, they distinguish between relationships of communication, authority (corresponding to our subordination relationships) and proximity (our contact relationships). They then set out a language allowing for the easy definition of organisations.

3.6   Individual organisations

Agents constitute a special, but essential, case of organisations. They are important not only because they are the starting point for the setting up of collective organisations, but also because they themselves appear to be the result of an organisation of lower-level components. For this reason, the structural analysis of an agent is similar to that of any organisation, apart from the fact that the components of an agent are generally not themselves agents but more or less specialised (horizontal or vertical) modules. However, we find there all the characteristics and all the parameters which we have previously examined in connection with organisations of every kind.

The term generally employed to describe the internal organisation of an agent is that of *architecture*, by analogy with the structure of computers. An agent can indeed be compared with a computer, with its organs of perception and action and its system of deliberation which resembles the input–output, memory storage and computation units of a computer. But this is a computer which is both less generalised (since the functioning of an agent, and even of a multi-agent system, can be simulated on a computer) and more evolved, since it is capable of pursuing its own objectives in an autonomous manner.

The resemblance between a computer and an agent should thus not be pushed too far, even if it does prove fruitful for anyone wishing to understand the organisation of an agent and to be in a position to construct an agent based on a given architecture, or even to invent new architectures. If computer architectures are relatively homogeneous, owing to the predominance of what is known as von Neuman architecture in almost all computers manufactured nowadays, the same does not apply to multi-agent architectures, which display a rich variety of solutions for designing agents equipped to produce the desired behaviour.

A cognitive agent naturally has a more developed architecture than that of a reactive agent. But the cognitive/reactive division certainly does not exhaust the debate over architectures. In the first place, there is a vast range of both cognitive and reactive architectures. More significantly, it is perfectly feasible to create reactive agents with architectures initially intended for cognitive agents, and vice versa. Apart from a few architectures such as those based on neuron nets, for which we are still not able to construct agents exhibiting very complex behaviour, most can be applied equally well to cognitive or reactive agents. Nevertheless, this assertion should be qualified by the recognition that certain architectures were developed within a specific framework, and therefore tend to be restricted to specific types of agents. For example, we shall see that blackboard-based systems tend to be reserved for cognitive agents, whereas subsumption architectures are used for reactive agents, even if in theory both could be used for agents of either type.

3.6.1   Table of main types of architecture

In an agent architecture, we find the general parameters which are valid for the structural analysis of artificial organisations: type of approach, subordination structures, pairing and constitution.

Among the totality of possible architectures obtainable by varying these parameters, only a small number have given rise to enough implementations to be capable of categorisation. We are speaking of *architectures based on horizontal modules* (or more simply *modular architectures*), *blackboard-based architectures*, *subsumption-based architectures*, *architectures based on competitive tasks*, *production rules*, *classifiers, dynamic systems*, *multi-agent based architectures* and *connectionist architectures*. They are grouped together in Table 3.7, along with their associated parameters. It may be noted that all the types of architecture (except perhaps the 'multi-agent' type) use a functional approach, whether it be horizontal or vertical.

3.6.2   Modular horizontal architecture

This type of architecture is certainly one of the most widespread. Whether we are dealing with theoretical work or practical applications, most architectures proposed for the definition of cognitive agents are based on the overall concept of horizontal modules linked by pre-established connections.

Modular horizontal architectures, which we shall refer to simply as modular for convenience, are conceived as being an assembly of modules, each carrying out a specific horizontal function. The most widely used modules are:

Table 3.7 Main agent architectures.

Type of architecture	Approach	Type of component	Subordination structure	Coupling structure	Constitution
Horizontal modular	Horizontal functional	Module	Hierarchical	Fixed (but progressive)	Predefined
Blackboard	Functional	Task	Hierarchical (Meta)	Variable	Predefined
Subsumption	Vertical functional	Primitive task	Hierarchical	Fixed	Predefined
Competitive tasks	Vertical functional	Task + primitive actions	Hierarchical (Competition)	Variable	Predefined
Production rules	Functional	Rule	Hierarchical (Meta)	Variable	Predefined
Classifiers	Vertical functional	Rule	Hierarchical	Evolutionary	Predefined
Connectionist	Vertical functional	Formal neuron	Egalitarian	Fixed (by weight)	Predefined
Dynamic system	Vertical functional	Stimuli command relationship	Egalitarian	Fixed (but progressive)	Emergent
Multi-agent	Object/ functional	Agent	Egalitarian	Variable	Emergent

- Perceptive and motor functions, if necessary
- Sending and interpretation of communications
- Beliefs base comprising modelling of environment and of other agents
- Management of obligations
- Expertise of skill domain
- Management of goals and decision making
- Planning of actions, and so on

In this type of architecture all links are fixed, that is, the data circulation mode is predefined by the designer. Figure 3.14 shows a typical example of such an architecture, characterised by a data flow which first ascends and then descends.

In the ascending phase, signals coming from the outside through sensors or letter-boxes, and comprising messages, are filtered in such a way as to obtain information of a more and more abstract nature, until it can be integrated into the modellings of the agent. The highest function is carried out by the decision-making module, which decides to act on the basis of the data it receives and in accordance with its own objectives. We then move into the descending phase, corresponding to

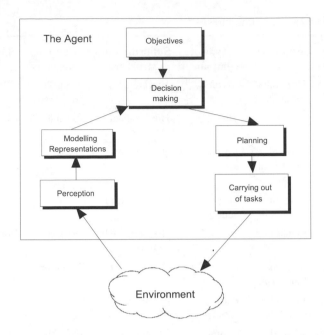

Figure 3.14 Characteristic representation of an agent with horizontal modular architecture.

the implementation of the decisions. The planning module determines the actions that need to be carried out to attain the selected objective. These are then transmitted to the execution module.

A large number of architectures proposed for cognitive agents, and in particular those which we shall put forward in Chapter 5, are essentially based on this model. For example, the Interrap system of J. Müller (1996) uses a horizontal breakdown. The main modules of this architecture (knowledge bases and controls) are themselves organised in levels.

3.6.3 Blackboard-based architecture

The blackboard architecture is one of those most widely used in symbolic cognitive multi-agent systems, and it has given rise to an abundant literature. Originally developed in the context of traditional artificial intelligence (that is, from the point of view of DAI, to create mono-agent systems) for speech recognition with the Hearsay II system (Erman *et al.*, 1980), blackboard-based architecture was soon appreciated within DAI as an architecture sufficiently flexible and powerful to be able to implement the reasoning and calculating mechanisms of the agents, notably with the DVMT system (Lesser and Corkill, 1983).

The blackboard model is based on a division into independent modules which do not communicate any data directly but which interact indirectly by sharing data. These modules, called *Knowledge Sources* or *KSs*, work on a space which includes all the elements required for solving a problem. The architecture of a blackboard-based system comprises three subsystems (Figure 3.15):

- *Knowledge sources (KSs).*

- The *shared base* (the 'board', properly speaking), which encompasses the partial states of a problem in the process of solution – hypotheses, intermediate results, and, more generally, all the data exchanged between the KSs. These bases are broken down into hierarchies (conceptual, partitive, causal and so on), which structure the modelling of the area of application as the space for hypotheses/solutions.

- A *control device*, which manages conflicts of access between the KSs. The latter intervene in an 'opportunist' manner, that is, without being triggered by a centralised control system. It is this part which has been most modified during the evolution of these architectures.

Control in blackboards

Although the blackboard model is very general, since it says nothing about the way these subsystems are organised, there have been numerous realisations, presenting different views on the control aspect of the system, which is in fact the most difficult. The control has, in essence, to decide what is to be done next, that is, it has to determine which knowledge source needs to be activated. To start with, in the initial implementations of Hearsay II, the control was 'wired up' within a procedure, and then it was very rapidly given the form of a set of rules. But it was only with the BB1 system of B. Hayes-Roth (1985) that the organisation of control in blackboards

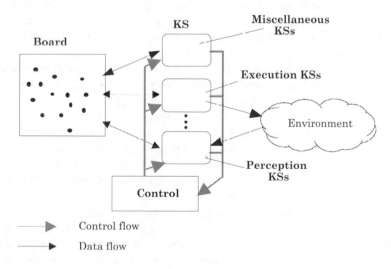

Figure 3.15 A blackboard-based architecture.

established its pedigree, the control system now being considered as a sufficiently important problem for it to have its own board. The BB1 architecture therefore includes two boards, the first for the processing of the problem in the domain, and the second for control management. This means it is possible to handle the activation of knowledge sources as if we were dealing with a separate problem.

To alleviate some of the efficiency problems inherent in approaches based on a BB1-type control board, and mindful that most control systems were in fact hierarchical, J.-P. Haton, H. Lâasri and B. Maître du Crin in Nancy tried to find an architecture representing a satisfactory compromise between expressiveness and efficiency. They wanted to be able to describe control in the form of KSs, without losing efficiency by comparison with a pure procedural control. This process of reflection gave birth to the Atome system (Lâasri and Maître, 1989; Lâasri et al., 1987), which has since been used in a large number of applications. We might make special mention of a system for aiding decision making in the management of repairs to the public highways in Nancy (Ferraris and Haton, 1992), and a real-time counter-measures management tool for fighter aircraft pilots (Lalanda et al., 1992).

For a good explanation of the blackboard concept as an independent system, its mechanisms and its various versions, see Engelmore and Morgan (1988) and Jagannathan et al., (1989).

Blackboards and multi-agent systems

If blackboard-based systems were initially considered as DAI systems, with each KS being perceived as an agent which interacts with the other KSs, this is no longer true today. Because of their very centralised control mechanism and their lack of local memory and thus of data locality, these systems are now regarded as practical architectures for the creation of 'intelligent' systems, and more particularly, for implementing the internal structure of symbolic cognitive agents. Many multi-agent systems have been implemented in this way in the United States (Lesser and Corkill, 1983; Hayes-Roth et al., 1988) and in Europe (Chevrier, 1993; Iffenecker, 1992; Cambier, 1994).

Blackboard architecture has numerous advantages, including first and foremost a remarkable flexibility in describing modules and articulating their functioning. Its interest lies in the fact that it is both opportunist and centralised, the links between the modules (and thus between the KSs) being capable of alteration. It is opportunist in the sense that the KSs are activated when configurations of the board interest them, following modifications triggered by other KSs. It is centralised through the intermediary of a control module which arranges the order in which the KSs will effectively be activated by trying to determine the course of action most appropriate to the state of the system.

The main drawback of blackboard architecture is its relative inefficiency, owing to the highly expressive character of its control. For this reason, this type of architecture has proved to be particularly useful during the prototyping phase of the creation of systems, or when the response times are not too restricting. Nevertheless, versions of BB1 have shown that, even in cases where it was necessary to have real-

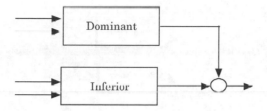

Figure 3.16   In a subsumption architecture, the superior modules will be dominant and, if necessary, will inhibit the output of the inferior modules.

time response times, precise management of the control could vastly accelerate its behaviour through correct decision making and the selection of important and urgent tasks at the right moment (Hayes-Roth and Collinot, 1993). The Guardian system, which monitors a patient in an intensive care unit, is a good example of this (Hayes-Roth *et al.*, 1992).

In any case, the advantages of this type of architecture are undeniable. Because of its very great flexibility, it is possible to implement any agent structure in terms of board elements and KSs. All other architectures can be modelled in blackboard terms, sometimes at the cost of a certain slowness in execution. The blackboard therefore represents a sort of 'meta-architecture', an architecture for implementing architectures.

3.6.4   Subsumption architecture

Subsumption architecture was proposed for the first time by R. Brooks for the setting up of tropistic-reactive agents (Brooks and Connell, 1986). In contrast to hierarchical modular architecture, which divides an agent into horizontal modules, subsumption[†] architecture breaks an agent down into vertical modules, each of them being responsible for a very limited type of behaviour.

The interactions between the modules are fixed, and are effected through the intermediary of a dominance relationship, defined at the design stage. The modules carry out their tasks in parallel, but if two modules are in conflict (that is, if two modules produce contradictory results), then only the data supplied by the dominant module will be taken into consideration. If the inferior module produces a result while the dominant module does not work, its effect will be taken into account, but if the dominant module also produces data, the latter will have priority as shown in Figure 3.16.

It is therefore possible to construct relatively complex systems using such an architecture. However, once again it is the designer who defines the assembly of modules and the dominance relationships that exist between them. Figure 3.17 gives a characteristic example of subsumption architecture for an explorer robot.

[†]Subsumption, from subsume, place beneath. Not to be confused with the use of the same word in the field of representation of knowledge, where it refers to a relationship of subsumption between concepts.

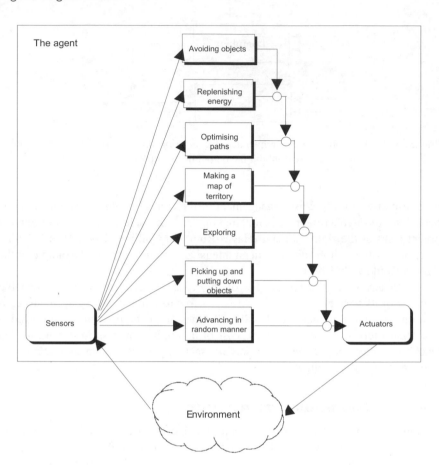

Figure 3.17 Model of explorer robot based on subsumption architecture.

This technique has mostly been used to describe reactive agents, but it would be possible to use it for cognitive agents by considering the more reflex modules as superior and the more cognitive modules as inferior and inducing a priority into the modules.

3.6.5 Competitive tasks

Whereas in the two previous modular architectures the links are fixed, other architectures have been proposed in an attempt to introduce a certain mutability into the links between modules, in order to obtain more flexibility in the choice of module selection. These modules represent vertical functions, what some refer to as 'behaviours' or 'tasks'.

In the competitive tasks structure, an agent is made up of an assembly of tasks, only one of which can be active at any time. These tasks are thus in competition for selection by a decision mechanism which takes account of various parameters: the weight accorded to the task at a given moment, the application context, data coming from outside, etc. This type of architecture is described very specifically in Drogoul and Ferber (1992). A task corresponds to a macroscopic action which displays a certain unity. For example, `lookforObject`, `recoverEnergy`, or `explore` can be considered as tasks, whereas `moveArm` or `changePosition` are actions which are too elementary to constitute tasks in themselves. These are *action primitives*, that is, the words of the language in which it is possible to define tasks. Figure 3.18 shows the procedure for selecting the current task. The selection module receives the readings for the various task parameters from each of the tasks, and selects the one for which the evaluation function, applied to the parameters, is the highest.

Once selected, the task is activated, and the previous current task is deactivated. But a deactivated task is not totally 'switched off'. In order to remain in competition, it exercises a monitoring activity which consists in receiving data from sensors and calculating the values of the selection parameters which depend on it. This is the type of architecture used in the Manta system for the simulation of ants (Drogoul and Ferber, 1994; cf. Chapter 7).

Other architectures have been put forward based on more or less the same principle. From an ethological point of view (McFarland, 1990, 1994), they all involve proposing an action selection mechanism for reactive agents to organise their behaviour, in response to the environmental stimuli they receive and the internal drives that motivate them (need for energy, reproduction, and so on). These

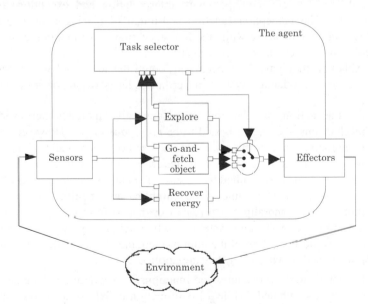

Figure 3.18   An agent based on competitive tasks. The task selector chooses the task which displays the highest value (obtained using an evaluation function).

problems will also be referred to in our discussion of the hybrid architectures (below), and in connection with the issues arising from the transition to the reactive act (cf. Chapter 5).

3.6.6 Production systems

Production systems certainly form a part of the best-known artificial intelligence architectures. A production system (or rule-based system) is defined as the combination of a database, a production rule base and an interpreter, the inference engine. Although there is a wide variety of syntaxes for the definition of production rules, they are generally given in the following form:

```
if <list of conditions> then <list of actions>
```

where `<list of conditions>` is associated with elements in the database and `<list of actions>` comprises elementary actions such as adding or deleting database elements.

Some actions can also activate execution commands for the agent directly. When a rule can validate each of the conditions on its list, it executes the corresponding actions. If several rules can be activated, we say that they are in conflict, and the inference engine control system activates the rule with the highest priority (depending on the rule's internal parameters, or quite simply on which rule comes first).

In the context of a multi-agent system, each agent is represented in the form of a production system, equipped with interpretation and execution functions (Figure 3.19). The perception function is limited to placing perceived data or messages inside the database while the inference engine is functioning, so that the rules base can take account of them directly.

Although they have long been considered the ideal tool for writing large knowledge bases, production systems nevertheless have two major drawbacks:

- As the action part of the rules generally includes action deletion mechanisms, the engine is said to be *non-monotonous*. However, in a non-monotonous engine, the result obtained is not independent of the order in which the rules are applied. It is therefore necessary to know the order in which the rules are applied to be sure of securing the desired result, which is contrary to the principle of the 'jumbling up' of rules. To deal with this problem, we generally group rules together to form rule packages. But in any case, if a production system is to be used efficiently it is indispensable to know the algorithms of the inference engine, that is, which rules are given priority and in what order they are applied.

- In contrast to the procedures and functions of programming languages, rules cannot be combined. While a Lisp function is defined as a combination of functions, the rules directly implement the relationship between the conditions and the actions, without its being possible to define abstractions

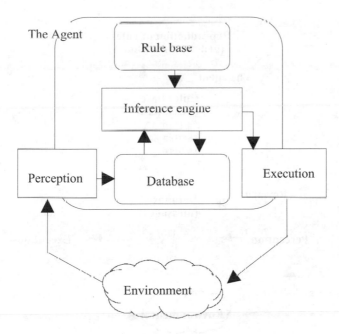

Figure 3.19   An agent based on production systems.

in the form of 'rules on rules'. The classic solution to this dilemma consists, as previously, in constructing rules packages bringing together a set of rules functionally linked to one another. But this package concept introduces a procedural mechanism which moves away from the initial virtues of the technique.

For this reason, the range of application of production systems is necessarily restricted, and programs created in this way should be carefully tested to verify that the systems are coherent. However, when the number of rules is small, or when the breakdown of the rules base into rules packages makes it possible to reduce the number of rules to be considered simultaneously, these systems do offer the advantage of supplying a simple form of writing for defining complex reasoning mechanisms. In the context of multi-agent systems, the knowledge bases associated with an agent are relatively simple, or at all events can be broken down into rules packages which then represent the modules of one of the modular architectures looked at previously.

3.6.7 Classifier-based systems

Systems based on 'classifiers' are special cases of production rules systems which were originally introduced by Holland (1968, 1978; Holland *et al.*, 1986) to design evolutionary autonomous systems.

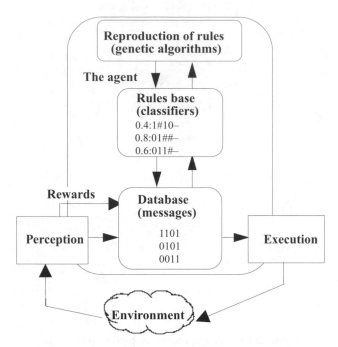

Figure 3.20 An agent designed around a classifer system.

A classifier-based system takes the form of a variation of a production system, in which the facts (called messages) are strings of characters with a fixed size generally taken from a binary 0,1 alphabet, and the rules (called *classifiers*) are pairs of character strings whose elements are taken from the same alphabet with the addition of a 'joker' character (#), which can be associated with any element. The rules are weighted in accordance with their probability of activation. Figure 3.20 shows such a system. The data coming from the environment are coded by the perception system in the form of a set of facts. The rules are applied to these facts and produce other facts which can, in their turn, activate other classifiers, or else produce actions in the environment via the execution system. Classifier-based systems would be no different from production systems if it were not for two mechanisms which have the effect of profoundly modifying their perspective, namely a credit attribution system and a system for reproducing rules by genetic algorithms.

The credit attribution system rewards the rules that have given rise to a 'good' action, that is, an action considered as having made it possible to arrive at a goal such as obtaining food, for example. The weighting of these rules is increased, whereas in the opposite case rules that have not brought any benefit to the agent have their weighting reduced. The most heavily weighted rules are given priority for activation. In addition, the system of reproducing classifiers through genetic algorithms is used to produce new rules based on the heaviest weightings by means of mutation mechanisms and cross-overs (Goldberg, 1989). These classifier systems are essentially used to create adaptative behaviours. For example, in Wilson (1991), animats situated in an environment learn through such a system to find their food in the fastest way possible.

3.6.8   Connectionist architectures

Connectionist architectures, which are based on the metaphor of the brain, are made up of a network of identical elements which are often called *formal neurons*, because of their resemblance (which is actually not that close) to the neurons of the nervous systems of animals. Each neuron determines its output function on the basis of the input values it receives from other neurons. The neuron transfer function is given by the equation:

$$y_j = f(\sum_i w_{ij}.x_i)$$

where the x_i are the output values of the i units, the w_{ij} are the *weights* of the connections linking the i neurons to the j neurons, and f is the activity function. The most classic activity functions are threshold functions or sigmoids, which indicate that a neuron is active (or more active) when the sum of the values which it is receiving at its inputs exceeds a certain level. There are a large number of neuron network models. The most classic are the layered networks. They assume that the neurons are grouped into sets, called layers, and that the inputs of the neurons of layer n are linked to the outputs of layer $n - 1$. In a network containing n layers, the first layer is directly linked to the sensors and layer n is linked to the actuators. The intermediate layers, called the internal or hidden layers, serve to memorise internal states. Figure 3.21 shows a three-layer network.

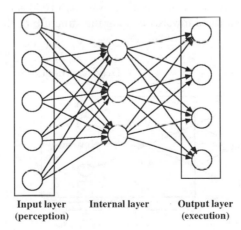

Input layer   **Internal layer**   **Output layer**
(perception)   **(execution)**

Figure 3.21   A three-layer network of neurons including an internal (or hidden) layer.

With regard to agent architecture, we can define the weights of the connections between neurons in three different ways:

(1) The first technique consists, quite simply, in defining these weights directly, or causing them to evolve through extremely simple techniques. When the architecture is very simple, this can sometimes be sufficient. Braitenberg, (1984) describes small situated autonomous robots which find their way around using a very small number of neurons whose architecture is given directly. For example, Figure 3.22 shows what is certainly one of the simplest architectures that can be created using neurons. With only two crossed neurons linking the sensors to the actuators, a small vehicle can be constructed which moves towards a light source, each neuron activating a motor in proportion to the power of the data received by the corresponding sensor. Several authors have taken this as their inspiration, in particular Beer and Chiel (1992) and Cherian and Troxell (1993), in the development of reactive agents capable of adapting to their environment.

(2) In the second technique, the network itself learns the weightings with the aid of a backprop mechanism. A set of input stimuli and an expected output response are submitted. The divergence between the expected response and the one the network gives is backpropped on to the weights of the connections between the different layers. While these techniques are well adapted to relatively static learning situations, like the recognition of faces or handwriting, they are not always suitable for mobile autonomic agents which have to learn a dynamic behaviour. Nevertheless, we can find this backprop technique in use in Lin (1992) in the definition of the behaviour of adaptative reactive agents.

(3) The third technique, which incidentally is developing rapidly, consists of causing the weighting to evolve with the help of genetic algorithms, which makes it possible to utilise environmental responses directly as reinforcement mechanisms, as in classifier systems (Todd and Miller, 1991). But there is also a trend towards making the structure of the neuron net evolve

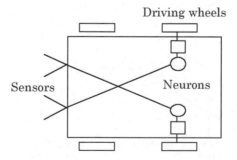

Figure 3.22 One of Braitenberg's little vehicles. It is capable of moving towards a light source, even though its control system consists of only two neurons.

directly through genetic algorithms by using learning to develop the hidden neurons required to accomplish the task by learning (Cliff *et al.*, 1993; Werner and Dyer, 1992; Werner, 1994).

3.6.9   Architectures based on dynamic systems

To say that dynamic architectures exist is a little presumptuous at present, since only one version of this type of architecture is actually in existence, that developed by L. Steels (1994) for the creation of cooperative autonomous robots. The principle specifically requires us to abandon the notion of architecture. The behaviour of the agent is implemented simply by directly describing the equations which link the values of the sensors (standardised for efficiency reasons) to those of the commands applied to the actuators.

For example, L. Steels uses a robot comprising an assembly of sensors and actuators which enable it to feel impacts or perceive obstacles using infrared light, to hear and emit noises and to perceive lights. Most importantly, it is enabled to move by direct action on the speeds of its right-hand and left-hand motors (Figure 3.23). For the robot to express a behaviour, it is sufficient to give the value at time $t + 1$ of the command parameter, on the basis of its value at time t and the value of all the other sensors at time t. For example, to tell it to advance, it is sufficient to give the movement equations for the speeds of the right and left-hand motors (RS and LS respectively):

$$RS(t+1) = RS(t) - \frac{RS(t) - RS_{Default}}{10}$$

and likewise for the left-hand motor speed. Thus, whether the motor is going too fast or too slowly, it will adapt little by little to its nominal speed, indicated by the parameter $RS_{Default}$ (which is equal to 150). When the contact sensor (a bumper, in

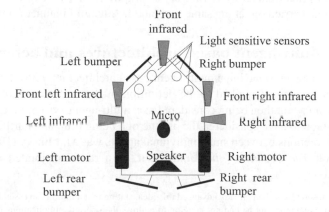

Figure 3.23   General outline of L. Steels's 'dynamic' robot.

the terminology of the robotics specialists) on the left touches something, the motors have to stop. With an architecture like that of subsumption, it would be arranged for the `avoidObstacle` behaviour to inhibit the `goStraightOn` behaviour. Here, however, the command values of the motors are directly modified by adding or subtracting numerical values so that the motors have a tendency to go in the opposite direction. The fact that touching something on the left means you go right is expressed as follows:

```
Behaviour 'GoRightIfTouchLeft' :
  If left-hand bumper is touched,
  then
    LS(t+1) = LS(t) - 300 * value (left-hand bumper)
    RS(t+1) = RS(t) - 400
```

It is then sufficient to add up all the motor values directly to obtain the desired behaviour. In this case, if the robot touches something with its left-hand bumper, it will go into reverse (since the reverse values are much higher than the nominal values for going forwards) with a small rotation movement taking its head to the right. In the ensuing moments, if the robot is no longer touching the obstacle, it will progressively regain its nominal forward speed, with the help of the forward movement equations. So all partial commands (`goStraightOn`, `avoidObstacle` and so on) are always added together, and the overall behaviour is the direct result of the sum of all the partial behaviours. L. Steels has applied this architecture to the creation of a pair of (real) cooperating robots, which stroll about in a natural manner to go and recharge their batteries and accomplish a 'useful' function for the designer.

Obviously, this approach is closely linked to the equipment used, since there are no intermediate representations on the basis of which it would be possible to isolate an independent behaviour. Nevertheless, and although this type of architecture is still in its very early stages, one can guarantee that it will soon have many skilled practitioners, by reason of its simplicity and its capacity for having several actions carried out at the same time and in a natural manner (cf. Chapter 5).

3.6.10   **Multi-agent based architectures and actors**

We refer to an agent as having a multi-agent based architecture when the concept of a multi-agent system is applied to the definition of the architecture of the agents themselves, an agent then being considered as a multi-agent system in its own right. The first person to have considered the psyche of a being (human or artificial) as the result of interactions between small individual agents was M. Minsky (1986)[†], in his famous book *The Society of the Mind*. In it, in a rather disjointed manner, he

---

[†]In fact, G. Bateson (1979) had already advanced this idea, stating that a mind is an assembly of parts or components in interaction, but he had not gone on to address the operative implications of this for any computing realisation.

describes a set of mechanisms resulting from conflicts and cooperations between small calculating entities which he calls agents. Each one is responsible for an activity, a memory, a recognised property of an object, without there being any real centralising system coordinating the whole. Hence, Minsky believes that the functioning of the psychological apparatus is not the result of a set of inferences relating to symbols, but rather the outcome of self-organising confrontations between autonomous procedures. Although very few systems have been designed on the basis of Minsky's work (and one might well wonder whether all his theories could really be implemented), his ideas have certainly influenced a whole school of thought (and especially the work of P. Maes about which we shall speak in the next section), which views the behaviour of an agent as resulting from a set of internal activities, such as can be associated with the functioning of a multi-agent system.

All work relating to actor languages and their use in multi-agent systems can be traced back to this trend to some extent. Initially, the concept of an actor appeared in Hewitt's work as early as 1973 (Hewitt *et al.*, 1973). This work really came into the public domain in 1976 or thereabouts, with the ground-breaking article *Viewing Control Structures as Patterns of Message Passing* (Hewitt, 1977), which developed a certain concept of programs, viewed as societies of specialists, solving a problem by communicating through the sending of messages. Hewitt demonstrated that his execution model made it possible to consider the control structures of traditional languages as patterns of communication between autonomous entities called *actors*. Since then, actor languages have mainly been studied, in particular under the influence of Agha (1986), Tokoro (Ishikawa and Tokoro, 1986) and Yonezawa (Yonezawa and Tokoro, 1987), as execution models for programming by competing objects. But some projects have been more concerned with the initial ideas promulgated by Hewitt (1991, 1985), which he reinforced with his concept of 'open systems semantics'. P. Carle (1992), S. Giroux (Giroux and Senteni, 1992) and J. Ferber (1987), while considering that actor languages are indeed very good tools for the implementation of parallel computations, nevertheless have reservations about their very originality. For in treating agents and multi-agent systems as natural extensions of the actor concept, they undermine the very notion of a multi-agent architecture.

But what is an actor? An actor is a computing entity which is made up of two parts: a structure which comprises the addresses of all the other actors it knows[†] and to which it can pass messages; and an active part, the *script*, which describes its behaviour when a message is received. The behaviour of each actor, which is executed independently and in parallel with the others, comes down to a set of extremely reduced actions: passing messages, creating actors and modifying its state (or determining a new behaviour for the next message). That's all! And it is enough, for any parallel computation can be expressed as a combination of these primitive actions.

[†]In terms of actor languages, these are called the *acquaintances* of an actor. However, we must not confuse this idea of acquaintance, which comes down simply to an address, with the management of acquaintances such as one meets with in multi-agent systems, which assumes an explicit representation of the characteristics of other agents (cf. Chapter 6, on the representation of an agent's knowledge).

Communication between actors is carried out by the passing of asynchronous messages, that is, the transmitter does not need the receiver to be ready to receive a message. But the most important original feature of actor languages is certainly the use of local continuations. When an actor A needs a response to a message which it sends to an actor B it does not wait for the response: it brings in a new actor C referred to by Hewitt as the customer, which undertakes to process the response and the continuation of the computation. This actor C thus acts *as* the local continuation of the computation initiated by the sending of the message from A to B. The use of local continuations imparts a very high degree of flexibility to computations expressed in actor languages, as the actors are freed from the need to wait for responses. Numerous actors' languages have been proposed. The best known ones currently operational are ABCL (Yonezawa, 1990), Mering IV (Ferber and Carle, 1991) and Actalk (Briot, 1989), this last being designed as an extension of Smalltalk (Goldberg and Robson, 1980).

In moving the concept of an actor closer to that of an agent, thanks to the use of organisational reflexivity, S. Giroux (1993) proposed that an agent should be considered as an ecosystem, that is, as an assembly of agents in interaction, and that an ecosystem should be considered as an agent. His system Reactalk, based on an extension of Actalk, provides agents with the possibility of adapting their behaviour according to the type of message they receive, and thus of being able to interact in synchronous mode as well, should it prove necessary. Nevertheless, these agents do not really display autonomous behaviours (they have no motivational systems) and they do not have representations of their environment, the idea of an ecosystem being taken rather as a metaphor. Nevertheless, this work shows that a continuity does exist between the concept of an actor and that of an agent. I had also proposed a system, Paladin (Ferber, 1989), written as an extension of the Mering IV language, in which the actors could pursue a goal and, if necessary, reason about their own skills and explain their behaviour to other entities in the system. The actors had genuinely taken on the status of agents, reflexivity here again providing the means of transition from an 'actor' level, on which the entities merely carry out computations, to an 'agent' level, where they have greater behavioural latitude and even reasoning capacities and motivations (Ferber and Carle, 1991).

Finally, it should be pointed out that L. Gasser, in his Mace system (Gasser *et al.*, 1987), drew much of his inspiration from Hewitt's ideas concerning actors. Furthermore, the Actalk language forms the basis for a large number of multi-agent platforms, the earliest of which was Mages III (Bouron *et al.*, 1990). The association between actors and agents has thus proved extremely fruitful, and there can be no doubt that there is more to come on the close ties that bind these two concepts.

4 Action and Behaviour

4.1 Modelling

4.1.1 The models ...

In science, a model is a stylised abstract image of a portion of reality. Scientific activity mainly consists in creating models of the objects and phenomena that science studies. These models can be very formal or simply provide a basic practical representation. For example, physics uses mathematical models to predict the movement of bodies or to determine the radiation from an electromagnetic source. Biology, on the other hand, uses data-transfer models, or simple images like that of the key and lock, to understand the functioning of the cell, reproduction and the evolution of an organism.

The advantage of a model is that it can be made more explicit, simpler and easier to manipulate than the reality it is supposed to represent. Model makers thus eliminate a large number of details that they consider unnecessary, in order to concentrate better on the data that they consider pertinent to the

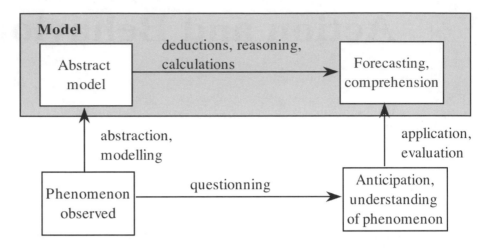

Figure 4.1   Models are created as an aid to predicting and understanding phenomena.

problem they wish to solve. For example, it is difficult to predict how a body will change position and its form under the pressure of various forces. But mechanics uses simple force models which, once conjugated, make it possible to give an accurate prediction of the movement of the body and the distortions it will undergo. It is because it has been possible to represent the body in terms of a dynamic model, and because we know how to use this type of model to predict the future, that the construction and use of such models has proved to be particularly useful.

Models are thus homomorphic images of reality, that is, a homomorphism exists between the object of study and the model, which means that the results from the model can be applied to the object itself, as shown by Figure 4.1.

The observed phenomenon is translated into the form of an abstraction, which can be manipulated (through algebraic transformations, numerical computations or simply logical inferences) to obtain results which can help us to improve our understanding or to predict future situations. It is through operations of this nature that it has been possible to compute the orbits of the planets around the sun and to gain a better understanding of the behaviour of wild geese.

4.1.2   ... and how MASs benefit from them

It might be wondered why multi-agent systems would need models. Are they not sufficient in themselves? Is not the programming code enabling the agents to perform their functions sufficient for the understanding of their behaviour?

Unfortunately, things are not that simple. With a multi-agent system, or for that matter any computing system sufficiently complicated, analysing the behaviour of a program on the basis of its implementation involves the following drawbacks:

(1) It is especially difficult to get into the core of a program and analyse its behaviour simply by looking at its implementation.

(2) The code of a program introduces a large number of details which are of no use in understanding its behaviour.

(3) Different implementations – in terms of languages and data structure selection – give rise to similar effects, while slight modifications to a program can have important consequences for its behaviour.

(4) As the agents are executed in parallel (whether this parallelism is simulated on a monoprocessor machine or actually executed on a multi-processor), it is even more difficult to understand their functioning on the basis of their code, owing to the non-determinism inherent in the parallelism.

(5) Last but not least, multi-agent systems are complex software, difficult to apprehend and to design. It is therefore necessary to reduce their complexity by bringing out their structure and analysing their different components separately, albeit without losing sight of the general organisation.

4.1.3 What should be modelled?

What are the essential characteristics of a MAS? What are the parameters which differentiate one from another? What precisely should be described? What is actually going on, and how is it going on? In other words, the fundamental questions are about what lies between the design and intelligibility aspects of the mechanisms set in play; between the expected consequences of their functioning and those that are actually seen; between, in other words, the viewpoint of the engineer wholly occupied with the cogs that make a system turn and that of the external observer analysing its behaviour. It is these questions that I shall try to answer in the rest of the book. We can distinguish four main concepts to which modelling appears to be particularly relevant:

(1) Modelling the actions of agents and their consequences in an environment. This environment may itself be complex and capable of autonomous evolution distinct from the consequences of the actions of the agents. This modelling makes use of type L3 languages (operative modelling) and type L5 (formalisation) (cf. Chapter 1).

(2) The functioning of an agent, with regard to both its observable behaviour and its internal mechanics, using type L3 languages (operative modelling) and perhaps type L4 (representation of knowledge).

(3) The interaction of agents with one another and, in particular, the different modes of communication which are the preludes to the organised forms of interaction – cooperation, coordination of action and resolution of

conflicts. This involves type L2 (communications) and type L3 (operative modelling) languages.

(4)   The evolution of the multi-agent system viewed as a whole, on the basis of experimentation and formalisation (type L5 languages).

A large number of models exist which can be applied to the understanding and design of multi-agent systems. Two large families can be distinguished: algebraic models, which tend to describe an agent in mathematical terms (type L5 languages), and operative models (type L3 languages), which use structures which are *a priori* more related to computing, even if some of them, such as finite-state automata or Petri nets, can themselves be formalised in algebraic terms. The former are fundamental, as they determine all subsequent developments by defining the foundations which will be used to make them possible, whether in respect of operative models, architectures, the mental states of cognitive agents or the definition of interactions between agents.

4.1.4 Agents and actions: deceptively elementary concepts

The question comes up all the time: what is an agent? What is an agent for its designer and for anyone observing it? How should we describe its behaviour, its architecture, its internal characteristics and what makes it behave the way it does? There are many answers, and in this chapter we shall not try to go beyond an initial outline: an agent will be considered simply as an entity which is permanently perceiving, deliberating and executing. So we are dealing with a very impoverished version of the concept of an agent, but it will be sufficient for use in the formal modelling of agents. We shall have occasion to develop it in the course of the following chapters.

In addition to the matter of agents, there is another topic which raises even more questions, that of action. How do we describe the fact that the world is evolving, that it is being transformed under the influence of our own actions and under the pressure of the myriad changes brought about minute by minute by the stars, by matter, by plants, animals and human beings, all of which and all of whom are affected by the consequences of these same changes? If action is the basis of our existence, it is equally the basis of multi-agent systems. In contrast to the classic conception of artificial intelligence, which postulates that the manifestation of intelligence rests on logical reasoning, multi-agent systems take as their point of departure not reasoning, but the behaviour of agents, the actions they perform in the world and the interactions which flow from them. Any analysis of multi-agent systems must then necessarily involve an in-depth study of the concept of action and the definition of a theory of action which makes it possible to deal with interactions and their consequences on society.

But what is an action? Although we are dealing with what we would all regard as an obvious concept, a precise definition of this term poses numerous problems, and depends on whatever quasi-philosophical blanket ideas we may hold on the subject.

E. Morin (1977) writes: *As far as we can go in conceiving the depths of the physical world, we find agitation and specific interactions. Immobility, fixed states and repose are local and provisional phenomena at the level of our timescale and of our perceptions.* Everything is in motion. The world is unstable and subject to changes which are the results of actions, and therefore of the interactions, reactions and feedback of agents in relation to one another. Atoms, chemical molecules, cells, multicellular organisms, animal and human societies and ecosystems are created by beings milling around in a permanent state of activity. They are the results of incessant movements and turbulent agitations whose starting points are the elementary actions of autonomous entities. But how can we describe this flux of animation, how can we find a rigorous way of representing the activity of an agent and the interactions between agents?

Action is first of all modification. Initially, there is a tendency to consider the world as being immobile, and to see agents' actions as modifying this stable state so that it subsequently takes on another stable state. Action is thus what modifies the global state of the world. Although this is one of the theories most in evidence in the field of artificial intelligence at present, we shall see that it is inadequate for taking account of interactions in which several agents can carry out actions at the same time and thus find themselves in a conflict situation. This is why other theories attempt to escape from the problem of action by eliminating it, either by having recourse to mechanical models of movement or by considering only sequences of events, without taking any account of the state of the environment.

Another problem concerns the reaction of the milieu to the actions of agents, and the fact that the same action can have different results. For action is also a gesture, an attempt to exert influence on the world, to modify it in accordance with our desires. And the consequence of this gesture is not always in accordance with the intention which has brought it about. The goal, the source of the intention, relates to an expected result; the gesture is a way of achieving it. But imponderables may interpose themselves between the gesture and the result, so that the result is not what we had computed it would be. For the universe is subject to laws from which we cannot escape. We propose, but the universe disposes. It combines all our gestures, all our efforts, and it produces a response which is the consequence of this combination, based on the laws of the universe within which these gestures have been made.

But if there are no gestures, the world does not remain in a stable state, as first impressions would lead us to believe. It is evolving, it is being transformed, and there is no reason to assume that any gestures are being made from outside, or that, as Aristotle claimed, there was a prime mover which set it in motion. So we must make a distinction between the gesture and the consequences of the gesture, between the act and the universe's response to the act. This is why we shall put forward a personal theory in favour of modelling action as a system of responses to the production of influences by agents. Action is thus no longer envisaged as the result of what agents do, but as the result of the reactions of the universe to the influences of agents.

4.1.5 Modelling action

There is more than one way of modelling actions and their consequences. Several more or less mathematical formalisms are available for taking account of actions, the activities of agents and the evolution of an MAS. Here are some of the formalisms we shall examine:

(1)   Action as *transformation of a global state*. The functional transformation of states model is certainly the most classical model, and we shall examine it first. All AI planning theory was developed within this framework, and most theories on multi-agent planning refer to it. It is thus essential to become thoroughly acquainted with it. It also serves as the basis for nearly all the other models of action, which are both related to it and distinct from it.

(2)   Action as *response to influences*. But the transformation of states model suffers from many limitations. To solve these problems, I shall put forward a model based on the concept of *influence*, which takes the form of an extension of the preceding model.

(3)   Action as *computing processes*. Action can also be seen as a set of events produced and consumed by computing. We can thus use theoretical tools, such as finite-state automata or Petri nets, to formalise the behaviours of agents and the environment.

(4)   Action as *local modification*. In local models, action is considered as being a local modification which is propagated along a net of automata. While these models pose numerous problems with regard to the description of agents, they provide an easy way of representing environments, particularly when cellular automata are involved.

(5)   Action as *physical displacement*. In geometrical and physical models, actions are considered as displacements within a geometrical space. This model is obviously very practical when we want to describe the actions of mobile agents.

(6)   Action as *command*. In the cybernetic model, action is a command. We are no longer interested in the transformations brought about by the agent in the environment, but only in what it perceives of this environment and in the commands it sends to its actuator organs in order to achieve a goal or satisfy an internal drive. This model is predominantly used to describe the behaviour of reactive agents.

Finally, I shall set out a personal model in which I attempt to synthesise the preceding models with a view to simplifying the description of multi-agent systems and making them easier to understand. It describes agents, their behaviour, and the environment as a set of interconnected components. This model, which uses the BRIC formalism, will be used throughout this book to describe the behaviours of agents and their interactions.

4.2   Action as transformation of a global state

4.2.1   A functional representation of action

The classic concepts of action used in artificial intelligence are based on an approach involving *states and transformation of states*. It is supposed that it is possible to characterise the (generally discrete) set Σ of the possible states of the world. An action *op* is defined as a transition of state, that is, as an operator whose execution produces a new state. Thus, starting from a situation σ_1 of Σ, the execution of the action *op* produces a new state σ_2 of Σ. For example, if in state σ_1 agent A is at location L_1, and the action $op = go(A, L_1, L_2)$ is applied, the resulting situation, σ_2, will show the agent displaced to location L_2 (on condition, of course, that the operator is applicable, that is, there is no obstacle to the accomplishing of the action):

$$\sigma_2 = Exec(go(A, L_1, L_2), \sigma_1)$$

where *Exec* is the operator of execution for the action operators, that is, a function of the type $Op \times \Sigma \rightarrow \Sigma^\dagger$.

A parallel can be drawn between this approach and that of a film strip. Each image represents a state of the world, and the actions describe the passage from one image to another. So it is the movement of the film that gives the illusion of continuity of movement.

4.2.2   STRIPS-like operators

But how are we to describe the situations, that is, the states of the world and the transformations? In 1971, as a response to some planning problems, Fikes and Nilsson (1971) put forward a representation, still known as the 'STRIPS-like representation' in honour of the first planner to have used it. In this representation, which is still the one most widely employed for planning problems in AI and DAI, a state of the world is described as a set of atomic formulae, whose conjunction is assumed to confirm the validity of the state. Let us suppose, for example, that we wish to represent a world in which a robot, Clifford, is capable of moving from room to room to fetch tools or other objects of a similar type, as demonstrated in Figure 4.2. We assume that Clifford is capable of directing itself in one of the four directions (north, south, east, west) and of picking up or putting down objects. We also assume that a room is an atomic place, a point in space, and that the positions of Clifford and the tools are relative to the rooms represented by their numbers. A state of the world is described by the set of atomic formulae which are true in

---

†An analogous example is given by the `Apply` function in Lisp.

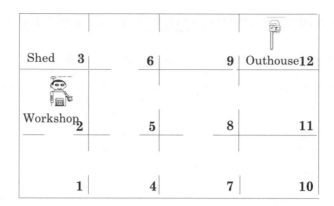

Figure 4.2 Clifford is an agent able to transport objects from one place to another.

this state[†]. For example, to say that Clifford is in room number 2 in state `s1`, it is sufficient to explain that the formula:

```
positionRobot(Clifford,2)
```

belongs to `s1`, and the same applies to the definition of the position of the tools, as well as to all the geographical relationships that may need to be expressed between these rooms when they are intercommunicating:

```
s1 = { positionRobot(Clifford,2), positionTool(Pliers,12),
       North(1,2), South(2,1), East(1,4),...}
```

[†]More precisely, it would be necessary to define a state not as a set of formulae, but as an algebraic structure for which the formulae are satisfied. To do this, it is sufficient to define each state as an algebraic structure, $\sigma = <D, R, F, C>$ where D is a set of elements called the domain of the structure, and represents the assemblies of entities in question, R and F are respectively the set of relationships and the set of functions defined on this structure, and C is a set of elements distinguished from D, the constants. We then say that a formula with the form $p(t_1,...,t_n)$ is satisfied in the state σ, which is noted down as $\sigma \models p(t_1,...,t_n)$, if and only if $<I(t_1),...,I(t_n)> \in R$. The same applies for the constants, where $\sigma \models c_i$ if, and only if, $I(c_i) \in C$, and where I is an interpretation function of the formulae. To manage a set Σ of states, it is sufficient to define Σ as a set of algebraic structures, $\sigma_i = <D_i, R_i, F_i, C_i>$ such that $\forall \sigma_i, \sigma_i \in \Sigma$, $D_i = D_j$ and $C_i = C_j$ (it is only the functions and relationships which can move between two states; the domains and constants remain unchanged). We then interpret the operations op as descriptions of functions of Σ in Σ, which associate a state, $op(\sigma)$, of Σ with a state, Σ, of Σ. This construction of states is used by E. Pednault (1986) for his ADL language, and one may also consult Jacopin (1993) for a presentation of some of the semantics associated with concepts of actions similar to Strips. In what follows, we shall stick to the simplified definition in which a state refers to a set of formulae. More details on the logical description of states may be found in the book by Genesereth and Nilsson (1987), which gives a simple presentation of the problem of definition of actions using a logical apparatus.

In this representation, the operators characterising the actions are described in the form of triplets:

```
op = <pre, del, adds>
```

where `pre`, `del` and `adds` are sets of atomic formulae. `pre` describes the precondition of the operator, that is, the condition which must be verified for the operator to be applied. `del` and `adds` are two sets of propositions which respectively describe the facts that need to be deleted from or added to the current state of the world to move into the following state. `del` and `adds` are thus what characterises the transformation involved in passing from one state to the next, and this transformation comes down to the deletion and/or addition of new propositions to the set of propositions describing the preceding state. For example, an operator allowing Clifford to go southward would be formulated as follows:

```
Operator goSouthward(x)
   pre: positionRobot(x, 11), South(11,12)
   del: position(x,11)
   adds: position(x,12)
end
```

The application of this operator to the initial situation s_1 produces a new state s_2 in which Clifford has moved into room 2 (or more precisely which does not include the formula `positionRobot(Clifford,2)`, this being replaced by the formula `positionPlace(Clifford,1)`):

```
s2 = Exec(goSouthward(Clifford),s1)
```

and thus

```
s2 = { positionRobot(Clifford,1),
       positionTool(pliers,12),
       North(1,2), South(2,1), East(1,4),...}
```

The operators do not describe everything about the initial and final states of a transition, but only what changes, and it is assumed that everything that does not move remains unchanged from one state to another.

4.2.3   Planning with STRIPS-like operators

In spite of its skimpiness, this action modelling is well suited to the problems of planning such as those that have been posed in AI since its beginnings. Indeed, a classic planning problem is based on a given initial situation σ_{init} and a given final situation σ_{fin} where we want to end up, both situations belonging to Σ, and a set of operators, *Op*, defined as above by functions of Σ in Σ. Solving a problem in such a context means finding the sequence of operators $X_1,...,X_i,...,X_n$ where the X_i are variables which are given their values in Op, such that:

$$\sigma_{fin} = Exec(X_n \circ ... \circ X_i \circ ... \circ X_1, \sigma_{init})$$

where the sign '∘' represents the functional composition. In this context, a planning problem can be formally described in the form of the quadruplet

$$PP = <\Sigma, \sigma_{init}, \sigma_{fin}, Op>$$

The solution to a planning problem is given by the production of a set of plans P, each plan, $p \in P$, being represented in the form of a sequence, $X_1,...,X_n$, of variables given their values in Op such that

(1)   The action associated with X_1 is applicable to the initial state, σ_{init}, or, to put it another way, σ_{init} is within the domain of the operator represented by X_1;

(2) $\forall i1 < i < n$, the operator represented by X_i, is applicable to all the states resulting from the application of X_{i-1}, that is, the state resulting from the application of X_{i-1} belongs to the domain of the action represented by X_i;

(3)   The application of X_n produces a final state in which σ_{fin} is present, which means that σ_{fin} is present in the arrival space (or co-domain) of the action represented by X_n.

Figure 4.3 represents the general form of a planning problem. Starting from the specification of the initial situations, goals and available actions, the planner finds a set of plans $\{p_i\}$, from which the plan p to be executed is selected. This plan is then transmitted to the executor, which undertakes to carry it out. In many systems, the planner only offers a single plan. In that case, the selector module can be deleted.

The best-known example in the planning domain is that taken from the world of cubes. The problem consists in stacking cubes one on top of another in a precise formation, starting from an initial stacking arrangement and moving only one cube at a time. Figure 4.4 gives an example of an initial situation and a final situation.

These situations are defined simply, in the form of a set of atomic formulae:

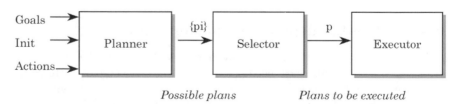

Figure 4.3 Planning is the production of a set of plans, only one of which will be carried out.

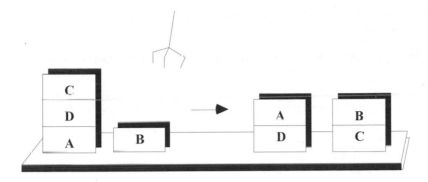

Figure 4.4   A cube manipulation example.

σ_{init} = { on(C,D), on(D,A), on(A, Table), on(B, Table)}
σ_{fin} = { on(A,D), on(D,Table), on(B,C), on(C,Table)}

The operators corresponding to the two classic actions of stacking one cube on top of another and putting a cube down on the table can be written as follows:

```
Operator place(x,y)
  pre: free(x), free(y), on(x,z)
  del: free(y), on(x,z)
  adds: free(z), on(x,y)
end

Operator placeTable(x)
  pre: free(x), on(x,y)
  del: on(x,y)
  adds: free(y), on(x,Table)
end
```

The operator place(x,y) indicates that for a cube x to be placed on a cube y, x must be free, y must also be free, and x must initially be on z. After the application of the operator, place(x,y), the state of the world is such that x is no longer on z but on y, and such that y is no longer free but z has become free. But how does a STRIPS-like planner function? As numerous variants exist, and it is not our purpose here to develop the full set of planning techniques, we shall confine ourselves to a brief illustration which should be sufficient for an understanding of the problems of multi-agent planning. Let us go back to the classic example of stacking cubes. Let us suppose that we want to go from an initial stacking order to a different one, as shown by Figure 4.4. The general planning technique consists in starting from the final state and looking for operators which would make it possible to obtain this state by applying a recursive technique. For a given final state, we take all the operators required to obtain this state, then we try to find out if they are applicable and to determine the consequences of their application. For example, to obtain the final situation

`{ on(A,D), on(D,Table), on(B,C), on(C,Table)}`

it is sufficient to apply the operators `place(A,D)`, `place(B,C)`, `place(C,Table)` and `place(D,Table)` to the preceding situation:

```
Operator: place(A,D)
  pre: free(A), free(D), on(A,z)
  del: free(D), on(A,z)
  adds: on(A,D), free(z)
end

Operator: place(B,C)
  pre: free(B), free(C), on(B,z)
  del: free(C), on(B,z)
  adds: on(B,C), free(z)
end

Operator: placeTable(C)
  pre: free(C), on(C,y)
  del: on(C,y)
  adds: free(y), on(C,Table)
end

Operator: placeTable(D)
  pre: free(D), on(D,y)
  del: on(D,y)
  adds: free(y), on(D,Table)
end
```

But are these operators actually applicable? Knowing that the initial situation is:

`{ on(C,D), on(A,Table), on(B,Table), on(D,A), free(C), free(B)}`

we can apply either the operator `place(B,C)` or the operator `placeTable(C)`. If we apply the former, we obtain the state

`{ on(B,C), on(C,D), on(A,Table), free(Table), on(D,A), free(B)}`

which prevents the application of the operator `place(C,Table)`, since C is no longer free and it is no longer possible to apply the operator `placeTable(C)`. It

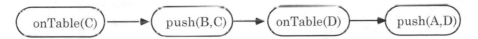

Figure 4.5   A linear plan for solving the problem of the cubes in Figure 4.4.

is therefore preferable to apply the second operator and obtain the state

```
{on(C,Table), on(A,Table), on(B,Table), on(D,A),
 free(C), free(B), free(D)}
```

We can therefore now apply either the operator `placeTable(D)` or the operator `place(B,C)`. These two operators are totally independent, since the application of one does not prevent the application of the other, and the final result is independent of their order of application. The application of these two operators in any order produces the state

```
{on(B,C) on(C,Table), on(D,Table), on(A, Table),
 free(B), free(A), free(D),free(Table)}
```

It now only remains to apply the operator `place(A,D)` to finish the construction of the plan (Figure 4.5).

4.2.4   Some plan categories

It is possible to classify plans into several categories, depending on the structure of the plans and the manner in which the goals interact.

We refer to *linear planning* if the goals can be satisfied independently of one another, that is, if they are such that the application of the operators does not lead to any conflict in the achieving of them. For example, the problem of the cubes in Figure 4.6 can be solved by a linear planner, for all the goals of the final situation

```
{on(B,A), on(D,C), on(A,Table), on(C,Table)}
```

can be separately achieved.

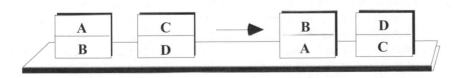

Figure 4.6   A problem which can be solved with the aid of a linear planner.

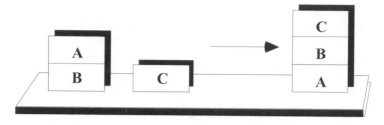

Figure 4.7   A non-linear planning problem.

For B to be on A, A must be placed on the table and B must be placed on A. In addition, for D to be on C, C must be placed on the table and D must be placed on C. These two lines of the plan are fully compatible. Each of the problems can be treated independently, as the actions serving to achieve one goal do not interfere with those which further the other goal. Of course, most current situations are not linear, for most goals are not independent. In that case, we refer to non-linear planning. For example, the problem in Figure 4.7, apparently simpler because only three cubes are involved, cannot be solved by a linear planner. Here the final situation is given by

```
{ on(C,D),  on(B,A),  on(A,Table)}
```

As soon as A is on the table, there are two possible actions which correspond to the final goal: either placing C on B or placing B on A. If we select the first possibility, we find ourselves in an impasse, as it is then not possible to place B on A. So the order of application of the operators influences the final result and the construction of the plan must take this order into account, whence the term *non-linearity*, which is associated with this type of plan and especially with planners capable of handling this situation.

Another kind of distinction which is certainly of interest in the case of multi-agent systems is that between *total plans* and *partial plans*. The former are made up of an ordered sequence of the operators to be applied. The plan for the example in Figure 4.4 is a total plan, for it is made up of a sequence of operators arranged in a *total order*. But as we have seen, there are several equivalent plans which allow the same result to be obtained, and which differ only in their order of execution. In this case, it is not necessary to impose a total order on the operators, and it is preferable to keep them in the form of a *partial order*, modelled on the form of a non-cyclical graph, as is shown in Figure 4.8. We thus obtain parallel branches of execution, from which we shall see that multi-agent systems can easily obtain a benefit.

When the plan is to be executed, a decision will be made as to how to go through this graph in such a way as to *linearise* the plan. Another appealing aspect of partial plans is that they are considered simpler to produce, even (and especially) if non-linear plans are involved. The principle is to delay the selection of the order in which the actions are to be applied for as long as possible. In this case, there are

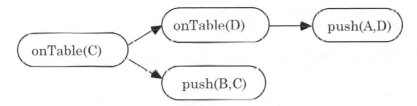

Figure 4.8 A partial plan corresponding to the example in Figure 4.6.

two stages to planning. In the initial phase, a partial plan is constructed, which takes no account of any possible conflicts. Then in the second phase this plan is refined so that any possible conflicts are detected and the plan is linearised. We shall take another look at the issues of planning in Chapter 8 in connection with applications involving several agents. The problems with these are decidedly more complex, and there are as yet few general models which allow them to be solved.

4.2.5 Limits of STRIPS-like planners

Planning by STRIPS-like operators assumes that the operators describe the transition from one state to another by making explicit only what is modified during this transition. We then say that this type of planning follows the STRIPS hypotheses (Waldinger, 1977):

(1) Only a single operator can be applied at any given moment to specify the way in which the transition from one state of the world to another is made. It is therefore not possible to carry out several actions in parallel.

(2) All consequences of the modifications effected by actions are explicitly specified in the adding and deleting part of the operators.

(3) An operator represents an instantaneous action. As we explained above, the action is not represented as it progresses (it takes no time), but only in the result of the transformations it brings about.

Clearly, these hypotheses seriously narrow down the possibilities for representing actions. The second hypothesis is especially restrictive. It states that all the consequences of actions must be directly coded into the operators. For example, let us suppose that we wish to represent that familiar schoolroom world, made up of taps and baths which fill and empty. The operation of *turning on* a tap can be written thus:

```
Operator openTap
   pre: tap (t) closed(t)
   del: closed(t)
   adds: flows(t, Water), open(t)
end
```

Now let us suppose that we have a world made up of a tap, T1, initially closed, and an empty glass, G1, which is just below T1. The initial state of the world is thus

```
S1 = { glass(G1), empty(G1), tap(T1), closed(T1),
       under(G1,T1)}
```

The application of the operator openTap produces the new state S2:

```
S2 = { glass(G1), empty(G1), tap(T1), open(T1),
       flows(T1,Water), under(G1,T1)}
```

in which it can be confirmed that the glass remains empty, even though the water is actually flowing! In fact, to deduce that a glass is being filled if it is under a tap from which water is flowing, we would need a supplementary operator in the form of:

```
Operator fillGlassUnderTap
   pre: tap(t), glass(g), under(g,t),
        flow(t,Water), empty(g)
   del: empty(g)
   adds: filled(g,Water)
end
```

and an additional piece of information telling us that the application of this operator is brought about by the application of the preceding operator. We would then have a representation with the capacity to manage the consequences of the actions.

Such an extension lies outside the scope of STRIPS-like planners, and few general planners are able to accommodate causality, although a great deal of research has been done into the problem of representing causal links (Shoham, 1988), which need a much more complex description of the action.

4.2.6 Limits of classic representations of action

In addition to the planning problems, this representation of action as a transformation of states displays numerous weaknesses as soon as we move away from the initial universe for which it was defined. They can be found on two levels:

(1)   the level of the language describing the action when we are restricted to STRIPS-like operators;

(2)   the level of the general design of the action considered as a transformation from one state into another.

The first limitation has often been recognised as terribly constraining, as it means that only very elementary actions can be described. To give some idea of the extent of the limitation, we need only observe that it is not possible to use this language to define an action such as: *place on the table all the cubes which are themselves on a cube*. Other languages have therefore been proposed to compensate for this shortcoming by improving the operators' capacities for description, while remaining capable of finding plans of action (for a summary of these descriptive languages, their possibilities and the problems they raise, see Jacopin (1993)).

The second limitation is more tricky, as it has been studied much less intensively. It is based on three postulates which cause problems in the case of multi-agent systems.

(1)   *Staticity postulate*. The Strips model views the world as *a priori* static, so that the only possible evolutions are the result of the actions of agents. To model a specific behaviour of the world (atmospheric changes or the evolution of river levels), it is therefore necessary to introduce explicitly such external agents as the atmosphere or the river. But what is more serious is that this system is incapable of taking account of Newton's first law: *A body remains at rest or moves with constant velocity in a straight line unless acted upon by a force*. Indeed, for a moving body pursuing a uniform motion in a straight line, the transition from one position to another does not require the intervention of an agent, for its different successive positions are simply the results of the motion. Now, STRIPS-like operators do not describe the motions of the objects of the world, but only the transformations obtained by the application of actions. So representations through transformation of states are pre-Newtonian in their expression, and any description of motion must use another technique.

(2)   *Sequentiality postulate*. Another drawback stems from the difficulty in translating simultaneous actions. For example, let us suppose that two agents, A and B, have to push a cube, as shown in Figure 4.9.

If we apply this model of action, and if we have available the operator move(x,   y,   d), where d is defined as a movement in the opposite direction, where agent x is situated, what will be the result of the application of these operations to the two agents A and B and to the cube C? Models based on the STRIPS approach assume that we will apply either move(A,C,+1) or move(B,C,-1), or vice versa. In the first case, the cube will first go to 3 then come back to 2, and in the second it will first go to 1 before returning to 2, perhaps crushing one of the agents in

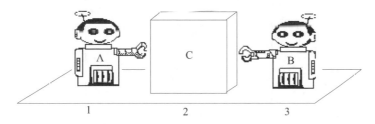

Figure 4.9   Two agents attempt to push a cube in opposite directions.

passing, but it will never remain immobile if the two agents are pushing in opposite directions.

(3)   *Universality postulate*. Actions are not described as they happen, but by their results. We do not distinguish the actions themselves, that is, what the agents are doing, from the consequences of those actions, which means that all the possible catastrophes that can occur have to be described in the actions. As they are dependent on the environment and on the laws of the universe, the action descriptions have to take account of all the possible scenarios, even those which result from an error, or from situations which are *a priori* unexpected. Thus, the action `Advance` for a robot must register the fact that it is possible for it to fall into a hole, for its path to be blocked by a wall, or for it to become stuck in sand. If a person can crush an ant in moving, it will be necessary to specify explicitly everything that could possibly be crushed by the movement of a person.

The sequentiality postulate in association with the universality postulate poses another problem when two agents are acting simultaneously. How can the consequences of a possible collision between two mobile bodies be described (Figure 4.10)? If the operator `Advance(a,dx,dy)` represents the movement of a body `a` over a quantum of space represented by its speed vector `<dx,dy>`, how can we describe the meeting between two moving bodies and its repercussions on their direction and speed?

There are obviously some solutions – computer scientists are rarely flummoxed. With the addition of supplementary reasoning to synchronise the actions (Georgeff, 1983) or reify the time, some of these problems can be solved at the cost of actions written in a more complex, and thus less natural way. But this is not always enough; it is sometimes necessary to increase the power of expression of the language, as E. Pednault does with ADL (Pednault, 1986). He so extends its power of description as to enable it to apply universal and existential quantifiers to the variables, as well as represent explicitly modifications in the functional values (`update` field in ADL).

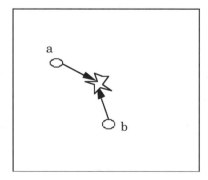

Figure 4.10   Two moving bodies, a and b, meet and cause a collision.

By also entering time as a parameter, ADL can characterise actions which happen at the same time t even if, as regards execution, the actions are applied sequentially. In addition, it offers the possibility of describing mechanisms resembling allocation of global variables in a programming language, which gives it the capacity to represent almost everything that can be coded in a computer language. To solve the collision problem, we can code into the body of actions the fact that, if there is another moving object in the same place, then there will be an impact (and possibly an explosion); that is, we can describe explicitly in the movement operators the tests for verifying whether there is an impact or not. But this would mean covering every detail relating to impacts and their consequences, which would quickly become very burdensome, and bring us back to the problem posed by the universality postulate. In addition, close attention must be paid to problems of synchronisation of actions, failing which collisions may be botched, a well-known problem for video game programmers.

But in all these cases we feel it is more a matter of 'tricks' of representation, involving the coding of any possible synchronisation of actions into the environment objects, than of seriously addressing the question of simultaneity of actions. In the context of multi-agent systems, the problem is patent. While we always assume that the actions of the different agents are carried out in parallel, we have no adequate formal structure to describe simultaneous actions easily, and thus to represent collective actions. The following section is devoted to the definition of such a formal structure.

4.3 Action as response to influences

4.3.1 General presentation

In this section, we shall put forward a model of action based on the principles of influences and reactions to influences (Ferber and Müller, 1996). This model makes use of certain elements from approaches based on the transformation of states, while extending that concept in order to be able to take account of the consequences of the simultaneous actions of agents and model phenomena stemming from interactions between agents. This model also makes it possible to describe actions considered as displacements in a physical space (which allows the integration of the formal structures of classical mechanics) as well as actions which have their origin in other spaces (such as the writing of a program, for example). There is more to this than extending the model of action by transformation of states; as we shall see, this classic model can be regarded as a special case in which the modifications to the world stem from only one agent. We are thus dealing with a general theory of action allowing us to represent its different aspects, a theory which nevertheless benefits from the studies carried out in each of the more specialised fields it encompasses, such as those of physical movement, local propagation by means of cellular automata, and even classic planning itself.

The problem with the preceding theories just discussed is that they amalgamate what is produced by the agents and what is actually happening, the gesture and the result of the gesture. These two notions only need to be separated for most of the problems previously encountered to disappear. An agent – whether it be a robot which pushes against a door or a person shifting position – is actually making a gesture. But the result of this gesture depends on other gestures made by other agents representing the environment's capacities for reaction. Gestures are what we call *influences*, that is, means of modifying the way things would have been without them, and the results of these gestures are obtained by application of the *laws of the universe*. The latter are the responses of the environment, which acts by combining all the influences it receives from agents, and then deducing from them a new global state in conformity with its own particular nature.

The advantage of the model put forward here is that it can serve as a global framework for integrating work developed in different fields. For example, in the domain of classical mechanics, the state of the world is given by the position and speed of a set of bodies. The influences are then the forces which are exerted on the bodies at a time t and the application of the laws of the universe simply consists in the drawing up of a balance sheet of the forces present and deducing from it, on the basis of the positions and speeds, the position and the speed of the bodies at the time $t + \Delta t$. In another field, that of control, the influences are described as modifications of the command variables of the system to be controlled, and the laws of the universe correspond to the response of the system to these input values. Finally, as we have said, if we confine ourselves to a mono-agent system, and if the only actions to be taken into account in the world are those carried out by the agent, then this model of action becomes identical to the state transformation model.

4.3.2   States

In order to simplify the presentation of the influence/reaction model, we shall present it as an extension of the Strips model. Nevertheless, it should clearly be borne in mind that this model of action is more general than it is presented as being here. A *state of the world* σ of Σ is described a set of atomic formulae with the form $p(a_1,...,a_n)$, where p is a predicate of arity n and $a_1,...,a_n$ are constants or functional terms not comprising variables. In this context, the situation σ_1 presented in Figure 4.9 can be described as:

```
σ₁ = { cube(C),agent(A),agent(B),place(C,2)
       place(A,1),place(B,3)}
```

But whereas classic theories include only a single structure, the state of the world, we are introducing another structure called *influence*, which represents all the gestures or attempts at actions performed by agents with reference to the current state of the world. These structures too are described with a set of atomic formulae defined with the assistance of a language equivalent to that of the states of the world, and we use Γ to refer to the set of these structures of influence described with the help of these formulae. Actions result from the combination of gestures into influences and from the reaction of the environment to those influences.

4.3.3 Actions and reactions

For reasons of simplicity, an operator will take on the appearance and syntax of STRIPS. It will be represented in the form of a triplet, *<name,pre,post>*, where *name* is an expression with the form $f(x_1,...,x_k)$ and where the x_i are the only variables authorised to appear in the *pre* and *post* forms. *pre* and *post* are sets of formulae with the form $p(a_1,...,a_n)$, where p is a predicate of arity n and the a_i are either constants or variables. The application of the operator produces a set of influences. *pre* describes the conditions which have to be verified for the operator to be applied, and *post* the set of influences which will be directly produced by this operator when it is applied. The application of an operator can be described by a function, *Exec*, which takes an operator and a current state and gives back an influence:

$$Exec: Op \times \Sigma \to \Gamma$$
$$Exec(op, \sigma) = \gamma$$

which is such that

$$Exec(<name,pre,post>,\sigma) = Post \text{ if } pre(\sigma) \text{ is verified}$$
$$\text{and } \{\} \text{ if not}$$

For example, the movement operators in Figure 4.9 can be described like this:

```
move = < name:  move(x,y,d),
           pre:   agent(x), cube(y),
           post:  push(y,d)>
```

and the attempt to move cube *C* by agent *A* starting from a situation σ_1 is then expressed as:

$$Exec(move(A,C,+1), \sigma_1)$$

and produces the influence γ_1:

$$\gamma_1 = \{ Push(C,+1) \}$$

An influence can result from the simultaneity of actions carried out in a given state of the world. The operator combining simultaneous actions, which is written as $\|$, simply unites the influences of the actions taken separately. The *Exec* function can then be extended to become a morphism of the action space equipped with the simultaneity operator bearing on the set of influences Γ:

$$Exec: (Op, \|) \times \Sigma \rightarrow \Gamma$$
$$Exec(a \| b, \sigma) = Exec(a, \sigma) \cup Exec(b, \sigma)$$

The laws of the universe are described with the help of a function *React* which specifies how the world is transformed from one state to the other and, in particular, how it reacts to influences.

$$React: \Sigma \times \Gamma \rightarrow \Sigma$$

There is a special description for this function for each type of environment. For example, in an environment in which cubes react to pushes by moving a distance proportional to the pushes, we could describe this function in the following manner:

```
React =
  < state: Place(c,x)
    influences: Push(c,d)
    do: delete{ Place(c,x)}
       add{ Place(c,x+dep)}
         with dep = +/{ d | Push(c,d)}
```

where '/' represents a reduction operator, making it possible to apply a binary operation to a set of values (example: $+/\{ 1 \ 2 \ 3 \ 4\} = 10$). This law is interpreted as such: the new state σ is equal to the former state σ from which all indications of place have been deleted, and into which have been added all the descriptions of localisation after the pushes being exerted on the objects of the world have been summed. So the result of the simultaneous execution of n actions is defined thus:

$$\sigma' = React(\sigma, Exec(op_1 \| .. \| op_n, \sigma))$$

So the solution to the problem in Figure 4.9 can be expressed in the following way: the two agents A and B carry out their actions simultaneously and produce a new state of influence, γ_1:

```
γ₁ = Exec(move(A,C, +1)||move(B,C, -1), σ₁)
   = { Push(C, +1),Push(C, -1)}
```

The application of the laws of the universe to the initial state, σ_1, produces the following new state of influence σ_2:

```
σ₂ = React(σ₁, γ₁)
   = { cube(C), agent(A), agent(B), place(C,2),
     place(A,1), place(B,3)}
```

The example of collisions between moving bodies given in Figure 4.10 is written in the same way. The operator of the movement is described without any reference to the collisions, which are left to the laws of the universe. The operator of the movement is thus written as follows:

```
advance =
   < name:  advance(a,dx,dy)
     pre  : moving body(a,x,y)
     post : trans(a, dx, dy)
   >
```

and the law of the universe is defined by the following React function which indicates that the two moving bodies produce an explosion if they are in the same position, and that otherwise they simply change position:

```
React =
   < state: place(a1,x1,y1), place(a2,x2,y2)
     influences: trans(a1,dx1,dy1), trans(a2,dx2,dy2)
     do:
        Delete{ place(a1,x1,y1), place(a2,x2,y2)}
        if x1 = x2 and y1 = y2 then
           Add{ explosion(a1,x1,y1), explosion(a2,x2,y2)}
        otherwise
           Add{ place(a1,x1+dx1,y1+dy1),
           place(a2,x2+dx2,y2+dy2)}
   >
```

Here is its meaning: if there are two moving bodies, a1 and a2, delete their position indication from the current state; if their positions are identical, then say that there is an explosion, otherwise add the movement influences to their initial positions. For example, if, in the initial state, two moving bodies, a and b, are at positions $(50,50)$ and $(70,70)$, the state σ_1 can be described thus:

σ_1 = { place(a,50,50), place(b,70,70)}

The application of the operators advance(a,10,-20) and advance(b,5,10) leads to the production of the influences

{ trans(a,10,-20), trans(b,5,10)}

and, by application of the laws of the universe, we obtain the new state

σ_2 = { place(a,60,-50), place(b,75,80)}

If, however, the movements involve moving the moving bodies with the help of the actions Advance(a,20,0) and Advance(b,0,-20), the influences will take the form

```
{ trans(a,20,0), trans(b,0,20)}
```

and, by application of the laws of the universe, we obtain

$$\sigma_2 = \{ \text{explosion(a)}, \text{explosion(b)}\}$$

because the moving bodies are in the same place.

4.3.4 Interest of the influences/reactions model for MASs

The main interest of the influences/reactions model lies in the fact that it makes a clear distinction between what properly pertains to the agents and the phenomena that take place in the environment. Differentiating between the influences produced by the agent and the reactions of the environment makes it easier to design heterogeneous multi-agent systems in which the agents have different structures and different internal organisations. All that is needed is to describe the set of influences which the agents can actually produce and use the environment as an integrator system in which the laws of the universe are the same for all.

4.4 Action as processes in computer science

Classic computer science never takes account of the overall state of the world. It conceives the (computing) universe as a set of activities which are being carried on in parallel and which are called processes. It is almost impossible to give a precise definition of what a process is, for we are dealing with a primitive concept, like that of an object or a machine. Let us say that, for the computer scientist, a process is a program in the course of execution. For the automation specialist, a process is a set of tasks which are carried out sequentially and in parallel, and for a theoretician such as Hoare, a process represents the behaviour of an object (Hoare, 1985). The concept is useful because it enables us to describe a behaviour when we are interested only in the initial and final states of actions considered as atomic. As they are carried out, these actions give rise to the production of observable events, the succession of these events making it possible to define a process from the point of view of the observer.

Although the concept of a process is a little fuzzy, nevertheless it corresponds to something fundamental as soon as we generalise its application to multi-agent systems. In considering the world as made up of a set of processes, we are no longer interested, as in the preceding section, in its global state, but in the set of entities which make it up, their behaviour and, above all, the interactions which take place between these processes. It is possible to represent a process in the form of a sort of flow chart, in which the squares correspond to the atomic actions and the arrows to the order of succession.

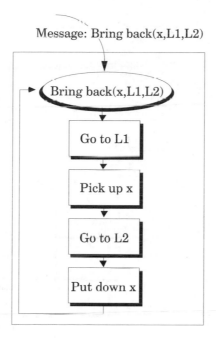

Figure 4.11   Clifford's behaviour represented in the form of a process.

Let us go back to the example of Clifford, which has to retrieve objects by going into a series of rooms, where it is assumed that it no longer has any problems in finding its way about. When Clifford receives a message of the form[†]

```
Clifford << Bring back(x,L1,L2)
```

which indicates that it has to go and get object x, which is in location L1, and bring it to location L2, it executes the process in Figure 4.11.

But what most interests us is the possibility of linking processes together so that they can be executed in parallel. For example, let us suppose that Clifford can accomplish other tasks, such as going to collect supplies from the stock of spare parts. Let us also suppose that Clifford can put the messages it receives on hold and deal with them as and when it is possible to do so. The process then results from the linking of three elementary processes: the one that is used for bringing back objects (Pr_1), the one that consists in fetching components from stock (Pr_2), and the one for managing messages on hold (Pr_3) (Figure 4.12). Pr_3 is executed in parallel to Pr_1 and Pr_2, which are mutually exclusive. Buffer is a component which serves to memorise messages and synchronise the receiving and interpreting of messages,

---

[†]The syntax and semantics of the messages are described below, in Section 4.11.2 and in Chapter 6.

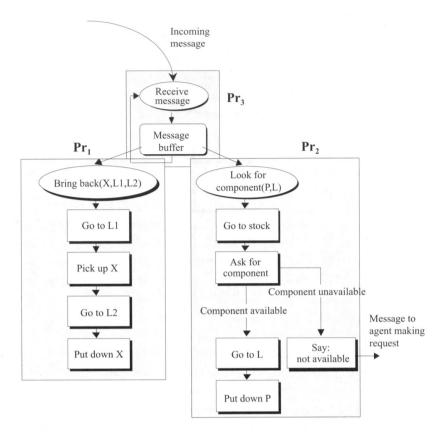

Figure 4.12   Clifford's behaviour is described here by a combination of three processes: two processes, Pr_1 and Pr_2, which are mutually exclusive, and a message managing process, Pr_3.

which are carried on concurrently[†]. It is also possible to link the behaviours of several agents in the same way, given that the messages produced by some go directly into the reception process of the others. There are many ways of representing processes. The most common are finite-state automata, register automata (or augmented transition networks) and Petri nets.

4.4.1   Representation of processes by finite-state automata

The interest of this concept of a finite-state automaton lies in the fact that, firstly, we can very easily describe the behaviour of an agent capable of memorising the state

†I shall use the terms *parallel* and *concurrent* without distinction of meaning when speaking of processes which can be executed simultaneously. In British and American usage, a distinction is sometimes made between these two terms, *parallel* being attributed to processes which are physically executed at the same time but on several different processors, and *concurrent* to the logical aspect of this simultaneity, whether the processes are executed at the same time or not. I shall not make this distinction here.

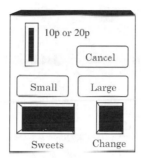

Figure 4.13   A sweet-vending machine. It accepts 10p or 20p coins and dispenses small sweets (price 10p) or large sweets (price 20p).

in which it finds itself and, secondly, the concept is backed up by a great deal of theoretical support and has been used in many computing fields such as computer architectures, automation, algorithmics, formal languages, compilation techniques, networks, etc.

States and transitions

A finite-state automaton is described by the aggregation of its states and by what is called its transition function, which specifies the subsequent state in relation to the present state and the data it receives upon entry. A finite-state automaton is represented in the form of an oriented graph in which the nodes are the automaton's states, and the arcs its transitions. On the arcs are indicated both the events which cause it to pass from one state to another and the actions which have to be undertaken when this transition takes place. For example, let us suppose that we wish to represent the behaviour of a sweet-vending machine like the one in Figure 4.13.

The vending machine accepts 10p or 20p coins and dispenses small or large sweets. When it receives too much money, it gives back change, and if 'Cancel' is pressed, it gives back the amount already inserted.

The machine can be represented as a black box with inputs and outputs (Figure 4.14). The inputs are the external events (insertion of a 10p or 20p coin, request for a small or large sweet, cancellation) and the outputs are the commands

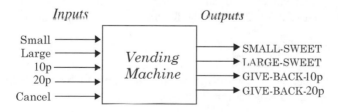

Figure 4.14   Representation of the vending machine in terms of inputs/outputs.

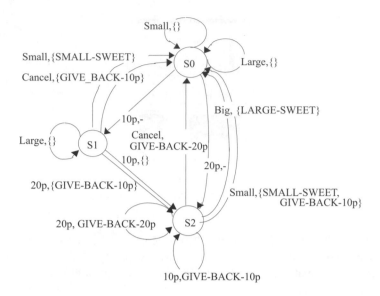

Figure 4.15 Graphic representation of sweet-distribution automaton.

which trigger the machine's operations (dispensing a sweet, giving change). The inputs and outputs are Boolean variables. We assume that only one of the inputs is valid at a given moment, but that several outputs can be true at the same time.

The automaton describing this machine is shown in Figure 4.15. It comprises three states, marked s_0, s_1 and s_2. State s_0 is the initial state, the one the machine is in when it is put into operation. States s_1 and s_2 represent the fact that the machine has received 10p and 20p respectively. Each transition is described by an <event, action> pair, which describes the event that initiates the change of state, together with the action which is carried out by the machine. Formally, a finite-state automaton with k inputs and p outputs is defined as an n-tuple:

$$A = <E,S,C,\psi,\phi,s_0>$$

where E is a finite set of events (described by words with k characters), S is a finite set of states, C is the set of commands equal to B^p (where B is the domain 0,1), s_0 is a specific element of S which is called the initial state, ψ is the *function of transitions*, that is, a function with the form:

$$\psi: S \times E \to S$$

and ϕ is the function of activity, that is, the function which issues a command and applies an operation when a transition takes place:

$$\phi: S \times E \to C$$

Table 4.1   Transition table for a finite-state automaton.

ψ,φ	Small	Large	10p	20p	Cancel
s_0	s_0, {}	s_0, {}	s_1, {}	s_2, {}	s_0,—
s_1	s_0, {SMALL SWEET}	s_1, {}	s_2, {}	s_2, {GIVE BACK-10p}	s_0, {GIVE BACK-10p}
s_2	s_0, {SMALL SWEET, GIVE BACK-10p}	s_0, {LARGE SWEET}	s_2, {GIVE BACK-10p}	s_2, {GIVE BACK-20p}	s_0, {GIVE BACK-20p}

For example, the automaton defined above to represent the behaviour of a vending machine can also be expressed as:

E = Small, Large, 10p, 20p, Cancel
S = s_0, s_1, s_2
C = <SMALL-SWEET, LARGE-SWEET,
       GIVE BACK-10p, GIVE BACK-20p>

The two functions, ψ and ϕ, can be represented by Table 4.1. The horizontal lines show the states and the columns the events, while the boxes contain the pairs formed by the subsequent state and the set of actions to be carried out.

Advantages and drawbacks of finite-state automata

Finite-state automata are very simple to operate and they make it fairly easy to describe the behaviours of simple logic systems. Computer architectures, in particular, use them frequently. It is actually possible to simplify them or to verify some of the properties[†]. However, they very quickly show their limitations when it comes to representing more complex behaviours, and most especially the evolution of a multi-agent system:

(1)   Their computation capacity is limited, owing to the fact that their number of states is finite. They cannot therefore remember a sequence of events of arbitrary length nor verify, for example, that a particular set of parentheses is well formed. This limitation rarely constitutes a problem, although it prevents the robots from memorising the route they have taken so that they can retrace their steps. If it is desired to go beyond this limit, the formalisation of finite-state automata will have to be extended.

[†]For more on this, consult any book dealing with computer architectures, such as Tanenbaum (1991), which discusses the definition of automata based on Boolean functions and their simplification using methods such as Karnaugh tables.

(2)   Automata can describe only sequential processes. For this reason, all computations and all parallel actions are practically out of the question for them. For example, it is impossible to represent an agent which is acting and simultaneously communicating with another agent without making use of very awkward automaton fusion mechanisms which rapidly become impracticable (a fusion between two automata with N states each produces an automaton with N^2 states). We then have to pass on to more powerful formalisms, such as those of the Petri nets described later (cf. Section 4.4.3).

(3)   Finally, all memorisation – for instance, memorisation of changes in value for registers – necessarily involves the transformation of one state into another. If the price of a sweet dispensed by the vending machine was £2.40 and the machine accepted 10p, 20p, 50p, £1 and £2 coins, the number of states would have to be considerably increased to take account of all the intermediate situations between 10p and £2.40, in steps of 10p, and all the additions that could be made along the way. For example, if we are in the 60p state and we put in 50p, we then go into the £1.10 state. The reader could try to draw the complete graph for this automaton! This one is still not very complicated! Here again, to get over this hurdle, we have to be able to extend the capacities of the formalism, and we shall now look at how this is done in register automata.

4.4.2   Register automata

All these limitations, and in particular the last one, have led to an expansion of the concept of finite-state automata which introduces registers which can contain any values, such as numbers, character strings, symbols, vectors, and so on. We then speak of *register automata* or *augmented transition networks* (or ATNs). This formalism makes possible a more extensive power of description, at the cost of losing some properties associated with that finite-state automaton (in particular, properties relating to synthesis and simplification).

Register automata are described, like finite-state automata, by a set of states and a transition function. The main difference is that we add to the states a set of registers which can be manipulated when transitions are triggered. This makes it possible to apprehend more complex behaviours than can be handled by finite-state automata. Register automata are defined as n-tuples of the form

$$AR = <E,S,C,\psi,\phi,s_0,R,D,T>$$

where the values E, S, C, ϕ and s_0 are identical to those for finite-state automata, D is a family of value domains, R is a set of registers r_i of values in one of the domains D_i, of D, and C is a set of Boolean functions which test the values of the registers. The function ψ is then slightly modified, since it is of the following type:

$$\psi = S \times E \times C \rightarrow S \times [R \rightarrow D]$$

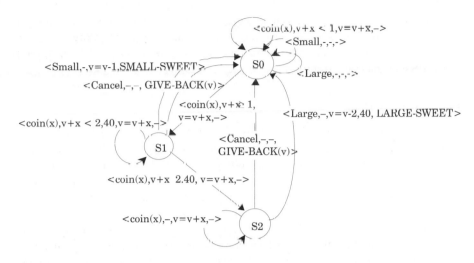

Figure 4.16   A sweet-vending machine modelled by a register automaton.

that is, its task is not limited to taking the automaton from one state to another; it also has to modify the values of the registers, the functional type $R \rightarrow D$ expressing the definition of a new set of register values.

Figure 4.16 gives the graphic representation of a register automaton describing the functioning of a sweet-vending machine accepting coins of any value, when small sweets are worth £1 and large sweets £2.40. We have added a register V which totals up the amount already inserted into the machine. The transitions are described by quadruplets:

```
<event, condition, modification of registers, commands>
```

which indicate the event initiating the change of state, the condition affecting the values of the registers, the modifications made to these registers if the transition takes place, and the commands carried out by the machine. The events now have parameters whose values can be set in the registers.

The obvious advantage of register automata is that they are much simpler than their finite-state counterparts once the number of states rises above a certain level. Thanks to their registers and the supplementary conditions associated with the transitions, they 'factor' data which in finite-state automata has to be distributed over several states.

4.4.3   Representation of processes by Petri nets

Finite-state automata, like register automata, can represent only sequential processes, and thus have serious limitations in dealing with those aspects of parallelism characteristic of multi-agent systems. For this reason, when agents become more complex, or quite simply when we wish to be more precise about what is happening during interactions between agents, we need more complex formalisms available to describe behaviours and organisations in which several processes execute concurrently.

General principles

One of the most formal, but also one of the best developed, models for representing multi-process systems is that of Petri nets. These can be considered as essentially asynchronous process-modelling tools based on a representation which is both graphic and mathematical. The graphic aspect makes it possible to visualise processes simply and facilitates the design and communication of behaviour models, while the mathematical formulation ensures that this formalism has rigorous foundations (cf. for example, Murata (1989)). Petri nets are used in a number of fields where it is necessary to represent mechanisms which are implemented in parallel: commands for industrial processes, communications protocols in networks, program and language semantics, prototyping of parallel systems, and so on. Finally, there is not one Petri net model but a whole family, so that it is possible to model mechanisms as complex as may be found necessary.

A Petri net is defined as an oriented graph comprising two sorts of nodes: *places* and *transitions*. This graph is constituted in such a way that the arcs can only link places to transitions or transitions to places, in accordance with the rules for the formation of augmented transition networks defined above. Places are graphically represented by circles and transitions by bars (Figure 4.17).

Unlike automata, Petri nets permit the representation of the dynamic aspects of processes by the moving of *tokens* from place to place. In ordinary Petri nets, those that form the basis for the entire family of Petri nets, these tokens are merely

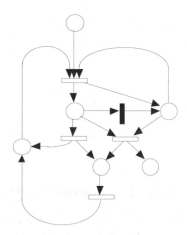

Figure 4.17   An example of a Petri net comprising six places and five transitions.

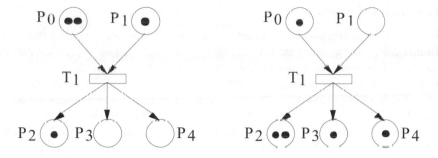

Figure 4.18   Example of transition crossing, before (a) and after (b).

simple and undiscernible elements which are represented as small black dots; while in other types of net, such as the coloured nets which we shall examine later, tokens are more complex structures, which have resemblances to Pascal-type records. The tokens move from place to place, following what are called *firing rules*.

We say that a transition T is *enabled*, if all the input places P for which there is an arc orientated towards T possess a mark. From among all the validated places one is taken at random which is then activated, and it is said that the tokens go through the transition. Firing a transition comes down to removing a token from each input place and adding one at each output place (the places P for which there is an arc from T towards P). Figure 4.18 shows an example of transition firing.

When there are several firing transitions enabled, the rule of drawing lots determines which of them should be fired, as demonstrated by Figure 4.19.

A *marking* is a distribution of tokens over places, and the initial marking is the initial distribution of tokens in the network.

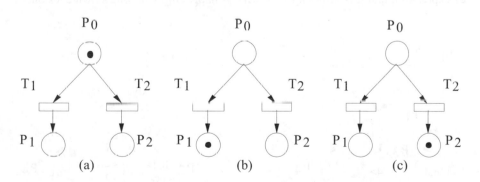

Figure 4.19   Transitions T_1 and T_2 being validated in (a); drawing lots for the transitions to be crossed produces marking (b) or (c).

Coloured Petri nets

If we want to distinguish between tokens, it is possible to use *coloured Petri nets*. In this case, we can associate a valuation with a finite domain, which we call the 'colour' of the token. It is also possible – and this is what we shall do below – to use tuples of coloured variables (in the form <a, a, b>, for example) to take the place of ordinary tokens (Jensen, 1992). The advantage of using coloured nets is that we can describe relatively complex dynamics with a small number of places and transitions. In this model, the transitions can be considered as kinds of rules, which can be activated only if the conditions associated with their input arcs are satisfied. They produce tokens corresponding to the data associated with their output arcs. The example in Figure 4.20 shows the firing mechanism. The transition T_1 can be fired only if a token exists with the form <x, x, n> at place P_0 and a token with the form <x, y> at place P_1. In the example, this is possible since a token <a, a, 2> exists at P_0, and a token <a, c> exists at P_1 in situation (a). These tokens are then deleted from the input places, and tokens corresponding to the indications for output arcs are produced at the output places. In the example, the tokens <a, c>, <3> and <c, c> are added to the list of marks for places P_2, P_3 and P_4(b) respectively.

There are a great many other Petri net models: object Petri nets, which assume that the tokens are objects which can themselves contain references to other objects, and whose domains can be modified (Sibertin-Blanc, 1985); predicate Petri nets; synchronous and delayed nets; and even continuous nets (David and Alla, 1989). In this book, we have selected coloured Petri nets, which have the advantage that they already have a high degree of modelling power while still offering possibilities for formal verification of their properties.

Modelling procedures using Petri nets

If Petri net models are fairly simple to understand, they still pose two problems. It is difficult to model a behaviour, owing to their great flexibility and the great power of expression; and it is difficult to see what is happening with one's own eyes once

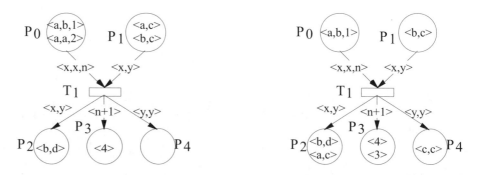

Figure 4.20 Crossing of a transition in a coloured net.

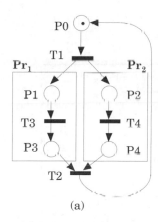

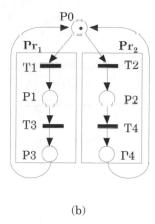

(a)   (b)

Figure 4.21 Pr_1 and Pr_2 are executed simultaneously in (a) and alternatively in (b).

the process being modelled starts to become complex. The first of these problems simply requires a little expertise. Petri nets are only another form of programming. Modelling a set of processes in the form of a Petri net should be treated as an art, in the same way as writing a program or laying down a specification. The second problem can be solved by defining a representation formalism at a higher level, the structure of which can still be transformed into a Petri net. We then have a more intelligible language, while benefiting from the formal properties associated with these nets.

The other interesting aspect of Petri nets is that we can integrate the formalism of finite-state automata as a sub-class of these nets. We then represent the states of the automaton in the form of places in the net, and its transition function as a set of transitions, each having only one input place and one output place. We then call them state-type machines.

Petri nets have a power of expression much greater than that of finite-state automata, for they can easily model a set of processes and describe any possible conflicts over access to resources.

For example, Figure 4.21 shows two examples with multiple processes which can be modelled by Petri nets. In the first case (a), the processes Pr_1 and Pr_2[†] are executed simultaneously. In fact, a token placed in P_0 fires the transition T_1 and occupies places P_1 and P_2 simultaneously. Then transitions T_3 and T_4 are executed independently of each another, but transition T_2 acts as synchronisation. It can be fired only if P_3 and P_4 both contain at least one token. Conversely, in the second case (b), the processes Pr_1 and Pr_2 are executed independently of one another, and if only one token exists in P_0, they will be mutually exclusive. The token in P_0 will go

---

[†]In these and subsequent examples, we have framed the processes to make the diagrams easier to understand. But the concept of a process does not form part of Petri nets in the strict sense, since they involve only places, transitions (and their associated arcs) and tokens.

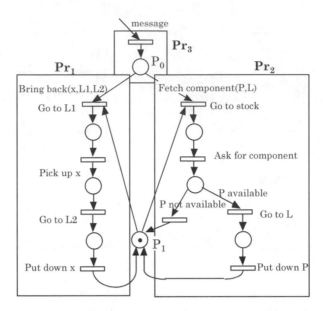

Figure 4.22   Representation of the behaviour of Clifford expressed in the form of a Petri net.

through either by Pr_1 or by Pr_2, and the other process will have to wait until the token has crossed all the transitions and come back into P_0 for the two processes to be executable once more. But if P_0 contains several tokens, the two procedures Pr_1 and Pr_2 may possibly be executed in parallel (Figure 4.22).

It is thus possible to give a precise description of the behaviour of Clifford as it was presented in Figure 4.12, where we assumed that Clifford could bring back objects and go and fetch components from stock while receiving messages. What we have in Figure 4.21 is a modification of the diagram in Figure 4.21(b). The two processes are mutually exclusive, the exclusivity being managed by place P_1, which initially contains a token. When a message arrives, it is stored in place P_0, and if P_1 contains a token one of the two processes, Pr_1 or Pr_2, is selected according to the nature of the message. If we are dealing with a `Bring back` message, then process Pr_1 is selected and activated, and the token from place P_1 is consumed, together with the message. The tokens thus pass from place to place until they reach place P_1. During this time, since P_1 does not contain a token, no other message can be taken into account by either of the two processes. But as soon as it recovers a token, that is, when Pr_1 and Pr_2 have been completed, and if P_0 contains messages, one of these two processes can be reactivated, depending on the form of the message.

The Petri nets we have just been looking at do not provide us with an easy way to represent mechanisms for giving priority to actions. It must be possible to indicate that something is *preventing* a transition, which cannot be done in the normal model. We can then add inhibitor arcs which link a place to a transition and which function in the opposite way to the normal arcs by preventing the firing of a

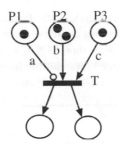

Figure 4.23   A Petri net whose arc (a) is an inhibitor.

transition if the 'inhibiting' place contains a token. In Figure 4.23, the arc (a) is an inhibitor, and the transition is blocked as long as place P_1 has a mark. Arcs (b) and (c) are normal arcs.

For example, a subsumption architecture model (cf. Chapter 3), which is based on the definition of a hierarchy between modules, can be described with the help of Petri nets with inhibitor arcs (Figure 4.24). It can be established that if the dominant module is activated, and there is therefore a mark at place P_1, then the transition T_2 is inhibited, which prevents the inferior module from functioning.

Modelling by means of Petri nets quickly becomes very complex, and it is then necessary to break the net down into separate modules. This is what we shall do through the definition of the BRIC formalism in Section 4.11.

4.4.4   Other factual models

There are many other models of concurrent mechanisms which can be used to describe multi-agent systems. In particular, CCS models (Milner, 1989) and CSP

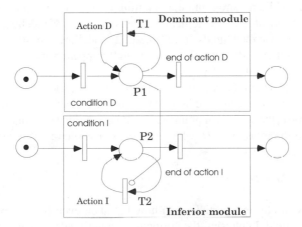

Figure 4.24   A subsumption architecture model using an inhibitor arc.

models (Hoare, 1985), which serve to describe formally the functioning of parallel and distributed systems in interactions, could be used more frequently in the context of multi-agent systems. Nevertheless, there is still a lot of work to be done, because these formal tools were developed in relation to distributed processes and the semantics of parallel languages, and they are not always very well suited to the problems of multi-agent systems, especially those of situated MASs in which agents carry out actions in an environment.

4.5   Action as physical displacement

Although developed at a much earlier date, the concept of action as used in physics has had little influence on the world of artificial intelligence, which has perhaps been too obsessed with logical formalisms. For physics, action is first of all what brings about movement, what changes the dynamic state of a body, that is, an acceleration. Newton's first law describes it well: *A body remains at rest or moves with constant velocity in a straight line unless acted upon by force* (Newton, 1985). Why not take inspiration from these principles to express the behaviours of situated agents for which the environment is conceived as a metric space? In fact, this approach can prove particularly fruitful in the case of reactive agents which have to plan their trajectory, avoid colliding with each other and, if necessary, be capable of meeting each other and moving together. We need only think of a squadron of aircraft in flight, or of the flow of cars along a main road, to have some idea of this mechanical application of action.

Indeed, when agents change their positions, whether they are mobile robots or vehicles attempting to avoid each other, their behaviour is naturally manifested as a movement in a Euclidian space. However, although it may appear natural to consider systems based on mobile robots as material solids moving in space over time, for a long while research into the planning of the movement of mobile robots was confined to symbolic and logical analysis. It is only recently that reactive techniques using potential fields have emerged, and they are still considered as almost 'revolutionary', although they can actually appear very simple, since they make use of vector analysis only.

It is indeed natural for reactive systems to turn to 'analogue' representations of reality, considering movements as additions of vectors in an Euclidian space (Figure 4.25).

If at time t_0 the agent is at point M, it will be at point M' at time $t_0 + \Delta t$, having thus completed the movement D, which makes it possible to write vectorially that:

$$\vec{OM'} = \vec{OM} + \vec{D}$$

The analogy with physical particles can now be taken even further by considering the concept of a field. In physics, the notion of gravitational, electrical and magnetic fields serves to explain the origin of forces and thus the movement of particles. We

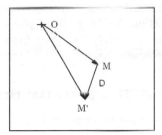

Figure 4.25   Geometrical displacement is a form of action which is expressed as a geometrical transformation in space.

generally distinguish between two types of field: scalar and vector. These fields associate a value with all points in space. For a scalar field, the value is a scalar, that is, a number which represents the intensity of the field at the point under consideration. In the case of a vector field, the value is a vector.

These fields can be combined or superimposed if fields of the same nature are involved. Such combinations are generally expressed in additive form by adding up the sizes of the fields at each of the points in space. If we give the names $U(p)$ and $V(p)$ to two fields defined by their values at any point whatever p in space, then the sum of the fields is a field, $W(p)$, whose value is simply the sum of the values at each point:

$$W(p) = U(p) + V(p)$$

It is also possible to combine fields of the same type by retaining only the highest value if we are dealing with scalar fields. In this case, the operation *max* is defined thus:

$$max(U(p), V(p)) = U(p) \text{ if } U(p) \geq V(p), V(p) \text{ otherwise}$$

Visualisation of the value of a scalar field on the basis of its position in a two-dimensional space gives a relief effect. The peaks are the places with the highest intensities and the valleys those where the influence of the field is less. The slopes of these mountains give what is called the *gradient* of a field, that is, its variation depending on the place, and determine the direction of the steepest slope associated with each point. The gradient is a vector function, which thus associates a field of vectors with the initial scalar field. If the scalar field defines a potential, then the gradient defines a force corresponding to the potential:

$$\vec{F}(p) = -\vec{\nabla}\, U(p) \tag{4.1}$$

where ∇ represents the operator gradient. These fields will determine the attractive or repulsive tendencies (which are often expressed in the form of forces) which cause the particles to move in a direction corresponding to the point in a field where there is the strongest attraction. So the gradient plays an essential role, since the steeper the gradient (the more rapidly one goes from a valley to a summit), the stronger the attractive or repulsive force.

4.5.1 Displacements in a potential field

This field concept is predominantly used in reactive systems to determine the behaviour of agents. It involves a relatively recent technique which has its origins in a radical critique of classical planning techniques for determining a path or a route to be followed (Latombe, 1991; Barraquand and Latombe, 1989). The general principle is to assume that the objects in the environment are emitting signals, whose intensity is proportional to the distance (or more generally to the square of the distance) to the goal. These signals are diffused throughout the space and define a potential, $U(p)$, for which it is possible to draw a vector force field, $F(p)$, based on Equation (4.1). We then assume that the goals define attractive potential fields, whereas the obstacles correspond to repulsive potential fields. So, the overall field U is defined as the vector sum of the fields of attraction and repulsion:

$$U(p) = U_{attr}(p) + U_{repul}(p)$$

These fields are generally defined on the basis of the distance to the goal or to the obstacles. The attractive fields can display an intensity proportional to the distance to the goal or, by analogy with 'natural' fields, proportional to the square of that distance:

$$U_{attr}(p) = k * dist(p, p_{goal})^2$$

The potential fields of the obstacles are often a little more complicated, for they serve only to prevent the moving body from coming into collision with the obstacle without its having too much influence on its long-distance trajectory. For this, it is sufficient to define an influence barrier, that is, a distance $dist_{influence}$ beyond which the influence of the obstacles is no longer felt.

$$U \ repul(p) = k' \frac{1}{dist(p, p_{obs})^2} \text{ if } dist(p, p_{obs}) \leq dist_{influence}$$
$$= 0 \text{ if not}$$

In this case, the intensity of the field increases very strongly as one approaches the obstacles (it is even 'infinite' at the obstacle's position). The movement of a robot can then be summarised as 'descending' the potential field by following the line of the steepest slope, the goal representing the valley and the obstacles the mountains which have to be avoided. This technique is thus very simply put into operation, and above all very easy to understand by virtue of its eminently visual character. In fact, if the movements of the robots are made in a two-dimensional space, it is possible

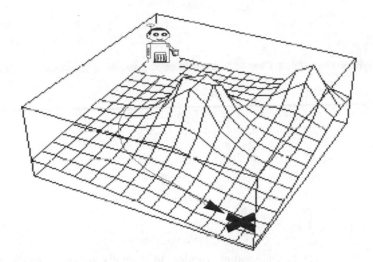

Figure 4.26   In a system of potential fields, the agent is attracted by the goal and repelled by the obstacles.

to represent these fields in three dimensions, with the height representing the intensity of the field. Figure 4.26 shows such a potential field for one goal and two obstacles.

We can see that the agent tries to find a trajectory offering the best compromise between the attraction of the goal on the one hand and the repulsion of the obstacles on the other. If we want the trajectory to pass closer to the obstacles, it is sufficient to make the repulsive fields more sloping and, conversely, to make them 'larger' if we wish to move away from the obstacles.

If potential fields have the merit of simplicity, they do unfortunately present several drawbacks, the main one being the existence of local minima. A robot faced with certain concave obstacles can be immobilised in a potential well, which prevents it from going backwards and thus from getting round the obstacle. A solution to this problem is to construct the attractive fields in a different way, by considering not the absolute distance between the goal and the points in space, but the minimal distance allowing for the skirting of the obstacles. This distance can be computed very simply on the basis of a 'wavefront expansion' algorithm (Barraquand and Latombe, 1989). Starting from the goal(s), we travel to all the points in space in parallel, increasing the value of the field intensity each time and going round the obstacles.

To construct such a field, we first need to 'digitalise' the space by breaking it down into a set of cells of equal sizes, each generally having the form of a square or, better, a hexagon (if we are dealing with a two-dimensional space, but we can easily generalise to a three-dimensional one). The algorithm is then distributed so that each cell acts in an autonomous manner. When a cell receives a new value which is lower than its own potential value, it stores it, and propagates that value, increased by one unit, to all the neighbouring cells:

```
Type cell
Fields
  potential: Number
  neighbouring: List of cells

Procedure value(x, v)
  if x.potential is not defined
  or if v < x.potential
  then
    x.potential: = v
    for every y in neighbouring x
      value(y,v+1)
    if not, do nothing
End
```

It is possible to get this algorithm working in a totally parallel manner and, if adequate calculators are available, to obtain the potential value at each point in space rapidly[†]. Readers who want to know more about displacement techniques for mobile agents, and particularly about techniques based on the concept of potential fields, can refer to the excellent book by Jean-Claude Latombe (1991).

We shall frequently see this technique applied to reactive MASs, like those used for the simulation of a world of ants (cf. Chapter 7) and for a situated agent which has to move in a world that includes obstacles (cf. Section 4.9.3). These techniques can be applied equally well to movements in a plane and to the diffusion of 'chemical' markers which act as fields of attraction for the behaviour of agents.

4.5.2   Appeal of this conception of action

This physical approach to action proves very fruitful in two cases:

(1)   Where it seems quite natural to treat actions as movements in a metric space. It is particularly useful for all multi-agent systems that conceive of agents as types of little robots moving about in an environment.

(2)   When actions depend on time and it is possible to use concepts of fields to describe the agents' tendencies to do something.

Vector fields offer fairly efficient management of the coordination of actions between multiple agents when the actions amount to movements in a physical

---

[†]This version functions very well, but does not permit us to know whether the computations have actually been carried out in parallel when the program ends. To obtain information on this, we must use rather more complicated algorithms which stamp the sources of the signals and give back the local termination values, as we shall see in Chapter 7 for task allocation algorithms. See Raynal (1987) for more detailed information on termination problems in wavefront propagation algorithms.

space. Their use in solving problems involving the coordination of the movements of several mobile agents, such as that of air traffic control, has proved particularly fruitful, as we shall see in Chapter 8. Nevertheless, vector fields have some drawbacks.

The first is that they are not naturally integrated into any logical conception of intention and action. How, indeed, can we connect the description of a state of the world which takes the form of logical formulae with actions in the form of movements in a space equipped with a field of potentials, and how can we plan these actions in such situations?

The second, more fundamental, difficulty with vector fields is that they are ineffective wherever situations cannot be represented in a metric space. For example, it is clear that we do not know how to solve administrative problems in this way. In particular, multi-agent systems based on cooperation of expertises (cf. Chapter 1) are unable to gain anything at all from such mechanistic models.

Finally, a third problem stems from the fact that it is difficult to take account of the overall evolution of a system when the agents are individually capable of deciding on their own actions. An agent, unlike a simple particle whose evolution is determined by the characteristics of the fields in which it moves, may have a real autonomy of decision, which makes any forecast as to the global behaviour of the system very difficult. Unless we reduce the capacity of these agents by making them all alike (and even very simplistic), there is really no theory capable of predicting the behaviour of a system in the presence of such autonomy. We then say that the global behaviour of a system *emerges* from all the local interactions.

4.6   Action as local modification

Contrary to notions which assume that each action effects a global transformation in the world, our common intuition apprehends action as a local modification. My deeds transform only the entities in my vicinity. If I drop a glass on the floor, I do not expect the orbits of the planets to be changed by this. Each action produces only a local disturbance, an alteration which is in contact with, or at any event at a finite distance from, the cause of that action. Even if it has sizeable consequences, such as a nuclear explosion, action can be seen as a local cause whose effects are propagated, by degrees, over a large part of space.

In contrast to the approach involving the transformation of states, which describes the world as a set of valid formulae, we assume here that the world is made up of a network whose nodes represent 'real' entities (parts of space, physical objects, beings, animals, persons; but also ideas, situations, events and tasks) and whose arcs correspond to the links between these entities: contact links, social relationships, dependencies and so on. Each node acts in an independent manner and modifies its own state in response to its perceptions. Here we come back to the basic idea of multi-agent systems as a foundation for the concept of action. Although there are few models which permit us to deal with this type of action in all its ramifications, there are theoretical and practical tools which, by reducing the objectives, enable us to go some way towards it.

4.6.1 Cellular automata

Cellular automata are dynamic systems, whose behaviour is determined wholly in terms of local relations. A cellular automata system is made up of a set of finite-state automata distributed over the nodes of a periodic network – generally a two-dimensional grid with a square mesh (Figure 4.27). Each automaton, called a *cell*, is linked to the automata which surround it, and its inputs are linked to the states of its neighbours. For this reason, the state of a cell at the instant $t + 1$ depends, not only on its preceding state, but also on the states of all its neighbours at the instant t. In addition, it is assumed that all the automata are identical, that they obey the same function of transition, and that their transitions are synchronous, that is, that they all change states at the same time.

One of the best-known examples of cellular automata is that of the 'life' game, thought up by John Conway, the functioning of which attempts to imitate the evolution of living organisations. This game was very well known in the 1970s, largely thanks to the publicity given to it by Martin Gardner, a scientific journalist on *Scientific American*, who wrote an article about it in October 1970.

A cell in the game of life can have only two states: 1 or 0, state 1 representing a living cell and state 0 a dead cell. The transition function of the automata is as follows:

- *Birth*: if the automaton is dead, it becomes alive (it passes to state 1) if precisely three of its neighbours are living. In all other cases, it stays dead.

- *Death*: if the automaton is living, it stays alive if two or three of its neighbours are alive. Otherwise it dies.

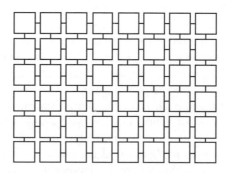

Figure 4.27 A flat cellular automaton with a connexity of 4.

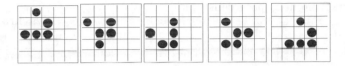

Figure 4.28 The displacement of a 'glider', a classic shape in the game of life, which identically reproduces itself at the end of four cycles by moving one square diagonally.

Figure 4.28 shows a possible evolution of the game of life over a few moments. The interesting thing about this game is that it showed that it was possible to have relatively stable dynamic configurations. One of them, the 'glider', identically reproduces itself at the instant $t + 4$, but changes its position by one square. It is fascinating to see from this game how such complex stable configurations can be generated by very simple local rules.

Nowadays, cellular automata are widely used to carry out simulations in physics, and more particularly in the context of fluid dynamics. Extensions of cellular automata to incorporate not just discrete, but continuous states have been used in relation to population dynamics. They are being more and more widely used to study the emergence of collective phenomena such as turbulence and chaos. The field of artificial life makes particularly intensive use of these techniques (Langton, 1988). In all domains where it is possible to characterise local rules based on proximity and geography, cellular automata can be put to profitable use.

4.6.2   Representation of a cellular automaton

The cell of an automaton is represented by a transition function, ϕ, which associates its subsequent state with its present state and with the state of its neighbouring cells. Each cell is therefore defined by a unique transition function, ϕ, defined as:

$$\phi(s_0, s_1,...,s_n) = s'_0$$

where s_0 is the state of the cell at time $t-1$, and the s_i are the states of the neighbouring cells at the same instant, and where s'_0 is the state of the cell at time t. It is possible to give an image of this in the form of a Petri net, as shown in Figure 4.29(a).

The inputs are provided by the states at time $t-1$ of the neighbouring cells which are buffered for each cell (the input positions of the net act as a buffer). The transition function of the cell is described as a simple transition which modifies the current state of the cell and propagates the new state to all the neighbouring cells. To make quite sure that all the cells function at the same time, they have to be synchronised. The terminals Synchro In and Synchro Out are dedicated to this function, respectively coming from and going to a synchronisation component shown in Figure 4.29(b). The Synchro Out inputs of the synchroniser are directly linked to the outputs of the same name from the cells, and the Synchro

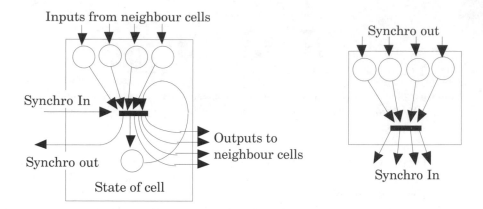

Figure 4.29 Representation of a cellular automaton cell (a) and its synchronisation system (b) in terms of Petri nets.

In outputs from the component go directly to the inputs of the same name in each of the cells. When the cells have completed their transition, they send a signal to their `Synchro Out` output. It is only when all the cells have sent this signal that the internal transition of the synchroniser can be triggered and a signal can be sent to `Synchro In` terminals of the cells, permitting them to effect their transition.

4.6.3   Cellular automata and multi-agent systems

One often wonders about the nature of the relationship between multi-agent systems and cellular automata. Are multi-agent systems types of cellular automata? Or vice versa? In spite of their resemblances, cellular automata are not multi-agent systems. If the environment of the MASs can easily be represented in the form of a grid of cells, the same is not true of the agents, which are autonomous entities able to change their position while still retaining their identities, and also able to modify the links they establish with other agents. Consequently, cellular automata can be considered either as 'degenerate' multi-agent systems in which the agents have become fixed; or, more positively, as good environmental models in which it is possible to define precisely the rules for the propagation of signals or, more generally, the laws of the universe.

For example, wavefront potential diffusion can, as we saw in the preceding section, be expressed quite easily in the form of a cellular automaton. The behaviour of a cell is then limited to taking the maximum value of the intensity of a signal given by its neighbouring values and decreasing its own value by a unit:

current cell value = max(values of neighbouring cells) – 1

When the net stabilises, the value of each of the cells corresponds to the intensity of the signal at this point.

4.7   Action as command

Control theory and cybernetics (Couffignal, 1963) have taken an interest in action from the specific points of view of industrial process control and the creation of regulated machines. The problem of action then consists in causing variations in a certain number of inputs, known as *command* variables, in a physical system to obtain specific output variable values. Thus, in a regulation problem, the output variables must reach and maintain fixed pre-set values.

Let us take the example of the automatic steering of a boat. To get to a specific point, the person steering the boat manipulates the helm so that the boat goes in the desired direction. This action is brought about by the prevention of the proper development of the liquid flows resulting from the boat's speed, which exerts a force on the rudder and modifies the movement of the boat.

But the water itself is agitated by movements and modifies the boat's course, which obliges the person steering to make a course correction by means of a retroaction mechanism, as shown in Figure 4.30.

Here the action of the person steering consists in controlling the physical system on the basis of information from his or her sensors (organs of sight) and correcting the behaviour of the boat by acting on the effectors (the rudder) to go in the desired direction.

So action is no longer merely a transformation of states of the world or a simple movement, but a complex activity entirely directed towards a goal, which takes account of the reactions of the environment and the corrections to be made to previous actions. This conception of action as command forms the basis of all systems of regulation and, in general, of all that has a bearing on the control of machines. Cybernetics, followed by the general theory of systems, has also sung the praises of this conception of action, with the work of N. Wiener (1948), L. von Bertalanffy (1968) or M. D. Mesarovic and Y. Takahara (1975).

The cybernetic view of action is clearly very important for MASs. The actions of the agents must take account of the reactions of the environment and be able to make necessary adjustments. Any action is carried out in an environment,

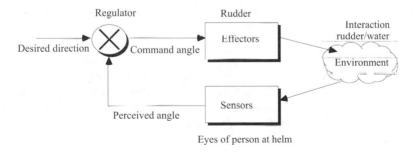

Figure 4.30   Cybernetics, and in particular command theory, treat action as a command which is applied to a system to regulate and control its functioning.

and presupposes the existence of a set of mechanisms regulating its execution which can correct any faults in its application. We shall see that agents themselves can be considered as cybernetic beings. But in spite of their interest, cybernetics and the view of action which it puts forward cannot express the wealth of interactions which take place between agents. However true it may be that an agent's capacity to act is ultimately no more nor less than its capacity to vary the command parameters of its effectors, that does not help us to address the question of interaction between agents. Such a perspective notably fails to make any provision for handling the simultaneity of actions, and no simple regulation technique is capable of describing coordination of actions, or of distributing tasks between several agents.

4.8 Tropistic and hysteretic agents

Having studied various different models of action, we can now move on to the description of agents and multi-agent systems. The approach used involves starting from the influence/reaction model, introducing agents as entities capable of producing influences and distinguishing, from among the states of the world, those which are useful for their actions. These models of agents owe a great deal to the work of Genesereth and Nilsson (1987) who were the first to come up with an algebraic representation of the structure and behaviours of agents. However, as they retained the concept of action as the transformation of states, they could provide only models of mono-agent systems, in which a single agent is responsible for the modifications it makes to the environment. In contrast, starting from action as the production of influences, it will be possible to introduce simultaneous actions, and thus display authentic multi-agent models.

Agents are entities capable of taking account of what surrounds them, which, for purely situated agents, translates into the capacity to *perceive* the environment and to act by *executing actions* which tend to modify the state of the multi-agent system (whether the agent acts directly on the environment or sends messages addressed to other agents), after having *deliberated* on what should be done. So we say that an agent is made up of three parts: perception, deliberation, execution, as shown in Figure 4.31.

Perception, for an agent, is the quality of being able to classify and distinguish states of the world, not only with respect to prominent features of the environment, but also with respect to the actions it is undertaking. We shall consider perception as a function which associates a set of values called *percepts* or *stimuli*[†] with the set of states of the world Σ. If P_a represents the set of percepts associated with an agent a then an agent's perception function can be defined as:

[†]The term *percepts* is preferred in relation to cognitive agents and *stimuli* in relation to reactive agents. Nevertheless, I shall use the two terms interchangeably to designate that which an agent perceives.

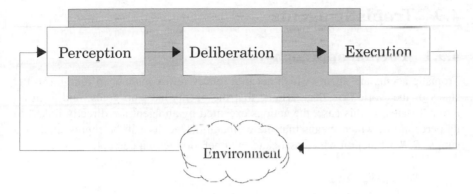

Figure 4.31   The structure of an agent: perception–deliberation–execution.

$Percept_a: \Sigma \rightarrow P_a$

which associates a percept with each state of the world. The execution capacities have been dealt with previously. They consist in producing influences which will be combined and dealt with by the environment in accordance with the laws that characterise it. Execution consists in applying an operator through the *Exec* function previously defined:

$Exec: Op \times \Sigma \rightarrow \Gamma$

where Op and Γ describe respectively the set of operations which can be carried out by the agents and the set of influences produced by the agents.

What is located between the input and the output, that is, between perception and execution, is called *deliberation*, and constitutes the most essential part of an agent, the part responsible for its actual behaviour and the part which is most complex and most closely studied. Whereas perception and execution capacities can often be considered as simple functions, the same does not apply to deliberation, for unless we are considering extremely simple agents, it is here that objectives, decision making and memory faculties are developed, together, in the case of cognitive agents, with the representations of the world and the concepts used to decide what action to take.

We can start by distinguishing two broad categories of agents: *tropistic agents* and *hysteretic agents*[†]. The former are characteristically elementary reactive agents which are always in the *here and now*, unable to memorise anything; whereas the latter have behaviours which can be as complex as we like, and use their past experience to anticipate the future.

[†]This distinction comes from Genesereth and Nilsson (1987).

4.9 Tropistic agents

4.9.1 Formal approach

Tropistic agents are agents which act in a totally reflex manner in relation to the states of the world. We thus assume that the agents have no goals, and even no internal states. In this case, the actions executed by an agent are directly linked to its perceptions, which means that the deliberation faculty can be represented as a simple *Reflex* function which associates an operation with a percept:

$$Reflex_a: P_a \rightarrow Op$$

A tropistic agent a in an action system $<\Sigma, \Gamma, Op, Exec, React>$, where $\Sigma, \Gamma, Op,$ *Exec* and *React* are defined as we have seen above, can thus be described as a triplet:

$$a = < P_a, Percept_a, Reflex_a >$$

that is, as a set of percepts, a perception function and a decision function which is limited to reacting in a reflex manner to the perceptions it receives.

If we give the name *Behave*$_a$ to the function which represents the behaviour of the agent a then this function simply combines the reflex and the perception of that agent to produce a new operation:

$$Behave_a: \Sigma \rightarrow Op$$
$$Behave_a(\sigma) = Reflex_a(Percept_a(\sigma))$$

4.9.2 A tropistic multi-agent system

The dynamics of a tropistic (and thus situated) multi-agent system are given by the evolution of the state of the environment, $\sigma(t)$, in relation to time. For an agent a the equation for this evolution is:

$$\sigma(t + 1) = React(Exec(Behave_a(\sigma(t)), \sigma(t)), \sigma(t))$$

The state of the environment is thus the result of the application of the laws of the universe to the influences produced by the application of the operation selected by the behaviour of the agent. When several agents, $a_1,...,a_n$ are acting simultaneously, we have to combine the influences produced by each of the agents:

$$Exec(Behave_1(\sigma(t))\|..\|Behave_n(\sigma(t))) = \bigcup_{i=1}^{n} Exec(Behave_i(\sigma(t)))$$

from which we derive the dynamics of the state of the environment:

$$\sigma(t + 1) = React(\bigcup_{i=1}^{n} Exec(Behave_i(\sigma(t))))$$

The evolution of a tropistic multi-agent system therefore consists of a succession of states, each one dependent both on the laws of the universe and on the behaviour of each of the agents. Figure 4.32 gives a graphic representation of a multi-agent system comprising three tropistic agents.

In the version we have given, this evolution is discontinuous: everything that happens between the instant t and the instant $t + 1$ is considered as 'instantaneous'. It would be possible to provide a continuous version, but for this the *React* and *Exec* operators should have a continuous expression.

4.9.3 Tropistic agents and situated actions

Although one might be inclined to think that, because of their simplicity, tropistic agents are not very useful, an entire area of research which stemmed initially from planning has been able to show that it is possible to define tropistic agents displaying relatively complex behaviour by utilising the environment as a reference point and a memory. We therefore say that the actions of a tropistic agent are situated, that is, they are related to its position and to the state of the world which it perceives. An expression has been coined for this concept: *situated action*. Introduced initially in 1987 by Suchmann (1987), taken up by P. Agre and D. Chapman (1987), supported by P. Maes (1990) and adapted for the multi-agent universe by Connah and Wavish (Wavish and Connah, 1990), situated actions constitute the most elementary model of reactive actions. The principle involved is very simple and is based on a stimulus/response-type diagram.

Perception plays an essential role in this model. Indeed, it is by means of characteristic indices situated in the environment that the associated action can be triggered. The notion of *index* is basic to the understanding of triggered

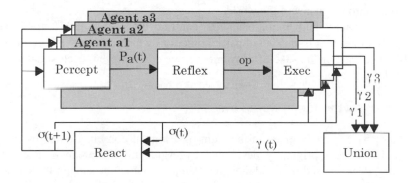

Figure 4.32   Graphic representation of an MAS comprising three tropistic agents.

actions. An index is a prominent feature of the environment which is helpful to an agent engaged in carrying out a particular action. If, for example, I know that in order to visit a friend, I have to turn right just after the chemist's shop, which is opposite the tobacconist's, this chemist's shop becomes an index triggering my action `turn right`. The existence of an index is always relative to the agent and its actions. There is no such thing as an index *per se*. For example, the chemist's shop becomes an index for my action of turning right only because I am on my way to visit my friend, and it loses its character as an index as soon as I have turned right. Likewise, a herbivore does not necessarily constitute an index for a predator. It takes on that character only when the predator is hungry, that is, when it has undertaken a hunting action and sees this herbivore as prey. So indices are action triggers in relation to an agent's circumstances. The percepts are then defined as combinations of indices significant for the accomplishment of actions.

The perception function can thus be defined as a combination of index-recognition functions where each partial index-recognition function, *PerceptIndex$_i$*, registers whether the index is present or not in the environment:

$$PerceptIndex_i: \Sigma \times Ag \rightarrow Bool$$

Bool represents the set of values {*True, False*}. In the case of Clifford, for example, the function which recognises whether or not there are pliers in the room where Clifford is will return *True* if they are in fact there and *False* if not. It is possible to compound these partial recognition functions with the help of logical operators such as $\wedge$ (and), $\vee$ (or) or $\neg$ (not). Perception is then defined as a combination of partial index test functions. For example, the percept

```
being-in-the-outhouse-and-spotting-pliers
```

is obtained if the two index-perception functions `being-in-the-outhouse` and `spotting-pliers` both return the value *True*. Situations are thus classified on the basis of the position of the agent, which assumes that the agents' positions are coded into the states of the world.

An agent's deliberation behaviour can thus be given in the form of a set of situated actions, that is, as a set of partial functions which associate a specific action with a percept. For the sake of convenience, we can represent each situated action as a rule:

```
if <percept> then <action>
```

where `<percept>` is given in the form of a logical combination of index tests. These ideas were originally developed by Agre and Chapman in a computer program, Pengi, based on a video game, Pengo, in which a penguin tries to amass as many diamonds as possible by moving through a labyrinth made up of ice cubes and inhabited by bees, which pursue the penguin and try to kill it by stinging it or

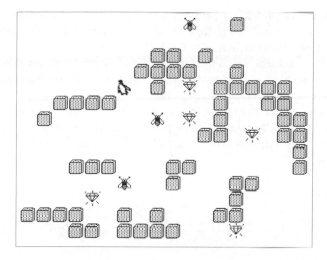

Figure 4.33   The Pengi game. The penguin has to amass as many diamonds as possible while avoiding the bees (taken from Drogoul *et al.* (1991)).

by projecting ice cubes at it. The ice cubes can actually be pushed by the bees and the penguin. They then move in a straight line until they touch another cube or the edge of the screen, and they kill the animals (bees or penguin) which are in their path (Figure 4.33). The interesting point in this game, as indeed in most action video games, is the fact that it is impossible to plan all the penguin's actions in advance. One has to react rapidly to situations as they arise using 'reflex mode'.

In Agre and Chapman's version, the penguin's actions are coded in the form of situated actions. For example, the action consisting in trying to squash a bee can be expressed as a rule[†] in the form:

```
Bee-killing rule-1
   if there is an ice-cube-beside-me
   and if there is a bee-on-the-other-side
     of-the-ice-cube-which-is-beside-me
   then
     push the ice-cube-beside-me
```

The first two premises of the rule indicate the premises triggering the action, and the conclusion specifies the action which is to be activated.

Although the behaviour of situated agents is very attractive in its simplicity, writing it poses numerous problems. The first relates to coherence. For example, if the penguin is near a diamond and it spots a bee situated on the other side of an ice cube, should it take the diamond or try to kill the bee first? The simplest solution is

---

[†]Although, strictly speaking, there are no rules in their system, it is easier to interpret it in this way.

to give an order of preference between actions, so that any possible conflicts are avoided. This order is often translated by attributing a priority coefficient to actions or by using a subsumption architecture (cf. Chapter 3).

Another problem lies in the fact that situated actions involve no conception either of an internal goal or of memory. An agent acts only on the basis of what it perceives here and now, and so it cannot take into account the state in which it finds itself. For example, let us suppose that we wish to write the behaviour of Clifford, which is being asked to take a pair of pliers from the outhouse to the workshop (Figure 4.2). One solution is to describe its behaviour with the help of the following set of rules, R1:

```
FetchPliers rule                                             (R1)
    if I am not in the outhouse
    and I am not carrying anything
    then go to the outhouse

PickUpPliers rule
    if I am in the outhouse
    and I am not carrying anything
    then pick up the pliers

GotoWorkshop rule
    if I am not in the workshop
    and I am carrying something
    then go to the workshop

PutdownObject rule
    if I am in the workshop
    and I am carrying an object
    then put down what I am carrying
```

Now, let us suppose that we want Clifford to pick up what it has put down. With the previous rules, as soon as Clifford is no longer holding anything, it goes to fetch a pair of pliers from the outhouse, and completely ignores the fact that it was carrying one a few moments ago. If, on the other hand, it 'knew' that it had been carrying a pair of pliers, it would not go back directly to the outhouse, but would look around to find the pliers again. One solution would be to code an internal state in the form of a Boolean variable, `in-the-process-of-fetching`, and to rewrite the set of rules in the following way:

```
LookforPliers rule                                           (R2)
    if I am not in the outhouse
    and I am not carrying anything
    and I am not in-the-process-of-fetching
    then go to the outhouse
```

```
PickupPliers rule
    if I am in the outhouse
    and I am not carrying anything
    then pick up the pliers
    and put myself into the in-the-process-of-fetching
    state

GotoWorkshop rule
    if I am not in the workshop
    and I am carrying something
    then go to the workshop

PutdownObject rule
    if I am in the workshop
    and I am carrying an object
    then put down what I am carrying
    and put myself into the not-in-the-process-of-
    fetching state

FetchPliersAgain rule
    if I am not carrying anything
    and I am in-the-process-of-fetching
    and I do not perceive the pliers on the floor
    then look around me for the pliers

PickupPliersAgain rule
    if I am not carrying anything
    and I am in-the-process-of-fetching
    and I perceive the pliers on the floor
    then pick up the pliers
```

Unfortunately, tropistic agents have no memory, which deprives them of any internal states! Should we kiss tropistic agents goodbye because of this? No, we just need to pay close attention to the way in which situated actions are coded, and ensure that an agent like Clifford is given the capacity to pick up the pliers again if it is not in the workshop. To solve the problem, all we need to do is go back to the set of rules R1 and add the following rule to it:

```
PickupPliersAgain rule                                (R3)
    if I am not carrying anything
    and I perceive pliers
    and I am not in the workshop
    then pick up the pliers
```

Thus, as soon as Clifford perceives a pair of pliers outside the workshop, whether it has just been carrying them or whether it has encountered them by chance, it will pick up the pliers and will go back to the workshop, without needing to have any internal states.

4.9.4   Flexibility of situated actions

What is most noteworthy about situated actions is their flexibility in accomplishing tasks and their ability to deal with unforeseen modifications to the world. For example, let us suppose that we first ask Clifford to bring a pair of pliers from the outhouse to the workshop as before, and that we *then* want it to go and fetch a hammer from the shed. One of the options, if we move away from the principle of situated actions, is to give the agent an internal Boolean variable, `pliers-put-down`, which, if it has the value 1, tells the agent that the pliers have been put down and that it can go and fetch the hammer. The rules for going to fetch an object are then as follows (set of rules R4):

```
LookforPliers rule                                             (R4)
    if I am not in the outhouse
    and I am not carrying anything
    and I am not in-the-process-of-fetching
    and not pliers-put-down
    then go to the outhouse


LookforHammer rule
    if I am not in the shed
    and I am not carrying anything
    and I am not in-the-process-of-fetching
    and pliers-put-down
    then go to the shed
```

Thus, Clifford from its internal state knows whether it has to fetch a pair of pliers or a hammer. This internal state constitutes a *representation* of the world (cf. Chapter 5): the variable `pliers-put-down` represents the fact that the pliers are actually in the workshop. Now let us suppose that, for one reason or another, there has been an error, and the pliers have not been put down. Clifford will set off to fetch the hammer, even though the pliers have not yet been brought to the desired location. One might consider this as an error or a bug in Clifford's behaviour, but it does not stem from anything it has done. It is merely applying its program to the letter. The error comes from a lack of congruity between its representation (the `pliers-put-down` value reads *True*) and the state of the world (the pliers have not been put down). Now, the point about tropistic agents is precisely the fact that they have no representation of the world, so that there is no danger of any lack of coherence (or any problems in managing it) arising from that quarter. To avoid the problem of incoherence, we can simply treat the matter as one of perception and look to the environment to provide the memory. We have only to ensure that Clifford first goes to the workshop to see whether a pair of pliers has been put down or not, and that its behaviour of looking for the pliers or the hammer is triggered on the basis of this perception. Which is what we achieve by encoding the 'fetch' rules in the following manner (set of rules R5):

```
FetchObject rule                                          (R5)
   if I am not carrying anything
   and I am not in-the-process-of-fetching
   and I am not in the workshop
   then go to the workshop

FetchPliers rule
   if I am not carrying anything
   and I am not in-the-process-of-fetching
   and I am in the workshop
   and I do not perceive a pair of pliers
   then go to the outhouse

FetchHammer rule
   if I am not carrying anything and I am not
   in-the-process-of-carrying
   and I am in the workshop
   and I perceive a pair of pliers // it is time to
   then go to the shed // fetch the hammer
```

Here it is the environment that is acting as a memory, by indicating whether the pair of pliers has been brought into the workshop or not, the perception of the put-down pliers playing the role of a Boolean variable for Clifford. The world 'knows' its own state, and it suffices that it be perceived. A representation is therefore unnecessary for Clifford, since it is enough for it to perceive the state of the world in order to act in a coherent manner. This advantage is counter-balanced by an increase in the number of movements Clifford has to make. Yet these supplementary movements, which allow him to make sure that the pliers are not in the workshop so that it does indeed have to fetch them from the outhouse, may prove advantageous when the world is evolving independently of its actions (for example, because there are workpeople who are using the tools it transports) and the orders it receives themselves turn out to lack coherence. The environment is thus a splendid memory which agents can use to their advantage, possibly by putting down marks which will act as indices for them in accomplishing future actions. The environment can record states and make it possible for agents with very limited cognitive capacities to carry out interesting tasks – like Tom Thumb. We shall see in a later chapter (cf. Chapter 8) that the environment's capacities for memorising can be used with profit to coordinate collective actions and so amplify the natural capacities of agents.

4.9.5   The goals are in the environment

Since they are able to act only on the basis of the state of the environment, we imagine reactive agents as either some kind of mechanical marionettes, thoroughly unstable, erratic, and lacking in interest, or as totally whimsical beings who are blown this way and that, at the mercy of the impulses they receive from the environment. It is difficult to comprehend that situated tropistic agents use the environment to carry out useful and sometimes relatively complex tasks. How in fact could a tropistic agent be capable of pursuing a goal? Displacement actions such as Clifford's going to the outhouse were previously considered as atomic. It was supposed that they were very simple and could be encoded directly. But if Clifford can no longer go from one room to another in a single action, how can it reach the room indicated? Many solutions exist, certain of which require no memorising and can be applied to tropistic agents.

Hard encoding

The first solution is to encode into Clifford's behaviour the sequence of rooms it must go through. For example, to get from the workshop to the outhouse, it has to go through rooms { 1, 4, 5, 6, 9, 12}, and to go from the workshop to the shed it has to go through rooms { 1, 4, 5, 6, 3}. But this technique needs far too much 'wiring'. It would be necessary to define all the possible routes allowing movement from one room to another, the number of which increases exponentially with the number of rooms. In addition, any modification to the environment would require the complete reprogramming of the agent.

Exploration and memorising

The second solution uses the technique of exploring a labyrinth by memorising the rooms passed through. Clifford only needs to explore all the rooms, listing all the choices it has made at any junction, and memorising the area it has already explored, to avoid going round in circles. Memorisation is a departure from situated actions, and this method is costly, because it could be necessary for Clifford to go through every room before it finds the outhouse. It is nevertheless useful in providing agents with representations of their environment so that they can optimise their movements.

Exploration and marking

The third solution is another labyrinth-exploring technique. But in contrast to the previous one it uses the environment to mark the rooms passed through. Clifford systematically puts down a mark each time it arrives in a new room, and places a cross in each room it goes through. If it gets into a dead end, it turns back, following the marks and picking them up until it gets back to a place it has not yet explored. In this way, it uses the marks to retrace its steps and the crosses to avoid going round in circles. This technique, which is based on situated actions, is nevertheless similar to the previous one. The marks play the part of the accumulated choices, and the crosses represent the memorising of the rooms already seen. It therefore displays the same drawbacks as the previous method, if we assume that the number of routes increases exponentially with the number of rooms. Moreover, the more exits there are per room, the greater will be the number of choices to consider, and the more difficult to go from one point to another. Finally, for a tropistic agent, any new displacement will call for new exploration as it will not have been able to memorise the routes already travelled.

Hill climbing

The fourth method is based on compass technique, and is therefore known as hill climbing by analogy with the technique used by mountain dwellers who climb by following the lines with the steepest gradients. If you know the geographical position of the room you want to go to, you simply take the direction that leads to it most directly 'as the crow flies'. It is obviously a very simple technique, and it works well when the environment is not too uneven. In this case, it is no longer necessary to explore all the rooms, when all you need to do is follow the compass. Obviously, as everyone knows, this technique does not always allow us to find our way around in a city, because of one-way streets and dead ends. The same is true for Clifford, which can easily find its way blocked. If it uses this technique and inadvertently enters room 11, its way will be irremediably cut off, and it will not be able to get into the outhouse.

Wavefront diffusion

The fifth method, which mitigates the deficiencies of the previous one, is a variant of the one which was developed to go round obstacles with the aid of potential fields (cf. Section 4.5). It is very simple and has proved useful for moving situated agents. Its principle resembles that of the diffusion of liquid in a container, with the source of the liquid corresponding to the goal one is trying to achieve. In contrast to a compass, the liquid 'embraces' obstacles and then indicates the route that must be taken to avoid barriers and dead ends. The environment is marked by associating an intensity with a portion of space. The source takes the value 0, and each time we move off we give the new portion of space a value incremented by one unit in relation to the preceding one. If it turns out to have been marked already, the lower of the two values is selected. Figure 4.34 shows a wavefront-like diffusion allowing Clifford to get to the outhouse. Clifford has only to follow the line of the steepest gradient, that is, to take the route along which the values are descending. So it will go from room 2 (value 6) to room 1 (value 5), then it will go to 4 (value 4), 5 (value 3), 6 (value 2), 9 (value 1) and finally to 12 (value 0). It thus takes the most direct route and avoids all the dead ends.

This marking technique has the advantage of not depending on the agent's position, but only on that of the goals. For example, if Clifford wishes to go from

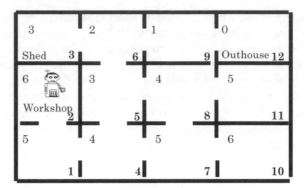

Figure 4.34 Wavefront-like diffusion in relation to the outhouse.

room 10 to the outhouse, it will follow the same marking. However, if it wants to go to the shed, it will have to propagate another marking starting from the shed. Clifford's movements between the workshop, the shed and the outhouse can be determined in their entirety by three markings, each corresponding to one of these sites. So this is a particularly attractive option for moving a tropistic agent in any space, and it has been used in numerous applications (Barraquand and Latombe, 1989; Drogoul *et al.*, 1991). Its mayor drawback lies in the potential complexity of the marking, which is proportional to the number of portions of space under consideration. When the goals are static, this poses no problems, but when it comes to simulating more dynamic activities in a multi-agent system, the propagation of the marks certainly becomes the activity requiring the most effort. Finally, because of very specific propagation phenomena relating to signals in nature (signal rebounds, noise, variations in intensities, and so on) and to the limitation of sensors, it is not always possible to use this technique in the case of situated robots in the real world.

We mentioned the Pengi game earlier, and how it could be tackled through routines triggered by environmental indices. In fact, it has proved to be simpler, more effective and more immediate to implement Pengi with the aid of a wavefront-like diffusion technique (Drogoul *et al.*, 1991). The penguin is attracted by the diamonds and repelled by the bees. Although the behaviours of the agents in the world of Pengi are elementary, the penguin is capable of playing in a completely correct manner, unlike a human player. Nevertheless, we might be inclined to think that a model based on local behaviours, without any planning, must have its limits (Figure 4.35(1)).

In this specific universe, the penguin can push only one cube at a time. It must not push the cubes directly in front of it, as this will create impassable walls (Figure 4.35(2). It cannot obtain a diamond through simplistic behaviour. The solution is to give it a slightly more sophisticated, aggressive behaviour towards the cubes. It must not push any cubes in the direction it is taking to get to a diamond, but rather perpendicularly to the attractive gradient[†]. This makes the definition of its

---

[†]Cf. Chapter 8 for a similar use of forces perpendicular to potential fields, in the context of avoiding a collision.

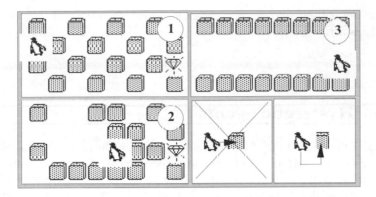

Figure 4.35　The penguin can extricate itself from very complicated situations (1), provided that it avoids pushing the cubes directly in front of it (2). For this, all it needs to do is to push the cubes perpendicularly to the direction of its goal (3).

behaviour slightly more complicated, but it means the problem can be solved without planning (Figure 4.35(3)).

Map making

The sixth and last method consists of giving Clifford a plan of the premises so that it can determine the path to take without moving. All it then has to do is plan a route using a STRIPS planning technique or one of the preceding methods. The map is thus used as a kind of virtual world, in which Clifford can anticipate all the actions to be carried out before it actually starts. This obviously assumes that Clifford has the considerable cognitive capacities needed to carry out such planning activity, which is impossible in the case of tropistic agents.

Which technique for tropistic agents?

In fact, only techniques using hard encoding, exploration and marking, hill climbing and wavefront-like diffusion can be applied to tropistic agents. They show that it is possible to give an agent a goal, provided that this goal can be defined in the environment. In fact, giving an agent a goal often means defining the objects or the places in the environment to which it has to become attached. These methods generally use environment-marking techniques, which enable agents to find their way about and achieve the goals assigned to them.

Researchers working on reactive agents should be given credit for having highlighted the importance of the environment in directing the action of agents with very limited 'mental' capacities. Certain faculties considered as being essentially cognitive, such as memory or apparently intentional behaviour, can easily be explained on the basis of indices situated in the environment. It is possible for a simple agent to carry out complex tasks with very poor cognitive skills if the environment is itself sufficiently complex to furnish the numerous indices it needs to guide its action[†].

4.10   Hysteretic agents

In spite of the interest they hold, tropistic agents remain relatively limited. If we want agents to be able to acquire experience personally or solve problems without having to mark the environment, they have to be given the capacity to retain information and thus to have memory. They are then called *hysteretic agents*.

4.10.1   Formal approach

The idea of a hysteretic agent, memorising a piece of information – and thus acting on the basis not only of perceptions but also of past experience – assumes that it can be characterised by an internal state s_a belonging to S_a the set of internal states of an agent a. Memorising information or an experience, then, is passing from one internal state to another. The capacity for deliberation is no longer described as a simple *Reflex* function, but as two functions, that of memorisation and that of decision. The memorisation function, *Mem*, takes a percept and an internal state and gives back a new internal state, whereas the decision function, *Decision*, takes a percept and an internal state and decides what operation to carry out. These two functions can be described thus:

$$Mem_a: P_a \times S_a \to S_a$$
$$Decision_a: P_a \times S_a \to Op_a$$

So perception can be defined, following the example of tropistic agents, as a function which produces percepts, derived solely from states of the environment. Perception can also be treated as dependent on the internal states of the agent, for example to characterise the phenomenon of the focusing of perception. In this case, the *Percept* function takes two propositions, a state of the environment and an internal state:

$$Percept_a: \Sigma \times S_a \to P_a$$

A hysteretic agent a in an action system $< \Sigma, \Gamma, Op, Exec, React >$, can thus be defined as an n-tuple:

$$a = < P_a, S_a, Percept_a, Mem_a, Decision_a >$$

[†]This concept is very topical in ethology (McFarland, 1990).

Behaviour is then more complex than in the case of a tropistic agent, since we are dealing with a function which associates a pair <state of environment, internal state> with another pair <set of influences, new internal state>:

$Behave_a: \Sigma \times S_a \to \Gamma \times S_a$
$Behave_a(\sigma, s) = <Decision_a(p, s), Mem_a(p, s) >$
$\qquad$ with $p = Percept_a(\sigma)$

4.10.2 A hysteretic multi-agent system

The model for situated hysteretic multi-agents flows easily from this. A multi-agent system made up of hysteretic agents is defined by the n-tuple:

$<Ag, \Sigma, \Gamma, Op, Exec, React, Cycle>$

where Σ, Γ, *Op*, *Exec* and *React* are defined as above, and where *Ag* is a set of hysteretic agents, each agent a_i being defined thus:

$a_i = <P_i, S_i, Percept_i, Decision_i, Mem_i>$

The dynamics of a multi-agent system comprising hysteretic agents are defined by $n + 1$ equations: a first equation describes the state of the environment, depending on the time and the behaviour of each agent, and the n others correspond to modifications in the internal states of agents.

$$\sigma(t + 1) = React(\bigcup_{i=1}^{n} Exec(Decision_i(p_i(t), s_i(t))))$$

$$s_1(t + 1) = Mem_1(p_1(t), s_1(t))$$

$$\ldots$$

$$s_n(t + 1) = Mem_n(p_n(t), p_n(t))$$
$$\qquad \text{with } p_i(t) = Percept_i(\sigma(t))$$

So the problem consists in determining the set of internal states of an agent and describing the two functions of decision and memorisation, in such a way that the agent's behaviour conforms with the designer's wishes and the desired collective phenomena are in fact put into place. Figure 4.36 shows the graphic representation of a MAS with three hysteretic agents.

4.10.3 Modelling of hysteretic agents by automata

To define the two functions of memorisation and decision, it will be simplest to reinvoke the concept of a finite-state automaton which we introduced in Section 4.4.1. We then identify the set of internal states of an agent with the set of internal states of the automaton, and the functions of memorisation and decision respectively

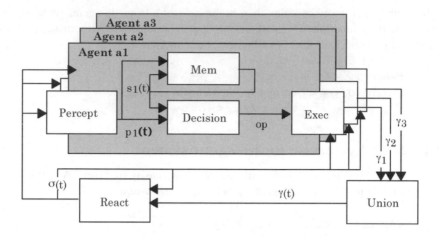

Figure 4.36 Graphic representation of the formalisation of a MAS with three hysteretic agents (i.e. agents with memories).

with functions ψ and ϕ of the latter. Events bringing about a change of state are given by the percepts arising from the function of perception.

Let us take the example of an explorer robot which has to search for ore and bring it back to its base. The robot first explores its environment, once it has been authorised to move off. If it notices some ore, it heads for the place where the ore is. Then it puts ore into its bucket until the bucket is full or until there is no ore left. When it has finished this filling operation, it heads back to its base. Figure 4.37 represents graphically the automaton associated with this agent. We have represented the percepts in the form of a vector of Boolean values comprising the following indices:

```
<authorisation-leave, ore-in-sight, on-ore-site,
at-base, bucket-full, bucket-empty>
```

For example, if the agent notices some ore and it still has an empty bucket, its percept will be:

```
<0,1,0,0,0,1>
```

On the diagram, the percepts are represented by the indices having a value other than zero. The set of internal states S_a of the agent a is equal to:

$$S_a = \{ \text{Ready to leave, exploring, tracking,} $$
$$\text{loading, return, unloading}\}$$

and the operations it can carry out are

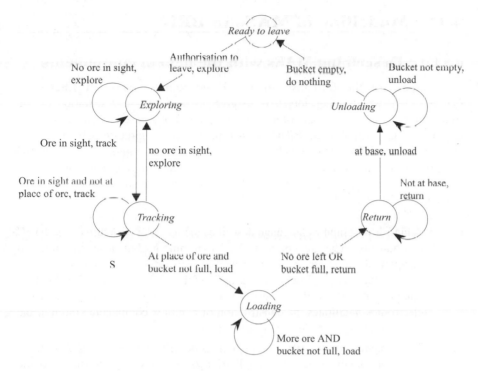

Figure 4.37   The behaviour of an explorer agent with a memory, represented in the form of a finite-state automaton.

$$Op_a = \{\texttt{explore, track, load, return, unload}\}$$

Although they are of interest, finite-state automata are relatively limited, for they cannot memorise non-Boolean values. The memorising capacities of such agents are thus constrained by the number of discrete states we know how to describe at the outset, as all the memorised information is within the states of the automaton. This limitation has consequences which are not unimportant. The agent has no easy way of counting the objects it sees. It cannot memorise the paths it has taken. It cannot know what its internal energy level is and so it cannot react by topping it up in some way. Even its own position has to be given through perception, since it is practically incapable of memorising this type of information. To solve these problems, it is sufficient to introduce registers, and model the agent with the help of register automata (cf. Section 4.4.2). Nevertheless, these models do not permit us to describe agents which do several things at the same time. For example, using a system based on finite-state automata, it is practically impossible to represent an explorer robot which communicates with other agents, or which plans its actions while it is carrying out plans already established. For this, we have to use a more powerful formalism, such as BRIC, which assimilates the concept of Petri nets.

4.11 Modelling of MASs in BRIC

4.11.1 Describing MASs with the help of components

The purpose of the formalism BRIC (Basic Representation of Interactive Components), which I developed, is to give an operative representation of the functioning of an agent, and of a multi-agent system, based on a component approach. The metaphor of BRIC is that of electronic circuits, which can be connected to one another relatively easily. Like electronic components, the BRIC components are attached to one another with the assistance of terminals and 'wires', along which messages are passed. The BRIC formalism is made up of two L3-type languages (cf. Chapter 1).

(1)   A high-level graphics language describes the modular structure of the BRIC components. The agents and the environment, but also the internal components of an agent, are described in the form of 'bricks' connected to one another, each 'brick' being defined by its interfaces and its own components. It is this language which, taking its inspiration from electronics, facilitates the construction of complex components through the assembling of more elementary components.

(2)   The behaviour of the basic components is described with the aid of a lower-level formalism using coloured Petri nets, which are well suited to the expression of parallelism.

A more complete presentation of this formalism is given in the appendix. We shall give only a rapid outline of it here. Each BRIC component can be considered as a module, that is, a software entity defined by the set of operations it can accomplish, which are illustrated in the form of input/output terminals (Figure 4.38). The components interact by means of communication links established between their terminals, an output terminal being linked to one or more input terminals of another component. The components are opaque modules. It is not possible to go in and modify the internal structure of a component directly. For this reason, the

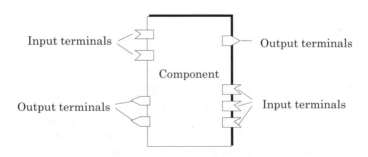

Figure 4.38   Structure of a component and its terminals.

components are all independent of one another, and the behaviour of a component cannot be changed by that of another. In software engineering terms, we say that their internal structure is 'encapsulated' by the messages that can be sent to them. The components function in a factual way. It is the messages passed along the lines of communication that trigger their activity. Each BRIC component acts in parallel with the other agents, parallelism being seen as a normal activity in the functioning of an agent, whether it is a reactive or cognitive agent.

The behaviour of these components can be defined either with reference to an assemblage of other components whose behaviour is already specified, and we then speak of a *composite component*; or directly, through an associated Petri net. In this latter case, we say that we are dealing with *elementary components*. Finally, it is also possible to introduce *primitive components*, whose behaviour is not described by a Petri net. The point of interest about these is that they can take charge of functionalities external to the agent or the system. For example, the basic activities of a mobile agent (for example, going straight on, turning left, following a gradient) can be described in the form of primitive components. BRIC components can be used to model agents and multi-agent systems. The significant thing about this approach is that it is recursive. An agent is a BRIC component, itself defined in terms of more elementary components. A MAS is then described as a set of interconnected components. This formalism is referred to constantly in the remainder of this book, and it constitutes the main operative description of the MASs. We shall deal with the general topic of modelling multi-agent systems in BRIC, leaving it until subsequent chapters to develop their special features. We shall model MASs using three types of agents: purely communicating agents, followed by purely situated agents, and finally communicating and situated agents.

4.11.2   Modelling of purely communicating MASs

Modelling of purely communicating agents

Purely communicating agents can be described in two different ways (Figure 4.39). The first way, (a), represents them in the form of a component with a single input terminal, the message receiver, and a single output terminal, the message transmission system. The receiver module is restricted to keeping messages in its queue and distributing them to internal modules representing the functions of memorising and decision making. Conversely, the message transmission module is responsible for collecting all requests and data coming from internal modules and sending them to the agents concerned. In the second system (b) the message reception and transmission modules have disappeared. Although this second form is less precise because of the absence of communication modules, we shall use it frequently for simplicity.

Modelling message routing unit

Communications are carried out through a message routing unit, which plays the role of a Post Office in being responsible for collecting and distributing messages

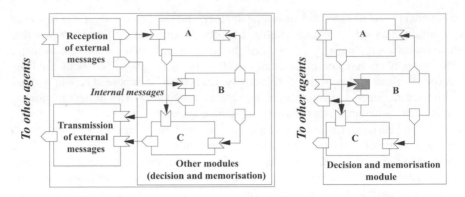

Figure 4.39 BRIC representation of purely communicating agents.

between agents. External messages transmitted by one agent to another are given in the form:

```
A << M(x1,...,xk)
```

where `A` is the addressee, `M` is the heading describing the type of message (cf. Chapter 6) and the x_i are the propositions of the message.

The message routing module is very simple, as it is limited to collecting messages from all the agents and transmitting them to the addresses of the agents concerned, as shown by Figure 4.40.

Modelling of communicating multi-agent systems

So it is possible to derive the structure of a communicating multi-agent system from this. Each agent (using representation (a)) has its output terminal connected to the

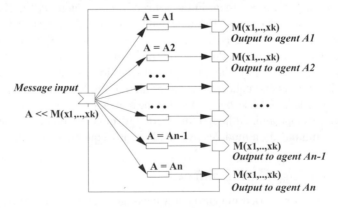

Figure 4.40 The message routing module.

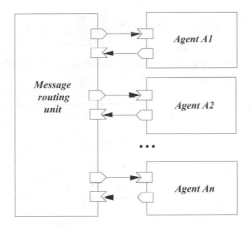

Figure 4.41   Architecture of a communicating multi-agent system.

input terminal for messages from the routing module, and its input terminal linked to the corresponding output terminal of this module, as shown in Figure 4.41.

4.11.3   Modelling of environments

Before going on to the modelling of situated agents, we first have to mention a key problem, the environment. This actually constitutes an essential part of situated multi-agent systems. Unfortunately, very little work has been done on modelling environments, and details relating to environments are usually lost in explanations of systems which have implemented them, or indeed completely buried in the code for their implementation. This is why we felt it was important to distinguish clearly between the various possible environment models, and to provide a precise model of our own espousing the concept of action by influences.

An environment can be represented in two ways. It can either be considered as a monolithic block, in which case we speak of a *centralised environment*; or it can be modelled as a set of cells assembled into a network to form a sort of cellular automaton constituting a *distributed environment*.

In a centralised environment, all the agents have access to the same structure. They produce influences which can be expressed as requests to the environment for actions, and it responds by sending back consumed or perceived elements, as demonstrated in Figure 4.42.

Centralised environments are much more widely used in systems where the propagation of signals is not too complex, that is, systems in which the number of possible stimuli is limited. Problems to do with hunting (prey/predators) are generally modelled with the aid of centralised environments, as are those relating to the representation of mobile robots (planes, land vehicles, boats) moving in an environment allowing only optical or electromagnetic detection. Systems which use such techniques include: Mace (Gasser *et al.*, 1987), Mice (Durfee and

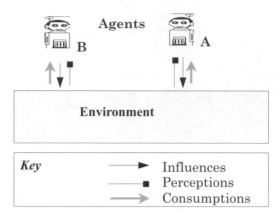

Figure 4.42 Schematic representation of a centralised environment. The agents can perceive what is going on around them in the environment, and can consume elements of the environment and influence its development by carrying out actions.

Montgomery, 1989), Craash (Zeghal and Ferber, 1993), Pandora II (Maruichi, 1989), Mages (Bouron, 1991; Bouron *et al.*, 1990). A distributed environment, on the other hand, is made up of a set of cells arranged in a network, like cellular automata. Each cell behaves like a centralised environment in miniature, managing the influences of the agents which are localised on that cell, and sending the consumed marks to the agents that ask for them (Figure 4.43). This technique is used mainly in MASs which effect a breakdown of the environment into small connected spaces as in video games such as war games.

The essential differences which mark out distributed environments from their centralised equivalents are the following:

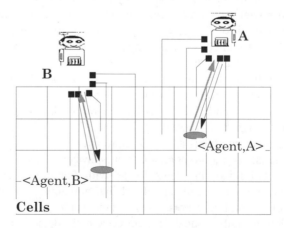

Figure 4.43 Representation of a distributed environment.

(1)   The state of the cell depends on the other cells which surround it, and thus also on the influences produced by the agents in the neighbouring cells.

(2)   The perception of the agents generally extends beyond one cell, which means it is not possible to transmit data on the state of a cell exclusively to the agent which occupies it.

(3)   Agents move from cell to cell, which means that the links which an agent maintains with a specific cell have to be managed.

(4)   Signals can be propagated from cell to cell. This propagation takes 'a certain amount of time', and so the displacement of the signals has to be synchronised with the movements of the agents.

Here we shall deal only with the modelling of centralised environments.

Modelling of a centralised environment

Since actions can be carried out in parallel, we must have a formalism which is capable of providing a support for this parallelism. BRIC is one of these, and I shall use it to introduce the various models of environment. Nevertheless, what is said here applies irrespective of the formalism used, and can be generalised to other representations. There are essentially two ways of modelling an environment:

- either we model the environment in an abstract manner, independently of the influences to which it can be subjected,

- or we particularise its characteristics to some extent by specialising it for a well-defined set of actions.

To model the environment, we must first know how to represent its different states $\sigma(t)$, and, in particular, how to represent the manner in which objects, agents and their positioning in the environment are symbolised. To this end, I shall make use of a classic technique similar to that which was introduced with the STRIPS-like representations of action. Objects and agents are given in the form of constants, and the relationships which exist between these objects and these agents are represented by a set of predicative formulae which we shall call *facts*. The variables will be denoted by lower case letters, and the names of the constants will start with a lower case letter. We shall assume that a fact exists for each agent, with the form `agent(a,p)`, where a represents the identifier of the agent (which must be unique within the system) and p the position of the agent (defined perhaps in the form of Cartesian coordinates on a flat surface or in space). For example, the environment shown in Figure 4.34 can be translated by the following formula, where `sig(R,x,y)` represents the level x of the signal from the outhouse into the room y:

```
{path(1,2), path(1,4), path(4,5), path(5,6), and so on
 sig(R,3,3), sig(R,5,1), sig(R,6,2), sig(R,0,Outhouse),
 sig(R,3,Shed), etc,..., agent(Clifford,2)}
```

Generalised environment

Centralised environments can be represented in BRIC in the form of a component which comprises two inputs and also three outputs (Figure 4.44). The input marked *Influences* receives the influences produced by the agents. These are combined with the state of the environment (place P_1) with the aid of two transitions, which represent the reactions of the environment. T_1 corresponds to reactions in the presence of influences from agents, and T_2 to what happens when the environment is left to itself. The outputs `Consumptions` and `Perception` correspond, respectively, to what is consumed (picking up of an object or absorption of food, for example) and perceived by agents during their actions. As with cellular automata, synchronisation inputs/outputs (`Sync. Reactions` and `End Reactions`), serve to synchronise the behaviour of the agents and the reactions of the environment. Place P_2 serves only as a time delay to make sure that the agents definitely perceive the new state of the environment.

The laws of the universe, that is, the definition of transitions T_1 and T_2, describe the reactions of the environment with and without influences. We should note that these laws can be defined with the aid of any description language.

Specialised environment

A point to note is that is is possible to represent each law in the form of a transition, and to associate a terminal with each type of influence. In this case, the behaviour of an environment can be described entirely in BRIC, and we then talk of a *specialised environment*. For example, let us suppose that an agent can do nothing in the environment except move, pick up an object or put one down. This amounts

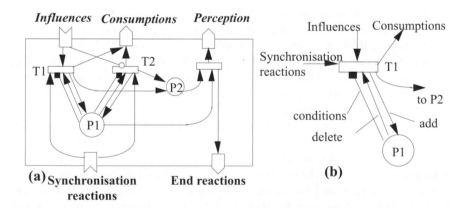

Figure 4.44 Representation of an environment in the form of a BRIC component (a). Place P_1 represents the state of the environment. The influences of the agents are compounded and processed on the basis of the current state by transitions (b) which describe the reactions with influences (T_1) and without (T_2). The *Consumption* and *Perception* outputs represent the elements of the world which the agents may perceive or consume.

to describing three influence terminals, one for movement, one for picking objects up and one for putting them down. The consumption and perception terminals remain unchanged, as shown in Figure 4.45.

Implementation of a specialised centralised environment

We have seen the representation of an environment in the form of a BRIC component, but what about its implementation in a programming language? All we need to do is return to the models we set out previously and to transform each component into the form of a module (for an implementation in a classic language) or a class (for an implementation in an object language).

With the centralised approach, the environment is implemented in the form of a global data structure shared by all the agents, which contains all the information relating to the positioning of the agents and other objects in space. Other properties with the power to modify the perception of the agents, such as the visibility of elements of perception, may perhaps be associated with this. Figure 4.46 shows the structure of a centralised environment, which is made up of two parts. One part comprises a dictionary, containing the description and positioning of each element of the environment (the agents and objects), and the second contains the procedures or methods of access to this environment.

We find here a direct representation of the modelling principles which we used previously. The dictionary of elements in fact represents the state of the environment, and the access procedures correspond, on the plane of computing implementation, to the inputs of the specialised model used by agents to pass on influences and modify the environment. So it is these procedures which will be instrumental in implementing the reactions of the environment.

Here again we see the procedures defined previously for our specialised model of the environment. In addition to the procedures `goTo`, `putDown` and `pickUp`, which correspond to the inputs already examined, the input procedure `observe` enables the agents to obtain information on the elements adjacent to

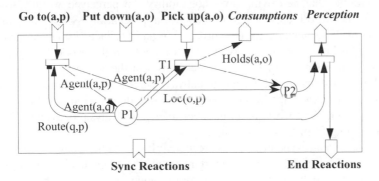

Figure 4.45   Modelling of a specialised environment. For the sake of clarity, the synchronisation mechanisms are not shown.

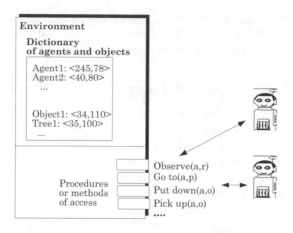

Figure 4.46 Implementation of a centralised environment.

them, within a radius *r* around them. This procedure returns the list of objects and agents, together with their positions, to the agent that has requested them.

4.11.4 Modelling of a situated MAS

Having described the environment, we can now go on to give a description of a purely situated multi-agent system. Let us begin with the agents. As with the environments, we can give either a generalised or a specialised model.

An agent can be described as a component comprising two inputs, perceptions and consumptions. A general model of an agent has only one output, which corresponds to the influences produced (Figure 4.47(a)). In a specialised model, we can represent each type of action in the form of an output terminal, as shown in Figure 4.47(b). The perceptions are filtered through the transition of perception, which does not consume its input marks (in effect, we are adopting the classic attitude that perceiving does not modify the perceived world). An agent perceives the world only when it receives a perception synchronisation. The reception of these *percepts* triggers processing and produces influences which are transmitted to the environment. When it has completed this work, the agent sends an end-of-action signal to the global synchroniser of the MAS.

We can suppose that the agent is always perceiving something – at least, the mark of its presence in the environment – and thus that it will always have something to do. An agent is never passive, since it is always processing at least one percept coming from the environment.

The global synchroniser is responsible for synchronising perceptions and actions (Figure 4.48). It is important to have a clear understanding of how significant the synchroniser is. We are talking about a clock, which stops actions carried out simultaneously from being interpreted as being totally separated in time. This clock does not tell the time, but ensures that, at a given moment, all the agents

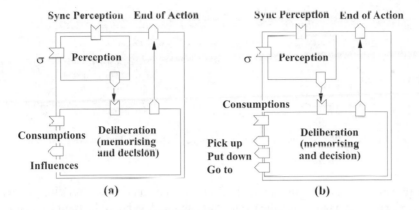

Figure 4.47 Representation of a situated agent in the form of a BRIC component. The generalised form (a) frees us from having to pronounce on the set of actions an agent can carry out, in contrast to its specialised form (b). The terminal σ represents data coming from the environment.

are treated as acting simultaneously, and that the environment reacts only subsequently, before handing over again to the agents in an endless loop. Figure 4.49 gives the time diagram for an MAS comprising two agents, the environment and the synchroniser.

When the synchroniser sends a `Sync Perceptions` signal, the agents `Agent 1` and `Agent 2` effect their perception. Each agent deliberates by processing the perceptions it receives, with reference to its preceding state, then transmits its influences to the environment. Finally, it sends an end-of-actions signal. When it has received all the end-of-actions signals from the agents, the synchroniser sends a `Sync Reaction` signal, which triggers the reaction of the environment to the production of the influences. Once this is over, the environment sends an end-

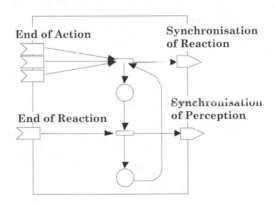

Figure 4.48 Synchroniser of a situated MAS.

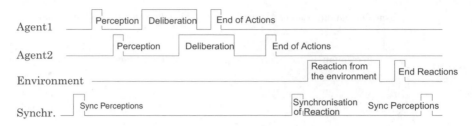

Figure 4.49 Synchronisation diagram for two agents and an environment.

of-reaction signal to the synchroniser, which reacts by sending a `Sync Perceptions` signal, and the cycle starts again. A general diagram for a situated MAS is shown in Figure 4.50, where both the environment and the agents are shown in their generalised form. We would need only to replace the centralised definition of the agents and environments by specialised versions to have a specialised model of a MAS.

4.11.5 Modelling of a complete MAS

The modelling of a system made up of agents which can both communicate and act in an environment is relatively simple, since it is sufficient to superimpose a situated agent's diagram on that of a communicating agent. But this apparent simplicity in fact conceals a more complex problem connected with the question of the

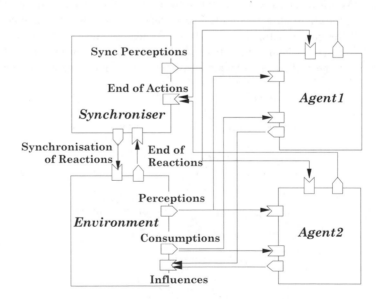

Figure 4.50 General diagram of a situated MAS with two agents.

synchronisation of situated actions in relation to messages. The communications have been modelled in an asynchronous manner, chiefly because of the Petri nets formalism which is naturally asynchronous, that is, the messages are transmitted in any order and we are not concerned about ascertaining how long it takes an agent to respond to a message. Situated agents, on the other hand, are totally synchronised by the environment, and this has made it necessary to introduce a synchroniser. The synchronisation problem can be solved in two ways. The first is purely and simply to ignore it by taking the view that communications have a rhythm of their own which has nothing to do with actions in an environment. But this does give rise to serious difficulties when agents have to collaborate in a common task in which time is an important parameter (real-time problems, for example). The second solution, which in my opinion is the more sensible one, is to synchronise messages with actions. The messages are transmitted at the same time as the influences, and received with the perceptions. In this case, the messages have a propagation time, treated as immediate by the model (although we can modify the message routing system to model a transmission period system, if we so wish). The synchroniser has only one extra terminal, End of Messages, which indicates that all the messages have been transmitted, and which links up with the index End Reactions (Figure 4.51).

4.11.6   An example: transporter agents

We are now going to show how it is possible to construct a simple reactive multi-agent system starting from the action model based on influences. The implementation of the environment in global terms is clearer in this case. The

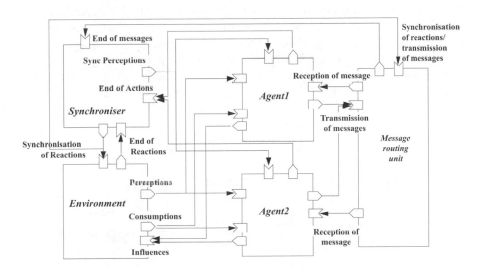

Figure 4.51   Model of system of communicating and situated agents. The synchroniser synchronises messages with actions.

example is that of Clifford (Section 4.2.2). Clifford has to go into the outhouse to fetch a pair of pliers and bring it into the shed. Let us assume that the outhouse and the shed are emitting signals, which are propagated in the form of waves going around obstacles. The environment is initially described by the following set of marks:

```
{path(1,2), path(1,4), path(4,5), path(5,6), and so on
  sig(R,3,3), sig(R,5,1), sig(R,6,2), sig(R,0,Outhouse),
  sig(R,3,Shed), and so on
  sig(H,0,Shed), sig(H,5,2), sig(H,1,4), sig(H,1,6),
  sig(H,3,Outhouse), and so on
  agent(Clifford, 2), pliers (Outhouse)}
```

The behaviour of the agent is limited to going to the outhouse by following the gradient of the signals which are emitted by this site (R signals), picking up the pliers and then going into the shed to deposit them there, following the H signals emitted by the shed. A model of the behaviour of this agent in the form of a situated agent can be given, whose only actions are to go into a neighbouring room, pick something up and put it down (Figure 4.52).

The perception module does nothing but filter the information which concerns the agent and construct percepts obtained by combining the indices agent(Clifford,x) which gives the position of the agent, pliers(y) which gives the position of the pliers, and sig(s,x,l) which gives the intensity x of a signal s at a position l (Figure 4.53).

The deliberation module is responsible for the agent's logic. The agent first follows gradient R, which takes it towards the outhouse. Then, when it finds itself in the outhouse, and if the pliers are there too, it picks them up (triggering off the action 'pick up', followed by the 'consumption' of the object). Then it goes towards the shed by following the gradients of the H signals. Finally, when it arrives in the shed, it puts down what it is holding (in this case, the pliers) and it stops. We are dealing with a relatively simple agent, which does not notice if it loses the pliers it

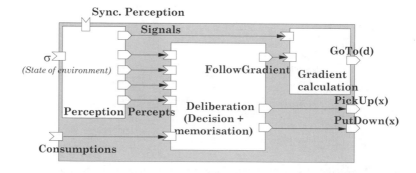

Figure 4.52 A reactive agent model based solely on perception.

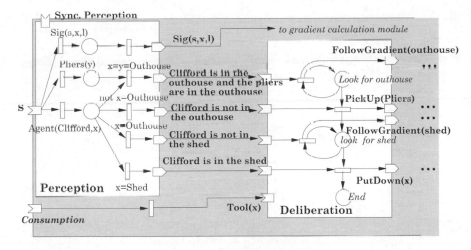

Figure 4.53   Internal structure of perception and deliberation components of transporter agent.

is carrying, and which comes to a halt if the pliers are initially not in the outhouse. When all is said and done, this agent can carry out only a single, extremely basic task (going to fetch a pair of pliers and carrying them from one site to another), which clearly limits its interest. Nevertheless, this example shows that it is possible to describe the entire behaviour of an MAS using the BRIC formalism. In the following chapters, we shall see that it is possible to construct much more elaborate agents which will demonstrate just how important this formalism is.

5 States of (Artificial) Minds

5.1 Mental states and intentionality

5.1.1 Introduction

Ordinary psychology consists of describing and explaining the behaviour of human beings on the basis of their mental states, that is, on the basis of their beliefs, desires, intentions and commitments. For example, if we say that 'Paul wants to give Marie a present, and he thinks Marie likes flowers', we may deduce from this that Paul is certainly going to offer Marie some flowers. Likewise, if Paul asks someone if he knows what time it is, we conclude from this that, first, he does not have information on what time it is at the moment when he makes this request, and, secondly, that he wants someone to give him this information.

Spontaneous reasoning of this kind, which is a feature of everyday life, and which we use to explain the behaviour of human beings, can give rise to the creation of theories. We then assume that what goes on in the head of an agent (whether this refers to an artificial agent, as in multi-agent systems, or a human person, in the sense in which the cognitive sciences can apprehend such a being) is the result of the interaction of a certain number of cognitive components, generally referred to as *mental states* or *propositional attitudes*.

For example, believing that it is raining, or that the cat is on the hearth, is having a certain disposition *about* the rain or the cat. Likewise, in wishing to go to the cinema, I am in a certain state of mind *about* the fact of going to the cinema. Desires, like beliefs, are thus mental states which refer to something concrete, as in the preceding examples, or indeed to another mental state. For example, if I believe that Paul wants a chocolate-filled pastry, my belief is connected to Paul's desire, that is, to a mental state, which itself refers to a chocolate-filled pastry. Mental states thus have this peculiarity of being *about something*, and this is why we talk of the *intentional* character of mental states.

The terms *intentional* and *intentionality* were coined by the scholastic philosophers of the Middle Ages. They are derived from the Latin *intendo*, which means 'I steer (or tend) towards'. They were then taken up by philosophers in a cognitive sense. Since consciousness is applied to something other than itself, it is by nature tending towards this something, and intentional. In effect, if I see an object, the belief that this object really is in front of me is a mental phenomenon which relates to this object. It is, moreover, in this respect that I can say that 'I see this object'. Likewise, if I want to go somewhere, this desire applies to the act of going to a certain place, and so to something other than this desire. Brentano, followed by Husserl (Husserl, 1950) maintained that intentionality represented the fundamental distinction making it possible to define the mental and the physical. All mental phenomena, and they alone, show proof of intentionality. Since then, Anglo-Saxon philosophers, in connection with what is known as the philosophy of mind, have seized upon this question to analyse what goes on in our minds, and to attempt to provide models for the relationship which exists between beliefs, commitments and intentions, to mention a few of the mental states mentioned above.

There is a wealth of problems connected with intentionality. We could formulate the essential question in the following way: what makes an agent do what it does? What are the internal elements it brings into play to give us the illusion that it has autonomy and that its behaviour follows a certain coherence in the exchanges which it carries on with the world and with other agents? Unfortunately, in spite of the attention currently being devoted to this concept, there is a striking lack of consensus with regard to the analysis of intentionality. The only point of agreement concerns the nature of the problem posed, and the solutions can be frighteningly technical in nature[†].

To this difficulty we may add another. The terms *intention* and *intentionality* may be accepted as meaning two distinct things. The first meaning, used in the field of philosophy, corresponds to the definition we gave previously, and refers to mental

---

[†]A good introduction to the problems of intentionality in AI can be found in Bachimont (1992), who sets out, in a relatively simple manner, the relationship that exists between philosophical theories of knowledge and the (partial) solutions provided by AI. On the other hand, a good way of approaching the question of intentionality in relation to the current cognitivist debate would be to read the excellent work by Pacherie (1993), which provides a very good summary of the different positions on offer. It might also be useful to read Searle (1985) and Dennett (1987) which list the important points of view in this debate.

states. The second refers to the common meaning of the notion of intention. We say that someone has the intention of carrying out an act (for example: going out, having a drink) if he or she actually wishes to perform this act. Intention is, as Thomas Aquinus explains, *an act of will, preceded by an act by which reason orders something to this end*. It is true that this confusion is made greater by the fact that the second accepted meaning is merely a special case of the first, and these two meanings are often present in the same work. Most of the time the term of *intentionality* is reserved for general problems relating to mental states and the term of *intention* for the will to act.

To avoid this confusion, we shall, for the remainder of this book (except where explicitly stated otherwise), use the terms *intention, intentional, intentionally* and *intentionality* only with the second meaning, that is, that of what leads an agent to act, preferring the expressions *mental states* or *cognitons* to designate the first meaning.

5.1.2   The cogniton concept

The term *mental state* is not very felicitous either, for it assumes a certain idea of sequential processing in the cognitive mode of functioning for an agent. In fact, the word *state* generally expresses an overall characteristic of a system. It gives the illusion that an agent, at a given moment, is in an easily quantifiable specific configuration. We then have the impression that if we say that an agent is in the *state of desiring* an object, its 'mind' will be in a specific configuration characteristic of a desire for an object. Now, this impression is totally false. We shall say simply that an agent is displaying the state of desire, if, somewhere in its cognitive structure, computing structures exist which are characteristic of desire, and which lead it to put its resources to work in such a way as to satisfy its desire, should that be possible. The mental state of desire (like that of belief, intention, commitment) is not actually a state but a computational structure representing a desire for something. If, by chance, an agent comes to desire and fear the same object, we shall not say that the agent is in a specific state of desire or fear, but that the two computational structures of desire and fear are present at the same time, and are acting in a joint (and opposed) manner to define the behaviours of the agent.

For this reason, I shall retain the term 'state' to describe any overall configuration of a system (this is the concept of 'state' as we saw it in regard to the concept of finite-state automata in Chapter 4), and in its place I shall use the neologism *cogniton*[†] to describe those computational structures which relate to something, and are therefore endowed with intentionality in the first meaning of the term, that is, that used by the scholars and by Husserl.

A cogniton, therefore, is an elementary cognitive unit, which is linked to other cognitons to form a dynamic mental configuration that evolves with time.

[†]This term is constructed from the term 'cognitive' and the ending 'on', which denotes something indivisible, an elementary particle, such as a photon or meson. It has been created by analogy with 'infon', the elementary information unit, developed by K. Devlin (1991) in relation to situational semantics.

Cognitons can be created, or can disappear, as consequences of the creation, or disappearance, of other cognitons in the cognitive apparatus of an agent. For example, if I believe that the cat is on the hearth, and then I perceive it on the table, I will revise my beliefs, considering that I have to give pride of place to what I see, as opposed to what I believe. The fact of having a belief at a given moment and then revising this belief on the basis of a perception forms part of the normal activity of the representational module, which draws up models of the world on the basis of information (percepts, informative messages) that it receives, together with knowledge it already possesses. In the same order of ideas, intentions are linked to the goals that motivate them, but are simultaneously connected with the standards and commitments that restrict them. If someone suggests a meeting on a date when you are not free, you either have to change the date of the proposed meeting or cancel your previous engagements, which will involve revising your beliefs and your intentions.

5.1.3   Types of cogniton

There are obviously a large number of cognitons. The three main ones encountered in most theories on mental states are beliefs, intentions and commitments. But there are many others which relate to the various elements that make it possible to understand the functioning of cognitive agents: for example, percepts, goals, desires, impulses, hypotheses and so on, are as essential to the definition of the behaviour of agents as commitments or beliefs may be.

It is possible to classify cognitons on the basis of the organic system to which they are linked. For example, intention and commitment are part of both the conative subsystem, since this deals with elements that make decisions possible, and the organisational subsystem, because they make it possible to manage action. Here is a non-exhaustive list of cognitons, and of the subsystems in which they act. When a cogniton appears in several, they are listed at the end of its description.

Interactional cognitons

Percept   Percepts represent perceptible information obtained through perception of the environment. This information is generally the result of development work carried out by sensors and pre-treatment systems, which we shall not be studying.

Information   A piece of information is a cogniton which represents a belief carried by another agent and transmitted through a message.

Command (or decision)   Commands are cognitons coming from the conative system and describing the operations which have to be carried out by the interactional system, which will be translated into actions by the agent affecting its environment.

Requests   Requests are actions carried out by an agent in order that another agent shall carry out an action (do something, reply to a question, etc.). Requests are thus relational actions, since they take place between agents. We shall see in Chapter 6 that the theory of speech acts provides them with a solid basis.

Norms   Norms are cognitons which actually represent the social demands and constraints imposed by the organisation on a specific agent. Norms can therefore be expressed in numerous ways. The most frequent is to attribute a set of tasks to an agent, to be accomplished in relation to the function (or the role) it has in its organisation. These norms are then known as social claims, for they play the same role as claims triggering action. Most standards are not acquired by the agent but installed by the designer when an agent is created.

Representational cognitons

Belief   Beliefs describe the state of the world from the point of view of an agent, and so the way it represents its environment, other agents and itself to itself. In particular, a clear distinction must be made between beliefs about oneself and beliefs about others. The former may be coherent with the state in which the agent finds itself[†], whereas the latter are only partial and perhaps erroneous.

Hypothesis   Hypotheses are possible representations of the world and of other agents which are not yet 'believed' by the agent. A hypothesis can serve to trigger actions aimed at transforming it into a belief.

Conative cognitons

Tendency/goal   Tendencies or goals (we shall not differentiate here) are essentially the results of impulses and claims. The question of whether or not they can be achieved plays no part in the definition of a goal. For example, I can have the goal of becoming a millionaire, even if I know that there is little chance of achieving this goal. But I shall nevertheless attempt to achieve it, for example by buying lottery tickets, and if I ever win the first prize, then this goal will have been achieved. Goals are always present, as long as what has led to the setting of the goal is itself valid. Goals (or tendencies) can be expressed as much in terms of attraction as of repulsion. They are, in fact, the core of the conative system.

Drives   Drives are the internal sources for the construction of goals. They correspond to claims from the self-preservative system, such as assuaging its hunger, attempting to reproduce itself and, in a general manner, everything permitting the survival of the individual or the species (vegetative and conative subsystems).

Claim   Claims are the external sources of goals. They intervene when an agent asks another agent for something.

Intention   Intentions describe what motivates an agent, what permits it to proceed to an act. Following Cohen and Levesque (cf. Section 5.8), we shall see that it is possible to get rid of the cogniton 'intention', on condition that we have the concepts of goals and of commitment, as well as the capacity to evaluate the importance of goals and their consequences (conative and organisational subsystems).

[†]It may be assumed that, in artificial systems, agents have true beliefs about themselves, and in particular about their skills, which is not true for real agents such as human beings, who often delude themselves and over- (or under-) estimate their capacities.

Commitment Commitments characterise the dependencies (duties, constraints, etc.) which bind cognitive agents in relation to themselves, but above all in relation to others, when they decide to carry out an action, perform a service or, in a general manner, when they have the intention of doing something (conative and organisational sub-systems).

Organisational cognitons

These cognitons provide for the monitoring of agents' actions. When an agent has a goal, it evaluates the different methods permitting it to achieve this goal, if it has any, or else it tries to break its goal down into sub-goals in such a way as to find a plan that will allow it to achieve its objectives. After having taken its decision, it sets to work, that is, it carries out the task corresponding to the selected method, this task being placed into a schedule of things to do and to monitor.

Method Methods are the set of techniques, rules, plans and programmes which can be brought into play by an agent to carry out a task and achieve a goal. A method describes the set of steps required to solve a problem or achieve a goal. For example, if we have to solve a problem, we can use the method we might call 'propose and revise', in which we first construct a partial solution without much detail, which we then proceed to develop. Methods often have the appearance of plans, that is, of sequences of actions to be carried out, with different levels of detail, to achieve a goal, as when Clifford has to determine how to achieve the goal 'pick up the pliers which are in the workshop'.

Task Tasks are encountered on two different levels. At the conceptual level, a task is the description of what has to be done to achieve a goal. For example, for the hammer to be in the shed and cease to be in the workshop, it is necessary, in succession, to go and find the hammer, pick it up, and transport it into the shed. Only high-level actions which can be carried out are involved. Nothing is said about the way they should be carried out. It is the methods which will be applied which will indicate how to go to the workshop, how to pick up the hammer and how to transport the hammer into the shed. On the organisational level, the tasks are also work units in the process of execution, that is, the instancising of the implementation of a method.

Sometimes, especially for reactive agents or simple cognitive agents, the terms 'tasks' and 'methods' are combined. If there is only one method for a defined task, then there is no longer any point in dissociating these two concepts, and so one can be used to denote the other.

Other cognitons

There are obviously many other cognitons characteristic of mental states, such as fears, desires, hopes, dreams, affects (feelings associated with another agent), etc.

We shall not be discussing them, since either they more or less form part of the preceding mental states (for example, desires are linked with drives and goals) or they relate to characteristics which do not interest us as far as artificial agents are concerned: fears, like dreams, affects and hopes, are not (yet) part of the structure of artificial agents.

5.2 The interactional system

It is through perception that the agent acquires information about the world to allow it to prepare its action by pursuing its goals. The perceptive system constitutes a door between the world and the agent, which gives it access to a certain 'conception of the world' in which its reasoning and its actions are significant.

In essence, all perception is individual and contributes to a personal representation of the world (Uexküll, 1956). For a dog tick, the world is reduced to three stimuli: diffuse heat, the odour of butyric acid and heat. This suffices for its needs, its behaviour being entirely determined by these elementary impressions. It climbs up towards the light until it can go no further, and as soon as it perceives the odour of butyric acid, coming from mammals, it drops down. If it falls on something warm, it has achieved its goal. It finds a spot devoid of hairs and it pierces the skin to suck blood. Then the cycle recommences. For more complex beings, their perceptive system allows them to recognise their prey and their predators, their reproductive sites, beings of the same species, etc. The perceptive system of an agent is linked to its cognitive and behavioural skills. An ore-prospecting robot must have ore-detecting mechanisms if it wants to accomplish its task. It may also perceive the obstacles that occur on its route (rocks, crevasses, trees, etc.) in order to avoid them. If it is also capable of perceiving that other robots are present, it can draw up exploration strategies allowing it to fulfil its function better by moving away from other robots looking for ore and, by contrast, moving nearer to those that have just found some. The range of behavioural responses thus depends on the extent of an agent's perceptions and recognition capacities. Mimicking the behaviour of another agent, for example, requires fairly well-developed cognitive capacities, but simultaneously, and above all, needs very complex recognition mechanisms, allowing an agent to recognise the posture and the gestures of another agent in order to be able to imitate them.

Since Aristotle, philosophers have always been interested in perception. Aristotle has a very realistic concept: perceiving is separating form from matter by abstraction. The being is thus 'informed' by this substance. The perceived object therefore acts directly on the perceptive system, the agent merely receiving this form passively and integrating it into its cognitive system (its Anima, as Aristotle calls it). Perception is essentially a physical modification, which leaves physical traces, 'phantasms', in the body (if you look at a piece of white paper, the eyes, or an internal part of the eyes, become(s) white by a sort of mimetic reflex of the perceiving in relation to the perceived). For a long time, and indeed right up to the time of Kant, philosophers maintained this causal concept of perception. The objects of the world acted mechanically on the various organs of the senses in such a way as to form 'ideas of sensations', the immediate objects of perception. Modern explanations are more technical but often start from the same idea. Sensations are immediate data originating from excitations coming from external or internal sensors which transform physical stimuli (vibration of the air, luminous energy, chemical compounds, etc.) into internal signals which are then processed by the set of primary perception systems that eliminate the noise, segment the signals and supply the secondary processing systems with the gross data on the basis of which they can effectively recognise significant forms.

It is still this concept, described as 'realistic', that predominates, in a naïve manner, in our everyday activity. We assume that we are directly perceiving the 'objective' properties of the bodies which surround us and which register themselves directly in our mind through a direct and immediate process. For this reason, the world for us is very much the way we represent it to ourselves. Snow really is white, roses really are red, tables really are flat, and so on. This purely passive idea of perception is so entrenched in us that it is difficult for us to think of our perceptive faculties as also being the result of development, and to grasp that we only really see what, in a way, we have already seen.

Perceptions are the fruits of constructions, which depend on prior perceptive layouts, which have been progressively put together by our interactions with the environment and with other agents which have reinforced our points of view. A body is 'red' because we are sensitive to certain frequencies of light, because the photons in this frequency range have been emitted by a light source and have not been retained by this body, and above all because we have already learned to distinguish through our culture, that is, through prior interactions with other members of our species, certain ranges of colours, differentiating red from pink and violet, for example (Bonnet *et al.*, 1990).

Current logic theories, like most systems of form recognition until the 1990s, are still based on the idea of passive perception of the world. Situational semantics, for example, merely repeats Aristotelian ideas while putting them into a more modern form. The world is made up of objects and situations which are already given, and the agent merely registers and classifies the information coming from its environment. The meaning of the phrases it pronounces thus refers directly (naïvely) to the objects of the world, and not to mental constructs built up independently (Barwise and Perry, 1983).

In contrast, results taken from the neuro-physiology of perception show that perception is the result of prior conceptualisation. For example, in peripheral visual systems, there are far more nerve paths going from the cortex to the lateral jointed body (a region of the thalamus which acts as the intermediary between the optic nerve and the visual cortex) than there are coming directly from the eye (Maturana and Varela, 1987). What an individual 'sees' is more what he or she receives from the brain than from the eye. Other mechanisms, such as that for perceiving movement in animals and people, make use of the principle known as

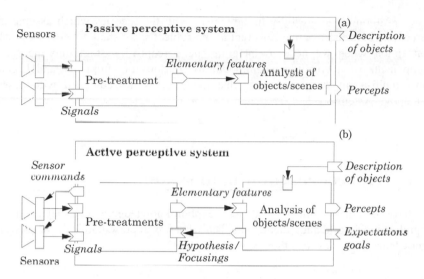

Figure 5.1   The perceptive system can be either passive (a) and, in this case, the data are analysed in a purely constructional manner, or active (b), by combining the constructional approach with a breakdown movement tending to generate hypotheses and focus perceptions.

'reafference', which links the movement of the individual and that of perception. By re-injecting what should be seen when he or she makes a movement, the individual analyses a visual change stemming from one of his or her movements as a fixed image, and analyses the movement of an object as a moving image. Other phenomena of the same order show that perception results from an active procedure, which takes previous perceptions and conceptualisations into account, and which implies an active exploration of the environment and of what the agent is trying to perceive.

Figure 5.1 shows the two types of system. In *passive perception* systems, the signals follow an approach which is entirely constructional. Elementary signals are pre-processed and then segmented to obtain *elementary features* leading to the recognition of objects, scenes, words or phrases. In active systems, by contrast, the perceptive system simultaneously receives the data coming from the sensors and the expectations and goals coming from the cognitive system. It can control its sensors in such a way as to maintain a coherent representation of its environment. One of the first perception systems combining the generation of hypotheses and their validation can be found in the work done on word recognition through blackboards (Erman *et al.*, 1980). We can obtain a general view of the problems of vision for the computer and the machine from Marr (1982) and Levine (1985). The main problems (and solutions) relating to active multi-sensory perception can be found in Ghallab *et al.* (1992), and Lesser and Corkill (1983) and Demazeau *et al.* (1994) deal with the use of multi-agent systems for the conception of active perception systems.

Although we are fully in agreement with the theories which assume that perception is itself an active construct of the subject's, we shall adhere to a passive conception when we need to integrate the perceptive system into the set of components of a cognitive agent, both for reasons of simplicity and because most multi-agent systems assume that their agents are equipped with passive perceptive systems.

5.3   The representational system

We have seen that cognitive agents have explicit knowledge, which they can use to apprehend the world and other agents. But what are 'representations', 'beliefs' and 'knowledge', and how can they be made explicit?

5.3.1   What is knowledge?

The concept of knowledge, as it has been developed in artificial intelligence, can be defined as all the information (learning, know-how, experience, memories, concepts, facts, and so on) needed by a human being (or a machine), organised in such a way that he, she or it can carry out a task considered as being complex. For example, diagnosing an illness, solving a mathematical problem, repairing a machine, handling a court case, managing a set of financial accounts, running a marketing campaign or translating a text are activities which, when they are carried out by human beings, call for a high degree of skill and make use of a large amount of information, organised with a precise aim in view.

For this reason, the term 'knowledge' is associated with a pragmatic dimension, that is, with specialist knowledge applied in a specific field to carry out a precise task. However, an agent's knowledge is not limited to that affecting the tasks it carries out. It is also necessary to include information concerning the world that surrounds it, that is, its environment and the other agents with which it communicates and interacts.

The concept of knowledge poses one of the central problems in philosophy and cognitive psychology, which can be expressed as follows: how can concepts be organised in such a way as to allow a human being or an agent to carry out tasks or to affirm adequate propositions?

We generally distinguish between *knowing something* and *knowing how to do something*. The former concerns the comprehension of beings which are perceived, and of phenomena which are continually encountered, but of which it is sometimes difficult to give a precise definition. The latter, by contrast, is not concerned with the definition of objects, but with the analysis of the relationships which exist between phenomena, so that laws of the universe can be modelled in order that their evolution can be predicted. For example, the attempt to define what movement is constitutes a complex philosophical problem, which was only partially solved by the philosophers of ancient Greece and of mediaeval times[†]. It was only when first Galileo and then Newton arrived on the scene that the realisation dawned that, if the problem was formulated in a different way, so that it was no longer necessary to try to define what movement *is*, it became possible to understand *how* moving bodies evolve, on the basis of the relationships between measurable variables such as distance, speed and time.

Scientific knowledge, like pragmatic learning, is knowledge relating to *how*, the important factor being to be able to act in the world, by anticipating the consequences of current states and of actions that we can carry out. The big general questions, such as 'What is life?', may well be particularly essential for us in order to orientate ourselves and to be able to respond to our existential questionings, but are of almost no interest to scientific learning. It is not interested in these questions. It needs only, on the basis of some relatively vague initial definitions, to build up a body of methods allowing it to understand the phenomena that occur during the lives of living beings, and so to be capable of explaining *what is happening*.

The same applies to knowledge. It is preferable, instead of trying to define precisely what 'knowledge' is, to put forward concepts and models making it possible to understand the phenomena of development and utilisation of what allows an agent to accomplish complex tasks.

Conceptualisation and reasoning

The problem of knowledge is closely related to those of *conceptualisation* and of *reasoning*. What, *a priori*, are the conceptual categories of thought and reasoning for an agent, and what, on the basis of these fundamental categories, are the different concepts constructed and the practical mechanisms which an agent employs so that it can orient itself in its environment, overcome difficulties, make judgements and solve problems, take decisions and achieve its ends?

In fact, we cannot speak of knowledge without speaking of the inferential power which is associated with it. Knowledge does not exist without the problems and the dissatisfactions which provide the motivations for it, without the actions which put it into practice, without the reason which gives it its internal dynamics. Conversely, if any conceptualisation necessarily reflects an intention to make use of this knowledge, no reasoning can be effected without a solid conceptual base. This is why reasoning and conceptualisation are the two facets of knowledge and of its use.

But does proper conceptualisation exist? Artificial intelligence has often asked itself this question. The search for the universal knowledge base containing all that humanity knows is one of the basic myths of AI, in which we can see the perennial aspiration of encyclopaedists, the project of being able to reduce all knowledge into a finite conceptual system (Lenat and Guha, 1990). Unfortunately,

---

[†]We can still also wonder what movement actually is. The Aristotelian position assimilating movement to a passage of power, or potentiality, to the act, or the realisation of this potentiality, is still current, with the concepts of potential fields and attractors in modern physics (Thom, 1988; Boutot, 1993).

there is no one simple definition of a concept. Everything depends on what we want to do with it, on the aspect of it that interests us.

For example, the concept of 'water', even though it might appear one of the simplest, is not so easy to sort out. Everyone can talk about water and can understand reasoning that uses this concept, and yet it remains decidedly difficult to provide a clear and unified view of it. In fact, talking about water means deploying a large number of concepts:

(1)   For someone who is thirsty, water is a liquid that one drinks and that allows one to quench one's thirst.

(2)   For the plumber, water is something that flows along pipes and that can escape from piping systems (leaks).

(3)   For the chemist, it is the molecule H_2O.

(4)   For the painter, it is a solvent and a dilutant.

(5)   For someone washing something, water removes dirt and rinses the washing-up.

Each of these definitions comes back to know-how, to a use of the concept in an appropriate context, which itself assumes a complete conceptualisation. For example, water as a chemical entity brings us back to the concept of a molecule, the molecules' capacities for coming together and separating, their composition, the overall effects that can be deduced from this, and so on. The number of such links is infinite, since all knowledge is bound together in a complex totality made up of an aggregation of individual points of view.

However, knowledge is not an individual affair. The isolated specialist does not exist. Although perspectives in the cognitive sciences – cognitive psychology and philosophy in particular – have put the emphasis mainly on the knowledge which an individual can amass for himself or herself in order to understand the ambient world and to solve the problems with which he or she is surrounded, an individual's knowledge is largely the fruit of interactions with other human beings. As the example of the wolf children shows, if an infant is isolated from earliest childhood and deprived of interaction with others of the same kind, it can never have the faculties of its species and become an accomplished individual. The lack of interaction, and therefore of knowledge, of communication and of the possibility to imitate the behaviour of others in its childhood removes the human element from its intelligence. But even without going to these extremes, we still have to recognise that a specialist is never alone. First of all, he or she is surrounded by all those who work in the same field. Mastering a speciality involves a long process of learning, during which he or she interacts with those giving instruction, but also with those who will become his or her companions and colleagues. And then, he or she is at the centre of a set of interactions with other specialists in neighbouring fields. The mason works with the plumber and the carpenter, the aircraft fuselage specialist collaborates with the engine designer and the aerodynamics expert. Knowledge is built up through working together, through contrasting points of view and exchanges of know-how. Numerous philosophers and sociologists who have carried out research on science and on scientific activity, such as Kuhn (1962), Latour (1989) or Lestel (1986), have shown the importance of social relationships in stabilising scientific concepts, and of the set of strategies used by researchers to take advantage of even the least significant of allies in producing what are claimed as being 'scientific facts'.

Knowledge in interaction

How, in fact, could we imagine a human being without all the communications he or she is involved in throughout life? How could we think of an individual's intelligence without thinking about the intelligence of his or her family or tribe, or of the society in which this individual developed?

The problem of knowledge has to be seen, not only in terms of a relationship between an agent and the world, but also in the light of the interactions taking place between agents, that is, the definition of the elementary conceptual categories and common concepts which agents have available for communicating and acting. Cognitive social psychology research has shown the importance of social considerations for the creation of conceptual categories. For an individual, being in harmony with his or her previous considerations, and with those of the group, involves modifications to the cognitive universe and, in particular, modifications to his or her categorisations and judgements.

For this reason, knowledge is, above all, the fruit of interactions between cognitive agents who or which, through a process of confrontation, objections, proofs and refutations (Lakatos, 1976) create concepts, construct theories and formulate laws. This process of creating by interactions takes place even in domains where one might think there were few controversies or polemics, such as mathematics. It is all the more powerful in sciences concerning areas which are at once more complex and more applied, such as the human sciences, economics, psychology, and the cognitive sciences in general. Kenetics can thus appropriate the following slogan:

> *There is no knowledge without interaction*

where the concept of 'interaction' includes both confrontations with the world and communications with other agents, knowledge then being defined as the result of the specific learning and know-how which the agents possess, this learning and know-how being the fruits of the confrontations of the individual with the world and the interactions the individual can have with other individuals.

These interactions are not only inevitable but also necessary. A specialist may have a profound knowledge of a specific domain, but he or she cannot know everything. His or her knowledge is limited, partly by the material difficulty of apprehending specialist knowledge covering several domains, but also because his or her knowledge does not necessarily form a homogenous and coherent whole.

In this respect, Carl Hewitt (1985) has described a type of organisation which he calls Open Information Systems, in which knowledge is not the sum of the knowledge of all the agents, but the result of the interaction of several micro-theories, that is, of learning and know-how associated with agents. Each micro-theory, although coherent in itself, may perhaps come into conflict, or even be in total contradiction, with other micro-theories coming out of the same organisation. When combined actions take place, the agents possessing these micro-theories then have to negotiate to determine which is the best joint action to undertake. For example, in a company, the marketing manager may have a skill which takes the following form:

```
R1:  increasing publicity will increase sales and
     so will bring profits to the company
```

which will come into conflict with that of the administration manager:

```
R2:  to increase the profits of a company,
     costs have to be reduced
```

In effect, applying rule R2 puts a veto, in advance, on the supplementary expenditure that marketing requires. These two rules, stemming from different points of view, are the expression of two divergent ways of thinking, one centred on the market and the other on the internal management of the company. When a decision has to be taken, these two micro-theories come into conflict, and the decision will arise from a resolution of this conflict, either because there will be a deliberate choice of one or the other, or through an attempt at a local synthesis which might be expressed, for example, in the form:

```
R3:  if the market is buoyant
     and the extra costs arising from publicity
     can be amortised by sales,
     then a publicity campaign can be launched.
```

If we stay within the same order of difficulty, we may find it interesting to note that this concept of micro-theories which cannot be combined to produce a coherent theory was adopted in connection with the CYC project for the representation of a large amount of knowledge common, more or less, to children aged between 6 and 10. When the project began, the knowledge was considered in an overall manner (Lenat and Guha, 1990). Theories which appeared inconsistent, and, above all, those whose effects were local, were then combined. Faced with the difficulties of making such theories coherent, Lenat and Guha, in their turn, took up the ideas on micro-theories in the work of McCarthy (1980) and Hewitt.

Now, a micro-theory is a specific entity, whose range of local, and whose application is relative to a context. For example, the naïve knowledge of physics corresponding to the fact that *something that is not supported falls down* is represented like this:

Theory: ∀x, ¬supported(x) ⇒ falls(x)

Obviously, this theory is local. It does not apply to balloons or to interstellar objects, and concerns only the objects that we encounter in our everyday lives. It is therefore a micro-theory, for its range is limited, but it will prove adequate for common reasoning in most of the situations we encounter every day.

All these concepts of micro-theories can be very well integrated into a multi-agent perspective. Owing to their essentially limited character, relating to a context, every micro-theory is representative of the knowledge of an agent. Or, more precisely, all knowledge associated with an agent has the value and the importance of a micro-theory. In a multi-agent system, no agent has total knowledge or possesses an overall truth relating to the world. All knowledge is therefore local, and all truth relative.

Nor can knowledge be reduced to learning. Even if artificial intelligence was for long the champion of declarative knowledge, of learning defined by itself, irrespective of its use, it has since realised, in connection with distributed artificial intelligence, that we cannot understand knowledge which has been experienced, that is, meaning, without referring to the behaviour of an agent situated in an environment and in relation to other agents. For this reason, more attention has been paid to know-how, to what is also referred to as an agent's skill and shrewdness, than to the 'book knowledge' that the agent may have.

In fact, theoretical knowledge relating to fluid mechanics is not much help in repairing a damaged water-pipe. On the other hand, it may well be useful to have carried out such repairs before or to have watched someone at work in such a situation. In other words, what is asked of a specialist relates more to all the experiences he or she has been able to accumulate in similar circumstances than to the extent of his or her actual learning. As Dreyfus (1992) points out, the rationalist tradition assumes that understanding a domain and knowing how to act skilfully in this domain come down to having an explicit theory concerning it. He demonstrates that the 'experts', that is, the most skilled people, are those who have the least explicit knowledge but who can call on the most experience, in that they have amassed enough capacity to recognise a characteristic situation. So, the more high-level knowledge is considered to be, the more it is actually specific and integrated into the actions of the individual who, moreover, is no longer consciously aware that he or she possesses it, this knowledge having become something completely obvious to him or her.

In these circumstances, what is knowledge? We have to start by distinguishing theoretical knowledge from practical knowledge, the former being based on an explicit body of rules, of formal models and of theories, the latter depending on the sum total of similar situations and similar actions carried out. However, it is obvious that in even slightly complex technical domains, that is, those for which the naïve models, like that of the fall of the bodies we considered above, are no longer of any assistance, we must call upon theoretical models which will take things further.

5.3.2 Representing knowledge and beliefs

Speaking of knowledge raises the thorny problem of how this knowledge is to be represented. Does a special level of representation exist, independently of any physical representation, or should we take account of the material carrier used for these representations? From the point of view of classic AI, knowledge can be represented in the form of a set of symbols expressing units of knowledge. This approach, which represents what is called the *symbolico-cognitivist* paradigm, is defined by the following three propositions (Andler, 1992):

(1)   Representations are independent of the underlying physical carrier.

(2)   Mental states are representational, or endowed with intentionality (in the philosophical sense), that is, they refer back to something external to the agents.

(3)   These representations are made up of symbols assembled into computer-based sentences or structures of any kind, and reasoning consists of manipulating these structures in order to obtain other structures from them.

To this classical school we must oppose the connectionist point of view, which assumes that knowledge is integrally distributed within a network of cellular automata in the form of numerical values attached to connections. Reasoning consists of propagating numerical values within this network, that is, modifying the connections established between the different elements of this network. We saw in Chapter 3 that these automata are used as formal neurons, that is, as little units which are limited to propagating numerical values. The interesting thing about this approach is essentially that reactive systems can be created which are capable of learning and of having adaptative behaviours by linking perceptions directly to actions, without any explicit intervention by cognitons. The systems which this brings about are sometimes capable of relatively developed performances (grammatical analysis, solving simple problems), but their preferred domain is perception (recognition of objects, faces, etc.) and articulation between perception and action (picking up objects, moving little mobile robots, etc.). The presuppositions are very different from those developed by the symbolico-cognitive school, as they are based on a sub-symbolic concept (Smolensky, 1992), the objective being to represent (or simulate) what happens in the nervous system of a living creature by using the forces of association of automata connected by weighted links.

Although not very highly developed at present, a third way exists, which we could call the kenetic or interactionist hypothesis, which postulates that an individual's knowledge can be considered as a multi-agent system in its own right, the concepts, ideas and representations then being agents of a specific nature which 'live' inside the agents. An agent's reasoning can then be seen as the result of the interactions of these noetic agents (Morin, 1991) in the way suggested by Minsky (1988) in his *Society of the Mind*. This approach is also defined by Dennett (1991), who tries to set out a theory of consciousness, taking as his starting point the idea that the cognitive system of a human being is fundamentally made up of independent entities which enter into competition and cooperate[†] to give meaning to the surrounding world. As in the case of the symbolico-cognitivist school, the cognitive elements are independent of the physical carrier but, as in the connectionist school, it is assumed, not that a meaning exists which is associated with a set of symbols, but that this meaning emerges from the interactions between the external and internal milieus of the agent, the latter being itself composed of autonomous entities in interactions (Varela *et al.*, 1993).

In this book, cognitive agents will be assumed to be created on the basis of cognitivo-symbolic models, as these are the ones developed to the greatest extent in distributed artificial intelligence for describing agents that have mental states. Even if it appears that the second school and, above all, the third one, could produce interesting results and provide new perspectives with regard to the comprehension of how knowledge is developed in multi-agent systems, these models are still essentially applied to reactive agents for which the problem of mental states is reduced to its simplest expression: the selection of pertinent actions in relation to the local perceptions of agents.

The symbolico-cognitivist hypothesis

The symbolico-cognitivist hypothesis therefore considers that the representations accessible to an individual are expressed in the form of symbols which refer directly to the entities of the world in which this individual is immersed[‡]. These symbols are articulated with the help of an internal language, a sort of 'mentalese', defined by a formal grammar and by the operations that can be applied to them. The syntax of these formal languages (generally derived from the logic of first-order predicates, to which modal operators are added) describes the set of grammatical rules by which the units can aggregate together to form symbolic assemblies by combining expressions or structures (graphics).

Reasoning therefore consists of manipulating these sets of symbols to form other sets through a process of *inference*. The operations making it possible to define such influences must be *valid*. They must respect semantic constraints and must be such that the inferences produced will themselves engender valid sets, that is, in correspondence with their semantic interpretations. This mode of reasoning, which forms the basis of the classic concept of the representation of knowledge, is based on the following five conditions:

[†]The term *cooperation* is ours. Although Dennett does not say much about the underlying mechanisms allowing these entities to interact, it is possible to read his book with a kenetician's eye, and to consider him as an ally, sharing the idea that knowledge can be considered as a multi-agent system in its own right.
[‡]It can be assumed that intermediate entities exist between the symbols and the entities of the world, as in the semantics based on the notion of possible worlds (cf. Section 5.3.3) or intentional logics like that of Montague (1974), but, apart from the odd variation of emphasis, the thought scheme is the same.

(1)   the existence of a set of symbols;

(2)   the existence of grammatical rules for the composition of symbols to form symbolic propositions or structures;

(3)   the existence of a reference world made up of clearly separated entities to which the symbols can refer;

(4)   the existence of an interpretation function which gives a meaning to the symbol, that is, which attributes a referent (or a class of referents) to each symbol;

(5)   the existence of a system of inference making it possible to produce new sets (propositions or structures).

Symbols

But what is a symbol? For the symbolico-cognitivist tendency, a symbol[†] is a specific element which refers to something else, which it correctly represents, and which is known as its *referent*. For example, words are symbols, which refer back to contents. The word John refers back to the real *John*[‡] whom I know, the symbol 2 refers back to the second element in the natural numbers, that is, to the successor of the successor to zero, and so on. The n relationships of the form p(a1,...,an) refer back to the contents represented in the form of sets of n-uplets. For example, to say that *John is a person*, which would be formally written in logic person(John), comes down to saying that *John* is part of the *person* set made up as follows:

$$person = \{John, Marie, Paul, Peter, Mark, \ldots)$$

Likewise, saying that John loves Marie, which is written love(John,Marie), consists of affirming that the couple *<John,Marie>* belongs to the set *whoLovesWho* made up of the couples *<a,b>* in which individual *a* loves individual *b*:

$$whoLovesWho = \{<John,Marie>, <Marie,Peter>, \ldots\}$$

In the symbolico-cognitive hypothesis, the intellect of a cognitive agent is made up of these symbols. Let us suppose that John has some knowledge of cats. He knows, for example, Molly, Tom and Sylvester, and he knows (or he believes – we shall return to this distinction later) that cats that purr are happy. So this supposes that his knowledge base is made up of the following symbolic expressions:

[†]We shall use the word 'symbol' in its cognitivist meaning here, that is, as a significant element referring back to a content, which makes it a synonym of 'sign' in linguistics. It must not be confused with the concept of 'symbol' as a mechanism and access support for spiritual and sub-conscious meanings.
[‡]It is important to be able to distinguish the symbol from its referent. We shall use different typographic forms for these two concepts: symbols (like computing entities) will be written in Courier type, while referents will be written in *italics*.

```
cat(Molly), cat(Tom), cat(Sylvester)
∀ x.[ cat(x) ⟹ (purrs(x) ∧ happy(x))]
```

Semantics and reference

As long as we have not described what these symbols designate, we are dealing only with syntactically correct simple aggregates. To elevate them to the level of symbols, a *semantics* has to be added to them, that is, the capacity to interpret these expressions in relation to what we call a model. For example, it is impossible to say whether the expression

$$\forall x \; \exists y \; P(x,y)$$

is true or false, as long as we do not know what the symbols ∀, ∃, P, x and y refer to, and from what these symbols derive their value. By contrast, if we say that the domain of reference of the variables is the set of natural integers and that P means 'less than or equal to', then it is possible to pronounce on the truth or falsehood of the preceding formula by considering that, in fact, any integer x can have attached to it at least one other integer, than which it is less or to which it is equal. This association between the symbols and the things of a domain D is defined by a function of interpretation. In our case, the function of interpretation I could be as follows:

$I(\text{Molly}) = Molly$
$I(\text{Tom}) = Tom$
$I(\text{Sylvester}) = Sylvester$
$I(\text{purr}) = Molly$
$I(\text{happy}) = Molly, Sylvester, John$
$I(\text{cat}) = Molly, Tom, Sylvester$
$I(\text{person}) = John, Marie, Paul, Peter, Mark, ...$
$I(\text{love}) = <John, Marie>, <Marie, Peter>, ...$
$I(\text{John}) = John$

To know if a proposition is true for an interpretation, I, which is denoted as $\models_I$, consists of verifying, for the atomic formulae, that the constants appearing in a predicate (or the list of constants) do indeed belong to the domain of interpretation of the predicate:

$\models_I P(a)$ *iff* $I(a) \in I(P)$
$\models_I R(a1, \ldots, an)$ *iff* $I(<a1, \ldots, an>) \in I(R)$

It is possible to combine the formulae with the help of operators such as ¬ (not), ∧ (and), ∨ (or), ⟹ (implies), and so on and, in this case, we verify the *satisfiability* of a formula by analysing its different components on the basis of the following rules:

Figure 5.2 In logic, symbols refer to objects and to situations of the world.

$\models_I \neg\phi$ *iff* $\not\models_I \phi$

$\models_I \phi \wedge \psi$ *iff* $\models_I \phi$ *and* $\models_I \psi$

$\models_I \phi \vee \psi$ *iff* $\models_I \phi$ *or* $\models_I \psi$

$\models_I \phi \Rightarrow \psi$ *iff* $\not\models_I \phi$ *or* $\models_I \psi$

$\models_I \forall x.\phi$ *iff* $I_{x/d}(\phi)$ *for every* $d \in D$

$\models_I \exists x.\phi$ *iff*

where $I_{x/d}(\phi)$ represents the interpretation of the formula ϕ in which it has replaced the variable x by the element d of the domain of interpretation D.

For example, the expression `cat(x) ∧ happy(x)` is true if in fact the interpretation of x simultaneously belongs to the set of cats and the set of the happy. For this reason, the formula `cat(Molly) ∧ happy(Molly)` is true, since *Molly* belongs simultaneously to *cat* and to *happy*. Likewise the formula,

$$\forall x.[\,\text{cat}(x) \ \wedge \ \text{purrs}(x) \ \Rightarrow \ \text{happy}(x)]$$

is true, since either `happy(x)` is true ($x \in$ *happy*), or `cat(x) ∧ purrs(x)` is false, that is, x does not belong to the intersection of *cat* and *purrs* (Figure 5.2).

The formalisation of the logic has made it possible to have general properties in logic systems, independent of the interpretations which one can have for the symbols. In particular, it is possible to show that, whatever the interpretation I adopted, the formula

$$\models \forall x.P(x) \ \Rightarrow \ P(x)$$

is true, which is denoted by deleting any mention of an interpretation in the sign $\models$. We then say that such a formula is *valid*.

Formal system and inference

Logical reasoning is based on the concepts of inference and of formal system. The concept of inference is very old (Aristotle is generally considered as being the inventor of logic), since it has always been considered as a general mode of reasoning. With the appearance of modern logics arising from the initial work of Boole, Frege and Russell, the inferential process became purely mechanical and 'formal', based on the concept of a formal system, which determines the laws of syntactical processing making it possible to assemble and produce in a coherent manner expressions based on more elementary expressions and considered as true. A formal system is composed of:

(1) a set of symbols, whose meaning is purely arbitrary, and which, in themselves, have no *a priori* link with what they represent;

(2) a set of grammatical rules making it possible to construct well-formed formulae for sets of more elementary formulae;

(3) a set of initial formulae, called axioms;

(4) a deductive mechanism making it possible to produce new formulae, called theorems, based on the initial axioms and on theorems already produced.

The deductive process follows an iterative mechanism, that is, the conclusions are obtained after a certain number of 'steps' of deduction. Each step in this process must follow a *rule of inference* which stipulates the way new formulae are produced. A rule of inference is written:

$$\phi_1,...\phi_n \vdash \phi_n + 1$$

which means that, on the basis of the formulae $\phi_1,...,\phi_n$, it is possible to produce the formula $\phi_n + 1$. The most famous and the most frequently used of the rules of inference is called the *modus ponens* and is written as follows:

$$\phi, \phi \Rightarrow \psi \vdash \psi$$

It stipulates that, if a formula exists with the form ϕ, and one with the form $\phi \Rightarrow \psi$, it is then possible to infer the formula ψ from this. For example, from it is raining and it is raining $\Rightarrow$ the road is wet, it is possible to deduce the road is wet in a single step.

One of the best-known logic systems in AI, which we have used to introduce the concept of a logic system, is that of *first-order predicate logic*. Initially conceived for the analysis of the foundations of mathematics, this logic makes it possible to represent certain, universal and timeless knowledge in a very elegant manner, that is, knowledge which expresses truths independent of any real statement situation. As we have seen, this type of knowledge stands against the concept of micro-theories considered earlier. Because its nature is too simplistic and it is incapable of handling concepts as common as time, beliefs, actions, doubts, etc., numerous other logic systems have been created. However, it is still frequently used, in particular due to the fact that it is often the base for other logics, which are therefore considered as extensions of predicate logic. In particular, the modal logic of beliefs, which is introduced below, is integrally based on first-order predicate logic.

Generally, the formal systems built up on the basis of this concept are *compositional* and *reductive*. These two terms, although generally used together, are not equivalents. We say that a semantics is compositional if the meaning of a complex expression is a function of the meaning of its constituents. It is reductive if primitive semantics exist, that is, symbols, whose meaning is not defined by the composition of the meanings of their constituents, but by a direct reference mechanism between the symbol and the thing referred to. Logic formalisms, and in particular first-order predicate logic and its modal extensions, are compositional (with certain limitations for modal logics, as we shall see below) and reductive.

Other formalisms exist for representing knowledge. The best-known alternative is based on the concept of a semantic network, of frames or of objects, these three concepts being interwoven relatively closely. A semantic network is a labelled diagram made up of nodes which represent concepts, and of arcs, which link these concepts to one another. This type of representation of knowledge is frequently used in the domain of the comprehension of natural language, where semantic networks render an account of the deep structure of sentences. One of the most current models nowadays is that of conceptual graphs, by J. Sowa (1984). Other languages for representing knowledge, based on the concept of objects or of frames, are currently used in artificial intelligence applications. An object is a computing structure described by a static aspect, which qualifies its state, and the links which it can maintain with other objects, and a dynamic aspect made up of the set of operations which are applicable to it. One can turn to Ferber (1990) for an introduction to programming and design by objects, and to Masini *et al.* (1989) for a general view on object languages and frame systems.

5.3.3 Logics of learning and beliefs

Believing something is admitting as a true proposition, a fact, a story, without actually knowing how true it is. In everyday language, we often use the term 'think that' to express a belief. For example, if one says 'I think that the postman delivered the post today', this means that one subscribes to the affirmation 'the postman has delivered the post today', but without being absolutely sure of it. In order to make sure, it is necessary either to confirm this fact by observation – by going to look in the letter-box – or to 'believe' people or things which have affirmed this proposition. For example, if you are on holiday and someone tells you on the telephone that 'the postman didn't deliver the post today', you have no way of going to verify this yourself, and you have to rely on what this person says about it. But it is not only people we have to believe in ordinary life. Inanimate objects also affirm statements which we have to believe and which we cannot always (or do not wish to) verify. For example, if the petrol gauge on your car is reading 'Full', this does not actually mean the tank is full of petrol. If the gauge is not working, the tank may be empty .... However, this belief may have consequences for your future actions. If you believe the tank is full, you can plan a long drive without filling up again, whereas if you think it is empty you will try to fill up as quickly as possible. If you believe the gauge is broken, you will use other methods to evaluate how much petrol you have left, perhaps by estimating your consumption on the basis of 'beliefs' regarding the distance travelled, trusting other instruments such as the trip recorder in your car or the distances shown on maps, etc. But you will not escape having to believe in certain propositions and rely on certain things.

The above considerations have only one purpose – to show, firstly, that all reasoning is based on beliefs and, secondly, that these beliefs can be verified only by methods involving interaction with other entities (the person on the telephone, the petrol gauge), whose reliability is itself the effect of other beliefs. In other words, 'facts' as such do not exist. There are only beliefs that have not yet been refuted.

From a more philosophical point of view, all learning relates to beliefs. It is always a matter of information obtained from something else or someone else, and this information may be subject to error. What we see is only an illusion conveyed by our senses, as the empiricists Hume and Berkeley well understood. The senses filter and translate reality, presenting things to us through a transformation process which sometimes deforms things. Information is also the object of a belief. What we learn from the newspapers is perhaps false (especially if the paper is dated April the first), or is quite simply no longer true because the newspaper only comes out every so often. Likewise, scientific laws and results, the very images of certainty, should be considered as adequate beliefs based on scientific – that is, refutable – propositions, which can be questioned at the appropriate time (Popper, 1963).

The concept of belief is associated with that of revision. Any information which is the subject of a belief can be called into question. This capacity of being able to call into question a fact, a deduction, a law or a judgement forms the basis of our capacity for cognitive adaptation, that is, the faculty which we have, as human beings, of accommodating our cognitive system to a world in perpetual evolution, this evolution being the fruit of the actions of the various agents intervening in our universe.

The same applies to the agents intervening in the context of DAI, which must be capable of questioning their information and revising their judgements. For example, in the pursuit problem (Chapter 1), the predators have to revise their beliefs concerning the position of the prey and decide on the action to be taken on the basis of this belief. If the reaction time and the communication propagation time is not negligible, the predators will sometimes have erroneous information, the situation of the prey having changed in the meantime.

Finally, beliefs are not universal. They are relative to an individual, a group, a society. What John believes is different from what Peter believes. One predator may have 'fresher' information than another, or an agent may have more specialised skills allowing it to appreciate the validity of a statement better. And, as we saw earlier in the context of knowledge, nothing indicates that all these beliefs are coherent. For this reason, the relativity of beliefs to individuals takes on major importance to multi-agent systems, as they emphasise the necessary localisation of data and the need to communicate in order to be able to transmit and compare beliefs.

Formalising beliefs

The study of beliefs in philosophy, and then in logic, is the fruit of a long tradition which goes back to the Greeks, although the idea that it was possible to formalise and to give a calculable form to beliefs dates from the beginning of the 1960s and the fundamental work done by Hintikka (1962). Those years witnessed considerable developments in formal theories relating to beliefs and knowledge. But the coming of multi-agent systems and, in particular, the rise of cooperative cognitive systems, led to a revival of interest in all these theories, which took account of the limits imposed by their effectively being put to work in computing environments.

The general principle of these logics is to define a set of axioms relating to beliefs, and then to give them a semantics by making them refer to elements of a mathematically defined structure.

But do we need a special logic for beliefs? Why not use first-order predicate logic? Indeed, one practical solution would be to use a specific atomic formula such as `believe(A,P)` to indicate that agent A believes proposition P. However, this formulation comes up against one of the essential properties of predicate logic, which is that it must be possible to substitute identical expressions in all the formulae where they appear. For example, if John believes that the author of *The Legend of the Centuries* is the author of *Notre-Dame*, and if it turns out that Victor Hugo is in fact the author of *The Legend of the Centuries* – which we can write like this:

```
Believe(John, author(authorOf('Legend of the
                  centuries'), 'Notre-Dame')
VictorHugo = authorOf('Legend of the centuries')
```

it then follows logically that John believes that Victor Hugo is indeed the author of *Notre-Dame*, which may not actually be one of John's beliefs. Thus, the property of substitution of identical elements leads to false deductions with regard to beliefs. The error stems from the fact that John's knowledge base, in which all his beliefs are located, constitutes a context which is 'opaque' to referencing. For this reason, if we wish to be able to handle the concept of belief, it is necessary to be able to free ourselves from the limits imposed by first order predicate logic and to use another logic capable of 'masking out' the contexts of beliefs.

These *epistemic logics*, which deal with knowledge and beliefs, use more esoteric formulations than employing a simple predicate `believe` or `know`, and extend first-order predicate logic to take account of all the subtleties of beliefs and knowledge. Beliefs and learning have numerous points in common. Traditionally, we distinguish between them by considering that learning is made up of true beliefs, that is, statements which are known by the agent and which are in conformity with the world. The concept of learning can thus be defined as follows:

```
know(A,P) = believe(A,P) ∧ true(P)
```

means that, if an agent knows P, then P is naturally true, which can be formulated:

```
know(A,P) ⟹ P
```

We shall therefore treat learning and beliefs together and will not distinguish between these two types of relationship with the world unless it proves to be necessary.

Possible worlds

The classic formulation of an epistemic logic is based on the concept of modal logic, and the semantic analysis of epistemic logics is based on the model of *possible worlds*. The latter, initially set out by Kripke (1991) for the logics of the possible and the necessary (*ontic* logics) was taken up by Hintikka for the formalisation of learning and beliefs.

The intuitive idea is to consider that each agent can conceive of a certain number of worlds which it imagines as conceivable. We then say that an agent believes a proposition if it is true in all the worlds it imagines. For example, if John believes that the petrol tank of his car is full, this means that he can conceive of several possible worlds – in some Napoleon died on Saint Helena, in others he died on the island of Elba, in still others he died in the Tuileries, John has no beliefs on the death of Napoleon – but in all these worlds his car's petrol tank is full.

To explain this idea, it is necessary to have a language for representing knowledge. In the classic manner, we shall make use of a modal language, that is, a language corresponding to that of propositional language or that of predicate logic, to which we shall add an operator for belief or learning – concepts we know as the modalities.

Henceforward we can write `believe(A,P)` to indicate that agent A believes proposition P, that is, that the modal operator `believe` is applied to the proposition P and indexed by agent A. For example, the sentence *John believes that Tina's tank is full* is expressed as follows:

```
believe(John,full(tank(Tina))),
```

where `Tina` is John's car. In terms of the semantics of possible worlds, this means that a set of worlds exists, called W, such that, starting from the world W_0, considered as the 'real' world, John sees (or imagines) only worlds in which his car's tank is full. Figure 5.3 represents this situation (we are also assuming that a rule exists with the form `∀x.empty(x) ⟹ ¬full(x)`).

In some of the worlds which John imagines, Tina is new, in others it no longer is. Sometimes, Napoleon died on Saint Helena, but in all cases he imagines only worlds in which Tina's tank is full, and it is for this reason that we can say that John effectively believes this proposition. John also believes something which is false. It is actually given, in the original world, W_0, that the tank is not full (it is even

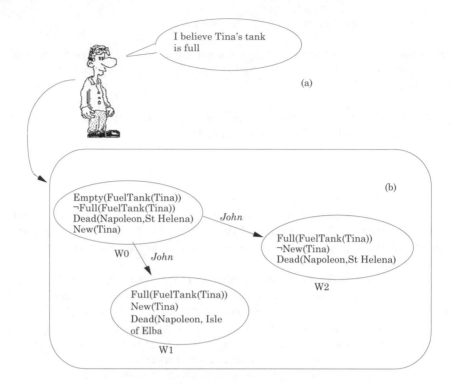

Figure 5.3 A model of possible worlds (b) corresponding to John's beliefs (a).

empty), but John does not see this. In more formal words, an interpretation in terms of possible worlds is called a *Kripke M* model, defined as an n-uplet

$$M = < W, I, R_1, ..., R_n >$$

where W is a set of possible worlds (or of possible states of the world, if you prefer), R_i is a relationship of accessibility associated with the agent i, and I is a valuation function which associates a truth value with a proposition and a world, that is, a function of the type

$$I: Proposition \times W \rightarrow \{True, False\}$$

The interpretation of a proposition containing a belief can then be given by a relationship of *semantic consequence* $\models$ where $M, w \models \phi$ means that ϕ *is true in the world w of the model M*. This relationship is defined recursively, therefore, in the context of a propositional modal logic[†]:

[†]We shall define here only the semantic relationship for a modal logic of which the statements are propositions. The extension of this type of semantics to predicative modal logics is immediate. Specifically, a presentation of this extension can be found in the book by Genesereth and Nilsson (1987).

$M, w \models \phi$ *if ϕ is a primitive proposition and $I(\phi, w)$ – True*
$M, w \models_I \neg\phi$ *iff $M, w \not\models_I \phi$*
$M, w \models_I \phi \wedge \psi$ *iff $M, w, \models_I \psi$ and $M, w \models_I \psi$*
$M, w \models_I \phi \vee \psi$ *iff $\models_I \phi$ or $\models_I \psi$*
$M, w \models_I \phi \Rightarrow \psi$ *iff $M, w \not\models_I \phi$ or $M, w \models_I \psi$*
$M, w \models_I$ believe(a, ϕ) *iff*
    for every world w_i such that $w\, R_a\, w_i, M, w_i \models_I \phi$

It is not enough to give a semantics to a modal operator. It must also be capable of characterising the different properties which are attached to these forms of knowledge. These can be defined by a set of axioms which characterise the inferential aspects of beliefs.

The first of these axioms, the *distribution axiom*, relates to the fact that an agent's beliefs or known facts follow the principle of the modus ponens. If an agent believes in an implication between two terms then, if it believes the first, it also believes the second. This axiom, which is often considered as the main element in the logics of learning and beliefs, can have several equivalent expressions:

believe(A, (P $\Rightarrow$ Q)) $\Rightarrow$ believe(A, P $\Rightarrow$ Believe(A, Q))   (*K*)
believe(A, P) $\wedge$ believe(A, (P $\rightarrow$ Q)) $\Rightarrow$ believe(A, Q)

The *non-contradiction axiom* characterises an agent's logical faculties. If it believes something, then it does not believe its opposite, which is denoted as:

believe(A, P) $\Rightarrow$ ¬believe(A, ¬P))   (*D*)

For example, if John believes his petrol tank is full, then he does not believe his tank is empty.

Cognitive agents can be considered as agents conscious of their own beliefs. This indicates that, if an agent believes something, then it believes that it believes it. This property is embodied by axioms of *positive introspection* and *negative introspection*:

believe(A, P) $\Rightarrow$ believe(A, believe(A, P))   (4)
¬believe(A, P) $\Rightarrow$ believe(A, ¬believe(A, P)   (5)

The learning axiom considers that everything an agent believes is true, and is denoted thus:

believe(A, P) $\Rightarrow$ P   (*T*)

This axiom is not adapted to beliefs. It is indeed possible to have false beliefs, and moreover this is what we have recognised as being one of the fundamental characteristics of beliefs. When John believes that his tank is full, it is possible that it is empty. In contrast, the concept of knowing, as it is used in logic, assumes that

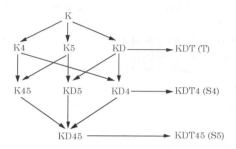

Figure 5.4 The different modal logics definable on the basis of axioms K, D, T, 4 and 5. An arrow, X → Y, indicates that all X theorems are integrally within Y. The names between () correspond to their usual denomination.

all things known are true, that is, that an agent cannot know something false. For this reason, the axiom of knowledge, which is one of the pivots of learning logics, will not be used in representing beliefs.

It is possible to mix these properties together and retain only the axioms which are desired. In this case, a different logic system will be obtained each time, in which certain deductions can be made and not others. Figure 5.4 (Konolige, 1986) represents the set of modal systems corresponding to these axioms, together with their dependency links.

The interesting thing about the semantics of possible worlds is that we can link the axioms of these modal logic systems to the properties of relationships of accessibility. Axiom K is indispensable, because it makes it possible to interpret modal propositions in terms of possible worlds. Axiom T is characteristic of a reflexive accessibility relationship. When it is also transitive, we obtain system S4. When we are dealing with relationships of equivalence, that is, if accessibility is reflexive, symmetrical and transitive, the corresponding axiom system is S5. Learning logics generally use S4 or S5 logics. By contrast, belief logics, which cannot accept axiom T, generally use KD45, the strongest of the belief logics.

The other interesting point about the semantics of possible worlds for multi-agent systems is that we can easily represent the mutual beliefs which agents can have in relation to each other and take into account a set of assertions such as:

```
believe(John,full(tank(Tina)))
believe(Marie,empty(tank(Tina)))
believe(Marie,believe(John,empty(tank(Tina)))),
```

in which Marie believes not only that Tina's tank is empty, but also that John believes that the tank is empty, whereas he actually believes that the tank is full.

First of all, this simply means that, in all the worlds initially accessible by John (that is, accessible from W_0), Tina's tank is full, and that, in all the worlds initially accessible by Marie, the tank is empty. The mutual beliefs can be described more precisely by saying that, in all the worlds accessible by Marie, the proposition:

```
believe(John,empty(tank(Tina)))
```

is true, that is, that in all the worlds accessible to John based on the worlds initially accessible by Marie, the proposition:

```
empty(tank(Tina))
```

is verified, as is shown in Figure 5.5.

Limits of semantics of possible worlds

Although frequently used in DAI to describe the beliefs and learning of agents, the semantics of possible worlds and the modal logics which are associated with it have given rise to several controversies. The first of these controversies concerns the *logical omniscience* of agents defined in this way.

The semantics of possible worlds absolutely proclaims one rule, called the rule of necessity, which indicates that any valid formula (that is, universally true whatever the model) necessarily forms part of the agent's beliefs, which are expressed in the following manner:

$$\text{for any agent } a, \quad \frac{\vdash \phi}{\vdash \texttt{believe}(a, \phi)}$$

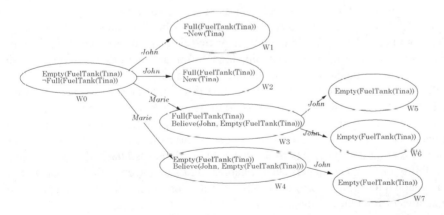

Figure 5.5   A model of possible worlds indicating the respective beliefs of John and Marie. The latter believes that John believes that the tank is empty, whereas he actually believes that it is full.

The drawback is that this rule, when it is associated with axiom K, means that the agent must be capable of deducing all the logical consequences of its beliefs and, in particular, those which stem from universally valid consequences. For example, if John believes that his car's tank is full, and if it is true that his car can travel 200 miles without needing any more petrol, then, according to the semantics of possible worlds, John must necessarily believe that he can travel 200 miles. But this is perhaps not one of John's beliefs, if he believes that his car can travel 300 miles without filling up. In this system, therefore, one may not believe something which is in contradiction to a fact which is universally true. False beliefs are therefore prohibited, and yet this is the distinctive feature of beliefs. Moreover, this semantics does not take into account the fact that the agents have a limited memory and limited processors.

So we cannot get out of these difficulties except by assuming that this semantics defines agents for which the deduction performances are 'ideal'. We shall also pay attention to limiting to a maximum the number of universally valid formulae, in such a way that undesired deductions cannot be engendered by the system.

Operational logics

The problem of logical omniscience is not the only difficulty with which modal logics are faced. There are also metaphysical problems concerning the existence of these 'possible worlds' and their construction. This is why other models of reasoning have been put forward in relation to beliefs and learning; these models are no longer based on the existence of these worlds but on the mechanical capacities of an agent to produce new assertions. We then speak of *operational* logic or *sentential* semantics, to indicate that the semantics of an expression is given in terms of the formal manipulation of a statement, and not by reference to a world model, whether this model deals with 'real' worlds or 'possible' worlds.

Each agent a is associated with a knowledge base Δ_a made up of 'ordinary' logic formulae (classic proportional logic or first order predicate logic) and a set of rules of inference, denoted Γ_a. Combinations, formulae and rules of inference make it possible to define the set θ_a, which comprises the set of initial formulae, together with those which can be derived by using the rules of inference of Γ_a, and which we call the *theory* of agent a. We use $\Delta_a \vdash_a \phi$ to denote the fact that the proposition ϕ is true in the theory θ_a, that is, that ϕ is a theorem deduced from the knowledge base of agent a. In this context, expressing that an agent believes a proposition ϕ comes down to saying that ϕ belongs to θ_a, that is, that a belief is attached to a deductive possibility of an agent. In particular, establishing that an agent believes that $\phi \Rightarrow \psi$ comes down to trying to prove that $\phi \vdash_a \psi$ in the context of the knowledge and the capacities of inference of the agent a.

This concept of beliefs has the advantage of taking much more account of the computational mechanisms which underlie the reasonings of agents. They do not pose the problems encountered with the semantics of possible worlds and, in particular, the problems of omniscience, since it is possible to define limited rules of inference (for example, by limiting the number of deduction steps that an agent can take or the type of deduction that it can carry out). The meaning is then seen more as a usage (Wittgenstein, 1951), that is, as the set of occurrences of this expression in the context of the set of proofs established when this expression is interpreted (Enjalbert, 1989). The model is then no longer given *a priori* but built up locally on the basis of partial interpretations local to each of the agents interacting. It was by using this approach that C. Lefèvre (1995) put forward a model of beliefs and learning based on a logical model arising from the typified lambda computation. This model solves the problems posed by the semantics of possible worlds while giving a solid formal base for different ways of believing. In this way, it is possible to distinguish between belief as proof and belief as reasoning, and so to offer the MAS designer different ways of tackling the problem of belief.

5.3.4   Adequacy and revision of beliefs

The first quality of a model is to be adequate, that is, to be in a relationship of correspondence with reality. Formally, adequacy comes down to saying that a morphism exists between the structure of the model and that of the real world. When this morphism does not exist, the model is inadequate. For example, a map of France provides no assistance if you are in the United States, because the structures of the two countries are too dissimilar. Likewise, a road map is not very useful when you are in a boat, because the angles and distances are not respected on it. The operations of vector addition which are essential for marine navigation are of no use for orientating yourself in a road network, whose structure is essentially that of a diagram.

The inadequacy of models is sometimes responsible for the difficulties we experience in acting. For example, many people were one hundred per cent certain at the end of the century that it was impossible for a 'heavier than air machine' to fly. The model which people had then, and which was based on the concept of weight, without the inclusion of the concept of aerodynamics, was inadequate, and no attempt to construct aircraft was made. Even the act of attempting to construct an aeroplane with a sufficiently powerful engine for the wind speed to produce a supporting force did not enter most people's heads, and only a few pioneers believed in heavier-than-air machines (Ferber, 1906).

A model is made up of beliefs, that is, data, whose validity can be called into question if new information is available. So to believe is to be capable of revising one's judgement if new information comes along to undermine what one thinks. When the robot Clifford moves, it has to keep updating the set of deductions it can carry out concerning the world. The positions of objects may be modified, and all the consequences linked with these objects have to be updated.

Default logic

For example, let us suppose that Clifford, which has a prehensile claw, has to reason concerning whether its claw is empty or not, to know whether it can pick up an object immediately. The general knowledge, valid for all robots which have claws, can be formulated like this:

```
clawEmpty(x) ⇒ canPickupObject(x)
```

However, this statement poses a problem. Let us suppose that initially Clifford has an empty claw, and that it therefore holds the fact

```
clawEmpty(Clifford)
```

in its knowledge base. It can therefore deduce the fact that it can pick up an object and that the formula

```
canPickupObject(Clifford)
```

is true. But as soon as it picks up an object, this statement is no longer true, because its claw is no longer empty. Other phenomena, for example if Clifford has broken its claw, can contradict the relationship which exists between the state of the claw and its capacity to pick up objects. The affirmation that the claw is empty is relative to a state of the world, and has therefore no universal validity.

Now, standard logic, such as first-order predicate logic, cannot take this type of situation into account. As soon as a proposition is affirmed, it cannot be called into question. We say that these logics are *monotonous*, because reasoning merely adds facts to the knowledge base, whose truth value cannot be modified, on pain of making the entire base incoherent. In order to reason about a world which is evolving, or which possesses only partial knowledge, it is necessary to have different logics available, capable of dealing with knowledge which can be revised, and is therefore able to call into question facts deduced at the start which prove to be no longer relevant.

Revising a knowledge base means correcting the expressions produced when certain facts are modified, that is, defining the progressive and incremental manner in which the beliefs of an agent change when facts are added to, or removed from, its knowledge base, allowing attention to be paid to the processing of data which are *incomplete*, *uncertain* and *evolutionary*. The development of the analysis of revisable reasoning has taken two main paths: firstly on the theoretical plane, by producing formal theories capable of taking account of revision operations, and secondly on the plane of the mechanisms making it possible to manage the adjustments between the consequences and the expansion of the coherence maintenance systems.

The logical processing of reasoning which can be revised is based on the definition of logics referred to as *non-monotonous*, considered as extensions of classic logics. These logics were not initially created in order to characterise reasoning which could be revised due to an evolutionary universe, but to formalise certain aspects of *common sense reasoning*, and in particular those which are related to the processing of typical knowledge and which can be paraphrased by 'generally all the A's are B' (Sombé, 1988). To take the famous example which allowed research in this domain to establish its pedigree, typically 'birds fly'. In the absence of any data to the contrary, it is possible to infer that Titi, which is a bird, can actually fly. Obviously this affirmation, which is generally correct, is not valid if Titi has broken a wing, or if we are talking about an ostrich.

The approaches which have been most fully developed in this area in recent years are *default logic*, Moore's *auto-epistemical logic* (Moore, 1988), and McCarthy's *circumscription* (McCarthy, 1980). Default logic, introduced by Reiter (1980), has the advantage of simultaneously being simple to understand and to put into operation in its most elementary versions and having been well studied.

The formulae for default logic are the same as those for classic logic. Default data, that is, data which are typical in nature, are given by specific rules of inference called default rules, which are written as follows:

$$\frac{\alpha : M\,\beta}{\gamma}$$

which means that, if α is a belief and the formula β is not incoherent with the others, then γ can be believed. Very frequently, the formulae β and γ are the same, and we then speak of normal defaults. The default rule relating to birds and their property of flying is expressed as follows:

$$\frac{\texttt{bird(s)} : M\,\texttt{fly(x)}}{\texttt{fly(x)}} \qquad\qquad (RD1)$$

It is possible to use default logic to represent the revisable reasoning of an agent. For example, if we wish to characterise the fact that normally a robot with an empty claw can pick up an object, it will be formulated as follows:

$$\frac{\texttt{clawEmpty(x)} : M\,\texttt{canPickup(x)}}{\texttt{canPickup(x)}} \qquad\qquad (RD2)$$

This rule expresses very precisely that 'if the robot's claw is empty and it is not incoherent to think that it can pick up an object, then it can do it'. Likewise, the relationship which links the gauge of Tina's tank (cf. Section 5.3.3) to the level of petrol can be expressed like this:

$$\frac{\texttt{gauge(x,full)} : M\,\texttt{tankFull(x)}}{\texttt{tankFull(x)}} \qquad\qquad (RD3)$$

The interesting thing about a default rule is that we can define links between the premises and the conclusions of a rule more loosely than in predicate logic. If a contradiction exists between the conclusion and other facts in the base, that is enough for the rule no longer to be applicable, and so the inference is blocked. For example, if Clifford's claw is broken, and if a rule exists with the form

$$\text{clawBroken}(x) \;\Rightarrow\; \neg\text{canPickupObject}(x)$$

together with the fact

$$\text{clawBroken}(\text{Clifford}),$$

then the system will deduce

$$\neg\text{canPickupObject}(x)$$

Rule RD2 cannot be applied, and it cannot be deduced from it that Clifford can pick up an object, even if the claw is empty.

Default rules such as RD2 or RD3 all indicate that a certain reasoning can be effected in the absence of contradictions considered as abnormal. For example, rule RD3 could be rewritten like this:

$$\text{gauge}(x, \text{full}) \;\wedge\; \neg\text{abnormal1}(x) \Rightarrow \text{tankFull}(x) \qquad (RD3')$$

where `abnormal1` represents a characteristic of abnormality which would cut across the relationship existing between the gauge and the tank. If we consider that, in the absence of supplementary data, the predicate `abnormal1` is false, which is what we obtain when we apply the hypothesis of the closed world where everything which is not known as true is false, then the preceding formula gives a very direct representation of default rule RD3. McCarthy's *circumscription* theory is a generalisation of this management of abnormality to any rule.

Justifications and TMS

The interesting thing about default logic and circumscription is that it is relatively easy to implement them with the assistance of coherence maintenance systems, better known as TMSs (Truth Maintenance Systems). TMSs are systems making it possible to manage the justifications of beliefs. When John affirms that Tina's tank is full, it is because he can read off the level on the petrol gauge, which acts as a justification of his belief. Obviously, this belief may prove false if the dependency link which exists between the petrol level and the gauge were to prove to have been broken. Justification forms the base for the beliefs and models which we can have in relation to the world.

TMSs are very simple computing mechanisms, initially invented by Doyle (1979), which manage the dependencies between facts and indicate whether a fact can be believed, yes or no, on the basis of the positive or negative justifications that can be associated with it. A TMS is a network of dependencies between data, the network nodes representing data which can be true or false, and the arrows characterising the dependencies between the data. These arrows can be either positive or negative. In the first case, they represent positive justifications between data (what are called 'arrows in' in TMS jargon) and in the second they are negative justifications ('arrows out'). A node is said to be valid if all the nodes on which it depends positively are valid and all the nodes on which it depends negatively are invalid. For example, the fact that Clifford can pick up an object if it is next to the object, if its claw is empty and if the object is not too heavy and if its claw is not broken can be expressed in the form of a diagram, as shown in Figure 5.6.

This diagram illustrates the eminently recursive character of coherence maintenance. Data are either primitive or dependent on other data. Each non-primitive fact is associated with a small 'processor', which computes the validities of the facts on which it depends. For example, the fact that the claw is empty depends on the indication of its sensor and on the state of health of the latter. Likewise, a claw is broken if it can no longer carry out vertical, horizontal or rotational movements. Nodes which do not depend on any other node are either premises or hypotheses. The premises are nodes, the data for which are always valid, whereas the hypotheses are nodes, the data for which are *assumed* to be valid. During the functioning of the TMS, it will be determined whether these nodes are effectively valid or not.

In the ideal case, where the network of dependencies has no cycle, a simple propagation algorithm is sufficient to manage the justifications. As soon as a fact becomes invalid, it invalidates all the facts which depend on it through a positive justification link, and it can make a fact valid which depends on it through a negative justification link if all the other negative justifications are invalid too. When a contradiction arises, a contradiction management system comes into operation and searches the set of hypotheses for those it needs to question to remove the contradiction. See Haton *et al.* (1991) for a good introduction to revisable reasoning, and Thibault (1993) for an application of coherence maintenance systems to a distributed perception system.

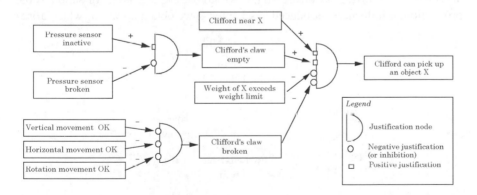

Figure 5.6   A schematic representation of a set of justifications. A non-primitive affirmation is true if all the positive justifications are true and all the negative justifications false.

Forecasts and adequacy

If a model has to be adequate, it must also provide some assistance in predicting what will happen by anticipating a future state of the world. On the basis of representations of the laws of this world and of 'psychological' knowledge on the behaviour of other agents, a cognitive agent can perhaps determine the facts and the events that may come about. This involves being able to determine the interactional input cognitons (percepts and data) before they are available. For example, if John 'knows' that Tina consumes 10 gallons of petrol in 100 miles, that he has just filled up, and that his tank contains 30 gallons, he can deduce from this that he can travel 300 miles before he will run out of petrol, and that after approximately 250 miles the petrol gauge will indicate that the tank is empty. To put it another way, John and Clifford can anticipate what they will perceive in the future. Figure 5.7 gives the layout of a forecasting system.

On the basis of perceptions or data relating to the current state of the world, on the basis of models of the actions which the agent can carry out, and on the basis of the laws of the world in which it believes and of supplementary factual beliefs, the provisional system supplies *expectations*, that is, percepts or data which should 'normally' be corroborated by the percepts and data coming from the perceptive system.

The forecasting procedure can be formally described in the following way. Let P_1 be a set of percepts (or data) describing a part of the current state s_1, let $M(Op)$ be the model of the action which the agent a is about to carry out, and let L and C be the sets of laws of the universe and of factual beliefs, then we have:

$$P_1 = Percept_a(\sigma_1)$$
$$P'_2 = Forecast_a(P_1, M(Op), L, C)$$

where P'_2 represents a set of expected percepts (or data) which should be perceived or obtained for the state σ_2. Looked at in another way, the agent carries out actions and the world evolves. For this reason, if we go back to the model of action as the production of influences introduced in Chapter 4, we obtain a state σ_2 which arises

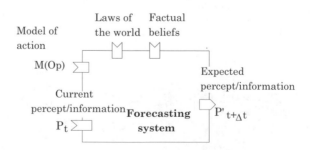

Figure 5.7 A forecasting system produces 'expected' percepts which subsequent perceptions or data will normally corroborate.

from the carrying out of the action Op and the influences γ_{others}, arising from other actions (coming from other agents):

$$\sigma_2 = React(\sigma_1, Exec(Op, \sigma_1) \parallel \gamma_{others})$$

This state can be perceived by agent A (or can give rise to data which A receives) in the form of a set of percepts (or data) P_2:

$$P_2 = Percept_a(\sigma_2)$$

If P_2 is in accord with P_2', no problem. We shall simply say that agent A has indeed anticipated state σ_2, and that all the laws of the world, its beliefs, its perceptive or informational mechanisms, together with its models of actions, are adequate. By contrast, if P_2' and P_2 are sufficiently different to be considered as incoherent (for example, if contradictions exist between these two sets of cognitons), then it may perhaps be necessary to revise the representational elements which brought about this false forecast. Figure 5.8 gives a diagrammatical representation of this revision procedure. It can indeed be seen that, if the forecast is adequate, then the divergence between P_2' and P_2 should be zero.

If the divergence is not zero, this means certain beliefs must be revised. It is therefore necessary to put revision strategies into place and to try to determine what the possible trouble-makers are. The problem lies in selecting the elements about which one has the most doubts, that is, the cognitons to which one attributes the least verisimilitude. Here are a few possible solutions:

(1)   *The sensors are in poor condition.* We can make sure they are functioning properly by checking that we obtain the expected percepts in known situations. For example, if John finds that his car is using too much petrol, he may first check the gauge by putting in some petrol and verifying that his

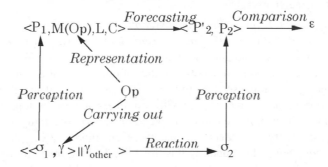

Figure 5.8   Forecasting diagram. When ε is zero, the forecasts are corroborated. The diagram commutes and we can say that the representations M(Op), L, C and the perceptual and informational systems are adequate.

gauge functions properly. In certain cases, an agent can ask another agent if they both have the same perceptions by posing the question: 'Do you see what I see?' The probability that the sensors of several agents have all broken down is so minimal that a simple question of this kind allows this factor to be eliminated very rapidly (collective illusion very rarely affects artificial agents).

(2) *The data supplied by the other agents are no longer correct or are insufficient.* In this case, we can try to check their quality by asking for these data again if this is possible, or else by trying to obtain supplementary data. If, in the pursuit example, one of the predators uses data supplied by another predator to know the position of a prey animal and does not discover it at the right place, it may perhaps request confirmation of this position from another predator, to find out if the information is wrong (and its beliefs had no foundation) or outdated, as the prey had fled (and the agent simply has to update its beliefs in the light of new data).

(3) *The factual beliefs the agent has available are erroneous or insufficient.* This is not always easy to check. These beliefs often depend on a large number of percepts, data and laws of the world. If we want to verify the quality of these beliefs, we shall have to verify all these elements, which may prove onerous and perhaps pointless. In general, it is easier to call into question the beliefs with the most suspect origins, while reserving the option of revising quasi-certain beliefs as a last resort. Nevertheless, other agents can be a great help here, by allowing the agent to compare its beliefs with those of others, to help in localising the cause of the forecasting error.

(4) *The action does not correspond to its model.* Two cases may arise. This can come from a fault in the modelling of the action. We must then try to revise this model by testing the action in other circumstances. But it may also quite simply be a question of a lack of skill. If I fire an arrow at a target and I miss it, it is not so much the model of my action that is poor, but my lack of skill in archery. So it is no longer a question of revising the model, but of practising an exercise.

(5) *The laws of the universe or the psychological models of other agents are no longer adequate, or are proving insufficient.* One way of making sure is to test these laws and models, that is, to carry out experiments (even very elementary ones) to verify the validity of our laws. For example, if John has a theory which causes him to believe that all pieces of wood float, he may be very perplexed when faced with certain exotic types of log, such as ebony wood, which sink. He can then update his theory by adding exceptions to it or, better, try to understand that there are hidden principles behind this phenomenon, which underly this theory and which relate to the densities of bodies and to Archimedes's law. This is the field of computer learning – trying simultaneously to establish general rules on the basis of specific cases and to cause these laws to evolve when new contradictory examples arise. This work can also be the subject of interactions between teachers and pupils

and, more generally, of dialogues between agents. However, you must not think that it is very easy to update beliefs relating to the laws of the world or to psychological models. On the contrary, it can easily be seen that, in numerous domains where beliefs are in fact signs of gullibility, the testing of models and of conceptions of the world is not something that happens by itself. The history of ideas demonstrates all the difficulties encountered by scientists in relation to religious and magical ideologies when their methods and responses called into question deeply entrenched concepts and required a profound rethinking of models. 'And yet it moves,' said Galileo. His condemnation symbolises how much work it takes to remove erroneous concepts.

(6)   Finally, there exists one last case, which does not involve any cognitons – neither knowledge of the world nor factual beliefs are false, neither the data nor the percepts. But the causes of the forecasting error are located, quite simply, in the complexity of the situation, the fact that there are too many parameters, and the near-impossibility of forecasting the behaviour of the system. Meteorologists, who have to deal with chaotic phenomena, are very familiar with this. Beyond a certain period of time, any forecast is bound to be wrong. Only crystal balls can predict the distant future ...

Much work remains to be done in this domain to produce a general description of the belief revision strategies which can be put into place independently of the specific mechanisms that may be used to update one's knowledge.

5.4   What to believe? Contents of representations

But to what contents should these beliefs refer? To what do the knowledge and beliefs of an agent refer, and what data does it need to act and to carry out its tasks? Beliefs, which can be formalised by propositions, as we saw in the preceding section, represent the world, that is, they can be interpreted by referring these propositions to models. The power of a cognitive agent resides essentially in its representational faculty, that is, in its capacity to draw up models of the world (of the environment and of other agents) in which it is immersed, making it possible to understand, explain and predict events and the evolution of phenomena. So there are a large number of models. Some are more scientific, for they take a methodical approach to making the model adequate, attempting to verify the model, or more precisely to show that it is refutable, but simultaneously resistant to the various tests to which they can subject it. Others are more 'intrusive' and do not resist methodical interrogation in the least. Newton, Bohr, Einstein, Freud, Marx, Piaget, Darwin, Watson and Crick are famous for having developed models allowing us to go a little further in understanding physical, biological, psychological and social phenomena. These models have been transmitted to us through our culture and we now effectively 'believe' that the movement of physical bodies in space follows certain trajectories, that our psyche contains a certain number of unconscious elements which can be revealed by dreams, that our cognitive development takes place through successive constructions, that we and the apes are descended from common ancestors, and that our individual organic characteristics depend on a strand of DNA. All these models have been drawn up through historical processes involving a large number of people, some of whom have become famous by positioning the cornerstones of these conceptual edifices.

We use models in everyday life. A map, for example, is a model of the terrain, which allows us to find our position and determine our route. Likewise, a house plan is a model of the house, which allows developers to coordinate their actions to build the house. In other words, the cognitive power of a being resides essentially in the capacity to construct adequate (theoretical or practical) models in relation to the world, making it possible for the being to act and to anticipate the future (to some extent).

These models can be grouped into two categories: *factual models* and *provisional models*. The former relate to the beliefs an agent has on the present state of the world and on the characteristics of the agents (including itself), and the latter relate to the laws and theories making it possible to anticipate the future states of the world and the behaviour of agents (and of itself). These two categories of models can then be put through a variety of forms within the dimensions of analysis of an agent. Thus, we can distinguish factual beliefs relating to society, to the environment, to others and to oneself, and theories and laws relating to society, to the environment (what we referred to as the laws of the universe in Chapter 4), to others and to oneself – these last two categories introducing veritable *psychological models*, that is, representations of the modes of behaviour that agents may attribute to one another.

Beliefs relate to the structure, the state and the laws of evolution of the world, the state and the behaviour of agents. According to the definition of functional dimensions given in Chapter 3, these beliefs can be analysed in accordance with the four dimensions – environmental (χ), social (σ), relational (α) and personal (ω) (the physical dimension (ϕ) relating to the implementation of the other dimensions). An agent's factual beliefs are formed on the basis of cognitons arising from its perceptive system and its previous beliefs. Perceptions and information are the main source for the construction of factual beliefs. The former serve to update beliefs relating to the physical characteristics of objects and of the world, and the latter make it possible to have a representation of the world and of other agents, without needing to perceive them and to be close to them. These beliefs are then combined to produce new ones, based on the concepts and theories available to the agent and on its reasoning mechanisms. Provisional models are given by the designer, or arise from learning processes.

5.4.1   Environmental beliefs (χ)

Along the environmental dimension, beliefs relate to the state of the environment, the characteristics of objects and agents (considered therefore as objects, that is, we are interested only in their external characteristics, such as their position, their form or their colour) and, in a general manner, in the set of characteristics which could be observed.

In the pursuit example (cf. Chapter 1), the predators may have a belief regarding the position of the prey animals which they are pursuing, and on that of the other predators. These beliefs allow them to move in the right direction, even if they neither perceive the prey animals nor receive information concerning them. In the example of the explorer robots, designed using cognitive agents, these factual beliefs relate to the positions of the ore, the base and the driller and explorer robots, as well as, more generally, the state of the world at large. The beliefs of Clifford, the robot transporting objects, are relative to the place where the tools have been stored and, perhaps, to the topology of the locations within which it has to move. In a distributed process control system, the beliefs relate to the state of the process and the value of the control parameters. Obviously, these beliefs, by their nature, can be erroneous, and can lead to false interpretations and absurd decisions. For this reason, it is fundamental to associate them with revision mechanisms, which can take into account the natural evolution of these data.

It is along this dimension that the laws of the universe in which the agent is immersed may be represented. Should this be the case, the agent then has available true provisional models, since it can attempt to project itself forward in time and anticipate the future state of the world. For example, to intercept a ball, you have to anticipate its next position, on the basis of its present position and an internalised model of its movement.

5.4.2 Social beliefs (σ)

The social dimension relates to the role and the functions which have to be performed within a society and, more generally, to the organisation and structure of the agent's group. It is therefore a question of general knowledge, just like environmental knowledge. But with the difference, as against the latter, that these beliefs are not orientated towards the world and the environment of the agent, but towards the society to which the agent belongs. As we saw earlier, this dimension has been little explored as yet.

It is also on this plane that we can find all the standards, constraints and social laws applicable to all the members of an organisation. For example, the Highway Code is a social law, which indicates what a driver should do when he or she is in certain situations. If I am at a crossroads and the lights are green for me, I deduce from this that they are red for the other directions and that I can cross without any harm coming to me, assuming that the other drivers respect this prohibition.

5.4.3 Relational beliefs (α)

The relational dimension concerns the representation of others. So these are beliefs concerning the skills, intentions, commitments, plans, methods, activities, roles and behavioural models of the other agents. These representations should be considered as kinds of 'hidden memories' which contain data on the other agents, thus enabling agent *A* to have data on agents *B* or *C* without having to ask them, and thus to be able to draw up partial plans and to anticipate the future state of the system. We can therefore consider that these beliefs are means of attributing to other agents cognitive and intentional characteristics which they perhaps do not have, and to make heterogeneous agents with different structural, cognitive and behavioural characteristics cohabit.

Skills

Skill is certainly the relational belief which presents the greatest interest in a multi-agent system composed of communicating agents. It enables us to respond to the question: *who can do what?* and thus to indicate what an agent can do. This information is utilised to be able to delegate work without having to issue continuous appeals for tender. In effect, as we shall see in Chapter 7, the distribution of work between the agents, which constitutes one of the fundamental activities of organisations, makes frequent use of this type of information. For example, the following rule:

```
If an agent A has to carry out a task T
and if it does not know how to carry out T,
but if it knows an agent B
which has the skill to carry out T,
then A can ask B to carry out T
```

makes it possible to delegate tasks on the basis of knowledge of the skills of other agents, and so to arrange that the system does not go awry if an agent has to carry out a task which it does not know how to, or cannot, carry out itself. It is possible to represent skills in many ways, but the two classic representations used most frequently are: keywords, and predicates and objects.

Representation by keywords assumes that a skill vocabulary exists, and that each agent is associated with keywords corresponding to its skill. For example, in the case of the robots on Mars, the speciality of the agents could be represented by keywords such as `transport`, `extraction`, `prospecting`, `powerRelay`, and so on.

But this representation mode is not sufficient if we wish to describe skills more precisely. So a number of systems, like the MACE system (Gasser *et al.*, 1987), use predicates which may include reasoning. Thus, to say that an agent is capable of inserting a component into a device, we will use the predicate:

```
capableInsert(agent, component, device)
```

and to express the fact that an agent is a specialist in the symbolic integration of an algebraic expression, we will use the following description:

```
capableSymbolicIntegrate(agent, expression)
```

However, this type of representation is relatively limited, for it does not allow us to describe the links that exist between different skills. For example, symbolic integration is a form of symbolic computation, which possesses many of its general characteristics and, in particular, the faculty of manipulating symbolic expressions as reasoning and as results, in contrast to numerical systems, which supply exclusively numerical results. To be able to describe this type of information, we use representations by objects, in the belief that skills can be described by structured symbolic diagrams, such as semantic networks (Lehmann, 1992) or Frames systems (Masini *et al.*, 1989). For example, the skill relating to symbolic integration can be expressed in the form of the following hierarchy:

```
CapableAction
   ...
  CapableCompute
    CapableNumericalCompute
      ...
    CapableSymbolicCompute
      CapableSymbolicDerive
      CapableSymbolicIntegrate
      CapableSimplify
      CapableFactor
      CapableSolveEquation
        CapableSolveLinearEquation
        CapableSolveTrigoEquation
        ...
```

We then assume that if an agent has the skill to 'solve linear equations', it also has the skill to solve equations, and so to carry out formal computation. This does not mean that it knows how to solve trigonometric equations, but that, *a priori*, it has general qualities enabling it to carry out certain computations; it seems competent to solve general equations, specifically linear equations, and possibly other types of equations. All these data can be used to delegate work to other agents and to diminish the number of messages during the task allocation phase (cf. Chapter 7).

Intentions and commitments

Intentions and goals indicate what an agent has chosen to accomplish. This allows us to reply to the question *who is going to do what*? As we shall see later, for an agent, intentions lead to the production of commitments to itself. For this reason, it is enough to know the commitments that agents have undertaken to themselves and to others to have a good idea of their possibilities of action. For example, if we wish to arrange a meeting with someone and we know our schedule and the other person's schedule, it is easier to find a date which suits both parties.

Plans/Methods

This information enables us to answer the question 'What are the plans of another agent?' If an agent *A* knows the plans of an agent *B* it can take them into account in drawing up its own plans. We shall return to this concept in the context of distributed planning, which we shall be looking at in Chapter 8.

Activities

This information enables us to answer the question *who does what*? It allows agents to have an idea of their contacts' workload, and to take it into account when they are trying to delegate work.

Roles

This indication refers back to the set of activities which an agent is assumed to know how to carry out within an organisation under consideration. As we saw in Chapter 3, the organisational structures are defined, in particular, by roles which translate the different functions which the agents must know how to perform within a specific organisation. Knowledge of roles – for itself and for others – permits an agent to know to whom to turn if it has to respond to a problem.

Behavioural model

Behavioural models make it possible to predict the mental state and the future behaviours of other agents, on the basis of a kind of folk psychology of other agents. These theories are based on what is called *attribution of intentionality*. For example, we can interpret the behaviour of a situated agent as if we were dealing with an intentional cognitive agent, and thus attribute mental states to it which it does not necessarily experience (Dennett, 1987). This problem refers back to that of intentionality as we set it out above.

5.4.4   **Personal beliefs (ω)**

Personal factual beliefs are types of relational beliefs which the agent has concerning itself; and they therefore include all the types referred to above. The essential difference lies in the fact that these beliefs can be made permanently true, and so behave like learning (in the sense the term is used in the theory of beliefs and learning). In fact, it is sufficient to arrange for these beliefs to engage directly with the other internal systems and to be automatically updated when skills, intentions, commitments, beliefs, and so on are modified.

It can therefore be said that an agent represents itself as if it were another: it objectivises itself. In this manner, all the representations defined in the relational dimension for the other agents can be made explicit within the agent itself and combined with other beliefs to produce reasoning.

5.5 The conative system

How does an agent decide to act as it does? What makes it carry out certain actions and not others? What are the causes of its action? What are the dynamisms of the mental activity which push agents to action? What are the motors, the mechanisms and the brakes affecting behaviour?

All these questions have been developed in numerous domains: whether we are dealing with philosophy, behavioural psychology, socio-psychology, psychoanalysis or ethology, the problem of internal and external causes of action has been debated and re-debated, and the numerous theories advanced bear witness both to the complexity of the subject and to the extent of our ignorance of the effective mechanisms which make an animal, and above all a human being, behave as they do. For this reason, while the propositions put forward are numerous, none of them enables us to take account of the extent of the problem. The creation of artificial agents raises this question once again, a question which is thousands of years old. It is not the aim of this book to recapitulate all the theories which may have been put forward on this subject, or even to summarise them – the propositions being so numerous, if we add the theories of animal behaviour to those concerned with human psychology.

Instead, we shall attempt to give a general model of the conative system, that is, of the assembly of structures and processes making it possible for both reactive and cognitive agents to act. This model can be considered as being general in this sense – that the ambition behind it is to integrate all the mental factors making it possible to design artificial entities capable of acting in an autonomous manner. Obviously, the conative system of a reactive agent will be cruder than that of a cognitive agent, but they will be designed in accordance with the same general plan. But before presenting this model in detail, we have to understand the context in which this model can be created and, in particular, how it is articulated in relation to the concepts of rational behaviour and autonomy.

5.5.1 Rationality and survival

Most theories relating to artificial intelligence assume the existence of a *rational agent*, that is, an agent whose actions are always the result of reasoned deliberation, and are of direct use in achieving the agent's goals. As Newell indicates, the principle of rationality consists of acting in such a way that 'if an agent knows that one of its actions enables it to achieve its goals, then it will select this action' (Newell, 1982). This theory of rationality has to be especially detailed in connection with multi-agent systems. Indeed, if rationality comes down simply to the internal coherence of the mechanisms brought into play by an agent so that it can achieve its objectives – which amounts to affirming that '*an agent which has goals behaves in such a way as to achieve its goals*' – any computer scientist will be forced to adhere to these principles, since this simply assumes that the designers of these agents are not completely mad, in that they are developing mechanisms which tend to respond to needs. But in that case all agents, whether they are cognitive or reactive, are rational, and this concept then ceases to be of interest, because it necessarily becomes universal.

But if we also postulate that rationality assumes both a reasoned development of, and a reasoned deliberation about, the goals which the agent consciously proposes to itself to achieve, which enable it, in particular, to explain and to justify its actions to anyone asking it to do so, then we arrive at a much stronger concept of rationality. We can say that an agent is rational if it adjusts its means to the ends which *it proposes to itself to achieve*, which can be summarised by saying that an agent which has the intention of doing P will do it if it has the skill for it:

```
intention(A,P) and canDo(A,P) ⇒ later(Execute(A,P))
```

We shall see (cf. Section 5.8) that Cohen and Levesque have developed their whole theoretical apparatus precisely in order to understand and formalise this principle of rationality, linked to the concept of intention and of the transition to the act.

If rationality underlies the work of a large community of researchers in both DAI and the cognitive sciences, the reactive school and, more specifically, the European and South American reactive school (I should say Franco-Chilean), which is sometimes called the second cybernetics (Dupuy, 1994), prefers to explain the behaviour of an agent on the basis of notions of autonomy and viability, following the work of von Foerster.

Etymologically, a system is referred to as *autonomous* (auto-nomos) if it is ruled by the laws which it has itself decreed. For H. Maturana and F. Varela, autonomy has a precise meaning. A system is autonomous if it is *autopoïetic*, that is, if it is made up of a set of components, whose transformations and interactions continuously reproduce the organisation of which they are the constituent parts (Maturana and Varela, 1980; Varela, 1989). In that case, the system defines an operational barrier between itself and its environment, between what remains unchanging in this permanent regeneration operation (the system) and what is transformed (the environment). Although we may find this definition completely captivating, and it is ideally adapted to the world of living organisms, it may be too restrictive in the case of multi-agent systems in which the agents are artificially designed, and whose individuality is given by the designer. For example, mobile robots can be autonomous, by reason of their independence as regards power and decision making; without this meaning they are autopoïetic.

To overcome this difficulty it is preferable, as F. Varela and P. Bourgine (1992) did, to consider autonomy on the basis of the concept of validity. A system is viable if the system's dynamics remain within a domain of tolerances. The behaviour of a viable agent therefore consists of determining a trajectory in the space of configurations which allow the agent to remain within its viability zone. If it leaves this zone – if, for example, it does not recharge itself with power before its minimum level is reached then it loses its autopoïetic capacities. It dies. An agent should therefore attempt to remain within this viability zone by nourishing itself, by fleeing (or attacking) predators, by avoiding accidents, and perhaps by carrying out the functional tasks for which it was designed, and all in an unknown and unpredictable environment. We shall see below that all the behavioural strategies which are brought into play for reactive agents tend towards this objective of viability – independently, therefore, of any hypothesis of rationality.

5.5.2   A model of the conative system

The conative system determines the action that the agent should undertake, on the basis of the data and knowledge available to it, in order to maintain a function, while preserving its structural integrity and its actions in such a way that the organisation of which it forms part also preserves its structural integrity. This problem is sometimes referred to in AI literature as the problem of *control* (Bachimont, 1992; Hayes-Roth and Collinot, 1993) or that of *action selection* (Tyrrell, 1993b). The key concepts of our model of the conative system are *tendencies*, *motivations* and *commands*, each having an associated cogniton.

In 1936, Albert Burloud (Burloud, 1936) developed a theory of psychological behaviour which took tendencies as its starting point. For him, a tendency was a dynamic form which determined an act, whether it managed it and fitted in with it or inspired and finalised it. By distinguishing between its physical and biological realisation, he placed the concept of a tendency at the centre of psychology and treated it as a scientific object. For our model, we shall take up Burloud's central idea that all behaviour is the fruit of a combination and an interaction of tendencies, which are the motors of mental activity and of the transition to the act. Moreover, as the motors of activity, all tendencies are the expression of a lack which the agent is seeking to reduce or, as the philosophers say, is like a spontaneous mental orientation of an individual towards an end.

For example, hunger is a lack of food, the desire for the other is expressed as a lack of the other, real or fantasised, fear is the anticipation of a lack of being, and so on. These lacks are not merely individual, but also inter-individual and social. When an agent cannot carry out a task which it has imposed on itself and it asks another to carry it out, then it transmits, through its request, a lack which the other will attempt to rectify. A satisfied agent, that is, an agent without a lack, is an inactive agent, even if this inaction is sometimes expressed by movement. For example, in the Manta system (cf. Chapter 7), the ants are sensitive to stimuli propagated by other agents which lack something. In particular, the larvae, when they are hungry, propagate stimuli which are considered as requests by the workers, which try to reduce the hunger of these larvae. These requests are combined with other internal and external motivations of the workers to constitute tendencies to act, which will bring about – after deliberation – an effective behaviour on the part of the ants tending to reduce these lacks of satisfaction. But an ant on which no claims are made and which has no internal motivation to act carries out an elementary behaviour which, in the case of the Manta system, consists of the ant's wandering about at random. More generally, satisfaction is translated by immobility, and lack of satisfaction leads to movement, directed towards a goal, imbalances in the homeostasis of the milieu or in the internal physiology of the agent being the internal motors of the actions of the agents. The source of the action therefore

> ### Definiton
>
> We shall consider tendencies as being the cognitons which impel or constrain an agent to act or which prevent it from acting.

resides in the lack of satisfaction of the agents and, in essence, finds its origin in individual or social imbalances[†].

Apart from the tendencies which impel an agent to act, there are also other tendencies which tend, by contrast, to limit the agent's action. For example, taboos and social norms tend to limit the repertoire of actions considered as acceptable. When a policeman indicates that a stationary car should remain immobile, its driver recognises this sign as an invitation not to act, and he therefore develops a tendency to stay where he is, which will be in opposition to the tendency to want to move off again. But this tendency, although restricting, can also be considered as resulting from a lack, or from the anticipation of a lack. If the driver moves off again, he risks being stopped by the policeman and receiving a fine, which will create a lack of freedom in him. In this case, the tendency not to move off again is obtained by a combination of a percept (the policeman's gesture) and a social norm (the interpretation of the gesture).

Tendencies themselves are the results of combinations of *motivations*, that is, more elementary cognitons (percepts, drives, standards, commitments, social and inter-personal requests) elaborated in the *motivational subsystem* of the conative system. Tendencies therefore become pivots of the conative system and of the transition to the act. For example, if an agent is hungry and finds food nearby, it will develop the tendency to take this food for itself. It is therefore the combination of an internal drive – hunger – and a perception – the sight of food – which provokes its desire and produces its tendency to act.

The form the resultant tendency will take then depends on its internal organisation. If we are talking about a reactive agent, this tendency will be expressed as a pair <hunger, value> where the value indicates the intensity of the hunger-type tendency and so the propensity to trigger the action(s) associated with the search for food. If we are dealing with a cognitive agent, this goal can be expressed in the form of a logical formula such as `Satisfied(a)`, where a is the agent that is hungry. In this case, this tendency is expressed as an initial goal or objective, that is, as the starting point and the criterion of satisfiability of the plans which agent a may draw up to achieve this objective.

[†]This theory should not be generalised too far to natural agents (animals, humans, etc.). It merely gives us a general perspective on the origins of action for both cognitive and reactive agents. The examples which are given here are intended to illustrate my words. They in no way constitute a human or animal psychological theory.

Depending on the beliefs, commitments, plans and constraints available to it, the *decisional subsystem* of the conative system evaluates these tendencies, selects those with the highest priorities and determines the means to be used to realise them. This decision making depends on the *personality* of the agents, as we shall see below, and leads to the definition of dynamic priorities between tendencies. The result of this deliberation takes the form of a set of decisions which are then transmitted to the organisational system for it to execute these decisions and carry out the corresponding actions and tasks. For a cognitive agent, in which the tendencies are expressed as goals, the decision making may give way to the drawing up of plans and to a breakdown of these goals into sub-goals.

Figure 5.9 shows the general structure of the conative system and its breakdown into two subsystems, motivational and decisional. We can see that the tendencies constitute the link between these two subsystems.

5.6 Motivations: sources of action

The reasons which push an agent into action constitute what we shall call *motivations*, which serve as the basic material for the constitution of tendencies. The hunger which impels an agent to find new energy resources or a request sent by another agent to ask it to help it are examples of motivations. These motivations are very numerous, and it would be difficult to give an exhaustive list of them. But by taking the four conceptual dimensions[†] of an agent described in Chapter 3 (personal,

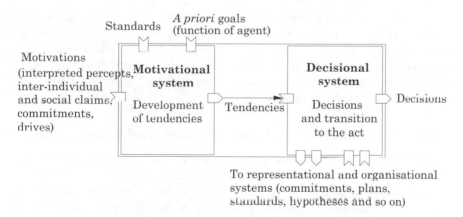

Figure 5.9 The conative system is made up of two subsystems: the motivational system, which develops tendencies on the basis of motivations, and the decisional system, which takes the decisions and undertakes the actions to be carried out.

[†]By definition, the physical dimension is neither conceptual nor directly the source of motivations. On the other hand, it is along this dimension that these motivations are realised.

environmental, social and relational), it is possible to group them into four categories: *personal motivations*, the object of which is the agent, and which tend towards the satisfaction of its needs or the discharging of the commitments it has imposed on itself, *environmental motivations*, produced by what the agent perceives, *social* or *deontic motivations*, which relate to claims expressed by the higher-level organisation and by the designer, and finally *relational motivations*, which depend on the tendencies of other agents.

One particularly active motivational source can be found in commitments. By promising to carry out an action for someone else or for itself, the agent undertakes to keep its promises, which become sources of motivation. Commitments therefore constitute basic elements for the creation of tendencies, on the same footing as hunger or sexual desire. These commitments are transmitted by the organisational system and developed by the motivational subsystem in the form of tendencies to act. The agent is free to follow its commitments or not, since the latter are expressed as tendencies, concerning which it is capable of deliberating. We shall call the set of motivations linked to commitments *contractual motivations*, and we shall find them in the personal, social and relational dimensions.

All these motivations are linked and they mutually reinforce one another. By virtue of hedonist principles, if an action does not allow an increase in satisfaction or the avoidance of adverse consequences, it will not be carried out. In a reciprocal manner, an action will be carried out only if it is in accord with the norms of the society in which the agent finds itself. So we see that the goals result from a set of motivations which have to find a compromise between the pleasure principle and that of duty, between what gives individual pleasure and what serves the organisation to which it belongs.

The relationship between drives and tendencies is more complex for more complicated agents. For a simple reactive agent, tendencies are the result of a combination of internal stimuli (which are called specific action potentials in ethology) and external stimuli or percepts. For more developed cognitive agents, processing mechanisms may intervene to combine the set of motivations together and produce 'high-level' tendencies.

5.6.1 Personal motivations: pleasure and constraints

Personal motivations simultaneously include those which tend to procure a certain pleasure for an agent, and which we call *hedonistic motivations*, and *personal contractual motivations*, which recall to the agent the commitments which it has made to itself and which allow the persistence of the objectives it has set itself.

Hedonist motivations are at the root of all living organisms: the search for satisfaction, for pleasure, or quite simply for a certain well-being, forms the basis for behaviour. For example, searching for food, making clothes and dwellings, or attempting to reproduce oneself, are behaviours linked with primary needs which are expressed in the form of drives: hunger, feelings of cold and discomfort, or sexual desire. We give the name 'drive' to any internal stimulus produced by the vegetative system, and from which the agent cannot remove itself. Moreover, failure to satisfy these drives may have unwelcome consequences for the agent and its descendants. For example, if the drives of hunger are not satisfied, the agent will fade away and die; if the drives of discomfort and security are not satisfied, the agent risks going downhill and being eliminated by bad weather and its predators; if sexual desires are not assuaged, it cannot be sure of leaving descendants behind.

So drives are associated with elementary needs, and are the mental representations of excitations stemming from the survival system and, more generally, from the agent's physical needs. They are transformed into tendencies (and into objectives for cognitive agents) on the basis of the perceptions and data the agent receives and the beliefs available to it. Drives are the basis for individual action, but they conflict, not only with contractual motivations, that is, with the agent's commitments, but also with each other, by reason of the fact that tendencies and the goals they engender are often contradictory. For example, for someone who pays attention to his appearance, wishing to be slim is a goal produced by the tendency to want to be desirable and to attract other people – feelings resulting from sexual drives. But these goals are in contradiction with the tendency to consume a good old-fashioned (and hyper-calorific) meal, which is produced by a drive for immediate taste gratification. The fact that it prefers to satisfy more or less long-term tendencies constitutes what we might call the agent's *'personality'*, and forms the object of the decisional subsystem. For example, a very 'determined' agent will be more likely to give preference to tendencies allowing long-term satisfactions to be obtained, whereas a 'weaker' agent will be more willing to satisfy tendencies allowing it to assuage its drives in the short term, even if the overall result proves to be less satisfactory.

As the basis for the behaviour of agents, drives form an area which has been the field of certain reflections on human action in psychology and anthropology. For example, the supporters of functionalism in anthropology and sociology propose that the structure of societies should be understood on the basis of elementary needs which must be satisfied (Malinowski, 1944). For them, the kinship system or the construction of shelters are cultural responses to elementary needs like reproduction or physical well-being. This theory frequently appears a little simplistic, but no doubt a rather more detailed kenetic analysis would make it possible to elaborate a more detailed theory; it would show how agents' actions modify responses to these elementary needs and produce emergent structures that modify the entire relationship between these needs and the social structures that result from them.

5.6.2   Environmental motivations: desire for an object

Percepts are, first of all, the essential motivations of reflex actions: by definition, a reflex is an immediate reaction to an external stimulus. The actions we saw in Chapter 4 are essentially implementations of relationships between perceptions and actions, without bringing in any intermediary explicit tendencies. In this case, the conative system is reduced simply to bringing the percepts into correspondence with

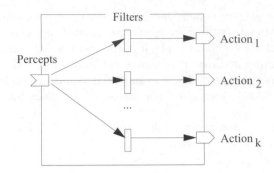

Figure 5.10 A conative system composed entirely of reflexes is restricted to linking percepts with actions. The filters select the percepts that concern them and trigger the associated actions.

the pre-programmed actions, as demonstrated in Figure 5.10, and the tendencies are merged with the percepts. The decisional subsystem is then limited to filtering percepts and triggering the associated actions.

But the importance of percepts cannot be limited to reflexes. They generally give assistance to other motivations and in particular to hedonist motivations, by reinforcing their intensity. For example, even if I am not very hungry, the presence of food may nevertheless trigger my appetite and my desire to ingest it. It is the presence of the visual and olfactory signs of food that actually triggers the desire for ingestion. So there is a reinforcement effect between the internal motivations of the individual, its drives, and the external stimuli it receives, the percepts. In ethology, since Lorenz we speak of *specific action potential* to designate the tendency to carry out an action. This specific action potential should be considered as a sort of level, which tends to trigger a fixed-action pattern. The latter, which we have called a task, is amplified, at one and the same time, by drives (specific endogenous excitations, in the terminology of ethologists) and the triggering environmental stimuli, the percepts. Figure 5.11 represents Lorenz's (1984) activation model, as he defined it himself, and as it can be redefined with the help of modern notations. The intensity of a tendency, that is, the propensity to carry out an action, is a (growing) function of the strength of the external stimuli (percepts) and of that of the internal stimuli (drives). The stronger the external stimuli, the less strong the internal stimuli need to be, and vice versa. The combination function is additive for Lorenz, but many models consider it to be multiplicatory. This motivational system forms the basis for most of the conative systems of reactive agents, as we shall see later on.

5.6.3 Social motivations: the weight of society

In deontic motivations, which are expressed in terms of the social dimension in the form of norms, we can distinguish between *functional claims* and *deontic rules*. Functional claims turn out to be the motors of most of the actions which are carried

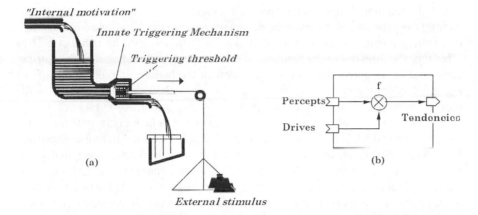

Figure 5.11   Lorenz's activation model in its original version (a) (drawing taken from Drogoul (1993)) and redefined with the assistance of systemic diagrams (b). The intensity of the tendency is a function of the strength of the external stimuli (the percepts) and of that of the internal stimuli (the drives).

out in connection with work. Why does the commercial traveller try to gain customers? Why does the judge pass sentence? Why is the librarian going to tidy the books? Why does the baker knead his or her dough? Why does the midwife help to bring children into the world? Why does the priest celebrate the mysteries of his or her religion? Quite simply, to fulfil their functions within society according to their social positions, and so to play their roles (professional or other) to the full and to carry out the set of tasks that are associated with them.

In the context of human societies, these motivations are linked to hedonistic causes, whether the advantages (or the adverse consequences) are immediate or far away. If we do not do our work, or if we do it badly, adverse consequences will follow: reduction in profits, loss of a job and of the means of subsistence, being looked down on by others, and so on. However, these functional motivations cannot be traced back entirely to hedonistic causes, for they take account of the needs of the society in which the agent finds itself. For example, although the tasks associated with sorting out the post in a business do not fill the person carrying them out with happiness, they are necessary for the proper functioning of the company and indirectly provide the person carrying them out with the means of subsistence.

In a multi-agent system, individual motivations are sometimes more restricted. For example, a database does not get any pleasure from giving information. It does this work entirely prompted by a functional motivation, because it has been designed expressly to carry out this type of task, the finality of its behaviour being located in the head of the designer. As this example shows, the functional mode operates entirely on the basis of goals which have been pre-set by the designer of the system or by the function which the agent has to fulfil within the organisation.

If functional motivations proceed essentially by responding to claims coming from the organisation (or the designer), deontic rules are linked to duty, that is, to the prohibitions and ideals which a society imposes on its members. They often take the form of laws or regulations, which specify what should be done or not done, and act as constraints that militate against the hedonistic motivations of the agent, by inhibiting actions before they are initiated (thou shalt not steal) or while they are in progress (stop at the red light).

Deontic reasons for an agent can be considered as hedonistic motivations for the society to which it belongs. For example, stopping at a red light is a constraint at the individual level, which can be justified by the social advantages that result from it, such as a reduction in the number of accidents. These norms can include the concept of sanctions, that is, the fact that performing a prohibited action may have unpleasant consequences. In this case, these norms are then reinforced by hedonistic reasons which lead the agent to avoid actions that might incur a penalty.

We have put deontic and functional reasons into the same class of motivation, because they are intrinsically connected. Both of them arise from social pressure which acts by commending or prohibiting certain actions. Duty is expressed as a path towards an objective coming from society, but also as a limit to the set of possible actions. Or better, it constitutes a model which transcends individual action. The reason for a sacrifice performed 'as a duty' cannot be found in the satisfaction of the agent, but actually lies in the set of idealised behaviours which are the mark of the developed moral values characterising a society (or a group of individuals) (Durkheim, 1897).

5.6.4 Relational motivations: reason is other people

We give the name *relational motivations* to motivations for which the motor of action is not within the agent but in the claims and influences coming from other agents.

For example, if an agent A asks an agent B to carry out an action P, the goal, for B, of carrying out P is a consequence of the request from A. B may do this for various reasons: because it cannot do otherwise (it does not know how to say no), because a concept of authority exists and A is its hierarchical superior, because B wants to please A, and so on. This is certainly the most important motivation in communicating multi-agent systems in which the agents cooperate by sending each other messages. As we shall see later, in the section dealing with intentions (cf. Section 5.8) and in Chapter 6, on communications, to communicate is to act. Communication is assimilated to an extension of individual action, and asking someone to do something is not really different from asking oneself to do something. The difference is essentially based on the dynamic character of the links which exist between the agents, and on the relationships existing between the agent making the request and the agent asked, the latter being able to refuse to respond to the requests of the former, even if it has all the qualities required to carry them out. The problem of intentionality, when there is interaction, is then based on the relationship which exists between the individual intentions of the agent making the request, the individual intentions of the respondents, and the relationships which connect them.

Conversely, receiving a request to carry out a service tends to provoke internal satisfaction, and thus a tendency to act. This action will consist of accepting or refusing the request (or even, perhaps, running away), but in all cases it will consist of responding to the original request. Relational motivations are therefore not foreign to deontic relationships. If agent A is subordinate to agent B, it will be obliged to do what B asks, owing to the social norms and constraints implied in the relation of subordination between A and B.

5.6.5   Commitments: relational and social motivations and constraints

Commitment constitutes one of the key concepts of collective action in the case of cognitive multi-agent systems. In making a commitment, an agent binds itself, through a promise or a 'contract', to carry out an action in the future, and thus to restrict the set of its future behaviours. For example, by agreeing to a meeting, one promises, firstly, to be at the appointed place at the time agreed for this meeting, but one also restricts one's use of time by not scheduling another meeting for the same time slot. So when a commitment is given, the promised action is 'programmed', and everything happens as if the behaviour of the agents could no longer be changed by anything.

In more general terms, commitment is a definition system for the social links through which a group stabilises its relationships to favour the organisation of actions. All human social systems are based on relatively complex commitment structures. Whether we are dealing with contracts, conventions, oaths or promises, whether we call this responsibility, fidelity or duty, whether they are discharged in the context of one's family, one's friends, one's professional relationships, or even the State as a whole, commitments are the basis of collective action. Through an entire network of tenuous dependencies, they construct a certain social organisation, from which even the societies that are apparently the most chaotic and the most violent cannot free themselves.

Commitment, in effect, is what makes it possible to reduce the degree of unpredictability in other people's actions, what makes it possible to anticipate the future, and so to plan one's own actions. For a commercial traveller for a company, for example, it is because he knows that his colleague will deal with a customer that he is free to go on to another deal.

Characteristics of commitments

An initial detailed analysis of commitment in the context of multi-agent systems was carried out by Alan Bond (1989), and to this we can add the work of Thierry Bouron (1992). Both define the characteristics common to commitments. We shall take up the results of their analyses and integrate them into our penta-dimensional definition of an agent.

Forms of commitments

The object of commitments is variable, for they apply to all the aspects of the social life of agents. Nevertheless, we can distinguish several scenarios, depending on whether the commitments relate to the carrying out of an action (I promise to pay you), the affirmation of a belief (I assure you it is true), the achievement of a goal (I do intend to go to Colombia this winter), social conventions (I agree to accept the internal regulations of this association) or a social role (I undertake to do everything in my power as Prime Minister). These different kinds of commitment can be classified in accordance with the object of their commitment and the systemic dimension in which the relationship between agents is carried on.

α   *Relational commitments.* This is the type of commitment most frequently studied in multi-agent systems. An agent makes a commitment to another, either to accomplish an action (or to try to achieve a goal, knowing that a goal can be defined as the condition of accomplishment of an action), or with regard to the validity of information. The commitment to carry out an action X made by an agent A to an agent B is expressed as a relationship of the pair <A,X> to B, which can be expressed as `commitDo(X,A,B)`. Likewise, when an agent A gives information to another agent, and if we assume that it is sincere, agent A makes a commitment to B regarding the validity of this information. In a similar way to the preceding case, we denote as `commitInfo(P,A,B)` the commitment by agent A to B with regard to the validity of the information P which, firstly, assumes that A believes P and, secondly, that its goal is that B should also believe P. Everything we subsequently say concerning commitments relating to tasks can be transposed, *mutatis mutandis*, to commitments relating to data transfers.

χ   *Environmental commitments.* These are commitments to resources. For example, ecological awareness is a form of environmental commitment, since it is a matter of carrying out actions which link us more directly, not to other people, but to our natural environment.

σ   *Commitments to the social group.* Two forms of commitment exist which are linked to the social group. The first consists in promising to carry out a task for the group. This type of commitment is similar to relational commitment, but with the difference that the commitment then relates to a group, and no longer to an agent. We shall denote as

   `commitDoGr(X,A,G)`

the fact that agent A undertakes to carry out action X for the group (or organisation) G. The second type relates to commitment to social conventions and to the acceptance of the constraints associated with a role in an organisation. Taking on responsibility in an association, or obtaining a job in a company, means making a commitment to the social group (the association, the company) to carry out all the tasks associated with this responsibility or this job. Let R be a role and G a group, the commitment to a role is formally defined like this:

```
commitRole(A,R)   ‾def
    ∀x ∈ Tasks(R),  commitDoGr(X,A,G)
```

φ   *Commitment of organisations to their members.* Although we can speak only in a metaphorical manner of the commitment of an agent to its physical components, the same does not apply to organisations which undertake to satisfy the needs of agents that are members of them. A company, for example, takes on a real commitment to pay its employees. So this type of commitment is the converse of the preceding type, since it is the group that takes on a commitment to its members: it can be formally expressed like this:

```
memberOf(A,G)  =def
    ∀x ∈ obligations(G),  commitDoOrg(X,G,A)
```

where `commitDoOrg(X,G,A)` indicates that an organisation G is undertaking a commitment to agent A to carry out task X.

ω   *Commitments to oneself.* In the same way that a commitment can be made to others, an agent can make a commitment to itself to carry out an action. For example, we individually commit ourselves to providing our bodies with the food they need. Likewise a 'good resolution' which one makes at the beginning of the year is a commitment to oneself. We shall denote as `commitDo(X,A,A)` the commitment made by agent A to itself to carry out action X.

Commitment as structuring of collective action

This is perhaps the principal characteristic of this concept. Commitments are not isolated, but form a dependency structure, which can be expressed like this: if A has made a commitment to B to carry out action X, B has perhaps also made a commitment to C for action Y, knowing that Y depends on X. This is what happens every day in the world of industry. The manufacture of a car, for example, depends on the satisfactory supply of the individual components, in other words, on actions carried out by sub-contractors and forwarders. The sub-contractors themselves have suppliers who have made commitments to supply them, on time, with the raw material they need. Certain tasks of B depend on A's commitment. If we write

   <B,Y> ← <A,X>

to indicate that there is a task Y of B's, which depends on the carrying out of X by A, this relationship forms a dependency diagram, as shown by Figure 5.12.

   This diagram shows the different forms of dependency between tasks. Certain tasks (for example, $<A,X_2>$) are dependent on other tasks carried out by the same agent (for example, $<A,X_1>$). A task can depend directly on several others, and we then speak of multiple dependency. For example, task Y_1 of B's depends on

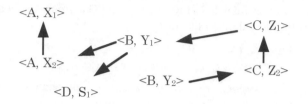

Figure 5.12   Diagram showing dependency between tasks.

the carrying out of task X_2 of A's and task S_1 of D's. We can see from the diagram that there are complex dependency mechanisms. For example, the carrying out of task Y_2 of B's is directly dependent on Z_2 of C's, and so indirectly dependent on Y_1 of B's.

This structure is interesting, for it shows that an agent can make commitments to itself. When A wishes to carry out X_2, it makes a commitment to carry out X1, which imposes on A the intention to carry out X1. In the same way, it is possible to introduce commitments concerning data into this dependency diagram, certain tasks depending on the validity of data and, conversely, data depending on the carrying out of certain tasks. For example, as we have seen for beliefs, going skiing depends on the validity of the information 'the level of snow is sufficient for skiing'. Another example is given by computation tasks characterised by the data they produce as results, on the basis of the data which are supplied to them as input. These output data are often the inputs for other tasks which depend on the original data supplied. For example, for an administrator, making a decision whether to invest or not depends on a set of parameters and, in particular, on the state of his or her accounts, obtained as a result of a computation task performed by his or her accountant.

Dependency diagrams can contain cycles; if they do, they cannot be executed. Tasks depending on one another are blocked by a deadlock, a problem well known in computer science relating to concurrent procedures. Only the correct diagrams, that is, dependency diagrams without cycles, can therefore be executed without blockages. The problem of deadlocks has been studied in great depth in relation to the creation of distributed systems.

Commitment as a motor of action

Commitment forms the basis of a large number of consequences for an agent. Undertaking a commitment to do something is making a promise to someone else that you are going to carry out a task; at the same time, it is making a commitment to yourself to do it – that is, if you are sincere, really having the intention to carry it out. We can denote this dependency between commitment and intention like this:

```
commitDo(X,A,B)  ⇒  commitDo(X,A,A) ∧
                     intention(A,X)
```

Likewise, the commitments between an agent and an organisation effectively bind the intentions of the agent.

$$\text{commitDoGr}(X,A,B) \;\Rightarrow\; \text{commitDo}(X,A,A) \;\wedge$$
$$\text{intention}(A,X)$$

So this means that there is a commitment to oneself which corresponds to any commitment to others.

Constraints on resources and coherence of commitments

Commitments impose constraints, not only on the intention of agents, but also on the resources used to accomplish their tasks. If an agent undertakes to carry out a task X which consumes resources, at the same time it limits the possibility, for the other agents and for itself, to carry out tasks using the same resources at the same time.

Owing to these constraints, certain commitments are contradictory. For example, making a commitment to go to the dentist on a particular date at a particular time and fixing a business meeting with a customer for the same date and time would be contradictory. As one of the purposes of commitments is to enable us to forecast and schedule the tasks to be carried out, it is sometimes possible to detect these local conflicts in advance before the situation materialises (cf. Chapter 8).

In multi-agent systems, we assume that cognitive agents are locally coherent in that they do not make contradictory commitments. Nevertheless, this does not mean that commitments are irrevocable. It is completely natural that an agent can go back on its decision, on condition that it informs the agents to which it is committed of this. For example, if you consider that the fact that you have to go to the dentist takes priority over the business meeting, you will try to reschedule it by informing the customer of this change to the agreement, which comes down to breaking the first commitment in order to make a second.

Validity and persistence of commitments

Commitments are persistent, that is, they endure until one of the following two conditions is met:

(1)   The object of the promise has been achieved.

(2)   The agent breaks the agreement to the commitment made.

The second case arises if the agent can no longer fulfil its commitment, either because it is no longer able to do so itself, or because it depends on other commitments and the agents it depends on have let it down. The possibility that a commitment can be broken forms part of the concept of commitment. For this reason, undertaking to do something also means committing yourself to warning others when the commitment can no longer be fulfilled.

```
commit(<A,X>,B)  ⇒ [eventually(¬canDo(A,X)
                    ⇒ inform(A,B,¬canDo(A,X))]
```

Likewise, when an agent A makes a commitment by giving valid information P to another agent, it simultaneously promises to let the other agent know if this information P ceases to be valid. We can express this characteristic formally like this:

```
commitDeed(<A,P>,B)  =def believe(A,P) ∧
    goal(A,[believe(B,P) ∧
        eventually(believe(A,¬P) ⇒ inform(A,B,¬P))]
```

Broken commitments can have a snowball effect and can lead to other cancellations. Setting up a fresh balance between commitments poses a complex problem of establishing a consensus within a system of distributed constraints.

Importance of commitments

It must be remembered that commitments are structures that are absolutely indispensable to teamwork in the case of cognitive agents capable of anticipating the future. They ensure a degree of stability for the world by giving agents a certain amount of confidence regarding the behaviour of other agents and a stable representation of the world. In fact, if agents did not make any commitments it would be impossible for them to have an adequate representation of a future state of the world and so to plan their own actions by anticipating the future. Without commitments, cognitive agents would find themselves in the position of reactive agents, which can take account only of the present situation.

The concept of commitment is, clearly, the indispensable correlation of the possibility of having cognitive agents which simultaneously have capacities for anticipation and a certain amount of free will in their decision-making power. Commitments often give rise to contracts between two agents, that is, a clear and precise definition, for each of the two parties, of the commitments they are undertaking. These contracts often result from a task allocation mechanism, as we shall see in Chapter 7.

5.7   Reactive undertaking of actions

The second part of an individual act is the decision and how it comes into play. This phase of the action, which is executed in what we have called the decisional subsystem, consists in determining, within the set of tendencies, those which are to pass from potential to act, and to give rise to the effective command for an action.

Several systems can be imagined. We can distinguish between those that take account only of the present state, by acting on the basis of information available to them in the here and now, and those that decide on action by projecting themselves into the future and evaluating the possible consequences of action, even if it means reappraising goals. We shall call the former *reactive undertaking of actions* and the latter *intentional* (or cognitive) *undertaking of actions*. We shall study the latter later, in Section 5.8, but for the moment let us devote our attention to the reactive undertaking of actions.

The concept of a reactive undertaking of an action is sometimes confused with that of reactive behaviour, the concepts of motivations and decision being intrinsically linked for these agents. Nevertheless, the problem of the undertaking of an action and of the organisation of actions into reactive systems is important enough for numerous researchers to have considered the question. It is often found in the literature under the term 'action selection problem'. The point is as follows. Having defined a repertoire of actions, how to implement these actions in a pertinent order according to the set of external and internal stimuli to which the agents are subjected? In the section dealing with environmental motivations, we saw how these two sorts of stimuli mutually reinforce each other to constitute tendencies to act. The action selection problem is incurred just after this. How can these tendencies be utilised to organise the behaviour of the agent? The literature on this subject proposes a large number of models, which are not without similarities with the models presented by ethologists. Moreover, in this domain, collaborations between computer scientists/robotics specialists and ethologists/physiologists, which have proved extremely fruitful, are becoming more and more frequent. It is enough to read the articles published following the conferences on 'Simulation of Adaptive Behavior: From Animals to Animats' (Meyer and Guillot, 1989; Meyer *et al.*, 1993; Meyer and Wilson, 1991) to be persuaded of this.

5.7.1   Consumatory acts and appetitive behaviours

Actions do not all have exactly the same impact on a reactive agent. A distinction is generally made between consumption actions and appetitive behaviours. The former are intended to discharge a tendency, whereas the latter are applied to the active phase of a goal-seeking behaviour. For example, in the case of taking food, if the consumatory act is `eat`, the appetitive behaviour will be `search for food`. Generally the consumatory act completes an appetitive behaviour, and this is why it is often called the *final action*. The interesting thing about this decision is that the appetitive phase can be produced in the absence of environmental stimuli, whereas consumatory acts depend entirely on the presence of the corresponding stimuli in the environment, which act as a kind of pre-conditions. Indeed, we cannot eat if there is no food, whereas we can go and search for food in its absence. Appetitive behaviours are therefore directed only by internal drives.

On the boundary between appetitive behaviours and consumatory acts are located the 'taxis' – that is, the behaviours which orientate and displace an animal

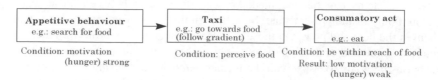

Figure 5.13 A typical task, or behavioural chain, having the goal of discharging an internal drive (for example, hunger) in a reactive agent.

so that it heads towards (or away from) a source of stimulation. When it is a question of approaching a goal, taxis often constitute the link between the appetitive behaviour and the final consumatory act. For example if, in the appetitive phase, the agent perceives food, it will head towards it by means of a taxis behaviour before finally consuming it. Taxis often make use of gradient-following mechanisms to achieve their goal (cf. Section 4.5). Figure 5.13 represents a typical behaviour for a reactive agent having the goal of discharging an internal drive. Each behavioural phase is conditioned by a triggering criterion. For the appetitive behaviour to take place, the agent must have a high level of drive. The taxi must effectively perceive the food and the consumatory act to be in a position to take this food. The result of such a behavioural chain leads to the diminution of the motivation that created it.

This type of behaviour is not merely the prerogative of animals, or of agents simulating animals (Meyer and Guillot, 1989). It forms the very basis of the behaviour of reactive agents.

For example, the explorer robots follow a pattern like this: an initial exploratory phase searching for ore, then an approach phase leading to the ore, and finally the consumatory phase, which leads the agent to pick up the ore and to return to base.

5.7.2 Action selection and control modes

The problem of decision making for a reactive agent, that is, of which action to select, can be stated in several ways:

(1)   What is to be done when several behavioural chains, like that which we have just seen, are in competition? For example, if the agent has to choose between eating, drinking or copulating.

(2)   What is to be done when the agent feels several different drives and receives a whole assembly of stimuli? In particular, what is to be done if, while it is looking for food, it perceives an attractive fellow creature with which it could mate?

(3)   Finally, how can attention be paid to the new environmental conditions, which are likely to call into question the agent's integrity or which prevent it from achieving its goal, such as the presence of a predator or an obstacle?

In order to answer these questions, T. Tyrrell (1993b) and G. Werner (1994) defined a certain number of criteria which a 'good' action selection model should be able to guarantee, of which the following are the principal ones. A good model should:

(1)   Be sufficiently general to respond in the same manner to all problems posed, and so avoid *ad hoc* models.

(2)   Demonstrate a certain persistence in consumatory acts, to prevent the agent's endless fickleness; prevent it, for example, from taking a little food, then a little water, then a little food, and so on, thus expending more energy in going from one point to another than in satisfying itself. To avoid this problem, it is sufficient to give the external stimuli an intensity which depends on the distance between the agent and the object it desires.

(3)   Prioritise on the basis of motivations. The hungrier an agent is, the more it must have a tendency to trigger a chain of actions allowing it to assuage this hunger.

(4)   Prefer consumatory actions to appetitive actions. It is not worth going elsewhere to search for what is already to hand.

(5)   Prefer to carry out chains of actions, and avoid excessively temperamental behaviours in which an agent is continuously beginning a chain of actions and never manages to complete any of them.

(6)   Interrupt an action if a new situation puts the agent at risk (predator or danger) or if the action proves to be manifestly impossible to complete (obstacle).

(7)   Demonstrate a certain opportunism, and be able to carry out consumatory acts which are not necessarily linked to the current chain of actions.

(8)   Use all the data available to display the behaviour best suited to the situation. For example, the agent should avoid going towards a source of food if a predator is nearby.

(9)   Allow several actions to be carried out in parallel, such as fleeing while sending out a distress signal.

(10)   Be easy to expand, to allow the designer to add new actions and new chains of actions to its repertoire.

(11)   Evolve through learning, by perhaps modifying options of behaviour in a more appropriate manner in the light of experience.

Certain of these criteria may appear contradictory: to want an agent simultaneously to be capable of persisting in its actions and to demonstrate opportunism seems difficult to reconcile within the same system. But several models allow most of them to be satisfied to a degree.

Situated actions and potential fields

The first of these models is that of situated actions, which we studied in Chapter 4. It is made up of a set of rules which link an action to a situation. Although this model tends mainly to enhance the value of environmental conditions, it is possible to add parameters to it corresponding to internal states, and so to define the current situation as a pair

<environmental conditions, internal state>

The Able system of D. Connah and P. Wavish functions in this way (Wavish and Connah, 1990). It is flexible enough to be used for several agents operating together. It can handle relatively complex situations like that which consists, for a (simulated) sheepdog, in driving sheep into a pen (Wavish, 1992). Nevertheless, situated actions suffer from numerous drawbacks: it is difficult for them to display real perseverance (except when some mechanisms are programmed in an *ad hoc* manner, but then that puts an end to the system's capacity for expansion), and, if they are able to be very opportunistic, it is difficult for them to be able to take decisions based on weight. It is a very complicated matter to program an agent with the aid of situated actions to make it carry out several different tasks. For this reason, situated actions are not considered as good action selection models.

The use of potential fields, like those we examined in Chapter 4, can solve a certain number of problems. By taking account of the distance between the agent and the source of the stimuli, these fields give an agent a certain persistence in its consumatory activities. In addition, they allow it to take account of new data, to be opportunist, and to handle several actions in parallel. For example, in the Pengi system which we introduced in Chapter 4, the penguin can simultaneously escape from the bees and search for the diamonds, while picking up new diamonds which are in its path in a very opportunistic way.

To take account of internal motivations, we only need to consider that the intensity of a signal is multiplied by a factor depending on these motivations. Nevertheless, potential fields, as they are very much linked to the environment, cannot always deal with all the problems of selecting chains of actions, and it is sometimes necessary to introduce other mechanisms to carry on an effective behaviour, like those we shall look at later. However, they have numerous qualities which are interesting for the implementation of multiple dynamic behaviours; later we shall see them in association with other task selection systems.

Hierarchical models

Numerous models have been inspired by work in ethology to implement effective action selection models. The most frequently studied are based on a hierarchical approach to behaviour, in which high-level behaviours are broken down into low-level actions. The most famous of these models we owe to an eminent ethologist, the Nobel prize winner, N. Tinbergen (1951).

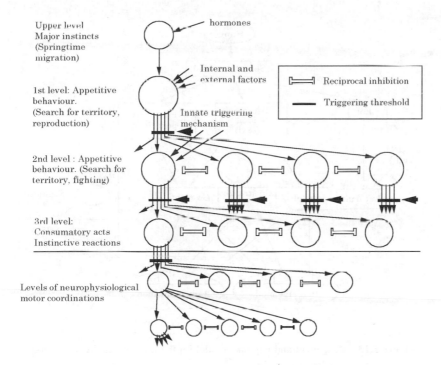

Upper level
Major instincts
(Springtime
migration)

hormones

1st level: Appetitive
behaviour.
(Search for territory,
reproduction)

Internal and
external factors

Reciprocal inhibition

Triggering threshold

Innate triggering
mechanism

2nd level : Appetitive
behaviour. (Search for
territory, fighting)

3rd level:
Consumatory acts
Instinctive reactions

Levels of neurophysiological
motor coordinations

Figure 5.14   N. Tinbergen's hierarchical system of instincts.

In this model, the organisation of behaviour takes the form of a hierarchy of nodes. To each of these nodes, which behave like types of formal neurons, is connected an innate triggering mechanism (ITM), a sort of pre-condition for the activation of the node. The nodes are triggered by the combination of stimuli coming from outside and the hierarchically superior nodes. When the total number of stimuli pertaining to the nodes exceeds a certain threshold, the node is 'released', and its activation energy is transmitted to the nodes on a lower level. The superior nodes correspond to general activities such as `reproduction` or `cleaning`, and the further one descends the more the nodes are involved with low-level actions, which go as far as relaxing muscles (Figure 5.14). Each node of a level is in conflict with the other nodes on the same level. If one of them is activated, then the others are inhibited.

This model is interesting for its pedagogical and explanatory aspects, but it was never designed for implementation in computing or robotics. At all events, hierarchical models, by giving too much importance to drives (internal stimuli), prevent opportunist reactions and make it practically impossible for a chain of actions to be interrupted. So in other words, the agent is 'concentrating' too hard on its goals, too 'deaf' to environmental stimuli.

This is why certain authors such as Rosenblatt and Payton (1989) and Tyrrell (1993b) put forward other models which are, at once, hierarchical in structure and

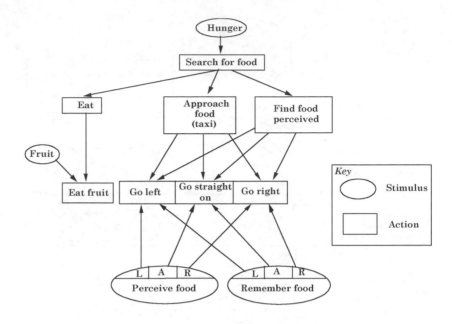

Figure 5.15   Rosenblatt and Payton's model for the task of searching for food.

non-hierarchical in decision making. These models are based on so-called free-flow hierarchies, in which the superior nodes do not decide which inferior nodes to activate, but simply define preferences regarding a set of candidates at a lower level. On the basis of the initial model from Rosenblatt and Payton, Tyrrell adapted it to give another, which he put into competition with other action models, which he tested in a world in which an agent has to carry out a certain number of tasks to survive, such as eating, drinking, escaping from predators and reproducing (Tyrrell, 1993a). Figure 5.15 shows the structure of such a model for the task of searching for food. We can see that the flow of activations descends from the upper levels to the lower levels, but without the latter being in opposition. It is only at the lower level that a selection mechanism selects the action with the highest activation value.

Even if we are dealing with a model which requires a very large amount of fine-tuning to ensure that appetitive behaviours do not end up totally dominating the consumatory actions, this model, according to Tyrrell, is the one that displays the best qualities, as against purely hierarchical models, or even ascending models like that of P. Maes.

Bottom-up models

Other authors, in complete opposition to hierarchical systems, attempt to find a route that makes use of the total elimination of any organisation in which any form of dominance can exist. This is the case, in particular, with the approach selected by P. Maes, with his ANA system (Maes, 1991, 1992) which stems simultaneously from neuron nets, from Minsky's multi agent approach, and from the model of competitive tasks. The ANA model is made up of a network of modules, each corresponding to an elementary action, such as `go towards food`, `drink water`, `flee creature`, and so on. Each action is described by its application conditions, its activation level, the links which it has established with its predecessors, its successors and the actions with which it finds itself in opposition:

```
Task go-towards-creature
   activation level: 56.3
   conditions: (creature-perceived)
   successors: fight
   predecessors: explore
   opposed: flee-creature
   code: code of commands to execute
```

The network for such a system is represented in Figure 5.16. The environmental stimuli and the internal motivations (fear, fatigue, aggression, hunger, thirst, curiosity) tend to activate certain actions by raising their activation level. The action with the highest activation level is selected, and its successors see their activation level slightly increased, which increases their chance of selection.

This system tends to separate appetitive actions from consummatory actions. The former are not connected with any internal stimuli, whereas the latter are. The successor links which exist between them are constituted and reinforced each time a consummatory act follows an appetitive action. Tyrrell tested the system of P. Maes in his simulated environment (Tyrrell, 1993a); and he observed that he did not obtain good performances when the network was very large. This phenomenon is essentially due to problems of selection between consummatory and appetitive actions, to the difficulty of taking proper account of multiple goals and, quite simply, to the plethora of choices between numerous candidate actions. So it would seem that a certain structure is necessary to ensure good action selection.

Nevertheless, taking up rather a neuronal technique, G. Werner (1994) puts forward an approach which, according to him, has all the advantages of Rosenblatt and Payton's method, without being based on a hierarchical approach, and which also makes it possible to carry out several actions independently. His model is actually based on a simple multiplicative combination of internal and external motivations, and so represents the motivational mechanism we saw earlier (Section 5.6.2). It comprises four sets of nodes: input nodes, which are connected to types of percept relative to the agent (`food-to-right`, `predator-ahead`, and so on) and to drives (hunger, thirst, and so on), output nodes which control elementary actions (`go-right`, `go-left`, etc.), nodes corresponding to a hidden layer (but one which is not used in the present examples) and, above all, a set of nodes, which represent what Werner calls commands and which actually resemble what we have called tendencies, that is, propensities to carry out one action rather than another.

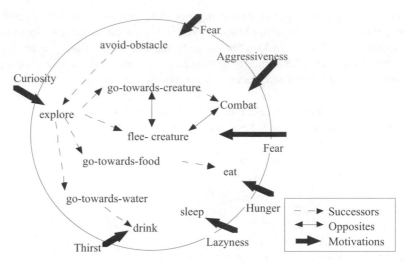

Figure 5.16 Activation network for tasks from the ANA system of P. Maes.

These commands are used as coefficients which intervene in a multiplicatory manner in the connections that link the input neurons to the output neurons (Figure 5.17). For this reason, the hungrier an agent is, the more it will have a tendency to head for food. Nevertheless, if there is water very close and it is a little thirsty, it will head for the water first if the product of the external stimulus coming from the presence of water and the drive of thirst is higher than the drive coming from the product of the stimulus from the food (which is situated further away) and the drive from the desire to obtain food. This shows that the agent's behaviour is simultaneously persevering (it does not change its views if the drive is sufficiently strong) and opportunist (if an external stimulus is sufficiently strong, it will try to respond to it).

Although the examples presented do indeed show that an agent can survive in an environment in which it has to find food, quench its thirst and escape from predators, G. Werner did not test his model in a sufficiently complex environment to know if his model can choose correctly between appetitive behaviours and consumatory acts, given that it looks as if the example he presents could be solved using taxis and consumatory acts alone. Nevertheless, it has the advantage of simplicity, and shows the importance of multiplicative factors in the combination of percepts and drives.

There is another ascending approach, that selected by A. Drogoul for the EMF model (Etho Modelling Framework) (Drogoul, 1993), which forms the base of the Manta system (Drogoul and Ferber, 1994) for simulating the activity of a nest of ants (cf. Chapter 7). Its problems are a little different from those of the other approaches, for it is one of the only two models introduced here (with the model from L. Steels presented in Section 5.7.3 below) which consider the agent, not in isolation, but socially, in interaction with other agents. In this model, founded on an

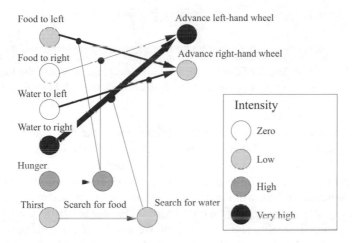

Figure 5.17 Werner's decisional system model for a reactive agent. The strength of the connections is indicated by the thickness of the arrows.

architecture based on competitive tasks (cf. Chapter 3), the emphasis was placed on its social adaptation capacities and, in particular, on its capacity for specialising an agent's skills over time. In contrast to other models, there is no difference in EMF between appetitive action, taxis and consumatory action, but there is a distinction of level between tasks and actions. An action here is a behavioural primitive, such as following a gradient, picking up an object or consuming food. A task is a set of such primitives carried out in sequence, following the pattern of a classic program. Nevertheless, a task can be stopped at any moment if the environmental conditions and the state of the agent make it necessary. Figure 5.18 presents a task composed of two primitive actions in the graphics language of the tasks editor of the Manta system.

As in other ascending systems, a task is triggered by a composite of internal and external stimuli. The special feature of the EMF model, as against other models, is that the system tends to specialise in the preferential triggering of certain tasks; in other words, the more frequently a task is triggered, the more chance it has of being triggered in the future. Figure 5.19 shows the control diagram for an EMF task. Internal and external stimuli are multiplied as in Werner's system, but the weight of the task also plays a part as a multiplicator effect to increase the sensitivity of the system to these types of stimuli. The comparator takes all the tasks, the level of activation of which exceeds a threshold S. The task selected then has its weight augmented by an increment.

In addition (though this is not shown in the diagram), a task which is being carried out has its weight reduced, in order to cause a 'fatigue' effect and to give the other tasks a chance to be selected. Quite apart from its adaptative characteristics for a set of agents, this model is particularly simple to put into practice and to use for programming other behaviours.

Figure 5.18   Graphic representation of composition of a food-taking task in the EMF model. The agent initially follows a stimulus gradient to the source of the food (taxis action) before consuming the food when it can do it directly.

Nevertheless, one of its major problems lies in the fact that it has difficulty in coming back to a task when it has been interrupted by the effect of opportunism. The agent 'forgets' what it was in the middle of doing. For example, if a hungry and thirsty agent is interrupted in its quest for food, it will not necessarily go back to this activity. What it will do, will depend entirely on the environmental factors and on its drives at the moment. This model shares this characteristic with most other systems, and it is notably similar to that of Werner, in that it combines drives and external stimuli in a multiplicative manner. But, as against this latter system, the tasks, which correspond to high-level behaviours (level 2 in Tinbergen's hierarchy), are chosen by a competitive selection mechanism. Because of its intrinsic qualities, it is a pity that Tyrrell has not been able to compare this model with that of P. Maes or Rosenblatt and Payton.

5.7.3   Action selection or dynamic combination

The mechanism of transition to an action by action selection, although shared by all the systems considered so far (apart from Werner's system), is considered very controversial by those who advocate the definition of dynamic systems. In fact, in competitive selection – often called the *winner takes all* strategy – the actions are necessarily incompatible with each other. When an action is selected, the others are *de facto* sent to sleep and it is impossible, not only to carry out two actions simultaneously, but also to execute a combination of these actions. Each of them is totally independent of the others.

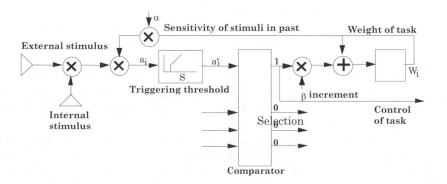

Figure 5.19   Diagram of control mechanism of a task in EMF.

In hierarchical systems, the order comes from the top, whereas in ascendant or distributed systems, the choice depends on the environmental conditions and the links the actions have set up between themselves. But in all cases, one action and one alone is selected at a given moment. For this reason, agents using this model cannot flee from a predator and go towards a food source at one and the same time. They do either one or the other, depending on the state they are in. Among the models looked at earlier, only the potential fields model and that of Werner are capable of combining actions, because they actually combine the tendencies which push them into acting. It was this limitation of competitive selection mechanisms that L. Steels was rebelling against by defining his dynamic system model (Steels, 1994) which we introduced in relation to architectures, in Chapter 3. This model can be illustrated by the diagram in Figure 5.20.

Primitive behaviours are functions (generally linear) of internal and external stimuli and of the implementer values (speed of left-hand or right-hand wheels, state of claw, etc.). The results of these functions are then added up, before being sent, as a command value, to the corresponding implementers. The formal definition of a command value y_j can thus be given by the following dynamic discrete equation:

$$y_i(t + 1) = \sum_{k=1}^{p} f k\, (x_1(t),...,x_n(t),\, y_1(t),...,\, y_m(t))$$

where the $x_i(t)$'s and the $y_j(t)$'s respectively give the value of the stimuli i and the implementers j over the time t. The interesting point about this approach is that we can combine behaviours defined in an independent manner and obtain a resulting behaviour which is the fruit of the composition of these behaviours. But the drawback of the L. Steels model, as we have said, is that it is still tied too closely to

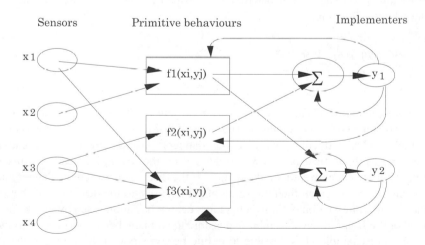

Figure 5.20   Model of a dynamic system of behaviour. The results of primitive behaviours are added up before commands are given to the implementers.

a defined material architecture. If you remove a sensor or if you add a wheel, these functions have to be given a completely new definition. There is no real modularity between the decisional levels defining the transition to an action and the levels of execution which bring these behaviours into play. In other words, it is the architecture that is responsible for the behaviour; strictly speaking, there is no behavioural model of an agent that is independent of its material organisation.

However, in certain cases it is possible to dispense with material representation, while still retaining the faculty of combining actions to define a behaviour. When actions can be expressed within a metric volume, which is often the case, it is possible to apply the laws of vector computation to them, and to combine behaviours as if we were dealing with vectors. For example, if the agent has to evade a predator and go searching for food at one and the same time, then it is possible to define three behaviours: going towards a goal, avoiding a danger by skirting around it, and fleeing if the danger becomes too grave (for example, if the predator is heading for the agent). To do this, it is sufficient to consider that the goals and dangers produce potential fields, that is, forces which are parallel to the gradients of these fields (Figure 5.21). Moreover, we can define the behaviour of skirting around as a displacement situated along a line of the same potential or, if you prefer, as a displacement perpendicular to the gradient (cf. Chapter 8).

These behaviours can then be combined to describe a whole set of behaviours, such as going towards food while skirting around a danger, but fleeing if the danger is too grave. This is the technique that K. Zeghal adopted in his `Craash` system for avoiding collisions between aircraft (Zeghal, 1993). Each plane considers the others as a potential danger. If two aircraft risk coming into collision, they attempt to avoid each other by skirting round each other, while still attempting to keep to their route trajectory, but if by chance the distance really does become too small, then they are free to flee from each other, even though this involves taking another direction. The overall behaviour, described by the vector $\vec{X}$, can then be defined by the equation:

$$\vec{X} = \frac{\alpha\vec{B} + \beta\vec{F} + \delta\vec{C}}{\alpha + \beta + \delta}$$

where the vectors, $\vec{B}$, $\vec{F}$ and $\vec{C}$ respectively represent the attraction towards a goal, flight, and skirting around a danger. The intensity of these vectors depends on the potential produced by the goals and the dangers. The parameters α, β and δ correspond to the critical factors which depend on the respective positions of the agent, the goal and, above all, on the danger. If the distance between the danger and the agent grows too great, then the value of β increases, to the detriment of that of α and δ. The combination of these behaviours cannot be summarised by the skirting around or the flight of agents, and it is possible to add new behaviours easily to the old ones. For example, it is possible to define behaviours of flocks (or patrols) in which agents try to form groups (cf. Chapter 8), which then superimpose themselves on the attraction, flight or skirting around behaviours. The advantage of this

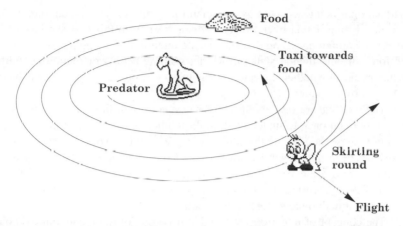

Figure 5.21   The behaviour of an agent can be given as the vector combination of elementary behaviours given in the form of vectors.

technique, by reason of its formalisation, is that we can define the behaviour of an agent in a totally abstract manner, without having to refer to specific sensors or implementers. In addition, the combination of these actions is totally modular, which makes the behaviour of an agent easy to expand. Finally, it is sufficient to use multiplicative techniques on the internal and external stimuli to benefit simultaneously from perseverance and opportunism. The vector combination of actions therefore *a priori* constitutes the best solution for the definition of reactive behaviours in the state of current knowledge.

5.8   Intentional undertaking of actions

After the reactive action modes, we can begin to study the concept of intention as it appears in work on DAI and in the cognitive sciences. The problem is both very simple and very difficult – how does an agent manage to do what it does in a more or less stable universe when the links it maintains with other agents can disappear at any moment? The response to this question, according to certain specialists in the cognitive sciences, lies in the intention, that is, in the conscious wish to carry out an act, in this mental disposition which pushes an agent to act in a certain manner by setting itself a goal for future actions.

We commonly explain what others do by assuming that they do it with a specific intention. Ambitions, desires, wishes and motivations thus serve to explain the behaviour of human beings. However, this is not necessarily a scientific attitude. In fact, explaining human behaviour by the concept of intention is often considered as popular psychology, that is, as a pseudo-theory made up of concepts and plans of reasoning which are used every day to explain the behaviour of the people around us, without their being accepted by the scientific community. For example, if Marie says to me 'I think Paula likes flowers', I can infer from this that she has a belief about Paula's preferences, and that she has the intention of giving her some flowers. I therefore attribute mental states to Marie, such as beliefs or intentions, without knowing precisely whether she actually has these mental states and if her behaviour is motivated by the latter.

The fact that we talk about popular psychology in this connection does not mean that the approach to understanding these phenomena is naïve in itself. Quite the contrary, these theories are the subject of a great deal of work, and several formal models have been put forward for a theory of the transition to the act by agents, whether we are dealing with human or artificial individuals (Pacherie, 1993). The key term of these theories lies in the concept of intention, that is, in what makes a cognitive agent undertake to carry out an action.

The concept of intention was (and still is) one of the most controversial in the history of psychology. Certain people – the eliminativists – purely and simply refuse to introduce this concept into their theories, claiming not only that it is useless, but also that it mindlessly confuses the issues. Others, in contrast, think of it as one of the essential concepts of psychology and that it should be given a central role, for it constitutes the keystone of the explanation of human behaviour in terms of mental states. Finally, the psycho-analytical school sees it as merely a vague concept which is handy in certain cases, but which should generally be replaced by desire and drives, which alone are capable of taking account of the overall behaviour of the human being in his or her aspirations and sufferings.

The concept of intention is not the only problem concerning the way cognitive agents come into play. In fact, although the philosophers of the eighteenth century considered decision making as a simple result of conflicts between weighted tendencies, with the strongest gaining an absolute victory and defining the action to be carried out, as for reactive agents, intention cannot be reduced to a simple conflict between tendencies arising from drives, demands and constraints. If the tendencies have their origin in the extremely simple elements of the agent's psyche, intentions assume a reasoned analysis of the present and future situation and of the possibilities for action. To a certain extent the cognitive agents are capable of predicting, the consequences of their choices, since they make decisions while keeping in mind the relationships of causality between events, that is, anticipating the future. It is this capacity to predict events that makes it possible to say that an 'intentional' agent is necessarily cognitive, since it bases its behaviour on a projection of future situations, that is, on a model of the world which it is capable of manipulating to evaluate the consequences of its acts and to choose the action to be undertaken. Moreover, this decision making is assumed to be 'rational', as we have indicated above, that is, subordinated to the objectives of the agent. It is, in fact, by means of conscious computation that the agent can compare final situations, that it can compute and compare the advantages corresponding to different situations and so draw up the balance sheet for the different possibilities opening up for it, so as always to select the solution that proves to be the 'best', with regard to the agent's goals and its options.

Several authors involved with AI and philosophy have suggested that the intention an agent has to carry out an act should be considered as one of the major characteristics of cognitive agents. DAI is not outdone, for intention is a very important concept for multi-agent systems, as it makes it possible to link goals with beliefs and commitments by having available a theory concerning the transition to an action of cognitive agents. Most theories concerning the concept of intention in connection with cognitive agents have emerged from the work on analytical philosophy first started by Searle (1985), Castañeda (1975) and, above all, Bratman (1987), and developed by researchers into artificial intelligence such as Allen and Perrault (1980) and especially Cohen and Levesque (1990a), who laid the foundations for a formal theory of intentional behaviours.

5.8.1 Logical theories of intention

A distinction is generally made between two types of intentions (Searle, 1985): the intention to act in the future and the intention to do something now. For example, if I say 'I intend to go to the West Indies this winter', the intention is directed towards the future (especially if the announcement is made in summer), and is the source of a behaviour, in particular of other intentions which I might formulate in order to achieve my initial goal: going to buy a plane ticket, obtaining information to help me find somewhere to stay (hotel, club, house to rent), and so on. The intention to do something now is relative to the immediate action. If I say 'I intend to pick up this apple', the action which follows from this must be carried out now, and does not imply any other secondary intentions, as it presides over the carrying out of my gesture.

In fact, these two types of intention do not coincide completely, and refer back to two different forms of intentionality. The first assumes a planning mechanism, whereas the second refers merely to the action execution mechanism. The first is the more interesting with regard to intentional agents, for it assumes a mechanism of anticipation and planning of future events characteristic of what are called intentional agents. This is all we are interested in, and we shall understand intention as being this mechanism of projecting into the future a state of the world not actually realised.

Intention lies within the framework formed by time, action and beliefs. An agent wishes to carry out an action, because it believes that what it is going to do will allow it to achieve a goal. For this reason, any theory of intention needs a good definition of an action, an event and a state of the world, and of how these events and states of the world are connected in time. Incidentally, this is generally the most complex part of theories of intention, and also what makes them most fragile, owing to the dual difficulty of manipulating temporal operators while taking account of all the aspects of the concept of action.

Bratman (1990) introduces what he considers to be the characteristics necessary to a theory of intentional action. In the first place, in order to come to fruition, intentions are at the origin of problems which agents have to solve. Intentions should also be coherent with each other, which implies that they should have inherent in them the admissibility of the adoption of other intentions. For example, if an agent intends to have a fried egg, and has only one egg, he or she cannot simultaneously intend to make an 'omelette'. Moreover, agents follow up the results of their actions, while remaining ready to replan their actions to fulfil their intentions. Finally, a distinction must be made between the results intentionally willed by an agent and those which are merely the involuntary consequences of the action.

Definiton

We say that an agent x has the intention of carrying out an action a which we denote as `intention(x,a)` if x has as its goal that a proposition P about a state of the world should be true (denoted `goal(x,P)`) and that the following conditions should be satisfied:

(1) x believes that P forms part of the consequences of a;

(2) x believes that P is not currently true;

(3) x believes that it is capable of doing a;

(4) x believes that a will be possible, and thus that P can be satisfied.

In addition, it is assumed that the intention will persist as long as the preceding conditions are verified, and that P forms part of x's goals, that is, that an agent will not abandon its intention 'for no reason'. For example, if an agent wants to go and fetch wood, and thinks the action is possible, that is, it thinks that a pile of wood exists, the location of which it knows, and that it knows a path which goes there, and knowing that it has the capacity to move, then it will have the intention of going there, this intention being at the root of its action of going to fetch wood.

However, this definition is based on the concept of 'believing an action is possible'. In the case of a static mono-agent universe, that is, one in which the only modifications of the state of the world depend on the agent, an action is *realisable* (or possible) if the conditions for carrying out this action are realisable at the present moment, or if a plan exists, that is, a series of actions that can be executed by the agent, which make it possible to verify the application conditions for the action the agent intends to carry out.

Let the world evolve, or let several agents be able to modify the world by their own actions, and it is not certain that the agent will actually be able to carry out its action fully. In that case, the conditions for realising an action are clearly less simple, for they are based on the possibility of anticipating how the world will evolve. For example, if I intend to go skiing, that means I think the necessary conditions are verified and, in particular, that there is snow. Now, if I intend to go skiing, not now but in a few months, that means I must be predicting that there will be snow at the right time, but nothing can ensure this situation for me. I may indeed think that going skiing in February at a ski resort in Savoie is possible (at any event, by default, or on a statistical basis). However, nothing can guarantee this possibility for me. If the season is particularly poor, the snow may not materialise on time.

The same applies in the case of multi agent universes in which the actions of others can modify the state of the world at any moment. To know if an action is possible, I have to take account, not only of my skills and the natural evolution of the world, but also of the actions, and above all the intentions, of other agents. For example, if the robot Clifford knows that the robot Charles intends to go and fetch a tool, it can take that into account in working out its own intentions, and can thus determine what to do using Charles's actions as if it were dealing with the result of its own actions, and assuming that the other will not abandon its actions in an unconsidered fashion.

For this reason, forming intentions is based on the regular elements of the world, that is, on the fact that the environment and the other agents *are committed* to the future actions they envisage carrying out. Any definition of intention in cognitive multi-agent systems is based on the possibility of planning joint actions involving multiple agents in an evolutionary universe.

Nevertheless, this definition poses a problem all the same. It says nothing about the fact that the agent which has the intention of carrying out the action has actually pursued this intention and is going to do everything in its power to realise this action. Having the intention to do something is also undertaking a commitment, to oneself at least, to try to carry it out. For this reason, formal theories concerning intention take the concept of commitment as a fundamental element in the transition to an action of a cognitive agent. The best-known work in this direction is that of Cohen and Levesque, together with Yoav Shoham's attempt at implementation.

5.8.2   Cohen and Levesque's theory of rational action

Philip Cohen and Hector Levesque defined a logic of rational action which has generated a lot of interest in the world of multi-agent universes, and which has led to a lot of research based on the formalism and the foundations of this theory. The details of this theory can be found in Cohen and Levesque (1990a, 1990b) with, in particular, the strictly formal definitions. We shall set out here only its most general characteristics, together with their consequences on the definition of intentional mechanisms.

The theory of Cohen and Levesque is particularly interesting for two reasons. It furnishes a uniform and practical notation to link concepts such as intentions, beliefs and action; above all, it puts forward a relatively integrated concept of rational action.

Notation

Cohen's and Levesque's formalism is based on a modal logic, that is, on a first order predicate system (with equality), augmented by a certain number of operators representing propositional attitudes or sequences of events. The two basic modalities of their logic are the belief and the goal. The first, `believe(x,p)`, means that agent x believes p, and the second, `goal(x,p)`, indicates that x's goal is that p should be achieved. Other predicates serve to manage the concept of action or, more precisely, that of event, for here action is considered simply as an event which makes it possible to satisfy a proposition. They therefore take no account of 'side effects' or of the consequences of actions. Nor do they consider problems of simultaneity, as shown in Chapter 4. These supplementary predicates are `agent(x,e)`, to signify that agent x is the only agent initiating the sequence of events e, e1 ≤ e2, which stipulates that e1 is a sequence of events preceding e2, and `happens(e)` and `done(e)`, which indicate that a sequence of events is just at the point of happening, or has just been completed.

In their formalism, no distinction is made between the concept of action and that of a sequence of events. Thus we shall speak of action or of events, without distinguishing between the two. These sequences can be structured with the help of operators similar to those from dynamic logic (Harel, 1979):

- a;b is the sequential composition of actions. This means that we first do a, then b, when a is completed.

- a|b is the non-determinist selection of actions. This means that we do either a or b.

- p? is an action which tests whether p is verified. If it is not verified, this action 'blocks' other actions, preventing the rest of the sequence from being carried out.

- a* is repetition. Action a is repeated infinitely, unless it is interrupted by a test failing to verify a certain property.

Starting from these basic operators, it is possible to construct more elaborate control structures in the following manner:

- if p then a if not b $=_{def}$ p?;a|¬p?;b, which means that the conditional is an action in which we carry out a as soon as p is verified and b as soon as p is false.

- while p do a $=_{def}$ (p?;a)* ¬p?, which means that a is repeated as long as p is true and that subsequently p is false.

- eventually(p) $=_{def}$ ∃e happens(e;p?) describes the operator eventually, which indicates that a sequence of action e exists, after which p will be true.

- always(p) $=_{def}$ ¬eventually(¬p) describes the operator always, which means that p is always true (literally, p will never be false).

- later(p) $=_{def}$ ¬p∧eventually(p), which means that p will be true later, that is, p is not true now, but will eventually be true.

- before(p,q) $=_{def}$ ∀c happens(c;q?) ⟹∃a(a≤c) ∧ happens(a;p?), that is, that p comes before q if when q is true p has been true previously.

It is also possible to introduce abbreviations such as

```
done(x,a)    =def completed(a) ∧ agent(x,a)
happens(x,a) =def agent(x,a) ∧ happens(a)
```

which makes it possible to represent the concept of action completed and accomplished by an agent a. The definition of all these operators is given by a modal axiomatics (in particular, the belief operator corresponds to an axiomatics, S5 – cf. Section 5.3.3) and by a semantics of possible worlds covering all belief operators, goals and constructions of sequences. On the basis of these definitions, it is possible to establish a whole set of consequences, such as this one:

```
eventually(q) ∧ before(p,q) ⇒ eventually(p)
```

that is, if q eventually is verified and if p is before q then p will necessarily be verified as well.

Intention and rational action

For Cohen and Levesque, the theory of rational action takes up Bratman's ideas, as we have summarised them above. Here, intention is conceived of as a choice and a commitment to one's choice. Their concept of a goal is rather specific. They do not use a formalisation of the intuitive concept of the word 'goal', but consider that the formula goal(x,p) means that p will be true in all possible worlds in which their goals will be achieved. They can thus dispense with the concept of a goal and consider only the consequences of goals.

Intention is therefore a kind of *persistent goal*, that is, a goal which an agent preserves as long as certain conditions remain in force. In their notation, a persistent goal is expressed as follows:

```
p-goal(x,p)  –def goal(x,later(p)) ∧
   believe(x,¬ p) ∧
   [before(believe(x,p) ∨ believe(x,always(¬p)),
   ¬goal(x,later(p))]
```

which is read as follows: we say that an agent x has a persistent goal p if it has the goal that p should be verified later, that it believes that p is not verified at the moment, and that it will abandon its goal if it believes that p is true, or if it believes that p can never be true. For this reason, persistent goals introduce the concept of commitment, although only implicitly. In effect, the agent will persist in its goal unless a specific condition is verified.

For this reason, if we suppose that one day agents will abandon their goals (they cannot remain engaged indefinitely and indefinitely attempt to achieve their goals), we can deduce from this that:

```
p-goal(x,p)  ⇒  eventually[believe(x,p)  ∨
believe(x,always(¬p))]
```

That is, if an agent has a persistent goal, it will eventually come to believe either that p is true or that p will never be true. On the basis of these initial definitions, Cohen and Levesque define the intention for an agent x to carry out an action a as a 'fanatical' commitment to accomplish the action a as soon as it can be performed (in effect, as soon as the agent believes that it can be performed), which can be written as follows:

```
fan-intention(x,a)  =def  p-goal(x,done(x,
   believe(x,happens(a))?  ;a))
```

This definition makes it possible to have an idea of the concept of intention, but it is too narrow. It concerns what Cohen and Levesque call 'fanatical' agents, which cannot cancel their goal once they have become committed to achieving it. An agent created with such a concept of intention will behave like those killer robots in science fiction films which cannot be stopped once they have received their orders, so becoming dangerous even for those who programmed them.

Cohen and Levesque therefore defined another type of goal, described as *relatively persistent*, that is, a persistent goal linked to a supplementary condition of satisfaction. The latter functions as a safeguard in the implementation of the action, what the authors consider as the *reasons* for an agent to carry out an action.

```
p-r-goal(x,p,q)  =def  goal(x,later(p))  ∧  believe(x,¬p)  ∧
   [before([believe(x,p)  ∨  believe(x,always(¬p))  ∨
   believe(x,¬q)],
     ¬goal(x,later(p))]
```

On the basis of this definition, it is possible to characterise a new concept of intention, relative to a condition q which is expressed as follows:

```
rel-intention(x,a,q)  =def
   p-r-goal(x,done(x,believe(x,
   happens(a))?;a),q)
```

In other words x intends to accomplish a, relative to condition q, and it has the persistent goal, relative to q, of accomplishing a as soon as it believes that this action can be carried out. These authors have also defined the concept of *vague intention*, or *abstract intention*. For example, the intention of 'becoming rich' is vague, because the agent does not necessarily have an immediate action available which will permit him or her to achieve this goal. The intention therefore relates to the satisfaction of a proposition and not to the implementation of an action. Having an intention in this sense therefore consists of believing that a sequence of action e' exists, such that it is subsequently possible to accomplish the action e which would satisfy p:

```
abs-intention(x,p)=def p-goal(x,∃e done(x,
                      [believe(x,∃e' happens(x,e';p?) ∧
                      ¬goal(x, happens(x,e;p?))]?;e;p?))
```

The theory in question

The most interesting thing about this theory is that it supplies a relatively simple and concise language and indicates that, on the basis of such a language, it is possible to define a theory of rational action which can be formalised and can thus provide the basis for a rigorous form of discussion. We can also see that numerous human or artificial situations can be translated into this form. For example, for a calculating agent which needs certain parameters, its intention consists of searching to find out whether an agent exists which possesses these parameters, as long as the initial problem has not been solved; this can be expressed like this:

```
rel-intention(Agent23,findParameters({p1,p2}),
  ¬found(problem1))
```

Several researchers have created multi-agent theories based on this formalism. For example, J. Galliers (1988) described a theory of cooperation actions using this technique and C. Castelfranchi and R. Conte created a theory of social intentions and influences (Castelfranchi and Conte, 1992; Conte *et al.*, 1991). However, this type of formalisation does display some loopholes:

(1)   Actions are considered as constructions of events, and not as operations applicable to the world. For this reason, this type of theory cannot take account of the modifications brought about by the actions of agents, and therefore proves inadequate for solving problems of planning (mono-agents or multi-agents) or, more generally, phenomena relating to interactions between agents. Nevertheless, with purely communicating agents, it is possible (and Cohen and Levesque (1990c) have done it) to introduce communications operators, and so to create an extension of their formalism in order to deal with interactions between agents. This extension makes use of the theory of language acts which we shall look at in Chapter 6.

(2)   It is difficult to prove such theories mechanically. Multiple modal operators, as well as the constructions of dynamic logic, do not make it easy to automate inference and permit a judgement to be made on the validity or invalidity of a formula. Everything has to be done 'by hand' by using semantic considerations regarding possible worlds, which is not very convenient.

(3)   Whatever Cohen and Levesque say on the matter, this is not in any way an operative description of the mechanisms brought into play for the undertaking of actions by a rational agent, but merely of the minimum conditions which must be satisfied before we can speak of intention in an agent.

For example, the concept of commitment exists only by default, and the undertaking of actions does not appear anywhere. One has the impression that the agent always has the desire to carry out the action, but one does not see when it accomplishes this action or if it accomplishes it explicitly. For this reason, an agent could be created based on the specifications of Cohen and Levesque – perhaps a little irrational, it must be admitted which would spend its time in having the goal of accomplishing actions without actually carrying them out. But it is not Cohen and Levesque who should be reproached for this, but rather the formalism, which does not permit taking into account the feasibility of the intention, and is therefore shown to be incapable of describing the undertaking of actions by an agent effectively.

In essence, this type of theory has the advantage that it clearly outlines some of the key concepts of intention. However, it has a tendency to be extremely simplistic with regard to the problems of action; in particular it does not take account of revisions of action or integrate the mechanisms for developing these intentions and the conflicts which can arise between motivations of various kinds and constraints. This theory assumes that a 1:1 relationship exists between the goals and the sequence of actions that can achieve the goals. It is caught out as soon as several methods exists of achieving the same objective – and yet this is most often the case.

For example, if a company wishes to publish a company news magazine, it can either try to publish it in house, using a micro-publishing system, or make use of the services of an outside publishing house. These two options achieve the same goal, although the means are different. Now, this type of theory says nothing about this decision making. It merely allows us, by explicitly encoding reasons for abandonment, to be able to call a goal into question if it is no longer suitable. For this reason, such theories of rational action should be expanded by considerations relating to the evaluation of goals and means, using techniques similar to those of games theory or decision theory.

It would be preferable to take account of the concept of intention on the basis of reactive mechanisms like those we examined in Section 5.7. This would make it possible to bridge the gap between reactive agents and cognitive agents, by showing that intentions, choices and commitments are the products of elementary mechanisms based on considerations of weights, thresholds and reinforcement. But this work has still to be done.

Any good theory of rational action should be able to integrate and coordinate, in a coherent manner, the concepts of goals, beliefs, decisions, undertaking of actions, commitments and communications, and the results of actions. In addition, it would be interesting if these theories could help in the creation of agents functioning on this principle.

The theory of Yoav Shoham, set out in his article on 'Agent Oriented Programming' (Shoham, 1993), corresponds to this objective by putting forward an 'agent-oriented' programming language, in the same way as there are 'object-oriented' languages. This involves considering that we program an agent with the help of high-level elements such as goals, choices, skills, beliefs, and so on, and that the types of message that agents exchange with each other also refer to high-level communication mechanisms in defining messages about data, requests, offers, promises, refusals, acceptances, and so on.

His language model is based on logics and semantics in terms of the theory of possible worlds. His two basic modalities are beliefs and commitment, represented respectively by `believe(x,p)`^{t} to say that agent x believes proposition p at time t and `commitment(x,y,a)`^{t} to mean that agent x has committed itself, at time t, to y, to carry out action a. All other modalities are derived from these two primitives. Choosing to carry out an action is defined as a commitment to oneself, and the capacity to carry out an action as the implication that the selection of p leads to p.

$$\texttt{choice}(x,p)^t =_{def} \texttt{commitment}(x,x,p)^t$$
$$\texttt{capable}(x,p)^t =_{def} \texttt{choice}(x,p)^t \Rightarrow p$$

On the basis of these initial concepts, he developed Agent0, a model of agents capable of carrying out actions, giving information to other agents and making claims on them. This architecture was extended and developed by Thomas (1994) to form the PLACA language for describing behaviours of cognitive agents. Although it is very interesting, since it represents an attempt to operationalise specifications of the type represented by that of Cohen and Levesque, this theory still remains a little simplistic, so demonstrating the difficulty of introducing a genuine 'agent-oriented' language and, more particularly, a theory of undertaking of actions for cognitive agents which could be operationalised. Other attempts to do this have been made. Let us mention, in particular, that by Chaib-Draa (1989), who developed, on the basis of the work of Cohen and Levesque (the work we have discussed here, plus their work on communication between agents based on language acts, which we shall be examining in the following chapter), a system allowing several agents to cooperate to solve relatively simple planning problems. Recently, a small number of researchers, grouped around H. Levesque, Y. Lespérance and R. Reiter, have taken up Y. Shoham's idea and have used personal bases to develop another, more complete logical approach to the programming of agents which directly describes the internal functioning of the agents (Lespérance *et al.*, 1995).

Rao and Georgeff (1992) formalised the idea of a cognitive agent by describing what are now called BDI architectures (Belief Desire Intention). A school grew up around this term, and since then all work relating to the creation of cognitive agents takes the form of variations on BDI architectures.

The current work by Wooldridge, in particular, is especially interesting, and reveals the current tendencies with regard to cognitive agents. It is no longer sufficient, on the one hand, to describe a logic, and on the other to create an architecture. It is now time to show that the designed architecture does effectively implement the specifications (Wooldridge, 1994).

Other logic theories have appeared linking intention and the creation of cognitive agents. We might refer, in particular, to the work of D. Sadek who, while starting from initial considerations similar to those of Cohen and Levesque, developed a theory of intention based on the predicates of beliefs, goals and uncertainties (an agent can be uncertain of the value of a proposition p). This work forms the basis for the current standardisation of FIPA on the communication language ACL (cf. Chapter 6) (Sadek, 1992).

Finally, we should mention M. Singh (1994), who has produced an authoritative work on the use of modal logics in the creation of rational agents.

Communications

6.1 Aspects of communication

In multi-agent systems, as for human beings, communication is the basis for interactions and social organisation. Without communication, the agent is merely an isolated individual, deaf and dumb to other agents, closed into its perception–deliberation–action loop. It is because agents communicate that they can cooperate, coordinate their actions, carry out tasks jointly and so become truly social beings. Communication is expressed as a form of interaction in which the dynamic relationship between agents is expressed through the intermediary of mediators, *signals*, which, once interpreted, will affect these agents. A large number of approaches to communication exist. Social sciences, and linguistics in particular, have developed a whole range of concepts which I shall be drawing on as I set out the main approaches to communication in multi-agent systems.

6.1.1 Signs, indices and signals

Communications are effected through signals, each signal characterising an index or a sign. Unlike ordinary language, in which these terms are almost synonymous (we say that a doctor diagnoses an illness through clinical signs or indices), linguistics and semiology, that is, the science of signs, make a very precise distinction between signs, indices and signals. A signal is the most primitive element. It can be defined as a mark, a trace, a modification of the environment on the mechanical plane (hearing, touching), the electro-magnetic plane (vision) or the chemical plane (olfactory or taste system), and may perhaps carry information for those capable of perceiving this signal. Signals are propagated by virtue of their own laws of propagation, and have no significance in their own right. To be significant, they have to fulfil two conditions: an agent with sufficient powers of perception to be sensitive to this signal (for example, as human beings we have hearing which is sensitive to atmospheric vibrations only within the passband from 30 to 16 000 Hz) and an interpretative system capable of converting this signal into a meaning, or, at the very least, into a behaviour. When this signal produces only a behaviour, we refer to it as a *stimulus*. This is the case for most animals and, as far as we are concerned, for all reactive agents. As we saw in Chapter 5, a signal, when it is received by such an agent, is capable of reinforcing a tendency. If the latter is sufficiently strong, the signal leads to an act. When the signal does not merely produce a behaviour but is inserted into a cognitive system, enabling it to render the signal intelligible, we say that the signal is a *carrier of meaning* and takes on the status of a sign. U. Eco (1988) defines the sign, above all, as *aliquid stat pro aliquo*, that is, something (a specific expression, a sound, a movement, a diagram, etc.) which refers back to something else (a situation, a physical object, an action, a procedure, another expression, etc.). The signals included in signs in themselves have nothing in common with the meaning they are intended to convey. We say, with Saussure, that linguistic signs are arbitrary, that is, that they are derived from a convention, and that their form is not linked to that to which they refer (Baylon and Mignot, 1991).

Several categories of signs exist. First, there are the linguistic signs which have arisen from a language, that is, a communication structure possessing, at one and the same time, an initial phonetic articulation, the sounds combining to form words, and a second, grammatical articulation, in which the words are assembled to construct phrases. Linguistic signs, which are the essential constituents of communications between cognitive agents, are associated with a significant form, which generally takes the form of a string of characters, a signifier, that is, a concept, an idea, the representation of something or of a mental state. But linguistic signs constitute only part of the universe of signs. Indices, in particular, form an important category of signs which are not constructed on the basis of a language endowed with a double articulation, but which refer back to the construction of hypotheses on a situation or a thing. For example, the tracks of animals are indices of their passage, the symptoms of an illness are the indices of an illness, smoke is the index of a fire. The cognitive process via which an agent passes from an index to a hypothesis is called *abduction*. It is characteristic of all investigative reasoning (we may think, in particular, of Sherlock Holmes, who could reconstruct the entire personality of an individual on the basis of a few indices) and of diagnosis.

6.1.2   Definition and models of communication

Many theories of communication exist, but they are essentially based on variations of the *theory of communication* which emerged from the telecommunications research of Shannon and Weaver in the 1940s (Shannon and Weaver, 1948). In this model, the act of communication consists of the sending of some information from a *sender* to a *receiver* (or *addressee*), this information being *encoded* with the help of a *language* and decoded upon arrival by the addressee. This information is sent via a *channel* (or *medium*), which may carry sound. The *context* is the situation in which the interlocutors are placed (this context can itself be broken down into the sender context and the addressee context). Figure 6.1 illustrates this model.

The initial model of this theory was very simplistic and totally bound up with technical matters, the problem then being to send data in such a way as to minimise any interference from the channel. Since then, this model has been improved a great deal by taking into account the mental states of the interlocutors, on the one hand, and the contents of the messages, on the other hand, by distinguishing between different communication situations and by classifying the functions performed by messages, as we shall see further on. The concept of communication has become structured in the meantime and, starting from the simple initial sending of information, we have moved on to more elaborate forms such as speech acts and conversational structures which place the emphasis on the concept of interaction in communications.

But communication is more than verbal exchanges. Indeed, this vision of communication as a sending/receiving process is not the only current theory. For researchers in the social sciences (ethnology, sociology and psychology) who have come together to form a school of thought referred to as the *Palo Alto school*, this concept is very much bound up with its technical origins. It relates essentially to conscious, voluntary, verbal communication, which is established between two human beings, and does not permit us to understand the fact of communication as a whole, that is, the set of significant interactions which is expressed between several beings. *Communication is then considered as a permanent social process integrating multiple modes of behaviour: words, gestures, looks, mimicry, interpersonal space, etc. Communication is an integrated whole* (Bateson *et al.*,

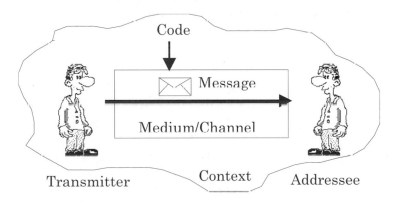

Figure 6.1   Classic model of theory of communication.

1981). In this case, messages no longer have any intrinsic significance: only the context is able to shed any light on the significance of modes of interaction.

Finally, in the context of the cognitive sciences, some call into question the classic model of communication defined on the basis of cognitivo-linguistic considerations, asserting that in this encoding/decoding mechanism, the code constitutes common knowledge background shared by the interlocutors. But does this common knowledge really exist in all cases? Is it really the same thing which is sent and interpreted? Isn't the code an illusion stemming from our naïve perception of forms of communication? Replying to all these responses in the negative, and placing the emphasis on the inferential mechanisms of interlocutors, Sperber and Wilson (Sperber and Wilson, 1986) put forward an outline of communication which is based on the interpretative aspect of communications: an utterance which has meaning is a pertinent utterance, that is, the 'minimal' utterance required for the sender to be understood, and thus to ensure that the addressee has as little difficulty as possible in understanding him. Each of the interlocutors sets up a set of hypotheses concerning the representations and objectives of the other. The speaker produces only the utterances that he considers necessary for the addressee to have an effective understanding of his communicational intentions. This concept of communication, which is still very little used in the world of distributed artificial intelligence, is nevertheless very interesting, for it is based entirely on inferential mechanisms and on the construction of models of the sender. Moreover, it assumes that the addressee has available a set of processing capacities which display close analogies with the various natural language comprehension systems developed by artificial intelligence (Sabah, 1989).

6.1.3 Communication categories

In spite of all the criticism it has attracted, the classic outline of communication has been considered sufficiently relevant by numerous linguists for them to integrate it into their own descriptions of speech acts by classifying ways of communicating with regard to the relationships which are expressed between the various agents involved in the act of communication. These relationships concern:

(1)   The sender–addressee link

(2)   The nature of the medium

(3)   The intention to communicate

Sender–addressee link

What is the relationship that binds the recipient of a communication to its sender? When the addressee is known to the sender, the latter can send him specific messages and so instigate individual communication. We then say that communications are effected in a *point-to-point* mode. It is this type of communication which is generally employed most frequently in cognitive agents.

We shall denote it as follows:

(id) <sender>: <addressee> << <utterance>

where <id> is the (optional) identifier of the message, <sender> is the agent sending the message, <addressee> is the agent to which the message is addressed and <utterance> corresponds to the contents of the message. For example, the following message:

(M1)   A : B << hello}

is a point-to-point communication which, for A, can be summarised as saying 'Hallo' to B. If the sender does not know the addressee, the message is sent, using a mode referred to as *broadcasting*, to an entire set of agents, the latter being linked to the sender by a relationship of proximity (nearness in the environment, connection through a network, and so on). This type of communication is frequently used in dynamic systems in which agents can appear or disappear. It is used, in particular, in task allocation protocols, like that for the contract net which we shall be talking about in Chapter 7. It will be noted that the addressee is replaced by the keyword All, or by the relationship of proximity linking the sender to the addressee. For example, the communication

(M2)   A : All << hello

consists of saying 'Hallo' to all the agents in the system, and

(M2')   A : {x | dist(A,X)} < d} << hello}

of broadcasting the same message to all agents for which the distance from A is less than a value d. In contrast to messages having an explicit addressee, broadcast messages are not necessarily the primitives of the system. They can actually be described by combinations of direct messages, provided an entity exists which is responsible for broadcasting. For example, the broadcast message

(M3)   A : {x | P(x)} << M

can be expressed as the combination of the following messages, M3' and M3'' :

(M3')   A : C << broadcast(M)
(M3'')   for all x of Receivers(C), C : x << M

where C is a broadcasting entity, a mediator, which merely assigns a message to all its receivers. For example, if a company decides to send out a mailing, it will turn to a company specialising in direct marketing, which will send its publicity message to all the people on its mailing list, with the specialised company now playing the role of the broadcasting entity.

Nature of the medium

The nature of the channel of communication also plays an important part in communication. We can distinguish between three sorts of message routing mechanisms: direct routing, routing by signal propagation, and public notice routing.

1.   *Direct routing* is the simplest mode: when an agent wants to send a message, the message is taken by the channel of communication, which carries the message directly to its addressee (or to all the potential addressees, in the case of a broadcast message), without the distance being taking into account (unless it is explicitly mentioned in the heading of a broadcast message) and without giving other agents the option of receiving it. The example in our daily life is that of postal or electronic mail. It is the type of routing which is most frequently practised by cognitive multi-agent systems.

2.   *Routing by signal propagation* is characteristic of the mode of communication of reactive agents. An agent sends a signal, which is broadcast into the environment, and whose intensity decreases as the distance increases. This decrease generally varies, either linearly or depending on the square of the distance. Thus at point x, the signal possesses one of the following $V(x)$ intensities:

$$V(x) = \frac{V(x_0)}{dist(x,x_0)} \qquad\qquad V(x) = \frac{V(x_0)}{dist(x,x_0)^2}$$

where x_0 corresponds to the source point of the signal. For this reason, the closer an agent is to the source, the stronger the signal will be. If this signal is considered as a stimulus, agents near the source will be more likely to take account of this signal than agents further away. This type of communication makes any direct communication difficult: any agent situated near the source can receive the signal and interpret it as it listens to it. To address a message to a specific addressee, supplementary data must be added. For example, in the real world, spoken communication calls for a whole set of supplementary indices (body posture, direction of look, prior call, etc.) for two people to be able to communicate directly and to arrange for a privileged channel of communication to be installed between the sender and the addressee.

The reduction in signals over time has a major impact on the organisation of a society of agents by defining the topological differences between agents. Spatial differences are then converted into social differences by the agents. If the agents are sensitive to the intensity of the signals, their behaviour will be affected by their respective positions in the environment. For example, let us assume that we have available a reactive multi-agent system, and that a stimulus S produced by a source at the point x_0, can trigger behaviour P in one of the two agents A and B. If A is nearer the source than B, since the intensity of the signal decreases as a function of

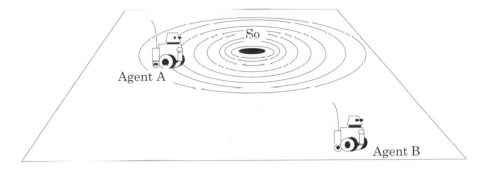

Figure 6.2 Agent A receives a stronger signal than does agent B.

distance, the level of the stimulus will be greater for A than for B, so that (all other things being equal) there will be a greater tendency for the behaviour P to be triggered in A than in B. In other words, we can say that the call of the stimulus is more urgent for A than for B (Figure 6.2). If a mechanism also exists tending to reinforce behaviours already triggered (for example, if the agents use a competitive tasks architecture with reinforcement – cf. Chapter 3), the simple fact that A is closer to a signal than B will produce a specialisation in the behaviours of the two agents. This is what is expressed by saying that *topological differences lead to social differences*. This characteristic is frequently used in reactive multi-agent systems as, simultaneously, a differentiation mechanism and a social regulation mechanism, as we shall see in Chapter 8.

3.   *The public notice routing* mode is less frequently used in multi-agent systems, though for no particular reason. It is typically the communication mechanism for 'small ads'. An agent, if it wants to communicate, places its message in a common space, called a noticeboard, a blackboard, or the ether (Kornfeld, 1979), which is visible to all agents (or all those in a specific class). This carrier mode combines the characteristics of direct messages (there is nothing to prevent an addressee's name being inserted in the heading) and those of direct messages.

However, it is very frequently used in architectures of the 'blackboard' type (cf. Chapter 3), where sources of knowledge are activated by events taking place on the blackboard, but it has not really been considered as a mechanism for routing communications between agents, except in the case of the Ether system (Kornfeld and Hewitt, 1980), where messages asking for solutions, hypotheses, proofs and refutations play an essential role in solving distributed problems.

The intention to communicate

Does the agent want to communicate or not? Is the action of communicating linked to an intention on the part of the sender, which in this way wants to obtain something from the addressee, or is it an incidental action, a process independent of the wishes of the sender? These two forms of communication, which exist in nature, can also be found in multi-agent systems. When two people converse, when a herbivore signals the appearance of a predator to the other members of its group, or when a person sends a letter to a third party, the communication can be described as intentional, in the sense that the sender resolutely decides to communicate something to its addressee(s). *Intentional communications* proceed from a choice. They express a wish, or, at the very least, a decision to act. *Incidental communications*, by contrast, are effected without the sender's taking any active part in them. Traces of scent or footprints, or body language of a human being – these are genuine messages for those who want to (or are able to) interpret them, but they are often communicated unconsciously by those sending them. These messages are epiphenomena arising from the presence of agents, or the state they are in, and can be utilised by those sensitive to them. We cannot speak of intention in this case. The herbivore has no particular desire to express its presence to a predator, but its scent, diffused into the atmosphere, or its footprints, are the result of its mere presence.

Incidental communications display two notable characteristics: their semantics is linked only to the state of the sender (without the sender necessarily being capable of controlling this communication), and their interpretation, which does not result from a code laid down in advance, is totally variable, and depends only on the addressee and on the meaning it gives it. In fact, although one can talk of the language of scents or of body language, the meanings of these signs refer back, in the last analysis, to the state of their originator, on the one hand, and the inferential capacities of the receiver, on the other. In this sense, incidental communications are entirely bound up with the interpretational inferences of the addressee (Sperber and Wilson, 1986). For this reason, these messages can be used by an animal to find others of its species, just as they can help a hunter to track it down. Although a semantics does exist (this sign refers to a state of the sender), there is no pragmatics intrinsic to the message (the sign can engender different behaviours in receivers). A clear differentiation can therefore be made between this type of message and intentional messages, the pragmatics of which can be analysed by the theory of *speech acts*, as we shall see later.

The intention to communicate is not a matter of all or nothing, but a graduated system which depends on the cognitive capacities of the sender. Studies of animal communications, in particular, have made it possible to discern the complex relationships existing between an individual's capacities of representation and the forms of communication it uses (Vauclair, 1992). J. Vauclair recalls that D. Dennett (1983) put forward a set of levels of intentionality, hierarchised in accordance with a scale of complexity which starts at 0 and goes up to a theoretical level n.

Intentionality of the order 0 describes situations in which the sender transmits a signal because it displays a certain internal state (for example, crying if it is hungry), or because it receives a specific stimulus (perception of a predator, for example), even if no receiver exists to receive this signal. The production of the signal is then based entirely on a stimulus/response relationship, and does not depend in any way on any deliberation on the part of the sender – which can be expressed by saying that:

> X sends message M because X perceives S

where S is a signal. In this case, we say that M is an *incidental message*. Intentionality of the order 1 assumes the existence of a direct desire on the part of the sender to obtain an effect from the recipient. For example, asking a question to obtain an actual response, or shouting to make an animal leave one's property, constitutes intentionalities of the order 1. We can express the relationship between the message and the intention in the following manner:

> X sends message M to Y because X wants Y to do P

Most so-called 'intentional' multi-agent communications are on this level. The higher levels deal with the beliefs produced by messages. In particular, order 2 supposes that the sender no longer directly wishes to obtain a response from the recipient, but wants to obtain a belief relating to a state of the world. Its logical form is as follows:

> X sends message M to Y because X wants Y to believe P

For example, an individual X may cry out, to make its assailant believe that it is going to attack. Order 3 can be described in the form:

> X sends M to Y because X wants Y to believe that Z believes P

where Z is a third party. The following forms can be traced back naturally to linked supplementary beliefs.

These different levels of intentionality are not external characteristics which can be determined by observation. In fact, if we see an agent X send a signal to Y and we observe a reaction of Y, we cannot infer any level of intentionality from this. It may quite simply be the case that X has an intentionality of the order of 0 and that Y is a reactive agent activated by the message from X, or that X has an intentionality of the order of 2 and that Y has reacted to the belief induced by the message from X. It is impossible to differentiate the two situations in a simple way. To be clear about it in our own minds, we need either to have access to the composition of X and Y and to know what their respective mental states are or to carry out complex experiments, as is done by animal cognition specialists (Vauclair, 1992).

Multi-agent systems do not generally include the entire range of possible communications. Table 6.1 shows the main language types, indicating their characteristics in terms of modes of communication, routing and intentionality.

Of course, it is possible to imagine other types of messages, such as point-to-point messages routed through propagation, but they are *a priori* of less interest, and are generally not implemented.

Table 6.1 Main modes of communication in multi-agent systems.

Types of message	Mode of communication	Routing	Intentionality
point-to-point symbolic message	point-to-point	Direct	Generally intentional
Broadcast symbolic message	General broadcasting	Direct	Generally intentional
Announcement	point-to-point/ general broadcasting	Noticeboard	Generally intentional
Signal	Broadcasting	Propagation	Incidental

6.1.4   What is communication for?

We have classified communications in relation to communication elements, and not in relation to what constitutes the essence of communication, that is, the function which it performs. According to Roman Jakobson (1963), who adopts a functionalist point of view of language, it is possible to classify modes of communication according to their functions. He distinguishes six of them: expressive, conative, denotative, phatic, poetic and metalinguistic functions. We shall divide this final group into paralinguistic and metaconceptual functions.

- The *expressive function* characterises the attitude of the sender of the message. It indicates the state this agent is in and what its intentions and goals are, and how it judges and sees things. In particular, this function makes it possible to synchronise agents, and so to coordinate their tasks, but also to make their beliefs common. This function can be summed up by the phrase: 'This is my state, this is what I think, these are my beliefs.'

- The *conative function* (from the Latin *conari*, to undertake, to try) refers back to the sender of the message, and corresponds to the concept of an order or a request which a sender addresses to an addressee. It should be pointed out that most of the messages in the crudest multi-agent systems perform this function. It can be summed up by one of the phrases: 'Do this' or 'Answer my question.' It is also associated with responses of acceptance and refusal. It is certainly the most obvious and the most important function in multi-agent systems. We shall study it in greater detail in the section reserved for the theory of speech acts.

- The *referential function* is centred on the context. This function is the guarantor for the sending of data relating to the facts of the world. A message which performs this function therefore relates to a state of the world or of a third party. 'Here's the way it is' is a phrase which characterises this function.

- The *phatic function* serves essentially to establish, prolong or interrupt a communication. It is used, in particular, to verify that the channel is functioning. The acknowledgment messages so popular in the protocols of distributed systems are essentially based on this function. It can be summarised by the expression: 'I wish to communicate with you, I am receiving your messages clearly.'

- The *poetic function* or aesthetic function is connected with the highlighting of the message itself. In multi-agent systems where the aesthetic aspect has not yet been tackled, the poetic function is not (or is scarcely) in evidence.

- The *metalinguistic function* relates to everything which concerns messages, language and the communication situation. This function is very important in multi-agent systems, for it allows messages to speak about other messages – about the communication situation – and also to harmonise the concepts, vocabulary and syntax employed by interlocutors. We shall distinguish between the *paralinguistic function*, which relates to messages which are going to be, or have just been, sent, and the *metaconceptual function*, which relates to the definition of a common linguistic and conceptual mould. The first relates to previous and subsequent communications by being concerned with the objectives of communication and the importance of messages. Phrases of the type 'Why are you asking me that?', 'I don't understand, can you be more precise?' and 'This is very important' are characteristic of this function. The second relates to the message code. Interlocutors are making sure that what has just been expressed has been properly understood and verifying the definition of the concepts employed. The latter is often the most complex objective to implement in multi-agent systems since it relates, in particular, to the development of joint concepts. We can summarise this function by the phrase 'by X I mean Y'.

A message performs several functions at one and the same time. In particular, every message has simultaneously an expressive and a phatic function. For example, a message taking the form:

(SM1) B : A << What are the X's such as P(x)

which performs a function which is quite clearly conative, also includes an expressive function, by indicating that the state of the sender B is that it wishes to know something. In addition, as for any message, a phatic function can be associated with it. In effect, by its very presence, SM1 indicates that B wishes to continue the dialogue. We shall use *principal function* for the function directly associated with the type of message utilised, and *secondary functions* for the other functions carried by this message. In the previous example, the principal function of M1 is conative, the expressive and phatic functions being secondary. On the other hand, a message taking the form

(SM2) `B : A << I think that P(c)`

is performing an essentially expressive function. Apart from the phatic function carried by any message, M2 performs a referential function, since we are talking about something (object C) to which we are attributing the property P. For example, a message taking the form

(M2.1) `B : A << I think that C is in position <x1,y1>`

is a possible example of the configuration of message SM2. It not only expresses the belief that B places in the positioning of C at `<x1,y1>`, but also the fact that C is *actually* in this position if B is not mistaken. There is also a secondary conative function, if we interpret this message as an attempt on the part of B to convince A to believe in the veracity of `P(C)`, that is, if it is interpreted by B as a message taking the form

(M2.2) `B : A << I wish to convince you that`
`C is actually in position <x1,y1>`

In this way, communication is expressed as a *cognitive contract* (Ghiglione, 1986) in which the sender assumes certain things to be known, and therefore puts forward some new data without recalling the old data. Grice (1975) issued some advice in the form of maxims on how to intervene in a conversation in the most concise and pertinent manner possible. For example, the quantity maxim lays down that a message should be as informative as possible, but not more than is necessary. The quality maxim states that only true information should be given, or at least information which the sender believes to be true. These maxims can be used in relation to multi-agent systems (Gleizes *et al.*, 1994), not as Grice understood the matter, to try to provide the best possible communication, but *a contrario*, as a point of departure for designing a communicational system. It will therefore be assumed that all agents communicate only information which they believe to be true (honesty postulate) and systematically reply to questions which are put to them (politeness postulate). The concept of a cognitive contract can be approximated to the concept of commitment which we saw in Chapter 5, and which relates to the fact that there is necessarily a joint substrate, so that two agents can communicate. This substrate is not necessarily fixed and laid down once and for all. Quite the contrary – current research into the social psychology of communication puts the emphasis on communication's faculty of producing and maintaining joint cognitive universes, that is, 'co-construction of references' (Ghiglione, 1989). Unfortunately, this concept of communication as a source for the construction of the cognitive model of the interlocutors, and of the language itself, sometimes seems a little too advanced for the technical resources available to us at the moment for the creation of multi-agent systems, as it assumes a certain plasticity of language – the possibility of playing on the polysemy of terms and on the connotations engendered by words and utterances – and poses the central problem of the symbol and its significance, a crucial problem which multi-agent systems cannot claim to be able to solve on their own.

6.2 Speech acts

There are theories which simultaneously seem to provide evidence for, and to constitute a major breakthrough with, previous concepts. This is particularly true for what we now call the pragmatics of discourse or, more simply, speech acts. This is a major language philosophy theory which is of great interest for the point-to-point analysis of symbolic communications in multi-agent systems.

6.2.1 To say is to do

When Austin's book *How To Do Things With Words* came out in 1962, it was something of a bombshell. For all linguists following the ideas of Ferdinand de Saussure, and for all language philosophers basing their views on logical positivism, studying language meant trying to understand the meaning of phrases by indicating how it was possible to use a combination of words to make a significant utterance. For theoreticians studying the semantics of language, that is, the study of the meaning of utterances, the important thing was to understand how a phrase could provide a satisfactory account of reality. For this purpose, they were essentially interested in knowing what degree of truth (or falsehood) there was in a *constative* phrase, that is, one that affirms something about the world. For this reason, theoreticians were interested only in the denotative function of language, that is, in the role of data transfer, and, by the same token, neglected the other aspects of communication, and in particular the conative function, which deals with the action on the addressee of the message. In this context, no one was really studying the question of finding out what language was for – or more precisely, as the title of Austin's book indicates, finding out whether things could be done with words. For Austin and his successors, the most important of whom is undoubtedly John Searle, enunciation – that is, the fact of producing an utterance – is an act which serves, above all, to produce effects on its addressee. When one says 'Pass me the salt' at table, one is not directly interested in the truth or falsehood of the phrase, but rather in the effect that this request can produce on one's interlocutor. More precisely, this phrase is neither true nor false, but it refers back to an action, which can succeed or fail. For this reason, the problem of truth loses its central place and leaves the field free for the criteria of success for the communication, that is, the pragmatics of communications.

But what is a speech act? Speech acts designate all intentional actions (in the operative sense of 'perform') carried out in the course of a communication. There are several types of speech acts. According to Searle (1979) and Vanderveken (1988), we can distinguish between the following main types of acts:

(1)   *Assertive* acts serve to give information on the world by asserting something (e.g. it's fine, John is 21 years old, rectangles have four right angles).

(2)   *Directive* acts are used to give directives to the addressee (e.g. give me your watch, wash your hands, what is the value of the third decimal point of π).

(3)   *Promissive* acts commit the locutor to performing certain acts in the future (e.g. I'll come to the meeting at five o'clock, I promise to send you some postcards).

(4)   *Expressive* acts serve to give the addressee indications of the mental state of the locutor (e.g. I'm happy, I'm sorry about yesterday, thank you).

(5)   *Declarative* acts perform an act by the mere fact of making the utterance (e.g. I declare the meeting open, I sentence you to two years' imprisonment, I curse you, I'm giving you the job).

Although it is of some practical interest, this classification is not always considered as being totally definitive. It still poses numerous problems, which are the subject of research in the domain of linguistic pragmatics (Récanati, 1981; Moeschler, 1989). In particular, how to classify conditional expressions (e.g. if you don't behave yourself, you won't get any pudding) or insults. Moreover, it is too general, and cannot be used just as it is for the creation of multi-agent systems. This is why we shall be obliged to put forward a more precise classification than the one above. This operation will be carried out in two stages. First we shall break down the directives into *interrogatives*, which serve to put a question in order to obtain information, and *exercitives*, which ask an agent to carry out an action in the world. Secondly, we shall refine our analysis by defining 'speech sub-acts', by specifying the object (or the action) to which the act relates and, above all, as we shall see further on, by characterising the conversational structure into which it is inserted.

6.2.2   Locutory, illocutory and perlocutory acts

Since Austin (1962) and, above all, Searle (1969), speech acts have been defined as complex structures made up of three components, considered as elementary acts:

- The *locutory* component concerns the material generation of utterances, by the emission of sound waves or by the writing of characters, that is, the mode of production of phrases with the help of a given grammar and lexicon.

- The *illocutory* component relates to the carrying out of the act, performed by the locutor on the addressee of the utterance. Illocutory acts, the most frequently studied acts in language pragmatics, are characterised by an illocutory force (examples: affirming, questioning, asking to do, promising, ordering, informing, etc.) and by a propositional content which is the object of the illocutory force. It is possible to represent these acts in the form

`F(P)`, where `F` is the illocutory force and `P` the propositional content. For example, to assert that *it is raining* will take the form

```
Assert(it is raining)
```

while the corresponding interrogation 'Is it raining?' will be represented like this:

```
Question(it is raining)
```

this expression indicating that a question is involved. Illocutory acts are often indicated by the presence of a verb, referred to as performative, which marks the type of act. For example, the phrase 'I ask you to come tomorrow' marks a directive illocutory act introduced by the performative `ask`. The *performative* concept is useful for multi-agent systems, since it is the performatives that will indicate the various types of speech acts that the agents can emit and interpret. For this reason, the utterances of the messages are expressed in the form

```
<performative>(<content>)
```

where `<performative>` is a keyword which designates the type of illocutory act associated with the message, and `<content>` is the propositional form.

● Finally, the *perlocutory* component relates to the effects that illocutory acts can have on the state of the addressee, and on his or her actions, beliefs and judgements. For example, convincing, inspiring, frightening, persuading, and so on are perlocutory acts. They are not introduced by performatives but should be understood as consequences of illocutory acts. For example, the phrase 'I affirm to you that the Earth rotates around the Sun' is an illocutory act of affirmation which can be taken, in a certain context of enunciation, as an attempt to convince the addressee that the Earth rotates, with the intention to modify all his or her beliefs. For instance, when John is asked to do something, the fact that he has understood that an exercitive is involved demonstrates that he has recognised the illocutory component of the act, and if John does in fact do what has been requested, then we can say that the perlocutory component has been satisfied.

All these acts are present in the same expression at different levels. This is why we can also speak of the locutory, illocutory and perlocutory aspects of expressions. When we discuss speech acts, we shall be implicitly referring to the totality of these three aspects, and not only to illocutory acts as Searle and a certain number of others do, even if they are one of the most important aspects.

6.2.3   Success and satisfaction

As we have seen, an utterance is not true or false, it succeeds or fails. For example, if agent A asks B to solve a differential equation, and B does not know how to do it, the request will fail. The same applies if B has not understood the request. In both cases, the speech act has not succeeded. Thus a speech act can fail to achieve its objective in several ways. It can do it:

(1)   *In the enunciation of the act*: because the message is not sent properly, because the locutor mumbles, because there is noise on the line or because the addressee does not understand the language used by the sender and the act will fail because it is not understood, or because the addressee will misunderstand.

(2)   *In the interpretation of the act*: the message is sent correctly and arrives at the right address, but the addressee does not interpret the sender's illocutory force correctly. For example, if, for the question:

     (M4) `A : B << Question(it is raining)`

the addressee, B, actually understands

     (M4') `A : B << Assert(it is raining)`

B will confuse a question and an assertion, which may lead him to produce a response which A will perhaps consider as bizarre:

     (M5) `B : A << Assert(I'll take my umbrella,`
                       `then)`

(3)   *In the actual fulfilment out of the act* brought about by the enunciation. The reasons for failure are legion. It is sufficient, for example, for one of the interlocutors not to have the skill to carry out this act. If A asks B to solve a problem involving differential equations and B does not know how to do it, this will constitute a failure. In general, a refusal by the addressee will cause any directive act to fail, that is, those that relate to a question or to a request to carry out an action. Likewise, promises are null and void if the senders are not capable of fulfilling their promises. The promise 'I'll give you your money back tomorrow' risks failure if the sender has not a penny in the world and has no way of giving this money back. Likewise, a prisoner who promises someone not in prison that he will come and see him tomorrow is extremely likely to fail to fulfil his promise if he is not released in the meantime.

Vanderveken (1988) proposes another classification with regard to the pragmatic aspect of speech acts by differentiating *success* from *satisfaction*. The conditions of success are those which must be fulfilled, in the context of an enunciation, for the sender to succeed in carrying out this act. A promise requires, as a condition of its success, that the locutor actually commits himself or herself to carry out the act corresponding to the promise. Likewise a declaration, such as 'I declare the meeting open' requires, as a condition of its success, that the locutor does have the authority allowing him or her to make this declaration. There is therefore success if the locutor carries out the illocutory act implicit in the statement. For example, as pointed out by C. Brassac (1992), the message

(M5) `A : B <<AskDo(P)`

is accomplished successfully and without error if:

(a)   the locutor A tries to make sure that his interlocutor B adjusts the world to the words (that is, the world should be in the state described by P)

(b)   with a certain position of authority

(c)   leaving B the option of refusing

(d)   B is capable of doing it, and

(e)   A locutor wants B to do it (desire is the psychological mode relating to the conditions of sincerity of directives).

On the other hand, the conditions of satisfaction relate to the perlocutory component, and take account of the state of the world resulting from this act. For this reason, the speech act associated with message M5 is satisfied if B carries out P. Likewise, a question is satisfied if the addressee responds to the question, an assertion if it is true, a promise if it is kept. The condition of satisfaction is stronger, since it takes account of the fulfilment of P. Satisfaction leads to success, but not vice versa.

6.2.4   Components of illocutory acts

To make it easier to understand illocutory acts, Searle (1969) describes the different types of speech acts through the set of conditions which he considers necessary and sufficient for their accomplishment:

(1)   Conditions of *departure and arrival* or of input/output. They relate to the fact that the message can arrive from the sender, who is not dumb, to the addressee, who is not deaf; clearly, a working channel of communication exists between the two interlocutors. In other words, the phatic function of the communication is provided for.

(2)   Conditions relating to the *propositional content*. Speech acts generally assume a specific structure for the syntax of the propositional contents which are associated with them. These conditions therefore relate to the grammatical and conceptual restrictions concerning the content of these propositions.

(3)   *Preparatory* conditions. They relate to what has to be true in the world for a locutor to be able to carry out a speech act. In the case of *exercitives*, that is, in the case of an utterance such as M5, these conditions are as follows:

  - B is capable of doing P
  - A believes that B is capable of doing P
  - Neither A nor B is certain that B will do P

It can be observed that these preparatory conditions are very similar to the logical definition of intention in Chapter 5. In effect, to communicate is to act, and there is nothing strange in the fact that the conditions for carrying out an intentional communication should be very similar to the conditions of execution of an intentional action. The essential difference stems from the presence here of two agents (to communicate, there must be at least two), whereas in the intentional action only a single agent was brought into play (one can act alone).

(4)   Conditions of *sincerity*. An act can succeed only if the locutor is sincere, that is, if the sender wishes to carry out what he is claiming to do in enunciating his phrase. In the case of a request for action, this means that A really wants B to carry out the action P. In the same way, if A makes a promise to B to do P, this means that he really has the wish to do P in the future. Finally, if we are dealing with an affirmation, A is assumed to believe in his assertion. These conditions, which are not always fulfilled by natural agents, are obvious for artificial agents.

(5)   *Essential* condition. This actually relates to what the locutor really wants to do when performing a speech act. If the locutor asks a question, it is because he wishes to obtain information. If he asks for something to be done, it is because he wants the action to be carried out. Rather than this essential condition, we prefer Vanderveken's concept of an illocutory goal, which corresponds to the main intention bringing about the performance of the act. According to him, there are five of these goals, corresponding to different types of speech acts: *assertive*, *promissive*, *directive*, *declarative* and *expressive* goals.

(6)   Vanderveken's *degree of power* (Vanderveken, 1988) corresponds to the intensity with which the act is carried out. For example, if we are dealing with an exercitive act, supplication is stronger than a simple request, for it assumes a stronger desire for accomplishment. Likewise, conjecture is weaker than assertion, which is itself weaker than a solemn assertion. However, we shall prefer, in what follows, to classify speech acts in relation to all these degrees of power, in a taxonomy relating to their role in communication configurations, rather than to characterise them by a simple numerical value, which is generally the mark of a superficial analysis.

Cohen and Perrault (1979) observed that all these conditions are not situated in the same plane – far from it. Whereas some of them relate to the locutory aspect of the message, others relate to the intentionality of the locutor, that is, to what the sender wishes to accomplish by sending a message. For example, the illocutory goal is directly relative to the sender's intention and the preparatory conditions to the knowledge that an agent has concerning another agent.

6.3   Conversations

The theory of speech acts, as developed by Austin, Searle, Vanderveken, Récanati and others, takes account only of the isolated act, the initial utterance, with its conditions of application, and the local effects which it can have on the interlocutors. It has absolutely no relevance to the sequence of interactions which is established between the interlocutors during their communications or to their reciprocal expectations. For example, an agent asking a question expects a response or a refusal; a promise subsequently leads to the fulfilment of the promise or to a failure to keep this promise by the locutor; and similarly an assertion leads to an acceptance such as 'I already knew that' or to a denial 'That's not possible'. In this way the concept of dialogue interaction is sometimes forgotten by speech acts. Nevertheless, one school of thought, essentially European, centred around Moeschler (1985) in Geneva and Trognon and Brassac (1988) in Nancy, has attempted to provide a theory of conversational linkages, based on an extension of the illocutory logic formalised by Searle and Venderveken (Searle and Vanderveken, 1985; Vanderveken, 1992). In this connection, speech acts are elementary units making it possible to analyse conversations. In particular, Brassac and Trognon demonstrated that it was possible to assign the illocutory force of a statement on the basis of future enunciations, and that the attribution of a speech act results from a process of co-interpretation of statements (Trognon and Brassac, 1992). This approach appears particularly fruitful in the context of human conversations, as it does not assume that there is, *a priori*, one possible interpretation of an utterance and one alone. On the contrary, a phrase acquires its meaning only through the set of reactions it excites in the interlocutors, the pragmatic significance, and thus the illocutory force, being reconstructed *a posteriori*. Nevertheless, this theory is still too advanced for the possibilities of multi-agent systems. We shall therefore put forward another extension of the theory of speech acts which is based on the definition of *communication protocols*, considering that any speech act assumes a certain possible linkage of enunciations, and that it engenders certain modifications in the mental state of the interlocutors. In fact, a speech act is practically never performed in isolation, and it is often the origin of other acts. For example, a promise such as 'I promise I'll come tomorrow' constitutes a commitment by the locutor to carry out a specific act, that of coming, at a specific time, tomorrow. Likewise, the request

(M5) A : B << Request(P)

is an act requesting an action, and is the origin of a whole series of subsequent actions: agreement or refusal by B to carry out P, perhaps the carrying out of the task P and the signalling of this to A. These consequences are important, for they lead to expectations on the part of the locutor. The latter, depending on the messages from B, may take measures concerning his or her own acts to be performed, and so will thus be able to anticipate the future. For example, if agent B agrees to do P, A may suppose that action P will be completed on date D + T, where D is the date when the action P begins and T is the normal time for carrying out P. For example, if A is the owner of a house, B a painter, and P the action of painting the lounge of A's house, the message M3, if it is accepted by B, may lead A to think that his lounge will have been repainted after a certain time. The definition of this time may itself be the subject of transactions or else refer to the normal performance time, that is, refer to a standard concept, shared by the interlocutors, of the normal characteristics of the task. An agent A who asks a question to an agent B that is, who sends a message taking the form

(M6) A : B << Question(what is the set {x | P(x)})

expects one of the following three reactions:

(1) The answer to the question:
     (M7) B : A << Answer(M6, a1,...an), where a1,...,an are the answers to the preceding question, that is, the values of x which satisfy P(x).
(2) A refusal to answer the question, perhaps accompanied by an explanation:
     (M7') B : A << RefuseIncompetentRequest(M6)
(3) A request for additional information (moving to the meta level, since it is necessary to speak of communication):

     (M7″) B : A << MetaQuestion(M6, Arguments(P))

The modelling of these conversations makes use, in particular, of the definition of *protocols*, that is, of valid sequences of messages. There are several ways of describing these protocols, but the most common use finite-state automata or Petri nets.

6.3.1 Conversations and finite-state automata

A conversation can be described as a series of states linked by transitions – communications which are exchanged by agents – and can be modelled in the form of a finite-state automaton (Winograd and Flores, 1986). Figure 6.3 shows the automaton corresponding to a conversation initiated by an exercitive.

Initially, the conversation is in state 1. Then A, by asking B to carry out an action P, initiates the conversation, which then passes into state 2. Several

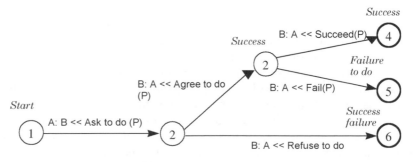

Figure 6.3 Automaton for description of a conversation starting with an exercitive.

possibilities then open up. B may accept, which commits it to A, or B may refuse (for example, considering it is not competent to carry out this action). It is also possible for B to move to the meta level by asking for additional information, but this is not taken into account in the diagram. Depending on B's answers, the conversation will pass into state 3 or 6, determining the possible sequences of communications. The conversation is considered as being completed when the automaton reaches one of the terminal states 4, 5 or 6.

On the basis of the observations of Winograd and Flores (1986) on the nature of conversations, it is possible to indicate the main properties that these communicational structures must possess:

(1)   Conversations begin by a major speech act (assertive, promissive, exercitive, interrogative, declarative and expressive) and are expressed as the result of an intention by an agent towards another agent.

(2)   At each stage of the conversation, there is a reduced set of possible actions. These actions are major or minor speech acts (examples: refusal, acceptance, and so on).

(3)   There are terminal states which determine the end of a conversation. When one of these states is reached, the conversation is considered as completed.

(4)   The performance of a speech act modifies not only the state of the discourse but also the state of the agents (beliefs, commitments, intentions) implied in the conversation. For example, when an agent B indicates that it cannot carry out an action P because it does not have the competence to do it, agent A can update its acquaintances by modifying the representation which it has of B. Likewise, when B undertakes to carry out P for A, it can add this promise to its list of commitments.

6.3.2   Conversations and Petri nets

Finite-state automata are of great practical value for specifying the structure of conversations when they appear in an isolated manner, that is, when a conversation can be summarised as a single process. However, agents are sometimes involved in several conversations simultaneously, and they have to manage these multiple conversations. It is then easier to describe the nature of these interactions by using the Petri nets introduced in Chapter 4. Moreover, the latter are very frequently used to model protocols in distributed systems (for example, Estraillier and Girault (1992)) and it comes as no surprise that they can be used to describe conversations between agents. This approach, which for the moment has not been developed very far in the context of multi-agent systems (except by Coria (1993) and Ferber and Magnin (1994)), none the less appears to show promise of a bright future.

Figure 6.4 shows a Petri net corresponding to the processing of an exercitive identical to that from the preceding section. Each agent is described by a Petri subnet, the positions in which correspond to the internal states of the agent (or of the task in hand, as we shall see later). The transitions correspond either to synchronisations due to the receipt of messages or to conditions of application of actions, such as the essential or preparatory conditions for the associated speech acts. Messages being routed are represented by supplementary locations which link agents A and B in such a way as to form a single net.

Locations DA and DB describe the initial states in which the agents find themselves before the beginning of the conversation, and locations FA1, FA2 and FB represent the end of conversation states. Starting from state DA, agent A sends a request to B and moves into state AR1, which represents waiting for a response. If B cannot do P, it sends a refusal to A, which then goes into state FA1, which indicates that A must look elsewhere to have P carried out. If B can do P, it sends an acceptance message to A, which again goes into a wait for a response state. During this time, B is in state BR, while trying to carry out the action P. If it can do it, it sends a notification of end of accomplishment, which places agent A in state FA2. If not, it indicates that it cannot do P. But in both cases it goes into the terminal state FB.

The interesting thing about this approach is that not only can we explain the exchanges between agents, we can also specify the internal states in which they find themselves, and so describe more precisely what is happening during a conversation. It will also be noted that all the characteristics linked with speech acts can be found here. For example, the states of success and of satisfaction of the initial request are illustrated in positions AR2 and FA2 respectively.

Petri nets even make it possible to model several simultaneous communications with several correspondents, using coloured Petri nets. In this case, it is no longer tokens that circulate in the locations and cross the transitions, but structures that represent conversations taking place. So that agents can orientate

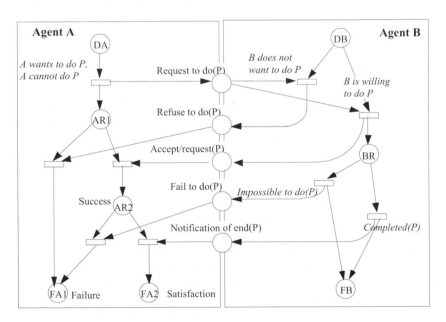

Figure 6.4 Modelling of a conversation using Petri nets.

themselves here, and not mix up the messages of several different conversations, each message is given a number in sequence, corresponding to the conversation to which it belongs. This is what we shall see in the following section, in which speech acts are modelled with the aid of BRIC.

6.3.3   A classification of speech acts for multi-agent conversational structures

It is difficult to give a general taxonomy for all speech acts which can be used by intentional agents, for several reasons. Firstly, the range of performatives required for the creation of a multi-agent system very clearly depends on the capacities of the agents themselves. If the latter are not capable of committing themselves, for example, promissives will be of no use. Secondly, it is not always easy to know if a specific act should be the subject of a new performative or if, on the contrary, the modalities in the propositional content should be used. For example, for an agent to be able to ask another agent to inform him or her each time he or she receives information relating to a given subject, is it necessary to define a new performative and send messages taking the form

(M20) A : B << RequestInformNewInformationOn(S)

or, in complete contrast, use a more general exercitive act and describe the action consisting of informing the other agent in the propositional content, even if this language may itself contain mentions of the performatives, in particular to describe conditional acts?

(M21) A : B << Request(if(info(x) & type(x,S)
             then Inform(A,x))

It is obvious that a choice in one direction or another will have a sizeable impact on the set of performatives, but also on the communication language used in the propositional form, and that these two 'languages' are complementary to one another. The bigger the set of performatives, the more the propositional content language can be simplified. Conversely, a reduced set of performatives will mean the description language has to cope with all the difficulties.

In spite of all these difficulties, we introduce here a classification of a set of speech acts intended for use in a multi-agent system. These types are defined by genus and species, that is, by classifying them hierarchically. On the most general level are the genera, that is, the principal acts defined by their generic characters. On the lower level are the sub-types corresponding to species, that is, to specialisations of these principal acts. Table 6.2 lists some elementary speech acts with their pragmatic categories and some examples of characteristic performatives. The sub-types are constructed by differentiation of this main type, through association with the object (or the action) to which the speech act refers. The performatives of the sub-types are obtained by concatenation of the performative of the type and the

Table 6.2 Some elementary speech acts.

Type of performative	Example of performative	Category
Request	`Request`	Exercitive
Interrogation	`Question`	Interrogative
Affirmation	`Assert`	Assertive
Offer of service	`OfferService`	Promissive
Indication of skills	`KnowHowDo`	Expressive
Proposition of hypothesis	`ProposeHypothesis`	Expressive

objects or the actions which specify the meaning of the act. For example, the performatives of the sub-types of *Request* will be formed by concatenating `Request` and additional reasoning such as `Request` for an action to be carried out, or `RequestSolve` to request a computation. This process will obviously be reiterated down to the desired level of detail. However, for reasons of simplification, certain performatives will be defined on the basis of shorter words which are easier to understand. For example, the performative `Advise` should in fact be written `InformRequestLetKnow` in accordance with our system of denomination.

We distinguish between two large groups of speech acts: *initiating* acts, which are at the origin of a conversation, and *response* acts, which intervene only in response to an initiating act. To these elementary acts we must add other types of more complex acts which are based on more developed conversational structures, such as the appeal for tenders or the different forms of collaboration, coordination of action and negotiation which we shall meet in the following chapters.

Elements of description of speech acts

Speech acts will be specified in two forms: a sheet summarises the data on the act, and a BRIC diagram describes the associated conversational structure. The sheets set out precisely the conditions of application of a speech act, from the point of view of the initiator of the act, and list the components of the illocutory acts, indicating the illocutory goal and the essential and preparatory conditions described by Searle and Vanderkeven, together with the conditions of success and satisfaction. They also include possible failures and their normal consequences. A sheet is made up of the following parts:

Format: describes the syntax of the message associated with the act. It takes the form `A : B <<F(P1,...Pn)`, where `A` is the sender agent, `B` the addressee, `F` is the performative indicating the speech act, and the `Pi`'s represent the reasoning of the performative representing the propositional content of the act.

Sub-acts: lists the set of variants of the act and their performatives.

Conditions: gives the conditions of realisation of the act, that is, its preparatory and essential conditions. They generally relate to the intentions and beliefs of the sender and to the skills of the two interlocutors.

Success: describes the normal consequences of the success of the act and the message which realises this condition.

Satisfaction: lists the post-conditions of satisfaction associated with the satisfaction of the act, as well as the message signalling the validity of this condition.

Failure: gives the 'normal' conditions of failure, that is, those entirely predictable if one of the conditions of realisation of the act is not satisfied. These failures, signalled by specific messages, generally have consequences on the beliefs of the sender and, in a general way, on his or her state. However, no mention is made of the request for explanation behaviours which are often associated with the causes of failures.

The conditions and consequences of these acts are specified with the assistance of basic predicates and cognitons. Here is a list of them:

Cognitons

`believe(A,P)`:   agent A believes the expression P. Beliefs are assumed to be reviewable. `believe(A,P)` in a predicative position means that agent A believes P, and in an action position that agent A is calling his or her beliefs into question in such a way as to believe henceforth that P is true, whatever may be the value of his or her previous belief regarding P.

`goal(A,P)`:   agent A has the goal that the condition P should be true.

`intention(A,P)`:   agent A has the intention of carrying out the action P.

`commit(A,B,P)`:   agent A is committed to do P for B.

`competent(A,P)`:   means that agent A is competent to carry out action P.

`believe(A,competent(B,P))` specifies that agent A believes that agent B is competent to carry out P.

Predicates

`compute(E)`:   represents the action of computing an expression, E. For example:

- `compute(2x+3 with x=5)` corresponds to the action of computing the expression $2x+3$ in which the value x is equal to 5;
- `compute({ x|descendants(LouisXIV,x} )` describes the action of computing all the descendants of Louis XIV;

`perceive(A,E)`:   indicates whether agent A perceives the object or situation E;

`exec(P)`:   indicates whether action P is executed or not;

`wantDo(A,P)`:   means agent A will be willing to do P in the future. This cogniton is equivalent to `eventually(intention(A,P))`, using the operator `eventually` introduced in Section 5.8, in the context of Cohen and Levesque's theory of intentions.

Exercitives

The exercitives essentially comprise two main speech acts: delegations (requests for action and requests for solutions) and subscription requests. These two speech acts are conversation initiators.

Delegation

Conversation associated with the act of delegation is, with the question, certainly the type of conversation most frequently used in multi-agent systems. Moreover, a model in Petri net terms has already been introduced (Figure 6.4). A request for action or for a solution to a problem is sent to an agent, which indicates whether or not it commits itself to carrying out this task. If it commits itself, then

(a)   either it subsequently sends back a notification of end of action, or the result, if solutions to problems are involved;

(b)   or it indicates that it has been impossible for it to fulfil its commitment, in spite of its promise.

In the corresponding BRIC diagram (Figure 6.5), it will be noted that the conditions of initiation of the act are not covered in this diagram, for they belong to the system of decision and task allocation of agent A, which selects the agent from which it wishes to request this service. Likewise, failures and satisfactions produce modifications in the mental state of an agent not described in this diagram.

Subscription

Subscriptions, or more precisely subscription requests, are a very important form of conversation, and unfortunately have not been studied in much detail in the work done on multi-agent systems. The principle behind them is simple: an agent A wishes to be informed when an event takes place, or to obtain all the information which an agent B may be able to acquire on a specific subject. For example, work involving exploration, monitoring or polling is based on this type of protocol, in which agents have the mission of referring back all data concerning information of this type. The subscription can be cyclical – A asks B to make a report systematically, at regular intervals – or event-linked (as soon as something new occurs). Figure 6.6 shows a conversation model for an event-linked subscription request. It can be observed that this type of conversation produces regular exchanges, until:

(a)   either the initiator of the conversation (agent A) sends an end of subscription

(b)   or the addressee (agent B) considers that it can no longer do its work, and stops sending the message.

Interrogatives

The interrogatives are used to ask questions, whose responses should not provide for a complex computation. The questions may relate to both the world – asking what an agent believes, or the mental state of the addressee – what are its goals, its commitments, its contacts, and so on. Figure 6.7 shows a model for an interrogative speech act.

Asking a question is relatively simple, since there is no possible commitment for the addressee: if A questions B, either B knows the answer, is willing to give it and gives it, or does not know it or refuses to respond.

Assertives

The assertives serve to give information on the world, and so to describe objects or situations. We can examine two levels of assertives: those where a message is sent upon request for information, and which are therefore subject to the logic of other speech acts, and those which attempt to make another agent share a belief. In the first case, success and satisfaction are linked. It is sufficient to respond to the request for the act to have succeeded – this is the case, for example, in the performative Respond, which is sent following a request for information. In the second case, on the other hand, the act is broken down into a data sending phase (which constitutes success) and a data acceptance phase (satisfaction), which proves that this information is compatible with the beliefs of the addressee. For example, a warning (e.g. there's a virus going round) leads to information being given without this resulting from a prior initiating act. This type of conversation, of which the performative Assert is characteristic (Figure 6.8), follows a quite simple protocol: A informs B, which accepts (Acquiesce) or expresses its disagreement (RefuseBelieve). In a more complex form, B could even refute what A says to it, and a dialogue could follow of the *argumentation* type, in which two agents are mutually trying to convince each other of the truth (or falseness) of an utterance. The works of J. Quinqueton, P. Reitz and J. Sallentin contain definitions of rational agents engaged in complex conversations relating, in particular, to argumentation (sequence of assertion, acceptance and refutations, or even silence) as a higher form of assertion (Quinqueton *et al.*, 1991).

In addition to the performative Assert, the assertives include the performative Inform, which is weaker than the preceding one, since it does not assume that an agent A which informs an agent B wishes B actually to believe the information it is sending to it.

Some other performatives

In addition to the main performatives which we have just seen, it is possible to define other performatives. Here are a few of them, which we shall simply list, without giving their detailed specifications:

Request: principal speech act consisting of requesting another agent to carry out a task: accomplish an action or solve a problem

Format: `A : B << Request(P)` with `P` a task

Sub-acts:

- `RequestSolve(P)` with `P` a problem

Conditions:

- `goal(A,C) ∧ believe(A,exec(P) ⇒ C) ∧`
  `believe(A,competent(B.P)) ∧`
  `believe(A,wantDo(A,P)) ∧`
  `[believe(A,¬competent(A,P)) ∨ ¬wantDo(A,P)]`
- `believe(A,¬eventually(C))`

Success:

- `B : A << Request(P) → commit(B, A, P)`

Satisfaction:

- `B : A << NotificationEndAction(P) →`
  `believe(A, C)` if `P` is an action
- `B : A << Result(P,R) → believe(A,R)` if `P` is a problem

Failures:

- `B : A << RefuseDo(P) → believe(A,¬competent(B,P)`
  `∨ ¬wantDo(B,P))`
- `A << FailureDo(P) →` ask for explanations

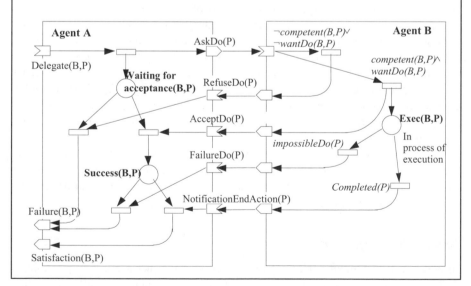

Figure 6.5 Conversational model of delegation of a task to another agent.

Subscribe: Principal speech act consisting of requesting another agent to inform the first agent of something, in accordance with one of the following modalities: at regular intervals, when an event occurs or when the addressee has new information of a certain type.

Format: `A : B << Subscribe(P,R)` with P a condition and R an expression

Conditions:

- `goal(A,believe(B,P) ⇒ believe(A,R))`
- `believe(A,eventually(believe(B,P))) ∧`
  `believe(A,believe(B,P) ⇒`
  `wantDo(B,B : A << Advise(R)))`

Success:

- `B : A << AcceptSubscribe(P,R) →`
  `commit(B,A,believe(B,P) ⇒`
  `¬wantDo(B,B : A << Advise(R)))`

Satisfaction:

- `B : A << Advise(R) → believe(A,R)`
- `B : A << RefuseSubscribe(P,R) →`
  `believe(A,¬wantDo(B,believe(B,P) ⇒`
  `wantDo(B,B : A << Advise(R))`

Failures:

- `B : A << RefuseSubscribe(P,R) →`
  `believe(A,¬wantDo(B,believe(B,P) ⇒`
  `wantDo(B,B : A << Advise(R))`

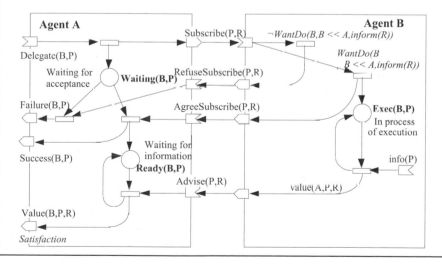

Figure 6.6   Conversational model of a subscription. The cancellation of the subscription is not indicated.

Question: principal speech act consisting of requesting information from another agent.

Format: `A : B <<Question(f,P)` where P is a datum and f a function

Sub-acts:

- `QuestionBoolean(P)` with P a propositional expression
- `QuestionReasons(E)` with E an expression without variables

Conditions:

- `goal(A,believe(A,R))` with:
  `R = f(P) ∧ believe(A,comptetent(B,f) ∧`
  `believe(A,¬comptetent(A,f)) ∧`
  `believe(A,¬believe(A,R)) ∧`
  `believe(A,wantAnswer(B,f))`

Satisfaction:

- `B : A << Answer(R) → believe(A,R)`

Failures:

- `B : A << RefuseAnswer(R) →`
  `believe(A, ¬wantAnswer(f) ∨ ¬competent(B,f)`

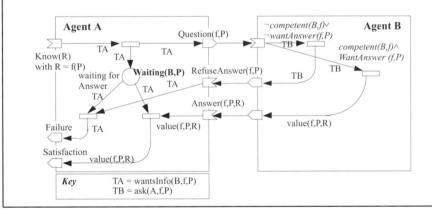

Figure 6.7   Conversational model of a question.

Promissives

`OfferService:`   an agent A proposes its services (example: carrying out a task) to an agent B which can refuse or not. This proposition commits A to B, and A normally has to carry out requests from B corresponding to its skills.

`Propose/Confirm/Refute/Hypothesis:`   this set of performatives can be used in distributed problem solving.

Affirm: principal speech act consisting of sharing a belief with another agent, that is, convincing a third party of the veracity of a fact

Format: `A : B <<Assert(R)`

Conditions:

- `Goal(A,believe(B,R)) ∧ believe(A,¬believe(B,R))`

Satisfaction:

- `B : A, Acquiesce(R) → believe(A,believe(B,R))`

Failures:

- `B : A, RefuseBelieve(R) →`
  `believe(A,believe(B,¬R))`

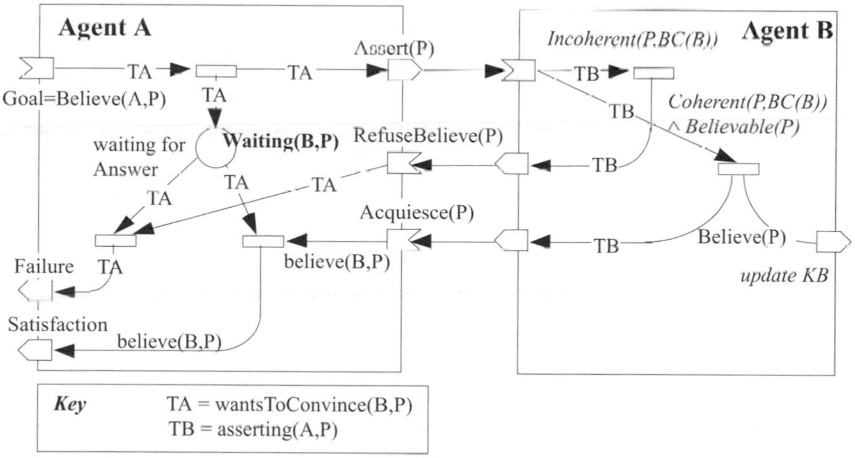

Figure 6.8 Conversational model of an affirmation.

Expressives

`KnowHowDo:` an agent A indicates its skills to another agent B. There is also the reverse performative, in which an agent explains that it does not know how to do something.

`Believe:` an agent A indicates to another agent B that it thinks that an expression is true.

This list makes no claim to be either definitive or exhaustive. We shall encounter a whole set of other performatives in the following chapters.

6.4   KQML

In the United States, a research project funded by the DARPA has the goal of developing a high-level communication standard based on speech acts, to allow cognitive agents to cooperate. Table 6.3 gives the list of performatives proposed for this language, which is called KQML (Knowledge Query and Manipulation Language). This is an ongoing project, and the descriptions which are given here may change with time. Although such an endeavour is certainly of interest, the KQML project displays loopholes. For Cohen and Levesque (1995), for instance, it has the following drawbacks:

- *Ambiguity and imprecision.* The meaning of the performatives is given in the form of simple descriptions in natural language, which often makes them vague and confused.

- *Useless and incoherent performatives.* Certain performatives are in fact not speech acts, for they do not have the power to satisfy the goals of the sending agent. This is particularly true for the performatives `achieve`, `broker` and `stream-all`, which cannot be understood as indirect speech acts, since they actually achieve goals belonging to other agents. Nevertheless, it is clear that any communication system should be able to call upon mediators, and it is therefore vital to take such acts into account.

- *Missing performatives.* In spite of the imposing number of performatives, an entire category of performatives is missing: the *promissive*. For example, it is not possible in KQML to express in a simple way that one is committed to a third party to accomplish an action.

All these reasons demonstrate that KQML is sorely lacking in specifications and formalisation. For this reason, anyone can claim to be using KQML, just because his or her agents are capable of sending each other requests and information. On the basis of these criticisms, Cohen and Levesque propose to define a minimum set of performatives by giving them properties of compositionality, to make it possible to define new performatives as combinations of more primitive speech acts. For this, and on the basis of their theory of rational action, considered in Chapter 5, they have developed a semantics for some of the most fundamental performatives of KQML.

Another communication standard is emerging in competition with KQML – the ACL language (Agent Communication Language) from the FIPA (Foundation for Intelligent Physical Agents), a standardisation body which began its operations in 1995 (*Fipa '97*). ACL, which comprises only about 20 basic types of communication, is also based on speech acts, but it differs from KQML in that it was directly created, using a rigorous semantic formula resulting from the work of David Sadek (1992).

Since Cohen and Levesque's criticisms, work has been done in connection with KQML which has produced more precise forms of semantics (Labrou and Finin, 1997), and the differences between KQML and ACL are tending to diminish, so that the factors they have in common now far exceed those which divide them.

Table 6.3   List of performatives defined in KQML.

Name	Description
achieve	A wants Y to accomplish an action
advertise	A indicates that it can do P
ask-about	A wants all expressions on P from the BC of B
ask-all	A wants all B's responses to a question
ask-one	A wants one response from B to a question
break	A wants to delete a communication
broadcast	A wants B to send a performative to all its contacts
broker-all	A wants B to collect all the responses to a performative
broker-one	A wants help in collecting the response to a performative
deny	A indicates to B that the performative no longer applies to B
delete	A wants B to delete an expression from its BC
delete-all	A wants B to delete all the corresponding P's from its BC
delete-one	A wants B to delete an expression P, from its BC
discard	A does not want the following responses from B
eos	End of a sequence of responses to a prior request
error	A considers that B's message is wrongly formulated
evaluate	A wants B to simplify the associated expression
forward	A wants B to delegate a performative
generator	Identical to standby for a stream-all
insert	A wants R to insert an expression in its BC
monitor	A wants R to update its responses to a stream-all
next	A wants the next response to a prior request
pipe	A wants R to redirect all the following performatives to an agent
ready	A is ready to respond to a prior performative from B
recommend-all	A wants all the agents which respond to a given performative
recommend-one	A wants one agent which responds to a given performative
recruit-all	A wants all the agents capable of responding to a performative
recruit-one	A wants one agent capable of responding to a performative
register	A indicates to B that it can accomplish an action
reply	A responds to an expected request
rest	A wants all the following responses
sorry	A cannot supply a more informative response
standby	A wants B to be ready to respond to a performative
stream-about	Multiple-response version of ask-about
stream-all	Multiple-response version of ask-all
subscribe	A wants B to update its responses to a performative
tell	Indicates that an expression forms part of the BC of A
transport-address	A associates a symbolic name with a transport address
unregister	A 'deny' of 'register'
untell	Indicates that an expression does not form part of the BC of A

Although these projects are interesting, I think specifications in terms of mental states pose a major problem. If we assume that communication standards like KQML are essentially intended to allow agents of various kinds to communicate with each other, then any theory based on mental states compels agents to conform to a specific architecture, which implements this theory precisely. For example, the theory of cognitons which we developed in Chapter 5 does not necessarily agree with that of Cohen and Levesque, which does not utilise the same primitives as that of Y. Shoham. For this reason, any communication standard based on the way an agent behaves restricts the integration options for agents which are really of different kinds. It therefore appears that if communications are no longer specified in terms of mental states but in terms of protocols, this has the advantage that the inherent nature of agents can be set aside, by focusing on the relationships which exist between communications. I may add that this is the approach which has been introduced in this chapter and which will be developed in the following chapters.

Collaboration and Distribution of Tasks

7.1 Modes of task allocation
7.2 Centralised allocation of tasks by trader
7.3 Distributed allocation of tasks

7.4 Integrating tasks and mental states
7.5 Emergent allocation
7.6 An example: the Manta system

If cooperation offers advantages in terms of quantitative efficiency and the emergence of quality, as we saw in Chapter 2, it also raises problems concerned with the distribution of tasks between agents. These problems are difficult, for they involve several parameters: agents' cognitive capacities and capacities for commitment; skills of the individuals concerned; nature of tasks; efficiency; cost of sending a message; social structures within which agents move, etc.

For this reason, the distribution of tasks and resources is both one of the major domains of multi-agent systems and one of their principal contributions to computer science in general. By emphasising distributed allocation of tasks and the concepts of contracts and commitments, multi-agent systems pose the problem of activity in terms which are both social and computational. This distinguishes them from the more classical forms used earlier, whether we are dealing with the allocation of machines or with the distribution of processes on processors. As we shall see, task allocation techniques use some of the results obtained from the field of operational research and distributed systems, while adapting them to their needs.

Distributing tasks, data and resources comes down to answering the question: *who has to do what, and using what resources, on the basis of the goals and the skills of the agents and the contextual constraints (type and quantity of resources, nature of environment, etc.).* With the coordination of actions, which we shall examine in Chapter 8, here is one of the main issues concerning the organisational function of a society of agents (cf. Chapter 3).

7.1 Modes of task allocation

Task allocation (or distribution) involves the definition of the organisational mechanisms through which agents can combine their skills to perform collective work. So we need to describe how tasks are allocated, knowing that the capacities of an agent depend as much on its intrinsic aptitudes (its available architectures, its cognitive capabilities and the types of communication) and the power resources available to it (computation time and energy level) as on external resources (tools, power sources) and environmental constraints.

Tasks requiring more resources, work or know-how than a single agent is capable of supplying should first be *broken down* into several sub-tasks, then *distributed* (or allocated) among the various agents. These two operations are obviously related, since the breakdown of tasks often has to take account of the skills of the agents, and so make the subsequent distribution easier.

7.1.1 Criteria for breaking down tasks

Bond, Gasser and Hill (Bond and Gasser, 1988; Gasser and Hill, 1990) introduced some criteria for breaking down problems. In particular, they indicate that, if problems can be naturally analysed by level of abstraction (working from the most general to the most detailed), it is also necessary to take account of other constraints such as control, data or resources. In fact, it is necessary to make tasks as independent of one another as possible, in such a way as to reduce the coordination required. In particular, we must try to minimise the quantity of data that tasks have to send to each other, and to make sure that tasks can make use of local resources, in order to diminish conflicts in connection with resources.

While breaking down activities are as important as those linked to distribution, the former are generally carried out by human beings. As far as we know, there are no computing systems that can automatically break down tasks. For this reason, research has essentially been concerned with the automatic distribution of tasks, and has rather left aside the problem of breaking them down into sub-tasks.

Nevertheless, we have described the various ways of approaching the breaking down of tasks (using object-oriented or function-oriented approaches in Chapter 3.

7.1.2 Roles

An automatic task allocation system should be capable of connecting agents needing information, or task realisation, the *clients*, and agents capable of supplying a service, the *suppliers* or *servers*. The same agents are frequently clients and servers at the same time, their status as clients or suppliers being generally determined in a dynamic fashion during the execution of a multi-agent system. We then say that an agent is taking the *role* of a client or the *role* of a supplier, without this being one of its intrinsic characteristics. Other roles can be defined, such as that of a broker or trader, which brings servers and clients into contact.

7.1.3 Forms of allocation

The breakdown of tasks can be managed by centralising the allocation process or by distributing it among all the agents concerned. In a *centralised allocation* mode, two cases may arise:

(1) If the subordination structure is hierarchical, it will be the superior agent that will order a subordinate to carry out the task. We can then speak of rigid or defined allocation. This allocation mode, characteristic of calling up a procedure in classic programming, will not be studied here. This type of distribution is met only in fixed organisations (Chapter 3).

(2) In contrast, if the structure is egalitarian, distribution then involves the definition of special agents – traders or brokers – which manage all the allocation procedures by centralising the requests from the clients and the bids for service from the servers, in order to match up these two categories of agents. This makes it possible to apply centralised modes to variable organisations.

In a *distributed allocation* mode, each agent individually tries to obtain the services it needs from the suppliers. These modes apply only to variable organisations, that is, to those which assume that the relationship between clients and suppliers can evolve over time without calling the general structure of the organisation into question. We can distinguish two distributed allocation mechanisms in predefined organisations:

(1) The *acquaintance network* mode of allocation assumes that clients have a representation of other agents and of their capabilities. We shall see that it is not necessary for agents to know the capabilities of all the other agents to be able to solve their problem, but only that the network formed by the set of contacts should be strongly connected (that is, that there is a path going from any agent to any other agent) and, obviously, coherent (that is, the

representations concerning the skills of an agent's acquaintances actually correspond to its effective skills).

(2) The *request for bids* mode of allocation is better known in distributed artificial intelligence under the name of *contract net*. It has the advantage of being very dynamic, and has proved to be particularly easy to implement. However, we shall see that, when it is implemented, problems inherent in the particularly dynamic nature of this mode have to be borne in mind.

To these modes, which are applied to predefined organisations, we should add the *emergent allocation* mode, less known in general and more characteristic of reactive systems in which communications take place in an incidental manner (cf. Chapter 6) by propagation of stimuli. Figure 7.1 summarises the principal task allocation modes. Obviously, a great many variants of these approaches can exist; in particular, there can be hybrids that try to synthesise the advantages of different approaches.

7.2 Centralised allocation of tasks by trader

The simplest case is that where only a single trader exists, with an acquaintance table indicating to it all the agents capable of carrying out a particular task T. This table can be updated directly by suppliers, which tell what their skills are when entering the system.

Figure 7.2 illustrates how the procedure works. When agent A needs to carry out a task T which it cannot (or does not want to) carry out itself, it asks the trader

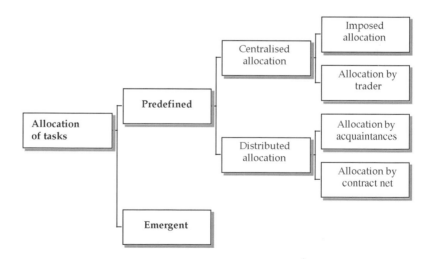

Figure 7.1 Principal task distribution modes.

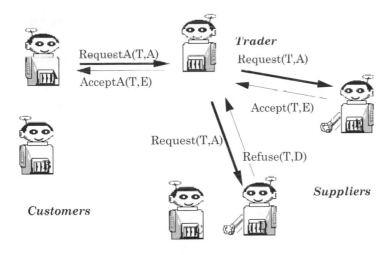

Figure 7.2 Centralised allocation of tasks.

to find an agent to carry out T. The trader then turns to the agents which are known to it to have the capability to carry out T. If one of them accepts, the trader sends the acknowledgement of acceptance to the client, otherwise it informs the client that it has not found anyone to carry out the task.

We are assuming in this process that a supplier which agrees to carry out a task is effectively committing itself to doing it, and will not back out when the contract is being concluded with a client, or while the task is being carried out. We shall also work on the hypothesis that the trader has a table of skills of the agents which is both complete and coherent, all agents A which have a skill being actually listed in this table, and that all references in this table are correct; in other words, for all pairs <A,C> in the table, agent A actually has skill C.

With these elements, the allocation protocol can be defined in the form of a BRIC element. We shall model only the trader, since the behaviour of the clients and suppliers follows the structures of requests (Request) and responses described in Chapter 6 on speech acts. This module, which entirely defines the behaviour of the trader, takes the client's requests and the supplier's responses at the input, and produces at the output requests for suppliers likely to support this request, together with responses for the clients. The communications between the trader, the clients and the suppliers use a set of messages corresponding to the following speech acts:

RequestA(T,X)   is a request from client X to the trader for task T to be carried out.

AcceptA(T,Y)   is the response from the trader to the client to indicate to it that agent Y undertakes to carry out task T.

Impossible(T)   is a response from the trader to the client to indicate to it that there are no agents which agree to carry out task T.

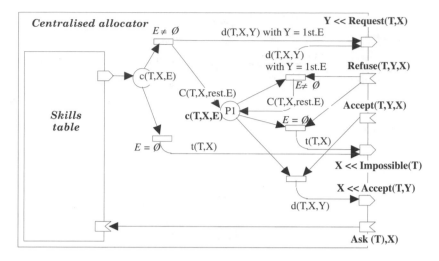

Figure 7.3 Description of centralised trader in BRIC.

Request(T,X) is a request from the trader for a supplier to carry out task P for client X.

Accept(T,Y,X) is the positive response of supplier Y to the trader's request. The supplier indicates to the client that it agrees to carry out task T for client X.

Refuse(T,Y,X) is the negative response of supplier Y to the request for allocation of task T for client X.

Figure 7.3 shows the representation of the centralised trader in BRIC.

When the trader receives a request on behalf of a client X to do T, it looks in its skills table and makes out a list of agents (which may be sorted in order of preference) capable of carrying out this task. If this set E is empty, then the trader responds with the message Impossible. Otherwise, it iteratively asks all the elements of E if it is possible for them to do T, using the location P_1 as a memory for all the suppliers still to be examined. If one of them accepts, the location P_1 is emptied of this task request, and the trader responds to the client X that supplier Y agrees to carry out T. This module uses the following three data structures:

s(T,X,E) gives the list of agents, E, having the skill to carry out the task, T, for the client. 1st.E sends back the first element in the list (identical to car in Lisp) and rest.E sends back the list, **E**, without its first element (identical to cdr in Lisp).

r(T,X,Y) requests the trader for supplier Y to ask it to carry out task T for X.

t(T,X) task T requested by X.

It is possible to improve this mechanism in several ways. The first is to optimise the allocation by priority selection of the most skilled agents, or those that minimise a cost function. For example, in the case of ore-gathering robots including driller and transporter robots, it is preferable to distribute transport tasks on the basis of the distance separating the transporters from the drillers, in such a way as to minimise the movements to be carried out. We can envisage two cases:

(1)   If the trader knows the evaluation functions used by the suppliers, it can sort out the skilled agents on the basis of the results of the evaluation and carry out its requests in this order. The protocol is not modified. It is merely necessary to assume that the trader's acquaintances manager sends back the set of suppliers sorted in order of preference.

(2)   If the trader does not know the evaluation functions, it should first ask each agent to formulate its proposition before actually selecting the one that is to be considered the best. This technique then resembles a contract net mechanism (cf. Section 7.3.2).

In our algorithm, the trader runs through the set of agents in a sequential manner, sending a request to the next agent only if the previous one asked has refused to carry out the task. It is also possible to define parallel algorithms. In this case, as soon as a supplier indicates that it agrees to carry out the task, the other suppliers are informed, so that they know it is no longer necessary to respond. This type of management is more precise, for it must be taken into account that agents can send in their acceptances in between times, and that they therefore must be capable of updating their commitments.

The interesting point about centralised allocation is that we can update the set of agents and their respective skills, and therefore favour the coherence of the system. In addition, the requirements for optimisation are more easily satisfied, the trader knowing the set of agents available, and it is easier for it to select the 'best' of the agents in relation to a given task request.

But the major drawback of this type of system is that it creates a bottleneck, and so considerably reduces the performance levels of the system as soon as the number of agents and requests increases. In fact, the number of messages the trader has to manage grows as the square of N, where N is the number of agents. If we consider that a rate, α, of potential clients exists (α is the number of clients/N ratio) which makes k requests per unit of time, and if we use β to refer to the rate of potential suppliers (that is, the number of suppliers/N ratio) for each request, then the number of messages M is equal to:

$$M = \alpha k N (2 + 2\beta N)$$

that is, to the product of the number of requests times the total number of messages which exist – on the one hand, between the clients and the trader, and on the other hand, between the trader and the suppliers. For example, if α equals 0.5 (half the agents are making requests), β equals 0.2 (20% of the agents are potential suppliers for each request, which means that the system is relatively redundant) and k equals 1 (there is one request per unit of time), we get the curve in Figure 7.4.

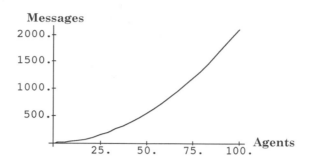

Figure 7.4   Number of messages processed by the trader, plotted against the number of agents in the system.

It can be observed that if, for 50 agents, the number of messages to be processed by the trader is in the order of 500, it changes to 2000 for 100 agents, which indicates that this method is not to be recommended for a large number of agents. In addition, if the system is distributed, all the messages must go via the trader, without taking account of the structure of the network.

Finally, a centralised system is very sensitive to failures. In effect, if the trader breaks down, the entire system falls to pieces. It is therefore necessary to provide complex mechanisms of assistance to try to avoid these problems, but that goes beyond the scope of this book. It is possible to improve this situation by using several traders. But this raises other problems, such as managing coherence between the different traders, which then becomes very complicated. When it is necessary for the system to distribute its allocation mechanisms, it is preferable to go to a true distributed task allocation mode.

7.3   Distributed allocation of tasks

7.3.1   Acquaintance network allocation

In systems of acquaintance network allocation, it is assumed that each agent has a skills table for the agents it knows, in the form of a dictionary such as this:

$$\{C_1:[A_{11},...,A_{1k}],...,C_n:[An_1,...,An_l]\}$$

where the C_i are the skills required to carry out a task T_i and the A_{ij} are the agents that know how to carry out this type of task. It is possible to represent this table in the form of a local table for each agent, with the rows showing the skills and the columns its acquaintances, that is, the agents it knows. Each square of the table then displays 1 or 0, depending on whether the agent in the column in question does or does not have the skill for the corresponding line. For example, an agent A which knows that it has skill C_3, that skill C_1 is available from B, and that D knows how to do C_3, has the following skills table:

$$
\begin{array}{c}
 \\
C1 \\
C2 \\
C3
\end{array}
\begin{array}{cccc}
A & B & C & D \\
\left[\begin{array}{cccc}
0 & 1 & 1 & 0 \\
0 & 0 & 1 & 0 \\
1 & 0 & 0 & 1
\end{array}\right]
\end{array}
$$

It is not assumed that each agent knows all the skills of the other agents, as this would violate the hypothesis of partial representation for multi-agent systems, and would place much too great a constraint on the creation and updating of such systems. We simply assume that the acquaintances tables are correct, that is, that their indications do correspond to the agents' real skills. We also adopt the hypothesis that the acquaintances tables of each of the agents are given once and for all and are not updated. We shall see, in Section 7.3.1, how to deal with the problem of updating acquaintance networks.

An acquaintance network can be represented in the form of a graph. The agents are the tips of the nodes and the arcs represent the skills which the agents know other agents have. In this way, this graph superimposes the various local acquaintances tables of the agents. For example, Figure 7.5 represents the superimposition of the following tables:

$$
\begin{array}{c}
 \\
C1 \\
C2 \\
C3
\end{array}
\begin{array}{cccc}
A & B & C & D \\
\left[\begin{array}{cccc}
0 & 1 & 1 & 0 \\
0 & 0 & 1 & 0 \\
1 & 0 & 0 & 1
\end{array}\right] \\
A
\end{array}
\qquad
\begin{array}{c}
 \\
C1 \\
C2 \\
C3
\end{array}
\begin{array}{cccc}
A & B & C & D \\
\left[\begin{array}{cccc}
0 & 1 & 0 & 0 \\
0 & 0 & 0 & 1 \\
1 & 0 & 0 & 0
\end{array}\right] \\
B
\end{array}
\qquad
\begin{array}{c}
 \\
C1 \\
C2 \\
C3
\end{array}
\begin{array}{cccc}
A & B & C & D \\
\left[\begin{array}{cccc}
0 & 1 & 1 & 0 \\
0 & 0 & 1 & 0 \\
0 & 0 & 0 & 0
\end{array}\right] \\
C
\end{array}
\qquad
\begin{array}{c}
 \\
C1 \\
C2 \\
C3
\end{array}
\begin{array}{cccc}
A & B & C & D \\
\left[\begin{array}{cccc}
0 & 0 & 0 & 0 \\
0 & 0 & 1 & 1 \\
0 & 0 & 0 & 1
\end{array}\right] \\
D
\end{array}
$$

There are essentially two modes of acquaintance network allocation, depending on whether agents are authorised to delegate their requests to other agents or not. So we shall refer to *direct allocation* or *allocation by delegation* modes.

Direct allocation

In the direct mode, an agent can have a task carried out only by an agent that it knows directly. The distribution mechanism is very simple, and is reminiscent of the behaviour of the single trader in the case of centralised distribution systems. The agent that wants to have a task carried out applies in turn to each of the agents it knows which have the desired skill until one of them accepts. If none of them accept, we reach a special state, which must be dealt with. Either we can consider that there is a fault in the system – but we must then make sure that in all cases there will be at least one agent which will agree to carry out the task – or we take measures tending to bypass the problem, by allocating a task to an agent in an authoritarian manner, or by recommencing operations through a contract net

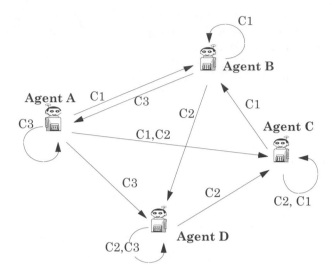

Figure 7.5 An acquaintance network superimposes all the local acquaintances tables in a single diagram, which represents what each agent knows about the skills of the other agents.

mechanism making it possible to select the agent that has the fewest reasons to refuse this task. If this fails, we can also appeal to a centralised system to allocate the task. The reservations associated with centralised systems are no longer appropriate in this case, as only a small number of requests will be sent to the centralised system, with usual requests going by way of the acquaintance network. In this case, the centralised system, which plays the role of a maintenance and repair agent rather than that of a real trader, proves to be very useful, for it can also serve to update the agents' acquaintances tables and thus reorganise the acquaintance network in order to accelerate the allocation process.

Here this allocation mechanism is not implemented by an agent distinct from the applicants but by a module directly integrated into the organisational system of the potential clients. There are therefore two types of connections: those that connect the allocation module to the motivational and organisational systems, and those that represent the messages which the client exchanges with other agents. The internal connections are defined by the following messages:

Allocate(T)   is a request from the motivational system to the allocation system for the latter to find someone to carry out task T.

Impossible(P)   is a response from the allocation manager to the motivational system of the agent which indicates that there is no agent which agrees to carry out task T.

Committed(Y,T)   is a response from the allocation module to the organisational module indicating that agent Y has undertaken to carry out task T.

External messages are defined by the following speech acts:

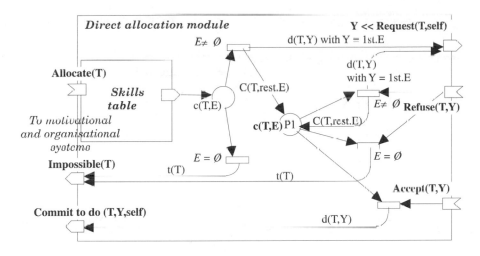

Figure 7.6 Representation of trader's request module using direct contacts.

Request(T,self)   is a request from the agent to a potential supplier agent for task T to be carried out.

Accept(T,Y)   is the positive response of the supplier Y to the client's request.

Refuse(T,Y)   is the negative response from the supplier Y to the request for allocation of task T.

The structure of the direct allocation module is represented in Figure 7.6. It returns to the main lines of the centralised allocation structure of the preceding section. It differs essentially at two points:

(1)   The parameter X, which previously represented the client, has disappeared from the trader's internal data structures.

(2)   The results – conveying acceptance or the impossibility of finding an agent – are sent back to the motivational and organisational systems of the client.

As in the case of the centralised allocation system, the order in which the agents are questioned is not necessarily neutral. Several possibilities can be considered, giving priorities to agents or involving a computation taking account of an agent's processing load and the characteristics of the task. The advantage of this allocation mode obviously lies in its simplicity. It simply assumes that clients have the capacity to know enough specialists for the tasks they cannot carry out themselves to be carried out by others. However, it turns out to be much too limited, as it cannot put suppliers into contact which are not direct acquaintances of clients. It is therefore necessary to introduce a mechanism which allows several agents to make indirect contact.

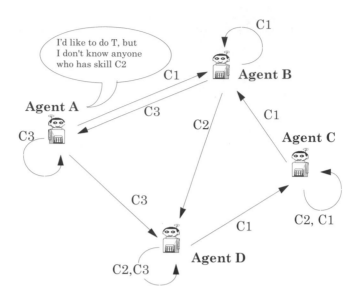

Figure 7.7   The problem of allocation by delegation in an acquaintance network.

Allocation by delegation

The technique of allocation by delegation makes it possible to link together clients and suppliers that do not know each other directly. In effect, this allocation mode allows a supplier which is asked to carry out a task to send it to another agent if it is not capable of doing it. For example, in Figure 7.7, agent A knows no one capable of carrying out a task which calls for skill C2. It therefore has to ask all the agents it knows to ask their own acquaintances with skill C2 to carry out the task T requested, this process having to be repeated until an agent is found which agrees to carry out this task, or until the entire network has been covered.

A search procedure of this kind is carried out on the basis of parallel graph search algorithms. There are essentially two approaches: searching in depth and searching across width. We are talking of algorithms which are very well known in distributed algorithmics (we could refer, for example, to Raynal (1987)), but they have to be adapted to task allocation.

Here we shall describe only the technique based on parallel searching, leaving it to the reader to translate its principles to the case of searching in depth. The general technique of parallel searching rests on diffusion algorithms which recursively propagate requests to all known agents except the requesting agent itself. However, attention must be paid to two constraints. It is first necessary, to verify that an agent is asked only once to carry out a task T and, secondly, to make sure that the procedure is completed, so that it may, if necessary, be envisaged that task T can be allocated in an authoritarian manner or a request for bids mode can be used. The first difficulty is resolved by marking the agents during the search, and the second by using a supplementary message Acknowledge, which is used to inform the agents upstream of the process of the fact that all the requests situated downstream of it have actually been carried out.

Each agent Z, when it receives an initial request from an agent Y concerning the carrying out of a task T for an agent X and requiring a skill C, first evaluates the task. If it has the skill and it accepts, it sends agent X an acceptance message, then sends agent Y an acknowledge message, to indicate the end of the process. Otherwise, it marks itself as having already analysed the request, and relaunches the request to all the agents it knows. When all have responded with an acknowledge message, it sends one to itself. When new requests are sent to it for the same task T it then simply sends an acknowledge message.

It is also necessary to manage the option of having several simultaneous acceptances. Owing to parallelism, two agents can actually accept the request and commit themselves to agent X. For this reason, the supplier which accepts does not have to commit itself, but simply has to book its commitment until the contract is concluded with the client. On the other hand, the client has to take account of the fact that it can receive several propositions, and it is assumed that it must accept only the first. Figure 7.8 illustrates the operation of such a system.

When agent A needs to have task T carried out, it asks all its acquaintances, B and C, to do T. As they cannot do it themselves, they delegate the request, to D and E for B, and to B and F for C. For this reason, B receives a new request, and merely sends an Acknowledge message to agent C. Since D cannot do it and has no acquaintances, it merely sends back the Acknowledge message to B. E, on the other hand, can delegate the request to F. Let us assume that F knows how to carry

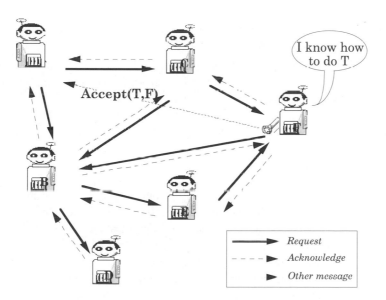

Figure 7.8   A system of allocation by delegation.

out task T and that it receives the first request from B. It sends A its agreement to do T, and it sends B an acknowledge message. When F receives a new request from C, it merely responds by an acknowledge message. If several acceptance messages reach A, it takes account only of the first, by noting that the task it has requested is under contract, that is, that F has committed itself to do it. The speech acts required for communications between agents are as follows:

Request(P,X,Y)   is a request from client X to the potential supplier for task P to be carried out, this request coming from applicant Y.

Propose(T,Y)   is the positive response from supplier Y to the client's request. It indicates that it is booking T and is waiting for either an agreement message or a refusal message.

Acknowledge(T,Y)   indicates either that agent Y agrees to do P or that it has received an acknowledge message from all the agents which it requested to do T.

OfferAccepted(T,X)   is a positive response from client X to the acceptance proposition from the supplier. The supplier can then commit itself to do P for X.

OfferRefused(T,X)   is a negative response from client X to the acceptance proposition from the supplier, which can delete P from its booked commitments.

To these messages we should add, as always, the connections between the agent's organisational and motivational systems. Here we shall find once more the internal messages between modules described in the preceding section, namely:

Allocate(T)   is a request from the motivational system to try to find someone to whom to allocate task T.

Impossible(T)   is a response to the motivational system indicating that it has not been possible to allocate task T.

Committed(T,Y,X)   is a commitment from agent X to carry out task T on behalf of Y. Each time an agreement is reached between a client and a supplier, the two agents memorise this commitment in a symmetrical manner.

The allocation by delegation mechanism can be written in the form of a set of four modules (Figure 7.9), which manage both the client and supplier parts of each agent:

(1)   A *request evaluation* module, which either proposes an offer or sends the request to the delegation module. If the agent has already received a request, it merely sends an acknowledge message to the agent sending the request.

(2)   A *delegation* module, which undertakes to send a request message to all its acquaintances and to receive all the acknowledgements. This module is activated either by a command from the preceding module or by a task allocation request coming from the agent's motivational system.

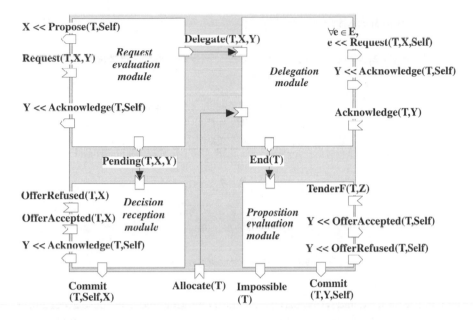

X << Propose(T,Self)

Request(T,X,Y)

Request evaluation module

Delegate(T,X,Y)

$\forall e \in E,$
e << Request(T,X,Self)

Delegation module

Y << Acknowledge(T,Self)

Y << Acknowledge(T,Self)

Acknowledge(T,Y)

Pending(T,X,Y)

End(T)

OfferRefused(T,X)

OfferAccepted(T,X)

Decision reception module

Proposition evaluation module

TenderF(T,Z)

Y << OfferAccepted(T,Self)

Y << Acknowledge(T,Self)

Y << OfferRefused(T,Self)

Commit (T,Self,X)

Allocate(T)

Impossible (T)

Commit (T,Y,Self)

Figure 7.9   System of allocation by delegation, broken down into four modules.

(3)   A *proposition evaluation* module, which merely accepts the first offer received from a supplier and refuses all the others.

(4)   A *decision reception* module, which commits the agent to carry out a task if the offer has been accepted and to put the pending offers refused in the trash.

The delegation module (Figure 7.10) merely sends the message `RequestD` to all its contacts and waits for their receipts. It counts the receipts received, thanks to location P_1. When it has received as many receipts as it has sent out requests, it sends an acknowledge message in its turn, unless it is the client, that is, the agent initiating the broadcasting. In that case, it sends back the message `End` to the proposition evaluation module.

The request evaluation module (Figure 7.11) undertakes to process a request. If it can carry out task T (and wants to), it proposes its services and then waits. Otherwise, it delegates this request to all its contacts, unless it has already received a similar request, in which case it simply sends back an acknowledge message. Location P_2 simply serves to memorise the fact that it has already responded to a request to do T for a client X.

The last two modules deal respectively with the reception of decisions coming from the client (Figure 7.12(a)) and the evaluation of propositions (Figure 7.12(b)). The latter, upon receiving an offer, indicates to the organisational system that the supplier is definitely going to commit itself, memorises the offer, with the

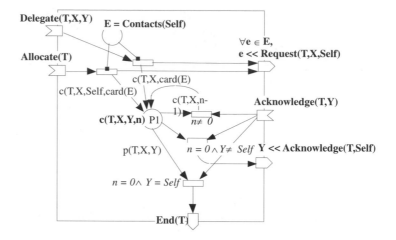

Figure 7.10 Delegation module.

help of location P_5, and refuses all the others. The former receives these acceptances or refusals, and sends the requesting agent an acknowledgement for having received a request. Finally, if the offer is accepted, it commits itself to its client. Location P_4 memorises propositions waiting to be accepted or refused, and location P_3, which serves as a sink, consumes the marks if the offer is refused.

However, this algorithm has some imperfections.

(1)   In the first place, no account has been taken of data relating to the acquaintances' skills to optimise the search. Each agent sends requests to all its acquaintances, whereas it could send priority requests to the agents it knows have this skill. But this optimisation, which seems insignificant,

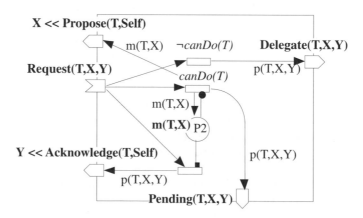

Figure 7.11 Request evaluation module.

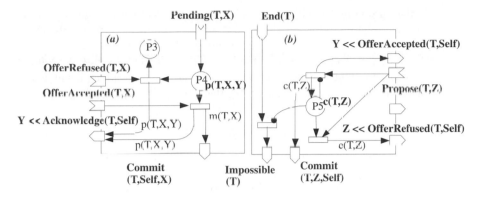

Figure 7.12   Decision reception module (a) and proposition evaluation module (b).

nonetheless conceals several little difficulties. First of all, the requests have to be differentiated. A direct request will initially be sent only to acquaintances having the skill, to ask them if they agree to carry out P, which will be followed by a general request which will be limited to delegating messages. For this algorithm to function, we must be sure that the representations of the agents are complete, that is, that if an agent B forms part of A's acquaintances, then A does actually know what B's skills are.

(2)   When an agent indicates that it accepts a task, it would be tempting to want to bring the whole process to a halt and tell all the other branches which are in the process of scouring the network that they can stop looking for a candidate. All that need happen then is for the agent which accepts to send an `AcknowledgeSuccess` message to the applicant, and for this applicant to send a `Stop` message to all the agents to which it sent a request and which have not yet returned a response. This modification, which can increase the number of messages to be sent between agents, is effective only if the `Stop` messages are faster, and have greater priority, than the others. Otherwise, this will merely complicate the mechanism.

(3)   This algorithm, like the preceding ones, takes no account of all the various skill levels of agents, in that it considers only the first acceptance. The agent does not ask for an 'estimate', on the basis of which it would be able to express a choice. However, the introduction of such a mechanism is relatively easy. It is sufficient to memorise the list of agents that agree to do the work, to conclude a contract only with the one that 'sounds best', and to indicate to the others that they have not been accepted. This technique then resembles those for requests for bids which we shall be examining in the following section.

(4)   Finally, attention must be paid to the way a task request is worded. If several requests corresponding to identical tasks are sent one after another, there is

a risk of confusion, with an agent believing it has already responded to the request relating to this task when it is actually a new one. In fact, the place in the request evaluation module systematically preserves all the requests it has received. To avoid these confusions, it is sufficient to word task requests by stringing together the description of the task, the initial applicant agent, and an order number. Requests are then all systematically differentiated.

Reorganisation of an acquaintance network

An agent's acquaintances can be considered as a kind of cache memory through which an agent can be in a position to have direct knowledge of the characteristics of other agents it may need. For this reason, acquaintance systems have the classic problems of cache memories and, in particular, the difficulty of maintaining coherence between the acquaintances and the state of the agents they represent. This is particularly true when an agent changes its capabilities, when a new agent appears in the system, or when one of them comes to leave it. In that case, the agent's acquaintance base has to be updated in such a way that it is coherent once again, which poses the difficult problem of reorganising an acquaintance network.

For example, let us assume that an agent A knows that an agent B has the necessary skills to carry out a task T and that, for some reason or another (a module of B fails, B has specialised in another task, etc.), B's skills are modified, and it no longer has the capacity to do T. The next time A asks B to do T, it will receive a refusal, whereas so far A has taken it for granted that B would do T every time A asked it to do so. This problem of distributed coherence can be solved in two ways:

- One way is to arrange for B to alert all the agents that know B to its change of state. But this raises two difficulties: (1) B would have to know that A knew B's capabilities, which would mean managing bilateral contacts between all the acquaintances, and (2) attention would have to be paid to problems of parallelism, which could lead to another request's coming to B before it had time to warn all the agents of which it is a contact.

- Alternatively, A's acquaintances table could be modified. When A asks B to do T and this request fails, A memorises the fact that B is no longer able to do T and restarts the procedure of looking for an agent.

There can obviously be many different kinds of acquaintance network. For example, we may wish to reorganise the network in a dynamic manner so that agents that do not know each other initially are put into contact. We can also improve the performance levels of the system by statistically managing the agents' acquaintances in such a way as to optimise the requests. Agents with which an agent is frequently contracted can be in its acquaintances table, while it discards acquaintances that are never used. It is then possible to arrange for the network to 'learn' to allocate the tasks it has to accomplish as it works. 'Good' marks can be given to agents that give satisfaction, and 'bad' marks to those that respond less well to requests. The Cascade system created by H. V. D. Parunak (1990), which controls a storehouse management system, works according to this principle.

What is to be done when new agents are brought into service in a multi-agent universe? Several techniques are available, and almost all of them stem from the technology of nets (for example, the Internet) or of distributed systems. With the check-in technique, in particular, new agents introduce themselves to a 'manager', but that means the manager has to know all the agents. This difficulty can be eliminated almost completely by defining a hierarchical administration system, as in computer networks, with each manager being able to control its region and its set of agents. We can also arrange that all new agents contact only some of the agents in the system – then, by using the acquaintance network (and in particular by using its system for reorganising acquaintances, if it has one), the data is propagated along the network. If the acquaintances graph does, in fact, have a great many connections, all the agents in the system can benefit from the characteristics of the new entrants.

7.3.2 Allocation by the contract net

The contract net is a task allocation mechanism based on a market-like protocol. Introduced by R. G. Smith (1979), this technique received an enthusiastic welcome from the community of researchers into distributed artificial intelligence, and numerous systems have used it. It is certainly a control structure which is very easy to understand and to use. However, we shall see that its simplicity conceals some difficulties which must be resolved if the contract net is to be used in a truly distributed context. The contract net is one of the computing techniques in which the conceptual aspect is associated with the implementation to introduce usable mechanisms which are easy to learn and to program, with results that correspond relatively well to expectations.

The contract net makes use of the protocol for the drawing up of contracts in public markets. The relationship between the client, or the *manager*, and the suppliers, or *bidders*, is chanelled through a request for bids and an evaluation of the proposals submitted by the bidders. The request for bids has four stages:

(1)   The first stage is devoted to the request for bids itself. The manager sends a description of the task to perform to all those it considers able to respond or to all agents of the system (Figure 7.13(a)).

(2)   On the basis of this description, in a second stage, the bidders draw up proposals which they submit to the manager (Figure 7.13(b)).

(3)   The manager receives and evaluates proposals and awards the contract to the best bidder in a third stage (Figure 7.13(c)).

(4)   Finally, in the fourth and last stage, the bidder which has been awarded the contract and which therefore becomes the *contractor* sends a message to the

manager, to signify that it is still prepared to carry out the required task (Figure 7.13(d)) and that it is therefore committing itself to do it, or else that it cannot carry out the contract, which triggers a re-evaluation of the bids and the awarding of the contract to another agent (taking us back to stage 3).

Algorithm with a single manager

We shall first analyse the protocols of the contract net when only one manager exists at a given moment, and then we shall look at the problems raised by generalising to

Figure 7.13 The four stages of the contract net.

any number of simultaneous managers. The types of message necessary for the realisation of this allocation system are as follows:

RequestForBids(T,X) is a message from the manager X to a potential bidder, to ask it to submit a proposition for the carrying out of task T if it is interested.

Propose(T,O) is the positive response from a bidder Y to a request for bids concerning task T. It then sends back a bid O which, among other data, includes the bidder's name.

NotInterested(T,Y) is the negative response of a bidder to the administrator, indicating to the latter that Y is not interested in doing T.

Award(T,C,X) is the message from manager X to a bidder to inform it that it has been awarded contract C relating to task T.

Accept(T,Y) is a positive response from bidder Y to the awarding of the contract by the manager.

Refuse(T,Y) is a negative response from bidder Y to the awarding of the contract by the manager, which re-activates evaluation and the awarding process.

Moreover, as in the other distributed allocation systems looked at earlier, the manager (which is also the client) displays classic connections with its motivational and organisational system, namely the request for allocation `Allocate`, the responses (`Impossible`, `Commit`) and the bidder's commitment (`Commit`).

An agent can be a manager and a bidder at the same time. These are two different roles, but the same agent can as easily take on one as the other. However, to make things clearer, I have found it preferable to break down this algorithm by making a distinction between the behaviour of the manager and that of the bidder. The requests for bids will be recognised in a single manner in the net, using a key made up of the description of the task, the manager responsible for issuing the request, and an order number local to this agent. For reasons of simplification, we shall identify the task with its number. Figure 7.14 shows the general architecture of the modules required to establish a contract net protocol.

The manager comprises two modules (Figure 7.15): the module (A) for the definition of the request for bids and for the reception of proposals being module A. The proposals are then selected by a second module (B) which is responsible for awarding contracts and receiving acceptances or refusals from the bidders. There are three locations in module A. The first, P_1, simply contains the identifier for all the agents of the system. The second, P_2, serves to count the responses to the request for bids to find out when it can go to the following stage, and location P_3 memorises all the proposals received. Module B contains only one location, which is used for defining the iterative awarding of contracts to the bidders. In this implementation of the contract net protocol, it has been assumed that bidders could refuse the contract sent by the manager. In numerous cases, it can be assumed that the bidders always accept contracts, which makes this module easier to write, since we can dispense with the acceptance and refusal responses from the bidders, as well as the

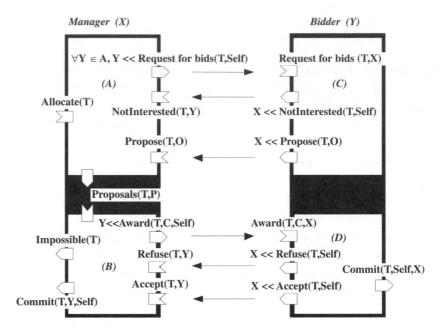

Figure 7.14 Flow chart of a contract net protocol. The manager is responsible for the task announcements and the reception of proposals (module A), then selects the proposals and awards a contract to the bidder that 'sounds best' (module B). The bidder draws up a proposal on the basis of the request for bids (module C) and decides to accept – or not to accept – the contract drawn up by the manager (module D).

iterative search of the list of proposals retained. The bidders also have two modules (Figure 7.16). The first (C) is intended for evaluating the request for bids and for drawing up a proposal, the second (D) for evaluating the contracts awarded by the manager.

Contract preparation language

The communication primitives we have shown above are rather elementary, but adequate to implement the essentials of the contract net. However, R. Smith has put forward a more complete language, which is on a higher level of abstraction (Smith, 1980), in which, as well as the description of the task and the contract number, the request for bids statement includes a *definition of the qualities required* for the task, the *form of proposal* and an *expiry date*. The definition of the required qualities means that agents that do not have these qualities can be eliminated rapidly, without it being necessary to carry out a meticulous analysis of the description of this task.

The form of the proposal indicates to the bidder what the criteria are that will be taken into account during evaluation, and so to facilitate the subsequent

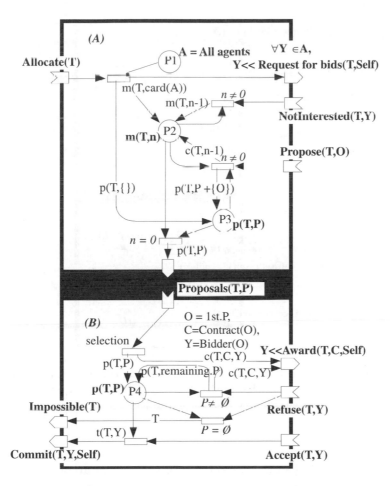

Figure 7.15 Diagram of the behaviour of the manager of a request for bids. Module A is used to issue requests for bids and to receive proposals, which are then sent to module B for the selection of proposals and the awarding of contracts.

evaluation work of the manager. Finally, the expiry date gives the limiting date after which proposals will no longer be retained.

Let us take the example of the ore-gathering robots. Having found a seam, an explorer robot plays the role of a manager and makes a request to all the robots capable of digging into loose ground to drill at its location. It asks them for their positions, so that it can select the driller nearest to it, but also asks for the list of their performance levels for different types of ground, knowing that only robots capable of digging in loose ground will be selected. Using R. Smith's notation to define messages between managers and bidders, here is how this contract net can be issued:

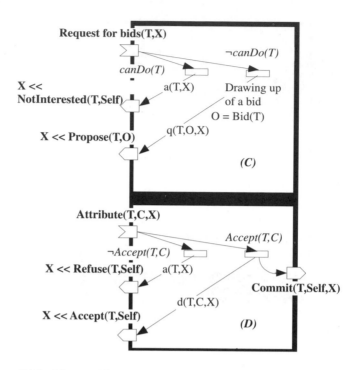

Figure 7.16 Diagram of the behaviour of a bidder. Module C is used to evaluate proposals and for drawing up a bid. Module D is responsible for the acceptance – or not – of a contract as it has been drawn up by the manager.

```
Message: RequestForBids
  To : *     // indicates broadcast message
  From : Explorer-25
  Contract : Drill-Explore-25-234
  DescriptionOfTask :
    TypeOfTask : Drill
  QualitiesRequired :
    MustHave : DrillingSystem
    MustBeAble : DrillLooseGround
  FormOfProposal :
    Position : <Lat, Long>
    DrillingQualities : { TypeOfGround : Performance}
  DateExpiry :
    20 July 2193 13 : 06 : 46
    End RequestForBids
```

The explorer robots will respond in their proposals by giving the characteristics requested by the manager:

```
Message : Propose
   To : Explorer-25
   From : Driller-18
   Contract :Drill-Explorer-25-234
   DescriptionProposal :
      Position: <47N,17W>
      QualiticoDrilling .
         { Sand : 0.5 Clay : 0.3 Shale : 0.8}
End Propose
```

The explorer will award the 'drilling contract' to what it considers to be the best proposal. The apparent simplicity of the algorithm introduced above should not mask a certain number of difficulties. These obscure points relate essentially to the evaluation of the proposal, to the access to the bidders, to taking multiple managers and personal commitments into account, to breaking down tasks into sub-tasks, and to the quality of the allocation obtained.

Evaluation of proposal

A bidder interested in a task submits a proposal containing an evaluation of its capacity to carry out this task. This evaluation can be expressed in the form of a simple numerical measurement or of a description including several criteria evaluated separately. In the application of this mechanism to load balancing in a multi-processor system, it is possible to measure the interest in a processor for a task by means of a simple numerical value that is proportional to the workload of the processor. The greater this is, the more the value of the proposal is reduced, and conversely. In other situations, it appears more difficult to characterise how interesting an agent is in relation to a task, and to measure its capacities to offer a 'good' service. In that case, it is up to the designer of the system to select his/her evaluation function well, together with the criteria which will be recognised as relevant by the system, for the performance of the contract net is closely connected to it.

Contacting bidders

In general, the contract net considers that all agents situated in the net are accessible to any of the net's agents, and that obtaining a list of them is not a problem. In particular, in the algorithm given above, we have intentionally indicated that the manager contacted all the agents. This was nevertheless, at the least, an idyllic concept, which does not deal with the problems of implementation in really distributed contexts, and which does not respond to the question: how can we access agents likely to submit a proposal?

Algorithms for searching the net in parallel can be used to access all the net's agents. Essentially, they resemble the algorithm used for allocation by delegation in an acquaintance network, but instead of asking agents whether they agree to carry out a task we ask them to draw up a bid and to submit this proposal to the manager. When the process is completed and the manager has received all the acknowledgements, whether they carry a proposal or indicate lack of interest, the manager knows that it has all the proposals and that it can start its evaluation.

This process is obviously very time-consuming and requires a great many messages, since it assumes that all the agents in the system have to be contacted individually. It also poses the problem of creating an acquaintance network, even if this net is simpler than in the case of allocation by delegation, since the agents are not expected to know their neighbours' skills but only to know that they have neighbours. Another solution consists in having all the agents memorised in an overall data structure maintained by a single agent, but then we are once again back with the problems of bottlenecks and sensitivity to breakdowns typical of centralised systems.

The solution most generally adopted by designers of contract nets consists in placing the agents on a 'bus' (Figure 7.17), that is, on a ring-shaped organisation, the functioning of which is very similar to that of the *token ring*.

The messages are then always carried in the same direction, and circulate from neighbour to neighbour, whether they are requests or proposals. One solution then is to consider that the requests for bids are placed on a tray. The bidders each read the requests for bids in turn, evaluate it and place their proposals on the tray. When the tray returns to the manager responsible for this request, it knows that everyone has responded, and it can choose from the set of proposals. This implementation is not very fast either, since evaluation is carried out sequentially and no attention is paid to the potential parallelism of the contract net to accelerate the process. Nevertheless, we shall see later that it has the advantage

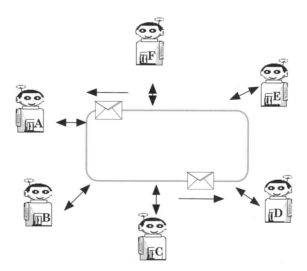

Figure 7.17 Implementation of the contract net by implementing the agents on a ring.

that we can define better allocations than those mentioned above. In order to increase the speed of computation and limit the number of messages, several partial improvements have been made which take account of the nature of the application. In particular, when the net is not very 'volatile', that is, the identity of the agents, their number and their skills show little variation – which is generally the case – it is possible to apply cache memory techniques, which come down to local management of a table of acquaintances by the managers, and indexing agents according to the tasks to which they respond. This technique was developed by Van Parunak (1990) to manage the automatic allocation of tasks in flexible workshops.

A type is associated with each task, and it is assumed that all the agents that know how to carry out tasks of a certain type will necessarily respond to the request by submitting a proposal. When a manager has to issue a request for bids for a new type of task, it broadcasts this request throughout the network, and memorises in its acquaintances table all the agents that respond to this type of task. When faced with a task of the same type, all it has to do then is to search this reduced list to attain the same efficiency. The acquaintances table then plays the part of a cache memory which optimises access. Sometimes the list amounts to a single individual, and the manager can then set up contracts directly, without going through a contract net protocol. If agents enter or leave the network, or if their skills are modified, it is assumed that they will inform the net of this by broadcasting the information to all the managers. Such a technique improves the response time and the number of messages sent, but its advantages are clearly perceptible only if the modifications are few in number compared to the number of requests for bids.

Limit date

Up until now, we have assumed that the manager waits for all the proposals before evaluating them. This obviously makes it possible to take more account of all the potentialities of the system by not forgetting any bid, but at the expense of two major drawbacks:

(1)   All the agents have to respond, even those that *a priori* are not interested in the request for bids. For this reason, the network could become saturated by too many messages which contain only very small amounts of information and carry only the message 'not interested'.

(2)   An agent that has broken down or is not functioning properly can block the system totally. If it does not send a response, the manager is kept waiting indefinitely.

All that need be done here is that agents should not send messages back if they are not interested or, obviously, if they cannot do what is asked. Secondly, each request will have a deadline for the receipt of proposals. Once this date has passed, the manager evaluates the proposals it has received, and all those arriving after this date are directly rejected.

Obviously, this solution raises other problems. This reaction time does have to be calibrated in such a way that the majority of the proposals have the time to return to the manager. If the deadline is set too early then numerous proposals will not be taken into account. If the deadline is too distant then the manager will be waiting pointlessly before beginning its evaluation. It is nevertheless possible to draw up an adaptative system. If too many proposals arrive after the deadline, the response time is increased, and if there is too long a wait after the final responses have been received, this time is reduced. In this way, agents will all respond with the same response time, so that the system will converge towards a well-adapted state.

Multiple managers and optimality

We have been considering the case of a single manager most of the time, but this is actually a degenerate case of the contract net, for several managers can be working at the same time and can issue their requests for bids simultaneously. It is therefore necessary to manage the fact that several managers can send two requests for bids to the same agent at the same time. They are liable to interfere with each other and to have a negative effect on the overall behaviour of the system. In the contract net, tasks are generally attributed only on the basis of the local knowledge of managers, without taking into account either what other managers want or the other proposals which may arrive later. Van Parunak (1987) in fact considers that, because this is a local process, the agents are ignorant in three ways: their ignorance relates to the temporal and spatial aspects and to the workloads of the bidders.

(1) *Temporal ignorance* comes from the fact that the bidders are aware only of the requests for bids already received, and not of those that are on the point of arriving. An agent may commit itself to carry out a task for which it is not really very well suited, and therefore miss contracts that would correspond better to its true qualities.

(2) *Spatial ignorance* comes from the fact that the managers cannot know about other requests for bids in progress, and the bidders cannot know about other proposals. For example, let us assume that two managers, A and B, send two potential bidders, X and Y, two requests for bids for two tasks, TA and TB, and that the proposals which result from this take the form below.

	TA	TB
X	90	80
Y	80	20

When these proposals are received, manager A will normally select X, for its proposal looks more interesting than Y's, and likewise B will choose X, because its proposal in this case is also much better than Y's. It follows from this that X will have a great deal to do while Y will remain inactive, whereas it would be preferable to award task TB to X and leave task TA to Y. If X knew about Y's proposal, it could reduce the quality of its proposal for TA, and if Y knew about X's proposal, it could improve its proposal for task TB. There are therefore algorithms in which all the bidders send their proposals to all the other agents, which makes it possible to obtain more fine-tuned proposals, which take account of all proposals from agents. However, these techniques are very time-consuming and require a great many messages, their complexity growing in an exponential manner with the number of agents in the system.

(3) *Ignorance of workloads* is due to the fact that the bidders have no information on other agents' workloads. For this reason, an agent that has work may be motivated to beat another that has practically nothing to do. To remedy this problem, Van Parunak proposes that agents should have information available on one another's workloads, so that they can modify their proposals and, if need be, be more 'aggressive' in order to win the contract.

Commitments, reservations and rejection of contracts

Parallelism raises another problem. Bidders can receive new requests between the time when they submit a proposal and the time they are awarded the contract or are rejected by the manager. The bidder is then faced with a difficult choice. It can either reserve space for all the tasks for which it submits proposals, and so risk finding itself without anything to do, or, on the contrary, it can submit new proposals without taking the previous ones into account, even if it may end up with too much work and be unable to meet its commitments. Each of these possibilities has advantages and drawbacks which it is expedient to analyse in the light of the type of application being considered.

(1) In booking tasks, an agent considers that the probability that it will be awarded a task is great. For this reason, it reserves the resources (in terms of time and space) required to carry out this task. When it receives a new request for bids, it takes account of the capacity reserved for tasks as if it had actually committed itself to doing them, and, should the need arise, envisages submitting proposals which will not be very interesting if the number of booked tasks is too great. However, it is taking the risk of seeing its proposals rejected, and thus of losing contracts, if it reserves too much capacity for tasks and does not become sufficiently 'competitive' in its proposals to acquire new markets. As a result, in this scenario, the risk is to end up without an adequate number of tasks to carry out. However, this method is not without advantages, in particular the simplicity with which it can be implemented. As soon as a proposal is submitted, the agent merely reserves the resources required to carry out this task, and computes its proposals taking into account the capacities reserved for tasks as if they represented actual commitments. Incidentally, this is the algorithm we

selected for the general presentation of the contract net. We can describe an agent functioning in accordance with such a principle as *prudent*, for it minimises the risks of overheating but increases the risks of lay-offs. This technique is particularly interesting if there are not many agents submitting proposals and if the risks connected with local overheating are not very great.

(2)   In contrast, by not taking account of proposals already submitted, an agent reserves no resources for the carrying out of tasks for which it submits proposals. It then risks finding itself with several contracts to fulfil, that is, with having too much work in relation to its capacities. The interesting thing about such an agent locally is that it is always more competitive, in relative terms, since it does not take account of the resources it will actually have to commit to other contracts. This method is obviously more advantageous than the previous one when there are a large number of agents likely to submit proposals, for the probability of being awarded a contract is lower. In order to resolve conflicts relating to the awarding of tasks, it is possible to arrange for a bidder which is awarded too many contracts to refuse tasks awarded to it. In this case, the manager must send out a new request for bids or, at the very least, re-evaluate the proposals which have been submitted to it and choose to sign a contract with another bidder. Our algorithm, incidentally, takes this eventuality into account.

(3)   Finally, it is possible to find a middle way by using the principles of support for decision making in determining the prospects for each task. To do this, we have to associate two values with the tasks – the probability of obtaining a contract and the estimated profit. The probability of obtaining a contract corresponds to the probability of being appointed to carry out the task. For example, if an agent X estimates that a proposal has a 20% likelihood of being accepted, it associates it with the probability 0.2. This evaluation corresponds to the advantages it can envisage. On the basis of considerations of this order, an entire branch of research into multi-agent systems is working on the use of micro-economic theories based on the concepts of the market and of utility, together with the games theory (Rosenschein and Zlotkin, 1994).

Influence of sub-contractors

A problem which has never been tackled by authors working on contract nets, and which has generally been dealt with by very few authors, is that of sub-contractors, or, more generally, of the enrolment of agents[†]. When a bidder X carries out a task T under a contract with a manager A it may decide to break this task down into sub-tasks, and it may not be capable of carrying out certain of these sub-tasks itself. It then has to behave like a manager, and issue a new request for bids for the set of

---

[†]To our knowledge, the only author to have spoken explicitly about these enrolment problems in the context of the contract net is T. Bouron (1992).

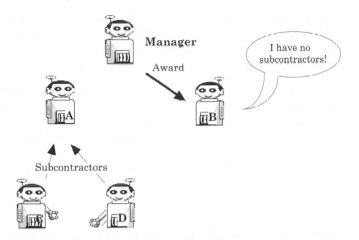

Figure 7.18   Problem of sub-contracting. B has no sub-contractor, whereas it has just been awarded the contract by the manager.

sub-tasks $(T_1,..,T_n)$ stemming from the task T. A bidder confronted with such a situation can issue this request only after having received the contract, or else can ask sub-contractors to commit themselves to carrying out these tasks first, before submitting proposals to manager A. Obviously, this is a recursive problem, and sub-contractors may decide to look for sub-sub-contractors, and so on.

Let us take the example of the furniture removers, where there are two types of agent co-existing – the 'carrier' robots, which know how to carry furniture, and the 'supervisor' robots, which organise the carriers into teams, sign contracts with the managers, coordinate the actions of the carriers, and ensure that the work is of good quality. Here the supervisors are playing the role of bidders in relation to the task of moving house, and the carriers than of sub-contractors, whose tasks are limited to those connected with carrying furniture. If a manager issues a request for moving the contents of a room, the supervisors can either respond directly to the proposal, and then issue the request for bids, or make up their teams first and then respond.

(1)   With the first solution, which we shall call *early commitment*, it is possible that the bidder (the supervisor in our example) will have problems if it does not find any sub contractor (worker) that is free and capable of helping. Figure 7.18 shows the problem that two bidders may be confronted with if they apply to the same sub-contractor. Bidder B, which has just been awarded a contract by the manager, is incapable of carrying it out, for it has no sub-contractor to help it, whereas A, which does have sub-contractors, has not been awarded the contract.

The problem here stems from the fact that B submitted its proposal without knowing if it had sufficient resources to be able to execute the contract. It is therefore stuck, and it has to break the contract with the manager, which obviously entails a lot of reorganisation. This type of allocation therefore functions well if resources are plentiful and if the risk of being without a sub-contractor is slight.

(2) The second solution obviously seems to be a correct solution to the preceding problem. To avoid not having a sub-contractor, it is sufficient to issue a sub-request (that is, a request for bids to find sub-contractors) before submitting a proposal. Any agent that cannot find sub-contractors will submit a proposal that will not attract much interest. If the opposite is true, a proposal can be submitted in complete confidence. We then say that the bidder is making a *late commitment*, since it first asks its sub-contractors to commit themselves to it, before it commits itself, in its turn, to the manager. But alas, this solution raises even more problems than the first, for it is necessary, first of all, to provide for a mechanism for managing the sub-contractors' commitments. If the proposal is not accepted by the manager, the sub-contractors must be informed that they are freed from their commitments. We are then confronted with problems similar to those we saw in the preceding section in relation to reserving capacity for tasks, and the solutions for resolving them are analogous. In addition, even if we assume that these problems are solved, we nevertheless find ourselves faced with a classic problem in resources management for distributed systems, the appearance of deadlocks when several processes have to access resources simultaneously – for example, if there are only six carrier robots for two supervisors, Bertram and Charles, and if, when the request for bids is received, the task requires four carriers. Each of the two supervisors may have bids from three carriers. In this case, neither Bertram nor Charles can respond positively to this request, whereas the number of workers is actually greater than that required for the task. The solution of such a problem involves the detection and the suppression of the conflicts producing these deadlocks. We shall deal with this problem in Section 7.3.4, which covers the general problem of the commitment of agents.

(3) A third solution exists, which is far from being ideal but which makes it possible to ensure a certain stability for the system and, above all, to avoid both deadlocks and non-execution of contracts. It consists simply in setting up relatively permanent teams of sub-contractors, which, for an agent, comes down to 'hiring' agents that it generally needs, and binding them to itself through a contract of exclusivity. The sub-contractors may respond only to requests from a single agent, their 'boss', refusing all work which does not come from this agent. In exchange, the boss undertakes to supply work for them. The establishment of these teams is therefore a more permanent affair than in the situations analysed above, the agents being part of a team for the implementation of a whole series of tasks. Team management is harder and easier at the same time than simply enrolling

someone for a precise task. It is harder, for it is necessary to manage the hiring and firing of the agents, while trying to respond to requests with the teams already in existence. But it is also easier, for all the modifications are local – to a team – and so have no consequences for other teams. In the example of the furniture removers, if the number of workers for carrying out a task is relatively constant, it will be easier to set up a team of furniture removers, rather than to manage the conflicts arising with each contract in relation to the defining of groups of sub-contractors. It is also relatively easy to adapt the hiring pattern to fit the tasks required if the work is fairly similar. It is merely necessary to take on additional agents if the need arises, and to make agents redundant when the work needs fewer sub-contractors, using a fairly simple regulation system.

What can be learned from the contract net

The contract net offers a task allocation mechanism which brings great flexibility to the manner in which the agreement between the clients and the suppliers is managed. However, this is not a model for the resolution of problems, but only for a protocol for the organisation and dynamic distribution of work. Like all protocols, it has no bearing on the content of what is exchanged. In particular, it assumes that a common language exists for the description of the tasks and the data to be sent. If R. Smith was able to give us some indications on how to constitute such a language on the basis of the concept of the description of attributes (cf. Section 7.3.2), other options are open, but at all events remain the responsibility of the designer of a multi-agent system.

Advantages

The advantages of the contract net are obvious:

(1)   We are dealing with an allocation mechanism which is simple to create and which can be designed on a distributed architecture. However, some precautions should be taken with regard to access to agents, the influence of multiple managers and the management of commitments.

(2)   It can be very dynamic, as there is absolutely no need to call on any acquaintances management. An agent need only be capable of registering with (check-in) and leaving (check-out) the network in order to take account of the arrival of new agents and the disappearance of old ones.

(3)   The task and the agent are matched up on the basis of a bilateral agreement between the client and the supplier, which makes it possible to take account of a large number of parameters, such as the agents' skills, the workload, the type of task to be carried out, the description of operations, the type of data to be supplied, the maximum authorised waiting period, the cost, the urgency, etc.

Drawbacks

Unfortunately, the contract net is not free from drawbacks:

(1)   If the design is simple, the execution is difficult, and generates a large number of messages. In fact, the number M of messages for a net such as we have given in BRIC is in the order of:

$$M = N + 2\alpha N = (1 + 2\alpha)N$$

where α represents the ratio of the number of bidders interested in a request for bids to the total number of agents in a system. It will be seen that as soon as the ratio approaches 0.5, which means that half of the agents are interested in each request, the total number of messages is in the order of N^2. For this reason, the contract net can be applied only to small societies of agents in which only high-level tasks can be dealt with by requests for bids, in such a way that the transaction times are not too prohibitive in relation to execution times. And indeed, who would be interested in a system for which all the computation time was taken up by distribution procedures and which therefore did not do anything productive?

(2)   We have also seen that the simplicity of the implementation is only on the surface and that, if we wish to benefit from a relatively high-performance allocation, either the number of requests for bids must be low or else a complex structure has to be implemented to manage the problems related to the parallelism of the processes. Incidentally, it is a shame that very little study has been done on performance evaluation for this type of allocation and on the theoretical and practical problems encountered in distributed implementation.

(3)   Finally, when tasks can be broken down further, it is necessary for the agents to have a decision-making strategy which allows them to choose between early commitment, late commitment and commitment by hiring.

The contract net system can therefore be applied only to small-size nets carrying out tasks broken down into very small elements, and in this case it offers considerable advantages in terms of simplicity and dynamism, as witnessed by their application in industry. We may, in particular, refer to Parunak (1990) for an introduction to the Yams flexible workshop management system and to the Flavors Paint Shop described briefly in Chapter 1.

7.3.3   **Variations and hybrid allocations**

The mechanisms which we developed before correspond to 'pure' approaches, whether we are speaking of the contacts system approach or that of using a contract net. It is obviously possible either to create variations of one of these approaches or to merge them to try to combine their advantages.

Contract net guided by proposals

The classic form of the contract net is guided by requests. It is the managers that ask the potential bidders to submit proposals concerning the tasks which the managers would like to see carried out. As we have seen, this form of allocation is more particularly adapted to low load situations, in such a way as to diminish conflicts, as well as the large number of messages needed for transactions.

It is possible to invert contract net protocol so that suppliers alert potential clients to their capacity. In this case, the system is guided by the proposals, that is, by the availability of the bidders. Although it is frequently used in the case of task distribution in distributed operation systems, this approach has been studied only to a very limited extent in the context of multi-agent systems. Nevertheless, if the suppliers inform the clients of their skills and their availability, this technique then resembles mechanisms for managing direct contacts, since the manager then knows the set of agents likely to be of interest to it.

Synthesis of contract net and acquaintance network

Managing tasks through acquaintances or through a contract net involves the same problems. What is needed is a system that can operate without the system designer having to say explicitly who must do what. In other words, a system that can ensure that tasks will be carried out by competent agents and at the same time that will arrange and take into account transformations such as addition and deletion of agents or modification of agents' capacities.

In an acquaintance network, the data characterising the skills or the state of an agent can be accessed directly by the clients, which can then make decisions without having to broadcast general advertisements. In a pure contract net, in contrast, it is assumed that the agents have no *a priori* knowledge of other agents. It is therefore necessary to ask all those that are interested to indicate their skills by means of a proposal.

We have seen that the acquaintance network is decidedly faster than the contract net (especially in direct allocation), since all that is needed is to ask the agents whether they know how to do the work, without there being any necessity to issue a request for bids. However, the acquaintance network lacks dynamism, since any modification requires a network reorganisation phase. It is possible to try to merge these two approaches in several ways in order to obtain the best advantage from them. Several ways exist in which acquaintance networks and the contract net can be combined.

(1)   The first consists of using the acquaintances system for 'small' tasks and the contract net for 'big' tasks. We have seen that the number one problem for the contract net relates to the number of messages, together with the possible waiting times before the manager can evaluate the proposals and award the contract. When large-scale tasks are involved, these waiting times can be accepted. But the same is not true for elementary tasks, which require only

a limited time to be carried out. In that case, we can use an acquaintance network for all requests that do not call for too much work (and an allocation error is not too serious, since the tasks do not take much time) and reserve the requests for bids for the more large-scale tasks.

(2)   In the second an acquaintance network can learn by using requests for bids every time this is necessary. For example, this can happen if there is a problem in the acquaintance network and a client does not find a supplier corresponding to what it wants, or again if new agents wish to enter the network. A contract net protocol can then be used to build and modify the acquaintance relationships.

Finally, a system of acquaintances can also be seen as a kind of cache memory of the contract net, or again as a compiled structure of the latter. The acquaintances act as a cache memory. Accessing them is faster, since it is no longer necessary to question the acquaintances about their capabilities but as a counterpart there must be a suitable way of managing any lack of coherence between acquaintances and agents which can arise, in particular, during reorganisations of the network. This is also a compiled version of the contract net, which makes it possible to avoid the request for bids and the cost of sending the associated messages. In this case, the reorganisation of an acquaintance network can be compared to a recompilation of a previously compiled structure.

7.3.4   Contracts and commitments

Concept of contract

A contract is defined as 'an agreement, by means of which one or more persons undertake to give, to do, or not to do, something'. This definition can just as easily be applied to contracts between agents. The supplier commits itself to a client to do everything possible to carry out the task, the attribution of which it has accepted, and the client commits itself not to propose the same task to another agent (even if sometimes this commitment is not always carried through). As we saw in Chapter 5, a set of commitments forms dependency structures. The fact that A can carry out its contract itself depends on another contract which B has accepted. This set of dependencies constitutes a network which structures collective action and enables cognitive agents to accomplish tasks by assuming that their suppliers will actually carry out the tasks to which they have committed themselves.

End of contract

A contract goes through a series of states, of which the main ones are as follows:

(1)   Initially, it is *in the course of allocation*. Whether we are dealing with a contract net or a system of allocation through acquaintances, no one has yet been selected to carry out the task, and the contract has therefore not yet been concluded.

(2)   The fact that the supplier agrees to carry out a task commits the latter to doing it, and so the contract is *concluded*.

(3)   If all goes well, the task is carried out normally and the supplier reports back that the task has been properly completed, and the contract is then in the *executed* state.

(4)   If, by contrast, an unforeseen event occurs during the execution of the contract because the supplier cannot fulfil its commitments, the contract is *broken*. In this case, the agent sends an `Impossible` message to its client.

What can the client do when a contract is broken? It is presented with several alternatives, and choosing one rather than another depends on its capacities, and on the nature of the task, T.

- If we are dealing with a task of small importance, the client for T may decide purely and simply to abandon it.

- If the task is important, and forms part of a more important task T_1, the client for T can (a) try to find another supplier, or else (b) tell the client for T_1 that it cannot execute T_1 either, which risks leading to a veritable cascade of broken contracts.

Breaking contracts can also lead to penalties. Thus, in the case of an acquaintance network, the client for T can delete this supplier from its acquaintances having the skills necessary for carrying out T. In a contract net, these penalties will compel the supplier to submit fewer bids in future for the execution of any tasks like T.

7.4   Integrating tasks and mental states

7.4.1   The SAM system

How can we integrate mental states, such as intentions and commitments, and allocation algorithms such as the contract net or acquaintances management? In order to answer this question, let us study the case of a system, SAM (Social Agent Model), developed by Thierry Bouron (1992). The interesting thing about his work is that it demonstrated the importance of collaboration mechanisms for the performance of the group. He applied his model to the very classical example of the pursuit by predators of prey, in which predators have to surround the prey animals, which flee by moving at random, as set out in Chapter 1. All the difficulties relate to the design of the predators and, in particular, to the way in which they cooperate to catch prey animals. So the idea is to design different cooperation strategies and evaluate them in relation to the performance levels for captures. In particular, his strategies consist of defining ephemeral *associations*, which last only for the time required to carry out the overall task.

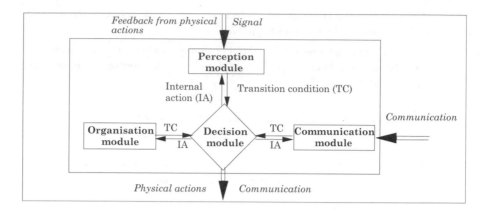

Figure 7.19   Organisation of a SAM agent.

T. Bouron developed a complete model for cooperation between agents, based on the concept of speech acts and that of commitment, and which integrates cooperation mechanisms such as the contract net. Agents are organised in such a way as to execute overall tasks, referred to by T. Bouron as social tasks, whose objective is to capture a prey animal. The agents are defined with the aid of a modular architecture (cf. Chapter 3) consisting of four modules – perception, organisation, communication and decision – as shown in Figure 7.19.

The first two modules handle perceptions and communications. The third, the organisation module, manages the commitments made by the agent. It contains a representation of the overall task from which its commitments stem, a description of the local task which the agent has been appointed to carry out in the context of the association and, as a minimum, the name and address of one other agent involved in this association.

The decision module is the most important of the four, as it determines the agent's behaviour, that is, the physical actions and the messages sent to other agents. This module is represented in the form of a finite-state automaton in which each decision is represented in the form of a transition which can be fired only if the agent is in the desired state and if all the conditions of application of the decision have been fulfilled. An agent's state is determined by a Boolean function relating to a set of variables of states called *statuses*. These variables, like the conditions and the transition actions, can be classified in several categories, as shown by Figure 7.20.

7.4.2   The hierarchy of architectures

In order to analyse the efficiency of cooperation of agents in a more refined way, T. Bouron defined a hierarchy which distinguishes between several levels of agents (Figure 7.21).

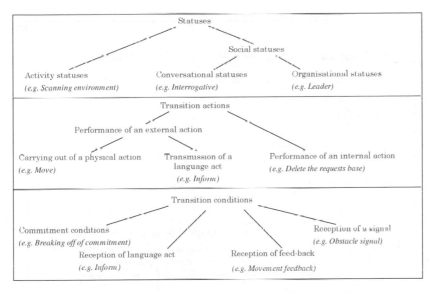

Figure 7.20   Statuses, actions and transition conditions of a SAM agent.

At the first level, the agents are merely mobile. They have only a perception capacity and cannot communicate with others. At the next level, the agents can communicate data to each other concerning the state of the external world, and can, in this way, increase agents' perception capacities. Level 3 introduces the contract concept. A *leader* is capable of recruiting collaborators to form groups of predators. Through the contract system, it is possible to define only groups which are of the 'right size', that is, where there are neither too many agents nor not enough agents which undertake to hunt a particular prey. The contract preparation technique is based on that for the contract net we presented above. At the next level, a delegation procedure is defined that authorises non-leader agents to delegate their contract to another agent if they discover a prey animal which is not yet being hunted. In this case, the agent disengages from its group and becomes the leader of a new group when the delegation of its current task has been completed. This mechanism makes it possible to increase the number of tasks taken into account by using committed agents as potential leaders of new groups. Finally, at the last level, a regrouping procedure allows several small groups which do not have enough agents to carry out their task to join together and unite their forces. This procedure is a response to the sub-contracting problem described in Section 7.3.2, which leaves groups incapable of carrying out the task to which they have committed themselves.

7.4.3   The results

This study is interesting, not only because of the definition of this set of architectures, which fit into one another, but also because of the experimentation aimed at analysing the performance of these systems.

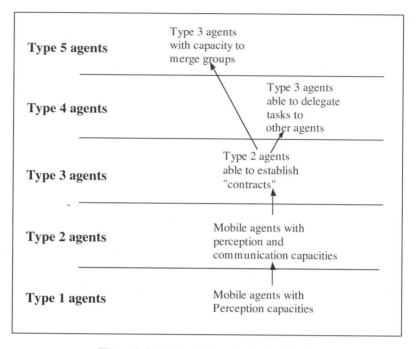

Figure 7.21 The different behaviour levels.

Figure 7.22 sets out the results obtained with these different architectures for a density of agents (number of predators versus number of prey animals) of 2. It can be observed that for this density the most complicated agents perform better than type 1 and 2 agents, since they can catch a higher number of prey animals in a shorter time. It should nevertheless be pointed out that type 3 agents, which have only contractual capacities, without mechanisms for delegation or reorganisation of groups, perform better here, for the density of predators is relatively high. For very low densities, agents of a higher type perform better; they can delegate tasks or regroup, so adding considerable interest by comparison with a simple contract net. However, it can be observed that the regrouping phenomenon is particularly interesting, if the time involved is not too long (less than 500 time units in simulations). On the other hand, delegation phenomena, which slow down the implementation of tasks, become more favourable beyond this, owing to their capacity to cover a larger area of territory. The graphs in Figure 7.23 give the mean number of movement actions carried out and the number of communications sent, plotted against the density of the agents. It can be observed that the collaboration techniques evolved are more costly in terms of communication, but they increase the number of movements made by the agents, which is a perfect illustration of how interesting cooperation is in terms of improving performances and reducing costs, provided, of course, we assume that it is more costly to move than to communicate.

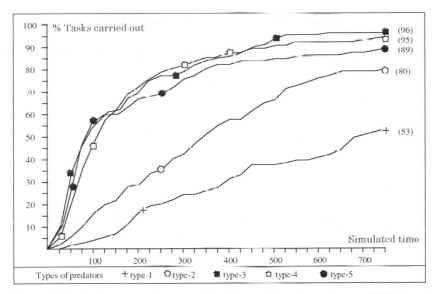

Figure 7.22 Performances of groups of predators as functions of types of SAM agents.

7.4.4 The implementation of architectures

In T. Bouron's SAM system, the behaviours of these various agents are defined in the form of finite-state automata, the states being given by the Boolean functions of the statuses. Unfortunately, as we indicated in Chapter 4, finite-state automata are not easy to put together, and they do not allow us to define the behaviours of agents in a modular fashion. For this reason, it is quite difficult to interpret the behaviours defined by T. Bouron. To make them easier to understand, we shall represent them here in terms of BRIC, which will make it possible to integrate them into the allocation mechanisms we looked at earlier. We shall introduce only the first three levels of SAM here.

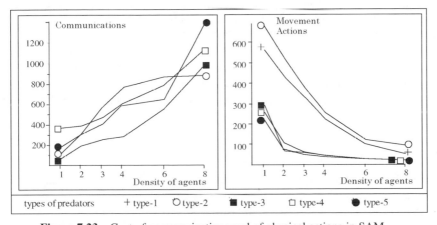

Figure 7.23 Cost of communications and of physical actions in SAM.

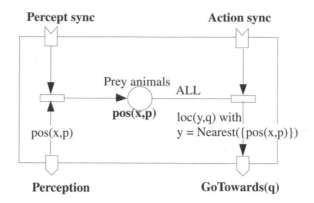

Figure 7.24 The behaviour of a level 1 agent is limited to going towards the nearest prey animal.

7.4.5 Level 1

The architecture of level 1 is extremely simple, since the agent is limited to selecting the prey animal that seems to it to be the nearest of all those that it perceives and to be going in its direction (Figure 7.24). Synchronisation inputs serve to model actions. We mentioned this in Chapter 4, with regard to the modelling of the architectures of agents in terms of BRIC.

7.4.6 Level 2

At level 2, the agents communicate their information to all the other agents. In the version we present here, we are assuming that the agents can subscribe if they wish to receive information from other agents.

Figure 7.25 represents a level 2 architecture in which we have omitted to mention the synchronisation terminals. The organisational system is broken down into two modules: one for subscriptions management (Figure 7.26(A)) and another for subscription requests (Figure 7.26(B)).

The control module implements the conative function, and is limited to receiving data from agents to which it has subscribed and percepts (Figure 7.27) and to triggering the corresponding actions. The agent requests a subscription if it does not perceive any prey, and discontinues its subscription when it does perceive a prey animal.

7.4.7 Level 3

Level 3 brings in the concept of a contract net, in addition to the management of subscriptions to data of level 2. If an agent perceives a prey animal, it goes towards it, becomes a leader and sends a request for bids to set up a team. Interested agents which have not already been recruited join such a team. The leader undertakes to

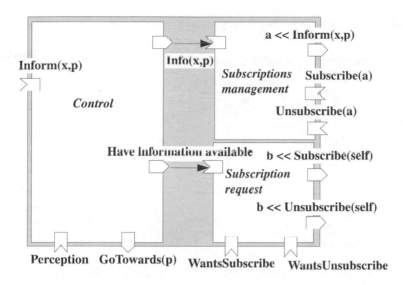

Figure 7.25 The behaviour of a level 2 agent can be broken down into a control module (which implements the conative function) and two subscriptions management modules.

give the position of the prey continuously and, when it is caught, the leader informs all the agents in the team that the task has been completed, which releases them from their commitment. Figure 7.28 shows the architecture of a level 3 agent. It is made up of five modules: a control module which implements the agent's conative function, two modules for processing the request for bids (manager module and bidder module) and two modules for managing, respectively, the team and commitment to a team.

These last two modules are particularly simple (Figure 7.29). The commitment manager merely memorises the fact that it is or is not committed, the control and bidder modules being able to access it to find out whether the agent is or is not committed.

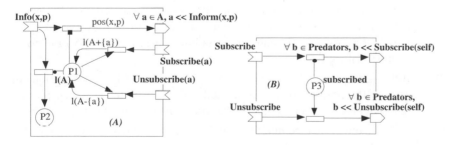

Figure 7.26 The two modules, management (A) and subscription request (B).

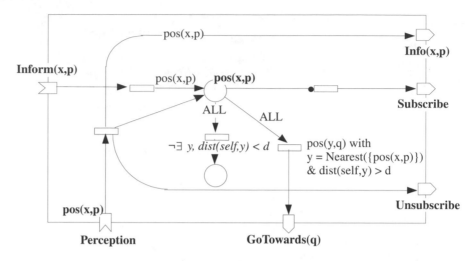

Figure 7.27 Control module (conative system) of a level 2 agent.

The team management module sends the position of the prey they are trying to capture to all the members of the team, as well as the end of task indication. In this case, the team is broken up. The definition of the team is given by the contract net modules. The latter, which are not shown here, differ from the modules we have examined previously only in the following points: the selection of the candidates does not lead to the recruiting of a single predator but three, to make up a team; the result is given in the form of a set of agents which undertake to pursue a prey animal; finally, the canDo test, which indicates whether a bidder is interested in the request for bids, is replaced here by a test relating to the distance of the bidder from the prey and by a request to the commitment module to find out if the agent is committed or not, as only a 'free' agent may join a team.

The control module (Figure 7.30) receives perceptions of prey, together with information coming from its leader if it forms part of a team. It takes its decisions on the basis of the following rules:

(1) If the agent is a leader (and committed – it is assumed that leaders are committed to their own teams) and if it perceives a free prey animal, then it moves towards it and sends information concerning its position to the members of its team.

(2) If the agent is not a leader, but is committed, and receives information concerning the position of a prey animal, then it goes towards this position, ignoring perceptions relating to other prey which it might perceive en route.

(3) If the agent is not committed and it perceives a free prey animal, then it becomes a leader and tries to set up a team by sending out a request for bids.

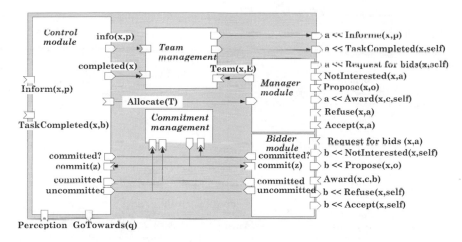

Figure 7.28 General diagram of an architecture for a level 3 agent which consists in a contract net system and a recruiting management module.

(4) If the agent is a leader and it perceives captured prey, then it sends a message indicating that the task has been completed, and it breaks off the commitment.

These rules, implemented in the BRIC control module, are sufficient for managing the behaviour of level 3 predator agents. Nevertheless, a certain number of simplifications have been slipped into the definition of this behaviour:

(1) We have taken no account of any possible disengagement by a member of a team from its commitment to its own chief. The only way for a team to break up is to succeed in capturing prey, so that the leader notices this and dissolves the team set up for this purpose. For this reason, when an agent is committed to a leader, it cannot go back on its commitments.

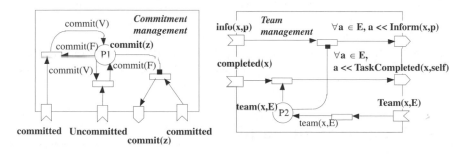

Figure 7.29 Modules for management of commitment to a leader and management of a team.

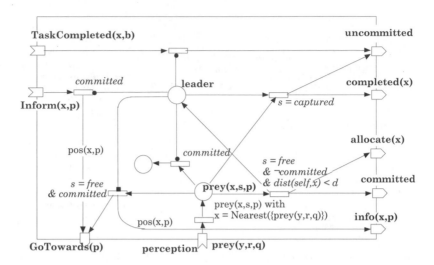

Figure 7.30 Control module of level 3 agent.

(2)   A bidder agent (that is, a non-leader) becomes 'blind' once it is committed, and the data it may perceive are not available to the other predators. This is why agents on a higher level delegate their data to all agents which are not committed so that they have more information available and improve their capture performance.

(3)   If leaders cannot recruit the right number of agents, they remain blocked until a team is set up. To remove this blockage, higher-level SAM agents can either break up an inadequate team or negotiate with other leaders that do not have a complete team to form a merged team.

However, this work makes it possible to understand how contract net techniques can be incorporated into commitment mechanisms and thus define agents capable of distributing their work and asking others to help them. In addition, we can observe that modularity is relatively well provided for. It would be very easy to modify the architecture of level 3 agents so that they could manage an acquaintance network. It is sufficient to alter the manager and bidder modules, to replace them by the client and supplier modules of an acquaintance system, for the overall behaviour of the agent to be reshaped without having to refashion the general architecture and the other modules.

7.5   Emergent allocation

So far, we have been interested only in the allocation of tasks by cognitive agents, capable of intentionally communicating with each other. This activity takes the form of dialogues between the agents to ensure that the work is carried out by a competent agent.

We may be surprised to realise that we can also speak of task allocation techniques in the case of reactive agents. One might indeed suppose that their limited capacities would not allow them to bring into play mechanisms as complex as the algorithms we have just analysed. And yet it is possible to ensure that, on the one hand, the tasks are distributed to the agents and, on the other, that the agents themselves specialise in one of the tasks.

Reactive allocation makes use of the concept of signals and not that of messages. Signals, as we saw in Chapter 6, are non-intentional forms of communication, sent by diffusion and propagation into the environment, the signal gradually decreasing in intensity with distance. These signals are therefore elementary forms of communication for which there is no one semantics. The same signal may induce two different behaviours in two different agents. The most characteristic example is the cry of a young animal. For those of the same species (depending on the species) it may trigger protective behaviour, whereas for a predator, on the contrary, it will give rise to a pursuit and hunting behaviour.

One of the most interesting things about these signals for the allocation of tasks is that their intensity decreases with the distance from the source. Indeed, the intensity of a signal which is propagated instantaneously is generally given by the equation:

$$I(x) = \frac{k}{dist(x,x_0)^2} \qquad \text{or} \qquad I(x) = \frac{k}{dist(x,x_0)}$$

where k is a constant that represents the maximum intensity of the signal at source, and *dist* is the function for computing the distance between two points. Although the second equation, which stipulates that the intensity of a signal decreases linearly with distance, has no immediate physical guarantor, it is often used in practice, because it is a simple matter to bring it into play. The degradation in the intensity of signals depending on the distance introduces a difference in the way agents perceive the signal. There are those that are near the source, and for which the signal will be strong, and those that are further away and therefore will receive only an attenuated signal. The task allocation principle is then based on the differentiated triggering of a behaviour, depending on the intensity of the signal an agent receives. For example, if an agent can carry out one of two tasks, T_1 or T_2, and these tasks are associated with the signals S_1 and S_2 respectively, it will carry out the task for which the stimulus (computed as the product of the intensity of the signal multiplied by an internal coefficient corresponding to the tendency of an agent to carry out a task) is stronger:

```
carryOut(T1)  if  S1 ≥ S2
carryOut(T2)  if  S2 < S1
```

When the intensities are identical, and to avoid the famous dilemma of Buridan's donkey, which could not choose between two piles of hay if it was an equal distance from the two piles, one of the two actions is selected at random. Tasks can also be activated in a random manner, with the intensity of the stimuli S_i defining the probability of activation of the tasks T_i. This differential activation introduces two forms of competition into multi-agent systems.

(1)   The first corresponds to an *intra-agent competition* which relates to the set of tasks an agent can carry out. For a reactive agent, decision making depends on three factors: the initial intensity of the signal, the tendency to carry out a task, the distance from the source and the agent's perception capacity. Two signals with the same intensity can be differentiated by the same agent on the basis of its own tendencies. For example, a predator with an empty stomach will not have the same interest in a signal indicating the position of a prey animal as it will have when it has just eaten. These four factors combine to give a stimulus whose intensity decides the selection of the task to be activated, with the task attracting the strongest stimulus winning the competition (cf. Section 3.6.5).

(2)   The second concerns the respective relationships of the agents to the source of the signal. As the relative intensity is greater when one is close to the source, the nearest agents will have a greater tendency to carry out the tasks linked to this stimulus than those further away. However, this competition is not without problems. What actually happens when two agents decide to respond to this stimulus and when only one agent is needed to respond to the request? In the example of the explorer robots, let us assume that a driller robot needs to have its ore transported to the base. To do this, it sends a signal `RequestTransport`, which is propagated and diminishes in intensity with distance. If several transporters receive the signal and decide to move to the source, which will actually be able to transport the ore? The obvious solution is first come, first served. If the transporters have the same locomotion capability, the one nearest the source will normally arrive first, and will therefore gain the reward of carrying out the task.

But this does not solve all the problems. Competition techniques do not always optimise the agents' behaviour. For example, let us assume that two drilling zones exist, relatively far away from each other, and that the two driller robots F_1 and F_2, positioned in these zones, need a transporter at the same time (Figure 7.31). If the transporters, A_1 and A_2, are situated nearer F_1 than F_2, they will both respond favourably to the request from F_1 and will head for F_1 (1). But, as A_1 is nearer to F_1 than A_2, it is this agent that will transport F_1's ore. A_2 will have had a pointless journey (2). But if F_2 still needs a transporter, A_2 will now be sensitive to its call and will head towards it (3 and 4).

We see that in this situation transporter A_2 headed towards F_1 first and found that it had already been assisted by A_1, and did not need it. It therefore travelled the distance $A_{2_0}F_1$ and then the further distance F_1F_2, instead of making the simple journey $A_{2_0}F_2$. This may prove costly if agents A_1 and A_2 are sufficiently far away.

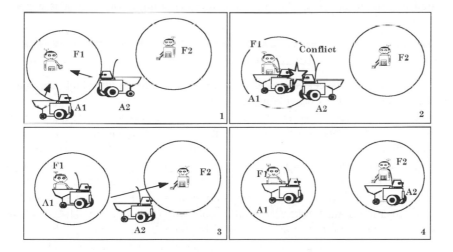

Figure 7.31   The different phases of a reactive task allocation system.

The non-optimisation of robot's route is unfortunately part of the reactive techniques: these generally do not tend to be the best ones, but they compensate for this deficiency by being very adaptable. It is clear, therefore, that this technique is totally independent of the number of agents brought into play; even better, the more agents are involved the more likely it is that there will be a response to requests for the implementation of tasks. If an agent is deleted, the system continues to function as if nothing had happened. No need for complex protocols or verification of end or, more generally, for any of the algorithmic paraphernalia we examined earlier.

There is a second problem. Reactive agents can be trapped in shadow zones for signals coming from other requests. In this case, the agent becomes deaf to the calls of other agents. This difficulty can be resolved in several ways. The first relates to the number of agents. The greater this is, the higher is the probability that some agents can respond to these needs. We can also eliminate this difficulty by continuously increasing the intensities of the signal sources as long as the sources have received no satisfaction. If we can cause the intensity to increase indefinitely, all the shadow zones will be covered one day, and the agents located there will be able to receive these stimuli.

7.6   An example: the Manta system

As a rule, reactive techniques are most frequently used for the advantage they confer in terms of simplicity and adaptability to conditions that change often. They provide for good task distribution on the basis of needs, but at the cost of a certain redundancy of means. The Manta system for modelling an ants' nest is a good example of this.

7.6.1 General description

The Manta system is characteristic of a reactive approach in which computer science and life sciences provide mutual support for one another. And indeed this project, which relates to the modelling, using multi-agent systems, of a colony of *Ectatomma ruidum* ants over the course of its evolution, sprang from an encounter between two areas of research: ethology and multi-agent systems. Experimental work has been directed, in particular, towards socio-genesis, that is, the constitution of a mature colony, starting from one or more queens, to the adaptation of a colony to its environment; it focused particularly on the division of tasks (polyethism) and the specialisation of the workers, as well as polygyny (Drogoul *et al.*, 1992). There was a particular desire to test an ethological hypothesis concerning the distributed aspect of decision making in an ant colony. Does the behaviour of individuals suffice to explain the generation and stability of the social forms observed (division of labour, polyethism based on age, dynamics societies' foundation, etc.)? Can it be shown that a society of agents can survive without calling on a centralised control system or on any hierarchical organisation? It was to answer questions of this nature that the Manta system was created. It highlights the fact that the organisation of labour in a colony of ants may result from a set of local interactions and controls, without it being necessary to call on the intervention of any kind of central regulating entity, the adaptative performances of the society being the result of the behaviours – which are bound to be elementary – of each of its members. In a multi-agent simulation system like Manta, the idea is to model the different entities active in an ants' nest in the form of reactive agents, without calling upon a pre-defined organisation or on any pre-established specialisations. We shall present only some of the outstanding features of this study here. The interested reader can refer to Drogoul (1993), which sets out the problems, the system and the experiments in all the necessary detail.

7.6.2 The system architecture

The agents

A colony of ants can be divided into three groups of agents: the 'beneficiaries' group, which comprises the eggs, larvae and cocoons, the 'carers', which include the queen, the workers and the males, apart from the 'miscellaneous', which brings together all the other 'active' entities of the nest, including, in particular, the food, the corpses of ants, and sources of light and humidity. The Manta environment is directly accessible on screen and represents an ants' nest similar to those used every day in laboratories. Figure 7.32 shows the screen used to define the nest and providing direct observation of the behaviour of the ant-heap. The control buttons on the right allow us to modify the topology of the nest, to add ants or other agents,

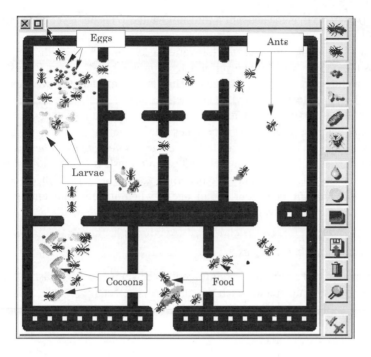

Figure 7.32   An ants' nest as visualised by Manta (as shown in Drogoul (1993)).

and to modify or inspect the state of the environment and the agents circulating there at any time. Each agent is represented in the form of a small automaton which has the capacity to choose from among a set of tasks in competition with one another, each task expressing itself in the form of a sequence of *behaviour primitives*, that is, a sequence of atomic actions that can be carried out by the agent.

Each stimulus from the environment is associated with a task (and with one only). An agent perceives only the stimuli associated with its own tasks. The stimuli are characterised by their *intensity*, that is, by the level of the signal corresponding to the stimulus at the position where the agent is. From an ethological point of view, the tasks represent fixed-action patterns. Each task is characterised by the stimulus making it possible to select it, by its *weight*, which specifies the relative importance of the task in relation to the others, by its *activation threshold* and its *level of activity*. The level of activity is given by the formula:

$$a_i(t) = \frac{w_i(t)}{\sum_{j=1}^{n} w_j(t)} x_i(t)$$

where w_i is the weight of the task, x_i is the intensity of the activating stimulus. For a new task to be selected, its level of activity must be higher than the activation threshold of the task and the level of activity of the current task, that is, $a_i(t) > \sigma_i$ and

$a_i(t) > a_c(t)$, where σ_i is the activation threshold and $a_c(t)$ is the level of activity of the current task.

Tasks are in competition. If several tasks can be selected, the controller chooses the one for which the level of activation is highest. Figure 7.33 shows the general architecture of such an agent. This is the mechanism we described in Chapter 3 on architectures based on competitive tasks.

When a task is selected, it becomes the current task, it executes its *activation behaviour,* and its level of activity takes the value of its level of activation. Conversely, when a task is de-activated it executes its *de-activation behaviour*. Each agent has a special task, which is selected when no task is selectable and when the level of activity of the current task becomes zero. This task, called the *default*, specifies the default behaviour of an agent when its environment is not very attractive, that is, low on stimuli.

Positive feedback processes

The behaviour of each agent is reinforced. The weight of each task is, in effect, increased by a certain amount each time task w_i is selected:

$$w_i(t+1) = w_i(t) + \delta \text{ if } w_i \text{ is selected}$$
$$w_i(t+1) = w_i(t) \text{ otherwise}$$

This reinforcement mechanism constitutes a positive feedback, expressed at the level of each agent, by making an agent more sensitive to the stimuli that correspond to the tasks it has already performed. For this reason, the more an agent carries out a task, the more it will have the tendency to carry it out again.

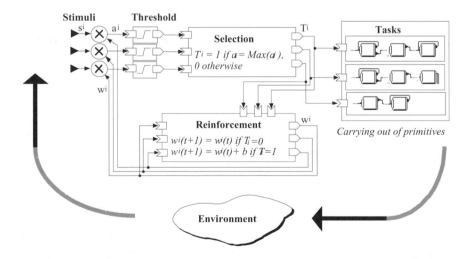

Figure 7.33 General architecture of a Manta agent.

The environment and communications

Communications are realised by the diffusion of signals into the environment. Each agent has a set of signals available whose emissions depend on its internal state. For example, a larva which is hungry will send forth a `hungryLarva` signal, which can be perceived by a worker and can perhaps trigger its `feedLarva` task. Signals are propagated in the environment, losing intensity with distance, as we saw above.

Negative feedback processes

The actions of the workers can be considered as regulating actions, aimed at maintaining the nest in homeostasis. In effect, most of them serve to satisfy the needs expressed by agents such as the eggs, the larvae or the cocoons, which required repeated care and large quantities of food (especially the larvae). Every time a worker satisfies a request, the level of the associated demand is reduced, and the signal corresponding to this request is also reduced. Let us take an example – by producing the `hungryLarva` signal, a larva expresses its need for food. But if a worker effectively succeeds in giving it food (by executing its `feedLarva` task), then its need for food will diminish and the intensity of the `hungryLarva` signal will be lower. For this reason, actions tend to reduce the intensity of demands and, as a result, to regulate their levels.

7.6.3 Experimentation

Task allocation and the division of labour

In the earliest versions of Manta (Drogoul and Ferber, 1994a, 1994b; Drogoul *et al.*, 1992), the emphasis was placed on problems of social differentiation, through the study of the appearance of a social organisation characterised by division of labour among workers which were initially identical. These experiments related to a population of 30 ants, 50 larvae, 50 eggs and 50 pieces of food distributed randomly within the nest. The ants here have only three possible tasks: to look after the eggs, the larvae and the food, by grouping these different entities together in piles of the same kind. Here is the code corresponding to the `careForEggs` task, which is triggered when an ant perceives the `Egg` signal at a sufficient level:

```
careForEggs
   followGradient(Egg)
   if there is a pile of eggs then
     take this pile
     followGradient(Egg) and avoidGradient(moisture)
     put pile down
otherwise stop careForEggs
```

In this program, the primitive `followGradient` causes the ant to follow the route with the steepest gradient, to take it to the source of the corresponding signal (here `egg`), whereas the primitive `avoidGradient` works in the opposite way by making the ant move away as far as possible from the source of the signal. The primitives `pickUp` and `putDown` are used to pick up and put down something where the agent is located. The simulation stops when all these elements have been fully sorted out and when all that is left is three piles. Although this example is not intended to simulate a real nest, two lessons can be drawn from it:

(1)   The mean distribution of the overall work time between the three tasks corresponds well with the initial distribution of the quantity of eggs, larvae and food, which indicates that the society as a whole adapts its means to the demand, and acts like a distributed regulation system.

(2)   The division of labour which appears within the nest is characterised by several functional groups (Figure 7.34):

   (a)   The 'egg nannies' (group 1, 8 ants), characterised by a high level of care for the eggs and a low level of inactivity.

   (b)   The 'non-specialised' ants (group 2, 8 ants), characterised by a high degree of inactivity, although overall they do contribute to other activities of the nest.

   (c)   The 'foster-mother' ants (group 3, 7 members), characterised by a high level of food preparation. The members of this group also show a high level of inactivity.

   (d)   The 'larvae specialists/inactives' (group 4, 3 ants), characterised by a high level of care for the larvae, and also a high level of inactivity and a very low level of care for the eggs.

   (e)   Finally, the 'larvae nannies' (group 5, 4 ants), which are very highly specialised in the care of larvae and display a very low level of activity in other domains.

This division of labour is obviously simpler than that observed in a real nest, because the behaviour of the ants has been simplified. Nevertheless, the structure remains very stable through all the experiments carried out, which confirms the operation of the negative feedback we spoke of above. The demands of the eggs and the larvae, in particular, are reduced by the work carried out by the workers in the miniature 'labour market' which an ants' nest represents.

Socio-genesis

Socio-genesis is the basic process through which a single individual (a queen) evolves towards a complete society by producing new individuals (eggs, larvae, cocoons and workers), searching for food and looking after the brood. Drogoul, Corbara and Fresneau (Corbara *et al.*, 1993; Drogoul *et al.*, 1993) showed that it was possible to reproduce the conditions of real socio-genesis artificially, as studied in laboratories, using *Ectatomma ruidum* ants. A variable quantity of food, which

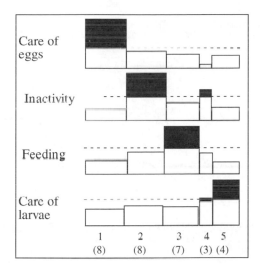

Figure 7.34   Sociogram of an ants' nest, showing the behavioural differentiation of the ants. The rows show the tasks carried out, and the columns indicate the time (as a percentage) taken by the different groups of ants to carry out these tasks (adapted from Drogoul *et al.* (1992)).

depends on the size of the colony, is supplied each day at the entrance to the nest. Each ant (including the queen) can carry out approximately 20 tasks.

When experimentation begins, a single queen is placed in an empty nest and the system is allowed to evolve by itself. It stops when one of the following conditions is verified: the queen dies of hunger, which signifies the end of the colony, or the population of the nest exceeds 20 or more workers, which indicates that the socio-genesis procedure has been completed successfully. About 78% of socio-geneses fail, which is quite close to the real results, in which about 86% of colonies never reach the stage of having 10 workers. In addition, the dynamics of an artificial society are very similar to those observed in reality. Figure 7.35 shows the socio-genesis process for a real colony, characterised by a marked discrepancy between the population of eggs and the population of larvae. Although the curves for a simulated colony are more regular (Figure 7.36), they display great similarity with the preceding diagram.

The main aspect this experimentation has succeeded in demonstrating is that the dynamics of a simulated society correspond quite well to those observed in reality, and show that it is possible to make the social organisation of a society of reactive agents evolve and stabilise, on the basis of simple behaviours with only a small number of primitives. It is therefore possible to dispense with a centralised control to regulate the activity and evolution of a society of autonomous agents. This type of birth control emerges only from the local interactions between the agents, and is conditioned only by the environmental constraints to which the agents are subjected, such as the restriction of food. Secondly, it has made it possible to

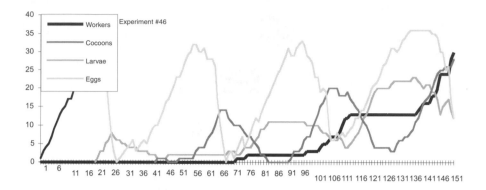

Figure 7.35 Evolution of brood in a natural colony (taken from Corbara (1991)).

corroborate the theoretical analysis corresponding to the double feedback mechanism – positive feedback which acts at the level of the agents and generates behavioural differentiation, and negative feedback which acts in a global manner through a mechanism of supply and demand similar to that of a market. Finally, the spatial component should not be neglected. It is largely responsible for the success and stabilisation of the society, and acts as a coefficient of amortisation in the overall dynamics of the society.

7.6.4   From ants to robot ants

Reactive robots may show proof of great flexibility in the elaboration of complex tasks and display relatively spectacular collective emergent behaviours based on some elementary principles. But can they be effectively used in the realisation of tasks which are useful for human beings? This was the task to which Lynne Parker (1994) addressed herself. Starting from R. Brooks's work on subsumption architecture, she developed a system of cooperative robots – Alliance – verifying its interesting aspects both on a simulation and on real robots at the same time. In one of her examples, several robots have to clean up some waste ground by clearing it of its rubbish, knowing that a set of tins of food has been dumped in one part of the area. In another, they have to remove the dust from (simulated) furniture and clean the floor.

Each agent has an architecture which seems to stem from a combination of subsumption and competitive tasks similar to that of the Manta system. As in the latter, high-level tasks are in competition with one another and are mutually incompatible. The robots can send each other signals, which indicate their state and the task they are in the process of carrying out – perhaps in order not to carry out tasks tackled by the others. The tasks are then defined in the form of a subsumption structure made up of a set of modules linked by inhibition devices. The tasks are selected by what L. Parker calls a 'motivational' system, which can be summarised

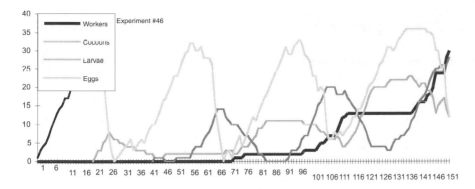

Figure 7.36   Evolution of a simulated colony (taken from Drogoul (1993)).

as a system for triggering through stimuli, as we saw with Manta. She has also developed adaptation mechanisms, consisting essentially of causing the threshold of task activation to vary, depending on the agents, that is, to reproduce a division of labour like that of the ants.

Even if this does not seem to be high-performance work in organisational terms in comparison with the social adaptation obtained with Manta, it must be recognised that the use of genuine robots entails a general degradation in the phenomena observed, essentially due to the faulty and incomplete data obtained by their sensors. This work allows us to validate, in a real environment, the hypotheses which we verified in the form of simulations with Manta, namely the possibility that a set of reactive agents could provide themselves with overall organisation and distribute work among themselves, without requiring a centralised coordinator.

8 Coordination of Actions

When Sidney, a repair robot, receives a request from the driller robot Theodore to repair its drilling head, it knows that this will take some time and will require a lot of effort. A drill cannot be replaced just like that. Sidney will have to ask another robot to help carry a new drill from the stores to the repair workshop. But the heavy-duty transporter robots are very busy just now. Sidney will have to ask Frederick, which organises the work rosters, to put it on the waiting list for applying for heavy-duty robots, and go and find Theodore in the meanwhile to take it to the workshop.

Some robots are busy moving the contents of a room which served as a store for small equipment. But the door and the corridor which give access to this store are not very wide, and two robots cannot pass each other except sideways. So the team has to get organised. Why not form a chain and pass objects from one robot to another?

In these two cases, taken from the same background, task management is a problem. In the first case, the work rosters and the waiting lists for applicants for heavy-duty transporter robots have to be managed. In the second, the actions of the robots have to be coordinated so that objects can be passed from hand to hand without their breaking and without causing a bottleneck. But how? This chapter is about solving problems like these.

8.1   What is coordination of actions?

When several agents are working together, it is necessary to manage a certain number of supplementary tasks that are not directly productive but serve to improve the way in which those activities are carried out. These supplementary tasks form part of the organisational system, and we call them *coordination tasks*. They are indispensable as soon as we have a set of autonomous agents which are pursuing their own objectives, since carrying out productive tasks entails a whole raft of coordination tasks, without which the former could not be accomplished.

8.1.1 Definitions

The coordination of actions was described by Thomas W. Malone (1988) as *the set of supplementary activities which need to be carried out in a multi-agent environment, and which a single agent pursuing the same goals would not accomplish*[†].

For example, at an aero-club where only a few planes land each day, traffic control is almost non-existent. By contrast, at JFK airport, where aircraft are taking off or landing every minute, air control is an activity of fundamental importance, carried out by technical personnel specially trained to prevent planes from colliding. Coordination activity becomes fundamental, and imposes restraints even on the original problem, transporting passengers, by limiting the number of aircraft in circulation. If the amount of traffic diminishes, then all this activity becomes pointless. If it increases, coordination problems become even more crucial.

In relation to cooperation then, the coordination of actions can be defined as the articulation of the individual actions accomplished by each of the agents in such a way that the whole ends up being a coherent and high-performance operation. It is a matter of arranging the behaviours of the agents in time and space in such a way that the group action is improved, either through better performances or through a reduction in conflict. So the coordination of actions is one of the main methods of ensuring cooperation between autonomous agents (cf. Chapter 2).

There are many examples of the coordination of actions, and they can be found in all domains of activity. Two vehicles which cross each other's paths at a

---

[†] T. Malone considers coordination tasks as being non-productive tasks, and therefore also includes those we have linked to the concept of *collaboration*, and in particular to the allocation of tasks (cf. Chapter 7).

crossroads have to adapt their actions to one another so as to avoid collisions. A trapeze artist who has to grab his partner's wrists at the end of his flight must compute very precisely the moment when he launches himself into the air. In performing their acrobatics, the aircraft of the Red Arrows team also have to coordinate their actions with enormous precision. Furniture removers moving a piano or construction workers who are building a house also have to coordinate their actions in such a way as to accomplish their task. The same applies to the musicians in a jazz or chamber music orchestra, who have to act in concert to ensure their different parts are coordinated in a precise and rigorous way, with a pleasing result to the ear[†]. Finally, computing procedures too have to synchronise their actions when accessing common resources, to guarantee that the system remains in a coherent state. Actions have to be coordinated for four main reasons:

(1)   The agents need *information* and *results* which only other agents can supply. For example, an agent building walls will need to obtain supplies of bricks; an agent supervising the activity of an industrial process at a given point will need information on the state of this process at other points. A software agent adding value to a communication network, such as a travel agency service, needs the services of other agents, such as those which reserve rooms and book seats on planes.

(2)   *Resources are limited.* We sometimes pay attention to the actions of others merely because the resources available to us are limited, and we find ourselves sharing them with several others. Whether it is a matter of time, space, energy, money or tooling, resources are needed to accomplish actions; they do not exist in infinite quantities (because there is limited space, vehicles are obliged to coordinate their actions to avoid each other). And coordination becomes increasingly important as resources decrease (for furniture removers, the heavier and bulkier the objects to be moved, the more they have to be careful to harmonise their actions). So resources have to be shared in such a way as to optimise the actions to be carried out (eliminating pointless actions, improving response times, reducing costs and so on), while still trying to avoid any possible conflicts (access conflicts, contradictory actions and so on).

(3)   We try to *optimise costs*. Coordinating actions also makes it possible to reduce costs by eliminating pointless actions and avoiding redundant actions. For example, if Sidney receives two different requests to fetch spare parts, it will be more profitable to combine these requests and make a single trip to fetch these parts. Likewise, if two people have to go to the same place they can use the same car and so save the petrol that would be needed for an additional journey.

[†]The interpretation of a piece of music, particularly when this involves improvising on a theme, also happens to bring into play the four forms of coordination examined here.

(4)   We want to allow agents having *separate but interdependent objectives* to meet their objectives and to carry out their work, perhaps while profiting from this inter-dependence. Figure 8.1 illustrates this situation in the 'cube world'. Two agents have to change one pile of cubes into another, moving one cube at a time. Several scenarios can happen:

   (a) If the objectives are compatible, and if the initial and final piles are fully independent (Figure 8.1(a)), we are then in a neutral or independent situation (cf. Chapter 2), in which the two agents can accomplish their actions in a completely independent manner.

   (b) If the objectives are compatible, but the cubes are placed in such a way that the agents have to take account of each other's actions, agents must avoid getting in each other's way and, if possible, assist each other for each to achieve its goals (Figure 8.1(b)).

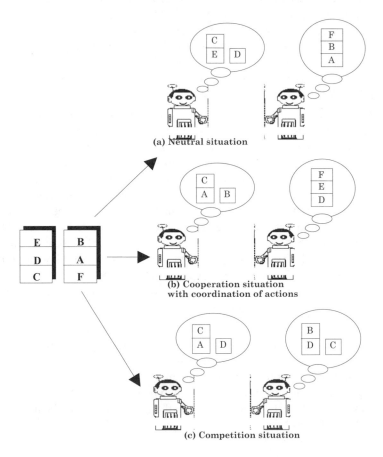

Figure 8.1   Some interaction situations. Only situation (b) is cooperative and, at the same time, requires coordination of the actions of the two agents.

(c)   If, ultimately, the objectives are incompatible, that is, the goals of one contradict those of the other (Figure 8.1(c)), then either we consider the system to be incoherent or we are faced with a competition situation (cf. Chapter 2).

In this chapter, we are interested only in cooperation situations requiring coordination of action, leaving aside neutral situations – by virtue of the fact that they pose no problems – and competition situations, which would require a study of another order.

8.1.2   Coordination as problem solving

The problem of the coordination of action raises several questions. They relate to the agents with which an agent should coordinate its actions, the time and place for the accomplishment of these coordinating actions, the detection of possible conflicts or synergies, and finally the way in which this coordination is carried out.

With what should actions be coordinated?

The first difficulty consists of determining with what an agent should coordinate its actions. In some cases, the answer is simple. For example, in air traffic control, a plane moving from one place to another should take account of all the aircraft that are too close to it, and with which it risks colliding. Identifying these agents then comes down to determining all those which are nearby, that is, perceiving aircraft which are situated near the plane and establishing their position and speed with precision. The case of air traffic control is not unique. On the contrary, it is a typical situation, which is encountered with all mobile robots in general and all anti-collision systems in particular. Coordination is thus based on the relationship the agents have with space and, in particular, on the perception of their relative distances and speeds.

Nevertheless, the definition of the agents with which coordination is necessary is often given by the problem itself. For example, two furniture removers, which have to synchronise their gestures to avoid dropping the furniture they are carrying, do not have to consider the question of with whom to coordinate their actions, since obviously it is with the other carrier.

Mutual dependence between actions

It is not enough to perceive and select the agents with which we should coordinate our actions. It is also necessary to manage the interdependencies between the actions of a set of agents. Three agents have to take mutual constraints and dependencies into account which two agents need not be aware of. For example, if three agents, A_1, A_2 and A_3, have to coordinate their actions, this means that not only must A_1 organise its movements with A_2, but also to coordinate them with A_3, which itself has to take account of the behaviour of A_2. For example, let us suppose

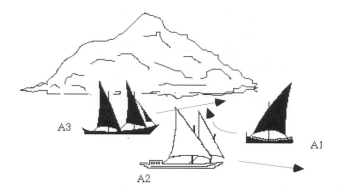

Figure 8.2 Avoidance of collisions between ships.

that three ships have to cross each other's paths at sea, as shown by Figure 8.2. If ship A_1 takes only ship A_2 into account, it may go to the right, but by doing this it risks colliding with ship A_3. Now A_3 cannot change course to avoid A_1 without being wrecked on the little island. For this reason, it has to maintain its course, and it is up to A_2 and A_1 to avoid it.

In a general way, if coordinated action exists, any action by an agent Ai depends on the actions of all the other agents $\{A_1,...,A_n\}$, whilst their actions in turn also depend on the actions of all the other agents. It is therefore possible to consider that coordinating the actions of a set of agents can be reduced to solving the following system of n equations and n unknowns:

$$\sigma_1(t + 1) = \theta_1(React(Exec(o_1(t)\|..\|o_n(t))))$$
$$...$$
$$\sigma_n(t + 1) = \theta_n(React(Exec(o_1(t)\|..\|o_n(t))))$$

where $o_i(t)$ represents the operation which the agent A_i carries out at time t, and the $\theta_1,...,\theta_n$ the dependencies between the actions of the agents. This system can also be expressed by the simple equation:

$$O(t + 1) = \Theta(React(Exec(O(t))))$$

where $O(t)$ represents the vector $<o_1(t),...,o_n(t)>$ of the operations selected by the agents $<A_1,...,A_n>$ at the time t, and Θ represents the vector of the dependency functions. Solving this equation therefore comes down to determining the set of behavioural functions (the sequence of selections of operations to apply) which are the solutions of this equation.

The difficulty lies in the fact that we do not know how to solve these equations in general, and so, except in special cases (and in particular those bringing moving agents into play, and in which the actions are movements in a Euclidian space), we must fall back on heuristic techniques. So a coordination theory remains a task for the future†. It could be based on the idea that behaviours are constraints, and the general heuristics might be to modify only the least constrained behaviours. Moreover, this is what we explained through the example of Figure 8.2. When there is a conflict owing to a limitation of resources, the behaviour of the most constrained agents is modified as little as possible and, by contrast, the least constrained agents are requested to take account of the other agents' actions and to act accordingly.

Relationships between actions

When the agents carry out their actions, certain actions are particularly sensitive, either because their simultaneous execution leads to conflicts or, on the contrary, because they lead to an improvement in performance levels.

F. von Martial (1992) has classified into two broad categories the relationships between actions when they are accomplished simultaneously by several agents, that is, what we referred to as operative relationships in Chapter 3. *Negative relationships* or conflictual relationships are those that hinder or prevent the simultaneous implementation of several actions. This negative aspect can obviously be due either to the incompatibility of the objectives or to the limitation of resources, as we saw in Chapter 2. *Positive relationships*, or synergetic relationships, on the other hand, are those that favour actions by making them benefit from one another, and so tend to greater efficiency than if the actions were carried out independently of each other. Figure 8.3 shows this classification of relationships. The *equality relationship* means that certain actions are not linked to a specific agent, and can be carried out by another agent. The *subsumption relationship*‡ indicates that action *a* of an agent A forms part of the actions *b* of an agent B and therefore that, in carrying out *b*, B at the same time carries out *a*. The *favour* relationship specifies that when an action is carried out, it favours the possibility of performing another action.

Detecting a relationship existing between two actions is of major importance in organising a set of actions, but is also a crucial problem for the organisation and improvement of the coordination of actions. Sometimes, especially if the actions are coordinated in a centralised manner and if conflictual forms are involved, relationships can easily be traced. On the other hand, if coordination is fully distributed, most of the relationships become difficult to recognise before the action takes place, and the difficulty of implementing genuine distributed planning methods is largely due to this drawback.

8.1.3 Characteristics of coordination systems

Several parameters are used to characterise the various forms of coordination of action. While Durfee, Lesser and Corkill (Durfee *et al.*, 1989) list only three (reactivity,

---

†When operations can be expressed in the form of vectors (speeds, acceleration) within a geometrical space, K. Zeghal (1993) proposes some premises for this theory.
‡This is an unfortunate term, since we also refer to subsumption architecture (cf. Chapter 3). I have adhered to it nevertheless, since it forms part of the baggage associated with von Martial's concepts.

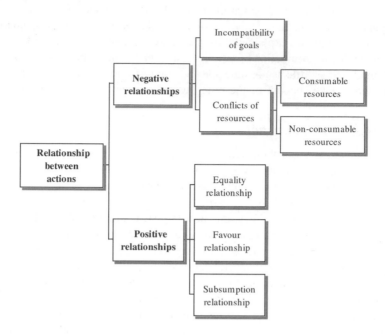

Figure 8.3   Types of relationships between actions.

predictability and the number of messages communicated), I propose eleven here, grouped into four categories: temporal and organisational characteristics, characteristics of realisation and characteristics of generalisation. Studying them will provide a better understanding of how interesting one or other mode of coordination may be.

A.   *Temporal characteristics*

Rapidity, adaptability and predictiveness characterise the relationship of the coordination system over time.

A.1   *Rapidity* relates to the system's capacity to react more or less promptly to an event, whether this event is foreseen or unforeseen. The less a system reasons, the more it is 'wired up', and the faster it is. The reaction time of a system obviously depends on the complexity of the computation, but also on other parameters, such as the number of agents, the number of tasks and so on.

A.2   *Adaptability* concerns the system's capacity to take into account unexpected events. The more adaptable a system is, the more it can react to unforeseen events or situations, and so the more it can be implemented in evolutionary contexts. Conversely, less adaptable systems are often more efficient in contexts in which all the data are known in advance.

A.3   *Predictiveness* relates to the faculty of anticipating the future, that is, of determining, with greater or lesser precision, the state of the world and of the other agents in the future. The more predictive a system is, the less it will tend to be rapid and adaptable. Predictive systems are especially efficient in contexts in which a great deal of information is available concerning future events and the way they have to be tackled. Conversely, systems which are not very predictive prove to be more interesting in contexts that evolve rapidly, or when we have few data on what is going to happen. Essentially, we distinguish between *anticipatory* modes, which try to determine the manner in which actions should be coordinated before carrying them out (planning) and *reactive* modes, which determine the order for actions and the manner of acting at the actual moment when the actions are carried out (reactive coordination, synchronisation). Obviously, these modes are merely the extremes, and all intermediate hybridisations are possible.

B.   Organisational characteristics

These characteristics relate to the manner in which the coordination of actions is organised, and to its centralisation.

B.1   The organizational structure can be described along a *centralisation/ distribution* axis, the most centralised organisations being generally the simplest to implement and the most coherent, and the distributed organisations being able to adapt more easily to unforeseen modifications in the environment and, in particular, to possible malfunctions of certain agents. We see again here the organisational characteristics which we developed in Chapter 3.

B.2   The *mode of communication* defines the way in which the agents gain knowledge of the actions of the other agents. If the agents are situated in an environment, they can perceive the actions of the other agents, either directly, by identifying their behaviour, or indirectly by means of traces and the propagation of signals. Since all coordination must necessarily go through communications, it is certain that the modes of communication play a determining role in the manner in which the agents are made to interact with each other; as usual, we see once again the importance of the cognitive/reactive dichotomy in communications, and thus in the way in which actions are coordinated.

B.3   The *freedom of action* left to an agent characterises the degree of independence in the behaviour of an agent with regard to the instructions which it may receive from a coordinator or in relation to the coordination protocol. The freer agents are to act as they see fit, the more they can adapt to special circumstances, but also the more they are in a position to create 'traps', that is, locally blocked situations, from which it is often difficult to emerge (cf. quality characteristics).

C.   Quality and efficiency characteristics

Quality and efficiency in the results obtained are certainly the two principal properties expected from a coordination method.

C.1   The *quality* of the coordination is obviously the main matter of importance in a coordination system. Are the behaviours optimal, or simply correct? Do they make the best use of the resources available? Are they capable of finding synergies, or do they exhaust themselves in pointless and redundant actions? We may also ask if the coordination techniques impair or improve the performances of the system. For example, how do the traffic lights required for regulating traffic and avoiding collisions between cars modify traffic? Do they improve traffic or, by contrast, do they cause confusions and bottlenecks?

C.2   *Avoidance of conflicts.* The quality of a coordination method also relates to its capacity for avoiding, and emerging from, possible conflicts. Some techniques unfortunately have the drawback of sometimes falling into 'traps', that is, situations which agents find difficult to escape from. For example, a traffic jam at a crossroads can become so solid that it becomes almost impossible to eliminate it. This trap corresponds to a deadlock, with each vehicle needing another to move before it can free itself. Clearly, it is preferable to avoid these situations, as far as possible, by using appropriate techniques. For example, giving priority to the right when drivers are driving on the right favours the occurrence of these deadlocks, whereas giving priority to the left would make it possible to eliminate many of these wasteful traps.

C.3   *Number of agents.* The quality of a coordination technique is also measured by the number of agents which it is capable of coordinating. Some cannot cope with more than a few units, whereas others can easily coordinate the actions of several hundred agents.

D.   Realisation characteristics

These characteristics relate to the means required for the realisation of a coordination system.

D.1   *Degree and quantity of data.* This characteristic concerns the quantity of data agents have to exchange to coordinate their actions. These exchanges can be carried out at two different times, either while plans of action are being drawn up in advance, if the agents are capable of using anticipatory techniques, or during execution. Preference is generally given to modes of coordination making it possible to reduce the number of communications necessary, to avoid information 'overflow'.

D.2   The *degree of mutual representation required* is, once again, a performance criterion. In fact, the more it is necessary to have information on the world and on others, the more information is needed to update this knowledge, and so the more difficult it is to make it appropriate to the state of the environment and that of the other agents. Conversely, the more information we have on others, the more we are in a position to predict the evolution of the system, and so to respond in a manner adapted to the actions of the different agents.

D.3   The *difficulty of implementation*. Certain techniques assume the existence of complex mechanisms, and are difficult to program and to finalise. Others, by contrast, prove to be very simple. All other things being equal, it is always preferable to keep to the simplest methods, if only because they are easy to design, realise and maintain.

E.   Characteristics of generalisation

These indicate to what extent a coordination method is general, by authorising some heterogeneity in the agents or by applying to different domains.

E.1   The *heterogeneity* of the approach, that is, the aptitude to define systems of coordination able to take account of agents which differ in their capacities of perception, reasoning and communication, and, therefore, in their capacity to be able to interconnect agents which do not have the same coordination mechanisms.

E.2   The *generality* of the method. Certain techniques are often better adapted to some domains (for example, coordinating the movements of autonomous vehicles) than others. If it is preferable to have general methods available, which can adapt to any domain, it should be remembered that the more general a method is, the less efficient it usually is.

Obviously, these criteria are not totally independent of one another. A very fast system, which is capable of coping with any situation, will generally not permit good long-term or medium-term forecasts to be made. Likewise, methods calling for a great deal of communication between agents and capacities of mutual representation will have difficulty in taking account of very heterogeneous agents.

8.1.4   Forms of coordination of action

On the basis of the above criteria, we can distinguish four main forms of co-ordination of actions, each of which can give rise to several variants (cf. Table 8.1):

(1)   *Coordination by synchronisation*. This is the most elementary and 'low-level' form of coordination. All coordination of action should precisely describe the sequencing of actions, which leads to a necessary synchronisation in their execution. We generally speak of synchronisation when there is a need to manage the concurrence of several actions and to

Table 8.1 Values of parameters in relation to forms of coordination.

	Synchronisation	Planning	Reactive	Regulation
Rapidity	Very good	Poor	Very good	Good
Adaptability	Very poor	Poor	Very good	Good
Predictability	Poor	Very good	Poor	Average
Centralisation/ distribution	Immaterial	Immaterial	Immaterial	Centralised
Mode of communication	Messages	Messages	Stimuli/marks	Immaterial
Freedom of action	Very limited	Limited	Great	Rather limited
Quality of coordination	Rather good	Very good	Rather good	Rather good
Avoidance of conflicts	Good	Good	Poor	Good
Number of agents	High	Low	Very high	High
Quantity of exchanges	Average	High	Low	Low
Mutual representations	Limited	Numerous	Limited	Limited
Difficulty of implementation	Average	Great	Small	Average
Heterogeneity	Low	Very low	High	Average
Generalisation	Poor	Average	Average	Average

verify that the result of the operations is coherent. The main problems and algorithms about synchronisation have their origins in distributed systems, and are used just as they are in the context of multi-agent systems. We shall therefore have very little to say about them.

(2) *Coordination by planning.* This technique, which is the most traditional in AI, is based on breaking actions down into two phases. In the first, we consider the set of actions to be carried out to achieve a goal and produce a set of plans. In the second, we select one of the plans, which we then execute. Because the environment can evolve, it may be necessary to change plans while they are being carried out, which therefore means that dynamic replanning options should exist. In addition, in multi-agent systems, the different plans drawn up by the agents may lead to conflicts of objectives, or conflicts over access to resources. Plans must then be coordinated in such a way as to solve these conflicts and so achieve the goals of the different agents. In general, planning techniques provide for high-quality

coordination, but prove to be incapable of taking account of unforeseen or extremely complex situations.

(3) *Reactive coordination.* This technique, which is more recent, considers that it is often easier to implement coordination mechanisms based on reactive agents than to plan the set of actions and their interactions before acting. In essence, these techniques make use, above all, of an agent's perception–action, that is, they are implemented *in situ*, and not *a priori* like those above. We can differentiate between several methods of reactive coordination which differ in their use of fields or routines (reflexes) in that they do or do not use limited representations of others, and do or do not use constraints and dependencies. Very reactive approaches do not necessarily provide for very high optimisation of all results, but they are capable of intervening in evolutionary contexts and, more generally, in situations where it is difficult to anticipate what will happen.

(4) *Coordination by regulation.* This is a method rarely described in the literature, but often put into practice in systems requiring limited coordination. The principle is to set rules of behaviour that aim to eliminate possible conflicts. For example, rules of priority will be laid down for vehicles at a crossing, in such a way as to avoid conflict. This technique is obviously inspired by the Highway Code and, in a general way, by all regulations used to define what is 'good' behaviour to avoid conflicts as far as possible.

8.2　Synchronisation of actions

To synchronise several actions is to define the manner in which actions are time-related, in order to time them in the right order and carry them out 'just at the right moment'. We therefore speak of synchronisation if the objective is to provide for some coherence in the system and to prevent interference between actions.

The problem of synchronisation of actions has been studied, above all, in the field of industrial automation or that of distributed operating systems. Synchronisation constitutes the 'low level' of the coordination of action, the point at which the basic mechanisms are implemented which allow the various actions to articulate themselves correctly.

8.2.1　Synchronisation of movements

As soon as several elements have to move together, their movements have to be synchronised. For example, a cyclist has to make sure that when his right leg presses down the right-hand pedal, the left foot relaxes, and vice versa. Coordination is therefore a matter of rhythm and of positioning actions in time, depending on

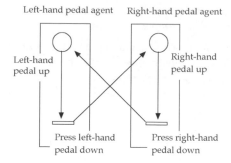

Figure 8.4   Synchronisation of actions of two legs of a cyclist.

events. If we consider each of the cyclist's legs as an agent, therefore, we have to synchronise the thrust of each leg in such a way that it can be executed only if the corresponding pedal is in the upper position.

Many formalisms have been developed to describe and solve the problems of synchronisation, but the best known and the most frequently used come from Petri nets (cf. Chapter 4). For example, the synchronisation of the cyclist's legs can be expressed very simply in the form of such a net (Figure 8.4). Each leg is represented in the form of a location and a transition, with the location representing the leg in the 'upper' position and the transition corresponding to the action of pressing down the pedal. In the initial state, we assume that only one of the locations is marked.

8.2.2   Synchronisation of access to a resource

When several agents have to share a resource, they have to synchronise their actions, to avoid their actions becoming incoherent. Let us suppose, as in Georgeff (1983), that two robots, Clifford and Charles, have to use the same machine, the first to manufacture nuts and the second to manufacture bolts (Figure 8.5). Clifford's behaviour consists of repeating ad infinitum the following series of actions:

```
Clifford's behaviour
   Go to machine
   Place piece of metal on machine
   Make nut
   Take nut to stock of nuts
```

That of Charles is not very different:

```
Charles's behaviour
   Go to machine
   Place piece of metal on machine
   Make bolt
   Take bolt to stock of bolts
```

Goal: make bolts

Goal: make nuts

Charles

Clifford

Figure 8.5   Clifford and Charles have to share the machine to make nuts and bolts.

The actions of the one can obviously interfere with those of the other. When Clifford is using the machine, Charles must not press any buttons and ruin the work of the other robot. For this reason, it is necessary to introduce synchronisation mechanisms, whose goal will be to place the user of the machine in a critical section and to make the other robot wait its turn. The concept of a *critical section*, with the associated techniques, is used by specialists in operating systems to indicate that a process is using resources and that it must not be disturbed during its work. To solve this problem, it must be arranged for each robot to wait its turn until it may use the machine. Figure 8.6 shows how this system can be modelled using Petri nets. The behaviour of each of the agents is modelled in the form of an endless loop, while occupancy of the machine is represented in the form of a single place. When a robot wishes to work on the machine, and the latter is available, it consumes the token and starts work. When it finishes making its component, it fires transition T_3, which gives the token back to the place E_4.

But how can this structure be implemented with agents? The simplest solution consists in considering the machine as an agent which responds to the robots' requests and lets them know when they can work. When a robot approaches the machine, it sends a request to use the machine, which responds with an acknowledgment (message Ok) which allows the robot to make its component. When it has finished, it sends a message End, which releases the machine and allows another robot to work. Figure 8.7 represents the behaviour of the agents Robot and Machine.

The solution given in Georgeff (1983) is a little different, as he uses communication mechanisms taken from the CSP system (Hoare, 1985); however, this solution has the drawback that it cannot be generalised for more than two agents, whereas the solution we have just set out can be generalised without any difficulty.

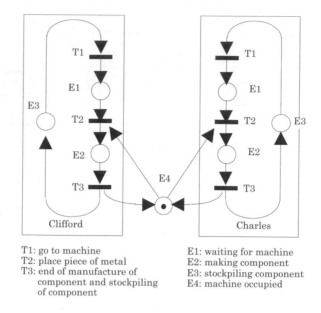

T1: go to machine
T2: place piece of metal
T3: end of manufacture of
    component and stockpiling
    of component

E1: waiting for machine
E2: making component
E3: stockpiling component
E4: machine occupied

Figure 8.6 Modelling of synchronisation of actions of Clifford and Charles to make nuts and bolts.

8.3   Coordination of actions by planning

By far the most classic method in DAI, coordination of actions by planning uses the results of single-agent planning, elaborated in the context of artificial intelligence, and extends them to situations in which several agents are involved. Before describing the problems of multi-agent planning, let us briefly recapitulate the classic techniques of single-agent planning.

8.3.1   Multi-agent planning

Multi-agent systems have not simplified the problems of planning – quite the reverse. If it is already difficult for a single agent to determine the series of actions it has to carry out, the introduction of additional agents has only made things worse. In the first place, multiplication can only aggravate the risk of modifications unforeseen by the planning system, which means the organ of execution must be more reactive, and may require a great deal of replanning. For the same reasons, interdependence between actions can only increase, which makes it more difficult to obtain a suitable order for the application of the operations – difficulties which we have already described in Chapter 4. Finally, the introduction of several agents which carry out their actions in parallel contradicts the hypothesis of sequentiality of application of operations which we find with STRIPS. However, being in the

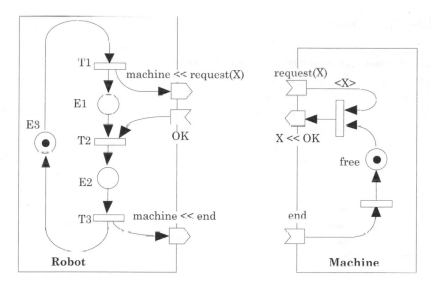

Figure 8.7 Description of behaviour of agents of Robot and Machine type making it possible to synchronise access to machine.

presence of a set of agents favours the execution of actions, since it is no longer necessary to linearise parallel plans; so synchronisation problems can have a natural solution.

Limitations of STRIPS-like models

The selection of a 'correct' representation of actions, which ensures that parallelism in the execution of actions is taken into account, becomes even more crucial than in the planning for single agents. 'STRIPS-like' action models, already limited for single-agent planning, display several difficulties in relation to multi-agent systems, because the actions of the agents have to be carried out simultaneously, and to the interactions that flow from this. For this reason, the hypotheses of STRIPS, and in particular those linked with the timelessness of actions and the sequentiality of operators' application, are excessive constraints when agents have to be made to interact with each other. However, owing to the great predominance of STRIPS-like principles of action in AI and the difficulty of putting forward any other powerful models of action with which it might be possible to make plans, numerous authors writing on distributed artificial intelligence continue to use STRIPS-like operators to describe the actions of their agents. Very conscious of the limitations of this model, Georgeff (1984, 1986) is the one among these authors who has contributed most to trying to introduce new ways of representing actions and applying them to multi-agent systems. However, as we shall see, these extensions are not without their own problems.

Action as a process

We have seen in Chapter 4 that actions can be represented in the form of processes. This is what Georgeff did in 1984, by proposing another approach to the representation of actions in a multi-agent universe, starting from this concept (Georgeff, 1984). A process is an abstraction which represents an action and which can itself be broken down into sub-processes until we reach the atomic processes which cannot be broken down. For example, `prepareSpaghetti-Bolognese` is a process which represents the set of specific measures for preparing Spaghetti Bolognese. For its execution, this process requires the execution of sub-processes such as `prepareSauce` and `cookSpaghetti`, which can be carried out simultaneously. The latter sub-process can be expressed in the form `takeSaucepan`, `fillSaucepanWithWater`, `heatSaucepan`, `putSpaghettiInSaucepan`, `TakeOutSpaghetti`. The action is thus a specific instantiation of the process which describes an order of execution for the various sub-processes which make it up. We saw in the same chapter that a process can be described in the form of an automaton, whose states represent the states of execution of the procss at a given time, and the transitions correspond to the passage from one state of the process to another. Each node is labelled by the set of permissible states for this state of execution. The arcs are labelled by the atomic transitions.

In this context, a plan is a word recognised by the automaton, and the set of possible plans for 'executing the process' corresponds to the set of words accepted by the automaton. For example, let us imagine the world of Figure 8.8, where Clifford can be located in five different places. Let us suppose that it wants to go to 5 to recover the tool. It can go there either through rooms 2 and 3 or through rooms 2 and 4. The process model associated with `goToRoom5` is expressed in the form shown in Figure 8.9.

Each state of the automaton represents a state of the world defined as a set of atomic formulae, and the transitions correspond to the possible actions the agents can carry out. The interesting thing about this concept is that processes can be combined in such a way as to form sequences, iterations and parallel compositions.

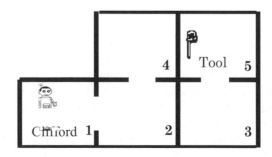

Figure 8.8 The robot Clifford wants to go to 5.

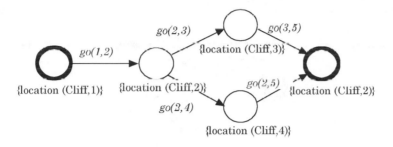

Figure 8.9   A plan by Clifford to achieve its goal.

For example, two processes P_1 and P_2 can be put together in a sequence, which is written $P_1;P_2$. To do this, it is sufficient to compute the intersection of the state of the world obtained upon leaving process P_1 with the state of the world obtained at the start of process P_2. Iteration consists of looping a process P to itself to construct a new process, P∗. Here too, we simply need to merge the initial state and the final state by computing the intersection of the corresponding states of the world.

Parallel composition is particularly interesting for multi-agent systems. To compose two processes, P_1 and P_2, in a concurrent manner, we can create an automaton P_3 obtained in such a way that any state of P_3 can be expressed as a combination of states of P_1 and P_2. In the example of the robot above, let us suppose that we wish to add another robot Charles which is initially in room 3, and which has the goal of going into room 5 and closing the door between rooms 3 and 5. The fact that Charles can close the door reduces Clifford's set of options. In fact, if Charles closes the door while Clifford is in room 3, the latter will no longer be able to go directly from room 3 to room 5. The process defining Charles is defined in Figure 8.10.

Unfortunately, if the idea of putting together automata may appear interesting *a priori*, it proves to be unusable in practice, because the number of states of an automaton P_3 resulting from the combination of two sub-automata, P_1 and P_2, is equal to the product of the states of its sub-automata. Thus, combining the models of the two processes, $P_{Clifford}$ and $P_{Charles}$, which have six and five states respectively, produces an automaton which has 30 states. For this reason, the size of the resulting automata grows exponentially with the number of agents, which imposes serious limits with regard to the applicability of such a system.

But the idea of considering actions as processes should not necessarily be abandoned for all that. Using Petri nets as models for processes, it is possible to combine them without having the problem of exponential growth in the number of states. In that case, the number of places in a combined net is equal to the sum of the number of locations in each sub-net, which gives us nets whose size is linear in terms of the number of agents.

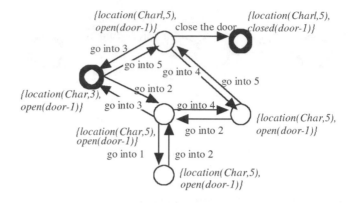

Figure 8.10 The process defining Charles.

To go back to our example of the robots, not only can we model Clifford and Charles as processes, we can also model the door which joins rooms 3 and 5. The actions of the agents are modelled in the form of Petri net transitions, and the conditions by places. These conditions are verified if there is (at least) one token in the corresponding place. Some tokens are completely consumed by actions, while others, in contrast, are preserved. The consumed (and generated) tokens represent transformations of state, whereas the preserved tokens represent characteristics necessary for actions, but not involved in the transformations. For example, the fact that the door is open is obviously a necessary condition for the robot to be able to go through the doorway, and this condition is not modified by this movement. The initial and final situations are given by the markings of the various places, and planning thus comes down to determining an order of activation for the transitions which makes it possible to go from an initial marking to a final marking. Bizarrely, no one (as far as we know - except A. El Fallah Seghrouchin and S. Haddad (1996)) has studied Petri net representation as a basic system for action analysis. Nevertheless, we shall use it in the context of multi-agent planning, for it gives us an easy way of presenting the problems which arise in connection with multi-agent coordination of action.

Multi-agent planning modes

Planning actions in multi-agent universes can be broken down into three distinct stages – making plans, synchronising/coordinating plans, and executing plans. As one or more agents can be used in each of these stages, it is possible to obtain a large number of different organisations, the general principle of which is given in Figure 8.11. A planning system is therefore made up of a set of agents able to plan and to synchronise or execute plans, with the same agent being able to carry out one or more of these tasks.

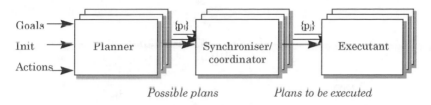

Possible plans   Plans to be executed

Figure 8.11   Multi-agent planning can call on several planners, several synchronisers/coordinators and, obviously, several executants.

The first step is to make the plans. To do this, we can call on a single agent, and we then speak of *centralised planning*, or, conversely, distribute the task of planning within each of the agents, and so obtain a system of *distributed planning*. In that case, each agent constructs a *sub plan* which meets its local objectives, without necessarily taking any account of the other agents. In this case, there is a good chance that these plans cannot be integrated with one another easily, and it then becomes necessary to coordinate them with each other. This task can either be delegated to a single agent, which will centralise all these sub-plans and will try to synthesise them in order to determine an overall plan, or left to the initiative of each of the agents, by asking them to coordinate their actions with each other and to solve their potential conflicts through techniques of negotiation.

For this reason, the three main classic modes of organisation in multi-agent planning are:

(1)   Centralised planning for multiple agents

(2)   Centralised coordination for partial plans

(3)   Distributed planning.

8.3.2   Centralised planning for multiple agents

Centralised planning for multiple agents assumes that only a single planner exists, that is, a single agent capable of planning and organising actions for all the agents, as shown in Figure 8.12. This agent generally also handles the synchronising of plans, together with the allocation of tasks to the other agents, whose role is therefore limited to being nothing but simple executants.

The techniques for the centralised construction of plans for multiple agents are on the same lines as those for single agents, and are generally implemented in three stages:

(1)   The first step is to look for a general partial plan, which can be expressed in the form of an acyclic diagram.

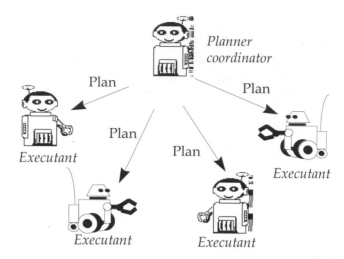

Figure 8.12   In centralized planning for multiple agents, a single agent – the planner – is responsible for producing an overall plan, the actions in which are then allocated to the executants.

(2)   We then determine the branches which can be executed in parallel, and we introduce synchronisation points each time two computation branches join together.

(3)   Finally, we allocate the execution of the tasks to the various agents concerned.

Let us return to the case of the cubes referred to in Chapter 4 in the context of single agents, and let us try to extend it to the case with two robots manipulating these cubes (Figure 8.13). In the case of centralised planning, we construct a partial plan as if there was only one agent, and the result from stage 1 gives an acyclic partial graph that displays two parallel branches of execution for the carrying out of the operations `putDownTable(D)` and `putOn(A,D)` on the one hand and `putOn(B,C)` on the other hand.

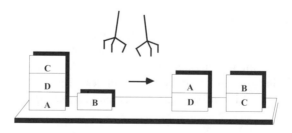

Figure 8.13   A problem involving the movement of cubes, but here we are trying to make two agents execute movements simultaneously.

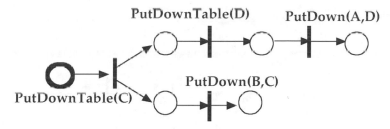

Figure 8.14 Plan for solving a cube problem.

Once the plan has been drawn up, execution points have to be positioned to prevent the agents from coming into conflict, and it must be ensured that the actions carried out along one computation branch are executed only if the preceding actions have actually been completed. For example, we can have `putDownTable(D)` and `putOn(B,C)` carried out simultaneously, since no interference is possible with the execution of these actions. It is then possible to create an execution diagram, in the form of a Petri net, which shows the parallelism between actions and the synchronisation points required (Figure 8.14).

The coordination problem therefore results in a simple combination of synchronisation and allocation of tasks. Two limiting cases may arise. Either the allocation is managed *a priori* by the planner (or some other centralising agent) which specifies which agent has to do what, or the allocation is managed in a dynamic manner at each new action. Obviously, it is possible to envisage a complete range of intermediate solutions between these two extremes.

(1) *Dynamic management of allocation.* Dynamic management of allocation can be carried out by a contract net mechanism, as we saw in the previous chapter. It is also possible to manage synchronisation and allocation of tasks at the same time, in a dynamic manner, by considering the executants as resources which, *a priori*, agree to carry out the work. For example, the problem of managing the cubes can be modelled by a Petri net, as shown in Figure 8.15. In relation to the execution diagram, we have added a supplementary place, which represents the resources (that is, the waiting pliers), and this place is linked to the start and the end of each action. This means that once the action is over, the resource is available again for another action, which elegantly solves the problem of the allocation of tasks.

(2) *Static management of allocation.* In static allocation management, the agents are distributed in advance, each knowing what it has to do and when. Coordination then comes down to simple synchronisation. Here too, Petri net modelling is very simple. We merely have to create as many places as there are agents, and link these places to the actions associated with each agent.

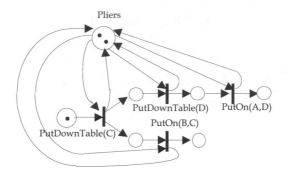

Figure 8.15 Execution of a plan with dynamic allocation.

8.3.3 Centralised coordination for partial plans

It is also possible to centralise only the coordination. In this case, each agent independently draws up its own partial plan, which it sends to the coordinator. The latter then tries to synthesise all the partial plans into a single coherent overall plan (Figure 8.16). It is then a question of unearthing potential conflicts and eliminating them, either by arranging actions in order or by determining the necessary synchronisation points.

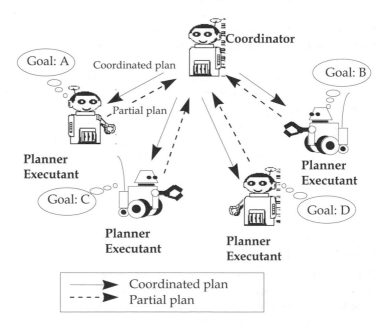

Figure 8.16 In centralised coordination for partial plans, an agent is responsible for merging and synchronising the partial plans drawn up independently by the agents.

Coordination by merging partial plans

Multi-agent planning is based on a successful merger of the partial plans coming from the various agents concerned, in such a way as to make them all into a coherent one. If the plans are represented in the form of Petri nets, merging two plans consists in joining the two diagrams representing the nets by identifying similar places. In that case, several options are available, depending on whether the plans are independent, positive or negative.

Independence of actions

There is no common location between the agents, and so it is impossible to merge the two nets into a single connected net. The agents' plans are therefore independent, and there is absolutely no modification of the execution of the actions of any of them.

Positive relationships between actions

The two plans contain actions which are in a positive relationship (cf. Section 8.1.2). It is therefore possible to merge the plans to obtain a single plan at least as good, in terms of performance, as the two plans carried out separately. The problem is then simply one of synchronising the execution of the partial plans in such a way as to manage the resources in conflict, without modifying the plans themselves. This can be done by intertwining the actions of the different plans, by establishing the order in which the actions are executed, and determining the sections where it is possible to carry out several actions in parallel, that is, to draw up an acyclic diagram representing the different actions to be carried out.

Let us assume, for example, that two robots each have to produce a pile of cubes, starting from a common set of cubes, as shown in Figure 8.17, and that each agent knows nothing of the goals of the other. The robots' goals are as follows:

```
Goals R1 = on(B,Table), on(A,Table), on(C,A)
Goals R2 = on(D,Table), on(E,D), on(F,E)
```

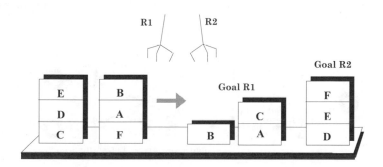

Figure 8.17   A problem of cubes with two agents.

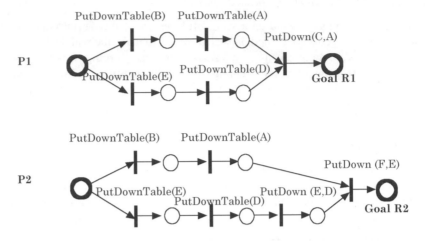

P1

P2

Figure 8.18 Partial plans of two agents.

If each robot has its own planner, it can draw up its own plan without taking account of the other. For this reason, the plans obtained by R_1 and R_2 may take the form of the (partially organised) plans P_1 and P_2 of Figure 8.18.

Merging plans P_1 and P_2 is relatively simple, since there are no points of conflict. So all a general supervisor has to do is to superimpose the two plans, which results in an overall plan P_G which is the synthesis of these two partial plans, as shown by Figure 8.19.

All that is needed then is to apply a static or dynamic technique for the allocation and synchronisation of tasks, such as the one we examined in the previous section.

Negative relationships and conflicts of resources

The solution of the preceding problem is relatively simple, since there is neither conflict nor synergy, but merely a non-empty intersection in the structure of the plans, with each agent being able to achieve its goals independently. Obviously this

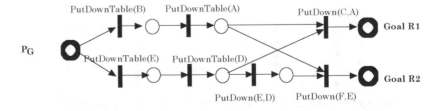

Figure 8.19 Synthesis of partial plans of R_1 and R_2.

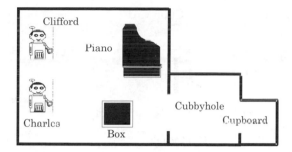

Figure 8.20   How can a box and a piano be put in position if we know that two agents are needed to transport the piano?

situation is merely a special case of the coordination of multiple agents. Let us assume, for example, that we have to deal with a situation like that in Figure 8.20, where several agents have to give each other mutual aid for actions to be accomplished. A small box is to be put at the back of a cupboard, and a piano at the back of a cubbyhole, with the cubbyhole giving access to the cupboard.

The two operators serving to define these actions can be written as follows:

```
Operator : placePiano
  nbr agents : 2
  pre : location(Piano,pa), empty(Cubbyhole)
  del : location(Piano,pa),
    empty(Cubbyhole)
  adds : location(Piano,cubbyhole),
    full(Cubbyhole)
end

Operator : placeBox
  nbr agents : 1
  pre : location(Piano,pb), empty(Cubbyhole),
    empty(Cupboard)
  del : location(Box, pb), empty(Cubbyhole)
  adds : location(Box,Cupboard),full(Cupboard)
end
```

Let us assume that Clifford decides to move the piano and Charles the box. Each has therefore only a single operator; if it has no knowledge of the goals of the other, Clifford will ask Charles to help put the piano away. But if it carries out this task, it will then no longer be able to put the box away in the cupboard.

So the problem consists of organising the actions of the two agents in such a way that they are carried out in the right order. Here again, as soon as a centralising agent exists, the problem comes down to merging the plans and

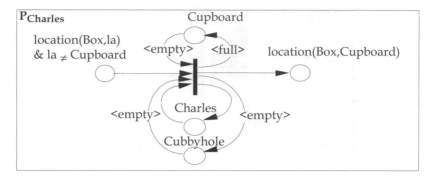

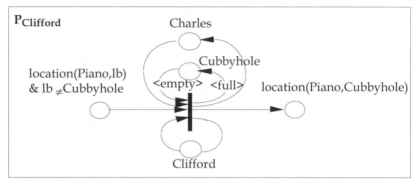

Figure 8.21 The partial plans of Clifford and Charles in the form of Petri nets.

determining a course in the execution of the plans which meets all the objectives. Figures 8.21 and 8.22 show the plans of the two agents respectively before and after the merger of the plans of Charles and Clifford, identifying the position of Charles and that of the cubbyhole as being identical on both plans.

Solving the problem therefore consists in finding a series of transitions to ensure that the two terminal states are accessible, that is, that the two terminal places each contain a token.

8.3.4 Distributed coordination for partial plans

General principle

Distributed planning introduces even more distribution of work by assuming that there is no centralising agent either for drawing up overall plans or for coordinating partial plans. In distributed planning, each agent individually plans the actions it intends to carry out, depending on its own goals. The difficulty therefore relates, not only to the resolution of potential conflicts which may arise during the execution of the plans, but also, as we explained earlier (cf. Section 8.1.2), to the recognition of

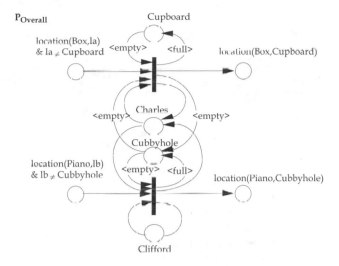

P_Overall

Cupboard

location(Box,la)
& la ≠ Cupboard   <empty>   <full>   location(Box,Cupboard)

Charles
<empty>   <empty>

Cubbyhole

location(Piano,lb)
& lb ≠ Cubbyhole   <empty>   <full>   location(Piano,Cubbyhole)

Clifford

Figure 8.22   Overall plan obtained following merger of partial plans of Charles
and Clifford.

the synergetic situations which can occur when the actions of one group may be useful for achieving the goals of others, so that the agents are of service to each other.

Figure 8.23 shows a distributed planning organisation. Each agent has goals and plans allowing it to attain its goals. The problem for the agents consists of exchanging information relating to their plans and their goals, so that each of them may achieve its objectives.

This is a very general problem, which is very difficult to tackle. In 1991, V. Lesser and E. Durfee attempted, with the PGP model (Partial Global Planning), to give a general framework for distributed planning for multiple agents (Durfee and Lesser, 1991).

In the partial global planning model, each agent has a knowledge base distributed over three levels. On the first level are the local plans, which organise the agent's future activities, with all the details needed: short-term or medium-term goals, costs, duration and so on. On the second level, we find the *plan nodes* (in Lesser and Durfee's terminology, a node is an agent), which are summaries of the local plans, devoid of unnecessary details. Finally, on the third level, there are the PGP (partial global plans), which contain general information on the developments in part of the global activities. A PGP is a data structure the agents use to exchange information about their objectives and their plans. A PGP contains information about the set of plans it is responsible for merging, the objectives pursued, what the agents are in the process of doing, the expected costs and results, and the way in which the agents should interact. An agent then exchanges PGPs with others and, starting from a model of itself and of others, it attempts to identify those agents whose goals form part of a group objective, called a PGG (Partial Global Goal), and to combine associated PGPs into a more general PGP to meet this objective.

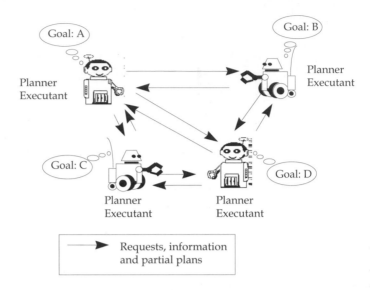

Figure 8.23 Distributed planning model. Each agent has goals and partial plans which it can communicate to other agents.

Conflicts over access to resources and construction of plans

We shall now illustrate the difficulty of merging local plans by giving an example, which does not come from the domain of MASs but which is drawn from everyday life. It has the advantage that it clearly shows the problems that arise when it is necessary, not merely to reorganise the order of actions, but also, for each agent, to revise its plan locally, depending on the plans of the others.

> *Julian decides to take his son, Hector, to the cinema. To do this, he intends to take the car and to leave just before the programme starts, which allows him to finish some work which is behind schedule before going, and then to put Hector to bed after coming back. But his wife Helen has to attend a meeting about her work, for which she absolutely must have the car.*

Here the two partial plans are in conflict, owing to the fact that access to a resource, the car, is limited, and that there are two imperative actions: Helen's meeting and Hector's bedtime (the latter requiring the presence of either Julian or Helen, it doesn't matter who), as shown in Figure 8.24.

How to solve this problem? Here is a 'human' solution.

> *Julian agrees to go by public transport and therefore to leave earlier. He will have to finish the work with which he is behind schedule in the evening, and will no longer be able to look after Hector. Helen suggests to him that she can do that when she comes back from her meeting.*

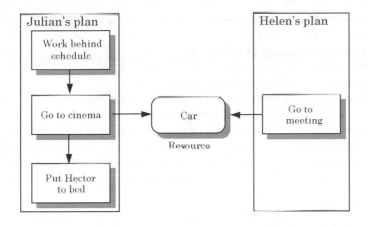

Figure 8.24   Original plans of Julian and Helen, before coordination.

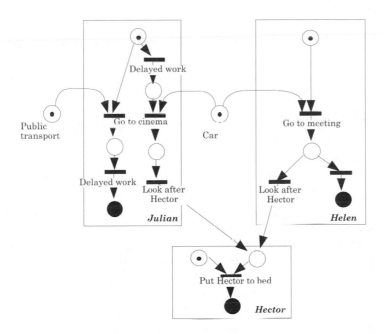

Figure 8.25   The set of plans for Julian and Helen, represented in the form of a Petri net.

In view of the fact that there are, not two, but three agents (Hector is an agent too) and that the car and the public transport services are acting like resources for the carrying out of actions, the problem and the solution can be presented as in Figure 8.25.

Starting from this net, it is easy to see that the final locations (circled in bold) can be reached only if Julian does in fact travel by public transport and Helen therefore undertakes to put Hector to bed. So, simply by using a technique that searches through markings in a Petri net (this is called 'reachability' problem in Petri nets), we can define a 'good plan' that will take account of the interactions between the agents and the available resources.

In fact, the problem generally consists in finding a good way of representing the plan. In essence, in the case above, it is only because there was a conflict over access to resources that Julian thought of an alternative to his first plan, deciding to go by public transport and only do the work with which he is behind schedule afterwards. This is the most difficult thing to do – to identify the conflicts, but also to identify the associated options, such as access to another resource not envisaged at first.

Difficulties, and some possible solutions

These general approaches based on partial plans are still subject to the following limitations:

(1) *Homogeneity hypothesis*. The agents are assumed to be homogeneous and to have the same reasoning mechanisms. It is assumed that, if put into the same conditions, all the agents will arrive at the same goal, which is obviously far from being the case in reality.

(2) *Limitation in number of agents*. The power of these plan merger techniques is limited to situations involving only a very small number of agents, owing to the difficulty of making the set of local plans converge into a coherent global plan in the presence of a number of constraints. In general, all these techniques have a complexity that grows exponentially with the number of agents and the number of possible choices for each agent.

(3) *Hypothesis of regularity of the world*. These approaches assume that the environment does not alter too fast in relation to the execution of the actions, and that the agents cannot easily change tasks. In other words, it is assumed that the agents undertake to carry out the actions they have planned. For this reason, these techniques are not very good at taking account of situations calling for a fast reaction, not planned, in the form of a reflex act.

(4) *Problems of time*. Finally, these techniques should be improved if we want them to take into account the effective duration of actions, and if we therefore want them to manage problems of simultaneity and of resources available only for a limited period of time.

In view of all these problems, and faced with all the difficulties that distributed planning involves, can we envisage any solutions that allow us to obtain coherent and applicable plans? In answer to this question, let us confine ourselves to giving some advice making it possible to arrive at practical solutions.

Hierarchisation of plans

We can hierarchise plans, and assume that their refinement will not lead to conflicts, by going back to the work done on hierarchical plans (see, for example, Nilsson (1980) for a presentation of hierarchical planning). If conflicts arise, we must then deal with them by making the best use of the heuristics presented below.

Commitment of agents

The concept of commitment is essential for multi-agent planning. If the world – and therefore the other agents – were totally unpredictable, if the world had no regular features, it would be impossible to carry out the slightest plan, since it would fail instantly. To understand this point of view, we have to get in touch with a chaotic world. For example, let us assume, as in the description by L. Suchman (1987) that we have to shoot some rapids in a canoe. We can, of course, sit down for a moment and try to find a plan which allows us to get through without difficulty. But, as soon as we enter the rapids, the currents quickly make us change our plan, and we then have to rely on our reflexes, our experience and our skill. The plan is no longer of any use. This concept tends to provide ammunition for the advocates of the reactive planning which we shall be studying in the next section. Fortunately, the world does not always behave like a set of rapids. We can plan our working day, for the environment does not change too much. Meetings are synchronisation points on which we can count if the agents are reliable and if they do not postpone their commitments (or only very rarely). In this case, planning is possible, for the world is relatively predictable, the commitments of the agents playing the role of the laws of physics to determine (partially) a future state of the world. For example, Clifford, which is in Dallas, has to go to Houston. It learns that Charles also has to go to Houston at the same time and therefore gives it a lift. So Clifford can take account of what Charles has just said – if Charles keeps its word, obviously – and therefore plan the journey on the assumption that the problem of transport has been solved.

Pragmatic strategies

We can also use pragmatic strategies, which determine a mode of approach to the world, knowing that some of them will certainly not lead to an optimum solution, but will prove easy and quick to implement, whereas others, more precise, will require larger amounts of resources. For example, we can assume that everything will go off well as long as there are no conflicts, and that we will not do any replanning unless conflicts are detected. In this case, we always execute our plans locally, without taking account of others, and it is only when we detect problems that we integrate the actions of others into our plans. This way of doing things is obviously bad, since it does not allow us to take account of the synergetic relationships between actions. It also has the drawback that it does not take enough account of others, so it has to rely a great deal on conflict resolution techniques each time a problem arises. Nevertheless, in situations where independence is the rule, where conflict situations are of minor importance and where the environment can be modified rapidly, this is a strategy that can be considered, and that has the advantage of being particularly easy to implement.

By contrast, we may prefer to adopt the strategy of the general commanding an army corps, and try to use all data available on others to take account of all the conflicts or opportunities that arise and replan as and when we obtain these data. Obviously, this technique corresponds to a search for an optimum solution, but it requires large amounts of computing resources to model the environment and the other agents and to try to predict their plans of action.

Between these two extremes, several approaches exist, but we have to realise that, with distributed vision, it is never certain (except in elementary cases) that an optimum solution can be obtained, and so we will have to use heuristics, even though we know that this can lead to failures even when a solution exists.

8.4 Reactive coordination

In contrast to the previous approaches, reactive coordination considers that it is often simpler to act directly, without planning what one wishes to do in advance. As we have already pointed out in earlier chapters, reactive agents are very simple, and have no representations of their environment. For this reason, all information relating to their behaviour is located in the environment, and their reactions depend solely on the perception they may have of it. Reactive agents, therefore, are situated (cf. Chapter 1) and operate in the present, that is, they do not memorise past events, nor can they anticipate the future. Although this simplicity often means they have no defence when they are used in an isolated manner, reactive agents derive their strength from working as a group, which enables them to carry out actions of which they would have been incapable individually. As we saw in the previous chapter, reactive agents are very sensitive to the spatial relationships that determine constraints and capacities for actions as well as define privileged cooperation relationships.

8.4.1 Coordination by situated actions

In Chapter 4, we saw how it was possible to define the behaviour of an isolated agent in terms of situated actions. But what about systems made up of several agents? For example, what happens if we ask several robots to carry out tasks, and how can they achieve their objectives simultaneously? We are evidently in a cooperation situation, and several scenarios may arise (cf. Chapter 2). If the agents have independent goals, the only problems they can encounter come from possible conflicts over access to common resources. We can then distinguish between two broad categories of situations:

(1)   The first group relates to access to the same portion of space by a set of agents. The objective, for them, is therefore to achieve their goals and still

avoid each other, as in the case of air traffic control. The most frequently used techniques in this context are those that relate to the use of potential fields defining attractive and repulsive behaviours.

(2)   The second group relates to the use of a limited resource, such as a common tool. It is then possible to use synchronisation mechanisms, similar to those we studied earlier (Section 8.2).

A special problem arises when the agents have dependent goals and the actions of some can improve those of others, and thus improve the performance levels of the entire group. The general principle consists of using the capacities of reactive agents to react to modifications of the environment, and often of marking this environment to coordinate the actions of agents with each other. For this reason, almost all techniques of reactive coordination, in essence, come down to the following techniques:

(1)   Use of *potential fields* or, more generally, *vector fields* to determine the movement of moving agents.

(2)   Use of *marks* to coordinate the action of several agents, these marks making it possible to use the environment as a flexible, robust and simple communication system.

8.4.2   On pack behaviour in anti-collision systems

One of the earliest behaviours situated reactive agents are asked to carry out is to learn how to move in a group while avoiding each other.

Elementary techniques

The first person to take an interest in flocking was Craig Reynolds. In 1987, he produced a flock model based on an extremely simple behaviour which every member of the flock observed (Reynolds, 1987). The aggregate behaviour of his creatures, which he called 'boids', is an emergent phenomenon which results from their interaction, each of them being content to adhere to the following behavioural rules:

(1)   Maintain a minimal distance from other objects in the environment, and in particular from other boids.

(2)   Adapt your speed to the mean speed of your neighbours.

(3)   Go towards the centre of gravity of neighbouring boids.

These rules are sufficient to enable the boids to adopt behaviour similar to that of a flight of migrating birds. In contrast to squadrons of aircraft, which have a leader, the boids move without any leaders and without any overall control. Their behaviour is particularly fluid, and appears very natural when they avoid obstacles, all together, while staying naturally grouped. Sometimes the flock splits up and forms two groups, which move independently of each other. And sometimes two sub-groups combine to produce a new group.

Collective robots

Reactive agents can demonstrate great flexibility in carrying out a task, and can display relatively spectacular emergent collective behaviours based on very elementary principles. In taking up the work of C. Reynolds and adapting it to real robots, M. Mataric, from R. Brooks's Mobot Lab at MIT, created veritable robotic packs (Mataric, 1992, 1994). Each robot has an array of high-level behaviours from which it selects, depending on the situation in which it finds itself: collision avoidance, following another robot, dispersion and distribution over a territory, aggregation and guidance towards a goal. These behaviours call on low-level primitives such as infrared perception of an obstacle, or distance computation using sonar. Here, for example, are the shadowing and aggregation behaviours.

```
Following behaviour
    If there is an object to the right alone
        then go right.
    If there is an object to the left alone
        then go left.
    If there is an object to the left and to the right
        then go straight on and measure the time.
    If there is an object to the left and to the right,
        which have been there for a moment, then stop.


Aggregation behaviour
    Weigh outputs for actions avoidance,
        shadowing, aggregation and dispersion
        and compute a movement vector.
    If I am at the head of the pack,
        then slow down.
    If I am at the tail of the pack,
        then accelerate.
```

According to M. Mataric, pack behaviour is very difficult to implement when real robots are involved, owing to the inherent dynamics of their mechanisms, together with the limitations of the sensors. You then have to adjust the weighting parameters and make sure the robots do not try too hard to move away from each other or, conversely, to form groups that are too compact and that would hamper their movements. Nevertheless, and on condition that these parameters are well adjusted, it is possible to make such behaviours emerge, whether the agents are simulated or real. However, one might be interested to know if the problems actually do stem from the sensors or if they come from an analysis of behaviours that is still too elementary.

Figure 8.26   The fish form into shoals in Ichtyus.

Shoals of fish

Although these approaches may be inspired by nature, they sometimes have only a distant connection with the way in which animals behave. Who among us has never been impressed by the collective behaviours found in the flocks of migrating birds, in shoals of fish, in packs of wolves or in herds of gazelles? How is it that animals can move like this in a group, and can sometimes form very complex patterns? How do they synchronise their actions to give the impression that there is a leader choreographing their movements?

It was to answer these questions that R. Mesle – acting under my direction and in collaboration with J.-P. Treuil and P. Fréon from Orstom – developed a program to simulate shoals of fish, called Ichtyus (Figure 8.26), showing how it is possible to understand their constitution and their evolution, entirely on the basis of distributed actions (Mesle, 1994).

A shoal of fish is a spatial aggregation of a certain number of individuals, based on an egalitarian approach, with all the members having the same influence. These shoals display particularly interesting collective behaviours, for their movements seem perfectly synchronised, as if they were all responding to the same signal, or as if there were some organ of command. Moreover, even though they act in a manner which is sometimes abrupt, the fish never bump into each other, all the movements always seeming to be well coordinated.

The distributed approach makes it possible to take account of this phenomenon. It is sufficient to consider each fish as being an agent, whose direction is a function of the influence of all its neighbours, that is, of the fish nearby, and to consider the collective behaviour as emerging from these interactions. Each fish computes the direction it must take as a function of its own previous direction and of the directions and locations of the surrounding fish by computing a vectorial sum weighted by distance, as follows:

$$\vec{V}_i(t) = Norm[b[c\sum_{j=1}^{n_i}\alpha_{ij}\vec{\mathbf{R}}_{ij}(t-1)+(1-c)\sum_{j=1}^{n_i}\beta_{ij}\vec{\mathbf{V}}_{ij}(t-1)]+(1-b)\vec{\mathbf{B}}(t)]$$

where c is a coefficient relating to the relative locations and speeds (the nearer c is to 1, the closer a fish is to the barycentre of its neighbours; the nearer it is to 0, the more closely the direction of the fish's movement is aligned with that of its neighbours); $\vec{\mathbf{R}}_{ij}$ is the (normalised) vector which links the position of i to j; $\vec{\mathbf{B}}(t)$ is a normalised vector, with a random direction; b is the coefficient which regulates the importance of noise in the movement of a fish (the closer b is to 0, the more random is the movement of the fish); *Norm* is the normalisation function of the vector v_i, and where α_{ij} and β_{ij} are the coefficients which depend on the distance of the fish i from the fish j. When the distance is equal to 0, the influence of the fish j on the fish i is at its highest (equal to 1), and it tends toward 0 when the distance from i to j is greater than, or equal to, a perception distance defined at the outset.

The result is impressive: starting from an initial situation in which the fish are positioned in a random pattern, and running a simulation going through several cycles (roughly from 40 to 100 cycles), we observe that the fish do indeed tend to form shoals, in which the agents coordinate their movements to go in the same direction.

Moreover, the presence of an obstacle does not worry them in the slightest. They avoid it in unison, as if they were acting on a word of command. All the fish avoid the obstacle, while still remaining grouped, without its being possible to pick out a leader, or even one single fish that triggers the movement.

Symmetrical fields of force

If herding behaviour can be explained by a simple vector combination, does the same hold true when several moving agents – aircraft, for example – have to coordinate their actions to avoid each other at considerable distances, while still trying to follow their flight plans? We saw in Chapter 4 that it was possible to model the movement of an agent on the basis of the attractive and repellent forces resulting from the combination of potentials corresponding to goals or obstacles. Can we generalise and use this method for moving agents? In this case, the agents are obstacles which modify the landscape of the potentials of other agents. Each of them constructs its own vision of the world, its own field of potentials, on the basis of the data it has available, that is, of what it perceives. The resulting potentials are therefore defined for each agent A_i as the sum of the attractive potential

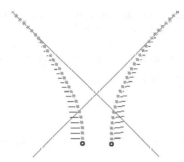

Figure 8.27   An unfortunate consequence of the use of fields of potential when the avoidance behaviour is reduced to an escape manoeuvre.

corresponding to the goal, with the sum of all the repellent potentials defined for the other agents to avoid.

$$U_i = Uattr_i + \sum_{j=1}^{n} Urep_i$$

The resulting force is then expressed as the gradient (that is, the derivative) of this potential at the point p:

$$\vec{F}_i(p) = -\vec{\nabla} U_i(p)$$

Even though this technique proves very simple to use, it nevertheless has a major drawback. Because the agents are moving, the potential fields are continually modified and the trajectories the agents are following sometimes become aberrant. For example, Figure 8.27 shows a typical situation introduced by the potential fields. Two agents following routes that cross each other attempt to avoid each other and to escape. To avoid agent A_2 agent A_1 moves off to the left, but agent A_2, similarly trying to avoid A_1, veers off to the right. Although these reactions are logical from the points of view of each agent, they lead to inadequate modifications in the trajectories. By simply using techniques based on the gradient of potentials, the agents are not able to take account of the movements of other agents, and therefore local decision making does not yield a global solution to the problem.

However, it is possible to solve this problem by introducing a new force, a *sliding force*, as was done by K. Zeghal[†] (1993); this allows us to embrace problems of spatial coordination while still staying with the same logic of force fields. The

---

[†]Working independently, De Medio and Oriolo (1991) on the one hand and Masoud and Bayoumi (1993) on the other hand have put forward similar techniques for dealing with the problem of avoidance between autonomous, moving agents in the context of robotics.

idea is very simple: in order to bypass an obstacle, it is sufficient to remain on a line which preserves the same potential value, and so to stay at the same distance from an obstacle. Mathematically expressed, force $\vec{F}_{ij}$, which is acting on the agent A_i, due to a potential coming from the agent A_j, is perpendicular to the gradient of the potential, which is given by the following equation:

$$\vec{F}_{ij}(p).\vec{\nabla}U_{ij}(p) = 0$$

Moreover, the intensity of this force at a point p is equal to that of the gradient generated by A_j:

$$\|\vec{F}_{ij}(p)\| = \|\vec{\nabla}_{ij}(p)\|$$

It is easy to illustrate this theory. The best way of bypassing an obstacle is not to run away from it, but to try to keep moving while always remaining at a distance greater than a limiting distance; mountaineers do this naturally when they try to keep on a line at the same altitude, an 'iso' line in their jargon. The intensity of this force is given as being equal to the intensity of the gradient at the same point; this means that, the further away one is, the less one tries to bypass an obstacle, and the nearer one is, the more one effectively has to move in a way that approaches the perpendicular of the gradient. Finally, we need to know on which side we have to try to bypass the obstacle. If this is (virtually) of no importance when we are dealing with a fixed obstacle or an agent not reacting to the presence of others, the same is not true when two agents react in the same way, as we saw in Figure 8.27. To go from an agent simply seeking to avoid an obstacle to an avoidance interaction between agents, it is sufficient to give the sliding force the direction defined by the difference in the speed vectors, as shown by Figure 8.28. The slightest little difference between

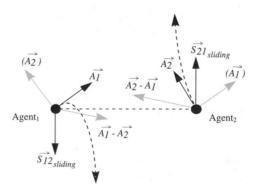

Figure 8.28 Symmetrical bypass by two mobiles. The sliding forms have a direction perpendicular to the gradient of the potential of repulsion and an intensity equal to that of the gradient, and their direction is given by the difference in the speed vectors of the agents.

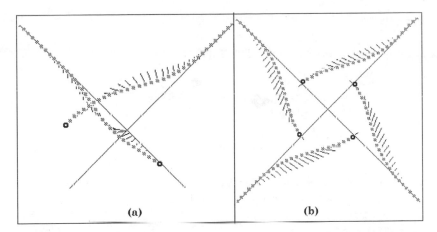

(a)   **(b)**

Figure 8.29   The introduction of an avoidance behaviour using sliding forces not only allows the solution of the problem posed by fields of potential (a) but also makes it possible to generate structures which emerge from the interactions, like that of the 'roundabout' (b). The latter appears when no priority rule is laid down (adapted from Zeghal (1993)).

the speed vectors of the two agents causes the speed vectors to go in opposite directions, which makes it possible to select the right direction for avoidance.

Interesting situations arise from this type of coordination of actions. When several agents have to avoid each other simultaneously, dynamic vortex structures appear spontaneously, giving the impression that the agents are turning around a roundabout (Figure 8.29).

K. Zeghal implemented this technique in the CRAASH system, which simulates the evolution of a group of aircraft which do or do not have collision avoidance systems (Zeghal and Ferber, 1993). He was also able to show that more than 50 or so civilian aircraft (Airbus, Boeing and so on) could all perform evolutions and could all land in automatic mode at the same airport without any collisions taking place.

8.4.3   Marking the environment

We have seen the importance of techniques using vector fields to define the respective positions of the goals, obstacles and agents, and so to allow the latter to coordinate their movements in space. But they are not limited to managing movement. They can easily be generalised for use in problems of coordination, with the marking of the environment constituting the key to the cooperative coordination of reactive agents.

What is a mark? A mark is a material sign or an imprint which serves to change the environment artificially in order to coordinate the actions of the agents. Marks can be put down, read and removed by the agents, but their effect can also disappear slowly by 'natural evaporation' into the environment.

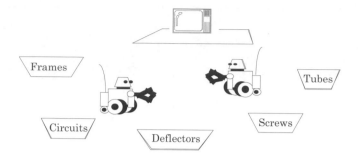

Figure 8.30 Robots have to assemble television components in a precise order, the separate components being located in separate racks.

Marks and synchronisation of actions

Connah and Wavish (Wavish and Connah, 1990) demonstrated how difficult it could be to design a set of cooperative reactive agents and, in particular, that it was not sufficient to add reactive agents 'at random' to bring about an automatic improvement in the performances of the system.

For example, let us suppose that we are trying to assemble dynamically the components to create a piece of electronic equipment such as a television set. In a room including a conveyor belt and five racks containing five types of television components (frames, tubes, deflectors, electronic circuits and screws), robots have to place the components in a precise order at the point of assembly (Figure 8.30). When these five components have been placed on the conveyor belt in this order, the television shall be considered completed and the task carried out (Hickman and Shiels, 1991).

The behaviour of each agent is defined in the form of a set of production rules, which implement situated actions (cf. Chapter 4). If an agent observes a particular situation, and, more especially, what is at the point of assembly, it triggers an action associated with the situation perceived. For example, if an agent notices that a particular component is already at the point of assembly, it can trigger the search for the following element.

```
Rule pickUp
    if I am not carrying anything
    and I am in front of a rack
    then I pick up what is in the rack
    and I go to the assembly point

Rule putDown
    if I am carrying something
    and I am at the assembly point
    then I put down what I am holding
```

```
Rule fetchDeflector
   if I am not carrying anything
   and I am at the assembly point
   and I perceive a tube at the assembly point
   then I go to the deflector rack

Rule fetchElectronicCircuit
   if I am not carrying anything
   and I am at the assembly point
   and I perceive a deflector at the assembly point
   then I go to the electronic circuits rack
```

The first two rules are general, but the subsequent ones must be prioritised. In fact, the rule `fetchElectronicCircuit` should take precedence over `fetch-Deflector` since, if there is a deflector, there is a tube as well, but the perception of the latter should not, for all that, trigger the fetching of another deflector.

With a single agent, everything is fine. It merely has to go to the point of assembly and confirm that there is nothing there, and it then heads for the frame rack, or else it goes directly to this rack, and, in this way, the components are added together in the right order. But what happens if there are just two agents? With the same behaviour, they risk putting some components down twice. In fact, when agent A sees that there is a tube at the point of assembly, it will naturally go and fetch a deflector. But if agent B arrives at the same point before A returns, it will also go and fetch a deflector, which will result in double the number of deflectors. B's behaviour is therefore redundant, and badly synchronised with that of A. This problem can be solved in several ways.

The solution presented in Hickman and Shiels (1991) consists in giving agents the chance to see what the other agents are carrying. If agent B sees that A is transporting a deflector, it will head for the electronic circuits rack, and so will not fetch another deflector. But this solution is not absolutely satisfactory and raises other problems. First, B must not only see that A is transporting a deflector, but also that it *has the intention* of fetching one when A heads for the racks, which contradicts the hypothesis of reactivity associated with situated actions. Moreover, this technique cannot be generalised easily. If there is a number of agents n, each one must see what the other $n - 1$ are carrying, and so be in a position to make a decision on the basis of a global perception of the configuration of the other agents – a hypothesis difficult to apply in a real situation, due in particular to the exponential increase in the number of rules.

Fortunately, simpler solutions do exist, consisting of marking what the agents are doing at the point of assembly. For example, if agent A decides to fetch a deflector, it will place a mark with the form `FetchDeflector`. This will ensure that an agent B arriving subsequently and seeing this mark, can go directly to the electronic circuits rack. This requires only a slight modification of the fetching rules to take the perception of marks into account. Here, for example, is the new electronic circuit fetching rule:

```
Rule fetchElectronicCircuit
   if I am not carrying anything
   and I am at the assembly point
   and I perceive a deflector at the assembly point
      or a FetchDeflector mark
   then I go to the electronics circuits rack
      and I put down a FetchElectronicCircuit mark
```

In this case, the marks act as indices for coordinating actions between the agents and prevent any possible inefficient actions. In this way, it is possible to use the marks to improve the performances of the agents, since they are both indices of collaboration and of coordination of actions.

Marks and improvement in performance

Using marks can also serve to improve the performance of a group and to form self-catalytic structures, that is, organisations which emerge from interactions. The earliest work relating to the use of such marks to solve the problem of ore-collecting was done by J.-L. Deneubourg (Deneubourg and Goss, 1989) and L. Steels (1989). A discussion of the possible approaches and their efficiency can be found in Drogoul and Ferber (1992).

The example of the explorer robots (cf. Chapter 1) can actually be used to understand how using the marks can serve to reduce the area the robots have to search, and so to improve their productivity. Let us recall that the problem of exploration, for the robots, consists in finding ore samples and taking them back to base. The behaviour of the robots can be described simply in terms of successive phases of exploration and transportation of samples to the base. In terms of situated actions, we could describe this behaviour in the following way:

```
Rule explore
   if I am not carrying anything
   and I do not perceive any ore
   then I explore in a random manner

Rule find
   if I am not carrying anything
   and I perceive ore
   then I take an ore sample

Rule takeBack
   if I am carrying ore
   and I am not at the base
   then return to base

Rule putDown
   if I am carrying ore
```

```
and I am at the base
then put ore down
```

We are assuming that returning to its base is not a problem for a robot. Let us suppose that the base emits a signal that is inversely proportional to the distance to it (or to the square of this distance), which allows each robot to find its way. The problem that remains is therefore only how to discover ore samples. If these are distributed in a random manner and the robots have no indicator of their presence, the robots will move in a random manner until they perceive an accumulation of ore, a sample of which they then take back to base.

The drawback to this technique is that it is relatively costly since, if the agents move in a random manner, the time taken to find a heap of ore is proportional to the exploration area. In this case, the actions of the robots are not absolutely coordinated, and all the work done by one robot in finding ore is completely wasted as far as the others are concerned. One method which can be used to improve the efficiency of the search is obviously that the agents can communicate the positions of ore found. Several solutions can be considered using reactive communications (cf. Chapters 6 and 7). Taking their inspiration from the way in which some ants identify the location of sources of food by depositing small amounts of pheromones, Deneubourg and Steels had the idea that the explorer robots could put down marks in the environment when they found ore and returned to base. These marks improve the process of prospecting for ore since, when a robot in the prospecting phase perceives a mark, it naturally goes towards this mark, and therefore goes all the way to the ore source. Accordingly, the behaviour of these robots is modified as follows (we modify the `explore` and `bringBack` rules and we add the `followMark` rule):

```
Rule explore
    if I am not carrying anything
    and I do not perceive any ore
    and I do not perceive any marks
    then I explore in a random manner


Rule bringBack
    if I am carrying ore
    and I am not at the base
    then return to base
    and put down a mark


Rule followMark
    if I am not carrying anything
    and I do not perceive any ore
    and I perceive a mark
    then I go towards this mark
```

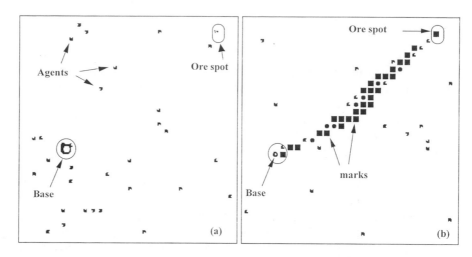

Figure 8.31 Use of marks by robots to bring ore back to base and improve their collective performance levels.

A robot that has found ore and that is returning to base will create a 'scent trail', that is, a sequence of marks deposited on the ground. The robots engaged in exploring will pick up the trail, and will therefore have a tendency to follow the traces, which will normally lead them towards the occurrence of ore. For this reason, over the course of time, more and more robots will be assisted in finding ore, and so mark the trail themselves by leaving marks; this will reinforce the robots' tendency to follow this trail, in a self-catalytical phenomenon typical of positive feedback.

Figure 8.31 shows the situation of a set of robots looking for ore samples and using marks to improve the process. This gives the impression that the agents are following a scent trail to locate the ore sample.

However, the use of marks can pose a problem. Their presence may lead the agents into an error. For example, if the seam of ore has been exhausted and if marks remain, then the agents will follow the marks and finish up at a location where there is now nothing left. So the marks themselves must be dynamic elements capable of disappearing when there are no more samples to collect, that is, the trail must be volatile and must vanish in time. Two solutions can be envisaged:

(1)   The first consists in using volatile marks. If the trail is not constantly reinforced by the depositing of new marks, the marks will disappear. This technique, which resembles what happens in nature with ants, merely requires the setting of the right parameters for the duration of the marks. If they remain effective too long, we shall be back in the situation above, where the robots are 'trapped' in their actions when these are no longer productive. If they are not effective for long enough, the marking mechanism will not have time to work for new ants.

(2)   We can also arrange for the agents to remove some of the marks. On their way back, instead of putting only one mark down, the robots will put down two. On their way out, when following the trail of marks, they will pick one up. In this way, if no ore is left, the robots caught out by the trail of marks will eliminate the marks put down earlier, which will have the effect of 'deleting' all the useless marks from the trail.

8.4.4   Coordination actions

In the preceding sections, we considered the use of marks deposited in the environment to coordinate the actions of reactive agents. But it is possible to coordinate the actions of such agents, even when there are no marks. We then have to add *coordination actions* which, in addition to the synchronisation mechanisms we looked at earlier (cf. Section 8.2), offer the possibility that the agents can help each other in their tasks (or simply not get in each others' way).

One particularly interesting problem is that of forming a chain for carrying objects. The moving of objects from one point to another is one of the fundamental activities of human organisations. Goods are generally not produced at the place where they are consumed, and so they must be transported. But how can these objects be transported from a point X to a point Y? There are essentially three basic transportation methods. The first is to carry an object directly from X to Y, over the entire distance. But as soon as distances become long and the quantities of goods to be transported become considerable, it proves more profitable to use mechanical means of transport, which allow large quantities of objects to be transported over long distances. These means of transport range from ox carts to cargo planes, via road haulage vehicles, railways, ships and wheelbarrows. The problem then consists in *loading* these transport systems, that is, we have a similar problem but involving much smaller distances, those separating the point of origin from the point where the vehicle is located. Either everything is carried in people's arms or intermediate technologies are used which enable goods to be transported over shorter distances. But there is another transportation method that can be used only if several agents are involved. This consists in *forming a chain*, that is, passing an object from hand to hand from its point of origin to its destination. By contrast to the first two methods, the object is not carried by the same person throughout its journey (or by the same system of transport). On the contrary, it is continually being passed on to someone else, and it is its transfer from agent to agent that moves it.

This method presupposes two things: firstly, that there are a large number of agents, and, secondly, that the object can be easily transferred from one agent to another. But the organisation of a chain and the gestures for transferring objects require a high level of coordination of actions for the objects to arrive safe and sound. This coordination can be described simply on the basis of the behaviour of the ore-gathering agents looked at above. When they go from the point of origin (X) towards the point of destination (Y) and they are carrying something, the agents pass on data on their load to any agent coming back from Y emptyhanded (Drogoul and Ferber, 1992):

```
Rule explore
  if I am not carrying anything
  and I do not perceive any ore
  and I do not perceive any agent with some ore
  then explore in random manner

Rule giveHelpingHand
  if I am not carrying anything
  and I do not perceive any ore
  and I perceive an agent with some ore
  then offer the agent my services
  and return to base

Rule bringBack
  if I am carrying ore
  and I am not at the base
  and no agent offers me its services
  then return to base

Rule exchange
  if I am carrying some ore
  and I am not at the base
  and an agent offers me its services
  then give my load to the agent
  and return whence I came
```

In this way it is possible to set up dynamic chains that are formed as soon as there is a sample of ore to be brought back. The agents coming back transfer their load to those going towards the source and go off to load up again. But in leaving they may be brought into contact with agents returning from the source, and may therefore take over their load and return to base. For this reason, it very soon happens that the agents are no longer covering the entire trail but are merely coming and going over short distances. A free agent takes over the load of an agent carrying some ore, transports it until it finds a free agent, and goes back toward the source, and does this continuously. If the number of agents increases, the agents no longer move from their positions, and now confine themselves to transferring their load from one neighbour to another, creating a veritable chain of agents. Figure 8.32 shows two examples of chains. The first (a) consists of only a single chain, since there is only one source of ore, whereas the second (b) forms a fork, because there are two sources. We may note that these chains sometimes include 'gaps', with agents moving between the segments.

The interesting salient point about this approach is to show that, with a very small modification in the behaviour of the agents, it is possible to build coordination structures with very interesting properties, such as that of producing 'open' stationary structures, which remain stable as long as they are provisioned with

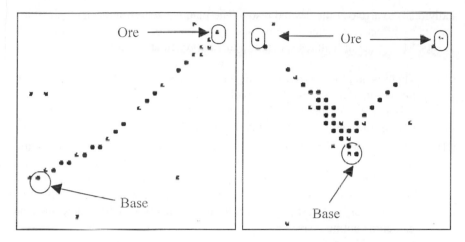

Figure 8.32   An example of chains. The first, (a), has only a single arm, since there is only a single source, whereas the second, (b), forks towards each of the sources.

'external' elements. In essence, they behave like self-catalytical structures, that is, open systems that remain stable beyond their point of equilibrium.

8.5   Solving by coordination: eco-problem solving

While all the techniques we have just studied assist in coordinating the actions of agents defined 'in advance', we shall see that it is also possible to use such approaches to solve classic problems by reformulating the problem. Eco-problem solving, in particular, is a method of problem solving which takes the opposite course to the classic techniques. Rather than formalising a problem in a global manner and then defining solution methods which apply directly to its definition, we assume that it is preferable to reformulate the problem in such a way that it is defined as a set of agents in interaction, which are trying to achieve their own goals individually.

8.5.1   Principles of eco-problem solving

In the context of eco-problem solving, to understand a problem is to define a population of agents, whose set of behaviours tends to end in a stable state which we call the solution of the problem. Each agent responds to the principles of autonomy and locality, that is, the actions it undertakes are, at one and the same time, the consequence of local perceptions and of the relationships it has established with other agents.

In the course of their behaviour, these agents sometimes carry out specific actions which, if they are memorised, correspond directly to the actions which might have been carried out by a centralised system (a planning program or an individual) to arrive at the desired result. The plan has therefore been obtained as a secondary effect (computer scientists call it a side effect) of the behaviour of the agents. The essential features specific to this approach are as follows:

(A)   There is no global exploration of the space covered by the possible states of the world. The states of the world are not used directly by eco-problem solving. Only the internal states of the agents and their perceptive relationship with the environment are taken into account.

(B)   These systems resist noise very well. A disturbance does not modify the solving mechanism. In fact, a disturbance is almost a normal occurrence in the evolution of the system, and is therefore taken into account without any difficulty. Incidentally, it is this characteristic that renders these systems very interesting in evolutionary universes, where new data are gathered continuously.

(C)   For this reason, this method involves very few combination explosions, which makes it capable of solving problems that are relatively large in size.

ECO is a general model of a problem-solving system based on eco-problem solving, which is made up of two parts:

(1)   A core which defines the protocol followed by the set of agents. This core is absolutely independent of the domain of the problem to be solved. It consists of an abstract definition of the agents of the system, known as *eco-agents*, and, above all, of the interactions between the different elementary behaviours of the agents. These very simple behaviours can be defined with the help of a states automaton, as we shall see below.

(2)   A part dependent on the domain of application, where the behaviours of the agents specific to the domain are encoded.

8.5.2   Eco-agents

Each agent has a set of predefined elementary behaviours, which involve it in a perpetual quest for a state of satisfaction. In this search for satisfaction, these agents can be obstructed by other agents. In this case, they attack these obstructors, which are obliged to escape. During this flight, they may be led into attacking other obstructors which prevent them from escaping, and this operation continues until the obstructors disappear.

Structure of eco-agents

Each eco-agent can be characterised by:

●   A *goal*, that is, another agent with which it has to be in a specific relationship, known as a *relationship of satisfaction*, for it to be satisfied.

- An *internal state*. An eco-agent can be in one of the following three internal states: *satisfied*, *looking for satisfaction* or *trying to escape*. The transition from one state to another is given by a table of characteristic transitions for a finite-state automaton (see below).

- *Elementary actions*, depending on the domain, which correspond to the satisfaction and escape behaviours of the agents.

- A *perception of obstructors* function, that is, a perception of the set of agents which prevent the current agent from being satisfied or escaping.

To this we must add the concept of dependencies, which is very frequently used in ECO:

- *Dependencies* are agents of which the current agent is the goal, and these dependencies can be in the *satisfied* state only if the current agent itself is satisfied. These dependencies are produced by the definition of the goals, and so by the establishment of the satisfaction relationships. We say that A is directly dependent on B if A is one of the dependencies of B (or if B is a goal for A). 'Being dependent on' is a relationship of a partial order, which can be stated like this: we say that A *depends on* B if B is directly dependent on A, or if another agent C exists, such that A is directly dependent on C and that C depends on B.

Behaviour of eco-agents

The elementary behaviours of an eco-agent are independent of the domain of application, and their interaction is defined in the core of ECO. These behaviours can be described as procedures[†]. Here is the simplified definition of these procedures:

(1) *The wish to be satisfied*: Eco-agents want to be in a state of satisfaction. If they cannot reach it, because they are prevented from this by obstructors, they attack the latter:

```
Procedure trySatisfy(x)
   if the goal of x is satisfied then
      for all the agents which are obstructing x
         escape(y, x, goal(x));
      as soon as there are no more obstructors,
         then satisfy(x)
```

The satisfy function depends on the domain of application, and has to be adapted for each type of eco-agent. It is responsible for carrying out the operation, the result of which will cause the agent to verify its condition of satisfaction. This action is made possible by the escape of the obstructors.

[†]In point of fact, as these functions are dependent on a type of agent, it is easier to represent them as methods of an object language.

(2)   *The obligation to escape*: When an eco-agent is attacked, it must escape. It must then search for a situation that satisfies the constraint c, which is used as the line of reasoning for the `escape` procedure. Here is its definition:

```
Procedure escape(x, y, c) // x escape y
with constraint c
   if x was satisfied, x becomes unsatisfied
   either p := findLocationForEscape(x,y,c)
     if P is NIL, then 'no solution',
   otherwise
      for all agents z which obstruct x in
      its escape towards p,
        escape(z,x,p)
     as soon as there are no more obstructors
     to escape,
       then Escape(x,p)
```

The functions `findLocationForEscape` and `Escape` are in their turn dependent on the application. The first searches for a location in the environment to which the agent can escape, and the second actually carries out the action of escaping.

Eco-agents as finite-state automata

Each eco-agent can be seen as a finite-state automaton with four states, two inputs and three outputs. The states of the automaton correspond to the states of satisfaction of the eco-agents. These four states are *satisfaction (S)*, *searching for satisfaction (RS = researching for satisfaction)*, *searching for escape (RF = researching for escape)* and *escape (F = escape)*[†].

The initial state is RS. The two inputs correspond to the two situations that can be observed by an eco-agent: attack by another agent, and the fact of having obstructors that prevent it from accomplishing its actions. The output commands correspond, on the one hand, to elementary actions (`escape` and `satisfy`) and, on the other, to an attack message sent to another agent. Figure 8.33 represents this automaton. The diagram for the automaton is given in Figure 8.34. Each change of state is characterised by a pair of input variables $<$Attack, Obstructors$>$, where a and σ denote input variables at 1, and $\neg$a, $\neg\sigma$ denote input variables at 0, the x value indicating indifference. A mark '–', indicates that no action has been carried out at output.

8.5.3   Simple examples of eco-problems

An eco-problem is defined by:

[†]Sometimes there are agents that have no goals. In that case, the automaton is slightly different, as the agents are not searching for satisfaction, and they have only an escape behaviour.

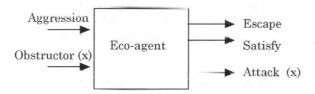

Figure 8.33 Representation of an eco-agent in the form of an automaton.

(1) A set of agents, each agent being characterised by a goal and a behaviour (made up of the automaton and the elementary actions depending on the application).

(2) An initial configuration, described by a set of agents positioned in their initial state (RS).

(3) A termination criterion defined as a function of the states of satisfaction of the eco-agents. In the majority of the following examples, this criterion corresponds to the satisfaction of all the agents present.

For this reason, the most complex stage in solving a problem in ECO is the determining of the set of agents and the way in which they are used. It calls for a method of analysis which differs radically from classic problem solving. Whereas the latter generally uses transition of state operators, eco-problem solving assumes that *it is the entities of the world and not the operators* which are interacting. *Indeed, this type of approach is to problem solving and planning what programming by*

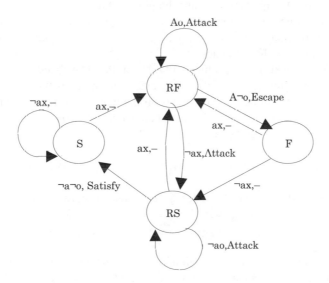

Figure 8.34 Diagram of states of an eco-agent.

object is to procedural programming. It is no longer the operators that are the centre of interest of the system but rather the objects to which these actions relate.

Cubes

The simplest and perhaps the most vivid example is given by the problem of the world of cubes, well known in planning. The idea is to invert two cubes in a pile, which is like exchanging the value of two registers. A cube can support only a single cube, and only one cube is moved at a time. Let us assume that we wish to obtain a state (b), starting from a configuration (a):

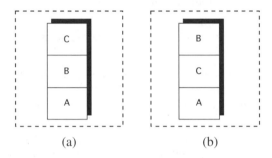

(a)   (b)

The classic solution consists in exploring a set of states generated by applying of the set of available operations to the initial configuration, as described in Chapter 4. If we explore this space with STRIPS-like operators, we are sometimes led into failure situations, in particular if we have placed cube B on C before making sure that C is on A. This failure means the planner has to backtrack and try another way out. To reduce the inconvenience caused by this drawback, some modern planners use, or find, heuristics to try to make the right choice, and so limit the number of times they have to backtrack.

In the context of eco-problem solving, on the other hand, the solution is to give the agents conditions of satisfaction relative to the final state which has to be generated. Cube A will be satisfied if it is on the table, cube B if it is on C, cube C if it is on A. Escape, for a cube, means being put down on the table. The set of relations of satisfaction is therefore:

```
{ on(B,C), on(A,Table), on(C,B)},
```

from which we deduce the dependency relationships between agents as follows:

```
{ B depends on C, C depends on A, A depends on Table}
```

Knowing that the table is always satisfied, we can deduce that cube A is satisfied. We are left with cubes B and C. Let us start with C, since B depends on C. B is an obstructor of C, since it is an obstacle to the direct satisfaction of C. For this reason,

C requests B to escape. But C is now an obstacle to B's escape, so B asks C to escape. The latter puts itself down on the table, which allows B to escape by putting itself down on the table. C can then put itself onto A and becomes satisfied; B can then put itself down on C, so terminating the solving process of the problem. It is then sufficient to memorise the trace left while executing actions to deduce a plan from it.

To write this example and to solve it using ECO, we first identify the different types of eco-agents, then associate a structure with them, and finally define the behaviours depending on the application, such as `escape` and `satisfy` In the world of cubes, two types of agents exist: the cubes and the surfaces, of which the table is the only example. Let us suppose that a cube can support only a single cube and that surfaces have an infinite location. Here is the definition of these types of agents:

```
Type Cube
  Sub-type of EcoAgent
  Fields
    above : Cube
    below : EcoAgent (Cube or Surface)

Procedure satisfy(x :Cube)
  x.goal.above(x)
  x.below.above(nil)
  x.below.goal

Procedure escape(x : Cube, p :EcoAgent)
  x.below.above(nil)
  x.below := p

Procedure satisfied?(x :Cube)
  if x.below = x.goal
then return(True)
else return(False)

Procedure findLocationForEscape(x : Cube)
  return(Table)
```

Now here are the procedures defining the obstructors of escape and satisfaction. A cube is obstructed in trying to escape if there is a cube on top of it, and it is obstructed in trying to satisfy itself if there is a cube on it or on its goal:

```
Procedure obstructorsEscape(x :Cube)
  if x.above <> nil then
  // list of obstructors returned
    return(x.above)
```

```
else
  return(nil) // otherwise nothing

Procedure obstructorSatisfaction(x :Cube)
  local r
  r :=x.above or x.goal.above
  if r <> nil then
    return(r),
  else
    return(nil)
```

The definition of the surfaces is much simpler. They are always satisfied, and as they are always free (we are assuming the table is infinite), they have no obstructors at all.

```
Type Surface
  Sub-type of EcoAgent

  Procedure satisfied?(x :Surface)
    return(True)
```

It will be noted that all these procedures correspond to simple actions. They do not call up any method of solution (and, in particular, they do not call up the core of ECO) and they directly reflect the data of the problem. The procedures obstructorsEscape and obstructorsSatisfaction, in particular, directly describe the constraints defined in the world of cubes, namely that we cannot put a cube down on the table unless it is free (it has no cube on top of it) and we cannot put a cube on top of another cube unless the two are free. One procedure, in particular, deserves our attention. This is findLocationForEscape. This procedure, which is very elementary, since it always returns the table, is generally the most complex to write, and the one where it is possible to add heuristics for faster solutions. We shall see some of these in the following examples.

Cubes with constraints

The problem of the cubes, as it has been described, may seem too easy. Indeed, all that is necessary is to put all the cubes down on the table, then replace them one by one to solve the problem. On the other hand, if we assume that the size of the table is limited, that is, if the number of cubes it can hold is finite, the problem is no longer so simple. This limitation involves constraints which oblige us to 'undo' situations, by assuming that, in order to escape, a cube may be led to put itself on top of another. Obviously, this escape may create an additional obstruction for the other cubes. The following situation is an example of this. To obtain the final configuration, the cubes have only three locations on the table (Figure 8.35). In (1), A is trying to satisfy itself (by going onto E) and requests B to escape, imposing on it the constraint that it must not put itself onto E. B can escape onto D, and attacks

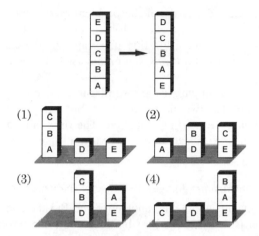

Figure 8.35   A problem of constrained cubes. The table can receive only three piles of cubes.

C, prohibiting it from going onto D. Thus, in (2), A is certainly free, but C is blocking its access to E, and it has to attack it again to achieve its goal. In the same way, in (3), B drives C away, prohibiting A as a destination for it.

In this problem, the procedure findLocationForEscape returns one of the eco-agents, selecting a free position on the table, then a different free cube from the constraint passed during the attack. *It is the only method that we have to modify the preceding problem.* The code for this is as follows:

```
Procedure findLocationForEscape(x : Cube, y :Cube)
   local set : list of EcoAgent
   set :=Table.locations
   for all z's in set
     if (z.on) = nil then
        return z
   // we search set of cubes
   for all z's of SetOfCubes
     if (z.on) = nil and (z <> y) and
        (z <> constraint)
        // constraint imposed by attack
     then return(z)
   return(nil) // no location for escape
```

The towers of Hanoi

The problem of the towers of Hanoi, in which a tower of discs has to be moved from one peg to another without a disc ever being being put on top of another disc of a smaller size, is the direct derivative of the problem of constrained cubes. In fact, what we have here is a special case of the problem in which an additional constraint is added during the search for a location to escape to. We can see the concept emerging here of a *family of problems*, the members of which are eco-agents with similar behaviours.

This problem is dealt with using a similar technique to that adopted for the cubes with constraints. The two classes of agents are (naturally) the discs and the towers, the latter being permanently satisfied. The discs are satisfied if they are resting on a disc of the next size up or on a free tower. Their behaviour is limited to two classic reactions:

(1)   *Satisfaction behaviour*: going onto a disc of the next size up.

(2)   *Escape behaviour*: going onto another tower. But the constraint attached to this reaction is that it is not possible to go onto the tower onto which the attacker (the disc that causes the escape) wishes to go. This constraint therefore makes it possible to eliminate the conflict problems that could arise if the larger disc went to the location to which the smaller disc wanted to go.

Moreover, as soon as the act of aggression has been completed, and the point of escaping therefore disappears, the satisfaction reaction comes back into operation. The disc A has as its goal (condition of satisfaction) to go onto disc 3. To do this, it attacks disc B, prohibiting it from going to 3. For this reason, B wants to go to 2. As it is being obstructed, it attacks disc C, prohibiting it from going to 1. For this reason, C can go only to 3. Once in position, it indicates to B that it can move, and B moves to 2. It then indicates that it has completed its attack on C, and C comes back on top of B. It also sends the message, to be passed on to A, that it can now move. This leads A to position itself at 3 and state that it has completed its attack on B. This leads B to want to go on top of A. But, as it is being obstructed, it is obliged to attack C, prohibiting it from going onto tower 3. C goes to 1, which frees B, which goes onto A. B ceases its attack on C, and C places itself on B, which completely solves the problem, the three discs being satisfied.

If we analyse the trace above, we can see that the obtained solution corresponds directly to the classic algorithm for the towers of Hanoi. This comment is based directly on an analysis of the behaviour of the towers, and was not something predicted earlier. This correspondence came to light when we looked at how the system works, and does not come from an *a priori* desire to carry out the same operation. When we find ourselves faced with such an observation, it is impossible not to formulate a certain number of comments and questions – these, in particular: What is the nature of the link between the behaviour defined and the well-known algorithm? Is this algorithm a stable state of behaviour, or has the algorithm not been programmed in a concealed way, or finally is it simply a coincidence for this particular example, a correspondence which cannot be generalised?

The problem of the towers of Hanoi is indeed very restricted, and any solution must involve either an exploration, with backtracks, of the states' space or

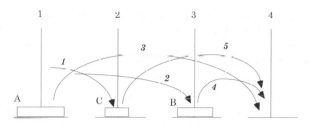

Figure 8.36   In a tower-of-Hanoi problem with more than three pegs, ECO automatically uses all the space available to it.

a behaviour which must be that of the algorithm. There is no other alternative. If, on the other hand, we reduce the constraints associated with this game (by increasing the number of pegs, for example), the behaviour then moves away from the perfect algorithm and variants begin to appear. For example, if we use four pegs with only three discs, the most perfect algorithm consists of placing disc C onto tower 2, disc B onto tower 3, then disc A onto tower 4, and finally stacking up all the discs one after another in the right order (Figure 8.36).

Studying systems as simple as those of the cubes or the towers of Hanoi shows how interesting this type of technique is. But it also demonstrates its limitations, since one cannot be certain, at the outset, of obtaining an optimum plan. However, it would certainly be possible to integrate learning techniques into this method, so that the behaviours of the agents could be modified locally and incrementally and the different reactions coordinated accordingly.

The n-puzzle

The teaser, far more than the towers of Hanoi, has inspired numerous planning studies. The n-puzzle (see for instance Nilsson, 1980) consists of a set of n movable tiles within a frame. One square of the frame is always blank thus making it possible to move an adjacent tile into the blank square. The objective is to change the initial configuration into the final configuration where all tiles are in a neat sequence. Its perfectly delimited universe, generating obvious constraints, is indeed particularly suited to the exploration of state-space or trees. The work which has progressed furthest to date, not merely in terms of reduction of the complexity of searches but also in terms of empirical results, is that of R. E. Korf, begun in 1985 with the use of the IDA* algorithm (Iterative-Deepening A*) (Korf, 1985) and continuing with the search algorithms RTA* (Real-Time A*) and its successors, including, in particular, LRTA* (Learning Real-Time A*) (Korf, 1988). Successful and interesting though it is, his work nonetheless remains faithful to the principles that have underpinned all attempts at solving the problem of the n-puzzle from the start, namely the more or less detailed exploration of state spaces, based on heuristic techniques.

The creation of the n-puzzle has shown that, even if the complexity of the functions relating to the problem increases considerably, it is not necessary to modify the functions of the ECO core. The algorithms used are linear in many manifestations of the n-puzzle problem, so the complexity grows linearly as the size of the n-puzzle increases. Moreover, this implementation in ECO opens up additional possibilities (such as having an n-puzzle game with multiple empty squares, solution of non-square n-puzzles, etc.), which is not at all the case for the exploratory approaches previously dealt with.

To solve this problem in ECO, we assume that the squares, like the tiles, are eco-agents. Whereas the former are always satisfied (the squares cannot move), the latter are only satisfied if they are in the square corresponding to the desired configuration. For example, the tile marked with the letter 'A' will be satisfied only if it is in the square with the coordinates (1,1). The function `findLocationForEscape` is a little more complicated here, for it has to consider which tile must be attacked in order to escape. A precise definition of the algorithm can be found, together with a proof of the completeness and the decidability of the solution, whatever the size of the n-puzzle, in Drogoul and Dubreuil (1992). As an example of the flexibility of the model, here is the solution to the problem of the corners: tile A wishes to take the place of E to complete the first line (Figure 8.37).

This mechanism, which uses the general properties of the problem, makes it possible to solve n-puzzles which are very large, some of which have never been solved on account of the cost of the computations involved. Figure 8.38 shows the average performance levels for the system, plotted against the size of the n-puzzle, each example being solved 100 times. The timing was carried out on a version of Eco written in Smalltalk-80 4.1, running on a SunSparc 10 workstation without a graphics display.

8.5.4   Evolutionary universes

ECO's possibilities are not restricted to problem solving. It has also proved to be a particularly well-adapted tool for the simulation of evolutionary universes.

As we pointed out earlier, combination methods are very sensitive to disturbance. In a system of eco-agents, on the other hand, external disturbance is treated exactly like any other datum of the problem. Any agent which perceives the disturbance reacts to it locally, as its behaviour dictates to it. It is in this context that the problem of the 'Misachieving baby' was implemented (Schoppers, 1987). During the solving of a problem from the world of cubes, a wicked baby moves cubes, parts of piles, even entire piles, as it sees fit (Figure 8.39). For example, in situation (1), cube B needs only to be put onto C to obtain the desired pile. At this point, the baby intervenes and moves the pile made up of cubes A and C, and puts it onto B (2). Cube A is no longer satisfied, and B is now obliged to attack the cubes on top of itself to be able to achieve its goal.

From the user's point of view, the definition of the problem is no different from that for the cubes examined previously. It is the core of ECO that takes charge of the dynamics of the system by managing the changes in conditions. It is sufficient merely to update the state of satisfaction (cube A is no longer satisfied) and, above

■ Blocked tile
■ Active tile

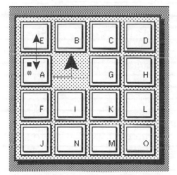

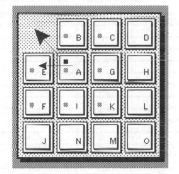

A attacks E, imposing on it constraint that it should not touch B (B is the tile on which A 'depends'). E has no other option but to attack A.

A attacks E again, this time imposing on it as a constraint that it should not escape into the blank space (its goal). So E attacks F, I, K, G, C and B are attacked in turn.

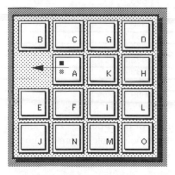

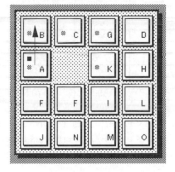

B, C, G, K, I, F and E having moved, A attacks the blank space with the aim of satisfying itself. The blank space escapes by exchanging its position with the tile which is attacking it.

A now attacks B, which is occupying its goal, without imposing any constraints on it. So B attacks C, which attacks G, and so on.

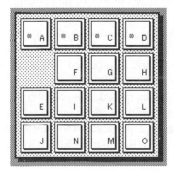

Figure 8.37   The problem of corners in the n-puzzle game, as managed in ECO.

Configuration		Solution		
Width	Tiles	Average time	Average length	Length per tile
n	N	Seconds	Number of movements	
3	8	0,2218	48,90	6,11
4	15	0,7547	142,10	9,47
5	24	2,4812	283,00	11,79
6	35	4,5146	482,00	13,77
7	48	9,6559	746,30	15,55
8	63	17,027	1 109,20	17,61
9	80	23,1532	1 455,20	18,19
10	99	35,4682	1 947,70	19,67
11	120	52,7616	2 483,10	20,69
12	143	65,7846	2 889,10	20,20
13	168	86,7198	3 361,90	20,01
14	195	106,9209	4 199,70	21,54
15	224	116,4785	4 881,50	21,79
16	255	165,8702	5 581,90	21,89
17	288	204,4582	6 267,10	21,76
18	323	230,687	6 947,60	21,51
19	360	271,5735	7 797,20	21,66
20	399	292,0156	9 004,70	22,57
21	440	340,8768	9 882,00	22,46
22	483	415,1151	11 093,70	22,97
23	528	477,3549	12 404,00	23,49
24	575	544,9122	13 340,10	23,20
25	624	625,5805	15 181,20	24,33
26	675	655,0309	16 514,00	24,47
27	728	782,0069	18 496,80	25,41
28	783	897,6368	19 999,40	25,54
29	840	1036,3034	21 229,20	25,27
30	899	1179,58	23 009,00	25,59

Figure 8.38 Experimental results of the solution of the n-puzzle. The values are the average values over 100 experiments for each example (adapted from Drogoul (1993)).

all, to re-initialise the obstructors and the escapers, while considering the situation resulting from the action of the mischievous baby as being a new initial situation.

The graph in Figure 8.40 shows the average number of movements of cubes (without counting those made by the baby), plotted against the frequency (P) of disturbances. Every time a cube is moved, the baby has one chance in P of causing a disturbance. For the problem to be solved, as described above, six movements are required if there is no disturbance. The operation was repeated 100 times for each value of P.

Even if the frequency of disturbance is increased, the solution is achieved rapidly. If the disturbances are more frequent than the actions of the cubes (P < 2), the system still reaches its final state when, at a particular moment (statistically becoming more distant in time as P approaches 1), the disturbance no longer affects any agents except those not satisfied. On the other hand, ECO's great success arises from the fact that the disturbance is sometimes positive. The baby may position the cubes in their state of satisfaction in a random manner. If the baby continues its

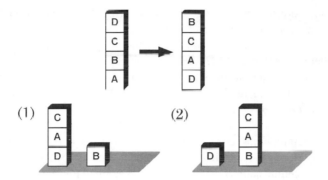

Figure 8.39   In a problem of cubes, a naughty baby interferes with a pile of cubes.

interference once the final configuration has been obtained, the system will recover its state of equilibrium naturally, which tends to make the system oscillate around this state. ECO therefore naturally induces a homeostatic system behaviour.

8.5.5   Formalisation

It is possible to give a formalisation for Eco, based on a criterion allowing us to know whether a sequence of operations has, in fact, achieved the desired goal.

The problems of planning have been studied in very specific detail by Chapman (1987), who provides both a formal planning model, a criterion making it possible to determine the validity of plans, and a planner designed as a computational realisation of this criterion.

The general idea is to describe a condition making it possible to decide whether a proposition, considered as a description of the final state, can be established by a sequence of STRIPS-like operators. It is possible to adapt this

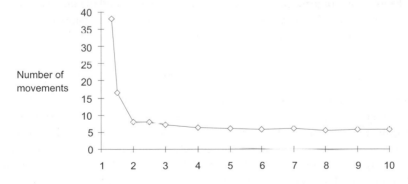

Figure 8.40   The number of movements of cubes required, plotted against the frequency of disturbance P.

criterion for eco-problem solving, by considering the satisfaction and escape operators as the principal plan construction mechanism.

Let $A = \{a_1,...,a_n\}$ be a set of agents which must be satisfied for the problem to be considered as solved, and Σ a set of states of the world, and if the satisfaction action for agent a_i leading to the state σ is referred to as $Sat(a_i, \sigma)$, with the escape action being referred to as $Escape(a_i, \sigma)$, then this criterion can be defined as follows (Bura *et al.*, 1991):

Criterion of satisfaction: The satisfaction of an agent a_i can be asserted in the final state of the world σ_f if it is directly asserted in the final state, or if it has been asserted in a preceding state σ_n and the agent has not had to escape into any state σ_b between the state σ_p and the state σ_f. For each state σ_b where the agent has had to escape, there must be a state σ_a between the state σ_b and the state σ_f which satisfies this agent again. For each state where an agent has to escape and can be satisfied at the same time, the agent carries out the operation that leads it to satisfaction.

Here is a more formal translation of this criterion:

$$\forall a_i \in A, \exists \Sigma, Sat(a_i, \sigma_p) \wedge (\forall \sigma_b \in \Sigma, (\sigma_p \leq \sigma_b) \wedge Escape(a_i, \sigma_b) \Rightarrow$$
$$((\exists \sigma_a \in \Sigma, (\sigma_p \leq \sigma_b) \wedge Sat(a_i, \sigma_a)) \vee Sat(a_i, \sigma_b))$$

This criterion makes it possible to understand how ECO functions in the preceding cases. For example, in the world of cubes (constrained cubes, towers of Hanoi and so on), the dependencies between agents form a partial order such that, to satisfy an agent, it is sufficient to move all the obstructors located between the agent trying to satisfy itself and its goal, that is, an agent already satisfied. As moving obstructors does not modify the status of agents already satisfied (it is sufficient to move all the cubes causing obstructions onto other piles), it follows that the criterion of truth is verified. This means that ECO can define a plan of action for all problems, whose final situation can be given in the form of a tree structure. This is true, in particular, for the assembly of lego-like structures, which assume that all the elements interlock with one another. Work is in progress on the more general application of this technique to more complex dependency structures.

8.5.6 Solving constraints by eco-problem solving

Reactive techniques are not limited to action planning. It is possible to use them to solve other problems, such as those encountered in the domain of the satisfaction of constraints. How, for example, can we best position a set of tasks on a set of machines? How can we draw up a timetable for a school, when there may not necessarily be a solution which simultaneously satisfies all the educational constraints and the preferences of the teachers? Solving problems of these types comes within the province of the satisfaction of constraints. Problems of constraints highlight two types of entities: variables and constraints. Solving a problem of satisfaction of constraints means being able to assign values to the variables that satisfy the constraints. For example, resolving the following system of equations:

$$3 * X + Y = Z, \quad Z > 2 * X, \quad 4 * X < 2 * Y$$

in which X, Y and Z are whole-number variables defined in the domain [1, 10], means finding the set of values that satisfy these constraints. A system of satisfaction of constraints could look like this:

```
X = 1, Y = 3, Z = 6
X = 1, Y = 4, Z = 7
X = 1, Y = 5, Z = 8
X = 1, Y = 6, Z = 9
X = 1, Y = 7, Z = 10
```

For a good introduction to problems of satisfaction of constraints, and in particular to programming by constraints, one can refer to Tsang (1993). Figure 8.41 shows a net of constraints for the above problem.

Starting from a point of view initially very different from that of the classic techniques based on the propagation of constraints and the implicit enumeration of solutions, K. Ghedira (1993, 1994) developed an original method of solving constraints which associates eco-problem solving and simulated reheating. The general idea consists in considering variables and constraints as eco-agents which are trying to find a state of satisfaction.

Constraints

A constraint is satisfied if its associated relationship is verified. Otherwise, an unsatisfied constraint requests one of its variables to change value. The diagram for the state of a constraint is given in Figure 8.42(a) and consists in four main

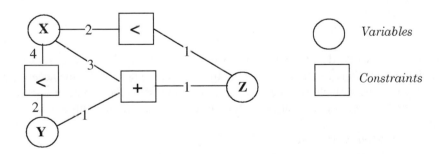

Figure 8.41   A small net of constraints solving the equation system with three unknown variables defined above.

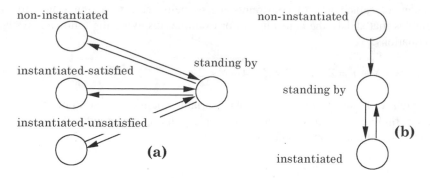

Figure 8.42 Diagram of states of a constraint (a) and a variable (b).

states: `non-instantiated`, `instantiated-satisfied`, `instantiated-unsatisfied` and `waiting`. The first corresponds to a state in which variables associated with the constraint are not yet instantiated, the second to a situation in which the constraint is both instantiated and satisfied, the third to the case in which it is both instantiated and unsatisfied, and the fourth to an intermediate situation in which the constraint is awaiting the verdict of a variable.

Variables

Variables try to find values belonging to their domain of definition. When requested to change value, a variable selects a value at random from its domain of definition, and asks its constraints for their opinion, that is, it asks whether these values satisfy them or not. On the basis of all these responses, it decides whether or not to accept this value, on the basis of a selection criterion depending on a mechanism founded on the concept of simulated reheating. Figure 8.42(b) shows the transition diagram of a variable. The decision function is based on the following procedure: let i be the current value of a variable v and j the new value, and let $S(i)$ be the number of its satisfied constraints; the variable will select the value j if:

$$S(j) \geq S(i)$$
$$S(j) < S(i) \text{ and } Rand(0,1) < e^{\frac{S(j) - S(i)}{T(k,v)}}$$

and will otherwise decide to keep the value i. The function $Rand(0,1)$ selects a random a value between 0 and 1, and the function $T(k,v)$ determines the acceptance tolerance of the variable v at the time k. In order to restrict the choice of a variable as the process goes on, the variable's tolerance decreases in line with time:

$$T(k+1,v) = T(k,v) - 1$$

the initial value of the function T depending on the number of constraints associated with the variable v. For this reason, the more selections a variable has already made, the less it will tend to accept a value that satisfies a smaller number of constraints. It will remain more and more 'set' on its previous selections, as if it was 'freezing' with time.

The interesting thing about this method is that it can easily be generalised to situations of partial satisfaction, that is, problems for which no global solution exists, leading to fast solutions. Moreover, theoretical work shows that it is capable of providing the best solution. Finally, slight modifications to the set of constraints do not call into question the set of situations already found. Lack of satisfaction will be transmitted step by step among variables and the other constraints, and the system will therefore favour solutions close to the solutions already found. Another approach based on a distributed concept of the satisfaction of problems was proposed in Liu and Sycara (1993), but at the moment it does not seem to produce such good results as that of K. Ghedira. Using the coordination of agents as a solution mechanism opens up new perspectives in problem-solving techniques.

$\mathbb{9}$ Conclusion

Kenetics proposes a new design concept for computer software. I have tried to show throughout this work a new additional way of solving problems, which is no longer based on a centralised vision of the world and the individual, but which thinks of everything in terms of interactions and the emergence of functionalities linked to these interactions. Multi-agent systems are proposing a quiet revolution, a simple change in attitude and perspective, but with radical consequences. It requires a certain open-mindedness to decide voluntarily to put aside global solutions in favour of taking a purely local view; everything we have learned, all our dominant paradigms regard taking an overall view as being the only way of solving problems. But the complexity of the world, and of computing systems in particular, is now so great that only perspectives that highlight local concepts and that place the greatest emphasis on the capacity of these systems for emergence and self-organisation will be capable of supplying viable and effective responses.

I have already participated, as a research worker and a lecturer, in the revolution brought about by object-oriented programming. But we need to go a little further, and give software components the behavioural autonomy they need. This is the price we must pay if we are to create these open, communicating and interactive systems in reality.

A brief glimpse of the future ...

What is the future of software, and how will tomorrow's programs be structured? To find the answers to these questions, let us take a little trip into the future – to the year 2045, for example. Here is what we might read in a computer magazine of the day[†] (something like *Byte* or *Dr. Dobb's Journal*).

[†]I published this text in 1989 (Ferber, 1989) in my PhD thesis. At that time, I treated it as science fiction. I now think it is the logical extension of the work described here, and that this can be seen as the predictable future of software engineering.

The way programs were structured in the twentieth century seems very strange to us now. Only a few old-fashioned individuals still produce programs like our grandparents. It is hard not to smile when we look at these strange systems which arbitrarily separated the data from the code and expressed themselves sequentially, forcing the human mind into weird contortions to adapt it to a machine. And the result was software which was virtually incapable of adapting to a context that was changing constantly. Evolution was impossible except through expensive code manipulations, which sometimes forced programmers to start again from the beginning.

In those days software was something inert, operated from outside, with no behaviour of its own. Some people tried to crystallise these programs into a rigid framework. These were called 'specifying' or 'proving' programs. Obviously, software created with specification techniques and program synthesis techniques ran correctly, but the problems were shifted elsewhere – into the drawing up of the specifications; these caused programmers to perform acts of mental gymnastics at least as complicated as those required for programming; above all, problems shifted towards making software evolve. Any modification required a considerable amount of work to ensure the independence of the changes made. In those days programming was an art, which called for adeptness and know-how, in order to avoid what was referred to at the time as a bug – that is, a programming error. Bugs, which have disappeared now – the Silicium Museum has preserved some rare and interesting examples – were the bane of programmers' lives, for their existence could bring the program to a complete halt. They didn't know how to create a software through self-organisation! They did not understand the techniques associated with emergence! They did not know how to use interaction with the environment as a factor in making programs more complex and more adaptable! Their technology was extremely rudimentary, and nowadays their ways look almost antediluvian to us.

Fortunately, things are very different now. Programs have become almost like living things, made up of a gigantic number of independent little units, endowed with a certain autonomy, which can communicate with each other, organise themselves, reorganise themselves, become more complex, and adapt themselves to their environment to carry out the tasks which they are given to do. This architecture is complex and continuously under review by all the units. They are organised into colonies, which display numerous analogies with both the neuronic structure of the brain and the structure of an animal or human society. So we can make programs 'grow', just as we make plants grow, or rear an animal. To obtain an application, we just need to insert a 'cutting' into a computing architecture and cause it to interact with other agents (programs and/or human beings) in an appropriate environment, causing them to adapt and to carry out the tasks for which they are specialised. It is now possible to 'graft' one program onto another, that is, to combine programs to make them cooperate. The result will not simply be the sum of the two programs, but the product of a special chemistry associated with the interactions taking place between the two initial units. In this way, we obtain original software, which no longer has anything but the most distant resemblance to those from which it arose – a little like a child in relation to its parents.

In the same journal, we might read the following advertisement:

New development: fast-growing software cutting for organisation and management of small and medium-sized companies

This cutting allows you to develop an integrated multi-organiser that will be responsible for decision making, management and communication for the company. It adapts itself to any 'Hyper Compatible' architecture with minimum three million Giga EO virtual[†]*. It can be installed into hardware very quickly. As for ordinary cuttings, you just increase its workload gradually, and it learns how to perform its task and adapt to your needs. Its new 'Multi World' organisation, which provides it with simulations of hypothetical internal interactions, means it can be fully operational after only a mere fortnight, instead of the two months an ordinary cutting needs. This revolutionary cutting integrates naturally with all those with eco-hetero-adaptation mechanisms.*

In the year 2045, every aspect of our current computing culture will look old-fashioned. Perhaps artificial intelligence will no longer exist as a separate discipline, except maybe as the study of 'psycho-socio-biology of artefacts'. It will have been completely merged and amalgamated with all the branches of computer science, where it will operate in collaboration with the physical, biological, social and psychological sciences. The structure of computers will be different. The very idea of a central processor will have disappeared completely. Every computing system will be made up of a network of many thousands of processors working together to make up the 'environment' in which the little units of the program will operate.

This vision of the future assumes that softwares can cooperate with us in harmony, sharing directly in all our activities. They will learn by observing us (but not controlling us I hope – we should not create Big Brother) and will become more integrated into processing procedures and routine tasks. But they will also be able to help us take decisions rapidly and efficiently. Following the example of human beings, who learn by 'osmosis', that is, by confrontation with reality, by imitating, by trying things out and by modifying behaviours 'to see what does what', the programs of the future will be in contact with us, watching and learning from the data flows which normally circulate between human beings. Today's simple tools will become tomorrow's collaborators. Computing agents will be as indispensable to us as a calculator or, for some people, a portable computer. These agents will

---

[†]EOs are 'Equivalent Octets' – a measurement used to describe memory organisations.

watch data circulating and will adapt to the way human beings function and the humans will adjust to the behaviours of the computing agents in return. They will dynamically reorganise and restructure themselves to improve and to adapt to the conditions of their environment. This type of system will then lead to the emergence of an eco-system of a completely new kind, a hybrid population of human and computing agents, learning to cooperate with each other to fulfil their destinies and live their lives.

APPENDIX A

BRIC

BRIC (Block-like Representation of Interactive Components) is a high-level language for the design of multi-agent systems based on a modular approach. A BRIC system consists of a set of components linked to each other by communication links. We shall confine ourselves here to the elements needed for an understanding of the components described in this book. Other extensions of BRIC are possible, but we shall not describe them here.

A.1   The components

A BRIC component is a software structure characterised externally by a certain number of input and output terminals and internally by a set of components. The input and output terminals play the part of an interface by receiving or sending messages from or to the outside world (Figure A.1). Every component is an instance of a class, which describes its internal structure. So the classes, just like object-oriented languages, serve to assemble together all the data common to a set of similar components.

The behaviour of these components can be defined either by assembling other components whose behaviour has already been established, and we then refer to *structured components*, or directly, through the medium of an associated Petri net. In this latter case, we say that these are *elementary components*. Finally, it is also possible to introduce *primitive components*, whose behaviour is not described by a Petri net, but which are interesting because they can be responsible for functionalities external to the agent or the system.

A.2   Composite components

A structured component is defined by the assembly of the its sub-components. The input terminals of the structured component are linked to the input terminals of the sub-components. It is also possible to combine the input (and output) terminals of the composite components with their sub-components, as shown in Figure A.2.

A.3   Constitution of elementary components

The behaviour of elementary components is described in terms of Petri nets. The net formalism normally used in BRIC is that of coloured Petri nets with inhibitor arcs.

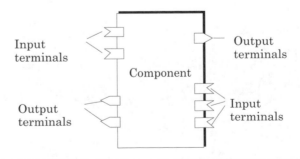

Figure A.1   Structure of a component and its terminals.

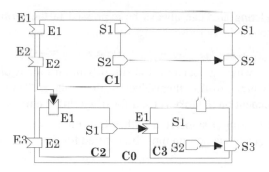

Figure A.2 A composite component.

But other formalisms can be used, such as those for synchronous nets or time-delayed nets.

The general form of a transition is shown in Figure A.3. A transition is defined by entry arcs, exit arcs and a pre-condition of activation.

(a)   The entry arcs associate a place with a transition. They are carriers of a condition, in the form of the description of a token, this description including variables. When the place contains a token corresponding to this description, the arc is validated. There are three categories of entry arcs:

    (1)   *Standard arcs*, denoted $a_1, \ldots, a_n$, trigger the transition only if they are all validated. These arcs 'consume' the tokens which act as triggers, and which are therefore deleted from the input places.

    (2)   *Inhibitor arcs*, denoted $i_1, \ldots, i_m$, inhibit the triggering of the transition if it is validated. These arcs do not delete tokens.

    (3)   *Non-consumer arcs*, denoted $b_1, \ldots, b_k$, function as standard arcs, the only difference being that they do not delete the input tokens. Non-

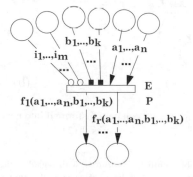

Figure A.3   General form of a transition in the BRIC formalism.

deleting arcs can always be expressed in the form of standard arcs, their sole purpose being to make diagrams easier to understand (Figure A.4).

(b)   Exit arcs, which associate a transition with an output place, produce new tokens, which position themselves in these places. These produced tokens are dependent on the tokens used for triggering the transition.

(c)   The pre-condition associated with a transition relates to the external conditions. This precondition must be verified for the transition to be activated.

A.4   Communication links

The components communicate by exchanging information (which we sometimes call 'messages'[†]) along communication links which connect output terminals to input terminals. Information is regulated by the Petri net firing rules, so *de facto* leading to a 'factual asynchronous' type of operation. The rhythm for the execution of operations is determined by the information sent and received by the components, the whole constituting an information propagation net. Information is transported through the net in the form of tokens. A token is either an elementary piece of information whose value is a mere presence or absence, or a predicate in the form $p(a_1, \ldots, a_n)$, where the a_is represent numbers or symbols in a finite alphabet.

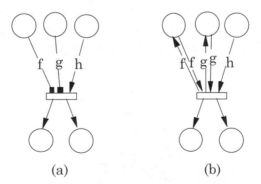

(a)   (b)

Figure A.4   Non-deleting arcs (a) can be transformed into nets comprising only consumer arcs (b).

[†]In order to avoid any possible conflicts of meaning with regard to the term 'message' as applied to communications between components or between agents, the former are referred to as 'internal messages' and the latter as 'external messages' whenever any confusion might arise.

A.5   Notation conventions and equivalents

In order to make BRIC components easier to comprehend, we shall make a certain number of assumptions concerning the notations:

(1)   We shall suppose that any exit arc from a place that is identified in the form $P(a_1, \ldots, a_n)$ will have as a condition of validity a description identical to the description of the place, unless otherwise specified. For this reason, it is generally not necessary to reproduce the description of an entry arc on a transition unless one is attempting to make a condition more precise. The external conditions associated with transitions (Figure A.5(a)) can be considered as requests for information. Figure A.5(b) shows an equivalent net, in which the external transition has been translated into the form of an access to an external component.

(2)   Names of the input terminals are taken to be place identifiers, since the input terminals are considered as places.

(3)   Any direct link between an input terminal of an incorporating component and an input terminal of an incorporated component is assumed to comprise a transition, in accordance with Petri net design rules. Nevertheless, and in order to simplify the diagrams, we can write direct links between these terminals by supposing that there is a 'virtual' transition between these terminals. Figure A.2 should therefore be rewritten, in the form of Figure A.6.

A.6   Translation in the form of Petri nets

It is always possible to convert a set of components into an equivalent Petri net, which represents a kind of 'expanded view' of the BRIC structure, by assuming that the input terminals of the components correspond to locations, while the output

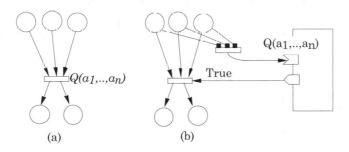

Figure A.5   External conditions can be translated into the form of a request for information from another component.

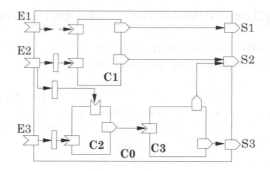

Figure A.6 Representation of intermediate transitions between input terminals.

terminals do not correspond either to places or to transitions, but serve only as 'conducting wires' to the output terminals of other components.

For example, the set of BRIC components from Figure A.7(a) can be represented by the equivalent Petri net for Figure A.7(b), the output terminals having disappeared and the input terminals being replaced by locations.

A.7 Example

Figure A.8 shows a component that takes up the well-known example of using object-oriented programming for a bank account (Goldberg and Robson, 1980), and which can be used to deposit sums (`deposit` terminal) or withdraw them

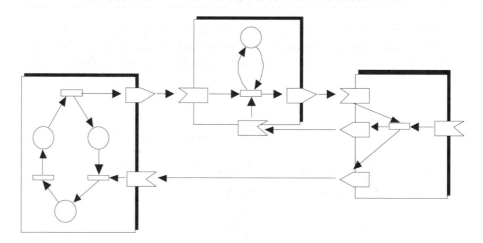

Figure A.7 The definition of a set of BRIC components (a) is converted into an equivalent Petri net (b).

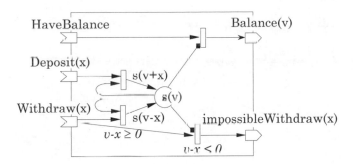

Figure A.8 A BRIC component representing a bank account.

(withdrawal terminal). It is also possible to consult the balance of deposits and withdrawals. The balance is represented by a place, S(v).

It will be understood that sums can be withdrawn only if they still leave the account open. Any attempt to withdraw a sum which exceeds the balance will trigger the production of the message impossibleWithdraw(x) at the output, where x is the amount one is attempting to withdraw.

Further readings and information on multi-agent systems

Books and monographs

Main books

Conte, R. and Castelfranchi, C. (1995) *Cognitive and Social Action*. UCL Press.
A book that makes a bridge between cognitive science and computer-based multi-agent systems.

Rosenschein, J. and Zlotkin, G. (1994) *Rules of Encounters: Designing Conventions for Automated Negotiation among Computers*. MIT Press.
The reference book on the game theory approach of multi-agent systems.

Monographs

Haddadi, A. (1996) *Communication and Cooperation in Agent Systems*. LNAI 1056, Springer-Verlag.

Jennings, N. (1994) *Cooperation in Industrial Multi-Agent Systems*. Vol. 43, World Scientific Press.

Müller, J. (1996) *The Design of Intelligent Agents, A Layered Approach*. LNAI 1177, Springer-Verlag.

Singh, M. (1994) *Multiagent Systems, A theoretical framework for intentions, know-how and communications*. LNAI 799, Springer-Verlag.

von Martial, F. (1992) *Coordinating Plans of Autonomous Agents*. LNAI 610, Springer-Verlag.

Collected papers

Avouris, N. and Gasser, L. (eds) (1992) *Distributed Artificial Intelligence: theory and practice*. Kluwer Academic Publishers.
Papers related to a summer school on MASs.

Bond, A. and Gasser, L. (eds) (1988) *Readings in Distributed Artificial Intelligence*. Morgan Kaufman.
The reference book on papers published before 1988.

O'Hare, G. and Jennings, N. (eds) (1996) *Foundations of Distributed Artificial Intelligence*. Wiley.
A good introduction to...

Bradshaw, J.M. (ed) (1997) *Software Agents*, AAAI Press, MIT Press.

Proceedings of main conferences and workshops

ICMAS (International Conference on Multi-Agent Systems)

The main international conference on MASs.

Lesser, V. (ed)(1995) *Proc. of the first international conference on multi-agent systems*. San Francisco: AAAI & MIT Press.

Tokoro, M (ed)(1996) *Proc. of the second international conference on multi-agent systems*. Kyoto, AAAI Press.

Demazeau, Y. (ed)(1998) *Proc. of the third international conference on multi-agent systems*. Paris: IEEE Computer Society.

Distributed Artificial Intelligence Workshop (United States)

The main workshop on multi-agent systems in USA.

Huhns, M. (ed)(1987) *Distributed Artificial Intelligence.* Pitman.

Gasser, L. and Huhns, M. (ed) (1989) *Distributed Artificial Intelligence,* Vol. II. Pitman.

Durfee, E. (ed) (1991) *Special issue on multi-agent systems, Systems, Man and Cybernetics.* IEEE, September 1991

Maamaw (Modelling Autonomous Agents in a Multi-Agent World) (Europe)

This is the main conference on multi-agent systems in Europe.

Demazeau, Y. and Muller, J.-P. (eds) (1990) Decentralized Artificial Intelligence, Vol I. *Proc. of the First European workshop on Modelling Autonomous Agents in Multi-Agent World.* North-Holland.

Demazeau, Y. and Muller, J.-P. (eds) (1991) Decentralized Artificial Intelligence, Vol II. *Proc. of the Second European workshop on Modelling Autonomous Agents in Multi-Agent World.* North-Holland.

Werner, E. and Demazeau, Y. (eds) (1992) Decentralized Artificial Intelligence, *Proc. of the Third European Workshop on Modelling Autonomous Agents in Multi-Agent World.* Vol III. North-Holland.

Castelfranchi, C. and Muller, J.-P. (eds) (1995) From Reaction to Cognition, *Proc. of the Fifth European Workshop on Modelling Autonomous Agents in Multi-Agent World* (Maamaw'93). Springer-Verlag.

Perram, J. and Muller, J.-P. (eds) (1996) Distributed Software Agents and Applications *Proc. of the Sixth European Workshop on Modelling Autonomous Agents in Multi-Agent World* (Maamaw'94). Springer-Verlag.

Van de Velde, W. and Perram, J. (eds) Agents Breaking Away, *Proc. of the Seventh European Workshop on Modelling Autonomous Agents in Multi-Agent World* (Maamaw'96). Springer-Verlag.

Boman, M. and W. Van de Velde, W. (eds) Multi-Agent Rationality, *Proc. of the Eighth European Workshop on Modelling Autonomous Agents in Multi-Agent World* (Maamaw'97). Springer-Verlag.

Intelligent Agents Workshop

A very interesting workshop which concentrates on logic based systems and intentional architectures of agents.

Wooldridge, M. and Jennings, N. (eds) (1995) Intelligent Agents, *Proc. of the ECAI-94 Workshop on Agent Theories, Architectures and Languages.* Springer-Verlag

Wooldridge, M. Mueller, J.-P. and Tambe, M. (eds) (1996) Intelligent Agents II, *Proc. of the IJCAI-95 Workshop,* Canada, August 19-20, 1995. Springer-Verlag

Mueller, J.-P., Wooldridge, M. and Jennings, N. (1997) (eds): Intelligent Agents III. *Proc. of the ECAI-96 Workshop,* Budapest, Hungary, August 12-13, 1996. Springer-Verlag. Lecture Notes in AI Volume 1193.

Singh, M., Rao, A. and Wooldridge, M. (eds) (1998): Intelligent Agents IV. *Proc. of the Fourth International Workshop on Agent Theories, Architectures and Languages.* Rhode Island, USA, July 1997. Springer-Verlag

Simulation of Adaptive Behavior

The main conference on the animat approach and the interrelations between biological sciences, robotics and computer science.

Meyer, J.A.and Wilson, S. (eds) (1991 From Animals to Animats, *Proc. of the First International Conference on Simulation of Adaptive Behaviour (Complex Adaptive Systems).* MIT Press.

Meyer, J.A., Roitblat H.L. and Wilson, S. (ed.) (1993) From Animals to Animats II, *Proc. of the Second International Conference on Simulation of Adaptive Behaviour (Complex Adaptive Systems).* MIT Press.

Cliff, D., Husbands, P., Meyer J.A. and Wilson, S. (ed.) (1994) From Animals to Animats III, *Proc. of the Third International Conference on Simulation of Adaptive Behaviour (Complex Adaptive Systems).* MIT Press.

Maes, P., Mataric, M., Meyer, J.A., Pollack, J. and Wilson, S. (ed.) (1996) From Animals to Animats IV, *Proc. of the Fourth International Conference on Simulation of Adaptive Behaviour (Complex Adaptive Systems).* MIT Press.

Simulating Societies

Proceedings of the Simulating Societies conferences which are dedicated to the simulation of social systems, mainly with multi-agent systems.

Gilbert, N. and Doran, J. (eds) (1994) *Simulating Societies, The Computer Simulation of Social Phenomena*. UCL Press.

Gilbert, N. and Conte, R. (eds) (1995) *Artificial Societies: the computer simulation of social life*. UCL Press.

Conte, R., Hegselmann, R. and Terna, P. (eds) (1997) *Simulating Social Phenomena*, Springer-Verlag.

Other workshops and conferences

Weiss, G. and Sen, S. (eds) (1996) Adaptation and Learning in Multi-Agent Systems. *IJCAI'95 Workshop Proc.,* Montréal, Canada, August 1995. Springer-Verlag.
A very interesting book on the subject of adaptation and learning in MASs.

Sycara, K. and Wooldridge, M. (eds)(1998) Agents '98 *Proceedings of the Second International Conference on Autonomous Agents*. ACMPress. *Scientific Journal Autonomous Agents and Multi-Agent Systems*, Kluwer Academic Publishers. *Adaptive Behavior*, MIT Press Journals.

Web sites

General sites of interest

AgentLink group (Europe Esprit Network of Excellence): http://www.agentlink.org/

FIPA (Foundation for Intelligent Physical Agents): http://drogo.cselt.stet.it/fipa/

Agents at stanford university (includes KQML): http://www.cs.umbc.edu/agents/ To get all agent and multi-agent related pages:

Mike Wooldridge agent related page: http://www.elec.qmw.ac.uk/dai/people/mikew/links/ Serge Stinckwich multi-agent related page: http://www.info.unicaen.fr/~serge/sma.html

Bibliographical References

Agha, G. (1986) *Actors: A Model of Concurrent Computation for Distributed Systems.* MIT Press.

Agre, P. E. and Chapman D. (1987) 'Pengi: an Implementation of a Theory of Activity'. In *AAAI-87*, p. 268–272, Morgan Kaufmann.

Allen, J. F. and Perrault, C.R. (1980) 'Analyzing Intention in Utterances'. *Artificial Intelligence.* **15**, p. 143–178.

Andler, D. (Ed.) (1992) *Introduction aux sciences cognitives.* Gallimard.

Atlan, H. (1979) *Entre le cristal et la fumée. Essai sur l'organisation du vivant.* Le Seuil.

Austin, J. L. (1962) *How to Do Things With Words.* Clarendon Press.

Axelrod, R. (1992) *Donnant, Donnant. Théorie du comportement coopératif.* Editions Odile Jacob.

Bachatène, H. and Estraillier, P. (1992) *A Modular Design on Stepwise Refinements of Coloured Petri Nets.* Research Report, MASI, University of Paris 6.

Bachimont, B. (1992) *Le Contrôle dans les systèmes à base de connaissances.* Hermès.

Barraquand, J. and Latombe, J.-C. (1989) *Robot Motion Planning: A Distributed Representation Approach.* Research Report, STAN-CS-89-1257, Department of Computer Science, Stanford University.

Barwise, J. and Perry, J. (1983) *Situations and attitudes.* MIT Press.

Bateson, G. (1979) *La Nature et la pensée.* Le Seuil. Engl. *Mind and Nature: A Necessary Unity.*

Bateson, G., Birdwhistell, R., Goffman, E. *et al.* (1981) *La Nouvelle communication.* Le Seuil.

Baylon, C. and Mignot, X. (1991) *La Communication.* Nathan.

Beckers, R., Holland, O.E. and Deneubourg, J.-L. (1994) 'From Local Actions to Global Tasks: Stigmergy and Collective Robotics'. In *Proc. of the Fourth International Workshop on the Synthesis and Simulation of Living Systems, Artificial Life IV,* R. Brooks and P. Maes (Ed.), MIT Press.

Beer, R. D. and Chiel, H.J. (1992) 'The Neural Basis of Behavioral Choice in an Artificial Insect'. In *From Animals to Animats: Proc. Of the First International Conference on Simulation of Adaptive Behavior (SAB '90),* Paris, J.-A. Meyer and S. W. Wilson (Ed.), p. 247–254, MIT Press.

Benda, M., Jaganathan, V. and Dodhiawala, R. (1986) 'On Optimal Cooperation of Knowledge Sources'. In *Sixth Workshop on Distributed Artificial Intelligence,* Boeing AI Center, Seattle, WA.

Bernard-Weil, E. (1988) *Précis de systémique ago-antagoniste. Introduction aux stratégies bilatérales*. Limonest, L'Interdisciplinaire.

Bertalanffy, L. v. (1968) *General System Theory*. New York, Braziller.

Boman, M. and van de. Velde, W. V. ed. (1997) *Multi-Agent Rationality. Proceedings of Maamaw'97*. LNAI Vol. 1237, Springer-Verlag.

Bond, A. and Gasser, L. (1988) *Readings in Distributed Artificial Intelligence*. Morgan Kaufman.

Bond, A. H. (1989) 'Commitment, Some DAI Insights from Symbolic Interactionnist Sociology'. In *Ninth Workshop on Distributed Artificial Intelligence,* Seattle.

Bond, A. H. and Gasser, L. (1988) 'An Analysis of Problems and Research in Distributed Artificial Intelligence'. In *Readings in Distributed Artificial Intelligence,* A. H. Bond and L. Gasser (Ed.), Morgan Kaufman.

Bonnet, C., Ghiglione, R. and Richard, J.-F. (1990) *Traité de psychologie cognitive, tome 1*. Dunod.

Booch, G. (1991) *Object Oriented Design with Applications*. Benjamin Cummings.

Bouron, T. (1991) 'What Architecture for Multi-Agent Systems'. In *AAAI '91 Workshop on Cooperation among heterogeneous intelligent systems*.

Bouron, T. (1992) *Structures de communication et d'organisation pour la coopération dans un univers multi-agents*. Thèse de l'université Paris 6.

Bouron, T., Ferber, J. and Samuel, F. (1990) 'MAGES: a Multi-Agent Testbed for Heterogeneous Agents'. In *Decentralized Artificial Intelligence (Vol II),* Y. Demazeau and J.-P. Muller (Ed.), North-Holland.

Bousquet, F., Cambier, C., Mullon, C. *et al.* (1993) 'Simulating the Interaction between a Society and a Renewable Resource'. *Journal of Biolog. Systems* **1**(2), p. 199–214.

Boutot, A. (1993) *L'invention des formes*. Editions Odile Jacob.

Braitenberg, V. (1984) *Vehicles: Experiments in Synthetic Psychology*. MIT Press.

Brassac, C. (1992) 'Analyse de conversation et théorie des actes de langage'. *Cahiers de linguistique française*. **13**.

Bratman, M. (1987) *Intention, Plans, and Practical Reason*. Harvard University Press.

Bratman, M. (1990) 'What Is Intention?' In *Intentions in Communications,* P. R. Cohen, J. Morgan and M. E. Pollack (Ed.), Cambridge, Bradford Book/MIT Press.

Briot, J.-P. (1989) 'Actalk: a Testbed for Classifying and Designing Actor Languages in the Smalltalk-80 Environment.' In *Proc. of ECOOP '89,* Nottingham, UK, p. 109–129.

Brooks, R. (1990) 'Elephants Don't Play Chess.' *Robotics and Autonomous Systems*. **6**.

Brooks, R. and Connell, J.H. (1986) 'Asynchronous Distributed Control System for a Mobile Robot.' *SPIE*. **727**, Mobile Robots.

Bura, S., Drogoul, A., Ferber, J. and Jacopin, E. (1991) 'Eco-résolution : un modèle de résolution par interactions.' In *Huitième congrès sur la reconnaissance des formes et l'intelligence artificielle (RFIA'91)*, Lyon, AFCET.

Bura, S., Guérin-Pace, F., Mathian, H., Pumain, D. and Sanders, L. (1993) 'Multi-Agents Systems and the Dynamics of a Settlement System'. In *Simulating Societies Symposium,* Siena, C. Castelfranchi (Ed.).

Burg, B. and Arlabosse, F. (1994) 'ARCHON : une plateforme industrielle pour l'intelligence artificielle distribuée.' In *Actes des deuxièmes journées francophones sur l'intelligence artificielle distribuée et les systèmes multi-agents (JFIADSMA'94)*, Voiron, Y. Demazeau and S. Pesty (Ed.), IMAG.

Burloud, A. (1936) *Principes d'une psychologie des tendances*. Paris.

Cambier, C. (1994) *SIMDELTA : un système multi-agent pour simuler la pêche sur le Delta Central du Niger*. Thèse de l'université Paris 6.

Cambier, C., Bousquet, F. and Dansoko, D. (1992) 'Un Univers multi-agents pour la modélisation du système de la pêche du Delta Central du Niger.' In *Premier colloque africain sur la recherche en informatique (CARI'92)*, Yaoundé.

Cammarata, S., McArthur, D. and Steeb, R. (1983) 'Strategies of Cooperation in Distributed Problem-solving'. In *Proc. of the 1983 IJCAI Conference*.

Carle, P. (1992) *Un Langage d'acteur pour l'intelligence artificielle distribuée intégrant objets et agents par réflexivité compilatoire*. Thèse de l'université Paris 6.

Castañeda, H.-N. (1975) *Thinking and Doing*. Dordrecht, Holland, D. Riedel.

Castelfranchi, C. and Conte, R. (1992) 'Mind is not Enough: Precognitive Bases of Social Interaction'. In *Simulating Societies Symposium*, Guildford, N. Gilbert (Ed.).

Castelfranchi, C. and Werner, E. (Ed.) (1994) *Artificial Social Systems, Proc. of Maamaw '92*. Springer-Verlag.

Chaib-Draa, B. (1989) *Contribution à la résolution distribuée de problème : approche basée sur les comportements intentionnels des agents*. Thèse de l'université de Valenciennes.

Chaib-Draa, B., Moulin, M., Mandiau, R. and Millot, P. (1992) 'Trends in Distributed Artificial Intelligence'. *Artificial Intelligence Review*. **6**, p. 35–66.

Chapman, D. (1987) 'Planning for Conjunctive Goals'. *Artificial Intelligence Journal*. **32**, p. 333–367.

Charest, J. (1980) *La Conception des systèmes : une théorie, une méthode*. Québec, Gaëton Morin.

Cherian, S. and Troxell, W.O. (1993) 'Neural Network Based Behavior Hierarchy for Locomotion Control'. In *From Animal to Animats 2, Proceedings of the Second International Conference on Simulation of Adaptive Behavior (SAB '92)*, Hawaii, J.-A. Meyer, H. L. Roitblat and S. W. Wilson (Ed.), p. 61–70, MIT Press.

Chevrier, V. (1993) *Etude et mise en œuvre du paradigme multi-agent : de Atome à Gtmas*. Thèse de l'université de Nancy I.

Cliff, D., Harvey, I. and Husbands, P. (1993) 'Exploration in Evolutionary Robotics'. *Adaptive Behavior*. **2**(1), p. 73–110.

Cohen, P. R. and Levesque, H. J. (1990a) 'Intention is Choice with Commitment'. *Artificial Intelligence*. **42**, p. 213–261.

Cohen, P. R. and Levesque, H.J. (1990b) 'Persistence, Intention and Commitment'. In *Intentions in Communication*, P. R. Cohen, J. Morgan and M. E. Pollack (Ed.), p. 33–69, MIT Press.

Cohen, P. R. and Levesque, H.J. (1990c) 'Rational Interaction as the Basis for Communication'. In *Intentions in Communications*, P. R. Cohen, J. Morgan and M. E. Pollack (Ed.), p. 508, MIT Press.

Cohen, P. R. and Levesque, H.J. (1995) 'Communicative Actions for Artificial Intelligence'. In *First International Conference on Multi-Agent Systems (ICMAS'95)*, San Francisco, V. Lesser (Ed.), MIT Press.

Cohen, P. R. and Perrault, C.R. (1979) 'Elements of a Plan Based Theory of Speech Acts'. *Cognitive Science*. **3**(3).

Collins, R.J. and Jefferson, D. R. (1991) 'Representation for Artificial Organisms'. In *From Animal to Animats*, Paris, J.-A. Meyer and S. W. Wilson (Ed.), p. 382–390, MIT Press.

Conry, S., Meyer, R.A. and Lesser, V. (1988) 'Multistage Negotiation in Distributed Artificial Intelligence'. In *Readings in Distributed Artificial Intelligence*, A. Bond and L. Gasser (Ed.), Morgan Kaufman.

Conte, R., Miceli, M. and Castelfranchi, C. (1991) 'Limits and Levels of Cooperation:

Disentangling Various Types of Prosocial Interaction'. In *Distributed A.I. 2,* Y. Demazeau and J.-P. Müller (Ed.), North-Holland.

Corbara, B. (1991) *L'Organisation sociale et sa genèse chez la fourmi Ectatomma ruidum Roger.* Thèse de l'université Paris XIII.

Corbara, B., Drogoul, A., Fresneau, D. and Lalande, S. (1993) 'Simulating the Sociogenesis Process in Ant Colonies with MANTA'. In *Towards a Practice of Autonomous Systems II,* P. Bourgine and F. Varela (Ed.), MIT Press.

Coria, M. (1993) 'Stepwise Development of Correct Agents: a Behavioural Approach Based on Coloured Petri Nets'. In *Proc. of the Canadian Conf. on Electrical and Computer Engineering,* Vancouver, Canada.

Corrêa, M. and Coelho, H. (1993) 'Around the Architectural Agent Approach to Model Conversations'. In *Proc. of the 5th European Workshop on Modelling Autonomous Agents in a Multi-Agent World,* Neuchâtel.

Couffignal, L. (1963) *La Cybernétique.* vol. 638, PUF.

Crozier, M. and Friedberg, E. (1977). *L'Acteur et le système.* Le Seuil.

Cyrulnik, B. (1989). *Sous le signe du lien.* Hachette.

David, R. and Alla, H. (1989) *Du Grafcet aux réseaux de Petri.* Hermès.

Davis, R. and Smith, R.J. (1983) 'Negotiation as a Metaphor for Distributed Problem-solving'. *Artificial Intelligence.* 20(1), p. 63–109.

De Medio, C. and Oriolo, G. (1991) 'Robot Obstacle Avoidance Using Vortex Fields'. In *Advances in Robot Kinematics,* S. Stifter and Lenarcic (Ed.), p. 227–235, Springer Verlag.

Delattre, P. (1968) 'Structure et fonction (Biologie).' In *Encyclopaedia Universalis*, vol. 15, (Ed.), p. 442–444.

Delattre, P. (1971) *Système, structure, fonction, évolution.* Maloine.

Delaye, C. (1993) *Structures et organisations des systèmes multi-agents autonomes et adaptatifs.* Thèse de l'université Paris 6.

Demazeau, Y., Boissier, O. and Koning, J.-L. (1994) 'Using Interaction Protocols to Control Vision systems'. In *IEEE International Conference on Systems, Man and Cybernetics,* San Antonio.

Demazeau, Y. and Müller, J.-P. (Ed.) (1990) *Decentralized Artificial Intelligence.* Elsevier North-Holland.

Demazeau, Y. and Müller, J.-P. (Ed.) (1991) *Decentralized AI 2.* Elsevier North-Holland.

Deneubourg, J.-L. *et al.* (1993) 'Self-Organisation and life: from Simple Rules to Global Complexity'. In *Second European Conference on Artificial Life.,* Brussels.

Deneubourg, J.-L., Goss, S., Sendova-Franks, A., Detrain, C. and Chretien, L. (1991) 'The Dynamics of Collective Sorting Robot-like Ants and Ant-like Robots'. In *From Animals to Animats,* Paris, J.-A. Meyer and S. W. Wilson (Ed.), p. 356–363, MIT Press.

Deneubourg, J.-L., Aron, S., Goss, S., Pasteels, J. M. and Duerinck, G. (1986) 'Random Behaviour, Amplification Processes and Number of Participants: How they Contribute to the Foraging Properties of Ants'. *Physica.* 22(D), p. 176–186.

Deneubourg, J.-L. and Goss, S. (1989) 'Collective Patterns and Decision-Making'. *Ecology, Ethology and Evolution.* 1, p. 295–311.

Dennett, D. (1991) *La Conscience expliquée.* Editions Odile Jacob. Engl. (1992) *Consciousness Explained*, Little Brown & Co.

Dennett, D. C. (1983) 'Intentional Systems in Cognitive Ethology: the Panglossian Paradigm Defended'. *The Behavioural and Brain Sciences.* 6, p. 343–390.

Dennett, D. C. (1987) *The Intentional Stance.* MIT Press.

Devlin, K. (1991) *Logic and Information.* Cambridge University Press.

Doyle, J. (1979) 'A Truth Maintenance System'. *AI Journal.* **12**, p. 231–272.

Dreyfus, H. (1979) *What Computers can't do: a Critique of Artificial Reason.* Harper.

Dreyfus, H. L. (1992) 'La Portée philosophique du connexionisme.' In *Introduction aux sciences cognitives*, D. Andler (Ed.), p. 352 373, Gallimard.

Drogoul, A. (1993) *De la simulation multi-agent à la résolution collective de problèmes. Une étude de l'émergence de structures d'organisation dans les systèmes multi-agents.* Thèse de l'université Paris 6.

Drogoul, A., Corbara, B. and Fresneau, D. (1993) 'MANTA: New Experimental Results on the Emergence of (Artificial) Ant Societies'. In *Simulating Societies Symposium,* Siena, C. Castelfranchi (Ed.).

Drogoul, A. and Dubreuil, C. (1992) 'Eco-Problem-solving: Results of the N-Puzzle'. In *Decentralized Artificial Intelligence III,* Y. Demazeau and E. Werner (Ed.), North Holland.

Drogoul, A. and Ferber, J. (1992) 'From Tom Thumb to the Dockers: Some Experiments with Foraging Robots'. In *From Animals to Animats: Second Conference on Simulation of Adaptive Behavior (SAB 92),* Hawaii, J.-A. Meyer, H. Roitblat and S. Wilson (Ed.), MIT Press.

Drogoul, A. and Ferber, J. (1994a), 'Multi-Agent Simulation as a Tool for Modeling Societies: Application to Social Differentiation in Ant colonies'. In *Artificial Social Systems,* vol. 830, C. Castelfranchi and E. Werner (Ed.), p. 3–23, Berlin, Springer-Verlag.

Drogoul, A and Ferber, J. (1994b) 'Multi-agent Simulation as a Tool for Studying Emergent Processes in Societies'. In *Simulating Societies: the Computer Simulation of Social Phenomena,* N. Gilbert and J. Doran (Ed.), p. 127–142, UCL Press.

Drogoul, A, Ferber, J., Corbara, B. and Fresneau, D. (1992) 'A Behavioral Simulation Model for the Study of Emergent Social Structures'. In *Towards a Practice of Autonomous Systems,*

Paris, P. Bourgine and F. Varela (Ed.), p. 161–170, MIT Press.

Drogoul, A., Ferber, J. and Jacopin, F. (1991) 'Pengi: Applying Eco-Problem-solving for Behavior Modeling in an Abstract Eco-System'. In *European Simulation Multiconference, ESM'91,* E.Mosekilde (Ed.).

Dupuy, J.-P. (1994) *Aux origines des sciences cognitives.* La Découverte.

Durfee, E. and Montgomery, T. (1989) 'MICE: A Flexible Testbed for Intelligent Coordination Experiments'. In *Proc. of Ninth Workshop on Distributed AI,* Orcas Islands, Seattle, M. Benda (Ed.), Boeing Computer Services.

Durfee, E. H. and Lesser, V. R. (1991) 'Global Partial Planning: A Coordination Framework for Distributed Hypothesis'. *IEEE Transactions on Systems, Man and Cybernetics.* **21**(6).

Durfee, E. H., Lesser, V. R. and Corkill, D. D. (1987a) 'Coherent Cooperation Among Communicating Problem Solvers'. *IEEE Transactions on Computers.* **C**(36), p. 1275–1291.

Durfee, E. H., Lesser, V. R. and Corkill, D. D. (1987b), 'Cooperation through Communication in a Distributed Problem-solving Network'. In *Distributed Artificial Intelligence,* M. Huhns (Ed.), Pitman.

Durfee, E. H., Lesser, V. R. and Corkill, D. D. (1989) 'Cooperative Distributed Problem-solving'. In *The Handbook of Artificial Intelligence,* vol. IV, A. Barr, P. R. Cohen and E. A. Feigenbaum (Ed.), p. 83–148, Addison-Wesley.

Durkheim, E. (1897) *Le Suicide.* PUF. Engl. (1997) *Suicide: A Study in Sociology*, Free Press.

Eco, U. (1988) *Sémiotique et philosophie du langage.* PUF. Engl. (1986) *Semiotics and the Philosophy of language*, Indiana University Press.

El Fallah-Seghrouchni, A. and Haddad, S. (1994) 'Représentation et manipulation de plans à l'aide de réseaux de Petri.' In *Actes des deuxièmes journées francophones sur l'intelligence artificielle distribuée et les systèmes multi-agents (JFIAD-SMA'94),* Voiron, Y. Demazeau and S. Pesty (Ed.), IMAG.

El Fallah-Seghrouchni, A. and Haddad, S. (1996) ' 'A Recussive Model for Distributed Planning'. in *2nd International Conference on Multi-Agent Systems*, M. Tokoro (ed), AAAI.

Engelmore, R. and Morgan, T. (1988) *Blackboard Systems.* Addison-Wesley.

Enjalbert, P. (1989) 'Notes préliminaires à une théorie opérationnelle du sens'. *Intellectica.* **8**, p. 109–159.

Enjalbert, P. (1993) *Théories du signe selon Umberto Eco.* Rapport interne, 93–10, Laboratoire d'algorithmique et d'intelligence artificielle de Caen, Université de Caen.

Erceau, J. and Ferber, J. (1991) 'L'intelligence artificielle distribuée.' In *La Recherche*, Juin.

Erman, L., Hayes-Roth, F., Lesser, V. and Reddy, D. (1980) 'The HEARSAY-II Speech Understanding System: Integrating Knowledge to Resolve Uncertainty'. *ACM Computing Surveys.* **12**.

Estraillier, P. and Girault, C. (1992) 'Applying Petri Net Theory to the Modelling Analysis and Prototyping of Distributed Systems'. In *Proceedings of the IEEE International Workshop on Emerging Technologies and Factory Automation,* Cairns, Australia.

Ferber, F. (1906) *Pas à pas, saut à saut, vol à vol.* Berger-Levrault.

Ferber, J. (1987) 'Des objets aux agents : une architecture stratifiée.' In *Sixième congrès RFIA*, Antibes, AFCET.

Ferber, J. (1989) *Objets et agents : une étude des structures de représentation et de communications en Intelligence Artificielle.* Thèse d'Etat, Université Paris 6.

Ferber, J. (1990) *Conception et programmation par objets.* Hermès.

Ferber, J. (1994) 'La Kénétique : des systèmes multi-agents à une science de l'interaction'. *Revue internationale de systémique.* **8**(1), p. 13–27.

Ferber, J. (1995a) 'Basis of Cooperation in Multi-Agent Systems'. In *Proc. of the 95 European Conference on Cognitive Science,* Saint-Malo, INRIA.

Ferber, J. (1995b) 'Reactive Distributed Artificial Intelligence: Principles and Applications'. In *Foundations of Distributed Artificial Intelligence,* N. Jennings (Ed.), Wiley.

Ferber, J. and Carle, P. (1991) 'Actors and Agents as Reflective Concurrent Objects: a Mering IV Perspective'. *IEEE Trans on Systems, Man and Cybernetics.* **21**(6).

Ferber, J., Carle, P., Mousseau, D. and Furet, T. (1993) 'Synchronisation de messages par utilisation de la réflexivité du langage d'acteurs Mering IV.' In *Actes des journées françaises sur les langages applicatifs, JFLA'93.*

Ferber, J. and Drogoul, A. (1992) 'Using Reactive Multi-Agent Systems in Simulation and Problem-solving'. In *Distributed Artificial Intelligence: Theory and Practice,* L. Gasser and N. Avouris (Ed.), Kluwer Academic Publishers.

Ferber, J. and Erceau, J. (1994) 'L'intelligence artificielle distribuée et la conception de systèmes multi-agents.' In *Intelligence Collective*, E. Bonabeau and P. Bourgine (Ed.), Hermès.

Ferber, J. and Magnin, L. (1994) 'Conception de systèmes multi-agents par composants modulaires et réseaux de Petri.' In *Actes des journées du PRC-IA*, Montpellier.

Ferber, J. and Müller, J.-P. (1996) *Influences and reaction: A model of situated multiagent systems.* Proceedings of 2nd International Conference on Multi-Agent Systems, Nara (Japan), M. T. (eds) (Ed.), AAAI Press, pp. 72-79.

Ferraris, C. and Haton, M.C. (1992) 'Un guide méthodologique pour l'acquisition des connaissances dans le cadre d'un système multi experts.' In *Actes des journées d'acquisition des connaissances*, Dourdan.

Fikes, R. E. and Nilsson, N. J. (1971) 'STRIPS: a New Approach to the Application of Theorem Proving to Problem-solving' *Artificial Intelligence.* **2**(3–4), p. 189–208.

Finin, T., Fritzson, R., McKay, D. and McEntire, R. (1994) 'KQML as an Agent Communication Language'. In *3rd International Conference on Information and Knowledge Management (CIKM'94)*, ACM Press.

Fodor, J. (1983) *The Modularity of the Mind.* Cambridge, Mass, MIT Press.

Forrester, J.W. (1980) *Principes des Systèmes.* Presses Universitaires de Lyon. Engl. (1968) *Principles of Systems.*

Fox, M. (1981) 'An Organizational View of Distributed Systems'. *IEEE Trans. on Man, Systems and Cybernetics.* **11**(1), p. 70–79.

Fresneau, D. (1994) *Biologie et comportement social d'une fourmi ponerine néotropicale.* Thèse d'Etat, Université Paris XIII.

Friedberg, E. (1993) *Le Pouvoir et la règle.* Le Seuil.

Fron, A. (1994) *Programmation par contraintes.* Addison-Wesley France.

Galliers, J. R. (1988) *A Theoretical Framework for Computer Models of Cooperative Dialogue*, Acknowledgeing Multi-Agent Conflict. PhD Thesis, Open University, UK.

Galliers, J. R. (1991) 'Modelling Autonomous Belief Revision in Dialogue'. In *Decentralized Artificial Intelligence 2: Proc. of the Second European Workshop on Autonomous Agents in a Multi-Agents World (MAAMAW'90)*, Y. Demazeau and P. Müller (Ed.), Elsevier North Holland.

Gasser, L. (1991) 'Social Conceptions of Knowledge and Action: DAI Foundations and Open Systems Semantics'. *Artificial Intelligence.* **47**(1–3), p. 107–138.

Gasser, L. (1992) 'An Overview of DAI'. In *Distributed Artificial Intelligence: Theory and Praxis*, L. Gasser and N. M. Avouris (Ed.), Kluwer Academic Publishers.

Gasser, L. (1995) 'Computational Organization Research'. In *1st International Conference on Multi-Agent Systems*, San Francisco, V. Lesser (Ed.), MIT Press.

Gasser, L., Braganza, C. and Herman, N. (1987a) 'Implementing Distributed Artificial Intelligence Systems using MACE'. In *IEEE Conference on Artificial Intelligence Applications*, p. 315–320.

Gasser, L., Braganza, C. and Herman, N. (1987b) 'MACE: a Flexible Testbed for Distributed AI Research'. In *Distributed Artificial Intelligence*, M.N.Huhns (Ed.), p. 119–152, Pitman.

Gasser, L. and Hill, R.W. (1990) 'Coordinated Problem Solvers'. *Annual Reviews of Computer Science.* **4**, p. 203–253.

Gasser, L. and Huhns, M. (Ed.) (1989) *Distributed Artificial Intelligence.* Vol II, Pitman/Morgan Kaufman.

Gasser, L., Rouquette, N., Hill, R. and Lieb, J. (1989) 'Representing and Using Organizational Knowledge in Distributed AI Systems'. In *Distributed Artificial Intelligence*, vol. II, L. Gasser and M. Huhns (Ed.), Pitman.

Genesereth, M. R. and Nilsson, N. J. (1987) *Logical Foundations of Artificial Intelligence.* Morgan Kaufman.

Georgeff, M. (1984) 'A Theory of Action for MultiAgent Planning'. In *AAAI-84*, p. 121–125.

Georgeff, M. (1986) 'The Representation of Events in Multi-Agent Domains'. In *AAAI-86*, p. 70–75.

Georgeff, M. P. (1983) 'Communication and Interaction in Multi-Agent Planning'. In *AAAI-83*, p. 125–129.

Ghallab, M., Grandjean, P., Lacroix, S. and Thibault, J.-P. (1992) 'Représentation et raisonnement pour une machine multi-sensorielle.' In *Actes des quatrièmes journées nationales du PRC-GDR intelligence artificielle*, Marseille, p. 121–167, Teknea.

Ghedira, K. (1993) *MASC : une approche multi-agents des problèmes de satisfaction de contraintes*. Thèse de l'ENSAE.

Ghedira, K. (1994) 'Partial Constraint Satisfaction by a Multi-Agent Simulated Annealing approach'. In *Int. Conf. of AI, KBS, ES and NL,* Paris.

Ghiglione, R. (1986) *L'Homme communicant*. Armand Colin.

Ghiglione, R. (1989) 'Le "qui" et le "comment".' In *Perception, Action, Langage – Traité de Psychologie Cognitive*, vol. 3, C. Bonnet, R. Ghiglione and J.-F. Richard (Ed.), p. 175–226, Dunod.

Giroux, S. (1993) *Agents et systèmes, une nécessaire unité*. Thèse de Doctorat, Université de Montréal.

Giroux, S. and Senteni, A. (1992) *Steps to an Ecology of Concurrent Computation*. Research report, University of Montreal.

Gleick, J. (1989) *La Théorie du chaos*. Flammarion. Engl. (1988) *Chaos: Making a New Science*. Penguin.

Gleizes, M.-P., Glize, P. and Trouilhet, S. (1994) 'Etude des lois de la conversation entre agents autonomes'. *Revue internationale de systémique*. **8**(1), p. 39–50.

Goldberg, A. and Robson, D. (1980) *Smalltalk-80: The language and its Implementation*. Addison-Wesley.

Goldberg, D. (1989) *Genetic Algorithms*. Addison-Wesley.

Grice, H. P. (1975) 'Logic and Conversation'. In *Syntax and Semantics,* Vol. 3, Speech Acts, P. Cole and J. L. Morgan (Ed.), p. 41–58, Academic Press.

Guha, R. V. and Lenat, D. (1990) 'CYC: A Midterm Report'. In *AI Magazine,*

Gurvitch, G. (1963) *La vocation actuelle de la sociologie*. PUF.

Harel, D. (1979) *First Order Dynamic Logic*. Vol. 68, Springer-Verlag.

Haton, J.-P., Bouzid, N., Charpillet, F. *et al.* (1991) *Le Raisonnement en intelligence artificielle*. InterEditions.

Hayes-Roth, B. (1985) 'A Blackboard Architecture for Control'. *Artificial Intelligence*. **26**(3), p. 251–321.

Hayes-Roth, B. and Collinot, A. (1993) 'A Satisficing Cycle for Real-Time Reasoning in Intelligent Agents'. *Expert Systems with Applications*. **7**, p. 31–42.

Hayes-Roth, B., Washington, R., Ash, D. *et al.* (1992) 'Guardian, a Prototype Intelligent Agent for Intensive-Care Monitoring'. *Artificial Intelligence in Medicine*. **4**(2).

Hayes-Roth, F., Erman, L., Fouse, S., Lark, J. S. and Davidson, J. (1988) 'ABE: a Cooperative Operating System and Development Environment'. In *Readings in Distributed Artificial Intelligence,* A. Bond and L. Gasser (Ed.), Morgan Kaufman.

Heudin, J.-C. (1994) *La Vie artificielle*. Paris, Hermès.

Hewitt, C. (1977) 'Viewing Control Structures as Patterns of Message Passing'. *Artificial Intelligence*. **8**(3), p. 323–374.

Hewitt, C. (1985) 'The Challenge of Open Systems'. In *Byte,*

Hewitt, C. (1991) 'Open Information Systems Semantics for Distributed Artificial Intelligence'. *Artificial Intelligence (special issue on foundations of AI)*. **47**(1–3), p. 79–106.

Hewitt, C., Bishop, P. and Steiger, R. (1973) 'A universal Modular Actor Formalism for Artificial Intelligence'. In *Third International Joint Conference on Artificial Intelligence.*

Hickman, S. and Shiels, M. (1991) 'Situated Action as a Basis for Cooperation'. In *Decentralized A.I.2,* E.Werner and Y. Demazeau (Ed.), Elsevier North Holland.

Hintikka, J. (1962) *Knowledge and Belief*. Ithaca, Kornell University.

Hoare, C. A. R. (1985) *Communicating Sequential Processes*. Prentice-Hall International.

Holland, J. H. (1968) 'Processing and Processors for Schemata'. In *Associative Information Processing*, E. L. Jacks (Ed.), p. 127–146, American Elsevier.

Holland, J. H. (1978) 'Cognitive Systems Based on Adaptive Algorithms'. In *Pattern directed inference systems*, D. A. Waterman and F. Hayes-Roth (Ed.), p. 313–329, Academic Press.

Holland, J. H., Holyoak, K. J., Nisbett, R. E. and Thaghard, P. R. (1986) *Induction: Processes of Inference, Learning and Discovery*. MIT Press.

Huhns, M. N. (Ed.) (1987) *Distributed Artificial Intelligence*. Pitman.

Husserl, E. (1950) *Idées directrices pour une phénoménologie*. Gallimard.

Iffenecker, C. (1992) *Un Système multi-agents pour le support des activités de conception de produits*. Thèse d'université, Université Paris 6.

Iffenecker, C. and Ferber, J. (1992) 'Using Multi-Agent Architecture for Designing Electromechanical Products'. In *Proceedings of Avignon '92 conference on Expert Systems and their Applications*, Avignon, EC2.

Ishida, T. (1989) 'CoCo: A Multi-Agent System for Concurrent and Cooperative Operation Tasks'. In *9th Distributed Artificial Intelligence Workshop*, Orcas Island, M. Benda (Ed.)

Ishikawa, Y. and Tokoro, M. (1986) 'A Concurrent Object-Oriented Knowledge Representation Language Orient84/K: its features and implementation'. In *OOPS-LA'86*, ACM Sigplan Notices.

Jacopin, E (1993) *Algorithmique de l'interaction : le cas de la planification*. Thèse de l'université Paris 6.

Jagannathan, V., Dodhiawala, R. and Baum, L. S. (1989) *Blackboard Architectures and Applications*. Academic Press.

Jakobson, R. (1963) *Essai de linguistique générale*. Editions de Minuit.

Jennings, N. (1994) *Cooperation in Industrial Multi-Agent Systems*. Vol. 43, World Scientific Press.

Jennings, N., Corera, J. M. and Laresgoiti, I. (1995) 'Developing Industrial Multi-Agent Systems'. In *First International Conference on Multi-Agent Systems*, San Francisco, V. Lesser (Ed.), MIT Press.

Jennings, N. and Wittig, T. (1992) 'ARCHON: Theory and Practice'. In *Distributed Artificial Intelligence: Theory and Practice*, L. Gasser and N. Avouris (Ed.), Kluwer Academic Publishers.

Jensen, K. (1992) *Coloured Petri Nets. Basic Concepts, Analysis Method and Practical Use*. Vol. 1, Springer-Verlag.

Konolige, K. (1986) *A Deduction Model of Belief*. Pitman.

Kort, R. E. (1985) 'Depth first Iterative-Deepening: an Optimal Admissible Tree Search'. *Artificial Intelligence*. **27**.

Korf, R. E. (1988) 'Real Time Heuristic Search'. *Artificial Intelligence*. **42**.

Kornfeld, W. (1979) 'ETHER: a Parallel Problem-solving System'. In *Proc. of 6th IJCAI*.

Kornfeld, W. and Hewitt, C. (1980) *The Scientific Community Metaphor*. AI Lab memo, 641, MIT.

Kripke, S. A. (1991) 'Semantic Considerations on Modal Logic'. In *Reference and Modality*, Linsky (Ed.), p. 63–72, Oxford University Press.

Kuhn, T. (1962) *The Structure of Scientific Revolutions*. University of Chicago Press.

Lâasri, H. and Maître, B. (1989) *Coopération dans un univers multi-agent basée sur le modèle du blackboard : études et réalisations*. Thèse de l'université de Nancy I.

Lâasri, H., Maître, B. and Haton, J.-P. (1987) 'ATOME : outil d'aide au développement de systèmes multi-experts.' In *Actes des sixièmes journées sur la reconnaissance des formes et l'intelligence artificielle (RFIA'87)*, Antibes, p. 749–759.

Lakatos, I. (1976) *Proofs and Refutations.* Cambridge University Press.

Lalanda, P., Charpillet, F and Haton, J. P. (1992) 'A Real Time Blackboard Based Architecture'. In *10th European conference on Artificial Intelligence,* Vienna, Austria.

Langton, C. (Ed.) (1988) *Artificial Life.* Addison-Wesley.

Langton, C., Taylor, C., Farmer, J. D. and Rasmussen, S. (Ed.) (1990) *Artificial Life II.* Addison-Wesley.

Langton, C. G. (Ed.) (1994) *Artificial Life III.* Addison-Wesley.

Lannoy, J. D. D. and Feyereisen, P. (1987) *L'Ethologie humaine.* Que sais-je?, Paris, PUF.

Lapierre, J.-W. (1992) *L'Analyse de systèmes.* Syros.

Latombe, J.-C. (1991) *Robot Motion Planning.* Kluwer Academic Publishers.

Latour, B. (1989) *La Science en action.* La Découverte. Engl. (1988) *Science in Action: How to follow Scientists and Engineers through Society.* Harvard University Press.

Le Gallou, F. (1992) 'Activités des systèmes, décomposition des systèmes.' In *Systémique. Théorie et applications*, F. Le Gallou and B. Bouchon-Meunier (Ed.), p. 71–100, Lavoisier.

Le Moigne, J.-L. (1977) *La Théorie du système général.* PUF.

Le Strugeon, E. (1995) *Une méthodologie d'auto-adaptation d'un système multi-agents cognitifs.* Thèse de l'université de Valenciennes.

Lefèvre, C. (1995) *Agents logiques communicants.* Thèse de l'université de Caen.

Lehmann, F. (Ed.) (1992) *Semantic Networks in Artificial Intelligence.* Pergamon Press.

Lenat, D. (1975) 'BEINGs: Knowledge as Interacting Experts'. In *Proc. of the 1975 IJCAI Conference,* p. 126–133.

Lenat, D. and Brown, J. S. (1984) 'Why AM and Eurisko appear to Work'. *Artificial Intelligence.* **23**, p. 269–294.

Lenat, D. and Guha, R. V. (1990) *Building Large Knowledge-Based Systems.* Addison-Wesley.

Lespérance, Y., Levesque, H, Lin, F. *et al.* (1995) 'Fondements d'une approche logique à la programmation d'agents.' In *Actes des troisièmes journées francophones sur l'intelligence artificielle distribuée et les systèmes multi-agents*, Chambéry.

Lesser, V. R. and Corkill, D. D. (1983) 'The Distributed Vehicle Monitoring Testbed: A Tool for Investigating Distributed Problem-solving Networks'. *AI Magazine.* **4**(3), p. 15–33.

Lestel, D. (1986) *Contribution à l'étude du raisonnement expérimental dans un domaine sémantiquement riche.* Thèse de doctorat, EHESS.

Lestel, D., Grison, B. and Drogoul, A. (1994) 'Les agents réactifs et le vivant dans une perspective d'évolution coopérative'. *Intellectica.* **19**, p. 73–90.

Levine, M. D. (1985) *Vision in Man and Machine.* Prentice-Hall.

Lin, L.-J. (1992) 'Self-improving Reactive Agents: Case Studies of Reinforcement Learning Frameworks'. In *From Animals to Animats: Proc. of the First International Conference on Simulation of Adaptive Behavior (SAB'90),* Paris, J.-A. Meyer and S. W. Wilson (Ed.), p. 297–305, MIT Press.

Liu, J. S. and Sycara, K. (1993) 'Emergent Constraint Satisfaction through Multi-Agent Coordinated Interaction.' In *Maamaw'93,* Neuchâtel.

Livet, P. (1994). *La communauté virtuelle.*

Editions de l'Eclat.

Lorenz, K. (1984) *Les Fondements de l'éthologie.* Flammarion. Engl. (1981) *The Foundations of Ethology.* Springer Verlag.

Maes, P. (1990) 'Situated Agents can have Goals'. *Journal of Robotics and Autonomous Systems.* **6**, p. 49–70.

Maes, P. (1991) 'A Bottom-Up Mechanism for Behavior Selection in an Artificial Creature'. In *From Animals to Animats: Proc. Of the First International Conference on Simulation of Adaptive Behavior (SAB'90),* Paris, J.-A. Meyer and S. W. Wilson (Ed.), p. 238–246, MIT Press.

Maes, P. (1992) 'Learning Behavior Networks from Experience'. In *Toward a Practice of Autonomous Systems, Proc. of the First European Conference on Artificial Life,* Paris, F. Varela and P. Bourgine (Ed.), p. 48–57, MIT Press.

Maes, P. and Nardi, D. (Ed.) (1988) *Meta-level Architectures and Reflexion.* North-Holland.

Malinowski, B. (1944) *A Scientific Theory of Culture and Other Essays.* Chapel Hill, North Carolina Press.

Malone, T. W. (1988) 'What is coordination theory?'. In *National Science Foundation Coordination Theory Workshop,* MIT.

Marr, D. (1982) *Vision: a Computational Investigation into the Human Representation and Processing of Visual Information.* Freeman.

Maruichi, T. (1989) *Organizational Computation.* Ph.D. Thesis, Keio University.

Maruichi, T., Ichikawa, M. and Tokoro, M. (1990) 'Modeling Autonomous Agents and their Groups'. In *Decentralized A.I.1,* Y. Demazeau and J.-P. Müller (Ed.), North-Holland.

Masini, G., Napoli, A., Colnet, D., Léonard, D. and Tombre, K. (1989) *Les Langages à objets.* InterEditions. Engl. (1991) *Object-Oriented Languages.* Academic Press.

Masoud, A. and Bayoumi, M. (1993) 'Robot Navigation Using the Vector Potential Approach'. In *Proc. of IEEE International Conference on Robotics and Automation,* Atlanta, p. 805–811.

Mataric, M. J. (1992) 'Designing Emergent Behaviors: from Local Interactions to Collective Intelligence'. In *From Animals to Animats 2, Proceedings of the Second International Conference on Simulation of Adaptive Behavior,* Hawaii, J.-A. Meyer, H. L. Roitblat and S. W. Wilson (Ed.), p. 432–441, MIT Press.

Mataric, M. J. (1994) 'Learning to Behave Socially'. In *From Animals to Animats 3, Proceedings of the Third International Conference on Simulation of Adaptive Behavior,* Brighton, D. Cliff, P. Husbands, J.-A. Meyer and S. W. Wilson (Ed.), p. 453–462, MIT Press.

Maturana, H. and Varela, F. (1980) *Autopoiesis and Cognition: the Realization of the Living.* Boston, D. Reidel.

Maturana, H. and Varela, F. (1987) *The Tree of Knowledge.* Boston, New Science Library.

McCarthy, J. (1980) 'Circumscription: A Form of Non-Monotonic Reasoning'. *Artificial Intelligence.* **13**, p. 27–39.

McFarland, D. (1990) *Dictionnaire du comportement animal.* Robert Laffont.

McFarland, D. (1994) 'Towards Robot Cooperation'. In *'94 Conference on the Simulation of Adaptive Behavior,* Brighton, MIT Press.

Mesarovic, M. D. and Takahara, Y. (1975) *General Systems Theory: Mathematical Foundations.* Academic Press.

Mesle, R. (1994) *ICHTYUS : architecture d'un système multi-agents pour l'étude de structures agrégatives.* Rapport de DEA, LAFORIA, Université Paris 6.

Meyer, J.-A. and Guillot, A. (1989) 'Simulation of Adaptive Behavior in Animats: Review and Prospect'. In *From Animals to Animats,* Paris,

J.-A. Meyer and S. W. Wilson (Ed.), MIT Press.

Meyer, J.-A., Roitblat, H. L. and Wilson, S. W. (Ed.) (1993) *Simulation of Adaptive Behavior: From Animals to Animats II*. Cambridge, MIT Press.

Meyer, J.-A. and Wilson, S. (Ed.) (1991) *Simulation of Adaptive Behavior: From Animals to Animats*. MIT Press.

Milner, R. (1989) *Communication and Concurrency*. Prentice-Hall International.

Minsky, M. (1988) *La Société de l'Esprit*. InterEditions. Engl. (1986) *The Society of Mind*. Simon & Schuster, New York.

Mintzberg, H. (1982) *Structure et dynamique des organisations*. Les Editions d'Organisation.

MIRIAD E. (1992) 'Approcher la notion de collectif.' In *Actes des journées multi-agents du PRC-IA*, Nancy.

Moeschler, J. (1985) *Argumentation et conversation*. Hatier.

Moeschler, J. (1989) *Modélisation du dialogue : représentation de l'inférence argumentative*. Hermès.

Montague, R. (1974) *Formal Philosophy*. Yale University Press.

Moore, R.C. (1988) 'Autoepistemic Logic'. In *Non-Standard Logics for Automated Reasoning,* Smets (Ed.), p. 105–136, Academic Press.

Morin, E. (1977) *La Méthode (1) : la Nature de la Nature*. Le Seuil.

Morin, E. (1991) *La Méthode (4) : Les Idées. Leur habitat, leur vie, leurs moeurs*. Le Seuil.

Morley, R. E. and C. S. (1993) 'An Analysis of a Plant-Specific Dynamic Scheduler'. In *Proc. of the NSF Workshop on Dynamic Scheduling.,* Cocoa Beach.

Moulin, B. and Cloutier, L (1994) 'Collaborative Work Based on Multiagent Architectures: a

Methodological Perspective'. In *Soft Computing: Fuzzy Logic, Neural Networks and Distributed Artificial Intelligence,* F. Aminzadeh and M. Jamshidi (Ed.), p. 261–296, Prentice-Hall.

Murata, T. (1989) 'Petri Nets: Properties, Analysis and Applications'. *Proceedings of the IEEE*. **77**(4), p. 541–580.

Newell, A. (1982) 'The Knowledge Level'. *Artificial Intelligence*. **18**(1), p. 87–127.

Newell, A., Shaw, J. and Simon, H. (1957) 'Empirical Explorations of the Logic Theory Machine: a Case Study in Heuristics'. In *Computers and Thought (1963),* F. Feigenbaum and J. Feldman (Ed.), p. 109–133, McGraw-Hill.

Newton, J. (1985) *Principia Mathematica*. C. Bourgeois.

Nilsson, N. (1980) *Principles of Artificial Intelligence*. Springer-Verlag.

Overgaard, L., Petersen, H. G. and Perram, J. W. (1994) 'Motion Planning for an Articulated Robot: a Multi-Agent Approach'. In *MAAMAW'94,* Odense, Denmark, Y. Demazeau, J.-P. Müller and J. Perram (Ed.).

Pacherie, E. (1993) *Naturaliser l'intentionnalité. Essai de philosophie de la psychologie.*. PUF.

Parker, L. E. (1994) *Heterogeneous Multi-Robot Cooperation,* Ph.D. Thesis, MIT.

Parunak, H. V. D. (1987) 'Manufacturing Experience with the Contract Net'. In *Distributed Artificial Intelligence,* M. Huhns (Ed.), Pitman.

Parunak, H. V. D. (1990) 'Distributed AI and Manufacturing Control: Some Issues and Insights'. In *Decentralized AI,* Vol. 1, Y. Demazeau and J.-P. Müller (Ed.), p. 81–104, North-Holland.

Parunak, H. V. D. (1993) *Industrial Applications of Multi-Agent Systems*. Research report, Industrial Technology Institute.

Pattison, H. E., Corkill, D. and Lesser, V. (1987)

'Instantiating Descriptions of Organizational Structures'. In *Distributed Artificial Intelligence*, M. Huhns (Ed.), Pitman.

Pavé, A. (1994) *Modélisation en biologie et en écologie*. Lyon, Aléas.

Pednault, E. (1986) 'Formulating Multiagent, Dynamic-World Problems in the Classical Planning Framework'. In *Reasoning about Actions and Plans*, Timberline, M. Georgeff and A. Lansky (Ed.), p. 425, Morgan Kaufman.

Perram, J. W. and Müller, J.-P. ed. (1996) *Distributed Software Agents and Applications*. LNAI Vol. 1069, Springer-Verlag.

Piaget, J. and Inhelder, B. (1966) *La psychologie de l'enfant*. PUF. Engl. Piaget J. Weaver H. and Inhelder B. (1972) *The Psychology of the Child*. Basic Books.

Pitrat, J. (1990) *Metaconnaissances. Futur de l'intelligence artificielle*. Hermès.

Popper, K. (1963) *Conjectures and Refutations*. London, Routledge and Kegan Paul.

Prigogine, I. and Stengers, I. (1979) *La nouvelle alliance*. Gallimard. Engl. (1984) *Order out of Chaos: Man's New Dialogue with Nature*. Random House.

Quinqueton, J., Reitz, P. and Sallantin, J. (1991) 'Les Schémas mentaux, un cadre conceptuel pour l'apprentissage à partir d'exemples.' In *Actes du congrès sur la reconnaissance des formes et l'intelligence artificielle*, Lyon, J.-P.Laurent (Ed.)

Rao, A. S. (1996) *AgentSpeak(L): BDI Agents Speak Out in a Logical Computable Language*. Proceedings of Maamaw'96, Eindhoven, Netherlands, W. V. d. Velde and J. W. Perram (Ed.), LNAI 1038, Springer Verlag, pp. 42-55.

Rao, A. and Georgeff, M. (1992) 'Social Plans: Preliminary Report'. In *Decentralized AI 3 – Proc. of MAAMAW'91*, E. Werner and C. Castelfranchi (Ed.), p. 127–146, Elsevier North Holland.

Raynal, M (1987) *Systèmes répartis et réseaux : concepts outils et algorithmes*. Eyrolles. Engl.

(1988) *Networks and Distributed Computation: Concepts, Tools and Algorithms*. MIT Press.

Récanati, F. (1981) *Les Enoncés performatifs*, Editions de Minuit. Engl. (1988) *Meaning and Force: The Pragmatics of Performative Utterances*. Cambridge University Press.

Regnier, S. and Duhaut, D. (1995) 'Une approche multi-agent pour la résolution de problèmes robotiques.' In *Actes des troisièmes journées francophones sur l'Intelligence artificielle Distribuée et les systèmes multi-agents (JFIADSMA'95)*, Chambéry.

Reiter, R. (1980) 'A Logic for Default Reasoning'. *AI Journal*. **13**, p. 81–131.

Reynolds, C. (1987) 'Flocks, Herds and Schools: A Distributed Behavioral Model'. *Computer Graphics*. **21**(4), p. 25–34.

Rocher, G. (1968) *Introduction à la sociologie générale. T1 : l'action sociale*. Le Seuil. Engl. *A general Introduction to Sociology, a theoretical perspective*.

Rosenblatt, K.J. and Payton, D.W. (1989) 'A Fine-Grained Alternative to the Subsumption Architecture for Mobile Robot Control'. In *Proc. of the IEEE/INNS International Joint Conference on Neural Networks*.

Rosenschein, J. and Zlotkin, G. (1994) *Rules of Encounters: Designing Conventions for Automated Negotiation among Computers*. MIT Press.

Sabah, G. (1989) *L'Intelligence artificielle et le langage. Tome 2 : Compréhension*. Hermès.

Sabah, G. (1990) 'CARAMEL: A Computational Model of Natural Language Understanding using Parallel Implementation'. In *Proc. of the Ninth European Conference on Artificial Intelligence (ECAI 90)*, Stockholm.

Sadek, D. (1992) *A Study in the Logic of Intention*. Proceedings of Conference on Principles of Knowledge Representation and Reasoning (KR'92), Cambridge, MA, pp. 462-473.

Schoppers, M. (1987) 'Universal Plans for

Reactive Robots in Unpredictable Environment'. In *IJCAI-87,* Milan.

Schwartz, E. (1993) 'A Coherent and Holistic Metamodel for the Functioning and Evolution of Viable Systems. An application to Human Societies'. In *4th International Symposium on Systems Research Informatics and Cybernetics,* Baden-Baden.

Searle, J. (1991) *The Rediscovery of the Mind.* MIT Press.

Searle, J. and Vanderveken, D. (1985) *Foundations of Illocutionary Logic.* Cambridge University Press.

Searle, J. R. (1969) *Speech Acts.* Cambridge University Press.

Searle, J. R. (1979) *Expression and Meaning.* Cambridge University Press.

Searle, J. R. (1985) *L'intentionnalité : essai de philosophie des états mentaux.* Editions de Minuit. Engl. *Intentionality: an Essay in the Philosophy of Mind.*

Shannon, C. and Weaver, W. (1948) *The Mathematical theory of Communication.* Urbana, University of Illinois Press.

Shoham, Y. (1988) *Reasoning About Change.* MIT Press.

Shoham, Y. (1993) 'Agent Oriented Programming'. *Artificial Intelligence.* **60**(1), p. 51–92.

Sibertin-Blanc, C. (1985) 'High level Petri nets with Data Structure'. In *6th European Workshop on Petri Nets and Applications,* Espoo, Finland.

Singh, M. P. (1994) *Multiagent Systems: a Theoretical Framework for Intentions, Know-How and Communications.* LNAI 799, Springer Verlag.

Smith, R. G. (1979) 'A Framework for Distributed Problem-solving'. In *Proceedings of IJCAI'79.*

Smith, R. G. (1980) 'The Contract Net Protocol: High-Level Communication and Control in a Distributed Problem Solver'. *IEEE Trans. on Computers.* **29**(12), p. 1104–1113.

Smolensky, P. (1992) 'IA connexioniste, IA symbolique et cerveau.' In *Introduction aux sciences cognitives,* D.Andler (Ed.), Gallimard.

Sombé, L. (1988) 'Raisonnement sur des informations incomplètes en intelligence artificielle.' *Revue d'intelligence artificielle.* **2**(3–4), p. 9–210.

Sowa, J. (1984) *Conceptual Structures.* Addison-Wesley.

Sperber, D. and Wilson, D. (1986) *Relevance: Communication and Cognition.* Blackwell.

Steeb, R., Camarata, S., Hayes-Roth, F., Thorndyke, P. and Wesson, R. (1988) 'Architectures for Distributed Air Traffic Control'. In *Readings in Distributed Artificial Intelligence,* A. Bond and L. Gasser (Ed.), Morgan Kaufman.

Steels, L. (1989) 'Cooperation between Distributed Agents through Self-Organization'. In *Decentralized AI.,* Y. Demazeau and J.-P. Müller (Ed.), Elsevier/North-Holland.

Steels, L. (1994a) 'The Artificial Life Roots of Artificial Intelligence'. *Artificial Life.* **1**(1).

Steels, L. (1994b) 'A Case Study in the Behavior-Oriented Design of Autonomous Agents'. In *Proc. of the '94 Conference on the Simulation of Adaptive Behavior,* MIT Press.

Stoetzel, J. (1978) *La Psychologie sociale.* Flammarion.

Suchman, L. (1987) *Plans and Situated Actions: the Problem of Human-Machine Communication.* Cambridge University Press.

Sutton, E. (1994) *Etat de l'art des algorithmes génétiques.* SGDN/STS/VST/5, Secrétariat général de la défense nationale.

Sycara, K. (1989) 'Multiagent Compromise via Negotiation'. In *Distributed Artificial Intelligence,* L. Gasser and M. Huhns (Ed.), Pitman.

Tanenbaum, A. (1991) *Architecture des ordinateurs*. InterEditions.

Theraulaz, G. (1991) *Morphogenèse et auto-organisation des comportements dans les colonies de guêpes Polistes dominilus (Christ)*. Thèse de troisième Cycle, Université d'Aix-Marseille I.

Theraulaz, G., Goss, S., Gervet, J. and Deneubourg, J.L. (1991) 'Task Differentiation in Polistes Wasp Colonies: a Model for Self-Organizing Groups of Robots'. In *From Animals to Animats*, J. A. Meyer and S. Wislon (Ed.), p. 346–354, MIT Press.

Thibault, J.-P. (1993) *Interprétation d'environnement évolutif par une machine de perception multi-sensorielle*. Thèse de l'université Paul Sabatier, Toulouse.

Thom, R. (1988) *Esquisse d'une sémiophysique*. InterEditions. Engl. *Semio Physics: A Sketch*.

Thomas, S. R. (1994) *The PLACA Agent Programming Language*. Proceedings of Agent Theories, Architectures and Languages, Amsterdam, M. J. Wooldridge and N. R. Jennings (Ed.), LNAI 890, Springer-Verlag, pp. 356-370.

Tinbergen, N. (1951) *The Study of Instinct*. Clarendon Press.

Todd, P. M. and Miller, G. F. (1991) 'Exploring Adaptive Agency II: Simulating the Evolution of Associative Learning'. In *From Animals to Animats: Proc. of the First International Conference on Simulation of Adaptive Behavior (SAB'90)*, Paris, J.-A. Meyer and S. W. Wilson (Ed.), p. 306–315, MIT Press.

Tokoro, M. (1993) 'The Society of Objects'. In *Proc. of the OOPSLA'93 Conference*.

Trognon, A. and Brassac, C. (1988) "Actes de langages et conversation". *Intellectica*. **6**(2), p. 211–232.

Trognon, A. and Brassac, C. (1992) 'L'Enchaînement conversationnel'. *Cahiers de linguistique française*. **13**.

Tsang, E. (1993) *Foundations of Constraint Satisfaction*, Academic Press.

Tyrrell, T. (1993a) *Computational Mechanisms for Action Selection*. Ph.D. Thesis, Edinburgh University.

Tyrrell, T. (1993b) 'The Use of Hierarchies for Action Selection'. *Adaptive Behavior*. **1**(4), p. 387–420.

Uexküll, J. v. (1956) *Mondes animaux et mondes humains*. Denoël.

Van de Velde, W. and Perram, J. W. ed. (1996) *Agents Breaking Away*. Proc. of the 7th European Workshop on Modelling Autonomous Agents in a Multi-Agent World, Maamaw'96. LNAI Vol. 1038, Springer-Verlag.

Vanderveken, D. (1988) *Les actes de discours*. Pierre Mardaga.

Vanderveken, D. (1992) *Meaning and Speech Acts*. Cambridge University Press.

Varela, F. (1989) *Autonomie et Connaissance*. Le Seuil.

Varela, F., Thomson, E. and Rosch, E. (1993) *L'Inscription corporelle de l'esprit*. Le Seuil.

Varela, F. J. and Bourgine, P. (Ed.) (1992) *Toward a Practice of Autonomous Systems*. MIT Press.

Vauclair, J. (1992) *L'Intelligence de l'animal*. Le Seuil.

Vernadat, F. and Azemat, P. (1993) 'Prototypage de systèmes d'agents communicants.' In *Actes des premières journées francophones sur l'intelligence artificielle distribuée et les systèmes multi-agents*, Toulouse.

Volterra, V. (1926) 'Variation and fluctuations of the number of individuals of animal species living together'. In *Animal Ecology*, (Ed.), McGraw-Hill.

von Martial, F. (1992) *Coordinating Plans of Autonomous Agents*. Vol. 610, Springer-Verlag.

Waldinger, R. (1977) 'Achieving Several Goals Simultaneously'. *Machine Intelligence*. **8**, p. 94–136.

Wavish, P. (1992) 'Exploiting Emergent Behaviour in Multi-Agent Systems'. In *Decentralized A.I. 3,* E. Werner and Y. Demazeau (Ed.), North-Holland.

Wavish, P. R. and Connah, D. M. (1990) *Representing Multi-Agent Worlds in ABLE.* Technical Note, TN2964, Philips Research Laboratories.

Weihmayer, R. and Brandau, R. (1990) 'A Distributed AI Architecture for Customer Network Control'. In *Globecom'90,* San Diego.

Weiss, G. and Sen, S. ed. (1996) *Adaptation and Learning in Multi-Agent Systems.* IJCAI'95 Workshop proc., Montréal, Canada, August 1995. LNCS Vol. 1042, Springer Verlag.

Werner, E. (1989) 'Cooperating Agents: A Unified Theory of Communication and Social Structure'. In *Distributed Artificial Intelligence, Vol. II,* L. Gasser and M. Huhns (Ed.), Pitman.

Werner, E. and Demazeau, Y. (Ed.) (1992) *Decentralized AI. 3.* Amsterdam, Elsevier North-Holland.

Werner, G. M. (1994) Using Second Order Neural Connections for Motivation of Behavioral Choices. In *Proceedings of From animals to animats 3: proc. of the third international conference on simulation of adaptive behavior,* Brighton, D. Cliff, P. Husbands, J.-A. Meyer, and S. W. Wilson (Ed.), MIT Press, pp. 154-161.

Werner, G. M. and Dyer, M. G. (1992) 'Evolution of Communication in Artificial Organisms'. In *Artificial Life II (1990),* Santa Fe, C. Langton, C. Taylor, J. D. Farmer and S. Rasmussen (Ed.), p. 659–687, Addison-Wesley.

Wiener, N. (1948) *Cybernetics.* Paris, Hermann.

Wilson, E.O. (1971) *The Insect Societies.* Belknap Press of Harvard University Press.

Wilson, S. W. (1991) 'Knowledge Growth in an Artificial Animal'. In *First International Conference on Genetic Algorithms and their Applications,* Pittsburgh, p. 16–23, Carnegie-Mellon University.

Winograd, T. and Flores, F. (1986) *Understanding Computers and Cognition: a New Foundation for Design.* Ablex Publishing Corp.

Wittgenstein L. (1951) *Le Cahier bleu et le cahier brun.* Gallimard. Engl. (1986) *Blue and Brown Books.* Harper Collins.

Wittig, T. (Ed.) (1992) *ARCHON: An Architecture for Multi-Agent Systems.* Ellis Horwood.

Wooldridge, M. (1994) This is MyWorld: The Logic of an Agent-Oriented DAI Testbed. In *Proceedings of Intelligent Agents, Workshop on Agent Theories, Architectures, and Languages,* Amsterdam, M. Wooldridge and N. Jennings (Ed.), LNAI 890, Springer Verlag, pp. 160-178.

Wooldridge, M. and Jennings, N. (1994) 'Towards a Theory of Cooperative Problem-solving'. In *MAAMAW'94,* Odense, Denmark, Y. Demazeau, J.-P. Müller and J. Perram (Ed.).

Yonezawa, A. (Ed.) (1990) *ABCL: An Object-Oriented Concurrent System.* MIT Press.

Yonezawa, A. and Tokoro, M. (Ed.) (1987) *Object-Oriented Concurrent Programming.* MIT Press.

Zeghal, K. (1993) 'Un Modèle de Coordination d'Actions Reactive appliqué au trafic aérien.' In *Journées francophones "IAD et SMA",* Toulouse, AFCET.

Zeghal, K. and Ferber, J. (1993) 'CRAASH: A Coordinated Collision Avoidance System'. In *European Simulation Multiconference,* Lyon.

Zeghal, K., Ferber, J. and Erceau, J. (1993) 'Symmetrical, transitive and Recursive Force: A Representation of interactions and commitments'. In *IJCAI Workshop on Coordinated Autonomous Robots,* Chambery.

Zlotkin, G. and Rosenschein, J. S. (1992) 'A Domain Theory for Task Oriented Negotiation'. In *Proc. of the International Joint Conference on Artificial Intelligence,* Chambery.

Index